"[A] meticulous and insightful acco
were drawn to the British side as poten̄tiaī nberators."

—Pulitzer Prize citation

"By the time British forces burned Washington, D.C., during the War of 1812, they had on their side hundreds of runaway slaves who acted not only as guides and sailors, but also as rebels committed to freeing family members and plundering their former masters. Drawing on overlooked sources, Alan Taylor presents a marvelous portrait of this 'internal enemy' and the slaveholders who, finding their worst fears realized, thereafter embraced sectional doctrines that led to civil war." —National Book Award citation

"*The Internal Enemy* reinforces Alan Taylor's standing as our leading historian of colonial and early national America. This deeply researched, beautifully written account of the slaves who sought freedom by escaping to the British during the War of 1812 illuminates a little-known episode in our nation's past and offers a dramatic instance of the persistent interconnections between American slavery and American freedom." —Eric Foner, author of *The Fiery Trial*

"Alan Taylor has added a remarkable chapter to American history, showing how the actions of black Virginians in the War of 1812 remade the nation's politics in ways that profoundly influenced the racialized lead-up to the Civil War. Taylor's meticulous research and crystal-clear prose make this essential reading for anyone seeking new insights into a troubled American past." —Elizabeth A. Fenn, author of *Pox Americana*

"Alan Taylor's brilliant new book illuminates the crucial role runaway slaves played in the devastating British campaign that led to Washington, D.C.'s burning. Deeply researched and movingly told, *The Internal Enemy* is a great historian's masterwork."

—Peter Onuf, author of *Jefferson's Empire*

"Explains how the loss of slaves, along with the perceptions that the government was doing little to stop their flight . . . sowed some of the Southern antagonism that led to the Civil War. . . . [Taylor] tells a captivating story through real accounts."

—Jean Marie Brown, *Dallas-Fort Worth Star-Telegram*

"*The Internal Enemy* is a comprehensive, scholarly work, made accessible by Taylor's skill as a storyteller. He focuses on individuals . . . [including] enslaved people, slave owners, political leaders, working-class white people, and British opponents—and by telling their stories, he brings the larger historical realities of the time to life."

—Kel Munger, *Sacramento Bee*

"One of the greatest works of American history I have ever read. . . . The elegantly written and carefully researched volume shatters a good deal of received wisdom and addresses an understudied phenomenon: the fate of the Southern slaves freed by force by the British."

—Stephen L. Carter, *Bloomberg View*

"An extraordinary story, and *The Internal Enemy* tells it in vivid prose and compelling, deeply researched detail. But Taylor never gets lost in details. He has important things to say—about slavery, about war and about America. . . . Taylor writes locally but thinks globally. . . . Indeed, it's hard not to be dazzled by the ease with which Taylor moves from the lives of individual slaves, to the history of a large planter family, to the fault lines of Virginia politics, to the national debate over slavery in the western territories, out into the Atlantic world to the history of the British Empire."

—James Oakes, *Washington Post*

"In his impressively researched and beautifully crafted *The Internal Enemy*, Mr. Taylor introduces us to far less familiar custodians of American liberty—slaves and former slaves like Bartlet Shanklyn, Jack Ditcher and Jeremiah West. . . . [H]e admirably contextualizes [the War of 1812] with a brilliant account of slavery in Virginia during and after the Revolution."

—Mark M. Smith, *Wall Street Journal*

"[An] exemplary work of history. . . . Full of implication, an expertly woven narrative that forces a new look at 'the peculiar institution' in a particular time and place."

—*Kirkus Reviews*
Best Books of 2013, starred review

"[R]evealing and engrossing. . . . This is a well-written and scrupulously researched examination of an important aspect of the struggle against American slavery."

—*Booklist*

ALSO BY ALAN TAYLOR

The Civil War of 1812:
American Citizens, British Subjects, Irish Rebels, & Indian Allies

The Divided Ground:
Indians, Settlers, and the Northern Borderland of the
American Revolution

Writing Early American History

American Colonies:
The Settling of North America

William Cooper's Town:
Power and Persuasion on the Frontier of the Early American Republic

Liberty Men and Great Proprietors:
The Revolutionary Settlement on the Maine Frontier, 1760-1820

THE
INTERNAL
ENEMY

—◆—

Slavery and War in Virginia,
1772–1832

ALAN TAYLOR

W. W. NORTON & COMPANY   New York   London

Burning of the Theater in Richmond, December 26, 1811,
colored aquatint by B. Tanner, 1812. (Courtesy of the Virginia Historical Society).

Copyright © 2013 by Alan Taylor

For information about permissions to reproduce selections from this book, write to Permissions,
W. W. Norton & Company, Inc., 500 Fifth Avenue, New York, NY 10110

For information about special discounts for bulk purchases, please contact
W. W. Norton Special Sales at specialsales@wwnorton.com or 800-233-4830

Manufacturing by Courier, Westford
Book design by Helene Berinsky
Production manager: Louise Parasmo

Library of Congress Cataloging-in-Publication Data

Taylor, Alan, 1955–
The internal enemy : slavery and war in Virginia, 1772–1832 / Alan Taylor. — First edition.
pages cm
Includes bibliographical references and index.
ISBN 978-0-393-07371-3 (hardcover)
1. Slavery—Virginia—Tidewater (Region)—History. 2. Slaves—Virginia—Tidewater (Region)—
History. 3. Plantation life—Virginia—Tidewater (Region)—History. 4. Virginia—History—War
of 1812. 5. United States—History—War of 1812—Participation, African American. 6. United
States—History—War of 1812—Naval operations, British. I. Title.
E445.V8T38 2013
975.5'03—dc23

2013009643

ISBN 978-0-393-34973-3 pbk.

W. W. Norton & Company, Inc., 500 Fifth Avenue, New York, N.Y. 10110
www.wwnorton.com

W. W. Norton & Company Ltd., Castle House, 75/76 Wells Street, London W1T 3QT

1 2 3 4 5 6 7 8 9 0

For Alessa, Chris and Gabriel

And
in memory of
Emory G. Evans

CONTENTS

List of Ilustrations and Maps   xiii

INTRODUCTION   1

1. REVOLUTION   13

2. NIGHT AND DAY   55

3. BLOOD   85

4. WARSHIPS   113

5. INVASION   145

6. LESSONS   175

7. PLANTATION   215

8. FLIGHT   245

9. FIGHT   275

10. CRISIS   317

11. AGENTS   351

12. FIRE BELL   389

EPILOGUE   419

APPENDIX A: *Corotoman Enslaved Families, 1814*   437

APPENDIX B: *Numbers*   441

Notes   443

Bibliography   557

Acknowledgments   585

Index   591

I do not wish, sir, to leave my master,
but I will follow my wife and children to death.
DICK CARTER, APRIL 22, 1814

LIST OF ILLUSTRATIONS AND MAPS

Maps

Page xvi: The Chesapeake Region, 1812

Page 288: The Chesapeake Campaign, 1813

Page 289: The Chesapeake Campaign, 1814

Page 356: The North Atlantic, 1815

Illustrations

Pages iv–v: "Burning of the Theater in Richmond, [December 26, 1811]," colored aquatint by B. Tanner, 1812.

Page 12: "Peter Francisco's Gallant Action with Nine of Tarleton's Calvary," engraving by D. Edwin, 1814.

Page 16, top: "View of Norfolk from Town Point," watercolor by Benjamin Henry Latrobe, 1798.

Page 16, bottom: "Rippon Lodge," watercolor by Benjamin Henry Latrobe, 1796.

Page 50: "But I did not want to go and I jumped out of the Window," engraving by Jesse Torrey, 1817.

Page 54: "Virginian Luxuries," tavern sign by unknown artist, ca. 1825.

Page 63: "An Overseer Doing His Duty, Sketched from Life near Fredericksburg," watercolor by Benjamin Henry Latrobe, 1798.

Page 84: "St. George Tucker," engraving by Charles B. J. F. de Saint-Memin, 1807.

Page 93: "Extraordinary Appearances in the Heavens and on Earth," watercolor by Benjamin Henry Latrobe, 1797.

Page 112: Gilbert Hunt (1773–1863), portrait by unknown photographer.

Page 119: "A Private of the Fifth West India Regiment," aquatint by I. J. C. Stadler, 1814.

Page 144: "Sectional Sketch of a Tellegraph on the Lever Principles," sketch by William Tatham, 1812.

Page 147: "Governor James Barbour of Virginia."

Page 174: "Admiral Sir John Borlase Warren, R.N.," engraving by R. N. Stipple, 1800.

Page 187: "The Conspiracy Against Baltimore, or the War Dance at Montgomery Court House," cartoon by unknown Maryland Republican, 1812.

Page 191: "Admiral Cockburn Burning & Plundering Havre de Grace on the 1st of June 1813; done from a Sketch taken on the spot at the time."

Page 210: "Vice Admiral Sir Alexander F. I. Cochrane," oil portrait by Sir William Beechey.

Page 214: "Lelia Skipwith Carter Tucker," oil painting by unknown artist, ca. 1815.

Page 216: "Joseph Carrington Cabell," from Alexander Brown, *The Cabells and their Kin* (1895).

Page 244: Caricature by Thomas McLean, 1831.

Page 252: "British Boats Landing at the Mouth of Lake Borne," pen and ink drawing by Rear Admiral Sir Pulteney Malcolm, 1815.

Page 274: "Admiral Sir George Cockburn," oil painting by John James Halls, 1817.

Page 278, top: "Tangier Island, with a plan of the Barracks, &c erected upon it by the 3d. Battalion of Regular & Colonial Marines," from the papers of Vice Admiral Sir Alexander F. I. Cochrane, 1814.

Page 278, bottom: "Colonial Marines Drilling at Tangier Island in 1814," modern painting of Gerry Embleton.

Page 307: "First View of the Battle of Patapsco Neck," engraving by Andrew Duluc, 1814.

Page 316: "View of the Capitol of the United States after the Conflagration," engraving by Jesse Torrey, 1817.

Page 341: "A View of the Town of St. George, Bermuda," aquatint by I. J. C. Stadler, 1815.

Page 344: "Philanthropie Moderne," cartoon by a French pro-slavery artist, 1830s.

Page 350: "Gabriel Hall," photograph by George H. Craig, 1892.

Page 365: "Halifax, from Dartmouth Point," acquatint by G. I. Parkyns, 1817.

Page 388: "Horrid Massacre in Virginia," woodcut by unknown Virginian, 1831.

Page 414: "The Noble Virginians Going to Battle," engraving by William Hillhouse, 1820.

Page 418: "George R. Roberts," anonymous photograph, undated.

THE INTERNAL ENEMY

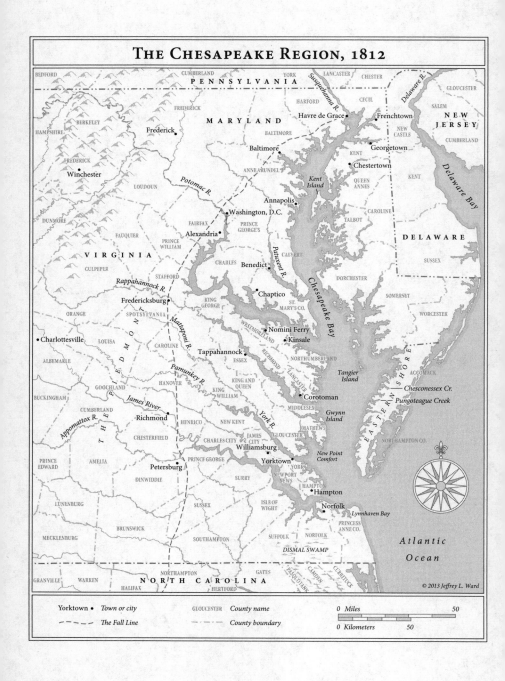

THE CHESAPEAKE REGION, 1812

BEDFORD

CUMBERLAND
YORK LANCASTER CHESTER
PENNSYLVANIA

HARFORD CECIL

GLOUCESTER

SALEM

MARYLAND Havre de Grace• •Frenchtown **NEW JERSEY**

FREDERICK

BERKELEY

HAMPSHIRE

Frederick•

BALTIMORE

NEW CASTLE

CUMBERLAND

FREDERICK

Winchester

LOUDOUN

Baltimore•

ANNE ARUNDEL

Georgetown
•Chestertown

KENT

Kent Island

QUEEN ANNES

KENT

Delaware Bay

Potomac R.

Annapolis•

CAROLINE

DUNMORE

FAIRFAX

Washington, D.C.•

PRINCE GEORGE'S

TALBOT

DELAWARE

FAUQUIER

PRINCE WILLIAM

Alexandria•

VIRGINIA

CULPEPER

CHARLES

Benedict•

CALVERT

Patuxent R.

DORCHESTER

SUSSEX

SOMERSET

Rappahannock R.

STAFFORD

ORANGE

Fredericksburg•

KING GEORGE

Chaptico•

ST. MARY'S CO.

Chesapeake Bay

WORCESTER

SPOTSYLVANIA

Mattaponi R.

WESTMORELAND

Nomini Ferry•

•Charlottesville

LOUISA

CAROLINE

Tappahannock•

•Kinsale

ALBEMARLE

ESSEX

Pamunkey R.

RICHMOND

NORTHUMBERLAND

LANCASTER

Tangier Island

ACCOMACK

Chesconessex Cr.

Pungoteague Creek

BUCKINGHAM

GOOCHLAND

HANOVER

KING AND QUEEN

James River

KING WILLIAM

•Corotoman

MIDDLESEX

EASTERN SHORE

Appomattox R.

Richmond•

HENRICO

NEW KENT

York R.

Gwynn Island

NORTHAMPTON CO.

CUMBERLAND

CHESTERFIELD

CHARLES CITY

JAMES CITY

GLOUCESTER

MATHEWS

PRINCE EDWARD

AMELIA

Petersburg•

PRINCE GEORGE

Williamsburg•

Yorktown•

YORK

New Point Comfort

DINWIDDIE

SURRY

NEWPORT NEWS

LUNENBURG

SUSSEX

ISLE OF WIGHT

HAMPTON

•Hampton

BRUNSWICK

SOUTHAMPTON

SUFFOLK

NORFOLK

Norfolk•

Lynnhaven Bay

PRINCESS ANNE CO.

Atlantic Ocean

MECKLENBURG

NORTHAMPTON

DISMAL SWAMP

GRANVILLE

WARREN

HALIFAX

NORTH CAROLINA

GATES

HERTFORD

CAMDEN

CURRITUCK

PASQUOTANK

Yorktown • *Town or city*

- - - *The Fall Line*

GLOUCESTER *County name*

········ *County boundary*

0 Miles 50

0 Kilometers 50

INTRODUCTION

Unfortunately, we have two enemies to contend with—the one
open & declared; the other nurtured in our very Bosoms!
Sly, secret & insidious: in our families, at our Elbows, listening with
eager attention; and sedulously marking all that is going forward.
—ROBERT GREENHOW, MAYOR OF RICHMOND, 1813[1]

O ne night in October 1814, on the Virginia shore of the Potomac
River, several young enslaved men stole a canoe and paddled
across the river to Laidloes Ferry on the Maryland shore. Abandoning the canoe, they took the larger ferry boat, for they needed a craft
big enough to carry away seventeen people. Returning to the Virginia shore, the men retrieved wives and children for a dash down
the river to seek a British warship as their portal to freedom. In the
morning, their masters discovered that the slaves were gone and, in
the words of one witness, "had taken many articles out of Mr. [Abra-
ham] Hooe's dwelling house in the course of the Night [and] all their
own articles & effects out of their houses." Armed white men rowed
a swift boat in pursuit down the river, but in vain, for the slaves had
reached the warship.[2]

During the War of 1812, Royal Navy warships pushed into
Chesapeake Bay and up the Potomac River to punish the United
States for declaring war against the British Empire. The Royal Navy
attacked the region as the home of the national capital, a heartland of

economic resources, and, in the case of Virginia, a hotbed of pro-war sentiment. The naval raids created an opportunity for the enslaved to escape and become free. Hundreds enlisted in the British service as sailors and marines or served as laundresses and nurses.

The ferry-boat escape aptly represented slave flight to the British during the War of 1812. First, this escape exposed the links of kin and friendship that constructed African American communities across several farms in a broad neighborhood, for the seventeen runaways had belonged to four different men, led by Abraham B. Hooe, who lost eleven slaves that night. Second, the runaways were especially valuable slaves: able, young, and skilled as artisans or house servants. Assessed at nearly $8,000 in total, the seventeen included two blacksmiths, two carpenters, a weaver, and two cooks. Third, most of these fugitives were young men, aged eighteen to thirty-five, with only one over that age, but the group also included two young women and three children. Indeed, the war enabled many enslaved families in the Tidewater to flee together. Fourth, this escape demonstrated careful planning and coordination as young men assembled kin and property and procured a craft big enough for all. They were far savvier than their masters had imagined.[3]

Five and a half years later, the leader of the escape wrote a letter to his former master, Hooe. In October 1814, Bartlet Shanklyn had been a prized blacksmith, thirty-five years old and worth $800: the most valuable of the runaways. In May 1820 he was thriving as a free man in Preston, a black township near Halifax in Nova Scotia, and he wanted Hooe to know it:

> Sir, I take this opportunity of writing these lines to inform you how I am situated hear. I have [a] Shop & Set of Tools of my own and am doing very well when I was with you [you] treated me very ill and for that reason i take the liberty of informing you that i am doing as well as you if not beter. When i was with you I

worked very hard and you neither g[ave] me money nor any satisfaction but sin[ce] I have been hear I am able to make Gold and
Silver as well as you. The night that Cokely Stoped me he was
very Strong but I showed him that subtilty Was far preferable to
strength and brought away others with me who thank God are
all doing well. So I Remain, Bartlet Shanklyn

 P.S. My love to all my friends. I hope they are doing well

As a free man, Shanklyn could, at last, make his own money. Virginia
slaves were third- and fourth-generation Americans who knew the
social value of a dollar as the measure of a man's merit. Indeed, the
runaway had become a better man than the master who had treated
him so "very ill" by keeping him down, for Shanklyn's prosperity did
not rely on enslaving others. "Cokely" was apparently a powerful
man, perhaps an overseer, who tried to restrain Shanklyn on the eve
of the escape, but the clever blacksmith had outwitted the foe to lead
family and friends to freedom. Slavery had taught the value and the
ways of "subtilty" to the enslaved, who had to mask their knowledge
and resistance. Rather than destroy the rebuking letter, Hooe showed
more greed than pride by submitting it as evidence in a bid for postwar compensation from the federal government. Hooe's choice preserved Shanklyn's words for future readers.[4]

 About 3,400 slaves fled from Maryland and Virginia to British ships
during the War of 1812. After the War of 1812, most of the refugees
resettled in Nova Scotia, New Brunswick, and Trinidad, while a few
scattered throughout the global British Empire. In their new communities, the refugees confronted discrimination, but they achieved far
more autonomy and material success than they had known as slaves in
the Chesapeake. In contrast to the earlier runaways of the revolution,
the War of 1812 fugitives have received little attention from historians.
Consequently, distortions persist, including the popular canard that the
British resold the runaways into a worse slavery in the West Indies.[5]

Fortunately, the experiences of the runaways are richly documented, especially in the postwar files submitted by their former masters seeking compensation. The files include depositions describing dramatic escapes, affidavits reconstituting slave families, and even a few postwar letters from runaways to relatives and former masters. By drawing on those largely untapped sources, this book examines the causes, course, and consequences of the flight by slaves to join and help the British. While focusing on the war years of 1812–1815, *The Internal Enemy* situates that conflict in a longer history of slavery and freedom in Virginia, the early republic's largest and most powerful state. Rather than offer a conventional military history of the Chesapeake campaigns, which other historians have already done, this book taps the unusually rich documents generated by war to reveal the social complexities of slavery in Virginia from the American Revolution through Nat Turner's revolt in 1831.

The fugitives demonstrated an initiative that transformed the War of 1812 in the Chesapeake. At the start of the conflict, the British sought only a few black men to serve as pilots and guides and balked at a larger flight that included women and children. During 1813, however, six hundred runaways stole boats and canoes to press themselves on the British, straining the capacity of the naval officers to feed the fugitives as well as their own crews. The officers gradually recognized that the refugees offered solutions to two key problems: a shortage of manpower and a lack of local knowledge. By welcoming the runaways, the British could strengthen their force with men and women who had a keen understanding of local waterways and paths.

Impressed by the numbers and zeal of the runaways, the British admirals persuaded their government to authorize a more aggressive war meant to disrupt the plantation economy. During 1814, the British shifted their strategy in favor of encouraging mass escapes, including women and children, for few enslaved men would come away without their families. The British enlisted 400 male runaways into a special battalion known as the Colonial Marines. These men became the best troops in the British force, for, unlike white men, they would not (indeed, could not) desert to enjoy freedom in the republic. Instead, the black marines had to fight to preserve their new liberty.

After taking in the runaways, the British became adept at nocturnal raids that frustrated the defenders of Virginia and Maryland during 1814. Masters dominated slaves by day, but slaves enjoyed more freedom at night. Familiar with paths through the woods, the enslaved could defy masters to gather for worship or to steal pigs and sheep for covert barbecues. While their masters and overseers slept, slaves also roamed to seek frolics, wives, and food. In the process, they sustained their own communities, which linked several farms owned by different masters. The runaways carried their networks and nocturnal expertise to the British, enhancing their capacity to wage war in the Chesapeake.

Strengthened by the runaways, the British could raid deeper into the countryside to procure the fresh provisions, especially livestock, desperately needed to feed the refugees and crews on board the increasingly crowded warships. The raids also allowed the black marines to plunder their former masters and retrieve family members. By bottling up trade while looting and burning farms and plantations, the attacks wrecked the Chesapeake economy. After exhausting militia resistance southeast of Washington, D.C., the British and the Colonial Marines could seize the national capital in August 1814, when they burned the White House and the Capitol.

The British commanders gloried in the intimidating power of their black recruits. In the Chesapeake region, the Colonial Marines played the part of forest fighters in a manner that resembled the Indian allies deployed by the British along the frontiers of the republic. Armed blacks and Indians haunted the overactive imaginations of the Americans, who dreaded darker-skinned peoples as ruthless savages. Rear Admiral Sir George Cockburn boasted that the Virginians "expect

Blacky will have no mercy on them, and they know that he understands bush fighting and the locality of the *woods* as well as themselves and can perhaps play at hide and seek in them even better."[6]

In 1814 at Corotoman Plantation in Lancaster County, British
raiders liberated sixty-nine slaves: the largest wartime loss by any
estate in the Chesapeake. Corotoman's owners included St. George
Tucker, who had played a leading role in defining freedom while preserving slavery in Virginia in the wake of the revolution. In 1796, he
drafted a famous plan for the very gradual emancipation of Virginia's
slaves. When the state legislature abruptly rejected the proposal, a
wounded Tucker retreated to a pro-slavery position and supported
the efforts by his son-in-law, Joseph C. Cabell, to compel harder
work from the Corotoman slaves and to sell the surplus. Cabell's
new regime angered the slaves, provoked stiff resistance, and culminated in their escape in April 1814.

In Virginia, the revolution had produced a tragic contradiction
by promoting greater equality for white men while weakening the
security of black families. The celebrated abolition of primogeniture
and entail increased the property rights of younger heirs. As Thomas
Jefferson intended, the new inheritance laws promoted, through the
divided transmission of property, the reduction of the largest estates
in Virginia in favor of a broader middle class of white men. But the
division of estates often separated enslaved wives from their husbands and both from their children. By diffusing slave ownership,
the new laws also broadened public support for slavery. As a consequence, emancipation efforts faltered in Virginia during the late
1780s, and they vanished a decade later, with Tucker's rejected plan
as an epitaph.

During the War of 1812, British warships gave hundreds of
slaves a precious new opportunity to reunite their families by fleeing
together. Because they longed to escape in kinship groups, the runaways rarely came from the distant interior. Instead, they fled from
the Tidewater farms along navigable waterways and within sight and

sound of the British warships. They escaped from a Virginia society that had been reshaped to their detriment by the American Revolution, so they turned to the British enemies of that revolution. After 1800, the British gained greater appeal as liberators by their efforts to suppress the oceanic slave trade, ameliorate slavery in the West Indies, and protect the new black republic of Haiti. By organizing regiments of black soldiers in the West Indies, the British also set a precedent for the Colonial Marines. Because slavery persisted in the British West Indies, the British were far from consistent liberators, but they had a better record on that score than did the Virginians. And as the enemies of the slaves' enemies in the War of 1812, the British became their friends.[7]

During the early nineteenth century, Virginians thought of blacks in two radically different ways. On the one hand, masters often felt secure with, and even protective of, particular slaves well known to them. But when thinking of all slaves collectively, the Virginians imagined a dreaded "internal enemy" who might, at any moment, rebel in a midnight massacre to butcher white men, women, and children in their beds. Virginians dwelled on lurid reports of massacres associated with the massive slave revolt in Saint-Domingue, a French West Indian colony that became the republic of Haiti in 1804. Virginians had not yet adopted the consoling myth, of the mid-nineteenth century, that their slaves were weak, happy, and docile.[8]

Prior to the War of 1812, Virginians frankly acknowledged that their exploitation and domination had bred an internal enemy who longed for freedom. In a long career as a politician, John Randolph heard many celebrated orators, including Henry Clay, Patrick Henry, and, of course, himself, but he assured a friend, "The greatest orator I ever heard . . . was a woman. She was a slave. She was a mother and her rostrum was the auction block." According to that friend, Randolph "then rose and imitated with thrilling pathos the tones with which this woman had appealed to the sympathy and justice of the bystanders, and finally the indignation with which she

denounced them." Randolph concluded, "There was eloquence! . . .
I have heard no *man* speak like that. It was overpowering!"

Her eloquence may have moved Randolph, but it did nothing
to stop her sale and separation from her children. If more honest
than the later sentimental defense of slavery, the trope of the internal enemy proved nearly as effective at preserving the slave system. Immediately after recalling the slave mother's vivid eloquence,
Randolph collected himself to launch a fiery defense of slavery:
"The question of slavery, as it is called, is to us a question of life
and death. . . . You will find no instance in history where two distinct races have occupied the soil except in the relation of master
and slave." Although sensitive to the evils of slavery, Randolph ultimately insisted that his race must triumph in an ongoing war against
the black enemy within. Most Virginians dared not emancipate
because they dreaded free blacks as even more menacing because less
supervised than slaves.[9]

Virginians argued that they could remain free only by keeping
blacks enslaved. If freed by the thousands, surely the emancipated
would try to destroy their former masters. Patrick Henry asserted,
"Our country will be peopled. The question is, shall it be with Europeans or with Africans." Colonel John Taylor feared that freedom
for blacks within Virginia would pit "two nations of distinct colours
and features on the same theatre to contend . . . for wealth and
power" until one crushed the other. Thomas Jefferson agreed that
the races were perpetual enemies who could never coexist in freedom
but instead would wage a brutal war, culminating in "the extermination of the one or the other race." Abandoning his usual optimism
about human progress, Jefferson denied that different races could
learn to live together as equals. He dreamed of gradually emancipating Virginia's slaves over two generations, but only if they could be
deported across the Atlantic as colonists in Africa.[10]

Mass deportation of freed slaves, however, was prohibitively expensive and economically ruinous for Virginia, so the Virginians felt stuck with their profitable but dangerous internal enemy. Jefferson famously declared of slavery, "We have the wolf by the ears, and we can neither hold him, nor safely let him go." Virginians had become trapped in a system of beliefs and behavior where neither their material interest nor their cultural convictions would permit them to escape from a terrible fear. Allowing themselves no way out, Virginians wove a cocoon of dread that became even more claustrophobic when the British threatened to make a common cause with the enslaved during the War of 1812.[11]

The pervasive dread ignored the considerable evidence that black people wanted equality and opportunity rather than revenge. When free, they offered to defend the state and nation that distrusted them so much. The Philadelphia journalist William Duane corrected his friend Jefferson, who had miscast blacks as alien and perpetual enemies. On the contrary, Duane reported, "The American born blacks, even in the Southern states where slavery is yet suffered, feel a sentiment of patriotism and attachment to the U.S. Those who doubt it know very little of human nature, and the force of habit on the human mind." Blacks wanted to be American citizens rather than to murder them.[12]

The war soured many Virginians on the Union because the national government did precious little to defend them and to prevent their slaves from escaping. After the war, Virginia's leaders cultivated a staunch states' rights position that informed their militant response to the Missouri crisis of 1819–1820. When northern congressmen proposed to restrict the western expansion of slavery, angry Virginians expressed a visceral dread of being trapped in a region with a restive black majority. They insisted that their own safety and prosperity required diffusing the threat of their internal enemy through the sale and migration of slaves westward. That insistence fed on their recent wartime experience with hundreds of runaways who had returned as British marines to attack their former masters. The war gave some substance to their long-standing fear of the internal enemy, and that southern fear put the Union in peril.

But the Union would not collapse until 1861, in part because the War of 1812 also generated a brand of racialized nationalism that could serve the South's interests. In newspapers and pamphlets, American writers demonized the British as race traitors who allied with savage Indians on the frontier and fomented bloody slave uprisings in the South. By arming and encouraging the supposedly barbaric red and black peoples, the British betrayed the white Americans, who claimed a unique capacity to enjoy freedom and sustain a republic. Fearing a persistent coalition of Indians, slave rebels, and British manipulators, the Americans pursued a more aggressive postwar expansion westward. They justified that expansion as essential to defend the republic from containment and subversion. So long as the conquests and cessions opened new lands to settlement by masters and their slaves, southern leaders could support the Union, even as they watched it more jealously for signs of being turned against them, for if they ever lost national power, Virginians dreaded a massive uprising by the internal enemy of their nightmares.[13]

1

REVOLUTION

*Whilst America hath been the land of promise to
Europeans and their descendants, it hath been the
vale of death to millions of the wretched sons of Africa.*
—St. George Tucker, 1796[1]

IN July 1774, on the island of Bermuda, Colonel Henry Tucker
wrote to his son, St. George Tucker, a law student in Virginia. A
leading merchant, the elder Tucker sympathized with the American
Patriots, who resisted new British taxes levied by Parliament without
the consent of elected colonial legislatures. Tucker assured his son, "I
think the Collonies ought to hazard every thing rather than to Submit to Slavery, . . . for if the Parliament of great Britain have a right
to dispose of the Americans' property as they please, call it by what
name you will there can be no greater marks of Slavery." The American Patriots sought to protect both liberty and property, which

Peter Francisco's Gallant Action with Nine of Tarleton's Cavalry, *engraving by D. Edwin,
1814. Widely circulated during the War of 1812, this engraving reminded Virginians of a
great hero of the revolution, a powerful blacksmith who single-handedly repelled a British
troop of mounted men. By depicting slaves cringing behind Francisco, the artist linked the
defense of liberty for white men to the preservation of slavery for blacks. During the War
of 1812, Francisco organized a special unit of older men, the "Silver Greys," dedicated
to patrolling Richmond to prevent a slave uprising. (Courtesy of the Virginia Historical
Society)*

they understood as interdependent. But the property of the colonists included thousands of people held as perpetual slaves deprived of their own liberty. In Virginia, a leading Patriot, Richard Henry Lee, staged a protest by parading his slaves around a courthouse while carrying banners that denounced Parliament's taxes as "chains of slavery." Masters like Lee and Tucker had a very weak sense of irony. Colonel Tucker might have seen greater marks of slavery had he looked at his own slaves.[2]

The tension between liberty and property became glaring in 1776, when the Patriots declared independence and sought to elevate their cause by embracing universal human rights. In Thomas Jefferson's celebrated preamble to the Declaration of Independence, Congress announced that "all men are created equal and endowed by their Creator with certain inalienable rights" including liberty. Similarly, Virginia's new state constitution announced "that all Men are born equally free and independent." Reconciling such sweeping promises with the practice of slavery would fall, in no small measure, to Colonel Tucker's son, St. George Tucker, who became a leading judge in Virginia thanks to the Revolution.[3]

Virginia

In 1771 Tucker had left home in Bermuda, at the age of nineteen, to attend the College of William and Mary in Williamsburg, then the capital of the royal colony of Virginia. Gregarious, bright, handsome, and clever, young Tucker readily made friends and shrewdly cultivated patrons among the Virginia elite: the proud gentlemen who governed the colony because they owned thousands of acres and scores of slaves. Tucker also impressed George Wythe, the learned lawyer and great moralist who opposed slavery and taught law at the college. As a young man, Tucker sought to navigate between the allure of power as a Virginia gentleman, on the one hand, and the appeal of Wythe's self-denying principles, on the other.[4]

Williamsburg lay in Virginia's longest-settled region, the Tidewater. Founded during the seventeenth century by English colonists, the Tidewater counties stretched around Chesapeake Bay: a vast estuary replenished by the many rivers of a humid climate. The bay extended about two hundred miles from south to north. On the western shore, the navigable Appomattox, James, York, Rappahannock, and Potomac Rivers formed low-lying peninsulas thrusting into the bay. The narrower Eastern Shore had shorter, smaller rivers on a long peninsula pinched between the Atlantic Ocean to the east and Chesapeake Bay to the west.[5]

The long, hot summers featured sudden and dramatic shifts in temperature and humidity, for Virginia lay at the volatile intersection of warm, moist air from the south and the colder, drier winds from the west and north. A thick haze usually covered the summer sky so that, a visitor noted, when the sun rose, "its disk was amplified & the whole sky, as it were, suddenly burst into a sheet of flame." During prolonged midsummer droughts, that fierce sun scorched the fields. Then a sudden thunderstorm might smash the plants with gales of wind and hail while filling the streams and rivers with torrents of rain, sweeping away riverside mills and crops. Thunderous and flashing with lightning, the storms terrified. Colonel Thomas Jefferson Randolph (Thomas Jefferson's grandson) owned thousands of acres and scores of slaves but dreaded any approaching thunderstorm. A slave recalled that Randolph would bellow, "Bring in the niggers!" and order them to crowd around him until the storm passed. The slaves "attributed it to his fear of God, on account of his sins."[6]

In 1775, Tidewater Virginia hosted only two significant towns: Williamsburg and Norfolk. While Williamsburg served as the colonial capital and home to 1,200 people, Norfolk provided the colony's lone major seaport. Located at the mouth of the Elizabeth River and near the ocean's entrance into Chesapeake Bay, Norfolk sustained 3,000 inhabitants and much of the colony's trans-Atlantic shipping. Although a vibrant place of business, Norfolk struck vis-

View of Norfolk from Town Point, *1798. In this watercolor, Benjamin Henry Latrobe, a British visitor and artist, depicts Virginia's leading port busy with shipping. (Courtesy of the Maryland Historical Society)*

Rippon Lodge, *Prince William County, 1796. Latrobe here depicts the home of Colonel Thomas Blackburn, a prosperous planter. (Courtesy of the Maryland Historical Society)*

itors as a swampy, hot, and humid sinkhole of ramshackle houses, narrow and muddy streets, and open, reeking sewage ditches. Annual outbreaks of malaria competed with frequent fires to afflict the town. White men owned the wharves, stores, and shops, but they slept fitfully owing to the hordes of mosquitoes and a dread of revolt by their slaves.[7]

The colonists exploited the long growing season (about 200 days) and the fertile soil to raise tobacco, which found a profitable market in Great Britain. They also benefited from the ready transportation offered by the sheltered bay and its web of navigable rivers. During the early eighteenth century, the wealthiest planters converted their profits into impressive mansions, often of brick, that loomed on bluffs beside the rivers. Their poorer white neighbors lived in log cabins with stone chimneys and wooden floors, while their slaves dwelled in log huts with stick-and-clay chimneys and earthen floors.[8]

By 1775, however, six generations of erosion and tobacco cropping had depleted the Tidewater soil, reducing harvests and curtailing profits. Unable to pay their debts to British merchants for imported tools and luxuries, the planters struggled to maintain grand appearances. Close inspection revealed, a visitor reported, "the shabbiness of their mansions," many with broken window panes stuffed with old newspapers. The common whites had even less to fall back on. A traveler described the Tidewater farms as "miserably poor. Here and there a hovel and the inhabitants of them look half starved."[9]

The Tidewater counties suffered by comparison to the newer, more vibrant settlements to the west, in the rolling hills of the Piedmont, where the well-drained soils sustained fewer mosquitoes, so the people suffered less from malaria. During the 1760s, the Tidewater population shrank as people moved west to exploit the fertility of newly cleared lands in the Piedmont, where the new farms and plantations tended to raise more wheat and corn and less tobacco, save in the southern portion, known as the Southside, between the James River to the north and the North Carolina boundary on the south.[10]

The marketing and milling of wheat promoted commercial towns along the Fall Line, where the Piedmont met the Tidewater. Millers tapped the waterpower in the rapids, and they loaded boats with barrels of flour bound downstream to the trans-Atlantic ships based at Norfolk. The new towns included Petersburg on the Appomattox; Richmond on the James; Fredericksburg on the Rappahannock; and Alexandria on the Potomac. Each developed a paved main street and a central square surrounded by the elegant brick townhouses built for leading merchants and lawyers. But the rough fringes of town featured muddy lanes, wooden shacks, dance halls, and many taverns, which hosted cockfights and bearbaiting. During the 1780s, Richmond became the center for Virginia's political, banking, publishing, and legal establishments. While the Tidewater represented Virginia's colonial past, the Piedmont anticipated the republican and commercial future.[11]

Beyond a few market towns, Virginia remained thoroughly rural and agricultural. The colony had dozens of counties, each with a court of local notables, who conducted local government, supervised the churches, regulated commerce, and administered justice. Every county had a small village where a cluster of shops and taverns surrounded a courthouse. Business surged once a month when circuit-riding lawyers and judges arrived to adjudicate disputes and try criminals. Court sessions drew curious crowds of rustic folk to gape, trade, gossip, drink, race horses, and wrestle. Their farms and plantations lay in the broad and woody countryside beyond the courthouse village. A visitor reported, "Now & then a solitary farm house was to be seen, a narrow wood building, two stories high, with gable ends & a small portico over the central door. A cluster of small, miserable negro huts, a canoe & a brood of little negroes paddling in the mud completed the landscape." Most of the houses were new, small, and hastily built of logs or planks. "It is impossible to devise things more ugly, uncomfortable, and happily more perishable," Thomas Jefferson declared. Zigzag fences of wooden rails surrounded the fields, while cattle and pigs roamed freely in the surrounding forest.[12]

People and goods moved more easily along the rivers and the bay than over land. The roads lacked signs, and the locals often proved misinformed about the best way out, so travelers got mired and lost along the muddy roads. Bridges were few and the ferries unreliable and unsafe. The bad roads discouraged foot traffic and carriages, so free people usually traveled on horseback. During a journey of 566 miles across Virginia, one traveler saw a single stagecoach and a lone carriage on the road. One weary traveler insisted that Virginia had "the very worst Roads in the U.S."[13]

The outside world of events, ideas, and news seemed distant, late, and elusive for the gentlemen who lived or sojourned in rural Virginia. In Amelia County in the Piedmont, Benjamin Henry Latrobe reported, "I felt myself almost out of the World. I found it impossible to get a letter to Richmond though only 32 Miles distant. Our latest Newspapers were a fortnight old." John Randolph lamented, "After you have read your old books (if you have them to read), you can get no new ones." But few common Virginians complained, for most wanted to be left alone by the outside world. While they welcomed visitors with warm and generous hospitality, the rural Virginians distrusted political decisions made beyond their own county. They could barely tolerate their own elected state legislature, and they dreaded the centralizing power of any government beyond Virginia.[14]

Somerset

In 1774 a crisis in the British Empire closed the courts of Virginia and threatened St. George Tucker's prospects as a new lawyer. During the 1760s and early 1770s, Parliament imposed new taxes and regulations which alarmed planters already struggling to pay their debts owed to British merchants. Jefferson complained that debts "had become hereditary from father to son for many generations, so that planters were a species of property annexed to certain mercantile houses in London." Jefferson had inherited such a debt incurred by his father-in-law, John Wayles, to buy slaves from a British firm. With hyperbole but sincerity, planters argued that they faced impending "slavery" from imperial taxes and mounting debts. George Washington insisted that the British meant to "make us as tame and abject slaves as the blacks we rule over with such arbitrary sway." Living among slaves, planters dreaded lapsing into dependency on a powerful and distant empire.[15]

While defending their liberty, the masters also fought to preserve the slavery of two-fifths of Virginia's population. Initially imported from Africa, the slave numbers had surged during the first half of the eighteenth century. Thereafter, natural increase by enslaved families sufficed to fill the demand in Virginia for their labor. By 1765, nine-tenths of the slaves had been born in Virginia. The planters' sense of a slave surplus grew as many diversified their crops, shifting from a reliance on tobacco, a labor-intensive crop, to more wheat and corn, which required fewer workers. By the 1760s, Virginia's leaders worried that they had more than enough slaves for the economy and too many for their security from revolt. To discourage more slave imports, the colony's legislature levied a heavy tax, but the imperial government vetoed it in defense of the interests of British traders. The imperial veto enabled the Virginians to claim a moral high ground and to feel threatened by British rule.[16]

That moral high ground proved slippery in 1772, when the highest court in Britain issued an antislavery ruling in the celebrated case of *Somerset v. Stuart*. Charles Stuart had brought a Virginia slave, James Somerset, to England. When Stuart tried to send Somerset away to Jamaica, the slave sued for his freedom with the support of an abolitionist attorney, who argued that colonial slaves became free when brought to England. The chief justice, Lord Mansfield,

ruled that, indeed, slavery had no just basis in either "natural law" or
the English common law, so it required a "positive law" passed by
Parliament to legitimate the system in England. For want of such a
law, Mansfield ruled that Stuart could not force Somerset to leave the
mother country for renewed slavery in a colony. During the same
year, Parliament considered but rejected a proposed statute to allow
slavery in England. Although technically narrow, Mansfield's ruling
became broadly interpreted as upholding Sir William Blackstone's
celebrated legal maxim that any slave became free upon setting foot
in England, deemed the great land of liberty.[17]

Widely reported in the American press, Mansfield's *Somerset*
ruling caused a sensation in the colonies. Although the ruling did
not apply there, colonial masters felt shocked by the implication
that their property system defied English traditions of liberty. Preferring to think of themselves as champions of liberty against British tyranny, Americans hated being cast instead as barbaric for their
colonial practice of un-English slavery. Indeed, British imperialists
derided their colonial critics as canting hypocrites who preached
liberty while practicing slavery. Ambrose Serle declaimed, "Such
men are no Enemies to absolute Rule: they only hate it in others,
but ardently pursue it for themselves." The *Somerset* ruling seemed
especially ominous for the colonists, given Parliament's controversial claim to hold legislative supremacy over the colonies. Virginia's
leaders feared that Parliament might eventually legislate against slavery in America.[18]

Some slaves sought to exploit the new loophole in the slave system. In 1773, a master advertised in the *Virginia Gazette* for the
recapture of a runaway slave couple. The master predicted that the
runaways would seek a ship for England "where they imagine they
will be free (a Notion now prevalent among the Negroes greatly to
the vexation and prejudice of their Masters)." As the slaves became
more restive, masters asked if they could preserve their property and
their lives if they remained ruled by an empire so indifferent to their

interests. When confronted by any sign of slave discontent, Virginians anticipated a ripening into bloody rebellion. Their terror grew as they read news of bloody uprisings in some of the British West Indies during the fateful year of 1772.[19]

The *Somerset* ruling also coincided with another imperial veto of Virginia's latest attempt to discourage further slave imports. That combination angered the colony's leaders, who feared being trapped with a growing surplus of slaves newly inclined to think of themselves as properly free. The empire seemed implicitly to stir up the discontent of slaves and to prevent Virginia from restricting the threatening growth of their numbers. Denouncing the British policy as hypocritical and menacing, Jefferson indicted the king for "exciting those very people to rise in arms among us, and to purchase that liberty of which he has deprived them, by murdering the people on whom he also obtruded them; thus paying off former crimes committed against the LIBERTIES of one people with crimes which he urges them to commit against the LIVES of another." Jefferson blamed the British for imposing on the colonies a slave system that afflicted the slaves and endangered their masters. Virginia's leaders interpreted the imperial taxes through the ominous prism of the *Somerset* ruling, the imperial vetoes, and the slave unrest in the West Indies. The traditional history of the American Revolution emphasizes the role of Massachusetts in resisting the British taxes, but Virginia proved equally important to the Patriot coalition.[20]

Virginians anticipated an invasion by British troops to enforce imperial control by recruiting slaves with the promise of freedom. In late 1774, James Madison, then a young Patriot, reported the discovery of a slave plot to welcome and assist British troops. "It is prudent such things should be concealed as well as suppressed," Madison confided in a private letter, for Virginians dreaded that any publicity given to a slave plot would spread the danger by emboldening other slaves to revolt. White men felt torn between the urge to announce their peril and their need to hide it. In June

1775, Madison warned a friend to beware of British efforts to foment a slave revolt: "To say the truth that is the only part in which this Colony is vulnerable . . . we shall fall like Achilles by the hand of one that knows that secret."[21]

Secret

Lord Dunmore knew that secret of the internal enemy. In 1772, as the colony's royal governor, Dunmore alerted his superiors that Virginians, "with great reason, trembled" because their slaves were "ready to join the first that would encourage them to revenge themselves, by which means a conquest of this Country would inevitably be effected in a very Short time." Initially, he balked at arming and emancipating the slaves because they were essential to Virginia's economy, and the British wanted to retain, rather than ruin, the colony. Dunmore hoped to intimidate the planters by merely threatening to arm and emancipate. His bluster became ominous on April 21, 1775, when his troops seized the public gunpowder supply in Williamsburg for removal to a British warship. Without that gunpowder, the planters feared they would lack the firepower to suppress a slave revolt, which rumors insisted was imminent. Galvanized by the seizure, Piedmont Patriots led by Patrick Henry took up arms and marched on Williamsburg to confront the governor, who escaped their wrath by fleeing to a British warship in June. By then in Philadelphia the Continental Congress of delegates from the colonies had taken charge of a conflict that had erupted at Lexington and Concord in Massachusetts in mid-April. Outraged by Dunmore's conduct, the Virginia delegates joined the New Englanders in urging a vigorous war to oust the British troops from the colonies.[22]

By calling Dunmore's bluff, the Patriot coup in Williamsburg forced him to convert his bluster into black soldiers. In early November 1775, his proclamation offered freedom to slaves and indentured servants who would help him suppress the Patriot rebellion. Rather than a blanket offer of emancipation to all, he promised freedom only to young men who would bear arms against the rebels. Instead of intimidating the Virginians into submission, however, his proclamation united almost all of the shocked whites as Patriots determined to win independence from British rule.[23]

By early 1776, about 800 enslaved men, and an equal number of women and children, flocked to Dunmore's encampments and ships. If Dunmore wanted men as soldiers, he also had to receive their families, although feeding and sheltering them all strained his resources. Dunmore organized the men into a special unit, the "Ethiopian Regiment," commanded by white officers, for he was no racial egalitarian. But American slaves sought to make him one, spreading far and wide his renown as a supposed liberator. In Pennsylvania, a master posted an advertisement seeking the return of a runaway: "As Negroes in general think that Lord Dunmore is contending for their liberty it is not improbable that said Negroe is on his march to join his Lordship's own black regiment."[24]

Slaves nurtured a wishful legend that the British king was their benevolent protector. As with peasant and enslaved peoples elsewhere, they had long believed that the monarch truly loved the lowly laborers. In Virginia in 1730, slaves insisted that the king had ordered freed all slaves who had become Christians but that their masters had defied their monarch by ignoring his order. Some restive slaves prepared to revolt, but the Virginians suppressed that plot by executing four leaders. In 1775 in South Carolina, slaves spread a similar rumor that the king "was about to alter the World and set the Negroes Free." This tradition of the liberator king prepared southern slaves to fight for the British and against their masters during the revolution.[25]

In Virginia, most of the runaways came from the Tidewater counties closest to Dunmore's ships and bases in the lower reaches of Chesapeake Bay. They escaped from riverside farms and plantations in canoes and boats stolen from their masters. Few ran the longer, overland gauntlet from the Virginia hinterland. Fearful of armed patrols and militia detachments, the interior slaves recognized, in the words of a Virginia newspaper, "the difficulty of effecting their escape, and what they must expect to suffer if they fall into the hands of the Americans." But that did not stop them from dreaming of freedom. On the upper Potomac River, far to the north of Dunmore's ships, George Washington's farm manager reported that among the slaves "there is not a man of them, but would leave us, if they believ'd they coud make their escape."[26]

Unwilling to accept that the escapes indicted their conduct and the slave system, the Virginians concocted their own wishful legend: that the British lured away the slaves only to resell them in the West Indies, where most would suffer conditions far worse than in Virginia. If the British were frauds instead of liberators, the slaves should cling to their masters as protectors rather than flee from them as exploiters. In speeches to their gathered slaves, masters warned of their West Indian peril and invited a renewed commitment to their servitude in Virginia. According to Robert Carter, his slaves dutifully answered, "We all fully intend to serve you our master and we do now promise to use our whole might & force to execute your Commands." But at least thirty of Carter's slaves ran away during the war. And there is scant evidence for the British selling any Virginia runaways into renewed slavery elsewhere.[27]

To discourage escapes, Virginians made examples of some captured runaways by giving them brutal public floggings, often accompanied by lopping off an ear. The authorities also hanged runaways caught bearing arms for the enemy. Their severed and rotting heads sat atop posts placed at crossroads as a warning to passing slaves. Other intercepted runaways died of disease in wretched jail cells while awaiting trial. Dunmore did not sell any runaways to the West Indies, but the vengeful Patriots did as punishment. Others they sentenced to a short life of hard labor in the mines of Fincastle County, where the prisoners dug the lead that became bullets for the Patriots to fire at Dunmore's men.[28]

The masters also threatened collective punishment on slave families for the decisions of their young men. In November 1775, the *Virginia Gazette* published an unprecedented appeal to Virginia's blacks, who previously had been excluded from any political decision. The essay warned them not "to provoke the fury of the Americans against their defenceless fathers and mothers, their wives, their women and children." The author recognized that few slaves would forsake their families. Historian Cassandra Pybus notes that runaways usually fled in "a series of premeditated and well-organized escapes by interconnected family groups"—as they would do again in the next war. Where families could not get out together, only a few especially desperate young men tried to escape to the British ships.[29]

Patriot propaganda depicted Dunmore as promoting a bloody and indiscriminate massacre of white people by slave rebels. In fact, he wanted only to weaken the Patriots and strengthen his own force with black troops. Indeed, his superiors in London had prohibited any promotion of a slave insurrection, lest it ruin the economy of a colony that they hoped to recover. And a slave revolt in Virginia would set a very ominous precedent for the British West Indies, which were especially valuable and dependent on slavery. To keep the West Indian colonies productive and loyal, the British played a restrained game with the slaves of Virginia. While welcoming and arming runaways, the British discouraged them from killing whites except as soldiers on the field of battle.[30]

Dunmore's military ineptitude soon undermined his credibility as a liberator. In December 1775, just a month after issuing his proclamation, he rushed his raw recruits into a premature battle. Attacking the Patriot militia posted south of Norfolk at Great Bridge, Dunmore's men suffered a crushing defeat. In a panic, Dunmore fled to his ships, evacuating Norfolk. He set up a new base on Gwynn Island at the mouth of the Piankatank River, where most of his refugees succumbed to an epidemic of smallpox, for Dunmore had neglected to inoculate his recruits. Abandoning his botched campaign in August 1776, he sailed away to the British headquarters at New York City, recently captured from the Patriots. He withdrew about 500 blacks, leaving behind another 1,000 who were dead or dying. Their fate provided great fodder for Patriot propaganda, which cast the British as duplicitous seducers of foolish slaves. Many of the ailing, however, died gruesomely when the vindictive Patriots set fire to their flimsy brush huts, ostensibly to stop the spread of their smallpox.[31]

Despite Dunmore's failure, Virginia slaves continued to seek freedom by fleeing to the British troops who returned to the Chesapeake in 1779–1781. Some runaways formed irregular armed gangs employed by the British to raid farms and plantations. In August 1781, a Patriot colonel on the Eastern Shore complained, "We have had most alarming times this Summer, all along shore, from a sett of Barges manned mostly by our own negroes who have run off."[32]

During the spring and summer of 1781, Lord Cornwallis led a British army up the James River to occupy and plunder Richmond. Cornwallis's army attracted 4,500 runaways, including twenty-three from Jefferson's estates, sixteen from George Washington's Mount Vernon, and some from St. George Tucker's Matoax Plantation. These runaways regarded the Patriot leaders as the enemies of their freedom.[33]

In September 1781, Washington marched his Patriot army south from New York to join a French fleet in trapping Cornwallis and his army at Yorktown. Running short on food, Cornwallis abandoned hundreds of refugees, many of them afflicted with disease and hunger. A Patriot officer saw "numbers in that condition starving and helpless, begging of us as we passed them for God's sake to kill them, as they were in great pain and misery." Tucker reported, "An immense number of Negroes have died in the most miserable Manner in York[town]." After the war, a British traveler visited the banks of the Elizabeth River, where he reported that "many Waggon loads of the bones of Men, women, and Children, stripped of the flesh by

Vultures and Hawks which abound here, covered the sand for a most considerable length."[34]

In October 1781, Cornwallis surrendered his army to Washington. That military disaster led the British government to negotiate a peace treaty that recognized American independence in early 1783. During the war, 6,000 Virginia slaves had fled to the British, but only about a third obtained their freedom by evacuation to the British colony of Nova Scotia. Another third died during the war, primarily of disease. The final third reverted to their masters after Cornwallis abandoned them. The British generals had fallen far short of the supposed promise made by the idealized king.[35]

Jefferson recovered six of his twenty-three runaways. One soon died, and Jefferson sold the others to punish their disloyalty and intimidate his other slaves. His friend James Madison proved less vindictive, freeing Billy, a recaptured runaway deemed "too thoroughly tainted to be a fit companion for fellow slaves in Virg[ini]a." Unlike Jefferson, Madison could not "think of punishing him by transportation merely for coveting that liberty for which we have paid the price of so much blood, and have proclaimed so often to be the right, & worthy the pursuit, of every human being." But most planters, including Tucker, followed Jefferson's lead in keeping or selling, rather than liberating, any recovered slaves.[36]

In 1783, the last British commander, Sir Guy Carleton, withdrew the troops and refugees, including 2,000 Virginia runaways, from New York to Nova Scotia. Feeling honor-bound by promises made to the fugitives, Carleton defied the peace treaty, which prohibited the British from taking former slaves away from America. Southern politicians howled in protest and demanded compensation, but the British government refused.[37]

Although painful to the affected planters, the losses proved negligible to Virginia as a whole. Largely confined to the Tidewater, the escapes had little impact on the larger Piedmont, where slave numbers continued to swell from births. At the end of the war Virginia had 236,000 slaves, up from the 210,000 at the start. Although briefly shaken, the slave system survived the war as important as ever.[38]

Virginia's leading Patriots owned large plantations, but they did not belong to the oldest, richest, and most prestigious families who had dominated Virginia during the colonial era: the Blands, Byrds, Carters, Harrisons, Randolphs, and Robinsons. Save for the prestigious Lee family, the leading Patriots held relatively recent fortunes by Virginia's conservative standards. Jefferson, Washington, Madison, George Mason, and Patrick Henry owed their wealth to their own commercial exertions and favorable marriages or to inheritance from their fathers rather than their grandfathers. Most of the newer elite lived in the developing Piedmont, while the older elite had dominated the stagnating Tidewater. Whereas the old elite planters were slow and reluctant Patriots, the Piedmont leaders aggressively pushed the revolution as an opportunity to advance themselves and their region. The new leaders proved more comfortable and adept at appealing for votes from common citizens, for the revolution could not be won without mobilizing farmers and artisans to fight the British and guard the slaves.[39]

The Patriot leaders persuaded common white men that the revolution would enhance their opportunities and status. A new republican ideology invested sovereignty in the people (provided they owned some property) rather than in a distant king. Downplaying the inequality of property, the Patriots promised a new equality of legal and political rights. Gentlemen would continue to govern Virginia but only by winning the consent of common voters. The revolution also enhanced opportunities for ambitious commoners by increasing the number of leadership positions as militia officers, county committeemen, and legislators. In addition, the Patriot leaders mollified the many Baptists and Methodists by disestablishing the elitist Anglican Church favored by the colonial regime. Thereby the revolutionaries elevated the evangelical churches to an equal standing. Above all, the Patriots exploited the popular backlash against

Dunmore's proclamation, for many small farmers owned or rented a slave or two. Most common men shared an interest in preserving the slave system.[40]

Enlistments in the Patriot army lagged, however, for most farmers preferred to stay home to tend their crops. When drafted to serve, some masters sent slaves as substitutes, promising freedom to those who survived the war. Desperate for soldiers, Virginia's leaders reluctantly accepted the slave substitutes despite the long-standing fear that, although blacks allegedly lacked the courage to fight, it was dangerous to teach them to bear arms. At least 500 Virginia slaves won freedom by serving in the Patriot army.[41]

After winning the war, however, Virginians quickly forgot the blacks who had fought for the revolution and fixated instead on those who had fought against it. In the postwar republic, Virginians defined blacks as alien enemies rather than potential citizens. During the 1790s, a French visitor to Virginia noted that "the American people, so excited about their own liberty, don't consider the liberty of others." He concluded that the revolution had increased the American contempt for the enslaved: "Doesn't this imply that it would have been better for the people in slavery if liberty had never been mentioned?" Convinced that they had fought resolutely for liberty, white men disdained slaves as degraded and dishonored by their own failure to win freedom. Jefferson defined his fellow southerners as "zealous for their own liberties, but trampling on those of others." Virginians so cherished freedom precisely because they denied it to others, but slaves were keen observers who wanted what their masters enjoyed.[42]

Patriarch

During the revolution, St. George Tucker had advanced into the Virginia elite. Initially, he assisted the war effort as a merchant, smuggling salt and munitions from Bermuda to Virginia. Impressed by his exertions, Patriot leaders commissioned Tucker as a major in the militia. During the last three years of the war, he fought against the British in Virginia and North Carolina. In 1781 the state legislature rewarded Tucker with appointment to the governor's Council of State: a prestigious and influential position.[43]

Although a beneficiary of the revolution, Tucker emulated the colonial great planters who defined the genteel style of high society in Virginia. Gentility required wealth, education, and good manners. Tucker had acquired polish and charm as a boy in Bermuda, and he received a fine education in the classics, natural history, and law at college in Virginia. His trading generated a little wealth, and a fortunate marriage provided the rest. In 1777, while attending church in Williamsburg, he met Frances Bland Randolph, aged twenty-five, the lovely and charismatic daughter of one elite family (Bland) and the widow of another (Randolph). A year later, their marriage endowed Tucker with many slaves and three plantations: Bizarre in Prince Edward County, Matoax in Chesterfield County, and Roanoke in Charlotte County. But the lands and slaves were mortgaged to secure a great debt owed to British creditors by her late husband. And, per the terms of his will, the land, slaves, and debt would pass to her three Randolph children—Richard then aged ten, Theodorick eight, and John six—once they reached legal maturity at twenty-one. In the interim, Tucker enjoyed the prestige and property of a great Virginia planter. Residing at Matoax on a bluff overlooking the Appomattox River, he acquired expensive furniture and dishes, entertained genteel visitors, and raised fine race horses.[44]

Already in decline before the revolution, the old elite suffered further losses during the war and still more during the postwar depression, when tobacco prices sagged. The scarce supply of money further deflated the value of land, slaves, and crops. Many planters lacked the funds to repair their properties ravaged by British raids. Meanwhile, the interest on their debts continued to mount. Tucker calculated that during the 1780s "barely one tidewater planter in twenty" made enough to pay the annual interest on his debts. Many old estates collapsed as lawsuits consumed the properties, leaving the losers with only the hollow pride of genteel poverty. A merchant sighed, "We have not only had a revolution in Political government but also in many people's private circumstances." Only lawyers and storekeepers seemed able to stay afloat.[45]

Struggling as a planter, Tucker resumed his legal practice in 1783. During the hard times of the 1780s, lawyering paid better than did the marketing of crops, for the courts filled with lawsuits brought by creditors against indebted planters. As his practice and fame grew, Tucker shifted away from the dispersed county courts to specialize in the more prestigious and lucrative business of the state courts in Richmond, the state capital after 1780.[46]

During Tucker's prolonged absences on legal business, Frances managed the three plantations and bore four more children—Ann Frances in 1779, Henry St. George in 1780, Theodorick Thomas Tudor in 1782, and Nathaniel Beverley in 1784—who grew up with their three Randolph stepbrothers. "The children are very well, but intolerable noisy and troublesome—it is a hard day's work to attend to them & the drudgery of the house," Frances informed Tucker. The pregnancies took their toll on her. In December she wrote her last letter to her again absent husband: "I am yet much disordered but I entreat you not to return till the court rises." Later that month she gave birth to a daughter named Elizabeth, but Frances never recovered, dying on January 18, 1788.[47]

Distraught and overwhelmed by his large family, Tucker sent the three Randolph boys away to boarding schools, and he moved with the younger children to Williamsburg, where he bought and expanded an old house for his new home. During his impressionable years as a student, Tucker had fallen in love with the old colonial capital, although it had become depopulated and dilapidated during the 1780s. At least it lay far from his painful memories at Matoax and closer to his new appointment as a state judge in Richmond. Better still, the new home was within walking distance of his other new post, added in 1790, as a law professor at the College of William and Mary, where he replaced his mentor, George Wythe, who had gone to Richmond to become chancellor of the state's new court of equity. One of Tucker's cousins insightfully observed that the inhabitants of Williamsburg "have something peculiarly courteous and engaging in their manners. Perhaps, republicans as they are, they still retain the air of the *old court* . . . unconsciously, and almost in spite of themselves." He perfectly described St. George Tucker, who had come home to Williamsburg: the past rather than the future of Virginia.[48]

Tucker had lost interest in managing the three Randolph plantations, which would soon pass to his stepsons, and he began to sell off his own rural properties acquired during the 1780s. "I never did or could pretend to be any Judge of the proper mode of managing a Virginia estate," he later explained. Tucker shrewdly invested his liquidated capital in bank stock and in the elite education of his sons, whom he expected to practice law rather than raise tobacco.[49]

In October 1791 he married another young widow with connections to old money and prestige. Lelia Skipwith Carter was the daughter of Sir Peyton Skipwith, a British-born baronet and great planter of Mecklenburg County. As the widow of George Carter, she also possessed a life estate in the great Corotoman Plantation of Lancaster County. By entering his second marriage, Tucker added the Skipwiths and Carters to his nexus of elite families, which already included, through stepsons, the Blands and Randolphs. The new marriage also introduced two more stepchildren—Charles and Polly—into Tucker's complex family.[50]

Constitutions

Adopted in 1776, Virginia's new state constitution dispersed power by keeping the counties strong while bolstering the state legislature at the expense of the governor. The new regime preserved the traditional power of the county courts and their local oligarchies. The counties elected the state legislators who formed two houses: the numerous and powerful House of Delegates and the smaller, more prestigious, but less important State Senate. The state leaders shifted the regional balance of power in the legislature in favor of the Piedmont. Each county, no matter how large or small, elected two men to the House of Delegates: a representation system that favored the older, smaller, and numerous counties along the Tidewater and in the Piedmont at the expense of the newer, larger, and fewer counties farther west.[51]

The Tidewater and Piedmont leaders insisted that their superior property in the form of slaves warranted enhanced political power. They did not trust the westerners, who owned few slaves, or the poor whites in general, to protect the slave system. The state constitution restricted the vote to white men who owned at least fifty acres of land or a town property of comparable value. About three-fourths of the white men qualified to vote, and they supported their leading men so long as they kept taxes low and the state government small.[52]

The state constitution weakened the governor and empowered the House of Delegates, which Jefferson characterized as an "elective despotism." Virginia's governor had no legislative veto, and his decisions required approval by a Council of State chosen by, and from, the legislators. One governor sighed that he was "no more than a reading and signing clerk to the Council." The joint houses of the legislature met to choose the governor annually, and he could serve for no more than three years in succession. The weak executive reflected the Patriots' disdain for the powerful colonial governors, especially the hated Lord Dunmore.[53]

The Virginians had escaped from the distant and centralizing power of the British Empire, but they distrusted the federal union of the states as a potential new threat to Virginia's cherished autonomy. In 1787 the proposed Federal Constitution provided for a stronger national government that could directly tax the people in the states. Virginia's "Anti-Federalist" majority feared domination by northerners who did not own slaves. In Virginia's ratifying convention, Patrick Henry explained that the Federal Constitution "put unbounded power over our property in hands not having a common interest with us." Henry feared that northern congressmen "might lay such heavy taxes on slaves, as would amount to emancipation." He concluded, "This government is not a Virginian but an American government." A true Virginian distrusted an American government.[54]

Led by James Madison, Virginia's nationalists (known as "Federalists") felt far more confident that their state would dominate the new Union. After all, Virginia was the nation's largest state, and demographic trends apparently favored growth to the south and west, regions assumed to have common interests with Virginia. Predicting that a stronger nation would better protect southern slavery, the Federalists praised the three-fifths clause, which bolstered representation for the slave states, and the fugitive slave clause, which required northern states to help recover runaway southern slaves. The latter clause rejected the principle of the 1772 *Somerset* case: that escaped slaves could claim freedom by fleeing to a state that did not sustain slavery by positive law. Madison also insisted that the federal military could help suppress slave revolts. In June 1788, Virginia's state ratification convention narrowly ratified the Federal Constitution, but Virginians remained wary of the new government.[55]

Manumission

The leading Patriots recognized the gap between their soaring ideals and their sordid practice of slavery. While Americans fought for liberty, Tucker noted, "we were imposing upon our fellow men, who differ in complexion from us, a *slavery* ten thousand times more cruel than the utmost extremity of those grievances and oppressions, of which we complained. . . . Should we not have loosed their chains, and broken their fetters?" Although Patrick Henry opposed a federal government that might meddle with slavery, he conceded that the system was "as repugnant to humanity as it is inconsistent with the bible, and destructive to liberty." But Henry never freed his own slaves due to "the general inconveniency of living without them." Slaves comprised so much property in Virginia that they could not be freed without impoverishing white men and ruining their creditors.[56]

During the 1780s, Virginia's evangelicals pushed the legislature to adopt some gradual plan for emancipation. They insisted that as republicans as well as Christians, Virginians needed to do right by their slaves. "The holding, tyrannizing over, and driving slaves, I view as contrary to the laws of God and nature," declared the Baptist preacher David Barrow, who regarded liberty as "the unalienable privilege of all complexions, shapes, and sizes of men." Citing the Golden Rule, Barrow wished that masters would be *"doing as they would others should do to them*!"[57]

The evangelicals welcomed blacks into their churches, where their emotional responses helped to inspire the relatively staid whites to lose their inhibitions and feel the Holy Spirit. A Methodist declared, "In general the dear black people, that profess Religion, are much more engaged than the whites." By 1790 the great majority of Virginia slaves had embraced Christianity fervently.[58]

By adopting their own, especially devout Christianity, the enslaved could resist psychological domination by their masters. Indeed, they could claim moral superiority and a better prospect of salvation in eternity. Mason Locke Weems, an Anglican priest, assured a visitor, "No people in the country prize the Sabbath more seriously than the trampled-upon negroes. They are swift to hear; they seem to hear as for their lives. They are wakeful, serious, reverent, and attentive in God's house." Many clergymen concluded that the truest Christians in Virginia were enslaved and should be freed.[59]

In 1778 the legislature did bar the importation of slaves into Virginia, imposing a hefty fine of £1,000 per violation and freeing any illegally imported slave. The ban allowed the legislators to display their antislavery sentiments without undermining the human property already in Virginia. Indeed, the restriction enhanced the value of the slaves within the state by reducing the competition of new imports. And the ban addressed the greatest fear of white men: that further growth in slave numbers would lead to a bloody revolt.[60]

In 1782 the legislature also enabled masters voluntarily to free their slaves: a legal process known as "manumission." Prior to the revolution, manumissions required the consent of the legislature, which was rarely granted from a reluctance to swell the numbers of free blacks. But the Patriots regarded that restriction as contrary to both liberty and the rights of property. They reasoned that a master should dispose of his own property as he wished even if he wanted to renounce it. However, because property rights trumped all, no indebted master could legally manumit without the consent of his creditors.[61]

Manumissions did increase after 1782, swelling the free black population from 2,000 in 1782 to 20,000 in 1800, and from 1 percent of all blacks in 1782 to 7 percent in 1800. Some of the freed moved into the commercial towns to seek work as artisans and domestic servants or as laborers on the docks, in the streets, and aboard boats. But most freed people remained in the countryside, working as hired laborers or tenant farmers. Very few acquired title to any land.[62]

A few manumitters were liberal critics of slavery, but many more were Quakers or evangelicals with religious scruples. Other masters simply wanted to reward a few favorite slaves for long service and to encourage others to work hard and remain loyal in hopes of their own eventual liberty. Most of the manumissions occurred in the older, economically stagnant counties of the Tidewater, especially on the Northern Neck (along the Potomac) and the Eastern Shore, where many planters had more slaves than they could employ. Masters with debts and few scruples sold their surplus slaves; only the solvent and the principled would manumit them.[63]

The greatest liberator was Robert Carter of Nomini Hall in the Northern Neck. An eccentric great planter, he experimented in radical religion, joining a Baptist church that included twenty-nine of his own slaves. Carter's spiritual quest led him to recognize slavery as a sin. In 1791 he began to liberate his 509 slaves, freeing about 25 a year until completing the process in 1812. His dismayed children saw much of their inheritance dissolve into freedom, and his neighbors denounced the freedmen for setting bad examples that ruined their slaves, who thereafter resented and resisted their bondage. An angry neighbor rebuked Carter, "It appears to me (witnessing the consequences) that a man has almost as good a right to set fire to his own building though his neighbor's is to be destroyed by it, as to free his slaves."[64]

Manumitters faced social pressure and harassment from their agitated neighbors. On the Eastern Shore, a Quaker named Robert Pleasants gave his former slaves plots of land to allow "them the full benefit of their labour." Lamenting the powerful prejudice "against Negroes being in any wise released from a state of absolute Slavery," in 1790 Pleasants reported that angry neighbors had "beat [the freedmen] without cause, and killed & destroyed their Hogs & other property." Instead of prosecuting the culprits, the county court fined Pleasants for allowing "his Negroes to go at large."[65]

The most defiant manumitter was Richard Randolph, the eldest stepson of St. George Tucker. Tall, handsome, and charming, Randolph inherited a plantation aptly named "Bizarre" in Prince Edward County. In 1793 the county court prosecuted him for enabling an alleged infanticide by his wife's sister, whom he was also accused of impregnating. Although cleared of the charges in a sensational trial, Randolph became embittered against his fellow planters.[66]

In June 1796, he sickened and died at the age of twenty-six. In his provocative will, Randolph asserted his moral superiority over his fellow Virginians, whom he denounced as hypocrites. In the will's searing preamble, Richard exposed the moral evasions of slaveholders by vowing

> to make retribution as far as I am able, to an unfortunate race of Bondmen, over whom my ancestors have usurped and exercised the most lawless and monstrous tyranny, and in whom my countrymen (by iniquitous laws, in contradiction of their own declaration of rights, and in violation of every sacred law of nature; of the inherent, inalienable and imprescriptible rights of man, and of every principle of moral and political honesty) have vested me with absolute property.

He rejected "the infamous practice of usurping the rights of our fellow creatures, equally entitled with ourselves to the enjoyment of liberty and happiness." His will freed seventy-two slaves and reserved 400 acres of land, a fifth of Bizarre, for their settlement on Israel Hill beside the Appomattox River. But Randolph was a prophet without honor in his own county, for no other master in Prince Edward County manumitted his slaves between 1782 and 1810. Instead, the planters continued buying, selling, working, punishing, and bequeathing slaves.[67]

Reaction

Most Virginians clung to the slave system as essential to their prosperity and security. In 1802 in Prince William County an elderly slave known as Old Dick recounted the story of his master Spencer Ball, who had married a daughter of Robert Carter, the great manumitter. According to Old Dick, "in a fit of religious enthusiasm," Carter "wrote a serious letter to Mr. *Ball*, exhorting him to free his negroes, or he would assuredly go to hell. Mr. *Ball*, whose property consisted in his slaves, and whose family was annually augmenting, entertained different notions; and with much brevity returned answer to the old gentleman's letter, 'Sir, I will run the chance.'" To provide for numerous heirs, masters risked eternal hell rather than impoverish themselves in life.[68]

Virginians disliked the growing number of free blacks, who allegedly lapsed into depraved lives of vicious larceny and drunken indolence: lounging in their cabins or wandering in the streets when not preying on the poultry, pigs, orchards, and gardens of their white neighbors. Examples of black freedom also encouraged slaves to bristle at their continued enslavement. In addition, white men suspected the freed people of harboring runaways and fencing goods stolen by the enslaved. Worst of all, free blacks might threaten the entire slave system by leading a revolt. A critic predicted, "They will furnish the officers and soldiers around whom the slaves will rally." By depicting the freed as active subversives, the Virginians contradicted the stereotype of them as indolent. But whether seen as lazy, thieving, or scheming, free blacks were cast as proof of the dangerous naivete of emancipation.[69]

To reduce their supposed danger, Virginians restricted the liberty of the freedmen, who could not vote, serve on juries, or join the militia and could only own a gun with the permission of their county court. They also had to register with the court and obtain a certificate for display to any suspicious magistrate or slave patroller. And no colored person could testify in court against a white who cheated or struck him or her. But, as with every racial law in Virginia, enforcement lagged behind the draconian letter of the law. The tax-phobic and antigovernment ethos of Virginia precluded creation of a professional police force and state bureaucracy needed fully to enforce the race laws. Implementation instead relied on the part-time, amateur local magistrates, who usually had better things to do on their own farms and plantations. And despite the laws, the freed had won important gains: the right to work for wages without corporal punishment and without the terror of legal sale hanging over their heads.[70]

During the mid-1780s, Methodists petitioned the state legislature to emancipate all of Virginia's slaves. That Methodist push galvanized pro-slavery counterpetitions from hundreds of masters who opposed abolition and demanded repeal of the manumission law, which saddled their counties with free blacks. The pro-slavery men claimed to defend the true legacy of the revolution: "We risked our Lives and Fortunes, and waded through Seas of Blood," to defend the private property of white men from any government meddling. Indeed, they denounced the would-be emancipators as "the Enemies of our Country, Tools of the British Administration" who allegedly sought the "sure and final Ruin to this now flourishing, free, and happy Country." In this view, any criticism of slavery threatened the freedom of white men, and emancipation would culminate in a race war of extermination: "the Horrors of all the Rapes, Murders, and Outrages, which a vast Multitude of unprincipled, unpropertied, revengeful, and remorseless Banditti are capable of perpetrating." The pro-slavery petitioners ultimately blamed the antislavery plot on insidious Britons: an equation promoted by the *Somerset* decision and the wartime alliance of runaways with British forces.[71]

Faced with the dueling petitions, the House of Delegates compromised in the fall of 1785. A small majority retained the manumission act, but the legislators unanimously rejected any state-mandated emancipation. Sobered by this defeat, the Methodists and Baptists, retreated from antislavery activity. Once a champion of abolition, the Methodist bishop Francis Asbury reconsidered in 1798: "I am brought to conclude [that] slavery will exist in Virginia perhaps for ages; there is not a sufficient sense of religion nor of liberty to destroy it." Most leading evangelicals sought respectability as middle-class men of property. Preferring neighborhood peace and acceptance, they marginalized any radicals who continued to agitate the issue. Becoming more conservative, mainstream evangelicals reframed their message, urging slaves to obey their masters and wait for freedom after death in heaven. Among the state's Christians, only

Quakers clung to antislavery principles, but they comprised a small and increasingly despised sect in Virginia.[72]

During the 1790s in Virginia, the kiss of death for antislavery came from news of a massive and bloody slave revolt in Saint-Domingue, a French colony in the West Indies. In 1789 the French Revolution divided the planter elite in the colony between supporters and opponents. In 1791, their contentions invited slaves to revolt, destroying a thousand plantations and killing hundreds of planters and overseers. Many more blacks died in the ruthless reprisals launched by the colonial government. In 1794 a radical regime in France sought to co-opt the rebels by emancipating all slaves throughout the French West Indies. Horrified by the news, white Virginians dreaded that the precedent might inspire their own slaves to rise in bloody rebellion.[73]

Although the Virginians had declared revolution a universal right for the oppressed, they shuddered when the enslaved claimed that right. Thomas Jefferson felt greater sympathy for the exiled planters than for the exploited slaves of Saint-Domingue. In 1797, Jefferson warned St. George Tucker, "If something is not done & soon done, we shall be the murderers of our own children [for] the revolutionary storm, now sweeping the globe, will be upon us." To fend off that storm, Jefferson favored emancipating and deporting Virginia's slaves over the course of two generations.[74]

Most Virginians, however, rejected Jefferson's plan for emancipation and African colonization as prohibitively expensive. If colonization could not work, emancipation would oblige Virginians to live beside an allegedly hostile black population. Indeed, they dreaded free blacks as more dangerous than slaves. After the revolution in Saint-Domingue, most Virginians concluded that their safety required bolstering rather than weakening the slave system. They had risked "the revolutionary storm" long enough.[75]

Heirs

Virginia's revolutionary reformers doubted that their republic could survive any further growth in the inequality of rich and poor among the free. Jefferson and Tucker worried that inherited wealth eventually would consolidate an aristocracy to threaten the new and vulnerable republic with counterrevolution. To promote greater equality, reformers looked to the gradual and private process of inheritance, rather than to a government-imposed redistribution of wealth. Jefferson assured Madison, "I am conscious that an equal division of property is impractical, but [given] the consequences of this enormous inequality producing so much misery to the bulk of mankind, legislators cannot invent too many devices for subdividing property." The reformers sought to abolish Virginia's colonial laws of "entail and primogeniture," which Tucker denounced as "the means of accumulating and preserving great estates in certain families." He deemed those laws "utterly incompatible with the genius and spirit of our constitution and government."[76]

Entail and primogeniture mandated that a great landowner pass on a landed estate (including slaves) intact to one heir, usually the first-born son, rather than divide that estate equally among all of the children. Perpetual in the male line, an entail barred any heir of any future generation from subdividing and selling or otherwise devising the property in parts. The owner had to preserve the estate for his eldest son and could not even mortgage it to borrow funds. The lone exception came when a generation had no male heir to inherit; in such cases, the daughters inherited jointly and divided the estate: considered a tragedy by a legal system that cherished the continuity of wealth in the male line. Aristocratic in design, entail and primogeniture sought to preserve a great estate through the generations. During the colonial era, Virginia's great planters emulated the English aristocracy by entailing three-fourths of the lands in the Tidewater. Very few entails could be broken by later generations without great expense to navigate through a complex legal thicket.[77]

Reformers denounced entail and primogeniture as the tyranny of a past generation overriding the rights of individuals in the present—and as a distortion of the natural equality of individual rights. Tucker derided entail as "the offspring of feudal barbarism." Pressure for this change did not come from the common farmers seeking greater equality. Instead, that pressure came from the younger sons of the great planters, particularly those in the Piedmont. They sought to manage their inherited lands more aggressively and commercially: mortgaging, buying, and selling to raise capital to improve their plantations. To prosper in a commercialized society, they needed to act more as capitalists and less as aristocrats.[78]

In opposing entails, Jefferson spoke from harsh experience. In 1774 he had petitioned the colony's legislature to break the entail on 1,200 acres that his wife had inherited from her grandfather, so that the couple could sell that property. The legislature agreed but Lord Dunmore vetoed the bill, compounding Jefferson's rage at the royal governor and the aristocratic tradition that he upheld. The revolution enabled Jefferson to break the entail, not just on his own estate, but those throughout Virginia.[79]

Despite resistance from the old elite, the legislature abolished entails in 1776 and primogeniture in 1785. Thereafter multi-geniture (the equal division of land among the children of an owner) prevailed in intestate cases (when the owner lacked a will). From these reforms, Jefferson expected two great boons. First, society would benefit from the increased equality brought by the division of large, landed estates among multiple heirs. Second, the heirs would become free to manage their properties by mortgaging, subdividing, and selling as they saw fit. The dual benefits attested that these bourgeois revolutionaries linked social benefits to individual liberties in a commercial society. The reformers insisted that, as individuals buying and selling in a free market, people could best achieve their full potential and best promote social equality.[80]

The reforms accelerated the decline of the old Tidewater elite through subdivision by inheritance and through their increased exposure to lawsuits by creditors. In 1795, Tucker predicted that the new "law of descents, by which lands are divided among the children, . . . would compel many to labour who now seem only born to consume the fruits of the earth." A decade later a visiting British diplomat mourned the decline of Virginia's colonial estates: "the abolition of entails has nearly ruined them all," for "present day estates are very much subdivided."[81]

Richard Randolph's younger brother, John, despised the decay of the colonial order wrought by the inheritance laws promoted by his stepfather, Tucker. No admirer of social equality, Randolph denounced the abolition of entail and primogeniture as ruinous: "Nothing . . . can be more melancholy than the aspect of the whole country on tide-water,—dismantled country-seats, ruinous churches, fields forsaken, and grown up with mournful evergreens,—cedar and pine." He mourned the decline of the old elite families: "They whose fathers rode in coaches and drank the choicest wines now ride on saddle-bags, and drink grog, when they can get it." He predicted worse to come: "The old families of Virginia will form connections with low people, and sink into the mass of overseers' sons and daughters; and this is the legitimate, nay, inevitable conclusion to which Mr. Jefferson and his leveling system has brought us." Unlike Tucker and Jefferson, Randolph saw aristocracy lost as a satanic bargain.[82]

Of course, Randolph had a special talent for hyperbole. While many old-style planters did lose their fortunes, the more entrepreneurial men of the new elite exploited the revised laws to borrow against their estates for capital improvements. At last Jefferson could sell his wife's entailed property for the cash needed to rebuild Monticello and expand his wheat fields. And Randolph underestimated his own adaptability to the new order, for he profitably rationalized his inherited estate at Roanoke. But he despised the new commercial discipline that he had to adopt to thrive in the new order.[83]

Division

Entails often had attached slaves to their estates, which barred the owners from selling them. Although certainly not meant to benefit the slaves, that feudal restriction inhibited the breaking up of their families by sale. Under the reformed laws, the division of estates tended to divide enslaved families among multiple heirs. The changes benefited younger sons, entrepreneurs, and creditors, but not the enslaved people treated as liquid capital.[84]

The reformed inheritance laws promoted a surge in the sale of slaves by owners seeking cash. During the 1780s, 40 percent of slaves advertised in the Virginia press had been sold at least once before in their lives: up from 24 percent during the 1760s. Virginia planters increasingly valued slave children for future sale. Richard Blow assured his son, "I think it useless to raise up families of them for any other purpose but to sell." Jefferson deemed "a woman who brings a child every two years as more valuable than the best man on the farm. What she produces is an addition to capital, while his labor disappears in mere consumption." Jefferson's grandson feared that Virginia was becoming "one grand menagerie where men are to be reared for market like oxen from the shambles." But he failed to recognize his grandfather's leading role in the revolution's transition to a more commercialized slavery.[85]

The wider inheritance and increased sale of slaves combined to multiply the number of slaveholders in Virginia. By 1800 about half of the white households in the Tidewater and Piedmont owned slaves, but usually only a few. Meanwhile, the number of great planters who owned more than 100 slaves had declined from the peak in 1776. The revolution had broadened slave ownership, which enhanced popular support for slavery, leading to the crushing political defeat suffered by Methodist abolitionists during the mid-1780s.[86]

An inherited slave or two became the prime social security for a widow or orphan in Virginia. In 1798 in Mathews County, the Episcopalian pastor Armistead Smith gave an enslaved child named Nancy to his daughter, Harriet, and her new husband as a wedding gift. By early 1814 the couple had died and their lone child, Sally, inherited Nancy, but she sued for her freedom, citing a legal flaw in the will. Smith denounced the "diabolical plan" and vowed to see "that the vile Strumpet at last may be defeated in her views & Justice be done by D[ea]r Sally." Focused on his granddaughter's security, Smith could see no justice in an enslaved woman's longing for freedom.[87]

After the revolution, the renting of slaves increased as a means for masters to profit from surplus slaves, in contrast to manumitting them, which brought no financial reward. Many widows hired out their inherited slaves to derive an income while avoiding the rigors of supervising and punishing them. Executors of estates also rented out slaves to support orphans until they came of legal age. During the 1790s a farmer could rent a prime male field hand for $31 per year, about a tenth of the cost of buying such a slave. And an adult woman cost only about $11 per year, compared to $200 for a purchase. As renters, common men could acquire slave labor more readily than by purchase. The surge in postwar hiring further spread slaves among the white households of Virginia. A careful study of Elizabeth City County (on the James River) found that over 80 percent of the farmers either owned or hired slaves.[88]

The rented slaves usually passed through multiple renters over the course of a decade, which complicated their attempts to form and keep families. Only 39 percent of the Elizabeth City County slaves lived in the same household for three consecutive years. The hired slaves often left relatively prosperous masters for poorer renters who lacked the means to feed, clothe, and shelter their laborers decently.[89]

The revolution also promoted a new spirit of commercial improvement that motivated the leading planters to rationalize their estates to seek higher productivity and greater profits. After determining the optimal number of slaves as a workforce, the improvers sold the surplus children. Because men made better field hands, masters often sold more young females than males. As a consequence, young men struggled to find wives and form families. Ruing their standing as especially liquid capital, slaves grimly declared that at any time the master could "put you in his pocket."[90]

The postwar era also increased the long-distance movement of slaves to harsher conditions on the frontier. By defeating western Indians as well as British troops, the revolution opened up vast tracts of backcountry land for settlement by migrating Americans. In Georgia, South Carolina, Tennessee, and Kentucky, the frontier enticed Virginia's young families with the opportunity to make their own farms by clearing the forest. Between 1790 and 1810, about 225,000 whites and 98,000 slaves left Virginia and Maryland for points farther south and west. While the frontier provided white opportunity, slaves bore the brunt of creating new farms in summer climes often even hotter and more humid than they had endured in Virginia.[91]

The forced migration disrupted slave families and communities. Given the dispersal of slave ownership in Virginia, most enslaved families had been divided among different owners in the neighborhood. When a master departed with his slaves, he compelled them to forsake wives, husbands, parents, and children on other farms and plantations. Austin Steward considered the forced migration of his master's slaves to be "the greatest hardship" that they "had ever met" because of "the separation from our old home and fellow-slaves, from our relatives and the old State of Virginia." Francis Fedric remembered "the heart-rending scenes" in Fauquier County when his master prepared to move to Kentucky: "Men and women down on their knees begging to be purchased to go with their wives or husbands . . . children crying and imploring not to have their parents sent away from them; but all their beseeching and tears were of no avail."[92]

Enslaved families also suffered from increasing sales to long-distance traders who served the voracious demand for slaves in the lower South. Before the revolution, Virginians sold few slaves beyond the boundaries of that colony. Between 1790 and 1810, however, at least 100,000 Virginia slaves moved south and west after sale to traders. The frequency and volume of interstate sales soared as cotton cultivation became profitable and widespread in the lower South. In 1803 a prime male field hand sold for about $600 in South Carolina, compared to $400 in Virginia: a $200 difference enticing to Virginia sellers and Carolina traders. The demand and the prices surged again in 1808, when the United States barred the import of slaves from Africa, a ban that rendered the lower South more dependent on Virginia for new slaves.[93]

John Randolph disdained the "base, hard-hearted masters" who sold "out of their families the negroes who had been raised among them," but few Virginians dared to be soft-hearted given their debts. Most preferred to see slaves sold beyond their state rather than freed within their borders. Unlike long-distance sales, manumissions generated neither revenue nor, Virginians feared, greater protection from revolt, for the freed usually stayed close to their family and friends in Virginia. One legislator explained, "I am for opening every outlet to such a destructive species of population and for barring up every avenue by which it may return."[94]

The sales divided enslaved families, separating children from parents and husbands from wives. William Grimes recalled, "It is not uncommon to hear mothers say, that they have half a dozen children, but the Lord only knows where they are." He spoke from experience, for Grimes was only ten when sold away to a distant master: "It grieved me to see my mother's tears at our separation. I was a heart-broken child . . . but I was compelled to go and leave her." Old

T. face page 43.

A. Rider delt.

"—but I did not want to go, and
I jump'd out of the window.—"

Designed and Published by J. Torrey Jun. Philad. 1817.

"But I did not want to go and I jumped out of the Window." *In this engraving, Jesse Torrey, a critic of slavery, depicted a December 19, 1815, episode in Washington, D.C. Imprisoned in a garret by slave traders, the mother sought to escape by jumping out the window, but she suffered paralysis from her wounds. Rendered worthless to the traders, she remained behind, but they took away two of her children for sale to the Deep South. From* A Portraiture of Domestic Slavery *(1817). (Courtesy of the American Antiquarian Society)*

Dick sadly recalled losing all of his children by forced sale over the years: "It was a hard trial to part with my little ones, for I loved them like a father; but there was no help for it, and it was the case of thousands beside myself." One historian calculates that forced migration and the domestic slave trade "destroyed about one-third of all first slave marriages in the Upper South" prior to 1840.[95]

In 1815 slave traders locked up a mother and two children in the garret of a tavern in Washington, D.C., in preparation for driving them to Georgia. Named Anna, the mother tried to escape and return to her husband and other children, who had been left behind. Jumping out the window, she shattered her spine in the three-story fall. The slave trader left Anna's worthless body behind but took away her children for sale in Georgia. A sympathizer mourned, "Thus her family was dispersed from north to south, and herself *nearly* torn in pieces, without the shadow of a hope of ever seeing or hearing from her *children* again!" The profits of masters and traders came at a high price paid by the enslaved.[96]

Wishful thinking asserted that the revolution's changes benefited slaves by dispersing them in smaller numbers among owners who knew them better. James Madison claimed that the Virginians had become kinder, gentler, and more generous masters to their slaves: "They are better fed, better clad, better lodged, and better treated in every respect," and "what was formerly deemed a moderate treatment, wd. now be a rigid one, and what formerly [was] a rigid one, would now be denounced by the Public feeling." Madison credited that better treatment primarily to "the abolition of entails, & the rule of primogeniture."[97]

In fact, dispersion through inheritance, sales, rental, and forced migration did little, if anything, to improve material conditions for the enslaved. On the issue that mattered most to the enslaved—the unity and security of their families—their conditions deteriorated after the revolution. In 1792, when restive slaves threatened to revolt in Northampton County, on the Eastern Shore, the governor, Henry

Lee, investigated. He concluded that the unrest derived from the masters' "practice of severing husband, wife, and children."[98]

Thanks to the revolution, common Virginians found it easier to buy or rent slaves, and to move west and south to make new farms. But the enslaved suffered for the democratization and commercialization promoted by the revolution. As the planters sought to service their debts, satisfy multiple heirs, and rationalize their estates, they treated the enslaved as commodities and often ignored their family bonds. As a consequence, few Virginia slaves could sustain stable households for life. By 1800 in Virginia most enslaved husbands and wives lived on different farms, rendering single-parent households the rule rather than the exception. Consequently, when British warships returned to Chesapeake Bay, Tidewater slaves would seize the opportunity to reunite their families by helping the invaders. Despite the disappointments of the last war, the liberator king offered hope for the enslaved.[99]

VIRGINIAN   LUXURIES .

2

NIGHT AND DAY

Black people were not like white people, . . . black people
worked in the night and white people in the day.
—PHIL, A SLAVE, KING AND QUEEN COUNTY, 1813[1]

IN JULY 1807 James Carter recalled the devastation of his family
by the accelerating sales of slaves in postrevolutionary Virginia.
Carter and his siblings had grown up near Fredericksburg, where
they worked as house servants for Mrs. Lucy Baylor Armistead, a
widow. In 1800 she remarried, taking Landon Carter as her husband and bestowing his last name on her slaves. Their merger rendered redundant most of her house servants, so the new couple
proceeded to sell off James Carter and his siblings, to the despair of
their mother. His brother Henry passed to a cruel taskmaster with
a harsh overseer, who killed the young slave with a hurled stone
when he tried to run away. Henry left behind a wife and infant
child. Next the masters sold Carter's sister Nelly to a Fredericksburg merchant whose "Greatist Speculation is on human flesh."

*Virginian Luxuries, by an unknown artist, ca. 1825. In this tavern sign, a New England
artist presents sexual and physical abuse as the essence of slavery in Virginia. (Courtesy of
the Abby Aldrich Rockefeller Folk Art Museum, Colonial Williamsburg Foundation)*

Resold far away, she vanished from her family's knowledge forever. Next the masters auctioned the youngest girl, Judy, in a tavern after displaying her to "Blood thirsty fellows." James Carter recalled, "My Mother and myself begged Mr. Carter not to sell this child out of Fred[ericksbur]g. He gave his word and honour that he would not but as soon as we left them he sold the child to thes[e] fellows." The family never heard from Judy again. At last, the masters sold James to a bank clerk in Alexandria, who resold him to a slave drover bound for the lower South.[2]

James Carter escaped from the slave drover and fled to Philadelphia, where he found an antislavery benefactor who helped Carter negotiate by letter with the Alexandria bank clerk, to whom ownership of the slave had reverted after his escape from the drover. In return for a hefty payment from his wages in Philadelphia, Carter obtained freedom and returned to Alexandria, where he supported his elderly mother. Although sixty-seven, Carter's father could still work, so his owner refused the son's offer of $100 for his father's freedom. At great cost, James Carter could reunite only a fraction of his shattered family.[3]

Carter felt betrayed because his ancestors had long served the Baylor family and, as mulattos, probably shared blood with their masters or overseers. But those traditional ties made scant difference when Landon Carter and his new wife needed money more than so many house slaves. James complained that although his mother "and Mrs. Armistead has been brought up together from Little Girls, she has sufferd all my Mother's children to be picked from her. My Mother's Family has served the Family of Mrs. Armistead upwards of one Hundred and 30 years." The postwar era ruptured the colonial bonds that, in some cases, had screened slaves from the full operation of market forces.[4]

Families

Some of the larger-scale planters tried to keep slave couples together, from a conviction that it improved morale and productivity. Married men worked steadier by day if they did not spend their nights traveling to visit or seek a wife on a distant farm. Thomas Jefferson instructed an overseer, "There is nothing I desire so much as that all the young people in the estate should intermarry with one another and stay at home. They are worth a great deal more in that case than when they have husbands and wives abroad." Jefferson gave presents to couples who married within his enslaved community and tried by purchases to unite couples who had "imprudently" married outside of "his family." But Jefferson also sold away any slaves who disappointed his expectations for obedience and work. For all of his "scruples about selling negroes," Jefferson did so as routinely as he promoted marriages. When a slave became disruptive, Jefferson would "make an example . . . in *terrorem* to others" by pointedly selling him to a "quarter so distant as never more to be heard of among us." Jefferson reasoned that a distant sale would impress the other slaves "as if he were put out of the way by death." Jefferson maintained his workforce at about 200 slaves from 1784 to 1796 by selling (or giving to relatives) 161 slaves.[5]

Selling and keeping operated as alternating currents in a system of discipline. The same masters who tried to unite couples also deployed the threat of sale to coerce their slaves to obey and work. William Grimes recalled, "My old master and mistress in Virginia had often threatened to sell me to the negro buyer from Georgia, for any trifling offence, and in order to make me dislike to go there, they would tell me I should have to eat cotton seed and . . . not have corn bread to eat as I did in Virginia." After catching a married man stealing wool, John Randolph reported, "I have punished the scoundrel exemplarily, and shall send him to Georgia or Louisiana at Christmas. He has a wife and three fine children." Randolph kept the wife and children, who did not have a merry Christmas.[6]

Chesapeake region slaves dreaded sale far from relatives and friends. Josiah Henson remembered "threats of being sold to the far south" as "the greatest of all terrors to the Maryland slave." In Norfolk, a visitor found that the slaves had "an invincible repugnance to being sold to the Southward," and he heard their mournful work song:

> *Going away to Georgia, ho, heave, O!*
> *Massa sell poor Negro, ho, heave, O!*
> *Leave poor wife & children, ho, heave, O!*

Although he owned slaves, George Tucker (a cousin of St. George Tucker) opposed their sale to the Deep South: "The sentence of banishment strikes them like the message of death. I have myself heard, with shuddering, their wild and frantic shrieks."[7]

When confronted with suffering slaves, some masters showed a deft ability to evade blame by, instead, congratulating themselves for a superior ability to feel the pain of inferiors. St. George Tucker's eldest son, Henry St. George Tucker, resided in Winchester in the Shenandoah Valley, where he practiced law. In 1804 the father sent to Henry a ten-year-old slave boy named Bob to work as a house servant. Bob felt devastated by the forced separation from his mother, as Henry reported to his own father:

> Poor little fellow! I was much affected at an incident last night. I was waked from a very sound sleep by a most piteous lamentation. I found it was Bob. I called several times before he waked. "What is the matter, Bob?" "I was dreaming about my mammy Sir"!!! cried he in a melancholy & still distressed tone: "Gracious God!" thought I, "how ought not I to feel, who regarded this child as insensible when compared to those of our complexion." . . . How finely woven, how delicately sensible must be

those bonds of natural affection which equally adorn the civilized and savage—the American and African—nay the man and the brute.

Despite discovering a shared humanity with the boy, Henry reiterated a stark polarity in which he stood as the superior: the civilized, American man in contrast to the savage, African brute. In that view, slave labor supported, rather than contradicted, the freedom of those who most deserved it.[8]

Most masters regarded blacks as carnal creatures lacking in sentiment and sensibility, so they would readily forget old loves and easily find new ones in their new homes. "Their griefs are transient," and their afflictions "are less felt, and sooner forgotten," insisted Jefferson. In fact, slaves cherished their families and longed to preserve their unity in the present and across the generations. In July 1774 at Robert Carter's Nomini Hall estate, an illiterate and elderly slave, Dadda Thomas Gumby, begged a favor from Philip Vickers Fithian, the Carter family tutor: to draw up a "List of his Children & their respective age." In return, Gumby and his wife showered Fithian with gratitude: "Thank you, thank you, thank you Master, was the language of the old Grey-headed pair." They did not own much, but they offered it all to Fithian: "Eggs, Apples, Potatoes, You shall have every thing we can get for you—Master!" Fithian demurred but Gumby persisted, for the tutor had done the greatest of favors for a slave who longed for a written record of his family in a bid to hold it together.[9]

The enslaved bitterly recalled the sale of a spouse as crueler than any beating. A woman declared, "Selling is worse than flogging. My husband was sold six years ago. My heart has bled ever since, and is not well yet. I have been flogged many times, since he was torn from me, but my back has healed in time." Charles Ball remembered his heartache upon sale away from his wife and young children: "I awoke in agony and cursed my existence. . . . As we passed along the road, I saw the slaves at work in the corn and tobacco-fields. I knew they toiled hard and lacked food; but they were not, like me, dragged in chains from their wives, children and friends. Compared with me, they were the happiest of mortals."[10]

Debt

The death of a master threatened enslaved families, for he (or she) almost always had many creditors and multiple heirs to satisfy. The heirs sold enough slaves to pay the debts and then divided up the rest. When the debts overwhelmed an estate, almost all of the slaves went on the auction block, and husbands and wives and their children usually passed to different and often distant owners. In 1824 the slaves at Monticello assured a visitor that "they were almost sure of not being torn away from [their families] to be transported elsewhere, so long as Mr. Jefferson lived." Two years later he died, leaving massive debts. An auction divided his slaves among multiple buyers, who often ignored family bonds. Peter Fossett recalled his traumatic shock at age eleven to be "suddenly, at the death of Jefferson, put upon the auction block and sold to strangers."[11]

In Campbell County, the Oxford Iron Works seemed to sustain the most fortunate of slave communities. The owner, David Ross, a Scotland-born entrepreneur, recognized and rewarded the abilities of his slaves, whom he described as suffering from overseers of "less understanding and sometimes less integrity than those poor blacks." Dispensing with a white overseer, Ross employed a slave named Abram to superintend the foundry. Because iron-making required special skills developed over many years, Ross provided positive incentives to the most able workers: extra food and good clothing. Needing a stable community of laborers, Ross tried to sustain the family cohesion that the enslaved longed for. Unlike other masters, he avoided selling any slaves, even those redundant for his operations, lest he alienate his skilled workers.[12]

But that apparently stable community lay atop a volcanic debt that erupted after Ross died in March 1817. Four months later, the Oxford Iron Works closed, and all of his slaves went on the auction block, passing to forty-seven different owners, who dispersed them to many newer ironworks farther west. Even the best conditions for slaves proved short-lived in a society that valued them as commodities needed to cover debts and provide inheritances.[13]

Conscience usually lost in the struggle with money for the fate of slaves. Widow McCroskey inherited her husband's debts as well as his slaves. Devoted to the house servants, she regretted her inability to keep them all. In November 1803, she wrote to St. George Tucker, who served as her legal advisor: "Every day, my d[ea]r friend, I am wounded by their coming to me to know what is to be done with them." Although she lamented the fate of the "poor young fellows that are to be the innocent victims of debt," she especially regretted that they would sell for only half of their appraised worth. After auctioning them, McCroskey updated Tucker:

> What a scene of distress have I waided thro this two days. Oh Heavens this trafick in human flesh, how I shudder at it. How wretched I have made my family and myself. Poor souls, three of them have had hard fate to fall in[to] the hands of the most cruel men in the country and I am the cause of it by selling them at public auction—but you say I must do so. . . . There was a negroe girl whose tears and intreaties made me make a bid for her, but I had her set up again.

The widow cast herself as the primary victim in the tragedy, punished by debt and her own superior sensibility over the sad fate of her slaves. But she feared debt and poverty even more than she hated to sell her slaves.[14]

Slaves anxiously watched their masters for signs of financial distress or deteriorating health and found the combination terrifying.

Josiah Henson recalled the death of his first master in 1795 as "a great calamity to us, for the estate and the slaves were to be sold and the proceeds divided among the heirs." The slaves felt "the frantic terror at the idea of being sent 'down south': the almost certainty that one member of a family will be torn from another; the anxious scanning of purchasers' faces; the agony at parting, often forever, with husband, wife, and child." Although only six years old, Henson was sold to a tavern-keeper who lived forty miles away.[15]

Overseers

The wealthier planters sought to increase their profits by enhancing the productivity of their land and labor. Careful record keepers and close supervisors, these agricultural reformers regarded time as money. In return for better food and clothing for the slaves, the improvers demanded faster labor over longer hours. They needed more work to realize their ambitious plans to dig ditches and drain swamps, erect new fences, shops, barns, and houses, and clear new fields to raise fodder for more cattle (in part to provide the manure needed to enrich the soil). Serving six days a week, with Sunday for rest, the slaves labored from dawn to dusk, with two brief breaks for meals. And they toiled in all weather conditions, save for a few of the coldest days in winter. Many masters lengthened the workday beyond dusk by requiring slaves to husk and shell maize or to sort and tie harvested tobacco deep into the night. The new work regime also stretched through the winter, previously a relatively slack time for slaves. The improvers kept their slaves busy and tired, from a conviction that idle hands made more trouble. The leading improver, Colonel John Taylor, advised selling trouble-makers "to some distant place" as "an object of terror" to the rest. He concluded, "Slaves are docile, useful and happy, if they are well managed."[16]

To enforce the more stringent work discipline, planters hired common white men to serve as overseers on the plantations. In

An Overseer Doing His Duty, Sketched from Life near Fredericksburg, 1798. *In this watercolor, Benjamin Henry Latrobe wryly contrasts the hard-working enslaved women supervised by a cigar-smoking overseer on a stump. (Courtesy of the Maryland Historical Society).*

addition to an annual salary of $200 to $300, the overseer received a share of the harvested crop: at least a tenth and up to a fourth. Obliged to work long hours, closely supervising often restive slaves, the overseer had to be strong, resolute, and handy with a club and cowhide whip.[17]

A leading improver, John Hartwell Cocke, owned Bremo, a 3,100-acre plantation in Fluvanna County (in the Piedmont). Although Cocke professed antislavery principles, he ran a very strict plantation, codifying his management principles in his "Standing Rules for the Government of Slaves on a Virginia Plantation." Cocke instructed his overseers: "It is the duty of a faithful, active & industrious agent to be the first on the ground in the morning & the last to leave it at night. . . . You are bound not only to give orders, but personally to see that they are well & faithfully executed." Cocke concluded, "Set the first example of strict attention to your duties & you may with the more justice & propriety inflict punishment upon others for the neglect of theirs."[18]

Cocke allowed extra meat and a few hours of free time on Saturday night "to such as had been the most faithful during the week." If deemed unworthy however, slaves lost their meat ration for the week and had to labor longer on Saturday night. Cocke also insisted that his overseers flog slaves who defied or slacked: "If you punish only according to justice & reason with uniformity, you can never be too severe & will be the more respected for it."[19]

Improving planters demanded a daunting consistency, restraint, rationality, and attention to detail. Cocke instructed his overseers, "Arrangement & regularity form the great secret of doing things well. . . . Have everything done according to a fixed rule." Inevitably, Cocke felt bitterly disappointed: "Overseers are too worthless generally & too prone to become good for nothing." Cocke fantasized about establishing an observatory "on one of my River hills from whence every body knew I could see every foot of my low grounds by turning my head, [then] the Corn & Tobacco wou'd grow a great [deal] better and thousands [of] things wou'd go on much better than they do now." He meant to employ a speaking trumpet to issue orders to all his workers, slave and free, from his hilltop observatory. Only a slave had to work harder to please Cocke than did an overseer.[20]

An overseer often felt caught between a demanding and meddling master and the resisting slaves. The master wanted the overseer to produce larger crops and make greater improvements while keeping the slaves reasonably content. Jefferson noted, "My first wish is that labourers may be well treated," but his second was that they work long and hard hours: "The man who can effect both objects is rarely to be found." Early and often, genteel planters derided their overseers as prone to steal, lounge, sleep with the slave girls, and whip too much. In a typical comment, Joseph C. Cabell described his overseer as "conceited & inclined to extort wages higher than he deserves. He is quite ignorant of farming."[21]

After a long absence, John Randolph returned to his plantation to find "everything in bad order." Noting "two negro girls, each with a mulatto child in her arms," Randolph concluded that the overseer, Mr. Pentecost, was the father. Pointing out the new mothers to some neighbors, Randolph demanded, "Look at these girls; they are my crop hands. See how their heads are combed; how oily their hair. Do they look like they had stood blasts of Winter or Summer's sun? No, Sirs; they have been in his harem." Randolph expected his field hands to show the wear and tear of the weather. After informing Pentecost's wife "of the infidelity of her husband," Randolph fired the straying overseer.[22]

Slaves balked at the speedup demanded by masters and overseers. The enslaved envied the leisure of white gentlemen, who so conspicuously ate, drank, and lounged to flaunt their status. No slave could miss the equation of freedom with leisure in Virginia, so they sought to be as free as they could by working as little as possible. An immigrant from England who became a Virginia planter, Richard Parkinson, denounced his slaves: "They are so lazy by nature, that they would do little or nothing, but take pleasure in fine weather, cook victuals, and play on music and dance all winter, if they had no master. I think them as unfit to conduct themselves as a child— thoughtless in the extreme and therefore requiring a severe master." When pushed too hard, slaves slowed down even further, although the overseer had the power of the whip, the slaves had the advantage of numbers and persistence, for overseers came and went. In 1803 a frustrated overseer complained that the slaves "Get much more Dissatisfied Every year & troublesome, for they say they ought all to be at there liberty & they think that I am the Cause that they are not." He concluded that the slaves "gives me all the trouble that they can which keeps me one half of my time in hot blood."[23]

Nonetheless, masters preferred slaves for plantation work because common whites took their republican equality so seriously. Despite belittling blacks as lazy, Parkinson deemed them "the best servants in America, since the establishment of independency" because "liberty and equality" had rendered white men "very saucy," relatively expensive, and often drunk. The difference lay in the power to whip work out of the enslaved. Parkinson explained, "The slave is your own, like your horse, and you may whip him as you please; but you have no command over a white man."[24]

Punishment

Masters and overseers inflicted pain to discipline and punish the enslaved. Charles Ball recalled the overseers' armament as "a twisted cow-hide, sometimes a kind of horse-whip, and very often a simple hickory switch or gad, cut in the adjoining woods." For an especially serious offence, such as stealing a pig, the overseer had the culprit stripped, tied by the hands, and suspended from a beam to receive at least a dozen bloodying blows to the bare back. The other slaves had to demonstrate their submission by helping to subdue, hoist, and whip the victim. Ball felt lucky to escape his first major flogging until age fifteen, for he described the "back of the unhappy Maryland slave" as commonly "seamed with scars from his neck to his hips."[25]

Most masters sought to avoid maiming or killing a valuable slave, but renters showed less restraint. In 1811, Thomas Chrystie of Hanover County hired out his slave named Bob to Philip Croxton. On May 18, Bob staggered back to Chrystie, who reported, "He has been beaten about the Head, Arms, & Hands with Sticks or billets of Wood so as to render his arms entirely useless for the present. In addition he has been whipt with a keen Cow Hide so as to leave upwards of one Hundred cuts on his back & Belly, which has brought on Fever & much Inflamation." Seeking "damages for the improper beating," Chrystie threatened Croxton with a lawsuit. As the renter of Bob's labor, Croxton could punish only so long as he did not cripple the slave, ruining his value.[26]

Masters or overseers handled most crime and punishment on their plantations without involving the legal authorities. The county court came into play when a culprit seemed too hardened to "plantation justice" or had committed too serious a crime for the neighborhood to ignore. Striking or murdering (or sexually assaulting) a white person demanded a trial. In these trials, the justices dispensed with a jury, but they appointed an attorney to defend the slave, and the law required unanimity by at least five judges to convict. The court could order a whipping, generally of thirty-nine stripes, supplemented by branding a hand. If subsequently convicted of another felony, the branded slave faced almost certain execution. When the court did sentence a slave to death, the state compensated the owner with the appraised value of his dead property.[27]

Local public opinion often proved surprisingly divided over the punishment of convicted slaves. Some rigid masters favored frequent executions as essential to cowing the slaves. But many other whites believed that an apparent justice and occasional clemency would best defend slavery by reconciling slaves to their fate. If previously deemed diligent, tractable, and honest, the accused could expect more sympathy. Public opinion also urged some mercy when the white victim had an especially vicious reputation for feeding his slaves too little or whipping them too much. And many white folk had religious scruples against executing blacks for theft: a crime where whites instead reaped only fines or imprisonment. Ultimately, the prevailing mood in a county carried great weight. When masters felt relatively secure, they petitioned the governor to reduce the sentence (usually to sale and transportation beyond the state), but when they felt threatened by a rumored slave revolt, most of the white folk wanted executions.[28]

Despite their bloodthirsty reputation as "the internal enemy," the enslaved bore their blows with remarkable restraint, rarely killing their tormentors. Between 1785 and 1831, the Virginia county courts convicted only 148 slaves of killing a white person: about three per year in a state with a white population in excess of 500,000. Far more often, slaves faced trial for arson or theft.[29]

Sometimes slaves did kill an overseer guilty of excessive brutality. In 1809, Miles King of Mathews County engaged John Mathews as an overseer. Apparently a vicious reputation preceded Mathews, for the pious King later discovered that the slaves had agreed "to kill him the moment they understood I had engaged him—Amen." On May 31, "in the Gum Swamp field in the noon of the day," Frank, Jack, James, and Edmund seized Mathews and crushed his skull and knocked out his teeth with blows from their iron hoes. They hid the corpse in a ditch but returned at night to retrieve "his mangled Body & carried it thro' the oat patch to a Canoe in the Creek where they tyed a Bushel Basket to his ankles with his feet in it & Loaded it with . . . some Rock Stones & carried him (aided by my Foreman Joe & ploughman Peter) into East river in the deepest water off Cully's point & there sunk him as they vainly thought *forever*!"[30]

On the night of June 9, the corpse bobbed to the surface and became entangled in the oar of a rowing white man, who drew the remains ashore. Alerted to the grim discovery, King had his "men and women, arrested and their arms tied fast and marched them to the spot where the body lay where they displayed Surprize & Horror! at again beholding the victim of their Cruel & Savage Rage." King made them all touch the body, from a folk belief that it would bleed anew when touched by a murderer: "'tis not possible to describe the fear manifested & one of them, old Billy, told me if I would forbear to make him feel it, he would tell the whole truth & out it came for all the field Negroes being present at the murder & Several corroborated Billy's tale in evidence at the Bar." King turned over six slaves for confinement and trial by the Mathews County Court, which sentenced the four killers to hang and the two accessories (Joe and Peter) to receive brands on the hand and thirty-nine lashes each. The heads of the executed were "stuck upon a Pole at the Court house as a warning to others."[31]

King predicted that the exemplary punishment would "most likely deter all the Negroes from a commission of the like crime for some years to come." But the murder had demonstrated careful planning and cast an ominous light on the nocturnal movement of slaves intimately familiar with the local lands and waters in a county along Chesapeake Bay, where the British warships had once dominated and might return to in a future war.[32]

Caves

Masters sought to feed their slaves the minimum necessary to keep them healthy and working. George Washington explained, "It is not my wish or desire that my Negros should have an ounce of meal more, nor less, than is sufficient to feed them plentifully." But no planter would consider it "plentiful" to live on the diet of his slaves. Charles Ball saw widespread hunger in the faces of his fellow slaves in Virginia: "A half-starved negro . . . his skin becomes dry, and appears to be sprinkled over with whitish husks, or scales; the glossiness of his face vanishes, his hair loses its colour, [and] becomes dry."[33]

The customary weekly ration for an adult slave was a peck of corn and a pound of salt meat (usually pork) or fish. The meat component was, at best, a fourth of what most white men consumed in Virginia. The fish tended to be herrings, and the meat usually came from parts disdained by whites: heads and feet. Rarely did masters provide any drink other than water. This monotonous diet ranked high in starch and painfully low in the protein needed by hard-working people. Only in the flush times of harvest did slaves get a little more meat and some alcohol to inspire extra exertions. Many masters encouraged slaves to supplement their diet by keeping poultry and raising vegetables, potatoes, and melons; but the slaves could tend these only at night and on Sundays. During their limited spare time, slaves also fished and hunted for small game, especially raccoons and possum.[34]

The slaves watched with envy as their masters consumed heaping helpings of eggs, chicken, pork, and beef, washed down with alcohol, tea, and coffee. No people more delighted in eating and drinking than Virginians. Watching with envy, the enslaved longed for more food, especially the prime cuts of meat, including ham and bacon. At night they roamed in search of orchards to plunder and a pig or sheep to kill. William Grimes recalled, "We used to steal meat whenever we could get a chance; and such was my craving for it, that if the punishment had been death, I could not have resisted the temptation." It required great ingenuity to pull off a surreptitious kill and hide the carcass from prying patrollers and overseers. "Is not cunning always the natural consequence of tyranny?" asked Francis Fedric, a former slave. As a young man in Maryland, Josiah Henson belonged to a planter named Riley, who stinted his slaves of food. Henson recalled "driving a pig or a sheep a mile or two into the woods to slaughter for the good of those whom Riley was starving. I felt good, moral, heroic." The clever young man who killed, hid, and shared a hog became the hero of his slave quarters.[35]

Slaves justified their thefts with a labor theory of value: they took a small part of what they had earned by work extorted by lazy masters. Richard Parkinson reported, "As I have travelled on the road, I have made it my business to converse with them, and they say, 'Massa, as we work and raise all, we ought to consume all.' . . . They say, 'Massa does not work; therefore he has not [an] equal right; overseer does not work; he has no right to eat as we do.'" Or they reasoned, in Austin Steward's words, that the stolen animals "belongs to massa, and so do *we*, and [so] we only use one part of his property to benefit another."[36]

By day, the slaves suffered from the master's power, but at night they became almost free. After dark, the master and overseer retreated to their families and homes. While the master slept, the slaves, particularly boys and young men, could roam and play. Parkinson noted, "Though you have them [as] slaves all the day, they are not so in the night. I compare them to cats. . . . All the black men I employed used to be out all night and return in the morning." They rambled to hunt and fish, attend dances, steal meat, or gather to worship Jesus. Above all, men sought their girlfriends or wives. Old Dick recalled, "A negur never tire when he go to see his sweetheart." Whites referred to the night as "Nigger day-time," and one master complained that slaves took "uncurbed liberty at night, [for] night is their day." George Tucker agreed: "The day was their masters; but the night is their own." By acting as if free by night, they avoided a full submission to the slavery of their days.[37]

Slaves found most of their pleasure at night or during the brief Christmas break. Henson recalled his youth in Virginia: "Slavery did its best to make me wretched, but, along with memories of miry cabins, frosted feet, weary toil under the blazing sun, curses and blows, there flock in others, of jolly Christmas times, dancing before old massa's door for the first drink of egg-nog, extra meat at holiday times, midnight-visits to apple-orchards, broiling stray chickens, and first-rate tricks to dodge work." At night and during Christmas, slaves felt a measure of hope. William Grimes declared, "If it were not for our hopes, our hearts would break; we poor slaves always cherish hopes of better times." In a perverse synergy, the release offered by nights, Sundays, and Christmas helped slaves to endure and so helped slavery to persist. A former Maryland slave, Frederick Douglass, noted that holidays served as "safety-valves, to carry off the explosive elements. . . . But for these [interludes], the rigors of bondage would have become too severe for endurance."[38]

By traveling at night, the enslaved gained an intimate knowledge of their landscape, particularly the forests and swamps and the paths and waterways that avoided the main roads watched by slave patrols. The same wild landscape that alarmed whites, especially at night, seemed more welcoming and secure to blacks. Reassured by that familiarity, slaves felt more attached to their home places than did the white folk, who proved all too ready to pick up and move in search of frontier opportunity. Even when freed, Virginia blacks preferred to stay near the intimately known world of their youth and family connections. In an experiential sense, Tidewater Virginia belonged to African Americans more than it did to the more rootless common whites. In the near future, the naval captains of the British king would cherish the slaves' intimate, nocturnal knowledge of the byways and waterways of Virginia.[39]

Sometimes the night became especially ominous for whites, as rumors of arson and revolt spread. The wooden buildings of Virginia often caught fire and burned down, arousing suspicions that a vengeful slave had slipped a hot coal into wooden shavings beneath a barn, kitchen, or house. After moving to Virginia, Philip Fithian adopted the local dread: "Now . . . I sleep in fear too, though my Doors & Windows are all secured!" Another traveler, Jesse Torrey, heard Virginians lament living in "a country where one cannot go to bed in the evening, without the apprehension of being massacred before morning!" Torrey noted that one master "retreated every night into an upper room, the entrance into which was by a trap-door, and kept an axe by his side for defence." The former slave Austin Steward noted, "The slaveholder is well aware that he stands over a volcano, that may at any moment rock his foundation to the center, and with one mighty burst of its long suppressed fire, sweep him and his family to destruction."[40]

Virginians also dreaded that, at night, their slaves were concocting poisons to slip into their coffee in the morning. When a white person suddenly sickened and died, the family suspected poison and often blamed an enslaved conjuror. In Halifax County, investigating magistrates opened a conjuror's box to find a mix of "palma-christal seeds, dirt-dauber nests, with dead spiders and snail shells." In a forensic experiment, they mixed the ingredients and fed the concoction to a cat, which quickly died. That evidence helped to convict and execute the conjuror for fatally poisoning a white woman who had been one of his patients.[41]

Masters and slaves contested the boundaries between night and day. A white man complained that a slave worked slowly by day but burst into activity at night, thinking nothing of walking seven miles to attend a dance, "in which he performs with astonishing ability, and the most vigorous exertions . . . until he exhausts himself." George Tucker agreed: "Look at these same fellows the day after one of these nocturnal wakes, and see how ready they are to fall asleep over their work." In King and Queen County in 1813 a slave declared "that black people were not like white people, that black people worked in the night and white people in the day." Recovering from the night's exertions, the slaves sought to work as slowly as possible through the day and to nap when the overseer was not looking. Pushing back, masters demanded more work by day and longer into the evening, particularly to pound corn. By exhausting slaves, masters hoped to curtail their roaming at night.[42]

Masters relied on slave patrols to enforce the laws against night meetings and roaming without a written pass from an owner. A straying slave could receive ten to twenty lashes or a brutal beating with fists and feet. In 1808 in Norfolk, a visitor saw a patroller accost a slave woman, demanding to know her owner's name. When she gave a saucy answer, he "began to box & kick her in a most cruel & unmerciful manner."[43]

But enforcement proved lax because the patrols were inefficient and irregular: often no more than once a month in times of apparent security. Drawn from the local militia, the patrollers spent much of the night visiting friends or taverns. In the dark the groggy (and sometimes drunken) patrollers struggled to distinguish friend from foe. In Alexandria, a resident reported a farcical scene involving novice slave patrollers: "We were somewhat alarmed last night by the noise they made in pursuing one of the citizens, whom they supposed to be some evil disposed person—while he, on the other hand, took them to be an armed band of negroes." And the patrollers rarely knew of the obscure paths through the woods used by the enslaved to evade surveillance.[44]

In alarming times of suspected rebellion, the patrols became more numerous and vigilant, briefly revealing and suppressing the black nocturnal world. In 1802 in Madison County, alarmed whites intensified their patrols, catching many black men roaming between 2:00 and 3:00 a.m.—deemed an especially suspicious time. One of the patrollers reported, "On being asked why they were out at such an unreasonable hour, some said they had been hunting the raccoon and opossum; and others replied that they had been visiting their friends and relations, which they could not do in the day-time." The local magistrates "found them guilty of being out of their quarters at an unseasonable time, and ordered them all to be severely flogged, which sentence was executed by the white men, in turns." Ordinarily safe, the nocturnal roaming became risky when white people suspected a plot against their lives.[45]

While masters tried to regain the night through armed patrols, some slaves sought to extended the night by running away. According to advertisements posted by their owners, most of the runaways were unmarried boys and young men: the slaves in the greatest danger of sale by their masters. The runaways tended to be especially daring and accomplished, for the advertisements dwelled on their skills and intelligence. Many fugitives were especially familiar with the roads and waterways to the wider world: boatmen, house slaves, and artisans rather than the field hands. Relatively few, the female fugitives often had recently been sold away from their old neighborhoods and sought to get back to their children and parents.[46]

Some runaways fled northward to escape across the state lines to the relative freedom of Pennsylvania or Ohio, but that was a very risky proposition. Even if an escapee made it through the gauntlet of slave patrols, suspicious whites, and professional slave catchers, he or she reached a northern community where, unless Quakers prevailed, most of the white people disliked blacks and enforced the federal fugitive slave law. More often, the Virginia runaway sought a time-out from slavery to visit a spouse or relatives in a nearby county; such fugitives rarely remained on the lam for long. Many runaways had better luck slipping away to a commercial town such as Richmond or Alexandria, where they found paying work by passing as free. This strategy worked best for skilled artisans who had free relatives in the town to provide haven. By selling their labor cheap, the skilled could find white protectors willing to evade the laws against harboring and hiring runaways.[47]

Running away often served as a short-term strategy to seek concessions from a master, particularly when he introduced a new overseer who demanded more work and inflicted stricter punishments. By bolting to hide in the woods, the runaways gave leverage to the rest to urge a more relaxed regimen, which usually then brought the fugitives home. Thomas Mann Randolph Jr. noted that when one slave ran, the others "felt pleasure at the idea of his running away, because the lost time would be an appeal to interest with the Master and overseer on future occasions manifestly in their favor."[48]

Some runaways became "outliers" by forming small refugee communities in forests and swamps within their home county. They relied on hunting, stealing, and rustling and on food slipped to them by family members. In 1813 the Gloucester County Court tried Sam, the slave of Lewis Williams, for stealing bacon, beef, salt, and herrings from a smokehouse. The court determined that "Sam has from his infancy been the most notorious villain that ever lived, he has been one half of his time for many years a Runaway—has been constantly engaged in stealing hogs, sheep, &c., &c.," despite at least one conviction and branding. He was finally taken in a "piney Swamp in this county," where "Sam & other slaves" had "been runaway, outlying & committing robberies for a great length of time." The four men and two women had dug holes to serve as "the hiding places of Bacon, &c." As an outlier, Sam enjoyed the meat denied to him as a slave, but as a convicted felon, for a second time, he died on the gallows.[49]

Some camps proved surprisingly substantial and enduring. The largest and longest-lived runaway community lay in the vast Great Dismal Swamp, south of Norfolk. Other smaller and briefer havens lay scattered throughout rural Virginia. In Buckingham County in December 1810, William H. Cabell sought a tougher law and "some exemplary punishment" against

> the practice very prevalent in this neighbourhood, and I understand in many others, of runaway slaves *collecting in numbers*, forming what they call Camp & to the great destruction of the [live]stock of the neighbourhood in which they may pitch themselves. These *camps*, as they are termed, are generally made under ground and covered with so much art that it is impossible to discover them in the day time, even should you walk directly over them. Few persons would give themselves the trouble to search for them in the night (when they are discoverable by the light of the fire below) in such difficult places as they generally chuse for the purpose, particularly when we consider the danger of the enterprise. The negroes go armed, and frequently a dozen in one camp or cave and therefore set at defiance the efforts of one or even 3 or 4 white men.

In these artificial caves in the forest, some runaways sustained and expanded the nocturnal world of potential freedom.[50]

Mixture

Visitors noted that Virginia's slaves often had the brown skin of mulattos rather than the dark skin of Africans. Despite laws and publications preaching a stark dichotomy of black and white, the

Virginians had bred an intermediate population of brown people. John Hartwell Cocke reported that Virginia's mulattoes "would be found by hundreds. Nor is it to be wondered at when Mr. Jefferson's notorious example is considered." As one of Jefferson's closest friends, Cocke was well informed. After Jefferson's wife died in 1782, he never remarried but instead kept a slave mistress, Sally Hemings, who bore him six children. As the daughter of a mulatto woman by Jefferson's father-in-law, Hemings was the enslaved half-sister of Jefferson's late wife. George Tucker marveled after reading Jefferson's insistence that blacks lacked physical beauty: "I own I was a little surprised at his derision after the stories I have heard of him."[51]

No law punished masters who raped slave women or kept them as concubines. Neighbors did little more than gossip so long as a master kept a low profile and did not marry a slave partner: a model of discretion set by Jefferson. White wives hated the interracial sex of their husbands, but pride kept most from pressing the issue on those who pretended to keep it secret. Instead, humiliated wives sought to punish the black women involved. Despite the risks, some enslaved women pursued white gentlemen as lovers in a bid for better treatment, small favors, and, perhaps, the manumission of their children.[52]

In Virginia, status followed the mother, consigning her children to slavery. William Grimes lamented that he was kept enslaved although he was "three parts white," the son "of one of the most wealthy planters in Virginia" and raised "in a land boasting [of] its freedom, and under a government whose motto is Liberty and Equality." The wife of Grimes's master was also the cousin of the boy's father. Apparently she hated him as a reminder of her cousin's betrayal of his white wife, for Grimes recalled, "She would beat me until I could hardly stand. . . . She is dead, thank God."[53]

After four generations of mixing, some slaves were virtually white, to the shock of travelers. At Monticello in 1796, a French visitor noted several slaves "as white as I am." At Norfolk in 1808, a

Scottish traveler noted a leading man whose slaves were "mostly his own Children," including one favored daughter, of especially light complexion: "She sleeps in the same bed with them [and] calls them father & mother while her Uncles, Aunts, &c. are serving at table. . . . So much for Virginia Manners!"[54]

Virginians worried that a mass emancipation would reverse the sexual power dynamic: instead of white men impregnating enslaved women, free black men would breed with white women to accelerate the making of a mixed race. In 1806 a legislator warned that if blacks "continue to mix with the whites as they have already done, as we daily see, I know not what kind of people the Virginians will be in one hundred years." Colonel John Taylor dreaded the emergence of "a body politick, as monstrous and unnatural as a mongrel half white man and half negro." Jefferson similarly worried that white Virginians were "in danger of falling into the ranks of our own negroes." Although he had contributed six children to the racial blending, Jefferson longed to whiten the republic by emancipating the slaves and sending them far, far away as African colonists, but it was already too late to separate the intermingled peoples of Virginia.[55]

Masters favored mixed-race people as their house slaves. Often on display to family and guests, house slaves enjoyed better clothing and food, for it would not do for them to appear hungry and ragged. But they lacked privacy and faced constant scrutiny, provoking considerable stress as they scanned the faces and heard the words of their masters, who expected the conspicuous performance of subordination. A traveler noted, "During the warm season in the more respectable families, two of these negroes attend in the parlour at breakfast, dinner, & tea each having a bundle of peacock feathers made up elegantly, which they keep constantly waving over the table to prevent the musquetoes from annoying their owners."[56]

Every day, the house slave risked losing his or her advantages by crossing some line known only to the master. In November 1802, St. George Tucker became disgusted with a young house servant named

Johnny and sent him away to his son, Henry St. George Tucker, who put Johnny to work as valet, groom, and cook. Initially pleased with Johnny's work, Henry soured on him in October 1803. Writing to Tucker, Henry reported, "Today, I have detected him wearing my clothes even. I cannot then hesitate about parting with him." By donning the new attire of his master, the house servant became too familiar and too close, so he had to be punished and sold away. His fall was sudden and complete.[57]

John Randolph developed especially close relations with his body servants, John and Juba. "People may say what they please, but I have found no better friends than among my own servants," Randolph declared. Given his fractious and volatile relationships with white men, we should take him at his word. Randolph considered Juba more intelligent than half the men in the president's cabinet. Randolph said of John, "I know not at this time a better man. . . . I have not a truer friend."[58]

But such unequal friendships could suddenly explode. In Randolph's absence to attend Congress, John drank heavily, quarreled with the overseer, and ran away. When caught, John suffered a great fall from grace. Randolph left him to rot in jail for three months and then sentenced him to three years of field labor before restoring him to the house. Then Randolph resumed praising John: "His attention and attachment to me resemble more those of a mother to a child, or rather a lover to his mistress, than a servant's to a master." John may, indeed, have been Randolph's Sally Hemings, given Randolph's aversion to marriage and special, but fraught, bond with John. Whether they had sex is unknowable and beside the point; emotionally John filled the subordinate but nurturing role of a wife to Randolph.[59]

No matter how cherished, even house slaves faced the harsh economic roulette of Virginia slavery. John Faulcon wrote to his father-in-law, John Hartwell Cocke, to express dismay at the heavy debts that compelled the sale of a trusted servant:

Had he been a common cornfield hand, a brute of a man, without any feeling than his sensual appetites, I might not . . . have
hesitated to hoist him on an auction block & have sold him to
the highest bidder—but I could not forget that he had been
raised in my father's family & amid scenes calculated to awaken
his sensibilities, that he had often exhibited evidences of feeling,
and that he had . . . some attachment towards myself.

Full of principle, Faulcon rejected an offer of $350 for the man.
When the price reached $400, however, Faulcon sold him.[60]

Monster

When closely examined, any system of slavery reveals surprising
diversity and multiple loopholes, for no set of masters could fully
and always hold themselves apart and above slaves with whom
they lived so closely. Slavery attempts perversely to treat human
beings—who invite personal relationships—as if they were inert
property defined by the law and the market. Such contradictions
proved especially powerful in Virginia during the generation after
the revolution, as the masters struggled to reconcile their libertarian principles with their practice of slavery. While the law and
newspaper essayists drew a clear and rigid line between black and
white, slave and free, lived experience proved far more kaleido-
scopic. Whites could rarely enforce the letter of the law, and slaves
often proved adept at evading it.[61]

As a complex and contradictory system, Virginia slavery offered
almost every conceivable human experience, just as the system sustained every shade of skin color from pale to dark. Some slaves
escaped to live in artificial caves; others fanned their masters with
peacock feathers. Some rebuked the impiety of their masters, while
others suffered brutal whippings for their temerity. Some wore rags
and ate refuse, while others donned the threads and ate the food of

their masters. Some killed their overseer with a hoe, while many more looked only to heaven for redress. Some flirted with their overseers, and others hated their sexual predation. Some plotted rebellion, while others turned informant. Some were trusted iron workers, while others were disdained as field hands. Some nurtured African traditions of conjuring, while others felt Jesus grip their souls—and many did both. Both masters and slaves included remarkably diverse individuals, all involved with one another in complicated relationships that shifted over time. They had to live together albeit in unequal ways. And while slavery enslaved blacks, it also imprisoned whites in a web of distortions and deceptions of their own making.[62]

Consider three letters received by Captain Benjamin Brand, a merchant in Hanover County. On January 6, 1809, John W. Tomlin could no longer control a restive slave and sought to sell him to an agreeable buyer: "Lewis says he will not live with me but will run away if I attempt to keep him; this is a considerable disappointment to me, as I have missed hiring [someone] else while depending on him. . . . He says several men want him, & as he appears to be an impertinent & obstinate fellow, I am willing to . . . let him apply to some of those who want him, which may save some trouble & satisfy the fellow." Lewis had won, for Tomlin doubted that a whipping could reclaim him. Elkanah Talley felt differently about Ned, who rambled into the village to spend Sunday nights, annoying both his master and Captain Brand. On September 10, 1809, Talley wrote, "Nothing would give me greater satisfaction than for you or aney other person in town to give him a pretty severe correction every time he is caught in town of a Sunday evening. There is two [sic] maney negroes resorting [to] that place of a Sunday & I think there ought a stop be put to such conduct." Finally, on May 7, 1810, Benjamin Lipscomb assured Brand that he had levied an execution on a debtor by seizing his "very likely young negro Fellow" and cast him "into prison for safe keeping" pending his sale at a public auction. In the three letters we see a defiant slave prevailing; another slave set up for a flogging; and a third converted into cash to settle a debt. The key variables in the three cases were the individual personalities, of both the slaves and the masters, and the volatile economic circumstances of the latter.[63]

Virginia slavery consisted of thousands of such diverse stories. But even at its "best" the system left every slave vulnerable to the whims of a master, the vagaries of the market, and the twists of fate. A master's death or bankruptcy could set her or his slaves adrift into cruel new uncertainties. Contrary to the apologists for slavery, the system provided far less security than did freedom.

In 1815 in Powhatan County, a pregnant slave named Jenny took her three young children down to the river and drowned them. The county magistrates convicted her of murder, but they delayed the hanging until she could give birth. In the interim, the magistrates considered conflicting testimony about her sanity: Was she crazy to kill three children to spare them from a life of slavery? Witnesses described a defiant woman who had often refused to work for her master, Peter Stratton, who "believed he had given her a thousand lashes on account of her neglecting her work." Some witnesses considered Jenny "a fool," but a jail guard "conceived her to be a very shrewd and sensible negro." Favoring her sanity and execution, Stratton offered in evidence that after she gave birth, he took away her baby as his property, and "she seemed to be much affected, and shewed a considerable degree of attachment to the Child." After this last loss, Jenny may have welcomed the noose.[64]

In November 1818 in Albemarle County, on a plantation near Monticello, a proud black man hanged himself in shame after receiving a whipping. The suicide shocked a neighbor, Thomas Mann Randolph Jr. (Jefferson's son-in-law), who had admired the "very sensible, lively, and likely young mulatto man." The unnamed young man had scrupulously avoided "any misconduct," but a new overseer "concluded that fear would be [a] safer security for good conduct than any determination to do right." To show that no slave could escape the whip, the overseer flogged the young man for leaving his tools behind in a field. He then "hung himself, 30 feet from the ground, in a tree near his Master's door, the same night." The death especially shocked because Randolph esteemed both the master and his overseer as "humane men" of "moral worth" who had whipped from a sense of duty. If they were not to blame, something bigger was. Randolph concluded, "What a hideous monster, among the various phaenomena of the social state, is our Southern system!"[65]

The suicide revealed to Randolph a terribly powerful social system that distorted the morality and justice of otherwise decent men. Slavery could not have endured without the support of attentive husbands, good fathers, pious church-goers, and conscientious citizens. Sobered by the death, Randolph sought to alter the monstrous system that held good men, as well as their slaves, captive. But the best he could do, upon becoming governor of Virginia, was to promote his father-in-law's very gradual emancipation program linked to the colonization of the freed in distant Africa: a non-starter in Virginia.[66]

Otherwise honorable men sustained an exploitative and encompassing economic system dedicated to property in humans, the pursuit of profit, the rights of creditors, and the interests of heirs. Seeing no other choice, most Virginians maintained slavery as their duty. One master confessed, "Surely, the Virginians are not barbarians. Habit may make them forget the situation of these poor wretches, who tremble under their hands, and even reconcile them, in spite of themselves, to the daily horrors which pass under their eyes." It is too easy for modern readers to feel superior by blaming slavery on the "bad people" of another time and region. Slavery reveals how anyone, now as well as then, can come to accept, perpetuate, and justify an exploitative system that seems essential and immutable. After all, we live with our own monsters.[67]

3

BLOOD

In the afternoon I passed by a field in which several poor slaves had lately been executed on the charge of having an intention to rise against their masters. A lawyer who was present at their trials at Richmond, informed me that on one of them being asked, what he had to say to the court in his defence, he replied, in a manly tone of voice: "I have nothing more to offer than what General Washington would have had to offer, had he been taken by the British and put to trial by them. I have adventured my life in endeavouring to obtain the liberty of my coun- trymen, and am a willing sacrifice in their cause: and I beg, as a favour, that I may be immediately led to execution. I know that you have pre-determined to shed my blood, why then all this mockery of a trial?"
—ROBERT SUTCLIFF, SEPTEMBER 25, 1804[1]

O N A SUNNY DAY in March 1798, blood fell from the sky onto an open book containing a code of laws for the state of Virginia. A jury in Culpeper County had convened in an open field outside of the courthouse, when the district attorney, a Mr. Voss, opened the book to instruct the jurors on their duty. At least forty bloody drops spattered the tome, splashing onto his clothing. Looking up

St. George Tucker, *1807, engraving by Charles B. J. F. de Saint-Memin. (Courtesy of the Tucker-Coleman Collection, Special Collections Research Center, Swem Library, College of William and Mary)*

into a clear blue sky, the jurors could see no source for the rain of blood. "Struck with the *Miracle*," the spooked jurors desisted from pursuing the inquest. Most were Quakers, which was unusual given their small numbers in Virginia and the official animus against them for their antislavery convictions.[2]

This "Curious Incident" survives in a notebook kept by St. George Tucker, who heard the story directly from Voss, a respected lawyer, in the presence of a former governor, a leading lawyer, and another judge. This apparently providential wonder fits oddly in Tucker's notebook, which he filled with scientific observations. A rationalist, Tucker adhered to deism, a tepid form of Christianity deprived of miracles and adapted to the Enlightenment science of the eighteenth century. Ordinarily, Tucker did not seek signs of divine prodigies and supernatural wonders.[3]

Tucker added no explanation or interpretation for the unusual entry of a bloody miracle, but he lived in an age of sudden and shocking revolutions. In addition to the American revolt against British rule, the French had recently toppled and executed their royal family, and, during the early 1790s, in Saint-Domingue, the slave majority had overthrown their white masters. That massive slave revolt compounded the powerful dread held by white Virginians that they lived among an "internal enemy" who might, at any moment, rebel. Haunted by Saint-Domingue, Thomas Jefferson declared, "Never was so deep a tragedy presented to the feelings of man. . . . It is high time we should foresee the bloody scenes which our children certainly and possibly ourselves (south of the Potomac) will have to wade through and try to avert them."[4]

Masters considered slavery an ongoing cold war that could turn hot on some dark night when a simmering plot would suddenly erupt into bloody retribution—perhaps with divine assistance. Although a slaveholder, George Mason conceded, "Every master of slaves is born a petty tyrant. They bring the judgment of heaven on a country." Jefferson expected "convulsions which will probably never end

but in the extermination of the one or the other race." And he feared
that the whites would lose. "Indeed, I tremble for my country," he
added, "when I reflect that God is just: that his justice cannot sleep
forever." Blood from the sky was an ominous sign for slaveowners
like Jefferson and Tucker. In 1798, Tucker especially worried about
a bloody slave revolt because the legislature had rejected his plan for
the gradual emancipation of Virginia's slaves.[5]

Plan

In a book, but not in the legislature, Jefferson had proposed gradually to emancipate the slaves and to deport those freed to an overseas colony. Most Virginians, however, recognized that colonization
was a fantasy. Even if they could afford to dispense with slave labor,
which they could not, the masters blanched at the logistical and
financial challenges of shipping thousands of people thousands of
miles away. Committed to low taxes and minimal government, Virginians lacked the means to finance or administer a massive project
of overseas colonization. Tucker calculated that Jefferson's colonization scheme would annually cost Virginia at least five times its revenue, and a fivefold increase in taxation was unthinkable.[6]

   In 1796, Tucker proposed an alternative plan for emancipation without state-sponsored colonization. Like Jefferson, Tucker
regarded slavery as incompatible with republican government,
and he also dreaded that a bloody slave revolt would destroy their
beloved Virginia. Unlike Jefferson, however, Tucker insisted that
whites and freed blacks could coexist within Virginia as unequals.
Bowing to white racial prejudice, Tucker proposed that the freedmen become lower-caste tenants without the rights to own land,
bear arms, vote, hold office, or marry a white person. He expected
that inferior status would pressure blacks gradually to migrate
southwestward to the frontier, saving Virginians the cost of sending
them to Africa.[7]

Tucker proposed a complex plan sufficiently gradual to avoid undermining the property rights of the living. He promised to perform a great magic trick: slowly to abolish slavery in Virginia "without the *emancipation* of a single slave [then living]; without depriving any man of the *property* which he *possesses*; and without defrauding a creditor who has trusted him on the faith of that property." His plan would free every enslaved female born after the legislature adopted it, but not until she turned twenty-eight, and no boys would ever be freed from the emerging generation. In the following generation, the children of the freed women, both boys and girls, would become free at twenty-eight, after serving a prolonged unpaid apprenticeship. Tucker predicted that it would take three generations (about a century) for Virginia to get rid of slavery under his plan, which he pitched as the rational "middle course, between the tyrannical and iniquitous policy which holds so many human creatures in a state of grievous bondage, and that which would [suddenly] turn loose a numerous, starving, and enraged banditti, upon the innocent descendants of their former oppressors."[8]

Tucker published his plan in Philadelphia and, in November 1796, submitted copies to both houses of the Virginia legislature. He naively believed that "a large majority of slave-holders among us would cheerfully concur in any feasible plan for the abolition of [slavery]." In fact, the House of Delegates abruptly and angrily rejected the plan. Because all legislation had to begin in that house, the State Senate could do nothing. The president of the senate, Ludwell Lee, politely assured Tucker, "You certainly judge rightly in supposing that, to an enlightened Legislature, no object can be more grateful than to restore, upon a plan not injurious to Society, the Freedom to a part of our Fellowman, which the God of Nature gave them." Lee expressed the ambivalence of Virginia gentlemen toward emancipation: they supported it in principle but could never discover "a plan not injurious to Society." Indeed, the rejection of Tucker's plan throttled any further appetite among the legislators for antislavery reforms. In 1799 a liberal legislator sadly concluded, "In truth the emancipation fume has long evaporated, and not a word is now said about it."[9]

A proud and sensitive elitist, Tucker had expected careful consideration of his plan by legislators deferential to his intellect, education, and high standing. Instead, he got a rude rejection because most legislators feared any public debate of emancipation no matter how gradual and incomplete. In 1790 a newspaper explained that "slaves have understanding enough to know, when so much noise is made by a part of the community about their emancipation, that the time perhaps may come when they shall be free—and that the time being spun out longer than they have patience to wait for, will be the cause of much bloodshed, by insurrections." Virginia's leaders insisted that white silence and black ignorance alone could spare both races from a bloodbath. But Tucker suspected that speaking no evil of slavery would instead hasten the bloody day of reckoning: "Actual suffering will one day, perhaps, open the oppressors' eyes. Till that happens, they will shut their ears against argument." As a consequence, he scanned the skies for signs of coming bloodshed.[10]

Alarm

In May 1792, alarming rumors insisted that in Northampton County (on the Eastern Shore) hundreds of slaves had accumulated an arsenal of muskets, spears, and clubs for a revolt. Allegedly they acted in concert with slave plotters across Chesapeake Bay who meant to "blow up the magazine in Norfolk, and massacre the inhabitants." In Mathews County (on the western shore) a magistrate alerted the governor to the "defenceless situation of most of the Counties in this State, & particularly those who have the Blacks in the greatest number." He begged for a shipment of weapons to enable the whites to "suppress their wrong intentions by a shew of force."[11]

In Northampton County, the magistrates arrested and whipped

a dozen supposed ringleaders but found insufficient evidence to convict them at trial. At most, a few slaves had denounced their masters and the slave patrollers, while many more blacks had attended nocturnal meetings for evangelical worship. On May 21, Colonel Smith Snead informed the governor that "only a few manifested by their conversation a desire of insurrection, but had no fixed plan of operation or time for execution; they had furnished themselves neither with arms nor ammunition." Nonetheless, rash talk could not be tolerated, so the magistrates ordered the dozen flogged and had three sold to distant Cuba as a warning to others. The magistrates also increased the number and repressive zeal of their slave patrols.[12]

The crackdown produced a backlash from defiant slaves, apparently encouraged by some white evangelicals. In July, Colonel Snead boasted that his slave patrols "prevented" the slaves from "meeting and strolling about from one place to another." But he added, "These measures were extremely irksome to the slaves, and abridged them of those privileges which they had been taught by many white people of this County to believe they were entitled to, and [the slaves] were determined if possible to prevent the activity of Patrollers, and destroy those enemies to their liberty." Armed with clubs, six black men ambushed a patrol, wounding one white man and bending his bayonet. The next day an overwhelming force of armed whites arrested five suspects, and the county court convicted three, who were hanged. "This I hope will be a sufficient terror, and teach them wisdom," Snead concluded.[13]

The alarm revealed the stark alternation in white attitudes toward slave revolt. Virginians ordinarily seemed inert and averse to any collective activity. "No people are more patriotic than the Virginians," announced a newspaper editor, "but they are characterized by a fatal apathy—the result of indolent habits, which ... defeats the operations of their acknowledged talents." John Randolph agreed that "we have quickness of parts enough among us in Virginia, but we want *application*." In addition to the debilitating heat and humidity, the Virginians felt preoccupied by their families, farms, and needy crops. Usually lax and inconsistent in enforcing restrictions on the slaves, Virginia's whites could suddenly burst into frenetic repression when they suspected a plot to rebel. The emotional volatility resembled the Virginia climate, where long, sultry stretches suddenly broke into thunder and lightning.[14]

Every crisis revealed that the Virginians were poorly armed, for during the long lulls most militiamen sold their guns or allowed them to rust. And local stocks of gunpowder had moldered away or been spent for hunting. When an alarm came, terrified militiamen suddenly begged their state government for arms and ammunition to stave off their peril. Once the alarm passed, however, the state leaders again curtailed expenditures and reassured voters that they should fear no new taxes to arm the militia. White men returned to tending their farms and families, indifferent to any larger, community effort. Once again the patrols dwindled, the arms rusted, and the slaves resumed their nocturnal roaming.[15]

During the long inert periods of relative security, tension slowly accumulated in the minds of white men until it erupted into alarm over something a slave said. In 1802 in Williamsburg a slave insulted a white man in the street, which led a witness to conclude "that an insurrection was in agitation." Surely only an impending revolt could embolden a slave to express such insolence. Terrifying rumors spread of covert, mass meetings to elect commanders, stash stolen arms, and mobilize a widespread network of preachers to coordinate a far-flung uprising.[16]

Springing into action, the county's magistrates and militia officers increased slave patrols and begged for more guns in anxious letters sent to the state leaders in Richmond. Meanwhile, the patrollers arrested, whipped, and interrogated enslaved men considered too bold and too outspoken. Pain and leading questions could elicit details from the suspects to confirm and elaborate on the dire suspicions. Peer pressure demanded that every young white man assist the patrols and take turns in whipping the suspects, which helped unite the majority in support of repression.[17]

Magistrates feared losing control as common whites whipped and questioned terrified suspects who confessed to wider and wilder plots. The local elite worried that enraged mobs might destroy too many lives to the detriment of their masters. One magistrate complained that the alarms put "power in the hands of ignorant and arbitrary Characters."[18]

During the crisis, white skeptics had to speak quietly and act discretely if they lacked high status. In 1802 near Petersburg, white men accused James Allen of harboring slave conspirators after he openly criticized the hunt for supposed rebels. The accusers grabbed Allen and whipped him to death in a failed bid to force a confession of complicity. Genteel critics avoided such overt violence, but they could be insulted and ostracized. In April 1802 flimsy evidence and an alarmed jury convicted Jeremiah Cornick, a slave, of plotting to burn Norfolk on Easter Sunday. Governor James Monroe considered pardoning Cornick until Norfolk's mayor, John Cowper, pointedly warned that public opinion demanded an execution. After the hanging, Cowper exulted, "I have no doubt, but this example will produce the effect that is wished."[19]

He sought a double effect: to intimidate slaves and calm whites. Leaders needed to restore order, so that whites and blacks could resume the work so urgently needed on farms and plantations. White men had to affirm that they could be trusted in a crisis to suppress the slaves, who once again had to lay low, speak softly, and work hard. So long as these alarms remained brief and killed few blacks and no whites, the outbursts helped to sustain the slave system by preventing larger plots from emerging. The alarms also accelerated the retreat from revolutionary principles. In 1793, a state senator and relative liberal, James Maud, rued that slave alarms promoted hostility to manumission: "The fancied negro insurrec-

Extraordinary Appearances in the Heavens and on Earth. *In this 1797 watercolor, Benjamin Henry Latrobe presents a "most perfect and singular" rainbow seen on his approach to Richmond. In the foreground he depicted black teamsters struggling with a troublesome horse. (Courtesy of the Maryland Historical Society)*

tions of which so much has been said in Virginia . . . originate in the minds of the worst of men for the worst of purposes, namely that of arresting the gentle army of humanity . . . outstretched for the relief of the slaves and with a design of procuring a repeal of the laws authorizing their manumission." In the wake of an alarm, hardliners blamed free blacks despite the scant evidence connecting any of them to the plots.[20]

Rarely can we tell how much fire lay behind the dense smoke of slave alarms. The tainted evidence cautions against the credibility of the full-blown, massive, and extensive plots to massacre whites. But it is just as hasty to regard the murky evidence as proof that slave plots were never more than repressive conspiracies by white men to maintain their control. After all, some slaves did arm themselves to assault the patrollers in Northampton County in July 1792. And eight years later a far bigger plot threatened to overturn slavery in and around Richmond, the capital of the state.[21]

Gabriel

A skilled blacksmith, Gabriel belonged to Thomas Henry Prosser, who lived six miles outside of Richmond. In the bustling town, Gabriel developed wide contacts with the urban artisans and country slaves who visited on Saturday nights and Sundays. In October 1799 a court ordered Gabriel to receive a whipping and a searing brand on his left hand as punishment for stealing a pig and fighting with a white man over it. Angered by the pain and humiliation, Gabriel longed for redress and freedom. Powerfully built, articulate, and charismatic, he could inspire men to take great risks. During the spring and summer of 1800, Gabriel recruited slaves for a bold plot to seize Richmond and demand their freedom. He initially attracted similar men: literate, versatile, and mobile slaves with artisanal skills. Masters naively expected little trouble from such men, assuming their loyalty in gratitude for their relative advantages. But after tasting a little freedom, the enslaved artisans longed for more, and such skilled slaves could best deploy words to persuade others to join them.[22]

Gabriel and his lieutenants traveled around Richmond and the surrounding countryside on Saturday nights and Sundays, when slaves enjoyed a measure of freedom. Pitching their plan at evangelical meetings, funerals, barbecues, and fish feasts, the plotters recruited primarily in Richmond and Henrico County, but they also enlisted supporters to the north and west in Caroline, Hanover, and Louisa Counties.[23]

Their recruiting pitch demonstrated familiarity with the republican rhetoric that got a heavy workout during the heated presidential election of 1800, when the Republican Thomas Jefferson challenged the Federalist incumbent John Adams. Deriding Adams as a pro-British monarchist, Virginia Republicans threatened secession and civil war if Jefferson lost the election. The electoral passions persuaded slaves that division among the white elite provided them with a rare opportunity to strike for their freedom. "We have as much right to fight for our liberty as any men," declared Jack Ditcher, one of Gabriel's lieutenants.[24]

Gabriel's supporters appealed to the masculinity of black men, who seethed at slavery for frustrating their longing to protect their women and children. Gabriel's lieutenants began by asking a potential recruit, "Are you a true man?" When the reply came, "I am a true hearted man," the lieutenant asked, "Can you keep a *proper* or *important* secret?" Black masculinity emphasized the ability to keep secrets from masters even under the torment of flogging and other tortures. When the recruit vowed to keep a secret, the lieutenant asked if he was "willing to fight the white people for his freedom." If "yes" followed, the recruiter concluded by asking if the recruit could kill a white man to prove that he was, indeed, "a true hearted man." Although seeking to protect enslaved women, these men excluded them from knowledge of the plot lest they disclose the secret to a master or mistress.[25]

The rebels' very American ideas of liberty and gender gave the lie to the insistence that the enslaved were an utterly alien people. Many of the rebels had familiar and complicating ties with particular white people. Gilbert explained that his "Master and Mistress should be put to death, but by the men under him (as he could not do it himself) because they raised him." To ease the minds of potential recruits, Gabriel promised to spare the lives of those whites who had displayed empathy for slaves: Quakers, Methodists, Frenchmen, and "all poor white women who had no slaves." Some terrible intimacies, however, produced a rage among other rebels, who longed to kill particular masters in revenge for whippings.[26]

The rebels planned, on Saturday night, August 30, to assemble 500 men armed with swords and pikes made from converted scythes. Once gathered on the western outskirts of Richmond, they would divide into three groups. The first and smallest group would set fire to the warehouses beside the river at the southeast end of town. They expected the alarm bell to draw to that quarter the town's white men, desperate to save valuable property from the consuming flames. Then the larger two rebel groups would seize the state arsenal, where they could procure firearms, and the state treasury, to gain money. They would also seize Governor James Monroe at the governor's mansion. With that hostage, guns, and money, the rebels hoped to negotiate for their emancipation. The plotters seem to have sought freedom for themselves and their families rather than for all of Virginia's slaves.[27]

The complicated plan invited something to go fatally wrong. On the appointed day, a violent thunderstorm lashed Richmond with sheets of rain, washing away many of the bridges. Blocked by the swollen streams and rivers, few rebels could make it to their rendezvous point. The confusion spread alarm among those in on the secret. A few fearful slaves sought to save themselves by revealing the plot to their masters, who alerted the militia officers. Called into service, the militia patrolled the roads and arrested suspects for interrogations, which identified Gabriel and other leaders.[28]

The trials commenced on September 11, and executions began the next day, for the justice inflicted was summary and harsh. Gabriel initially eluded arrest, slipping away down the James River on a schooner, but on September 23 magistrates arrested him in Norfolk. Following a quick trial in Richmond, he died in front of a huge crowd on October 10, when a noose snapped his neck. By December 1, twenty-seven men paid with their lives for trying but failing at revolution. They met their deaths with a defiant resolve that alarmed a watching John Randolph: "The accused have exhibited a spirit, which, if it becomes general, must deluge the Southern country in blood. They manifested a sense of their rights, and contempt of danger, and a thirst for revenge which portend the most unhappy consequences." An unusually sympathetic white man, John Minor, concluded, "My heart bleeds for them, and yet this degree of severity is necessary." Only a measure of terror could maintain slavery in Virginia.[29]

Governor Monroe needed to execute some plotters to appease local whites and terrify the enslaved, but he also worried that over-kill would play badly in the northern press. Randolph noted that the only blood shed by the rebellion was "that which streamed upon the scaffold." Given that no whites had died, excessive hangings would make Virginians seem bloodthirsty. With the presidential election looming, Monroe's friend Jefferson also wanted to limit the executions lest they sway some northern voters in favor of Adams. Writing to Monroe, Jefferson urged, "There is a strong sentiment that there has been hanging enough. The other states and the world at large will forever condemn us if we indulge a principle of revenge." Monroe slowed the executions, and Jefferson won the presidency.[30]

In January 1801, Monroe recommended, and the state legislature approved, a new policy of selling some convicted slaves outside of the United States. Known as "transportation," distant sale got rid of a dangerous slave and punished his family while reducing the expenses borne by the state, which had to compensate the master for the appraised value of an executed slave. The new transportation law spared eight of Gabriel's convicted plotters from the noose. Slave traders took them far away to Louisiana, then a foreign colony.[31]

Chains

The crisis inspired St. George Tucker's cousin, the young lawyer George Tucker, to publish an appeal to the state legislature. Dwelling on "the danger arising from domestic slavery," George Tucker insisted that Gabriel "has waked those who were asleep, and wiped the film from the eyes of the blind." At last, Tucker hoped, Virginians might make the necessary sacrifices to emancipate their slaves. He noted that the rebels had been enlightened and emboldened by overhearing the republican rhetoric of free men. Such slaves would no longer submit without trying their strength in revolt. In fleeing to Lord Dunmore during the revolution, "they sought freedom merely as a good; now they also claim it as a right." Should the British return as enemies, they would "hold out the lure of freedom" and "have, in every negro, a decided friend." Tucker astutely predicted that the British could "convert a willing multitude into a compact and disciplined army." Therefore, he concluded, Virginians should begin to free their slaves or "see our folly [culminate], in one general wreck of property and life."[32]

Avoiding appeals to humanity and morality, George Tucker narrowed his argument to the most urgent concern of Virginians: their safety from revolt. To appease the still greater dread of freed blacks, Tucker explicitly rejected his cousin's alternative of freeing but retaining slaves as a lower caste, lest "a foreign enemy" exploit their discontent at inequality. His program would tax masters to raise the revenue needed to buy adolescent slaves and transport them to some distant frontier. Few Virginians, however, would accept increased taxes or the notion that white, wage laborers could replace the deported slaves. Like Jefferson, George Tucker proved insightful about the problem of slavery but proposed an absurd solution.[33]

Nonetheless, the governor and legislators sought to keep open their future options for emancipation by procuring a distant haven for potential freedmen. In June 1801, Governor Monroe wrote to President Jefferson to request the federal purchase of some foreign or frontier territory to serve as a Virginia colony "to which persons obnoxious to the laws or dangerous to the peace of society may be removed." Monroe's opaque wording perfectly expressed the confusion of the legislators, who could not agree on whom they intended to deport. At a minimum, they wanted a place to dump future slave convicts, but the legislators also hinted that Virginia might someday free some slaves if provided with a faraway place to send them.[34]

Monroe also had to be circumspect lest his letter become public and, so, violate the Virginian code of silence regarding emancipation and revolt. Carefully avoiding the terms *slave, rebellion,* and *emancipation,* Monroe instead referred to "a subject of great delicacy and importance," which "involves the future peace, tranquility and happiness of the good people of this Commonwealth." Sharing that caution, Jefferson replied with comparable circumlocutions. In a succession of cryptic and noncommittal letters stretching into early 1802, the governor and the president produced a farce, for neither could grasp precisely what the other meant to do. In the end, Jefferson ruled out a black colony on the American frontier because white settlers coveted those lands. Jefferson wanted a white man's republic to cover the continent without "either blot or mixture on that surface." He favored shipping blacks to Africa or the West Indies, but neither the United States nor Virginia could afford to fund an overseas colony, so nothing came of the ambiguous proposal by the legislature. Monroe revealingly told Jefferson that emancipation would have to be "without expense or inconvenience to ourselves."[35]

Unable to free slaves "without expense or inconvenience," Virginia's legislators preferred to blame the rebellion on masters' alleged indulgence of ungrateful slaves. Monroe expressed surprise that the slaves would rebel, "for their treatment has been more favorable since the revolution." Rather than abolish slavery, the legislators decided that safety lay in greater repression, so they funded more arms for the militia, tightened the laws restricting slave movements, and established an armed "Public Guard" to patrol the streets of Richmond and protect the arsenal, treasury, and governor's mansion. Any blacks caught on the Richmond streets after a 9:00 p.m. curfew could be stripped, whipped, and cast into an iron cage for the rest of the night. Likening the slaves to a dangerous beast, a Virginian concluded, "If we will keep a ferocious monster in our country, we must keep him in chains."[36]

In January 1801 the legislators did buy and free two slaves. On the fateful night of August 30, 1800, Pharoah and Tom had revealed the plot and later testified against the rebels. "Sound policy dictates that rewards should be held out to those who have rendered essential service to our country," reasoned the legislators. In the end, Gabriel's revolt emancipated two slaves but at the cost of twenty-seven other lives.[37]

During the ensuing five years, the legislators continued to tighten restrictions on the enslaved. No slaves could hold worship meetings at night unless their master also attended and no Quaker presided. Seeking greater security in black ignorance, the legislators exhorted masters to prevent their slaves from learning literacy. Public pressure kept pace, ostracizing the few remaining liberals who had formed societies to support schools for blacks. Almost all of the societies had disbanded by 1805, when a former member in Alexandria declared, "We are in fact dead; and I may say, I have no hope of reanimation."[38]

Most Virginians believed that blacks were more dangerous when free than when enslaved. Although few free blacks had anything to do with Gabriel's plot, they became the usual suspects blamed by Virginians, who insisted that the freed set alluring examples of indolence that inspired slaves to seek freedom through revolt. "It is the free blacks who instill into the slaves ideas hostile to our peace," declared the legislator Thomas B. Robertson. Banish the free blacks and the slaves would become docile and resigned to their proper fate. Robertson explained, "If the blacks see all of their color slaves, it will seem to them a disposition of Providence, and they will be content." By blaming the freed for the revolt, Virginians could evade faulting themselves and their slave system.[39]

To restrict further growth in the freed population, the hardliners also pushed to ban manumissions. In response, moderates insisted that manumissions provided a safety valve that reduced the threat of slave revolt. Addressing his colleagues, John Minor warned, "What will be the situation of the blacks if you shut this only door through which they can enter the sacred ground of liberty? They will be fixed in the deepest state of damnation, despair without hope. In such a situation, they will prefer death to existence." Dismayed by the sacrifice of revolutionary principles, Minor lamented, "In past days these walls have rung with eulogies on liberty. A comparison between those times and the present is degrading to us. We may be equal in intelligence and virtue, but not in the love of liberty."[40]

In reply, the hardliners insisted that natural law principles were dangerously incompatible with a slave system that they could not safely abolish. "Tell us not of principles," declared Robertson. "Those principles have been annihilated by the existence of slavery among us." While regretting slavery in theory, the hardliners defended the system as a necessary practice. One legislator tellingly referred to blacks as "the melancholy race of men, whose fate we may deplore, but cannot redress." Maintaining slavery had become the hard but immutable duty of Virginians.[41]

In early 1806 the legislature rebuffed a complete ban on manumission by just two votes. Then, by a 94 to 65 vote, the legislators passed a supposed compromise: masters could still manumit, but the freed had to leave the state within one year or face renewed slavery. As intended, the law had a chilling effect on manumissions. For example, in the town of Petersburg, masters freed 173 slaves between 1782 and 1806 but none during the following five years.[42]

Slaves longed for freedom but also to remain among their family and friends. In the dispersed slavery of postrevolutionary Virginia, few families belonged entirely to the same master; therefore, the freed would suffer exile far from their enslaved kin left behind in Virginia. Manumitted without his wife and children, John Winston moved to Pennsylvania, which he soon regretted. Petitioning the legislature for permission to return to his family in Virginia, Winston explained that he could no longer "sacrifice ... his domestic happiness" for his "love of liberty." Many blacks also balked at living among strangers in the northern states, where prejudice and discrimination prevailed. Masters rationalized that true humanity kept their slaves at home in Virginia instead of casting them adrift as free people in the cold uncertainty of the North.[43]

Ultimately the new law worked in tandem with a decisive shift in public opinion against freeing any more slaves. As a boy in Bedford County, Jeremiah Bell Jeter grew up with slavery: "Slaves were my nurses and the companions of my childhood and youth. To many of them I formed a strong and enduring attachment." He despised the harsh treatment inflicted by his neighbors on their slaves: "They were poorly fed, thinly clothed, hardly worked, cruelly chastised for slight or imaginary offenses, and in some cases, murdered." Bolstered by his evangelical faith, Jeter vowed never to own another human, but he married a woman who had inherited slaves. He then decided that blacks were unsuited for freedom: unable "to support themselves, . . . the free negroes were, in general, in a worse condition than the slaves." Moreover, his slaves wanted to stay in Virginia: "If sent, they must be forced to leave their wives and children, belonging to other masters, to dwell in a strange land." Jeter concluded that he had to keep them: a decision shared by thousands of other Virginians.[44]

Virginia's leaders rallied around the new consensus that slavery was wrong in principle but essential in practice. Colonel John Taylor deemed slavery "incapable of removal. . . . To whine over it, is cowardly; to aggravate it, criminal; and to forbear to alleviate it, because it cannot be wholly cured, foolish." In sum, masters had a duty to rule their slaves with an iron fist within a velvet glove. While providing better housing, clothing, and food, masters demanded steadier work and longer hours.[45]

Trade

During the late 1790s in national politics, most southerners rallied to the Republican opposition led by Thomas Jefferson and James Madison, who denounced the expansion of national power by the

Federalist administration of John Adams. Although the Federalists did not challenge southern slavery, many southerners worried about the future uses of federal power if state sovereignty eroded. The Federalists also offended southerners by defending trade with the rebels in Saint-Domingue.[46]

In 1800, Jefferson won the presidency, and the Republicans captured control of Congress thanks primarily to southern voters. Jefferson won 82 percent of the electoral votes in the South compared to only 27 percent in the North. Southerners also comprised most of the Republican majority in the House of Representatives that convened in early 1801. Virginia provided more than a quarter of the Republicans in that house: twice as many as from any other state. Attentive to those who had elected him, Jefferson refused, as president, to meddle with slavery, reasoning "that no more good must be attempted than the nation can bear." In 1805, he noted having "long since given up the expectation of any early provision for the extinguishment of slavery among us." He helped to defeat a proposal in Congress to restrict slavery in the new territories of the Louisiana Purchase. His administration also sought to isolate and impoverish the new republic of Haiti (the renamed Saint-Domingue), which he dreaded as a dangerous example to American slaves: "The existence of a negro people in arms, occupying a country which it has soiled by the most criminal acts, is a horrible spectacle for all white nations."[47]

In 1802 Jefferson's postmaster general, Gideon Granger, dismissed the free blacks employed in his department, reasoning that they threatened the security of the slave states. He assured a southern congressman,

> After the scenes which St. Domingo has exhibited to the world, we cannot be too cautious in attempting to prevent similar evils. . . . Everything which tends to increase their knowledge of natural rights, of men and things, or that affords them an opportunity of associating, acquiring and communicating sen-

timents, and of establishing a chain and line of intelligence, must increase your hazard. . . . By traveling from day to day, and hourly mixing with people, they must, [and] they will acquire information. They will learn that a man's rights do not depend on his colour.

Having concluded that blacks must *not* discover that "all men are created equal," Jefferson's postmaster general persuaded Congress to restrict postal work to white men.[48]

Jefferson and other southern Republicans did push to ban the importation of more Africans as slaves. They reasoned that the natural increase in the current slave population sufficed for expanding the plantation economy westward, and they feared that new slaves from Africa were especially prone to revolt. In March 1807, acting on Jefferson's recommendation, Congress outlawed the import slave trade, effective January 1, 1808: the first year the Federal Constitution permitted such a ban. The overwhelming vote, 113 to 5, in the House of Representatives attested to broad support in the South as well as the North. But the new law manifested no commitment to antislavery within the nation and no bar to the booming interstate trade in slaves. Indeed, by eliminating foreign competition, Virginians could sell more slaves to the lower South. The sellers also expected to sleep more securely as the domestic slave trade diffused their surplus slaves at higher prices to the south and west. By banning the import slave trade while expanding the interstate slave trade, the Virginians hoped to render slavery safer and more profitable.[49]

Poison

In the spring of 1806, shortly after the state legislature limited manumissions, a murder shocked the people of Richmond. On Sunday, May 25, 1806, George Wythe became violently ill after drinking his morning coffee. It had been laced with arsenic. The same poison gripped his black cook and housekeeper, Lydia Broadnax, and a mixed-race boy, Michael Brown. A liberal who lived by his principles, Wythe had freed both and readily shared coffee with them despite their darker complexions. Broadnax slowly recovered, but Brown died on June 1, and Wythe on June 8, after two weeks of torment. He was eighty years old.[50]

Leading Virginians revered Wythe as the most learned and ethical of men. "He lived in the world," observed John Randolph, "without being of the world, and . . . was a mere incarnation of justice." Able, modest, polite, erudite, and principled, Wythe had become the leading lawyer and legal educator in Virginia. Since 1789, he had presided as chancellor over the state's court of equity.[51]

He was a rare Virginian to argue that the races could peacefully live together in freedom as equals. After Wythe's wife died in 1787, he freed their slaves, a decision made easier by a lack of children expecting an inheritance. To demonstrate the potential of blacks, Wythe adopted and educated Michael Brown as a gentleman. Unable to accept Wythe's disinterested motives, gossips insisted that he had fathered the boy, with Lydia Broadnax as the mother. In fact, Brown had other parents.[52]

Brown and Wythe did share the same murderer, another member of their household: a young white man named George Wythe Sweeney. As Wythe's grandnephew, Sweeney resented Wythe's good treatment of Brown. Dissipated and indebted, Sweeney sold books pilfered from Wythe's library, and he forged Wythe's signature to fraudulent checks. Fearful that Wythe would discover the frauds, Sweeney poisoned him, Brown, and Broadnax. Shocked Virginians asked who was safe if the best of men could be poisoned by his own relative. Something seemed to have gone badly awry in the postrevolutionary generation.[53]

In September 1806 in Richmond, the state attorney general prosecuted Sweeney for murder, but the jury acquitted him for want of a witness who could testify to seeing him put the poison in the coffee. Broadnax had seen the fatal deed, but Virginia law forbade hearing any testimony by a black against a white. Sweeney killed the most revered of Virginians with impunity because the state refused to consider the truth when spoken by a black person.[54]

Wythe's murder represented the passing of the revolution in Virginia, for thereafter few leading men spoke of natural rights as universal. In his last court case, *Wrights v. Hudgins*, Wythe had ruled against a master, Houlder Hudgins of Mathews County, and awarded freedom to Jacky Wrights and her three young children. The ruling took both narrow and broad grounds. At a minimum, Wythe regarded the Wrights as properly free because they were light in complexion and descended from an Indian woman who had been unjustly enslaved early in the eighteenth century. But he also advanced a more explosive argument that, in freedom cases, the burden of proof should fall on the master because slavery was unnatural and unjust. Wythe cited Virginia's bill of rights, which had declared, in his words, that "freedom is the birth-right of every human being." With this ruling, Wythe tried to reverse the drift in Virginia toward asserting racial inequality as natural and slavery as perpetual. His ruling threatened to expose masters to widespread litigation by slaves seeking their freedom. While burying and honoring Wythe, Virginians hoped that a legal appeal would soon bury his last, dangerous ruling. For that reversal they looked to the presiding judge of the Court of Appeals: St. George Tucker.[55]

Race

After the abrupt rejection of his gradual emancipation plan by the legislature in 1796, Tucker nursed his wounded pride by retreating into a public silence about slavery. Dreading further humiliation, he restricted his antislavery thoughts to private conversations with trusted friends and to letters sent to northern correspondents. In 1797

a Quaker abolitionist solicited Tucker's support for a renewed appeal
to the legislature, but Tucker sadly replied that adding "my name to
it, I fear would prejudice rather than serve the cause." Making peace
with slavery, he closed ranks with other Virginia gentlemen, dismiss-
ing his emancipation plan as a "Utopian idea" in 1803.[56]

Tucker was not about to free his own slaves unilaterally, for he
had too much invested in human beings to renounce their value. In
December 1796, two days after submitting his ill-fated emancipation
plan to the legislature, he hired a slave trader to sell a mother and her
three daughters. Pleased with the prices obtained, Tucker did more
business with the trader over the ensuing four years. With the proceeds, Tucker bought bank stock, which he reserved as a trust fund
for his daughter Anne Frances. In 1815, he appraised his Williamsburg structures, including a rambling mansion ninety-feet long by
thirty-two feet wide, at $1,500, but he appraised his fifteen slaves at
$3,000: twice the value of his real estate. Few gentlemen could free
their slaves without sacrificing their prosperity, social standing, and
ability to pass both on to their children. Whenever Tucker deemed
any slaves redundant, he sold them, or he gave them to his children.
Tucker set aside his antislavery convictions to benefit his heirs.[57]

Tucker gradually embraced the consoling fictions that blacks
were incapable of freedom and happiest under the benign rule of
paternalistic masters. Such slaves were, he explained, "better clothed,
lodged, and fed, than if it depended upon themselves to provide their
own food, raiment, and houses." Slavery also restrained them from
"falling into vicious habits, which emancipated blacks appear too
prone to contract." His son Nathaniel Beverley Tucker described
the family's mission as "to feel and to act toward these poor creatures as to humble and dependent friends." By 1806, paternalism
rather than emancipation had become the mission of genteel masters
in Virginia.[58]

As a judge, Tucker dealt with the freedom suits brought by
mixed-race slaves seeking liberty by claiming descent from an

unjustly enslaved woman: either an Indian or a white indentured servant. Troubled by this litigation, in 1795 the state legislature banned critics of slavery, especially Quakers, from prosecuting such suits on behalf of slaves or from serving on the juries. Thereafter, the number of freedom suits dwindled, but Wythe's provocative ruling in *Wrights v. Hudgins* threaten to revive and expand them.[59]

As a law professor, Tucker eloquently expounded on the natural rights of all men, and on the injustice of slavery, but as a cautious jurist he felt constrained by statutory law and public opinion. Attentive to his social standing, Tucker could ill afford to alienate the masters of Virginia. In November 1806, as chief justice of the Court of Appeals, he demolished Wythe's broader ruling that freedom was the birthright of everyone in Virginia:

> I do not concur with the chancellor in his reasoning on the operation of the first clause of the Bill of Rights, which was notoriously framed with a cautious eye to this subject, and was meant to embrace the case of free citizens, or aliens only; and not by a side wind to overturn the rights of property, and give freedom to those very people whom we have been compelled from imperious circumstances to retain, generally, in the same state of bondage that they were in at the revolution, in which they had no *concern, agency,* or *interest.*

With one stroke, Tucker dismissed blacks from any share in the revolution and its fruits: the Bill of Rights and republican citizenship. He rewrote a history in which at least 500 Virginia slaves had fought as soldiers for the Patriot cause. In the process, Tucker renounced the antislavery principles that he had learned as Wythe's student.[60]

While protecting the rights of property over brown and black people, Tucker also sought to liberate any white-appearing people held in slavery by preserving Wythe's narrower ruling: that the Wrights deserved freedom because of their white skin and Indian maternal ancestor. "This is not a common case of mere *blacks* suing for their freedom; but of persons perfectly *white*," their lawyer reminded the court. Rewriting colonial as well as revolutionary history, Tucker declared, "All *white persons* are and ever have been FREE in this country. If one *evidently white* be notwithstanding claimed as a slave, the proof lies on the party claiming to make the other his slave." Tucker insisted that the burden of proof fell on masters only when the petitioning slaves seemed white in the eye of the judge beholder.[61]

Tucker contributed to the emerging pseudo-science of racial difference. Citing his readings in natural history, Tucker offered a guide for how judges could discern black ancestry in cases where skin color seemed ambiguous. When "the characteristic distinction of color either disappears or becomes doubtful," the descendants of Africans retained "a flat nose and woolly head of hair." Likening them to animals, he insisted "that a man might as easily mistake the glossy, jetty cloathing of an American bear for the wool of a black sheep, as the hair of an American Indian for that of . . . the descendant of an African." In the absence of documented ancestry, Tucker concluded that a presiding justice "must judge from his own view. He must discharge the white person and the Indian out of custody . . . and he must deliver the black or mulatto person, with the flat nose and woolly hair to the person claiming to hold him or her as a slave." The apparently white persons got the benefit of the doubt, while people perceived to have African traits remained enslaved. The other justices supported Tucker's dual ruling: in favor of freeing the Wrights but against the natural freedom of blacks. The only partial caveat came from Judge Spencer Roane, who doubted that judges could so readily tell race by sight given the many mixed-race people of Virginia: when "these races become intermingled, it is difficult if not impossible, to say from inspection only, which race predominates in the offspring."[62]

In 1796, Tucker had vowed, "The abolition of slavery . . . is *now* my *first*, and will probably be my last, expiring wish." A decade later,

he defined a stricter color line meant starkly to demarcate white freedom from black slavery. Joining the reaction against Gabriel's plot,
Tucker helped to redefine slavery in more purely racial terms. Along
with Jefferson, Tucker retreated from the revolutionary flirtation
with universal human rights. Ultimately, both men converted the
scientific reasoning of the Enlightenment from a philosophical call
for equality into a biological mandate for inequality.[63]

Some Virginians could see the lie. The chief justice's cousin,
George Tucker, owned slaves, but he still recognized their natural
equality as humans. Noting Jefferson's case for black inferiority,
George Tucker lamented, "There is no excuse for his remarks. I am
afraid, indeed, that his opinion is but too popular here, as I have heard
several masters ready to justify their severity to these poor wretches,
by alleging, that they are an inferior race, created only to be slaves.
What a horrible doctrine . . . and what a pity that any gentleman of
Mr. J's reputation for talents, should lend it the countenance of his
name." George Tucker might have said the same of his distinguished
cousin, but most Virginians followed where Jefferson and St. George
Tucker led. Thereafter, slaves could expect little from a people whose
revolution had grown cold and hollow. Instead, many of the enslaved
would seek freedom from the returning warships of the liberator
king. With his ruling in 1806, St. George Tucker increased the prospect that blood would spatter the land of Virginia.[64]

4

WARSHIPS

————ᴄᐫᴏ————

In addition to the danger to be apprehended from foreign enemies,
we have in the bosom of our Country an enemy more dangerous
than any we can expect from the other side of the Atlantick.
—THOMAS M. BAYLY, 1812[1]

I N EARLY APRIL 1812, in Montgomery County (in the Piedmont),
two magistrates, John Floyd and Henry Edmondson, interrogated Tom, a black man who confessed to murdering his master on
March 23. As Tom's interrogator, young John Floyd unwittingly
prepared for his role as Virginia's governor nineteen years later,
when he would confront Nat Turner's slave revolt. In 1812 Tom
had killed his master to impress a slave woman named Celia, who
longed for a slave revolt: "She said they could not rise too soon for
her, as she had rather be in hell than where she was." The magistrates asked Tom, "Have you any knowledge of other negroes . . .
who are disposed to rise in order to kill their masters?" In reply, he

Gilbert Hunt (1773–1863). An enslaved blacksmith in Richmond in 1811, Hunt
helped to rescue white people caught in the Richmond fire. For his courage, Hunt received
freedom and went to Liberia, but he later returned to Richmond. His actions in 1811
belied the myth that slaves set the fire. Taken by an unknown photographer, this image
is from the end of his life, during the Civil War. (Courtesy of the Valentine Richmond
History Center)

knew of thirty or forty, allegedly "instigated to kill their masters" by a conjuror.[2]

Tom then broached an even more terrifying prospect: "The negroes in the neighborhood said that these British people was about to rise against this Country, and that they intended to rise sometime in next May. . . . That they said they were not made to work for the white people, but they (the white people), made to work for themselves; and that they (the negroes) would have it so." Noting a recent deadly fire in a crowded Richmond theater, Tom added, "The negroes in the neighborhood said they were glad that the people were burnt in Richmond, and wished that all the white people had been burnt with them. That God Almighty had sent them a little Hell for the white people, and that in a little time they would get a greater." Pressed for his source for an impending British invasion, Tom explained, "It was heard from the poor people in the neighborhood, and by hearing the newspapers read."[3]

Often the reports of Virginia slave plots reveal the overreaction and ventriloquism of panicked whites, but this transcript seems far closer to the words of a slave, and Tom had, in fact, killed a master. Tom also resisted some of the leading questions posed by the magistrates such as, "Did you ever hear them say whether they intended to murder the white women and children, or not?" The indiscriminate murder of women and children was a staple of the white fantasy version of slave revolt. But Tom answered, and his interrogators noted, "I never heard them say [so]." Floyd and Edmondson concluded "that a deep and extensive plan is now in agitation against this country" because "the negroes are under an impression that it is now in their power to liberate themselves." On May 18 the magistrates hanged Tom and compensated his owner's widow with $450.[4]

Aside from Tom's murder of his master, however, the Montgomery County slaves were guilty of talk rather than action, for they intended to await the arrival of a British invasion force. Far from relying on British agents, blacks got their news from newspapers and the conversations of poor white people. The Virginia code of silence about slavery in public forums seems especially pointless given the ease with which blacks overheard the political talk of white folk, who openly worried that the British would return in armed force to liberate Virginia's slaves. That threat seemed more ominous to the planters because the British recently had adopted a moral crusade to restrict slavery, providing a better fit with the longing by American slaves for a liberator king.[5]

Empire

During the decade after 1800, the British became the global champions for suppressing the slave trade and ameliorating slavery. They linked that cause to their military struggle against Napoléon's domination of Europe, as proof that their empire promoted freedom around the world. On February 23, 1807, Parliament abolished the overseas slave trade, effective January 1, 1808. That abolition sacrificed a powerful economic interest, for the slave trade and the plantation colonies were then booming. The prime minister, Lord Grenville, praised that abolition as "one of the most glorious acts that had ever been undertaken by any assembly of any nation in the world." While banning the slave trade, however, Parliament did not liberate the 600,000 slaves already in the British West Indies. Indeed, to protect the British planters from foreign competitors, the imperial government pressed other nations to bar the slave trade to their colonies. By leading a global push to ban the slave trade, British diplomacy both protected the British West Indian sugar producers and claimed a high moral ground. Although the United States barred slave imports at the same time, British diplomacy and the Royal Navy did far more to enforce the ban than did the Americans.[6]

Parliament's ban demonstrated the powerful growth of antislavery sentiment within Great Britain. During the 1780s and 1790s, English Quakers, Methodists, and evangelical Anglicans had built a mass movement to abolish the slave trade. Seeking to moderate the brutal slavery in the West Indies, the reformers reasoned that, if deprived of new slaves, the planters would have to stop driving their current slaves to early graves. The activists then hoped that ameliorating the conditions for the slaves eventually would lead to their emancipation. Infused with middle-class values as well as Christian zeal, they insisted on the right of every individual to realize his potential by reaping the rewards of his own labor. By appealing to the Christian consciences of common people, the antislavery activists secured thousands of signers to petitions addressed to Parliament.[7]

The political mobilization stunned the West Indian planters, who insisted that abolition would ruin the sugar production that generated so much profit for merchants and revenue for the empire. The trade's defenders attacked the antislavery activists as dangerous radicals in secret cahoots with the French revolutionaries. During the 1790s the slave revolt in Saint-Domingue also put the activists on the defensive as planters insisted that any antislavery discussion provoked bloodshed in the West Indies.[8]

Antislavery gained more political traction as British nationalism after 1800, when Napoléon seized power in France and sought to restore slavery and the slave trade in his empire. Activists toned down their moral and religious appeals in favor of a military security argument: that abolishing of the slave trade would strengthen the British Empire at the expense of the French. The abolitionists insisted that Saint-Domingue had demonstrated the vulnerability of all West Indian colonies to revolt so long as they remained slave societies. Consequently, the empire would inevitably lose the British West Indies if those colonies continued to fill with restive Africans. In Parliament, Henry Brougham asked, "When fire is raging to windward, is it the proper time for stirring up everything that is combustible in your warehouse, and throwing into them new loads of material still more prone to explosion?" So recast, antislavery served imperial power as well as moral principle, ennobling Britain's dual struggle to expand her global empire of commerce and defeat Napoléon.[9]

Imperial officials deployed antislavery measures to tighten their control over the West Indian colonists, who opposed the slave trade ban and other measures to ameliorate slavery. The planters already rued the empire's decision in 1795 to establish eight regiments of black troops to defend the islands. Stretched thin fighting the French in Europe, the British could not afford to send more white troops to die of tropical diseases in the West Indies. Turning to slave soldiers, the British promised equal treatment, uniforms, and pay with white troops. In 1807 the imperial government offered freedom to those who performed honorably through their full term of service. But the equality remained incomplete, for only white men could serve as officers in the West Indian regiments.[10]

The West Indian planters did not want their slaves to see black men bearing arms. One planter complained, "Compared to slavery, the restrictions of military discipline are an exquisite freedom; and the negro who has once tasted it cannot be expected to return quietly to the yoke, and again expose his back to the whip." Soldiering would ruin slaves and perhaps slavery. The West Indian planters also recognized that the black troops strengthened the empire at the expense of the colonial legislators. Because the West Indian legislators blocked the enlistment of local slaves, the empire bought Africans to serve in the black regiments: not exactly what the abolitionists had in mind. After the British abolition of the slave trade, the army stopped buying slaves but impressed into service the black men found on board slave ships intercepted by the Royal Navy.[11]

The black troops quickly proved their worth to the empire. In addition to suffering far fewer losses to disease, they rarely deserted, for they had everything to lose by slipping away into a slave society. Their discipline and courage also impressed their officers, who clamored for more black, and fewer white, troops to defend the West Indies. By 1803 the approximately 8,000 black troops comprised most of the "British" force in the West Indies.[12]

Ultimately, Britain's black troops had a contradictory impact on slave society in the West Indies. On the one hand, they saved that society from French-inspired slave revolts, preserving the British West Indies as plantation colonies. On the other hand, by treating black soldiers as the equals to white soldiers, the imperial government weakened the racial justification for slavery.

In 1797 the black regiments helped the British to conquer the Spanish colony of Trinidad, an island at the southeastern end of the West Indies. Relatively large and fertile, Trinidad was economically underdeveloped but promising as a plantation colony for raising sugarcane. British planters longed for the opportunity to cultivate the island with imported slaves, but they faced parliamentary opposition from abolitionists, who balked at boosting the slave trade to meet the voracious, new demand for labor in Trinidad. Warning of a foreign invasion and internal revolt there, James Stephen insisted that developing a slave colony was "scarcely less irrational than it would be to build a town near the crater of Vesuvius." A member of Parliament, Stephen had lived in the West Indies, where he came to hate slavery as an immoral menace to British rule. The abolitionists also found tacit support from planters in the older British colonies who disliked the prospect of competition from new plantations on Trinidad.[13]

Responsive to the old planters and new activists, the Privy Council and prime minister barred any further importation of slaves into Trinidad after 1805. In early 1812, Stephen also secured a Privy Council order imposing, for the first time in a Crown colony, a systematic registration of the slaves in Trinidad. Abolitionists reasoned that a registry (with an annual reporting of deaths and mutilations) would compel the planters to treat their slaves better, but the planters resented any interference in the management of their plantations, so they did their best to frustrate the registry.[14]

A Private of the 5th West India Regiment, *1814. Aquatint by I. J. C. Stadler after Charles Hamilton Smith. (Courtesy of the Council of the National Army Museum, London).*

While allowing the old plantations with slaves to persist on the island, the British officials sought to develop a new farming sector with free black settlers. By West Indian standards, Trinidad already had an unusually large proportion of "free coloureds": 20 percent of the population in 1810. The antislavery imperialists sought to prove that the West Indies could thrive with free peasants, rather than slaves, producing cacao and sugar. The reformers also argued that free blacks would defend the colony from invasion—in contrast to slaves, who would welcome invaders as liberators. The British foreign minister, George Canning, declared, "We have our choice, whether to make Trinidad a new sugar growing, negro driving colony, productive indeed, but weak, and exposed, and inviting attack in proportion—or to create there a place of military strength, a fortress for the defence of our other colonies, and to lay the foundation of a new system of colonization for future military purposes."[15]

By promoting the growth of a free black society, antislavery activists hoped to encourage eventual abolition throughout the West Indies. Stephen predicted that, if endowed with "free, strong and faithful hands to defend it, . . . Trinidad may become at once an example, and a protection; a farm of experiment, and a fortress to the rest of our Sugar Colonies." But he warned against "the fatal error of giving to it, in its infancy, a Legislative Assembly." To defend the reform policies, the Crown appointed a governor and a council but allowed no elected legislature for Trinidad. Imperialists recognized that white legislators would defend slavery and suppress free blacks. The colony's free blacks agreed, petitioning the Crown against granting an elected assembly to Trinidad. Imperial consolidation went hand in hand with initiatives to protect blacks from white planters. Excluded from the American Revolution by their geopolitical situation, the white West Indians could only seethe as the empire tightened its power over them in the name of protecting blacks. Virginians felt blessed to have escaped that imperial power through revolution, but their slaves had new reasons to look to the British as potential liberators.[16]

During the global war against France, the British aggressively redefined their empire in benevolent and humanitarian terms. Imperialists posed as the protectors and benefactors of darker-skinned peoples deemed capable of becoming free and Christian under the tutelage of their British superiors. The new breed of imperialists cast local planter elites as selfish exploiters of slaves and as obstacles to Christian uplift and the consolidating power of the empire.[17]

However sincerely held, the new principles served the imperial drive to dominate and exploit foreign peoples as supposed inferiors. And colonial practices often contradicted the lofty principles espoused in Parliament and the imperial cabinet. In Trinidad in 1801–1802, the governor, General Thomas Picton, favored developing the island as a traditional sugar colony worked by imported slaves. He also used torture to elicit confessions from slaves and free people of color. But the government sacked and prosecuted Picton, replacing him with a governor who clung more closely to the imperial script by protecting free blacks while denying a legislature to the white planters.[18]

The empire's contradictions naturally led Americans to denounce the British as dangerous hypocrites who built their global power on hollow pieties. Citing British massacres in Ireland and India and their military assistance to Native Americans, one Virginian denounced "those half-Indian, scalping assassins, those degenerate, ferocious Disgraces to civilization, the British, the enemies of virtue, liberty and America." American masters regarded their West Indian counterparts as the victims of an imperialism rendered more insidious by its new moralism. Virginians feared the arrival of that imperialism on their own shores, as warships pushing into Chesapeake Bay with black troops on board. In turn, however, the alarmed talk of Virginians alerted listening slaves that they might become free by escaping to those ships.[19]

Sailors

On June 22, 1807, a British frigate, HMS *Leopard*, intercepted an American frigate, USS *Chesapeake*, in the Atlantic about eight miles beyond the mouth of Chesapeake Bay. The British captain, Salusbury Humphreys, demanded permission to board the *Chesapeake* to seek deserters from the Royal Navy. The American captain, James Barron, refused, so the *Leopard* unleashed three devastating broadsides at close range, crippling the *Chesapeake*, killing three sailors, and wounding another sixteen. The ill-prepared American crew could discharge only one cannon before Barron surrendered. The victorious Humphreys sent across a search party, which returned to the *Leopard* with four sailors deemed deserters. The victors then released the ravaged *Chesapeake* to return to Norfolk for repairs. As a warning to other sailors, the British hanged one of the deserters and cast the other three into prison in Halifax, Nova Scotia, the Royal Navy's primary naval base in North America.[20]

Captain Humphreys acted on orders from his admiral, Sir George Cranfield Berkeley, who meant to stem the American practice of harboring deserters from the Royal Navy. The admiral also enforced the British insistence that no man born anywhere within the empire could ever renounce his duties as a subject. Allegiance began at birth and ended only in death. No matter where a "natural-born subject" emigrated, he remained obligated to serve the king in time of war. The imperial government asserted that no legal process of naturalization could remake a British subject into an American citizen.[21]

British officers routinely stopped and inspected the merchant ships of their own and other nations to impress seamen into service in the Royal Navy. A relatively small homeland surrounded by the sea, Britain required thousands of sailors and marines to work a powerful fleet meant to keep European enemies away. The navy also protected the trade routes of a vast, overseas empire, which funneled a lion's share of the world's colonial commerce into British ports. During the long, hard war against the French Revolution and, later, Napoléon's empire, the Royal Navy had grown to a mammoth scale that demanded over 100,000 seamen.[22]

Many British sailors evaded naval service by seeking berths in the booming American merchant marine. Because the United States remained neutral in the global war, American merchants picked up trade on routes too dangerous for French shipping. By evading the British blockade of France and her colonies, the American neutral trade benefited Napoléon at the expense of the British Empire. The profits of this trade induced the Americans to build more ships, doubling the tonnage of their merchant marine between 1792 and 1807. Lacking enough American-born sailors, the merchants paid premium wages to attract the sailors of other nations, and Britain offered veteran seamen keen to serve under another flag. American shippers paid $15 per month for able sailors, compared to just $7 in the British navy. That discrepancy pushed sailors away from Britain and pulled them onto American vessels. By 1807, at least two-fifths of the 50,000 sailors working American merchant ships were British by birth, and the Royal Navy wanted them back.[23]

Crisis loomed as the empire and the republic competed for a limited pool of sailors in a world at war. The British insisted that they retrieved only their own subjects from American merchant ships, but Royal Navy captains defined American citizens narrowly and British subjects broadly. Often a naval captain simply took the best sailors who spoke English, which included hundreds of Americans as well as thousands of Britons.[24]

Led by Jefferson and Madison, the governing Republicans asserted America's right to create citizens by naturalization. They also insisted that the American flag vested every merchant ship with national sovereignty, rendering their crews properly immune to foreign impressment. American diplomats conceded only the wartime right of a belligerent to stop and search ships for munitions bound to an enemy's port, so they protested when the British extended those searches to reclaim supposed subjects.[25]

The British countered that as the world's dominant naval power, they set and enforced international law on the high seas. Embroiled in a massive war against France, the British demanded greater understanding and restraint from the Americans. Claiming to defend the world, including the United States, against conquest by Napoléon, the British urged the Americans to repatriate British sailors and tolerate the occasional impressment of the American-born.[26]

Given the weakness of the American navy, Britons marveled at the high pretensions of American diplomacy. To save money, the Jefferson administration had reduced the navy to about a dozen oceanic warships, compared to more than 500 in the powerful Royal Navy. For coastal defense, the Republicans relied on cheap and paltry gunboats that could not venture far from shore. Most Republicans balked at building a stronger navy of bigger ships, for fear that they could never compete with the British and would only invite a preemptive strike, like that recently inflicted on neutral Denmark by the Royal Navy. Consequently, the Americans could only seethe as British warships hovered off the major seaports to board and inspect every passing vessel to impress sailors.[27]

To sustain their coastal patrols, however, the British warships needed provisions and water bought from the American ports. When the warships sent boats into American seaports to make the purchases, many of the seamen ran away, and mobs of sailors and laborers protected them from retrieval by their officers. The seaport magistrates did little or nothing, for they either applauded the desertions or feared the mobs. Such incidents confirmed the British prejudice against the American republic as anarchic.[28]

When British officers and diplomats protested, Secretary of State Madison invited the British to forsake impressment at sea in return for an American promise to retrieve naval deserters. In effect, American officials winked at the desertions and mobs as the means to pressure the British. That tacit collusion enraged the British as the consummate mix of republican weakness and perfidy. A British diplomat complained, "I came to treat with a regular government, and have to deal [instead] with a mob and mob leaders."[29]

To recoup their losses from desertion, British naval officers impressed more sailors from the ships leaving or entering American ports. A British diplomat conceded that it was "highly grating to the Feelings of an independent Nation to perceive that their whole Coast is watched as closely as if it was blockaded, and every Ship coming in or going out of their Harbours examined rigorously in Sight of the Shore by British Squadrons stationed within their Waters." In a vicious cycle, Americans enticed deserters, while Britons impressed more Americans, fueling a mutual and deepening animus on British warships and in American seaports. In June 1807, that cycle culminated in the attack by the *Leopard* on the *Chesapeake*.[30]

"Panack"

On June 23, 1807, the return of the battered *Chesapeake* to Norfolk sparked "a General Panack," in the words of one resident. The inhabitants assumed that the British would next attack American seaports, beginning with Norfolk. Infuriated by the sight of dead and bloodied sailors, the defiant citizens convened a mass meeting that resolved to deny communication and supplies to any British warships. Hundreds of angry men promptly surrounded the Norfolk home of the British consul, John Hamilton, to demand the surrender of a visiting naval lieutenant as "an Atonement for the Blood shed on board the Chesapeake." Only the intervention of American naval officers and the Norfolk magistrates saved the visitor from the lynch mob and his schooner from burning. In nearby Hampton, another mob smashed 200 water casks intended for the British frigates in the nearby bay.[31]

It was all so republican for mobs and a mass meeting of local citizens to act without waiting for direction from their governor or president. Indeed, the state and national leaders had to scramble to catch up. Virginia's governor, William H. Cabell, called out 700 militiamen to guard Norfolk and nearby Princess Anne County, and he appointed Brigadier General Thomas Mathews to command them. President Jefferson committed the national government to pay for their support, and he issued a proclamation barring supplies to, and contact with, the British warships.[32]

At the mouth of Chesapeake Bay, Captain John Erskine Douglas commanded two Royal Navy frigates and two larger "ships of the line." The Americans could counter with only the battered *Chesapeake* and four petty gunboats. Confident in his superior firepower, Douglas wrote a menacing letter to Norfolk's mayor, demanding the immediate restoration of supplies and communication with the British consul. Douglas threatened to blockade Norfolk's shipping until the mayor submitted to the ultimatum. In mock honor of the captain, the Virginians called the crisis "the Douglas war."[33]

On July 4, primed with patriotic speeches and alcoholic toasts, Mayor Richard E. Lee responded to Douglas with republican bombast: "The day on which this answer is written ought of itself to suffice to prove to the subjects of your sovereign that the American people are not to be intimidated by menace. . . . We are prepared for the worst which you may attempt." But Lee knew better, for on the same day he privately warned Governor Cabell, "The militia of this section of the Country are almost defenceless." The men lacked arms, training, discipline, and able officers. Jefferson's military advisor in Norfolk, William Tatham, reported, "I wish to God some old officer was sent among us who would introduce order, economy, & discipline, in lieu of shew, puffs, & good eating & drinking. If feasts, popular toasts, fine speeches, patriotic professions, & self important airs were weapons . . . we should drive all our Enemies *into the red sea*!" After a parlay with Douglas on his flagship, Lee left in a huff, feeling insulted by the British officers, who tended "to cast sarcasms, and to treat with derision and contempt the feelings of the American people and the measures which had been adopted." The officers mocked the combination of republican boasting with military weakness.[34]

The crisis deepened as Douglas landed sailors to seek supplies and draw water from isolated shores. On July 16 in Princess Anne County, a militia patrol captured two British midshipmen and three sailors. Another patrol fired on a second landing party, which rowed away, leaving behind water casks and muskets.[35]

While five Britons entered captivity in Virginia, five slaves from Princess Anne County sought freedom by stealing a canoe and a fishing boat to escape to HMS *Triumph*. Eager for information and to tweak the Virginians, the naval officers welcomed the refugees. An alarmed General Mathews warned Governor Cabell that the British welcome had "made a deep impression on the minds of our people, and will no doubt increase their resentment." In addition to fearing the mass escape of more slaves, the Virginians dreaded their potential return as armed emissaries of bloody revolt.[36]

In mid-July, Douglas sailed away, transferring command to Captain Thomas M. Hardy, who saw the runaways as a chance to intimidate the Virginians. Hardy opened a back channel to the British consul in Norfolk with the covert help of Henry Jackson, "a Black Pilot, whose whole conduct toward us since the 22nd June has been Exemplary." A free black, Jackson carried to Hamilton a letter from Hardy conveying his plan to awe the Virginians into cooperation:

Now, Sir, I feel it my duty to point out the risk that the Inhabitants of Virginia may incur by totally excluding His Majesty's Squadron from their Shores, and from Supplies of every description. This Morning . . . a small boat was observed not far from the *Triumph* apparently in want of assistance. I sent a Boat immediately to her relief and found in her three black Men, who call themselves free . . . & they told me that many hundreds of the same description of persons were ready to come on board, provided boats for that purpose could be procured, and one [man], who seems very intelligent, told me that more than two thousands of the people of Colour would join if I would only land the Soldiers.

Hardy wanted Hamilton to pass on this threat of mass flight and slave revolt to intimidate the Virginians. Although he had no intention of provoking bloodshed, Hardy hoped to bluff the Virginians into reopening his communications with, and supplies from, their shores. He sought to deploy the "internal enemy" in the minds, rather than against the bodies, of the Virginians.[37]

In reply, Hamilton warned that Hardy was playing with fire: "nothing would, at this Juncture, have a more general tendency to increase the popular irritation in this quarter than the Idea of any facility being offered to the Escape of the Negroes, at all Seasons with the inhabitants of the Sea Coast an object of peculiar Jealousy and anxious apprehension." Far from intimidating the inhabitants, Hardy's threats would enrage them into overt hostilities, so Hamilton urged the captain to receive no more runaways and return the five already on board his ship.[38]

Jefferson also wanted to reduce tensions, so he ordered the release of the five captured British sailors, who came back to their warship on August 1. Hardy then forced his five runaways to return to their masters. In 1807 the British were not yet prepared to liberate American slaves. By initially welcoming the five runaways, however, the Royal Navy had planted a seed of alarm in the minds of Virginians, who expected the worst in the event of a future war. Captain Robert Barraud Taylor of Norfolk brought the slaves from Hardy's ship back ashore to their masters. Five years later, on the eve of war with the empire, he warned Virginia's governor that "Sir Thomas Hardy [had] received a communication from the slaves that they were ready to unite with the British so soon as they hoisted their war flag."[39]

During the *Chesapeake* crisis, British sailors deserted from their warships, while runaway slaves fled to those vessels in search of freedom. A land of liberty for white men, the American republic sustained slavery for African Americans, who continued to hope for a liberator king. Depending on race, one person's floating prison was another's portal to freedom.

Declaration

Nationwide, during June and July 1807, the attack on the *Chesapeake* outraged Federalists as well as Republicans. Protest meetings adopted angry resolutions demanding preparations for war, while mobs raged in the seaport streets, smashing British boats and the windows where British diplomats resided. In Philadelphia, the British consul also complained that a musical mob sang "Indecent Tunes . . . before my House late at Night."[40]

But the republic was better prepared for singing than fighting because the Republicans had curtailed the nation's military in order to cut costs and diminish taxes. Reduced to a mere 3,287 men, the army struggled to patrol a frontier of 10,000 miles and a coastline at least twice that long, extending from Louisiana, on the Gulf Coast, to Maine, on the Bay of Fundy. For want of warships, soldiers, fortifications, and cannon, the seaports were exposed to British naval attack. Jefferson, however, had to do something in light of the crisis, so he ordered the gunboats repaired, and he directed the state governors to prepare 100,000 militiamen for federal service. A reserve of militia amateurs cost far less than a real army of professional soldiers on active duty. By threatening British Canada with invasion by a militia army, Jefferson hoped to pressure the empire, but his Secretary of the Treasury conceded that the men could come only from the northern states because "none can be spared from the negro country." The southern militiamen had to stay home to guard against a slave revolt. The Republicans planned a war to liberate Canada while defending slavery in America.[41]

Neither the British nor the American government wanted war. Jefferson dreaded that the immense costs would swell the national debt and require increased taxes, which would sap his popularity. And the British preferred to concentrate on their pressing struggle against Napoléon. To limit the controversy with the republic, Britain's rulers agreed to pay reparations, return the three surviving

American sailors taken from the *Chesapeake*, and renounce searches of neutral warships. The British, however, refused to relinquish their power to stop and inspect neutral merchant ships to impress sailors and enforce a blockade on French-dominated Europe.[42]

Unable and unwilling to declare overt war, the Republicans settled for waging an economic war. Factory workers in Britain and planters in the West Indies would starve, Jefferson reasoned, if the Americans stopped exporting their wheat, flour, fish, pork, and cattle. In December 1807 he proposed, and Congress adopted, an embargo on all maritime commerce; no American ships could leave port, and no foreign ships could export any American produce. The Federalists denounced the embargo as self-destructive and for a bad cause: to retain British subjects on American ships.[43]

The embargo failed because Jefferson overestimated the British dependence on American imports and underestimated the importance of exports to the American economy. In Latin America, the British found alternative sources of food and a new market for their manufactures. And British merchants could hardly believe their good fortune: that the foolish Americans had abandoned maritime commerce. Meanwhile, the American seaport economy withered, idling thousands of sailors, laborers, and artisans. Unable to export their grain and livestock, farmers glutted the domestic market and suffered from a great fall in the prices paid for their produce.[44]

The unpopular embargo revived the Federalist Party in the Northeast, a region that heavily relied on maritime commerce. The Federalists insisted that Jefferson's supposed cure was far worse than the British disease of meddling with ships and sailors. Because the trans-Atlantic trade had been so profitable, the Federalist merchants had become resigned to writing off the loss of some vessels and men to British seizure, but the shippers reaped only losses when Jefferson locked up their vessels for over a year. Northeastern Federalists charged that Jefferson's southern-dominated party actually designed the embargo to impoverish New England and diminish its political clout in the Union. Accusing Jefferson of favoring Napoléon, the Federalists celebrated Britain as the global champion of true liberty against French despotism and Republican hypocrisy.[45]

The Federalist revival fell short in the presidential election of 1808, when Madison won the right to succeed Jefferson. The Federalist presidential candidate carried New England (save for Vermont), but the southern, middle, and western states remained solidly Republican. By early 1809, however, most northern Republicans had soured on an embargo that had weakened them by reviving the Federalists. To hold their party together, the Republicans in Congress terminated the embargo on March 4, 1809, Jefferson's last day in office.[46]

Embarrassed by the failed embargo, President Madison sought to prepare the nation for war against the British, whom he accused of "trampling on rights which no Independent Nation can relinquish." Madison insisted that the British imperiled the nation's sovereignty by impressing sailors and assisting the Indians who resisted America's western expansion. To bolster a native alliance deemed essential to Canada's security, the British armed the Indians, who opposed American troops at the Battle of Tippecanoe in northern Indiana in late 1811. Anticipating a tough reelection campaign in 1812, Madison hoped that a war against the British and their Indian allies would unite the fractious Republicans. In the House of Representatives, the president got vigorous support from the Speaker of the House, Henry Clay.[47]

On June 18, 1812, Madison signed the declaration of war authorized by Congress. In both houses, the vote largely broke along party lines, for every Federalist opposed the declaration, which 81 percent of the Republicans favored. The greatest opposition came from the Northeast, where the Federalists were strongest and where many Republicans felt dismayed by the paltry military preparations for war. Support for the declaration primarily came from Pennsylvania, the South, and the new western states of Ohio, Kentucky, and Tennessee: all Republican strongholds.[48]

Despite the nation's military weakness, most Republicans felt that they had to declare war or lose their credibility. Identifying their party with the nation, they feared that inaction would discredit the republic as impotent, which would doom true liberty by inviting the voters to restore the elitist Federalists to power. By winning some quick victories, the Republicans hoped to unify a divided country and discredit the Federalist opposition. By declaring military war on Britain, the Republicans escalated their political war on the Federalists. Domestic partisanship shaped the conflict as much as did the international crisis. Tarred as Tory obstructionists by the Republicans, the Federalists sought revenge by frustrating the invasion of Canada.[49]

Flames

A doctrinaire southern conservative, John Randolph was a rare Virginia congressman who opposed the war. Randolph feared that a bloated military would lead to higher taxes, a compounded national debt, enhanced presidential power, and hordes of parasitical patronage seekers. He also dreaded that a British invasion would provoke a bloody slave revolt in the South: "While talking of Canada, some of us were shuddering for our own safety at home. He spoke from facts, when he said that the night-bell never tolled for fire in Richmond that the mother did not hug her infant more closely to her bosom." He noted the "repeated alarms of insurrection among the slaves—some of them awful indeed" during "the last ten years."[50]

Indeed, the crisis with Britain coincided with a surge of alarms in Virginia. After the June 1807 confrontation between USS *Chesapeake* and HMS *Leopard*, the Virginians shifted into their anxious mode, prone to overhear slaves talk of burning towns and murdering masters. In May 1808 in Richmond, a visitor noted that any noc-turnal ringing of the fire bell "always produces a very great alarm in this Country" from an "apprehension that it may be the Signal for, or Commencement of a rising of the Negroes." In November in Nor-folk, alarming rumors led the mayor to call out the militia to patrol the streets, search all "the negro houses," and interrogate suspects. "Unfortunately no single negro has been identified as concerned in this affair," complained one frustrated militia officer.[51]

In December 1808, many Virginians expected a revolt during the Christmas holiday, when the slaves enjoyed a five-day release from work and could more freely travel and gather. During that brief annual relaxation in the slave regime, masters chronically wor-ried that the slaves might meet, plot, and rebel. In the Piedmont on December 21, Peggy Nicholas, the wife of Congressman Wilson Cary Nicholas, reported, "Through the mercy of providence we have once more escap'd the horrors of a Massacre. The Negroes have plan'd to rise on Christmas day. A Negro Woman by some means . . . discover'd the secret and gave information against three fellows in Nelson [County] who were immediately secur'd and whip'd. Two of them have confess'd the fact, the third wou'd not, but they say, they are all to be hang'd immediately. The whole Country is in alarm."[52]

Richmond's magistrates also claimed to have "satisfactory evi-dence, verbal and written" for "a general insurrection of the Blacks" during the Christmas holiday. The magistrates had discovered an ominous letter dropped in the street and allegedly written by "J. B.," a supposed slave rebel, to his shadowy commander, "General T. R." The author claimed to have covertly recruited 100 enslaved men with the promise of plunder "when Richmond shall be ours." Armed with stolen muskets, old swords, and clubs, the rebels planned to divide into four divisions and then set fires throughout the town. J. B. urged his general, "Keep every thin[g] silent till that fatal night which will show to the world that slavery will no longer exist in Virginia." The stilted letter reads like the ventriloquism of a white man assuming the role of an imagined slave rebel. Apparently the author sought to shock the magistrates into enforcing the restrictions on black movement and nocturnal meetings—which they did.[53]

In May 1810 in Isle of Wight County, a magistrate, Richard W. Byrd, warned the governor of an impending "insurrection of the blacks." The alarm began when an enslaved boy allegedly told a militia man, "You will all have to use your muskets enough before long, and if you knew what I know it would be well for you." That cryptic statement sufficed to spook the local whites, who had the boy arrested, flogged, and interrogated. After twenty-five lashes, he confessed to having heard that some North Carolina slaves armed "with clubs, spikes, and axes" were preparing to "come over here to help the Virginia negroes." Suddenly every unusual black statement heard by whites became pregnant with menace. One slave allegedly said "that there would be an Earthquake here on the same night; that he was entitled to his freedom, and he would be damned if he did not have it in a fortnight." Another slave told his owner "that if she knew what he did it would make her heart bleed." But the county court could convict only one slave of conspiracy, and the evidence against him was so flimsy that the governor opted to sell and transport, rather than to execute, the convict.[54]

The Isle of Wight alarm spread up the James River to Richmond. On the night of June 9, 1810, a visitor, Elizabeth Kennon, found militiamen "parading all over the City, to preserve the inhabitants from the horrors . . . this eventful night will produce (for this is the night it was said the blacks intended to begin their struggle for liberty)." An astute observer, Kennon did not share the widespread alarm, "for I believe the blacks are, in this City, under more apprehension [of the] consequences which will ensue, than the whites are." Recalling the bloody suppression of Gabriel's revolt ten years before, the slaves understood that they paid a heavy price when whites panicked. Kennon aptly expected that "as they know so many men are under arms, they will keep close in their houses, and say to the white people . . . if you will let me alone, I will let you." No revolt erupted.[55]

On the night of December 26, 1811, the worst fear of Virginians seemed realized when a deadly fire consumed the Richmond Theater. The audience of 600 included dozens of fashionable men and women who had gathered to see a new play, *Father, or Family Feuds.* The flames spread so rapidly through the packed theater that people struggled to escape, trampling and suffocating the slow. Others died or suffered crippling injury by jumping from the windows on the upper floor. John Campbell recalled, "My ears were stun'd with cries & shrieks and screams! . . . I saw numbers that were carried away half burnt up." Another witness reported seeing "the wretched half burned females . . . crawling on their hands & knees in all directions from the smoking ruins in a state of frenzy." The seventy-two dead included the state's governor, George William Smith. "Never, never, in the whole course of my Existence have I been so afflicted by any Event," Dr. Philip Barraud assured St. George Tucker.[56]

According to a witness, the Richmond whites initially believed "that the house was intentionally set on fire" as "the signal for *insurrection*, and that those who escaped the fury of the flames, might have to encounter an enemy more destructive than fire itself." The deadly fire had erupted during the Christmas holiday, when masters most feared a slave revolt. Eventually, however, evidence revealed that a candle carelessly placed too close to the stage set had caused the blaze, but Virginians associated the tragedy with their image of a slave revolt: nocturnal flames and the indiscriminate death of women and children. So the theater fire compounded the unease in Virginia as Congress debated declaring war on the British Empire.[57]

In most of the suspected plots, we merely hear the careless talk of hopeful slaves seizing upon wishful rumors of outsiders coming to liberate them. White folk, however, dreaded any such talk, lest it eventually embolden slaves to convert hope into action, rumor into rebellion. Far better, they thought, immediately to show their power to punish and thereby force the slaves back into quiet submission rather than to await better evidence. If the plots were flimsy, the fear was real and powerful in the minds of Virginians. During the panic of December 1808, Peggy Nicholas begged her husband to move their family westward: "I am as usual on these occasions terrified almost to death and really believe if I am oblig'd to stay here on Christmas day that I shall die with terror. . . . Gracious God, what is there in this country to make amends for all this terror?" But like most Virginians, Wilson Cary Nicholas was too indebted and entangled in slavery to move away from that terror.[58]

Freedom

In London in 1812, an American diplomat, Jonathan Russell, met with Viscount Castlereagh, the British foreign minister. Russell denounced the impressment of white men as a crime far worse than the enslavement of Africans: "as the negro was purchased, already bereft of his liberty, . . . while the American citizen is torn without price, at once, from all the blessings of freedom." Russell declared "astonishment, that while Great Britain discovered such zeal for the abolition of the traffic in the barbarous and unbelieving natives of Africa, . . . that she should so obstinately adhere to the practice of impressing American citizens, whose civilization, religion, and blood so obviously demanded a more favorable distinction." Russell argued that a supposed racial superiority should spare white men from a practice that resembled the slavery best reserved for the "barbarous" Africans.[59]

British imperialists and American Republicans offered competing stories of freedom, each shaped by a different formula for class and race. The British boasted of their global struggle against Napoléon's despotic empire and the international slave trade. The Republicans countered that they defended American liberty against the encroaching might of a tyrannical British Empire led by a haughty king and

arrogant aristocrats. The Republicans celebrated the equality of
white men in their shared superiority over other races. British officials, however, defended their class hierarchy and doubted that common whites were innately superior to Indians and Africans.[60]

Republicans denounced impressment as the enslavement of white
Americans, which they considered extraordinarily cruel because no
people more cherished or deserved freedom. Castigating Britain,
an orator demanded, "Does she care about liberty[?] Is it for liberty's sake, that thousands of men are torn from their homes, their
friends, and every thing dear to them, and forced to linger out a miserable existence, in worse than barb[a]rian slavery?" Republicans
denounced the British for blurring the proper racial line between
servitude and freedom. An American mariner complained that British naval officers would "muster the crew, and examine the persons
of the sailors as a planter examines a lot of negroes exposed for sale."
In Georgia on the eve of war, a British shore party pursued a white
deserter into a store. The owner bellowed, "Why, I declare to god,
these Britishers think to treat us like niggers!" Those provocative
words rallied a mob that drove off the British party. Although nearly
a fifth of American seamen were people of color (including three
of the four sailors taken from USS *Chesapeake* by the British), one
would never know it from the Republican rhetoric, which treated
sailors as white.[61]

Republicans regarded the whipping of impressed white Americans as the greatest of British racial crimes. A mariner complained
that impressed sailors "were stripped, tied up, and most cruelly and
disgracefully whipped like a negro slave. Can any thing be . . . more
humiliating to the feelings of men born and brought up as we all are?"
Leading the push for war, slave-state congressmen sought to liberate
white men from a bondage, which they deemed fit only for blacks.[62]

Republicans warned that, if the United States allowed the British to impress and whip white Americans, the nation would lapse
into renewed dependence on the empire: a collective condition they

also called "slavery." In July 1812 in Charlotte County, Virginia, the citizens insisted that accepting British impressment would "be a surrender of National independence" and "immediately preparatory, to Slavery & despotism, not to be endured by free Men." In August 1812, John Campbell, a Virginia legislator, asserted, "War has been declar'd to save the nation from slavery & disgrace & the sword of vengeance will now drink the blood of those who have been seeking our downfall." He sought to rescue a republic for white men from a dependence he wished to reserve for blacks.[63]

During the War of 1812, the Republicans waged a racial crusade against the British, damned for allying with scalping Indians and rebelling slaves. Republicans denounced the British alliance with Indians and use of black troops as cynical ploys to destroy the white man's republic in America. The *Richmond Enquirer* shuddered, "They employ the Indians! They burn down our villages and houses! They train the infatuated blacks to arms!" Republicans insisted that the British inverted the natural racial hierarchy by elevating brutish Indians and blacks at the expense of white Americans and their free government.[64]

The racialized pro-war rhetoric outraged African Americans who suffered far worse from the "tyrants of America" than did the sailors impressed by the British. A former slave noted that although "Britain has got three thousand American citizens in slavery on board her ships of war: Has not America, likewise, got in slavery 2,000,000 of the former citizens of Africa?" Masters kept them "almost naked, starved and abused in a most inhuman and brutal manner in her fields & kitchens." Britain's sailors received pay and did not suffer from the sale of their loved ones. Reverend Lemuel Haynes, a free black in Vermont, also found hypocrisy when President Madison spoke "feeling[ly] on the subject of the impressment of our seamen. . . . Yet, in his own state, Virginia, there were, in the year 1800, no less than three hundred forty-three thousand, seven hundred ninety-six human beings holden in bondage for life!"[65]

British officials claimed to defend "rational liberty" against the fraudulent version practiced in the American republic. Elite Britons insisted that their mixed constitution provided as much freedom as any people could sustain. By contrast, the American republic struck them as a school for demagogues and anarchy. Britain's rulers sought to fend off reformers who called for a broader electorate and equal political rights. Because British reformers cited the United States as a model, the ruling traditionalists had to discredit the republic.[66]

Where Republicans saw Britain as an imperial bully, British leaders insisted that they defended the world's freedom against Napoléon's brutal and expansionist dictatorship. Admiral Sir John Borlase Warren assured his sailors that they fought for "the Noblest Cause that ever called for the Efforts of Men, the Preservation of the *Liberties, Independence, Religion*, and *Laws* of all the remaining Nations of the World, against the Tyranny and Despotism of France." By keeping the French despot far from North America, Britons argued that they deserved American gratitude rather than protests and war. One Royal Naval officer castigated the Americans for "declaring war against us at a most critical period, when we were not only making a desperate struggle for our existence as a nation, but also to liberate other powers from the iron grasp of Bonaparte; and fighting in the cause of liberty itself." The British considered the American declaration of war as a vile betrayal of global freedom by vicious ingrates.[67]

The British also cast the American Republicans as canting hypocrites who nattered on about liberty while keeping slaves. Captain William Stanhope Lovell of the Royal Navy noted, "Republicans are certainly the most cruel masters, and the greatest tyrants in the world towards their fellow men. They are urged by the most selfish motives to reduce every one to a level with, or even below themselves, and to grind and degrade those under them to the lowest stage of human wretchedness. But American liberty consists in oppressing the blacks beyond what other nations do, enacting laws to prevent

their receiving instruction and working them worse than a donkey."
During the war, a British officer debated a captured Republican, who
poured "forth an uninterrupted stream of eloquence in the cause
of liberty and equality" until the Briton silenced him by "casting
the stubborn fact of domestic slavery in his teeth." American slavery enabled the British to mock republicanism as tyranny perfected
rather than as liberty protected.[68]

Of course, the naval officers were inconsistent in their antislavery principles, for some owned West Indian plantations and all
held some racial prejudice. Even as they empathized with American
slaves, British officers referred to black men as "Sambos" and called
their children "pickaninnies." These officers denounced slavery to
discredit the Americans rather than to promote racial equality. But in
self-defense, the officers could reply that slavery was less hypocritical when conducted by men who did not pretend to be republicans.[69]

Indeed, the British regarded the Americans as doubly damned for
owning blacks while preaching the equality of white men. To Britons, it seemed odd that race mattered so much, and class so little, in
America. After hearing Jefferson describe blacks as racially inferior,
a British diplomat countered that "the black race is, however, as sus-
ceptible of refined civilization, and as capable to the full of profiting
by the advantages of education as any other of any shade whatever."
Because class mattered as much as race for British leaders, they could
consider blacks as potentially the equals of common whites in a society properly ruled by an aristocracy of superior birth, manners, education, and wealth.[70]

Rejecting that British critique, American slaveholders insisted
that they had inherited a great evil without any responsibility for it.
They blamed the British for the mythic original sin of forcing slaves
upon reluctant colonists. Therefore, Republicans despised the British
criticism as a ploy to instigate slave revolts and thereby destroy the
world's only true republic.[71]

Noting the West Indian Regiments, Virginians feared that a British invasion would bring black men in red coats to their shores to provoke a massive slave revolt. In June 1812, William Tatham warned the governor that when the British invaded Virginia with black troops, "I need not shew you that a powerful deluded multitude of domestic Enemies will join them." Norfolk's militia commander, Robert Barraud Taylor, warned the governor that the slaves took a suspiciously "deep interest in a rupture between England and this Country." Richmond's mayor, Robert Greenhow, worried, .

> Unfortunately, we have two enemies to contend with—the one open & declared; the other nurtured in our very Bosoms! Sly, secret & insidious: in our families, at our Elbows, listening with eager attention; and sedulously marking all that is going forward. They know where our Strength lies; and where & in what point we may be most easily assailed. The Standard of Revolt is unfurled! And whenever practicable, those deluded Creatures, regardless of Consequences, have flocked to it and enrolled into military Bands. We perhaps may have a Sanguinary set of desperadoes to contend with.

In June, the Northampton County militia commander informed the governor, "The inhabitants have lately had their fears much increased by some proofs of an intended insurrection in this place. . . . Our jail is now full of those suspected to have been the leaders & the presumption of their guilt is every day strengthened by additional evidence. Many have been heard to declare that they would be ready to destroy the whites in the event of war."[72] The specter of foreign invasion renewed Virginians' dread of their "internal enemy."

Some British naval officers did regard American slaves as potential allies. In 1807, Admiral Berkeley had assured his superiors that in a war, they could rely on a revolt by the "Slaves and people of Color in Virginia, etc., whose nightly shouts at this moment are 'God bless King George.'" Looking to the king for liberation, they "only wait the Signal to embody and hoist the British flag." Berkeley predicted that American troops would be hard pressed "to prevent the explosion of this Volcano in their own bowels."[73]

In London, however, the imperial rulers proved far more cautious. Loath to play with the fire of a slave revolt, they hoped that hints alone would intimidate the southerners, hampering their war effort. In 1812 the imperial rulers did not anticipate that hundreds of runaways would flee to their warships. Nor did they know that the mass flight would demand a British escalation of the war meant to liberate thousands of slaves.

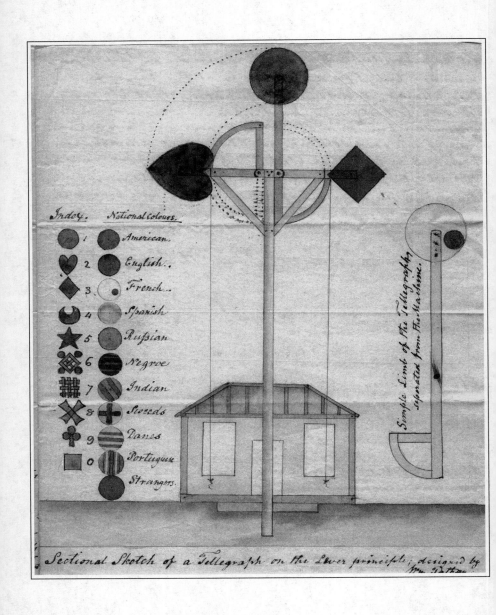

Index.	National colours.	
	1	American.
	2	English.
	3	French.
	4	Spanish
	5	Russian
	6	Negroe
	7	Indian
	8	Sweeds
	9	Danes
	0	Portuguez
		Strangers.

Simple Limb of the Tellegraph separated from the Machine.

Sectional Sketch of a Tellegraph on the Lever principle; designed by Wm Wethen

5

INVASION

*No nation upon Earth, that nearly approached us in populousness,
was so weak & incapable of Carrying [on a] war, as we are.*
—WALTER JONES, 1814[1]

I N JUNE 1812 in Richmond, Virginia's leaders awaited news of
war. They included John Campbell, a young and able politician
who recently had joined the Council of State. On June 12, Campbell
reported to his brother, "We wait here in hourly expectation for the
declaration of war. The sound of military music is now ringing in my
ear." Nine days later, the local militiamen discharged their cannon to
signal that the president and Congress had, at last, declared war on
the British Empire. Campbell noted, "The Cannon is now roaring
whilst I am writing. . . . We are all *noise, bustle & talk* here. War!
War! War! The hour has arrived so long expected."[2]

On the Fourth of July, hundreds gathered in Richmond's Capitol
Square and the main street for a carefully staged political theater of

William Tatham, Sectional Sketch of a Tellegraph on the Lever Principles, *1812. A military advisor and engineer, William Tatham proposed this optical telegraph, based on a French prototype, to convey alarms from the coast to the state government in Richmond. Note that the sixth of the "National Colours" was a symbol for the "Negroe," indicating their potential threat to Virginia. (From the James Barbour Executive Papers, courtesy of the Library of Virginia)* resolve and unity. Thomas Ritchie, editor of the powerful *Richmond Enquirer*, exulted in hearing "the spirit stirring fife, the pealing drum, the hum of the delighted multitude that thronged the Square, and the steps and windows of the Capitol." At noon, the state's new governor, James Barbour, exhorted the crowd to remember "the glories of the revolution" and "to bury all inferior party distinctions in the love of the country." The governor then led the militia commanders, state legislators, and leading citizens and ladies inside the Hall of Delegates to hear a spirited reading of the Declaration of Independence. In the afternoon, the militiamen and their bands entertained the crowd with military maneuvers and patriotic music. At dusk, the home and shop owners illuminated their windows with candles in a vivid display of pro-war solidarity. Campbell exulted that the city's main street "appear'd bespangled with myriads of stars." Ritchie insisted that the festivities lacked the raucous disorder of previous celebrations in Richmond: "No jarring, no riots, no mobs, not one pane of glass broken even by a boy." Surely, that unity and self-discipline boded well for the war against the British. But appearances can be deceiving.[3]

While Ritchie shrewdly managed power from behind the curtain, Governor Barbour barged into every spotlight to perform his boisterous eloquence, which earned him the nickname of "the Thunderer." Tall, handsome, and bombastic, he gave pro-war speeches to anyone who would listen, exhorting the militiamen to fight to the death to defend Richmond: "I am sure you will say with me that it would be infinitely more desirable to be buried in its ruins than save a life rendered infamous by a pusillanimous retreat." Delighting in attention, Barbour wore a specially designed general's uniform of exquisite elegance, for he expected to command the militia in the field. Campbell reported that during the Fourth of July celebration, Barbour "was in his glory. He pranc'd here & there and every where."[4]

Thirty-six years old, Barbour became governor in early January

Governor James Barbour of Virginia. *(Courtesy of the Library of Virginia)*

1812, replacing George William Smith, who had died in the Richmond Theater fire. Despite modest origins and a limited education, Barbour had thrived as a lawyer and politician, thanks to support from his Orange County neighbor, James Madison, and the Richmond power broker, Thomas Ritchie. Conventional on issues of race, he lamented slavery as an evil but did nothing to free his slaves or anyone else's.[5]

Leading Virginians did not know whether to mock Barbour's vainglory or applaud his zeal. Campbell eventually warmed to Barbour as far more decisive than the dithering state legislators: "Barbour takes it *rough, roll & tumble*, some times right & some times wrong. He is quick as lightning . . . & is willing to do every thing in his power, I believe, for the country." A leading lawyer, William Wirt, reported that "a party of mischievous boys" tweaked the governor for giving pompous speeches to every passing militia company. Making a bustle before the governor's mansion, they drew out Barbour, who asked, "What do you want?" The boys replied, "A speech." According to Wirt, Barbour "felt the ridicule & retired in dismay. But after all he is a good fellow."[6]

Barbour recognized Virginia's vulnerability to a British invasion from the sea, for the Tidewater's rivers and bay could bring enemy warships deep within the state at multiple points. Save for Norfolk, none of Virginia's harbors had any significant fortification or garrison of U.S. troops. Barbour dismissed the ruinous Fort Powhatan, Richmond's main defense on the James River, as "literally nothing but a scarecrow." The Council of State supported Barbour, but the tax-averse legislators rebuffed his requests for more authority and funds to bolster the state's defenses.[7]

The jealous and penny-wise legislators served constituents who wanted to be left alone by their government, which did not bode well for the sacrifices required by war. United on the Fourth of July, the Virginians divided thereafter into rival regions: Tidewater, Piedmont, and the West. The Tidewater and Piedmont representatives agreed on little beyond defending slavery and marginalizing the West, which was weaker, poorer, and whiter. The Piedmont and western delegates coalesced only to minimize the funds and men committed to defend the Tidewater, which faced the greatest danger of British attack. In every region, the militiamen tried to minimize their active service rather than neglect their farms and shops. Common farmers, artisans, and shopkeepers, the militiamen preferred the patriotic bombast of the Fourth of July to the grim realities of war: periodic deadly combat and long stretches of exposure in filthy, disease-ridden camps.

Militia

Virginians expected the federal government to defend their state against invasion, while they guarded against the internal enemy. What good, they asked, was the Union if it would not defend every state? Alas, in 1812 the same sort of southern Republicans who governed Virginia also led the United States. As national leaders they had no greater stomach for taxes to fund a strong military than did their counterparts in Virginia. In 1812, the overmatched secretary of war, William Eustis, struggled to rebuild an army that had withered during the Jefferson administration. Throughout 1812, low bounties and poor pay discouraged enlistments, which lagged far behind expectations. Common men could make more on the farm or in their shop than by risking their lives to disease or bullets in the army. "I know our people," a Virginia congressman privately observed, and "their selfish feelings far outweigh their public spirit & principles," for "the enjoyment or acquisition of *property* are the ruling & universal passions."[8]

Putting a premium on invading Canada, the Madison administration lacked enough troops also to defend the long American coastline. In July 1812, Eustis enraged Virginians by ordering most of the state's new recruits to march away to the northern front. Barbour protested, citing "the great dangers to be apprehended from our black population if not from their violence at least great loss might occur by their desertion." But the federal order to march stood, leaving the defense of Virginia to a mere two companies of U.S. troops posted at Norfolk. To supplement them, Eustis did authorize Barbour to mobilize 500 militiamen for federal service at Norfolk. The rest of Virginia's indented coast lay undefended.[9]

If British raiders landed, the commanding colonel of a county could call into service all of the local militia. Composed of every able-bodied white man between the ages of sixteen and forty-five, the militiamen were better known for drinking whiskey than for obeying orders, for they lacked training beyond a festive annual muster at their county courthouse. Congressman Walter Jones described the Virginia militia as "very badly equipped, worse disciplined, & still worse commanded" in "a system that looks well dressed by the patriotic puffs of the newspapers & orators." When called out, the men appeared "in driblets" with only "a few muskets without flints or moulds, bayonets without sheaths, cartridges to the amount [of] five or six per man, of which one third, upon examination, have proved unfit for use."[10]

Proud of their republican equality, the militiamen often defied their officers. One county commander reported that his major "was often compelled to appeal to weapons or Shelter to Escape the assault of his own men [at] the Battalion Muster Last Fall & again this Last Spring. What few of the men did meet produced an open war Between them and their Major and his friends, & Bloodshed and Battery has been the consequence." The men had scant reason to respect their bumbling officers, who often were old and inept and owed their commissions to the cronyism of their county court. One frustrated junior officer declared, "Were all the County Courts in Virginia to lay aside the slavish respect . . . for seniority" in favor of merit "there would not be seen so many doll-babies at the head of Regiments and Battalions." John Campbell lamented, "Nine-tenths of the Colonels are as ignorant as Asses and the Generals are, if possible, worse."[11]

The brief mobilization of 1807 had given way to renewed budget-cutting by the legislature, which left the militia woefully unprepared for the next crisis. Throughout 1812 and 1813, Barbour received panicky reports from local militia officers begging for weapons. Soldiers had sold, lost, or neglected the arms issued during the previous great alarm, just five years earlier. In York County, the commander reported that "not more than one man out of five or six has a musket." Everywhere officers denounced the wretched quality and poor design of the arms made by the state arsenal in Richmond. A cavalry officer complained, "The Swords are so extremely long & heavy that men of ordinary strength cannot wield them." Another declared, "Many of the pistols have bursted or been broken . . . by firing." When men had working guns, they often discovered that the heat and humidity had ruined the gunpowder in their cartridges.[12]

Dispersed among many careless hands, the weapons corroded or vanished by sale. Some reformers proposed to concentrate the arms in county arsenals for better storage and repair, but Barbour worried that the proposal was "subject to the objection which has been perpetually presented when the propriety of this mode of saving the arms has been discussed in the Legislature, viz. the peculiar species of population we have among us." The legislators dreaded that any concentration of arms at the county level would tempt seizure by slave rebels. When in doubt, Virginians dispersed authority and weapons, to the detriment, however, of their ability to resist invasion.[13]

The militia also suffered from class tensions because the prosperous could evade service by hiring substitutes. In June 1812, Joseph C. Cabell served in the State Senate when drafted in his home county for service at sickly Norfolk. A friend in the U.S. army, Isaac A. Coles, joked that he would join Cabell "on the swamps of the Chesapeake to fight the English & Moschetos together." Cabell's wife, Polly, did not find that funny, for she wailed through the night, begging Cabell "not to kill her by going into the army." A sickly gentleman, Cabell also wanted no part of service, but he worried that hiring a substitute would embarrass his political prospects. The former governor William H. Cabell reassured his younger brother: "Hire a substitute without hesitation" to avoid "the certainty of destruction to yourself from the climate. . . . Put Polly's mind at ease & let her be as silent as possible on all these topics." Applying the logic of Virginia localism, William reasoned, "If you lived in Norfolk and the Town was besieged, or if the part of the Country in which you reside should be invaded . . . it might be necessary for you to turn out, but there is no such necessity as yet." To avoid publicity in his home county, Joseph followed St. George Tucker's advice to hire a substitute through a friend in another county: "Do this without naming me—or suffering the thing to leak out." By promising $100 on top of the regular pay, the friend procured a substitute to serve for six months (in addition, he would receive monthly pay from the state).[14]

Common men, however, could not afford to hire substitutes, so they had to leave their farms and shops. Because armies and navies moved more freely and aggressively in the warm months, military emergencies conflicted with the peak period for agricultural work. Common farmers faced ruin if they failed to plant or harvest in time. Artisans suffered nearly as much, for militia pay was always late and far less than they could make at their shops. And men who sickened and died in the service left behind impoverished widows and orphans. One set of officers lamented, "The cries of women and children are so afflicting as to melt the Hardest Heart." Their men were tempted to desert "when they reflect on the exposure of their Families to the internal enemy, [and] when they see ruin staring them in the face by the total neglect of the agricultural preparations."[15]

Common men resented having to defend the plantations of the rich from the flight of their slaves. In Princess Anne County (near Norfolk), sixty-six militiamen considered it "entirely repugnant to Liberty, our Laws & Constitution that they should be compelled to perform the servile Duty of guarding the private Property of a few Citizens who are, at the same Time, sleeping in their Beds with nothing to interrupt their Repose, but an Apprehension that they may lose a few Slaves." These men refused "to become Slaves to their Neighbors." Living amid slaves, the Virginians became hypersensitive to any implied dependence or inequality, which they likened to slavery.[16]

In the western mountains, poor whites prevailed, for slaves and plantations were few. Although most disliked black people, the westerners balked at having to leave home to defend the eastern planters from a slave revolt. The western men also detested the eastern domination of the state government and the exclusion of landless white men from the right to vote. For years, the Tidewater and Piedmont legislators had blocked democratic reforms and appropriations for economic development in the western counties. A western populist, Colonel John Stokely, warned Barbour that the militia resented "paying taxes & fighting the Battles of their Country" when they "have no voice in the choice of either Civil or Military Officers. Often have I heard the poor Fellows murmur at this Privation & justly too according to my opinion." They felt reduced "to slavery or to a situation little superior to it." Stokely exhorted the governor to pay "respect to the Poor & virtuous Plough Boys as well as to those whose wealth intitles them to Live in Idleness & Invites them many times to ruin & to wickedness."[17]

Another western legislator, Noah Zane, insisted that the easterners needed the hinterland militia to protect them, for "at this time they were afraid to lie down at night lest they would be burned up by their Negroes before morning." Zane added that if the easterners "treated their Negroes properly there would be no danger from them." Zane's talk inspired a listening militia officer, John Richardson, to add that "if the Negroes was to rise in rebellion against their masters in the Eastern counties he would not turn out in support of the latter or any set of people that would deprive him of his Just rights." Zane warned Richardson that "it would not do for him to express himself that way in old Virginia." Indeed, Governor Barbour promptly sacked Richardson as a militia officer for his indiscreet words.[18]

As a Piedmont slaveholder, Barbour opposed the political reforms sought by the western populists, and he feared their antislavery grumbling. For Barbour, localism took a back seat when the eastern counties needed western help: "We are one Family and when any member thereof is assaulted it is entitled to the resources of the whole . . . & if by untoward circumstances a portion of the Commonwealth has a species of population thrown upon them without their consent by which they are particularly exposed to danger it has the strongest claims to the aid of the other portions of the state which have been happily exempted from such Calamity." Barbour regarded Virginia as one big family to defend slavery, although that imagined community had refused to extend political equality to the poorest westerners.[19]

Barbour also rejected the widespread complaints that the rich man's war had become the poor man's fight: "The solace to murmurs of this kind is to be found in the reflection that the road to wealth is accessible to all. The wheel of fortune is in perpetual rotation & he who today occupies the lowest Station in the Wheel in a short time may exchange situations with the one who enjoys the highest." If a common man did not like militia service, he should become rich and buy his own substitute. By deploying the American promise of social mobility, Barbour sought to defuse the class tensions aroused by a militia service that bore down hardest on the common man.[20]

Examples

The patriotic enthusiasm of the Fourth of July faded during the late summer and fall of 1812, as Virginians began to count the military costs and to rue the political divisions of war. Undermanned, underfunded, and badly led, the American invasions of Canada culminated in embarrassing defeats. The worst humiliation came at Detroit in August, when General William Hull surrendered his garrison to a smaller enemy force without firing a shot. Virginians blamed Hull's cowardice on his origins in New England: deemed a region devoted to money and Federalism rather than honor and Republicanism. But in December, Virginians felt ashamed of their own bombastic, cowardly, and inept general, Alexander Smyth, who botched an invasion of Canada from his base at Buffalo, New York. Longing for peace Colonel John Taylor denounced the wretched war effort characterized by an "appalling debt, a legion of officers without an army, a few detachments of raw soldiers without generals, a ruined commerce, [and] a people divided into two parties neither of which is very willing to take the field or to pay taxes."[21]

And then the British brought war to Virginia. On February 4, 1813, five British warships entered Chesapeake Bay and began to seize and burn merchant ships. By March 6 the British had seventeen warships in the bay: more than the entire American navy then at sea. Within the bay, the Americans had only a few small gunboats and a single frigate, the USS *Constellation*, which took shelter behind the forts that guarded the entrance to Norfolk's harbor. Governor Barbour and the Council of State ordered another 2,000 militiamen into service, primarily at Norfolk.[22]

Dread of an impending slave revolt rippled throughout the Tidewater in the panicky talk and letters of Virginians. In Gloucester County, Major Nathaniel Burwell reported, "We are threatened with an insurrection of our Negroes. Ten have been apprehended and are in jail for examination." Fearing *"our worst enemy,"* Richmond's mayor insisted that he had proof "that the Slaves of this City, probably in conjunction with free persons of colour, have conspired and are conspiring to burn the City, possess themselves of the public arms, and probably to murder the white Inhabitants indiscriminately." John Campbell warned "of the whole state being convulsed *by an insurrection.*"[23]

On the night of March 2, 1813, in the Kingston Parish of Mathews County, in the Tidewater, eight enslaved men and one boy rendezvoused outside of Parson Armistead Smith's gate. Harry, Abram, Humphrey, Yeoro, Billy Goodchild, James, Wharton, Sci, and Hugh belonged to eight different owners, attesting to a neighborhood cooperation among the slaves of scattered farms. Harry had brought along Sci Gillett, a boy of sixteen, which troubled the other men, who declared "that Boys could not be trusted." Harry replied, "He has been raised with me. I know him and can trust him."[24]

Passing quietly by the church, they reached the store of John Ripley. Breaking in, they awakened Ripley, who leveled his musket, but it misfired. The intruders overwhelmed him with fists and sticks, "calling him a Damm'd American Bugger." Their "Captain," Harry, put a sword to Ripley's "Breast, declaring that if he breathed or spoke a single word they would stab the sword through him, calling themselves Englishmen." These self-made Englishmen sought revenge for past rebukes at the store, for they accosted Ripley, "saying you have refused to let us have a little water and fresh Provision, now damn your country we will let you know what it is to refuse us and if you speak a word we will stab the sword through you and put every person to the sword as we go." Rebels against the American Buggers, these slaves identified with the English as liberators.[25]

The black Englishmen then heard a warning. Ripley recalled, "A person came into the yard and gave a whistle, they then all retired from the House," taking away $1,900 in gold and silver found in his money box. After each man claimed $6, Humphrey buried the rest. But John Patterson became suspicious when his slave Harry spent "more money in the course of a few days than it was likely he could have acquired by honest means." Patterson's overseer seized Sci Gillett, the weakest link in the gang. Hauled into Patterson's office, Sci confessed and named the others in hopes of saving his own life. All were jailed, with the informant kept in a distinct cell lest he "be murdered by the friends or relations of some of the parties concerned." By some mix of pain and persuasion, the magistrates induced Humphrey to lead them to the stash of gold and silver.[26]

On March 18, 1813, the magistrates of Mathews County tried the eight men for burglary. Convicting them all, the judges sentenced them to hang and appraised their worth at from $310 for Humphrey, evidently the oldest, to $472 for Yeoro. Before any would hang, however, their fate became entangled in another incident from James City County to the south.[27]

Before dawn on March 23, 1813, the armed schooner *Sarus* lay anchored in the James River near Jamestown. Three black men in a stolen boat rowed out from the shore and "asked if the ship was an English Ship." "Yes," replied the mate, so Anthony, Tassy, and Kit scrambled aboard and vowed to fight the Americans. Given cutlasses, the delighted refugees "declared that their overseer was the first they intended to kill and all Americans they could catch." Anthony, Tassy, and Kit promised to recruit "from one to two thousand other negroes to join them in killing the Americans." But the crew suddenly clamped all three into chains, for the *Sarus* was an American privateer rather than a British warship.[28]

Eight days later, Anthony, Tassy, and Kit went on trial for their lives for having conspired "to rebel and make Insurrection." Meanwhile, newspapers published an inflated account, insisting "that 2000 negroes were embodied and exercised in squads at night." As the property of a widow, Lucy Ludwell Paradise of Williamsburg, these three young men were especially vulnerable to imminent sale and relocation. Indeed, in January 1812, their erratic mistress had been committed to the Williamsburg insane asylum, where she would spend the last two years of her life. By running away and seeking British help, Anthony, Tassy, and Kit had sought to determine their own fate. Instead, they fell into the hands of judges who convicted and sentenced them to hang. Each of their corpses would cost the state $400 in compensation due to the widow Paradise.[29]

Per Virginia law, the magistrates of James City County and Mathews County forwarded their trial transcripts to the governor and Council of State in Richmond for review. The state leaders had the power to affirm the death sentences or to commute some or all of them to sale and transportation. Economy-minded, the state leaders wanted to buy only the minimum number of corpses needed to appease white fear and to promote black intimidation. Determined to transport most of the convicts, the council solicited recommendations from the county magistrates.[30]

In both counties, the leading men favored clemency for most of the convicts. The magistrates wanted slaves to fear them as powerful but also to respect them as just: a tough balancing act. While

dreading slaves collectively as a menacing abstraction, "the internal enemy," Virginians could balk at hanging particular local slaves
whom they had long known. In a petition to the Council, the leaders
of James City County discounted testimony from the privateers as
outsiders. Asserting superior familiarity with the convicted slaves,
the magistrates defended Anthony, Tassy, and Kit as submissive and
ignorant—all too easily manipulated by cunning outsiders. The petitioners insisted "that these offenders were compleatley entrapped by
the witness and others on board the vessel who[m] from their ignorance of words perhaps and by leading questions which were put to
them were induced to say what they never designed to execute & . . .
would never have thought of, had the subject not been first mentioned to them." The magistrates could not believe that the three
were covert rebels plotting to butcher their white neighbors.[31]

The petitioners knew the three as "runaways & had been so for
several months before, from some disagreement between themselves
& their overseer." They had hidden in the forest until, wary of the
"inclement weather," they sought out the vessel so that "they could
ultimately make their escape from this country & so gain their liberty." Remarkably, the petitioners advanced these considerations, in
a matter-of-fact tone, to mitigate the conviction rather than to condemn the convicted. They understood if they did not like, that sometimes slaves ran away, hid for months, and sought some avenue to
freedom. Rather than hang such men, to the utter distress of their
families, the local whites preferred to sell and exile them.[32]

On April 17 the Council of State decided that Humphrey and
Harry should hang in Mathews County, but to sell and transport
the other six convicts there, and all three in James City County. That
limited clemency saved the state $2,700 because a slave trader paid
$300 apiece for the nine. The total fell $850 short of their appraised
value, which the state had to pay to their former owners, plus the full
$625 value of Humphrey and Harry.[33]

The governor carefully instructed the sheriff of Mathews County:

"By way of making the example more terrible you will cautiously conceal the fact of reprieve till the criminals are all under the gallows and the two doomed to death shall have been executed." Only after scaring the other six out of their wits could he disclose their partial reprieve. By a show of power and clemency in the right proportion, Virginia leaders hoped to reassure alarmed whites and to reconcile intimidated blacks to their lives as slaves with powerful but just masters.[34]

Throughout Virginia, the leading men struggled to remain vigilant without overreacting. Despite all the agitated talk of menacing plots, the Virginians prosecuted very few slaves for conspiracy to rebel during the war. And they convicted fewer still, for the judges usually acted with a scrupulous skepticism of the wildest charges. In 1813 in Lancaster County some slave talk alarmed the local militia commander, who had three slaves arrested for "having consulted and advised rebellion, murder and insurrection." Billy, Grandy, and Tamer belonged to Mary Ann Haggeman, a widow: a situation that aroused fears that the slaves lacked sufficient oversight. But the county court discharged them as innocent after a trial on April 20. Seven months later, the same county court acquitted another slave accused of setting fire to the county jail.[35]

Despite the many rumors of a slave revolt, imagined as the indiscriminate massacre of whites, none erupted in the Chesapeake region during the war. At best, some blacks discussed their options when the local militia marched away to defend the shore. The closest thing to a plot developed in Fredericktown, Maryland, in August 1814, when eight slaves met to "talk of arming themselves with knives" and to choose a captain as their leader. Arrested and tried, seven were convicted of conspiracy. The Frederick County Court sentenced three to the state penitentiary and ordered four others "whipped and sent home to their masters." A local witness aptly dismissed this plot as "perfectly contemptible, both in numbers and means of mischief."[36]

During the war Virginians executed only three slaves for con-

spiracy: the two in Mathews County in 1813 and a third in Powhatan County in 1814—and the Powhatan episode fell far short of a
true plot, for there was only one supposed conspirator: an enraged
slave who resisted punishment by brandishing an axe. Reluctant to
destroy valuable human property, the Virginians could find little evidence for the supposed midnight plots to murder indiscriminately.
Virginians had far better reason to fear plots to escape to the British
warships as Sci Gillett did in March 1814, a year after his pardon for
testifying against Humphrey and Harry in Mathews County.[37]

Union

On February 6, 1813, shortly after the British warships entered
the bay, Governor Barbour received a letter from James Monroe,
who warned that the federal government could do nothing more to
defend Virginia. Dismayed by the federal neglect and spooked by the
British invasion on February 13 the legislature authorized enlisting
1,000 men to form a state army to defend Virginia. Kept on duty
and subject to discipline, the state regulars promised greater reliabil-
ity and less expense than the chaotic militia amateurs. A state force
also would reduce the need to draft men from the militia for active
service in disease-ridden Norfolk. Instead, the hinterland militiamen
could stay in their own counties to tend their farms and watch the
slaves.[38]

But the Madison administration insisted that the Federal Constitution reserved to the nation the power to raise a standing army.
Desperate for federal recruits, the president's men rightly feared that
few Virginians would enlist in the national service on the cold northern frontier if, instead, they could serve closer to home in a state
force. In addition, Madison and Monroe feared setting a precedent in
Virginia that the Federalist governors in New England could exploit
to create state armies to resist the National government. How could
the Madison administration deny them what it allowed to Virginia?

As an alternative to a state force of regulars, Monroe promised to organize and enlist a national regiment posted at Norfolk and officered by Virginians commissioned by the president. The secretary of war also retained a Virginia militia general, Robert Barraud Taylor, in overall command at Norfolk.[39]

In late March, Barbour reluctantly suspended the state regular corps and called the legislature into session to complete the repeal. A majority of the Council of State agreed, but two members dissented, staking out a defiant, states' rights position that anticipated Virginia's political future. Strict constructionists of the Federal Constitution, Nathaniel H. Claiborne and Peter V. Daniel argued that it barred the states only from keeping armies in peacetime. During a war or rebellion, they insisted, every state retained the sovereign power to raise professional troops for self-defense. Claiborne maintained that Virginia needed such a force to suppress a slave "insurrection, an event the most awful and which we have every reason to fear, from the known disposition of the enemy." He claimed that "the spirit of revolt has been recently discovered to exist to an alarming degree among our slaves." The dissenters argued that Virginians could not trust the federal government to protect them from internal rebellion. Most of the state legislators, however, supported Barbour by repealing the state defense force in May.[40]

Although Barbour stood by the Madison administration, he privately resented its failure to defend Virginia: "The inattention of the General Government to the defence of the State has been to me inexplicable." John Campbell added, "The *General Government* has left us to *paddle our own Canoe.*" Virginians grew more uneasy about the Union under the strains of external war and internal fear.[41]

They felt trapped in a contradiction: the federal government could not protect them but would not allow them to defend themselves more efficiently with state regulars. Instead, Virginia had to rely on disorderly, expensive, restive, and sickly militiamen who longed to run home. And the reliance on militia drafts increased the tensions between the Tidewater folk, who wanted reinforcements from the interior, and the Piedmonters, who dreaded serving in the disease-ridden low country and opposed paying higher taxes for defense. Campbell noted, "The *low-landers* curse and abuse us for not keeping a standing force in every point that is exposed, and the *high landers* think we are playing the very devil *with* the Treasury. So here we are between Scylla and Charybdes in the midst of a storm and the Lord have mercy on us." He did not expect the British and the slaves to do so.[42]

By concentrating the federally authorized force at Norfolk, the state government left the rest of the Tidewater exposed to British coastal raids. On the Northern Neck, Walter Jones warned, "If all the petty resources of the State are collected at Norfolk, the Enemy knows that there are four other equally productive peninsulas, within a few hours Sail, which they may ravage with little or no hazard." The British exploited the superior mobility of their ships, which sailed far faster than the militia could march over the bad roads, through the thick forests, and around the many streams and rivers of the Chesapeake. "They have *wings*, we have only *heels*," noted a frustrated Virginian. Rowing ashore in barges, armed British sailors and marines landed to loot exposed farms and plantations. Once the local militia assembled in threatening numbers, the raiders quickly withdrew with their plunder to the safety of their warships.[43]

The British raiding threatened the shaky finances of Virginia and Maryland. As the naval squadron roamed up and down and across the bay, the warships drew out thousands of alarmed militiamen who had to be paid and supplied, at a great and growing cost, while their farms and plantations suffered in their absence. During 1813, Virginia's military expenditures quadrupled to $433,363, which amounted to 52 percent of the state's budget (compared to 23 percent in 1812). The increase burdened taxpayers without generating enough revenue fully to arm and pay the militia in the Tidewater counties. In Princess Anne County the British burned a mill when the local militia lacked the ammunition to resist. On the Eastern Shore the militiamen ran out of provisions, and their commander worried that he would have to disband them: "In that case if the British did not destroy us, our internal enemy, the blacks, might do it with facility."[44]

The British raids and blockade wreaked havoc on the Chesapeake economy, which relied on exporting tobacco, corn, wheat, and flour. John M. Garnett lamented that Virginians were "closely blockaded by his Satanic majesty's shops and unable to sell a bushel of corn or wheat." Thomas Jefferson estimated that, on the James River alone, the blockade had trapped 200,000 barrels of flour worth a million dollars. As a wealthy planter, Jefferson could stand the losses far better than the common farmers, who also faced militia drafts to serve in Norfolk, where death by malaria threatened to complete the ruin of their families.[45]

The hinterland militia dreaded swampy Norfolk as a death trap for newcomers. A western legislator complained, "From the pure atmosphere of their native hills, they are removed to a foetid air and a noisome bogg." Westerners regarded the Tidewater climate as "more dreadful to them than the Bayonet of the foe." In the Piedmont, during the summer of 1813, John Randolph heard "the shrieks of agonizing wives that yet ring in my ears," because anyone "who would go to Norfolk at this *season*, would be reckoned a *mad*, and certainly a *dead* man." The Piedmont people also feared "the danger from *an internal foe*, augmented by the removal of so large a portion of our force" to distant Norfolk.[46]

The Piedmonters longed to stay home to guard against a slave revolt. After the governor called militia away from Frederick County, Virginia, James Singleton warned that "from the nature of our population, there are perhaps few parts of the state in which a beginning of the modes of midnight murder may be more justly apprehended." Any departure by the militia seemed to excite seditious words from the local slaves, as whites heard more clearly what they listened most intently for. One visitor reported that "the blacks in some places refuse to work, and say they shall soon be free, and then the white people must look out." In Amelia County in July, a slave robbed a white woman, which caused a sensation because 120 of the local militiamen had recently marched away to Norfolk, leaving "a great number of their families exposed to the attacks of that unfortunate race, the blacks."[47]

In Hanover County in December 1813, a Mr. Bowles went to serve at Norfolk, leaving behind a wife and infant daughter. One dark and rainy night, a slave broke in allegedly to rape Mrs. Bowles. While the intruder sat down to wash his feet, she seized an axe and brought it down "with such tremendous effect upon his skull, that he fell dead from his seat." His brains fell neatly into the basin at his feet. The episode unnerved Virginians, who expected white men instead of women to kill wayward slaves. Rather than praise Mrs. Bowles for courage and strength, the official story credited a sudden infusion of divine energy that temporarily transcended her proper weakness as a woman. Although she had been strong and decisive, the mayor of Richmond, Robert Greenhow, described "the rescue of a forlorn, helpless female, from the fell designs of a fiend! A monster in human shape!! Her mind in a moment endued with power; and her arm nerved with supernatural strength." The Council of State discharged her husband from militia duty to return home, thereby restoring gendered order to his household.[48]

During 1814, Barbour sought more militia from the interior to defend the Tidewater, provoking greater protests from the Piedmont. The Caroline County magistrates insisted that their slaves had "uttered threats" and committed "in one instance an outrage," when they heard that the local militia had been ordered to march away to the Northern Neck. Similarly, the bankers of Lynchburg demanded the retention of their militia after discovering a plot for "a general rising of the blacks in this quarter." The bankers conceded that "a plot was not actually developed, yet it . . . has lately been the subject of frequent conversations among them."[49]

Ruing the crippling dread of his constituents, Barbour doubted that the slaves would rebel when so many militiamen were moving about the region under arms. Slave revolts, he insisted, would "never manifest themselves at a time like the present when all are on the alert and every man with an efficient arm in his hand." But the governor reluctantly conceded that "a sufficient number of the militia should be left in each County to secure the police & quiet of the people against internal disturbance." That political restraint reduced the reinforcements desperately needed to defend the beleaguered Tidewater counties.[50]

Barbour also faced angry protests from the militiamen posted at Norfork, who bristled at the rigorous drills and severe punishments imposed by their commander, General Taylor. A friend noted that Taylor sought "to reclaim the character of the Virginia Militia. . . . The Task is Herculean and, I fear, with the Habits & Genius of our people, next to impossible." During the spring, Taylor made some progress in training his men, but disease depleted and demoralized his force over the summer. Scores ran away to tend their farms and reassure their wives. In July, Taylor warned that desertion had "become so frequent as to threaten the dissolution of the army."[51]

Taylor and Barbour also took heat for rearranging militia companies under new officers chosen for their merit rather than their local popularity. Although officers disdained serving at Norfolk, they felt dishonored when sent home in favor of some rival. And the militiamen disliked the strange new officers who demanded extra drill and inflicted more punishments than did their familiar, neighborly officers. Disgruntled officers denounced Taylor's system as a threat to republican principles of equality and local control. In early December 1813, to secure reelection as governor, Barbour abandoned Taylor's unpopular militia reforms. Feeling undercut, Taylor resigned his command, sadly concluding "that the hope of introducing skill, regularity, & economy among militia troops is idle & illusory."[52]

County

In March 1814, Governor Barbour commiserated with Colonel Leaven Gayle over the failure of the United States to defend Mathews County from British raids: "Our situation is to the last degree unpleasant and embarrassing. The constitution of the United States has very wisely confided the General Defence to the General Government," but because the administration had repeatedly "refused its interposition," the "People of Mathews have been doomed to feel more than their proportion of the evils of war." Those evils included the burglary, a year before, by restive slaves posing as "Englishmen."[53]

Intersected by many streams and small rivers, Mathews County presented a cluster of peninsulas exposed to the enemy's amphibious raids. Land-bound by the enemy's control of the bay, the militiamen struggled to cope with their more mobile enemy. "After they have Landed & laid their destructive hands on our property [it] will be too late," lamented Colonel Gayle. To fend off the powerful warships, Gayle's men had only two small cannon, and lacked ammunition for them.[54]

The Mathews militia also suffered from a political and class division among the officers, pitting those with higher external status against those with deeper local roots. Governor Barbour and the Council of State worried that the Mathews militia regiment lacked energetic leadership. Colonel Gayle was a genial mediocrity, privately derided by the county clerk as "the most uninformed man upon earth" and possessing "no military talent whatever." His major, John Billups, was even worse: an elderly drunk who rarely showed up for duty. In March 1813 the council pushed Billups to resign and eventually elevated Captain Christopher Tompkins to fill the vacancy. While keeping Gayle on as a figurehead, the state leaders relied on Tompkins to manage the defense of Mathews County.[55]

A prosperous merchant, Tompkins had a better education and wider horizons than any other captain in the county, but those qualities exposed him to populist charges of elitism. Claiming to uphold the revolution, a critic adopted the pseudonym "Seventy-Six" to warn the governor that Tompkins was one "of the most gainsaying, hard-hearted, stiff-necked, rebellious Federalists that ever disgraced the unsullied soil of the U.S. of America." The critic insisted that "a very large majority" of the Mathews militia were "Whigs & Republicans" who despised Tompkins and would defy his orders.[56]

By choosing Tompkins as major, the Council of State rejected the competing nomination by the county magistrates of Langley B. Eddins, the most senior captain. A poorly educated and hard-drinking good-old-boy, Eddins owned a substantial farm of 165 acres worked by five mature slaves, but that property compared poorly to Tompkins's 330 acres and sixteen slaves. At a time when a carriage was an expensive status symbol, Tompkins owned one but Eddins did not. Captain Eddins did, however, enjoy the patronage of the county's leading magistrate, Houlder Hudgins (who had lost his white slaves in the famous case of *Wrights v. Hudgins* in 1806). Hudgins had considerable local clout thanks to his 811 acres, thirty-six adult slaves, carriage, and his especially extensive family network, for "Hudgins" was the most abundant surname in Mathews County. In 1812 only one other taxpayer had the last name Tompkins—compared to the four Eddinses and the fifty-two Hudginses. As a relative newcomer, Tompkins had broader external connections to Richmond but shallower family roots in Mathews County.[57]

Fiercely defending their traditional power over local appointments, the Mathews Magistrates resented the governor and council as dangerous innovators and centralizers for imposing Tompkins as the major. Tompkins reported, "Mr. Houlder Hudgins addressed the other members with considerable warmth, observing by the way that it was the greatest insult that could be offered to our Bench, that the Executive should take upon themselves to dictate to the Court." Hudgins added, "Captain Eddins sometimes got *merry* with his friends, which for his part, was considered rather a Virtue than a Vice."[58]

By commissioning Tompkins, the council outraged the Eddins family and their Hudgins connections. One of the captain's relatives refused to perform guard duty "& said that he would kill the first man that dared attempt to carry him." Despite enemy warships nearby, Captain Eddins told the assembled militiamen "that they were not bound to obey any officer except Col. Gayle." Delighted to avoid duty, the men dispersed until Gayle ordered them to reassemble, but he refused to arrest Eddins for mutiny, as Tompkins demanded. Eddins then headed to Richmond, bearing a remonstrance signed by most of the county's magistrates and militia officers who insisted that by overriding seniority the executive had dishonored the bypassed officers. But the council stood firm, so Eddins resigned his captain's commission in a huff. In April 1814, however, the Hudgins faction reaffirmed its local popularity by winning both Mathews County seats in the state legislature.[59]

The turmoil in the militia came at a bad time, for in early 1814 the Royal Navy seized New Point Comfort at the southeastern tip of Mathews County as a watering station. The crew on a frigate or ship-of-the-line consumed two to three tons of water per day. Landing at New Point Comfort, the British dug wells to procure water. The local militia could neither defend nor retake the isolated point because attackers from the mainland had to cross a long, sandy spit exposed to naval fire. Barges mounted with a small cannon at each bow hovered along the spit to support a shore party of 200 men, a mix of working sailors and guarding marines. From the top of the point's lighthouse, a British officer could watch for any threatening movements within three miles. Occasionally, from the far side of the sandy spit, the militia fired at the occupiers, but the long shots fell short. Having filled their casks, the British departed, after posting a

placard on the lighthouse with a doggerel poem to mock the impo-
tence of the Virginians, known as "Buckskins": "Let the Buckskins
do as they will, We will get a plenty of water still."[60]

The militia watched the British from a guard post on the far side of
the sandy spit. The guards served primarily to keep slaves from running across to freedom and to entice British deserters to bolt across
the spit to America. Fear of desertion discouraged the British officers
from venturing their men beyond the point, a restraint that, Major
Tompkins explained, "affords us more serenity than anything else."[61]

Through the winter of 1813–1814, the militia guards suffered
from exposure to the biting winds and driving rains, for they lacked
decent clothing and proper tents. At best, the men could huddle
around fires in front of their brush huts. Most of the guards became
too sick for duty, reducing the county's able-bodied militia to just
100 men. Reverend Armistead Smith reported, "Our poor Militia are
worn out with fatigue, constant Duty day & Night." He considered
them "cowed and dispirited.[62]

Feeling abandoned by their state and national governments, the
Mathews men despaired of resisting the British. In February, Smith
reported, "Every thing has been in a constant state of confusion &
alarm. Every Business of every kind has been at a stand & I never
laid myself down to rest at night but expected before the morning to
be alarmed with the horrid raps & thunderings of the Enemy at the
doors." John Patterson predicted that "the [militia] camp in a short
time will become depopulated & the whole Country left to the free
will of an invading foe." Patterson warned that the Mathews people
soon would "tamely submit & place ourselves at the mercy of our
old Masters & instead of looking up to our own Government for
protection take the Oath of allegiance & ask a safeguard of [our]
invading Foe." In mid-March, Barbour belatedly ordered eighty-
two men, drawn from two other counties, to march to the partial
relief of Mathews County.[63]

Despite the militia guards, some local slaves escaped to the enemy in stolen boats. A few runaways bolted in January and February 1814, and seventy did so in March, as the weather warmed and the waves stilled. On March 12, Colonel Gayle reported, "The desertion of our slaves have increased within the last ten days to an astonishing degree & in a short time all the lower Country immediately connected with this place must be ruin'd. They comprise the principal capital of this Section of the State & the chief dependence of the widow & orphan." A slave or two provided social security for many of the common white people in Mathews County. Averse to working his own fields, Reverend Smith worried that the British would "pillage & plunder me . . . of every species of property, particularly our negroe property on which our principal Dependance rests."[64]

The runaways compromised the county's security by identifying militia weak points and hidden shipping to the British. Visiting a warship under a flag of truce, a Mathews militia officer discovered "that they knew our force very well, and could at any time land double our number and take the County, if there was an object for doing so." On the night of May 1, three barges filled with Britons dodged the militia guards and ascended the East River to capture an especially valuable schooner, the *Grecian*. Tompkins lamented "that some Negro had got off to the Brig in the early part of the Night & gave information as to the position of the schooner."[65]

The runaways stole the ubiquitous canoes and small boats of the watery county, where so many people lived by seeking fish, crabs, and oysters in the rivers and bay. Tompkins explained, "Tis a curious fact that no spot can be found in this county more than a mile from tidewater; hence the impossibility of securing the canoes without guarding them, and I expect that one Thousand is the smallest number we have in the County, for not only every white person but almost every negro has a canoe." Empowered by a new state law passed in January 1814, Tompkins divided the county into districts, each with a compound guarded by five sentries to watch the boats every night. The owners could borrow their boats by day, but had to return them at dusk. When a negligent owner kept his canoe one night, nine slaves stole it and escaped to the British.[66]

In October 1814, more than 300 men signed petitions protesting the local enforcement of the boat law: "Manifest Oppressions and injustices have been done to your Petitioners" who "have been deprived of their Canoes, which were a means of the greater part of their Support during the greater part of the Summer and fall." Fiercely libertarian, common Virginians resented any new exercise of government power to restrict their freedom.[67]

A month later, the Mathews County proponents of the boat law sent a counterpetition to the legislature. Although only eighty-four men signed the pro-restriction petition, they included Tompkins, Gayle, and Reverend Smith (whose daughter had married Tompkins). They cited the great exception to the state's libertarian tradition: the laws requiring all white men to cooperate in keeping the slaves in order. The signers reasoned, "The principal capital of Virginia consists of Land & Slaves and upon this capital the payment of Taxes to support the Government both in time of War and Peace is predicated." Therefore, they concluded, "Every man in the community subject to the payment of Taxes has an interest in the security of the slaves." Rather than weaken the boat law, the Tompkins faction sought the authority for militia officers "to destroy any canoe or light vessel" belonging to anyone who ignored the regulations.[68]

The dueling petitions revealed a class division between the opponents and the proponents of the boat law. According to the Mathews County tax list for 1812, the pro-restriction men had more slaves to lose than did their opponents: 7.2 per proponent versus 1.5 per opponent. Indeed, most of the opponents owned no taxable slaves, while over four-fifths of the proponents owned at least one. The proponents had also suffered greater losses to wartime escapes: thirteen of them had lost a total of thirty-three slaves, compared to the eighteen runaways lost by just eight of the opponents. Perhaps most telling of all, 37 percent of the proponents owned a carriage, but only 3 percent of the opponents owned one, which attested to their lower status and greater reliance on canoes.[69]

The exceptional opponent who proved the rule was Houlder Hudgins, who had lost ten wartime runaways and owned a carriage and thirty-six taxable slaves. But Hudgins resented Tompkins's rising power, so the old judge rallied the local majority with a populist appeal meant to embarrass his younger rival. Hudgins had also moved his remaining slaves west to Kentucky, far from harm's way for the duration of the war, so he neither needed nor wanted the interfering protection offered by Tompkins and the boat law.[70]

Relatively wealthy, the proponents of the boat law denounced their local opponents as "a few restless men residing immediately on those water courses, owning little or no property except a Canoe & giving nothing in support of the Government, extending their Ideas no farther than their own convenience." Such men lacked any "immediate interest in the Security of the Slaves," and some of them were even "disposed rather to favour than prevent their escape" because "influenced by what they call a leveling principle," deemed essential to defend "their *rights and privileges as free men*." Under the duress of war in a slave society, common whites worried that poverty might compromise their freedom. As the war dragged on, class fissures widened among the whites of Virginia.[71]

By failing to defend the long, exposed Atlantic seaboard, the federal government unwittingly cast the apple of discord into Virginia, exposing an array of internal divisions. The hinterland people dreaded militia service at Norfolk, while the rest of the Tidewater felt abandoned to British raids by a state government beholden to the Piedmont. For want of federal troops, Virginia had to rely on militiamen called out by the hundreds whenever the British threatened a particular county. The repeated emergencies strained the politics, finances, and economy of the state. Striving to bring order to the chaos, Governor Barbour sought greater state control over a better-trained militia. But his reforms aroused fierce resistance from traditionalists who preferred the laxer and more decentralized ways of Old Virginia. Lying behind all the friction lay the dread of an internal enemy prone to become "Englishmen" to fight the "American Buggers."[72]

Wie Pinx   Ridley Sculp

6

LESSONS

———⌒∿⌒———

*It was now that the slaves began to desert to us, and by their
local knowledge we were afterwards enabled to carry on a system of
harassing warfare which, in the end, obliged the inhabitants to throw
themselves upon our mercy, instead of the protection of their militiamen.*
—LIEUTENANT JAMES SCOTT, MAY 1813[1]

IN JULY 1807 a fourteen-year-old slave named Willis fled from his
master in Princess Anne County by stealing a boat and rowing
out to a British warship anchored in nearby Lynnhaven Bay. Willis
expected a warm welcome, for war seemed imminent after the recent
British attack on the USS *Chesapeake*. Initially, the British took in,
fed, and clothed Willis and four other fugitives, but in early August
the Royal Navy Commodore sent them back to their masters in a
bid to defuse tensions with the Virginians. Instead of dwelling on
that betrayal, Willis later recalled that "he had been to the British
once & that they treated him well & he wished his master had let
him remain." In 1814, Willis escaped again to a British ship along
with "many other negroes in the neighbourhood."[2]

Willis's persistence demonstrated the allure of the British as

Admiral Sir John Borlase Warren, R.N., *an engraving by R. N. Stipple, from* The Naval
Chronicle *(London, 1800), vol. 3. (Courtesy of the Navy Department Library, Washington, D.C.)*

potential liberators among the restive slaves of the Tidewater. In March 1813 in Mathews County, the slaves who broke into John Ripley's store called themselves "Englishmen." In July 1814 in Calvert County, Maryland, a white farmer sought water by visiting a spring. Noting the slaves gathered there, he hid behind a tree and overheard "the negroes belonging to the said John J. Brooke huzzaing for the different British admirals." Two days later, three of those cheering slaves fled to the warships. A later Chesapeake slave, Frederick Douglass, recalled looking longingly at sailing ships scudding along the bay as "freedom's swift-winged angels" and vowing, "This very bay shall yet bear me into freedom." Willis had felt the same way.[3]

By their enthusiasm for the British as liberators, the Chesapeake slaves made it so, flocking to them in unanticipated numbers that would compel a major rethinking of British strategy. At the start of their first Chesapeake campaign in 1813, the British officers were reluctant to take on more than a few black men as pilots and guides. During their second campaign in 1814, the British would seek and welcome hundreds of runaways, including women and children. Willis and other runaways would not take no for an answer.

Admirals

During 1812 the British proved slow in mustering their naval might against the Americans. Committed to a massive conflict against the mighty Napoléon, the Royal Navy was stretched thin around the globe. To command the undermanned North American squadron, based at Halifax, the Admiralty assigned Vice Admiral Sir John Borlase Warren, who was better known for his lavish style of life than for his devotion to active service. Thomas Grenville of the Admiralty considered Warren "good for nothing but fine weather and easy sailing." But Warren had some experience as a diplomat, and the imperial government empowered him to negotiate peace with the Americans. Keen to concentrate on fighting the French, the British wanted promptly to stop the distracting American war. In June, the empire suspended the Orders in Council, which had restricted American trade with Europe, hoping thereby to mollify the Americans enough to restore peace. Instead, they continued to fight to break up the British alliance with Indians and to seek an end to the impressment of sailors.[4] In sum, Warren held two conflicting assignments: as a diplomat charged with seeking peace and as an admiral obliged to inflict the pain of war.

The Admiralty expected too much from Warren, who had too few warships to blockade the long American coast and protect the vulnerable British trade with the West Indies against American privateers. Warren's squadron also suffered from a shortage of skilled seamen, which reflected the strain of a prolonged global war on the limited manpower of Great Britain. His standing with his superiors in the Admiralty eroded when some of the powerful American frigates slipped out to sea, where they captured or destroyed three British frigates. Used to defeating the French and Spanish, no matter the odds, the British felt shocked at their losses to the Americans. The defeats threatened British morale far beyond their paltry strategic significance. Rather than take the blame, the Admiralty heaped it on Warren.[5]

In December 1812 the British leaders decided to escalate the war against the Americans, to punish them for rejecting a quick peace. Napoléon's recent crushing defeats in Russia also persuaded the imperial government that it could afford to divert additional ships and men from Europe to fight the Americans. By the summer of 1813 the Royal Navy had doubled the number of warships in American waters to 129: five times the strength of the American navy. The Admiralty directed Warren to take his warships into Chesapeake Bay to smite Maryland and Virginia, deemed the heart of American resources and the political base for the pro-war Republicans. By blockading trade capturing merchant ships and privateers and by raiding farms and villages, the British hoped to compel the Americans to pull back their troops invading Canada to defend the Chesapeake country instead. After a year's restraint, the British meant to teach the Americans a bloody, burning lesson: that they should never provoke the empire.[6]

To promote greater aggression, the Admiralty sent Rear Admiral Sir George Cockburn to serve as Warren's second-in-command. Forty years old, Cockburn was in the prime of his health and nautical career, in contrast to Warren, who had seen his best days. As the son of a wealthy merchant, Cockburn had learned the self-righteous values of self-discipline and hard work, which distinguished his character from the aristocratic Warren. Cockburn entered the Royal Navy as a teenage midshipman. Zealous, able, and courageous, he won the esteem of his superiors, particularly Britain's greatest admiral, Lord Horatio Nelson, who became his patron. In 1795, at the precocious age of twenty-three, Cockburn took command of a frigate posted in the Mediterranean. In later operations along the Dutch coast, Cockburn developed an expertise in amphibious operations, experience which subsequently served him well in the Chesapeake.[7]

Supremely self-confident, he was a flamboyant performer of command who delighted in military pageantry. Another officer described Cockburn as "very fond of Parade & shew, 60 men therefore to parade every morning" with "the Band playing 'God Save the King.'" A great wit and remarkably calm under fire, he inculcated an *esprit* among his subordinate officers, who found his dash and activity contagious. Cockburn also encouraged and promoted talented young officers, who became deeply devoted to their patron. One midshipman fondly recalled "that undaunted seaman, Rear-Admiral George Cockburn, with his sun-burned visage, and his rusty gold-laced hat—an officer who never spared himself, either night or day, but shared on every occasion, the same toil, danger, and privation" as the petty officers.[8]

Devoted to his king and empire, Cockburn disdained the Americans, for indirectly helping the French and for harboring British deserters. He shared the contempt of all British officers for the American declaration of war as cowardly and treacherous because made at a critical moment in the empire's desperate struggle against Napoléon. One officer complained that the Americans "snarled at us like curs, when a bull is being baited; for while we were tossing the [French] dogs in front, they took the opportunity of biting our heels." The British officers longed to punish the Americans for their temerity. Once humbled by defeat, surely they would reject the Republicans, restore the Federalists to power, and accept British leadership in commerce and diplomacy.[9]

Raids

While ravaging the Chesapeake shores and shipping, admirals Cockburn and Warren were supposed to avoid great risks, for the empire could ill afford any losses of men or ships. Instead of mounting mass assaults on strongly fortified positions, the admirals were supposed to make smaller and safer raids on poorly defended places. British leaders remembered the catastrophic defeats on land that had cost them Burgoyne's and Cornwallis's armies during the last unhappy war in America. To avoid repeating the humiliations of the American Revolution, the British avoided major battles and probes deep inland where their precious men might get ambushed in the woods, picked off by riflemen, and surrounded by superior numbers. One officer concluded, "To penetrate up the country amidst pathless forests and boundless deserts, and to aim at permanent conquest is out of the question." The British came to harass rather than to conquer America.[10]

The British perceived the vast American landscape as an unconquerable foe. Coming from a mild, rainy, compact, and cultivated island, they felt awed by the bigger, wilder land and volatile climate of the Chesapeake. "Low, flat, sandy banks covered with pines is all we see," Rear Admiral Edward Codrington reported from his warship. The naval officers regarded the riverside farms and plantations as pleasant oases in the midst of "the boundless forests" of massive trees that stretched around and behind them. And the British suffered from the blistering summer sun and clouds of mosquitoes. Lieutenant James Scott recalled faces "bloated, swelled, and disfigured by the smarting, itching incisions of . . . these bloodthirsty devils. The heat was suffocating." And the sudden, violent storms of summer sometimes capsized barges and smaller warships. After one storm of thunder, rain, and wind, a naval captain reported, "we saw immense trees torn up by the roots, [and] barns blown down like the card houses of children." Codrington concluded, "This Chesapeake is like a new world." It was a strange and frightful new world for men of the sea from a distant island.[11]

Rather than invade the daunting land, the British usually kept close to the security of their warships during the campaign of 1813. Cockburn insisted that the Americans' "Rifles & the thickness of their Woods . . . constitute their principal, if not their only, Strength." When the British did venture inland, their operations often went badly awry owing to faulty information. "We have [a] nasty sort of fighting here amongst creeks and bushes, and lose men without show. . . . It is an inglorious warfare," lamented a British officer. In August, Sir Sidney Beckwith sadly reported that his troops became confused when fired upon while "moving thro' the thick wood" about four miles from the bay. After his spooked men shot three of their own by mistake, Beckwith decried "the extreme imprudence of risking such Troops" in the American woods. A Tidewater man happily noted, "The enemy does not like to put his feet on our shores, as many parts thereof are covered with pine & they know not what force we may have."[12]

Instead, the admirals exploited the superior mobility of their ships to mount hit-and-run raids before the land-bound American militia respond in force. To maximize impact and minimize risk, the warships roamed up and down the bay, alarming all shores and making, in Warren's words, "sudden & secret attacks at those points in which the Enemy is most vulnerable." The American secretary of the navy aptly attributed the British strategy to "our extensive and navigable waters and their great naval superiority."[13]

By targeting shipping and exposed villages, the British took many prizes while suffering few casualties. "Never was there a finer opportunity to make our fortunes," one officer exulted. While the big ships of the line and frigates kept to the deeper waters in the middle of the bay, the shallower-draft sloops and schooners probed up the rivers, "searching out, capturing, and destroying every vessel or craft floating on the waters," as Lieutenant Scott put it. The British burned the older ships but loaded the better ones with loot and sent them off to Bermuda and Halifax for sale, with the prize money divided among the capturing officers and crews.[14]

Barges filled with armed sailors and marines also landed to plunder exposed farms, plantations, and villages, but the British fled to their ships as soon as the local militia assembled in threatening numbers. In a game of cat and mouse, the British warships and barges would approach a point, attracting a concentration of alarmed militia, before sailing away to an unguarded point to raid. Scott exulted, "Our business was generally achieved before they could possibly reach us, from the circuitous track they were obliged to pursue. . . . The poor militiamen were fairly worried out of their lives, [for] they knew no repose by night or by day" as the British raiders "were here, and there, and everywhere." One British officer aptly called the strategy a "species of milito-nautico-guerilla-plundering warfare."[15]

Civil War

The dirty secret of the Chesapeake operation was that the Royal Navy depended on local help to sustain the blockade, for their crews needed fresh water and provisions from the farms and plantations along the shore. The British also relied on American pilots to guide them around the treacherous shoals and up the shallow rivers. In addition, the naval officers paid informants to reveal the strong and weak points of the American defenses. Deftly deploying flattery, trickery, and money, Cockburn cultivated suppliers, guides, pilots, and spies. He learned much simply by reading the American newspapers, which reported military deployments in surprising detail. A visitor noted that the admiral routinely received "newspapers, smoking from the press, and every other information they could obtain to our strength, dispositions of force, &c."[16]

Many Americans readily sold their wares and principles for British gold. Loading their vessels with cattle, poultry, sheep, hogs, and vegetables, they sailed straight for British warships while flying a white flag. By Cockburn's prearrangement, the British "captured" the ships, took off the cargo, but then generously paid the captains and released their ships to return home with a phony story. One canny captain damaged his sails, "to shew when he went home, that he had been fired at and compelled (sorely against his will!) to go along-side one of the enemy's ships." In another trick, the merchant captain hid a cargo of provisions beneath a load of lumber. After buying the food, Cockburn gave the obliging captain a pass to sail unmolested through the British fleet to another American port to sell the lumber, thereby making a double profit.[17]

On islands and exposed points where resistance was futile, the inhabitants sold livestock and provisions to the raiders. In April 1813 the British landed in force on Spesutie Island, Maryland, and threatened to burn homes. "This had the desired effect & we procured a prodigious quantity of everything," Major Marmaduke Wybourn reported. In August on Maryland's Eastern Shore, a militia commander complained that the illicit trade with the enemy "was so great, as to be highly criminal."[18]

The British cooperated with the tender consciences and cunning evasions of their new friends, who wanted to keep secret their assistance to the enemy. A British officer explained, "The plan agreed on was this: they were to drive [their cattle] down to a certain point, where we were to land and take possession; for the inhabitants being all militiamen, and having too much patriotism to sell food to 'King George's men,' they used to say, 'put the money under such a stone or tree, pointing to it, and then we can pick it up, and say we found it.'" Sometimes the raiders left payment in a cupboard for the poultry or livestock of a cooperative farmer.[19]

The British suffered some stinting periods of short rations but in general, their squadron derived plenty to eat from the shores of the Chesapeake. Lieutenant Scott concluded, "Fish, flesh, and fowl were obtained in abundance on the Chesapeake station." Warren exulted, "I never saw a country so vulnerable, open to attack, or that affords the means of support to an enemy's force, as the [United] States." In late 1813 the official newspaper of the Madison administration, the *National Intelligencer*, warned that the enemy could not be defeated "while we continue to feed his armies and fleet." In pursuit of profits, many Americans supplied the national enemy.[20]

In addition to the slaves, the Americans faced another internal enemy: themselves. A Baltimore newspaper lamented, "Certainly no country was ever cursed with so many traitors as we have." Because the American law of treason required at least two witnesses to an overt act of war, prosecutors failed to convict any of the accused suppliers of provisions and information to Cockburn. At best, officials could harass the suspected traitors with arrests and brief stints in jail pending trial.[21]

By driving up the costs of war and ruining those who resisted, the British hoped to promote political divisions and perhaps even a civil war within the United States. Warren predicted, "It is possible that the increasing Demands for cash & consequently Taxes may occasion convulsion & Disorder among the several States." He reasoned that Americans had to learn harsh lessons before they would renounce their unjust war and oust their bumbling Republican leaders, embracing instead the pro-British Federalists. Another officer

explained that the Americans needed to "experience the real handi-
caps and miseries of warfare. . . . So it is with democracy at war. Burn
their houses, plunder their property, block up their harbours, and
destroy their shipping," then but only then "you will be stopped by
entreaties for peace."[22]

Although waged by distinct governments, the War of 1812 was
also a civil war between kindred people sharing the same language
and cultural heritage. Indeed, combatants often struggled to tell
friend from foe. A British officer of marines recalled that during
night attacks on the Chesapeake shores, the British sailors had to
wear "white bands round their arms & hats, to distinguish English
from Americans."[23]

Americans and Britons waged the war with familiar words as
well as with weapons. Appealing to similar values of freedom and
Christianity, the two sides employed persuasion to weaken their
enemy by making converts. Admiral Warren complained that American captors politically seduced their British prisoners: "every art [is]
practiced to persuade them to become American Citizens, which,
from the peculiar situation of the two Countries speaking the same
Language is more easy to accomplish than in any other part of the
world." While the Americans enticed deserters from the Royal Navy,
the British worked to divide the Americans by rewarding Federalists
and punishing the Republicans. British sailors could become Americans by deserting; Federalists could become British allies by supplying the blockading ships.[24]

Both sides regarded the war as a second act in a drama launched
by the American Revolution. During the new war, some British officers called the Americans "rebels," as if they had not truly
won their independence and the revolution was not yet lost to the
empire. Because of the cultural overlap between Americans and
Britons, similar people fought on both sides. British immigrants
lived throughout the United States, and British forces included
many sons of the Loyalist refugees from the revolution. "It is quite

shocking to have men who speak our own language brought in wounded; one feels as if they were English peasants, and that we are killing our own people," declared one British officer posted in the Chesapeake. He added, "There are numbers of officers, of the navy in particular, whose families are American, and their fathers in one or two instances are absolutely living in the very towns we are trying to burn." For example, the British general Sir Sidney Beckwith had cousins in Virginia.[25]

Although a fierce supporter of the war, St. George Tucker had relatives from Bermuda holding high commands in the British military. His nephew John G. P. Tucker became a colonel in the British army and fought against the Americans on the Niagara front. During the war, Colonel Tucker wrote to his uncle, "Altho we are *politically* the most determined Enemies, yet our private feelings can never cease to impel us to acts of friendship & kindness" provided they did not contradict "the *first* duty which we owe to our Country." He signed, "Your affectionate nephew." Another Tucker nephew commanded HMS *Cherub*, which helped to capture a powerful American frigate, but he suffered severe wounds in the battle. St. George Tucker and his brother Thomas felt tormented by the tension between their intense family ties and their equally fervid patriotism. Thomas consoled St. George: "How lamentable, how distressing, my beloved brother, that friends so truly dear to us shou'd be engaged in the service of the enemy. I have always depreciated the consequences of a war in which the nearest & dearest relatives are engaged on opposite sides, & liable to become the murderers of each other."[26]

Irish-born Americans particularly experienced the conflict as a civil war. Although they had immigrated to the United States to escape British rule, the Irish faced impressment when found on board American merchant ships. Worse still, once the war began, British officers threatened to hang as traitors any former subjects captured bearing arms against their king. British officers perceived the American navy as filled with "traitors to their country [who] were supposed to be more than half the force opposed to us"—in the words of Major Wybourn. In sum, the British officers treated Irish Americans as rebels in a civil war between the empire of their birth and the republic of their choice.[27]

A naturalized American citizen, John O'Neill hated the British as "the oppressors of the human race, and particularly of my native country, Ireland." O'Neill fought fiercely to defend his home on May 3, 1813, when the British raided Havre de Grace, Maryland. The rest of the local militia quickly fled, leaving O'Neill alone to resist 150 Britons until they wounded and captured him. After burning his house, the victors threatened to hang O'Neill as a traitor, although he had resided in the United States for fifteen years. Three days later the British relented, releasing him on parole rather than make a popular martyr of a respectable man. Admiral Warren subsequently (and implausibly) insisted, "I was not informed of this man being an Irishman, or he would certainly have been detained, to account to his sovereign and country for being in arms against the British colors." Warren could not admit that he had compromised his empire's policy of punishing any former subject captured in the enemy's service.[28]

The conflict also verged on a civil war within America because of the bitter partisanship pitting Federalists against Republicans. Each party denounced the other as betraying the republic to assist a foreign enemy. Republicans cast the Federalists as latter-day Tories who served the British, while the Federalists denounced the Republicans as stooges for the French dictator. By frustrating the war effort, the Federalists sought to expose the Republicans as fools for declaring war. By winning the war, the Republicans hoped to discredit the Federalists and cast them into political oblivion. The *Baltimore American* explained that in time of war "there are but two parties, *Citizen Soldiers* and *Enemies—Americans* and *Tories*." Recalling the

The Conspiracy Against Baltimore, or the War Dance at Montgomery Court House. *Crafted in 1812 by an unknown Maryland Republican, the cartoon lampoons the state's Federalists including the newspaper editor and publisher Alexander Contee Hanson, Jr. depicted with the devil's horns at center. He looms over Robert Goodloe Harper shown playing a harp, as a pun. In the group to the left, the dancing man with a distinctive hat, a military* chapeau de bras, *is General Henry Lee, a former governor of Virginia, who suffered crippling wounds in the Baltimore riot. (Courtesy of the Maryland Historical Society).*

revolution's brutal suppression of the Loyalists, Thomas Jefferson boasted that Republican mobs would silence the Federalists. In Norfolk, a mob fulfilled Jefferson's prophecy by tarring and feathering a Federalist before dumping him in a creek.[29]

The partisan fury peaked in Baltimore, a booming seaport of 41,000 people, most of them Republicans. In late June, Republican mobs tore down the Federalist newspaper office of Alexander Contee Hanson Jr., dismantled ships suspected of trading with the enemy, and destroyed the homes of free blacks accused of British sympathies. A defiant Hanson fortified a new office with armed guards, including the former revolutionary war generals James Lingan and Henry Lee (also a past governor of Virginia). In late July, the Federalists fired into an attacking mob of enraged Republicans, killing one and wounding others. The city magistrates jailed the Federalists, but the rioters broke in the next day to batter their foes. Watching women cried, "Kill the tories!" and the rioters sang:

> *We'll feather and tar ev'ry d[amne]d British tory,*
> *And that is the way for American glory.*

Stabbed in the chest, Lingan died. Eleven others, including Lee and Hanson, suffered crippling injuries. A few token prosecutions convicted only one rioter, and he merely paid a small fine. A juror explained "that the affray originated with them tories, and that they all ought to have been killed, and that he would rather starve than find a verdict of guilty against any of the rioters."[30]

Pride

British naval officers considered pride the worst of American sins. Adhering to a hierarchical code of strict discipline, the officers disdained the pushy and boastful Americans, who seemed to recognize no superior. When compelled to postpone an attack, Warren lamented that "any Delay on our side in attacking them has only added to their pride & presumption": a most distasteful development. But Lieutenant Scott warned the Americans that "severer trials awaited their pride." Rather than simply defeat the Americans, the officers longed to humble them.[31]

By ravaging the Chesapeake shores, Cockburn hoped to disgrace the Americans and discredit their republic. In March 1813 he assured Warren that "the whole of the Shores and Towns within this Vast Bay, not excepting the Capital itself will be wholly at your mercy, *and* subject, if not to be permanently occupied, certainly to be successively insulted or destroyed at your Pleasure." The British raids would, Lieutenant Scott explained, expose the inability of the Madison administration "to afford the necessary degree of protection, justly expected by the inhabitants of every country whose government ventures to decide upon a state of warfare." After plundering one Virginia farm, a witty officer left a note written in sheep's blood to pledge that President Madison would pay the owner for the stolen livestock taken "for the use of the British navy."[32]

British officers detested most Americans as greedy cheats, long on cunning but short on scruples. "They will do anything for money," a captain concluded. According to Rear Admiral Codrington, after the British occupied an American town, a resident boasted, "I'm as brave as Julius Caesar" and "I've as fine a house in this city, and shan't quit it for you or anybody." A British officer replied, "Oh, ho! You've a fine house here have you? Well, I'll soon rid you of that encumbrance, for I'll burn it directly." Falling to his knees, the American "rascal" begged, "Mister if you won't burn my house, I'll do what ever you please." Codrington concluded, "This is the picture of the people in general. They are meanly inquisitive, arrogantly impertinent & cruelly tyrannical where their power is uncontrouled, and yet they bend the neck to the yoke of coercion as if nature formed them for slaves."[33]

Hardened by war and proud of their discipline, the British officers mocked the Americans as dishonorable amateurs full of false bravado and real cowardice. Major Wybourn dismissed the United States as "a country of *Infants in War*." Used to fighting in the open, the British disdained the American preference for long-distance sniping from behind cover as cowardly and effeminate. In one battle report, Cockburn derided his foes: "no longer feeling themselves equal to a manly and open Resistance, they commenced a teasing and irritating fire from behind their Houses, Walls, Trees, &c." The British denounced as cheating the expedients of untrained and poorly equipped American militiamen. A British officer declared, "They fight unfairly, firing jagged pieces of iron and every sort of devilment — nails, broken pokers, old locks of guns, gun-barrels — everything that will do mischief."[34]

The Americans especially infuriated the British by deploying floating, explosive mines, known as "torpedoes," cast adrift to strike and
destroy warships in the night. Although the torpedoes proved inef-
fective, they offended the British as cowardly and treacherous. Citing
the "dastardly" torpedoes, the British felt justified in conducting their
punishing and plundering war against the American coast.[35]

Republicans denounced Cockburn as an indiscriminate plunderer,
and some historians have mistaken his strategy as "total war." In fact,
he was highly discriminating in his targets, for Cockburn sought to
teach Americans the perils of their pride, and as a paternal teacher he
had to reward the deserving as well as punish the stubborn. Cockburn carefully investigated the political allegiances of the leading men
dwelling along the shore, for he meant to harass Republicans and spare
Federalists. A visitor to Cockburn's flagship returned to report that
the admiral "appears well informed of the *political* character of many
persons and places on the shores of the bay." In one raid on a Maryland town, Major Wybourn told a woman, "the question they generally asked when they went to any place was, how they voted at the
elections, and inquired . . . if her uncle, meaning Mr. Henderson, voted
for the war." Apparently he had voted Republican, for Wybourn had
Henderson's stable and coaches burned. In general, Cockburn's men
plundered and destroyed the buildings of anyone who resisted (usually Republicans) but protected the property of those who submitted.[36]

In mid-April 1813, Cockburn sailed up Chesapeake Bay to
"teach a salutary lesson" to his American students on the shores of
Maryland. On April 27 his men raided Frenchtown, near the head of
the bay. A brief militia resistance exposed the town's storehouses to
looting and burning, but Cockburn spared the private homes. Turning west, he attacked Havre de Grace after noticing a new battery,
whose crew "hoisted the American colours, by way of bravado."
Determined to humble every display of American pride, Cockburn
led an assault on May 3. A brief and futile resistance by a few militiamen (including John O'Neill) qualified the village for a thorough

Admiral Cockburn Burning & Plundering Havre de Grace on the 1st of June 1813; done from a Sketch taken on the spot at the time. *At the right of center Cockburn leans on his sword while his marines and sailors loot the village. Note the British barges in the background. (Courtesy of the Maryland Historical Society)*

plundering (and some burning) of homes as well as stores. Cockburn explained that he sought to bring the people "to understand and feel what they were liable to bring upon themselves by building Batteries and acting towards us with so much useless Rancor."[37]

Turning east, Cockburn attacked Fredericktown and George-town, along the Sassafras River of Maryland's Eastern Shore. On May 6, Cockburn warned that if the inhabitants "offered any useless or irritating opposition, they must expect the same fate as that which had befallen Havre [de Grace] and Frenchtown; but if they yielded, private property would be respected, the vessels and public property alone seized, and that whatever supplies might be required would be punctually paid for." The local magistrates wanted to submit, but a fiery militia officer ordered his men to shoot at the British landing party. After routing the militia, the British plundered and burned both towns, sparing only a few houses with especially charming women or with owners who paid a ransom in cattle. A local Federalist blamed the "imprudent & foolish conduct" of the Republican militiamen who fired a few shots and then ran away, exposing the abandoned villages to the raiders.[38]

Preferring discretion to valor, the people of nearby Charlestown surrendered rather than risk their homes. To prevent militia resistance, the town fathers "buried their cannon & knocked down a little fort," as a relieved Federalist reported. Lieutenant Scott concluded that the British had opened "the eyes of the whole neighborhood . . . to the folly of irritating resistance."[39]

Cockburn played the benign protector when Americans submitted. Later that month a British frigate ran aground near Annapolis, but the militia wisely declined to open fire. Sending a message ashore, Cockburn assured the inhabitants that their "prudence . . . in not firing on the frigate which grounded near their city saved it from destruction." Similarly, on Kent Island in August, Cockburn compensated the passive inhabitants for some thefts made by rowdy sailors, whom the admiral had flogged. And, "from Motives of Humanity," he protected a shipment of coal bound by merchant ship from Virginia to New York "for the use of the New York Hospital."[40]

On his flagship, HMS *Albion*, Cockburn delighted in hosting genteel and cooperative Americans. A guest gushed to a newspaper that he had been "treated with great politeness and attention by the commander, Ad[miral] Cockburn, who unites the gentleman with the seaman." Cockburn entertained grandly, for another visitor recalled "every eating & drinking Vessel was of Silver. The Table lighted by 8 silver Candlesticks which reflected from large Mirrors around his Cabin, made the Scene quite dazzling." Major Wybourn recalled that Cockburn hosted a "large party of Americans who had been civil to our boats on the Maryland shore." The officers "shewed them great attention, so much so that after a superb supper they began to find *we* were nearly all alike, for they had been told strange stories of us; we made them all completely drunk except one Methodist & . . . after breakfast they went on shore highly delighted."[41]

Cockburn and his officers played the gallant with the women in captured villages and ships. After reporting the sack of Frenchtown, a Baltimore newspaper conceded, "It is justice to the enemy to say, they treated the women and children with considerable attention and respect." At Havre de Grace, a sailor robbed a milliner of her dresses but was, in Lieutenant Scott's words, "deservedly mortified by the Rear-admiral obliging him to return the spoils . . . to the forlorn damsel, with an impressive rebuke." At Charlestown, Major Wybourn reported finding "a train of boarding school misses with governesses & teachers, about 40. These we shewed great humanity to & spared a village on their account."[42]

Britons claimed to be truer men than the cowardly Americans who had failed to protect their families. On the Eastern Shore, Cockburn's raiders surprised a genteel house "full of joyous girls" celebrating a birthday. Initially terrified, the girls soon felt reassured, Scott wrote, by the "courtly demeanour of the Admiral, and [his] promises of protection restored the roses to their smiling countenances, and they learned that the enemy and the gentleman may be combined." Scott added, "Every male biped of the household stole off on the first intimation of our arrival, and left the fascinating innocents completely at our mercy." British officers won a delicious victory every time they obliged American women to praise their humanity and to rue the cowardice of their own men.[43]

Villain

In June, Warren and Cockburn received reinforcements from Europe: 2,650 soldiers and marines. But they were a motley crew of men deemed expendable from serving with the British army in

Spain. At the bottom of the barrel were 300 captured Europeans, mostly French, who agreed to serve the British in America rather than linger in confinement.[44]

The admirals thought that they had enough men to attack Norfolk's first line of defense at Craney Island, where the Americans had built a battery and posted their gunboats. On June 22, Cockburn and Warren sent fifty barges laden with troops to land on the muddy island to overwhelm the battery, but the American fire smashed at least two barges and drove the rest away. Suffering heavy casualties, the British accused the Americans of massacring some helpless men. Then Admiral Cockburn and General Sir Sidney Beckwith squabbled over who was to blame. A pox on both, concluded Sir Charles Napier: "Cockburn thinks himself a Wellington, and Beckwith is sure the navy never produced such an admiral as himself—between them we got beaten at Craney." For once, Cockburn's impetuous, attacking style had failed, producing casualties that the British could ill afford to replace.[45]

Embarrassed by defeat and angered by the supposed massacre, the British sought a quick and easy victory on a more vulnerable American position at nearby Hampton. At dawn on June 25, the warships bombarded the shore batteries, while barges landed about 900 troops to the west. Fearing capture, the 500 defenders broke and ran into the woods and on to Yorktown, defying their commander's orders to stand and fight. In their haste to escape, they threw away knapsacks, canteens, tents, and guns.[46]

The French mercenaries in the British force vented their anger and lust on the hapless civilians who remained in Hampton. Defying their own frightened officers, the mercenaries looted homes, committed a few rapes, and killed one sick old man (named Kirby) in his bed. Then at least thirty mercenaries deserted to join the Americans. The number of rapes remained murky because, one magistrate reported, "women will not publish what they consider their own shame; and the men in Town were carefully watched and guarded."[47]

The Virginians converted their small military defeat into a major propaganda victory. In lurid prose, they exaggerated the atrocities and blamed them on the British commanders. In the most provocative version, Governor Barbour announced "that many of the Females had been violated in the most Brutal manner, not only by the troops, but in some instances by the Slaves that had joined them." A negative fantasy tempting to Virginians, the raping slaves had no basis in evidence from Hampton.[48]

By dwelling on the perils of women and the duty of men to seek revenge, the Virginians refuted the British claims to superior civility. The *Richmond Enquirer* exhorted, "Men of Virginia! Will you permit all this? Fathers and Brothers & Husbands, will you fold your Arms in Apathy and only curse your despoilers?" On the Fourth of July in Richmond, the Republicans offered a toast: "That barbarity, which has inspired one sex with terror, has only inflamed the courage of the other." In the Chesapeake, the propaganda war pivoted on who could best claim to defend America's women.[49]

Deeply embarrassed, the British commanders blamed the mercenaries and cited the alleged massacre at Craney Island as the trigger for their rage. Beckwith deemed them "a desperate Banditti, whom it is impossible to control." Despite their shortage of troops, Beckwith and Warren shipped the mercenaries away to Halifax and then back to Europe. The commanders primarily acted to stem their rampant desertion rather than to punish them for their crimes. But the Virginians also lacked moral consistency, for they welcomed deserting mercenaries despite their atrocities at Hampton. Indeed, the Virginians preferred to blame the mess on the British commanders.[50]

The Republican press and politicians cast Cockburn as an archfiend who ravaged one and all. Describing the sack of Havre de Grace, one writer insisted, "Cockburn stood like Satan in his cloud, when he saw the blood of man from murdered Abel first crimson the earth, exulting at the damning deed, and treating the suppliant females with the rudest curses and most vile appellations—callous, insensible, hellish." A second writer concluded "that there breathes not in any quarter of the globe a more savage monster." A third declared, "He should be lashed naked through the world with whips of scorpions." Some Americans renamed their chamber pots after Cockburn. In Virginia, an Irish American offered a $1,000 reward for Cockburn's head and $500 for each of his ears. By casting the admiral as a monster, the Republicans denied that he could ever teach them lessons by discriminating in his targets.[51]

Cockburn felt both amused and outraged by his American reputation. In December he thanked a subordinate for sending him an American pamphlet: "The Book against me which you sent has afforded some amusement to those who have had time to read it & Sir John Warren is now going through it." The abuse increased Cockburn's determination to teach more lessons to the Americans. Employing the then-common British name for them as "Jonathans," Cockburn explained, "My Ideas of managing Jonathan, is by never giving way to him, in spite of his bullying and abuse."[52]

In general, the British sought to minimize civilian casualties while seeking out property for destruction. Farms and plantations and villages burned, but the Chesapeake campaign lacked the bloody massacres of civilians and prisoners that characterized the war raging in Europe. Compared to the brutality of the Napoleonic wars, particularly in Spain, the Chesapeake campaign of 1813 was remarkable for claiming the life of only one captured civilian: Mr. Kirby. The only confirmed rapes also occurred at Hampton.[53]

In July 1813, after plundering and wrecking Hampton for ten days, the British withdrew to their warships and reverted to sailing up and down the bay to harass weak points in both Virginia and Maryland. In late August, Warren sailed away to Halifax with half the squadron and all the soldiers to save them from desertion and malaria, which peaked in late summer. A month later, Cockburn withdrew most of the rest of the squadron to Bermuda to refit through the winter. The admirals left behind Captain Robert Barrie with a rump force: one ship of the line, two frigates, and five smaller vessels. Barrie's little squadron guarded the mouth of Chesapeake Bay, attacking the merchant ships and privateers that tried to exit or enter. Through the cold, stormy fall and winter, Barrie and his men kept up this hard duty, capturing or destroying eighty-nine ships by February 4, 1814.[54]

Barrie also harassed the Virginia shores with petty raids. On September 21, he landed seventy marines and eighty armed sailors on the shore of Lynnhaven Bay, to attack an American observation post at the Pleasure House: a popular bayside tavern before the war. Most of the militiamen fled, but Barrie captured nine and then burned the compound. He dared not pursue the fleeing militia because, he explained, "we were extremely ignorant of the nature of the Country . . . interspersed by Swamps and Thickets": a common British lament in 1813. He assured Cockburn that the fall raids were "a sad annoyance to the Militia as the weather is very severe and the Troops are all sickly." He delighted in reports that the militiamen "complain bitterly of being kept to such hard duty in harvest time." Cockburn congratulated Barrie for "keeping my Yankee Friends on the Fret. We ought not to allow them any Peace or Comfort."[55]

Despite the miseries inflicted on the Americans, the close of the campaign left the British frustrated with their opening foray in the Chesapeake. Despite capturing many merchant ships and damaging some villages, the British had failed to inflict a crippling blow that would compel the Madison administration to call off the invasion of Canada and sue for peace. Used to victory and proud of their gentility, the British officers also felt embarrassed by their defeat at Craney Island and by the atrocities at Hampton.[56]

But the British officers expected greater victories in 1814 thanks to the local knowledge gained in 1813. They had mastered the bay by making maps and placing buoys, and they had learned the shores and made valuable contacts with cooperative suppliers. Scott boasted that the British achieved "a better knowledge of the navigation of the Chesapeake than the American pilots themselves; indeed the Americans were fully persuaded that some of their own countrymen had turned traitors and guided us through its intricacies"—as indeed they had. Cockburn insisted that a decisive blow could be struck in the Chesapeake region if the British could deploy more men.[57]

Deserters

During 1813, desertion weakened the already undermanned British force. In late March, thirty sailors stole three boats to desert to the militia at Hampton. In early August, many more bolted from a camp on Kent Island, Maryland, where a narrow and shallow strait allowed easy access to the mainland. By August 23, nineteen British deserters, including a midshipman, had reached Easton on Maryland's Eastern Shore. In late August, eighteen British sailors landed to seek some pigs in the bushes near Cape Henry beach, when seven "took to their heels and made off," reaching the safety of an American militia guard.[58]

The Republicans celebrated every deserter as a triumph that proved the moral superiority of the republic over the empire. Desertion apparently revealed the prime weakness of the coercive empire: the alienation of its common sailors and soldiers, who longed "to quit their floating dungeons" to embrace the liberty of Americans. "If one hundred men are sent to shore, another hundred must be sent to watch them," the *Richmond Enquirer* boasted.[59]

The Irish in the British service proved especially prone to desert often with the help of Irish Americans. In late April, during the British occupation of Spesutie Island, Major Wybourn discovered that four of his "best men" had deserted, persuaded by "an old Irish rascal who had been a labourer 14 years among the Yankees on this island." Wybourn led a pursuit party, but the deserters escaped by wading across to the mainland, where "the four villains tossed their hats up, saying they were now Americans & tried to persuade" the pursuers "to join them." To Wybourn's relief his men "d[amne]d them for traitors & rascals & came back."[60]

America enticed British deserters as the land of prosperity, liberty, cheap alcohol, and the same mother tongue. Employing "Jack," the nickname for the common sailor, Lieutenant Scott lamented, "The captivating sounds of liberty and equality . . . have led astray many a clearer head and sounder judgment than falls to the lot of poor Jack." The "land of freedom and plenty" allured men weary of "the regular and strict discipline absolutely necessary in a man-of-war." Cockburn ordered his captains to minimize contact between their common sailors and American civilians "in order to avoid Corruption, Seduction, or the Seeds of Sedition being sown" among the crews. The British commanders had the unenviable task of fighting an enemy while closely guarding their own men.[61]

After a battle, the naval officers screened their new prisoners to cull anyone suspected of British birth or recognized as a deserter from the British service (even if he had been an impressed American). Most of those so detected were Irish by birth and Americans by choice. British captains also raided villages suspected of harboring deserters. At best, retaken deserters could expect a flogging followed by a return to hard duty on a warship. At worst, they were hanged from a ship's yardarm as a warning to others. The Irishman Patrick Hallidan deserted from Kent Island on the night of August 15 in a stolen boat. Recaptured and convicted by a court-martial, he was hanged on August 28. Most deserters, however, got away into America.[62]

Already shorthanded when the campaign began, the warships suffered considerable attrition from sickness, a few combat deaths, and many desertions. In September 1812, Cockburn's captains enumerated the crews for eight of his largest warships: they fell short of their full complement by 198 seamen and 56 marines (who were red-jacketed and musket-armed "sea-soldiers"). The desertions impaired the efficiency of the warships, and the remaining men bore a heavier workload, which increased their temptations to escape.[63]

The British needed able-bodied men who would resolutely fight the enemy rather than desert to him. A potential, partial solution lay in the hundreds of slaves who fled in stolen boats and canoes to seek refuge on the warships during 1813. Unlike the British sailor and marine, who anticipated a better life in the republic, the former slave would almost never desert. Cockburn sought to replace many of his white marines with black recruits: "They are stronger Men and more trust worthy for we are sure they will not desert whereas I am sorry to say we have Many Instances of our [white] Marines walking over to the Enemy."[64]

Promoting slave escapes also seemed the perfect turnabout to punish the Americans for enticing Britons to desert. Codrington explained, "For surely if the Americans whilst at Peace with us encouraged the desertion of our Seamen & paraded them in triumph before our officers who were treated with the grossest insults, it is not unbecoming us to receive deserters from them when in open hostility against us, let their colour be what it may, using those deserters as soldiers or sailors according to the example they themselves set us. I hope, indeed, we shall punish them severely in this way." British desertion helped to persuade the officers to embrace blacks as essential allies in the Chesapeake war.[65]

Fugitives

Americans dreaded that the British would promote a slave revolt to massacre white families, but the imperial government had, in fact, ruled that out. The imperial leaders heeded anxious West Indian planters, who bitterly opposed, as a terrifying precedent, any British promotion of a slave revolt in America. Britons also feared that Americans would exploit any slave-committed atrocities for propaganda that might make trouble in Parliament.[66]

On March 20, 1813, the British secretary of state, Earl Bathurst, codified the official policy in orders to Sir Sidney Beckwith: "You will on no account give encouragement to any disposition which may be manifested by the Negroes to rise against their Masters. The Humanity which ever influences His Royal Highness must make Him anxious to protest against a system of warfare which must be attended by the atrocities inseparable from commotions of such a description." Bathurst did, however, authorize the Chesapeake commanders to recruit a few guides, enlist them "in any of the Black Corps," and take them away as free men at the completion of their service. Bathurst emphasized, "You must distinctly understand that you are in no case to take slaves away as slaves, but as free persons whom the public become bound to maintain." The Chesapeake commanders were supposed to minimize contracting "engagements of this nature, which it may be difficult for you to fulfill." Leery of costs and complications, Bathurst wanted only a few black men useful as guides and no women and children.[67]

During 1813 the British naval officers first encountered Tidewater slaves as watermen paddling dugout canoes and small boats for fishing, crabbing, oyster-raking, and transporting goods. Their masters employed them to catch fish and crabs to feed the rest of their slaves. The oysters and better fish could also be marketed for cash in the seaports. Many Chesapeake slaves also worked as sailors on the sloops and schooners that carried cargoes up and down the bay.[68]

The watermen connected the naval officers to the enslaved communities on shore. On June 25, 1813, a white man saw a slave named Anthony fishing in the James River when a British boat came up and took him on board. Two weeks later, three young men escaped from Anthony's neighborhood in a stolen dugout known as a "periauger"; two of them shared Anthony's owner. Evidently Anthony had spread the word that the British would welcome young, male runaways who could help them. In late August on the Eastern Shore, Sam "was fishing on that day & must have seen the British fleet which came down the Bay on that day." During the following night, "many negroes were missing from the said neighbourhood at the same time as well as canoes & boats." The runaways included Sam.[69]

In addition to watermen, "outliers" made early contact with the British. Every Tidewater county had defiant malcontents who had escaped to hide out in makeshift camps in a forest or swamp. The appearance of British warships in the bay invited the outliers to flee to the warships. In March 1813 they included the three James City County runaways—Anthony, Tassy, and Kit—who mistook an American privateer for a British warship.[70]

Three other outliers, Joshua, Arnold, and Will, came from North-ampton County, on the Eastern Shore. In July 1813 they also mis-took an American privateer for a British warship. Severely flogged by the crew, they were dumped on the shore, where they resumed hiding out in the woods. Peggy Collins, a free black woman, secretly fed them. She later remembered that Arnold "seemed from the marks on his back to have been dreadfully beaten & that he begged her to ask his master to let him come home, that she did so & his master consented that he should come home & he would not whip him." Joshua, Arnold, and Will returned to their masters, but neither the whipping nor the apparent pardons remade them into docile slaves. In May 1814 they organized a bigger and better escape, leading away thirteen other slaves, including Joshua's wife and two children. In a stolen canoe, they paddled away on a night that "was clear & calm" so they "could hear distinctly . . . the drum & fife & fiddle from the shipping then lying opposite in the bay." They deployed a clever ruse to distract the leading master, for Peggy Collins recalled that they "had a great dance the night they went away & said [if] they would dance & be merry, Master wouldn't think they were going to the British."[71]

In early 1813, the British attracted runaways primarily from the Virginia shores near the mouth of the bay, where the warships initially concentrated: from Princess Anne County to the west and

Northampton County on the Eastern Shore. The commander of the Northampton County militia, Lieutenant Colonel Kendall Addison, offered to pay ransom if Warren would restore the runaways to their masters. Warren pointedly replied that the fugitives had become free by taking protection under the British flag on his ships. "At liberty to follow their own inclination," they could not be sent back for any ransom. By flocking to the warships, the runaways pressured Admiral Warren into making decisions that fudged his restraining orders from Earl Bathurst.[72]

More runaways came forward on foot when British raiders landed to attack the Maryland villages. In early May, eighteen runaways followed a British foraging party back to HMS *Sceptre*. Reluctantly taking them on board, Cockburn sought further orders from Warren, who again directed their retention as free people. In late May, Warren reported to the Admiralty that his warships had received about seventy refugees "to whom it was impossible to refuse an asylum." He added, "The Black population of these Countries evince, upon every occasion, the Strongest predilection for the cause of Great Britain, and a most ardent desire to join any Troops or Seamen acting in the Country, and from information which has reached me, the White Inhabitants have suffered great Alarm from the discovery of Parties of the Negroes having formed themselves into Bodies and especially with Arms in the Night." In such reports Warren urged a new British policy of encouraging and arming runaways as the best means to intimidate their masters.[73]

The number of escapes surged during the summer and fall as word spread that the British officers welcomed runaways. In July, Lieutenant Colonel Addison reported to the governor, "The Negroes are frequently going off to them. Already we have lost from this County about one hundred & twenty Negro Slaves. Thus situated, sir, you can readily conceive our apprehensions."[74]

In early November, Captain Barrie's warships visited the Potomac, attracting many runaways in stolen boats. On Virginia's Potomac shore, Major John Turberville reported that 100 slaves had fled "owing principally to the neglect of those whose duty it was in securing the boats, canoes, &c." Walter Jones worried, "The Spirit of defection among the negroes has greatly increased. . . . No doubt remains on our minds that concert and disaffection among the negroes is daily increasing and that we are wholly at the mercy of the Enemy." Jones feared that "clandestine Elopement" soon would ripen into "open Insurrection."[75]

As growing numbers reached the British warships, the officers struggled to feed, clothe, and shelter them. In early September, Warren observed,

> It is with great Difficulty that larger numbers have been pre-vented [from] joining us; 150 have come down in a body near the shore of the Potowmac just after we had left it. I could not refuse those which have got on board the ships in Canoes—men, women & children—amounting to about 300 as they would certainly have been sacrificed if they had been given up to their masters & destroyed our Influence among them, for at present every Slave in the Southern States would join us if they could get away.

In reports sent to London, Warren walked a fine line, insisting that he did nothing to attract the runaways but could not turn them away, although entire families came, including the women and chil-dren that Bathurst did not want.[76]

Captain Barrie also recognized the military potential of "the poor devils (the negroes) that were continually coming along side in canoes." On November 14, 1813, he added, "The Slaves continue to come off by every opportunity, and I have now upwards of 120 men, women and children on board . . . and, if their assertions be true, there is no doubt but the Blacks of Virginia & Maryland would cheerfully take up Arms & join us against the Americans." Although many masters had come under flags of truce to speak to their slaves, "not a single black would return to his former owner." By the end of 1813, at least 600 Chesapeake slaves had escaped to the British, who sent many on to the naval base at Bermuda.[77]

Bermuda

During the war, Bermuda became the primary support base for the British squadron blockading the American coast. A cluster of low-lying islands about 600 miles southeast of Virginia, Bermuda was fourteen miles long, about a mile wide, and covered with cedar trees. From a distance, it made a delightful first impression on naval officers. Lieutenant Scott reported, "Bermuda assumes the aspect of a paradise when approached on a fine day. . . . The numerous islands reposing on its glassy lakes, and reflected as in a mirror by the clear blue sea, lend a degree of enchantment to the scene scarcely credible." But first impressions proved deceiving, for the ships had to penetrate a long, twisting channel through rocks and around shoals to reach the harbor of St. George's. And the town quickly depressed the officers as a grubby den of indolence and greed where the merchants and landlords charged exorbitant rates for their goods, provisions, and lodging. Admiral Cockburn dismissed Bermuda as "a vile Place." Upon sailing away, Admiral Sir Pulteney Malcolm declared, "Thank God I am clear of Bermuda." No naval officer would have predicted that Bermuda had a future as a tourist mecca.[78]

The refugees saw relatively little of Bermuda because the leading colonists wanted no more blacks, lest they tip the balance in the population, then approximately equal between the races. In August 1813 the legislature's leaders denounced the "very considerable number of Negroes . . . lately imported into these Islands from the Coast of the United States" by British warships. The legislators feared "the most

pernicious effects in this Colony" because "our black population is
the principal cause of the Decrease of the white Inhabitants, whose
total extinction would be the ultimate consequence."[79]

But the colonial law of Bermuda did not apply to one of the
islands—called Ireland—which belonged to the Royal Navy and
where most of the refugees had to live and work. During the war
the British expanded the fortifications and dockyard to service and
repair the many ships operating along the American coast. Because
white workers were in short supply, the dockyard hired refugees as
laborers and carpenters. Each received a bounty, rations, and two
shillings in daily pay, but he had to sign an indenture to serve for at
least one year. In October 1813 the dockyard employed 100 black
men and about 25 women and children. They lived in huts at the
dockyard or on board a hulk anchored in the harbor: HMS *Ruby*.[80]

Some Chesapeake blacks balked at the hard work of the dockyard, which struck them as differing too little from slavery. A British
officer concluded that "they considered work and slavery synon-
ymous terms." Admiral Cockburn informed the newly liberated
that they had "a right to the Wages earned by their Labor, yet that
they are not on this account to suppose themselves entitled to be
maintained in Idleness and to be fed, cloathed, and Lodged without
working . . . and that they are in all respects precisely treated herein
as His Majesty's English born Subjects." The British officers invited
the runaways into the partial freedom of the working class.[81]

Each dockyard worker received a daily ration which proved inad-
equate also to feed a wife and children, who demanded their own.
A stickler for regulations and hierarchy, the dockyard commander,
Andrew Fitzherbert Evans, had scant patience for complaints from
blacks. He would provide rations to women and children only
if they picked oakum: a tedious task. Work for food without pay
seemed too familiar to them as slavery, so the women also demanded
$4 a month. Evans nearly burst a blood vessel: "I am sorry to add
that they evince a very riotous disposition and appear averse to any

kind of Controul, professing as they have been led to believe that
they are free men [and women] and subject to no restraint but their
own Caprice." Commiserating with Evans, Cockburn denounced
the "riotous and improper Inclinations amongst these foolish and
ever discontented People." But the naval officers eventually compromised, for by April 1814, the women and children were paid
as well as fed for picking oakum. The Royal Navy officers had to
learn, through trial and error, how to work with the runaways who
expected true freedom.[82]

Scouts

Black scouts improved the daring and performance of shore raids
and eased the British dread of probing deeper into the countryside.
Experienced at dodging slave patrols, the slaves had an intimate
knowledge of the intricate Tidewater landscape of swamps, forests,
and waterways. Along the James River in 1813, Lieutenant Scott
wisely made friends among the enslaved: "Our means of security
were afterwards greatly increased by the assistance of the negroes.
Though several snares and ambushes were laid for me during our . . .
services in the Chesapeake, I escaped them through the agency of my
invisible friends." Black guides also revealed hidden herds of livestock or storehouses filled with provisions and munitions. Masters
struggled to keep secrets when runaways flocked to the invaders.[83]

   With the help of their new guides, the British gained possession
of the night. They usually launched their shore raids after dark,
while the militia and planters slept and when the slaves were the special masters of the paths. Lieutenant Scott recalled,

   The opportunities afforded us of safely traversing the enemy's
   country at night, by means of these black guides, placed a powerful weapon in the Rear-Admiral's hands. . . . The country within
   ten miles of the shore lay completely at our mercy. We had no

reason to doubt the fidelity of our allies. . . . By their assistance
we were enabled to pass the enemy's patroles, make the circuit
of their encampments, and cut off the post beyond it. The face of
the country (generally thickly wooded) was propitious to these
nightly excursions. . . . Before these useful auxiliaries came over
to us, our nightly reconnaissance was necessarily circumscribed.

Formerly wary of the Chesapeake landscape, the British gained confidence after they recruited runaways for guides.[84]

As the land became more visible to Britons, it became murkier to
slaveholders. In 1814 on Maryland's Eastern Shore, a militia officer
rued that four local blacks led a British raiding party "into an intricate position at or about midnight," and we "could not ascertain any
other mode by which information so accurate as the enemy certainly
evinced, could have been obtained." In addition to guiding Britons,
blacks could mislead Americans. Called out to repel a British raid, a
Maryland militia patrol got lost and offered a slave $5 to show them
the road back to Baltimore. He promised to do so after first completing his errand "for some gentleman." When the slave returned,
he brought British troops, who surrounded and captured the lost
militiamen.[85]

Proclamation

Admiral Warren urged his balky government to permit the recruit-
ment of black troops in the Chesapeake: "The Black force could be
augmented to any amount & being organized upon our Modes could
be managed & kept within bounds and the Terror of a Revolution
in the Southern States increased to produce a good Effect in that
Quarter." While keeping the blacks under military discipline, Warren could intimidate southern whites. With black troops, the British
could "penetrate to Washington & Destroy the Dock yard & City."[86]
Sir Charles Napier endorsed and expanded on Warren's proposal.

An especially bold army officer who commanded a regiment in the Chesapeake campaign, Napier wanted to recruit and arm thousands of runaways. Slaves, he insisted, would flock to his standard because they regarded the British as "demigods" and their masters as "devils." Napier requested weapons for 20,000 recruits, a set of white officers, and 100 drill sergeants. After landing on the Eastern Shore, Napier would "strike into the woods with my drill men, my own regiment, and proclamations exciting the blacks to rise for freedom, forbidding them, however, to commit excesses under pain of being given up or hanged." Napier planned to establish a free-black colony that would attract runaways from throughout the United States. Then his black army would march on Washington, D.C., to dictate a peace that would abolish slavery in America. Lacking Napier's romantic imagination and bold optimism, the British rulers in London preferred a smaller black force more closely controlled by naval officers.[87]

In September 1813, Earl Bathurst authorized the Royal Navy to enlist Chesapeake runaways "into H[is] M[ajesty]s's land or sea service." Although Warren had proposed the new policy, implementation fell to his more aggressive successor, Vice Admiral Sir Alexander Cochrane, who took command of the North American squadron on April 1, 1814. In operations against the French in the West Indies, he had recruited and armed runaway slaves. Eager to escalate the war in the Chesapeake, Cochrane wanted to vigorously recruit runaways. Recalling a prewar visit to Virginia, he concluded, "From what I saw of its Black Population they are British in their hearts and might be made of great use if War should be prosecuted with Vigor."[88]

Cochrane hated the Americans, in part because they had killed his beloved brother in the battle of Yorktown during the revolution. In 1814 that hatred became an asset to a government resolved to punish the Americans for prolonging the war. "I have it much at heart to give them a complete drubbing before peace is made," Cochrane promised. "They are a whining, canting race, much [like]

Vice Admiral Sir Alexander F. I. Cochrane, *an oil portrait by Sir William Beechey. (Courtesy of the National Maritime Museum, Greenwich, England)*

the Spaniel and require the same treatment—must be drubbed into good manners." Humbling American pride remained a top priority.[89]

A hyperactive schemer, Cochrane suggested bribing some Americans to kidnap Republican congressmen: "A little money well applied will attain almost any object amongst such a corrupt and abandoned race." He would hold the Republican leaders as hostages until their government released all of their British prisoners. A skeptical Cockburn replied, "I do not think any Yankee Senator or Member of Congress worth half the Money you seem inclined to give for them, but I will try what is to be done in the way you mention." As with so many of Cochrane's plans, however, realization lagged far behind his imagination. Sir Pulteney Malcolm complained, "Cochrane is all zeal. His first resolves are generally correct, but . . . his head is so full of schemes that one destroys the other." Cockburn, however, worked well with a commander who shared his aggressive personality and ambitious goals.[90]

To obtain black recruits, Cochrane had to commit to their future as free men. On April 2 he addressed a cleverly worded proclamation to "all those who may be disposed to emigrate from the United States . . . with their Families." He promised to honor "their choice of either entering into His Majesty's Sea or Land forces, or of being sent as FREE Settlers to the British Possessions in North America or the West Indies, where they will meet with all due encouragement." To deny the charge that he promoted a slave revolt, his wording avoided explicitly addressing slaves while emphasizing the word *FREE* as their future state as British friends. In a private report, Cochrane explained that he sought to harass the masters "and bring the consequences of the War home to their own Doors."[91]

From his headquarters at Bermuda, Cochrane sent 1,000 printed copies of the proclamation to Cockburn for distribution along the shores of the Chesapeake. Incredibly, many American newspapers, including the Madison administration's own *National Intelligencer*, also spread the word by reprinting the proclamation, albeit with hostile commentary. The *National Intelligencer* insisted that the proclamation was a scam to lure credulous slaves away for British sale "to a bondage more galling than the light servitude they now endure." Whatever masters read, they talked about, which slaves overheard and interpreted in their own way.[92]

Cochrane issued the public proclamation on his own authority rather than on behalf of the imperial government: "in it I keep Ministers out of sight and take the odium and responsibility upon myself." But in January 1814, Henry Goulburn, Bathurst's undersecretary, privately had authorized Cochrane to welcome runaways "into His Majesty's Service" or to become "free Settlers in some of His Majesty's Colonies." Goulburn sought to entice the many "Negroes and coloured Inhabitants of the United States" who had "expressed a desire to withdraw themselves from their present Situation."[93]

In March, Cochrane had sent an advance copy of the proclamation to the Lords of Admiralty, but they carefully avoided taking a public position, pro or con, lest they bear responsibility for the new policy. In May, Bathurst reminded his Chesapeake commanders that the government opposed any effort to promote a slave revolt. Cochrane replied, "I entirely Agree with your Lordship that no steps should be taken to induce the negros to rise Against their Masters. My views go no farther than to afford protection to those that chuse to Join the British Standard."[94]

Bathurst had preferred to attract only men, but his officers recognized that few would enlist unless promised a haven for their families. Captain Joseph Nourse explained that most of his refugees were women and children, "but there would be no getting the men without receiving them." Bowing to that reality, the British government authorized the Royal Navy to "receive on board His Majesty's Ships the families of such Persons, and in no Case to permit their Separation, the Assistance given to their families in the British Service being understood to be one principal Cause of the desire to emigrate, which had been manifested by the Negro population."[95]

In addition to welcoming runaways who reached their ships, the officers aggressively went ashore to entice slaves to come away with them. As a central goal of the 1814 campaign, Cochrane ordered Cockburn to seek out and liberate slaves of both genders and all ages: "Let the Landings you may make be more for the protection of the desertion of the Black Population than with a view to any other advantage. . . . The great point to be attained is the cordial Support of the Black population. With them properly armed & backed with 20,000 British Troops, Mr. Maddison will be hurled from his Throne." Cockburn promptly directed one captain, "You are to encourage by all possible means the Emigration of Negroes from the United States."[96]

The new strategy reflected the lessons learned by British commanders in the Chesapeake during 1813, when they had struggled to keep white men from deserting and had failed to keep hundreds of slaves from fleeing to their ships. Making a virtue of necessity, the commanders recognized that the runaways offered invaluable local knowledge and potential as sailors and marines. Bending their orders from London, the admirals gradually embraced the many black refugees, including women and children. The commanders then persuaded their government to authorize recruiting blacks for war. By their courage, persistence, and numbers, the runaways enabled the British to adopt a new, far more aggressive strategy for 1814. Black initiative transformed the British conduct of the war in the Chesapeake.[97]

In early 1813 the Royal Navy officers did not intend to emancipate more than a few slaves, but scores of Tidewater slaves acted as if the British were liberators, escaping to them in stolen canoes and boats. Put on the spot, the naval officers took in the runaways: reluctantly at first but with growing zeal over time. The officers warmed to their new role as liberators as a chance to highlight American hypocrisy about liberty. By protecting runaways, the officers claimed moral superiority over the enslaving Americans. By the end of 1813 the naval commanders also realized that the blacks could provide invaluable services to the British campaign. The runaways had made themselves essential to the officers' self-image and to their drive to humble the Americans along the shores of the Chesapeake.

7

PLANTATION

*I never did or could pretend to be any Judge of the
proper mode of managing a Virginia estate.*
—ST. GEORGE TUCKER, OCTOBER 11, 1807[1]

A T DAWN on April 22, 1814, Dick Carter, a forty-five-year-old
slave at Corotoman Plantation, discovered that his wife and
children had boarded a British barge about to depart from the mouth
of a nearby creek. Dreading separation from his family, he ran toward
the barge, waving his hat and calling on the sailors to wait. Urged
to stay by the plantation's manager, Carter yelled back, "I do not
wish, sir, to leave my master, but I will follow my wife and children
to death." In the nick of time, he reached the barge, and the sailors
hauled him on board and rowed away to the British brig, *Jasseur*.[2]

Explaining Dick Carter's escape to a British warship certainly
involves the grand history of a war: the actions of Congress and
Parliament, of president and prince regent, of militia generals and
Royal Navy admirals. Their interacting decisions brought warships

Lelia Skipwith Carter Tucker, *oil painting by an unknown artist, ca. 1815. Lelia Tucker
was the second wife of St. George Tucker, the mother of Charles and Mary "Polly" Carter,
and the mother-in-law of Joseph Cabell, who married Polly. (Courtesy of the University of
Mississippi Museums)*

Joseph Carrington Cabell, *from Alexander Brown*, The Cabells and Their Kin *(1895). (Courtesy of the Virginia Historical Society)*

into Chesapeake Bay and barges to Carter's Creek and weakened the resistance by the local militia. But Carter made his own decision, which came in response to what his wife and children had already chosen. Their choices derived from the more intimate history of one plantation, which induced many, but not all, of the resident slaves to risk their lives and futures on escaping to the British. Located in Lancaster County on the north shore of the Rappahannock River at its juncture with Chesapeake Bay, Corotoman was an especially large and famous plantation with a substantial slave community. During the preceding decade, however, Corotoman had been roiled by divisions among the owners over how best to exploit the slaves.

Marriage

Thanks to his second marriage in 1791, St. George Tucker managed the dower right of his new wife, Lelia Skipwith Carter, on behalf of her two children, Mary (known as Polly to the family) and Charles, by her first husband, George Carter. Once they reached adulthood, the two children would each receive a third of the estate, and when their mother died, they would divide her third. Meanwhile, Tucker remained responsible for the whole. Corotoman had been the palatial headquarters of the colonial era's premier grandee, Robert Carter, aptly known as "King Carter" for his wealth, power, aggression, and arrogance. By his death in 1732 at the age of sixty-nine, Carter had accumulated multiple plantations, totaling nearly 300,000 acres and employing at least 700 slaves. Thanks to an entail, his eldest son, John, received the core plantations, including Corotoman, which subsequently passed to King Carter's great-grandson, George, who married Lelia Skipwith, before dying in his prime in 1788.[3]

As Carter's widow, Lelia felt overwhelmed by her responsibility for Corotoman, a 7,000-acre estate with about 200 slaves, and Tucker disliked running any plantation: "I never did or could pretend to be any Judge of the proper mode of managing a Virginia estate." To a son-in-law, Tucker explained, "the complaints of the negroes, waste of every kind, idleness and neglect were beyond calculation. All these things Mrs. Tucker, who suffered a perfect purgatory there, will tell you." Staying away in distant Williamsburg, Tucker hired a Lancaster County man, George Gresham, to supervise the estate. Given a good harvest, the plantation produced a small profit, but most years yielded disappointing crops and financial losses.[4]

Tucker seemed satisfied, so long as he received annual shipments of apples, hams, and other provisions for his household. He also drew on Corotoman for an occasional horse or house slave, brought to work for him in Williamsburg. In 1805 Gresham sent to Tucker a promising young slave named James to become a cook. A realist, Gresham considered James "the best of anay one that is on the Estate tho he can be as ill behaved as anay one on the Estate." Gresham recognized that the most talented slaves also tended to be the most defiant. If a house slave disappointed, Tucker exiled the culprit to work as a field hand at Corotoman. Tucker wanted the plantation to remain out of sight and out of mind while providing for his material needs.[5]

Joseph C. Cabell initiated a revolution at Corotoman after he married into the Tucker household. The son of a prestigious family in Amherst County within the Piedmont, Cabell was a sickly adolescent but precocious student at the College of William and Mary from 1796 to 1798. Two years later, he returned to study law with Judge Tucker, who admired Cabell's talents and prospects. To improve his precarious health and broaden his horizons, Cabell toured Europe between 1803 and 1806, visiting England, France, the Netherlands, and Italy. In May 1806 he returned to the United States, determined to marry an heiress and launch his career as a Virginia planter and politician. Twenty-seven years old, he had no time to waste. His brother and mentor William H. Cabell exhorted, "It may not be amiss *now* to tell you that you will stand in need of some addition to your fortune. . . . Some of your old fellow students have hinted [at] a short course; as they suppose you have become too old ever to marry *for love & affection*, they have recommended your looking out for some rich old maid: the richer & older the better." Joseph had a more appealing target in mind: a rich young maid he had met as a student in Williamsburg, Polly Carter Tucker.[6]

His attentions almost came too late, for Cabell reached Williamsburg in October 1806 to find that a classmate and friend named Brent was calling at the Tucker household as a rival suitor. But to Cabell's delight, Brent returned to their shared room in a tavern to announce his rebuff by Polly. "My mind at this observation must have resembled the face of a certain ventriloquist in Paris, who I saw smile on one side, and weep on the other," Cabell reported. Both young men "slept together that night, after taking an oister supper together and parted the next morning in perfect friendship," as Brent took the stage to Richmond. Cabell then walked up the street to call on Polly at the Tucker house: "In a few minutes all agitation had disappeared & we were all in high talk."[7]

Within three days, Cabell had won Polly's affection and her mother's consent, but the judge proved a harder nut to crack. Although he liked Cabell, Tucker doted on Polly and did not like losing her to marriage so soon, for she was not yet twenty-one. The judge also felt protective of her Carter inheritance and did not trust any young gentleman with full control over that property. Tucker promised to approve the match only if Cabell entered into a premarital contract to preserve her Corotoman inheritance intact, negating his power as a husband to sell its slaves or lands. Although Tucker had publicly championed the abolition of entails in Virginia, he privately upheld a version for wealthy young women, for he had seen too many ruined by reckless husbands who squandered estates on drink, gaming, and foolish investments. Regretting the "inequality and injustice of our laws in respect to females," he observed, "A woman in possession of a fortune in Lands, Slaves, & money Marries. The instant she does so, her slaves and money are Exclusively her Husband's. If indebted, they go to the payment of his debts, without reserve. If he dies indebted the whole may be taken to pay his debts." Tucker had imposed such a premarital contract in 1802, when John Coalter had married the judge's daughter, Anne Frances, so he expected Cabell to follow suit. By acting as his stepdaughter's protector even after marriage, Tucker resisted the American Revolution's promotion of greater liquidity for capital and its weakening of patriarchal power over children. By seeking his daughter's security, Tucker indirectly protected the slave community at Corotoman by, in effect, entailing them to Polly's children.[8]

Cabell, however, expected complete control over his wife's inheritance. A fiery gentleman of the postrevolutionary generation, he bristled at Tucker's attempt to impose a patriarchal restriction. Cabell exhorted Tucker to imagine "the feelings with which a young man of spirit and honor ought to be inspired by such a proposition." Both Tucker and Polly needed to invest an "unbounded confidence" in Cabell's management of her property, for he would never accept "the appearance of a humiliated dependent." Instead, he demanded a free hand to "change the nature of her property and wield it to the advantage of our family accordingly as times, circumstances, and views in life might require." Writing to his older brother, Joseph posed as a young republican resisting an old patriarch who had "made a little aristocratic parade" of his antiquated power. Cabell boasted that if Tucker continued to "resist, it will be in vain; for the girl is mine, by all the thirty thousand gods of the Romans. No two lovers ever felt as we do, ever since the days of Pyramus & Thisbe"—so Cabell wrote a week after initiating the courtship.[9]

After the revolution, genteel courtship and marriage assumed a more romantic gloss, which rendered couples more equal in the exchange of emotions. But the sentimentality gave the husband greater power over the household property at the expense of the wife's protection by her lineage. Cabell defined marriage as "not only a union of affections, but as complete a union of fortunes as the parties can possible effect," but he made clear that the husband alone would run the estate: "Who could manage the interest of my wife better than myself?" The new ostensibly romantic mode of marriage promoted male control of his wife's property in a free market.[10]

William H. Cabell demanded that his brother hold firm, lest Joseph appear weak in the masculine realm of Virginia politics:

> I am opposed to marriage settlements on principle . . . they are
> *degrading* in the estimation of our fellow citizens—and what-
> ever my attachment to any woman might be, I would renounce
> her, I would renounce even an Angel, if I could only procure
> her by submitting to terms which are contrary to principle &
> degrading & humiliating in [the] estimation of myself and oth-
> ers. . . . I had rather you should be deprived of the use of both
> hands than that you should put either of them to an instrument
> that would seal your shame.

A Virginia gentleman had to live by a code of masculine honor
policed by his peers. William would share the shame if Joseph submitted to an old-style patriarch entangling a wife's estate.[11]

In early November, Cabell followed Tucker to Richmond, where
the judge attended to his duties. They continued their high-stakes
game, exchanging polite but firm notes reiterating their property
positions at the risk of the marriage. In the end, Tucker accepted a
sop: a mere letter from Cabell declaring that should he die before
Polly, she could recover her inherited property "as well Slaves &
personal Estate, as real, without the forms & Ceremonies of Law . . .
in the same manner as if no marriage had taken place between them."
This formula placed no limit on Cabell's ability to sell her property
during his lifetime, so if his investments went bad, there would be no
estate for her to recover.[12]

On January 1, 1807, in Williamsburg, Joseph and Polly married,
and for nearly two years they lived in the rambling Tucker house
to the delight of her parents, but Cabell longed to establish his own
household. "My wife and I are rich, and we do not mean to live as if
we were poor," he boasted. Eager to launch a political career, Cabell
decided to move to Nelson County, where he had prospering brothers, and the Cabell name carried great clout. During 1808–1809,
Cabell built a new home, "Edgewood," on a plantation near the village of Warminster. In 1809 he won election to represent Nelson in

the House of Delegates and, a year later, secured a promotion to the State Senate, where he also represented four other Piedmont counties. During the winter sessions of the legislature, Cabell resided at a Richmond inn, while his wife stayed with her parents in Williamsburg. In the summer, the Tuckers returned the favor, escaping the Tidewater heat to sojourn in the cooler hills at Edgewood. Cabell shrewdly cultivated a close relationship with his mother-in-law, Lelia, who could help him manage the more difficult Tucker.[13]

Management

Cabell toyed with moving to Corotoman, for absentee owners rarely reaped profits, but the plantation lay isolated on a point far from any genteel town. A friend reported, "This place is almost as much out of the world as it would be on the western side of the Allegany [mountains]." Cabell noted, "The theater for farming is the best I ever saw, but the place is insulated, and the society bad." He concluded, "I fear my little wife has been too much accustomed to town to feel very contented on a plantation with negroes." The location would also imperil their health with summer fevers. William warned his brother, "I am certain you & Polly would both die in less than six months at Corotoman—suppose you or she should be sick, cut off from all medical aid, & in fact from all the world."[14]

Corotoman also was not yet fully Cabell's to manage because of Lelia's lifetime dower right to a third of the plantation and the co-ownership of Polly's younger brother, Charles. By dividing the estate, Cabell hoped to complete his ownership to at least a third, but that division had to wait until Charles turned twenty-one years and returned from his studies in Europe. While impatiently awaiting Charles Carter's return, Cabell had to cooperate with Tucker, who controlled both Lelia's and Charles's shares in the plantation. And Tucker's diffidence kept Corotoman in a limbo that generated more uncertainty than profit. In September 1807, when pressed by Cabell for financial information, Tucker revealed how little he knew: "It is utterly impossible for me at present to give you a List of my Receipts for the Corotoman Estate, or even a tolerable estimate of them. . . . My wife, until her marriage with me received almost nothing. . . . For several years, perhaps 8 or 10, I never received any part of the Tobacco made, or received for rents." To render Corotoman profitable, Cabell wanted to take charge and implement the agricultural reforms of Colonel John Taylor.[15]

By rationalizing operations at Corotoman, Cabell meant to maximize the profits from labor and land. In 1807 he began by ousting the seventeen white tenant farmers on part of the estate. Deeming a third of the 206 slaves redundant, Cabell wanted to hire out, remove, or sell the surplus elsewhere. This reduction would then compel more work out of those who remained: "The removal of the superfluous hands is a measure of great importance; for indolence, loss of labor & waste must accompany such a crowd of idlers." No sentimentalist, Cabell treated slaves as investments, so he shifted and sold them to increase his profits, slighting their family relations as of little concern. When the estate manager, George Gresham, balked at the proposed changes as disruptive, Cabell wanted to fire him.[16]

Tucker worried that Cabell's ambitious plans would aggravate the tenants and slaves and drive away a good manager. Dreading any agitation, Tucker preferred to cultivate a family cocoon of serenity withdrawn from the world of commerce and politics. Tucker expected more trouble under a new steward, for the estate would be "not so well managed, nor the negroes so well taken care of and happy." So Tucker asked Cabell, "Would it not be better to put up with some Errors rather than part with such a man[?]"[17].

Tucker's waffling irritated Cabell, who confided to a friend, "I have met with *substantial* opposition in the form of difficulties, inconveniencies, &c., &c., from *the same person* who came athwart me on a former occasion. . . . He refusing to yield his hold on the soil, at the same time that he never has & never will visit [Corotoman] and personally attend to the management of the property."

With eloquent self-pity, Cabell added, "We parted in Richmond with all the exterior of good humor & friendship, but I fear this affair will be the cause of alienation in the end. . . . Was ever [there a] poor devil, doomed in secret & silence, like me, to contend against unnecessary and capricious difficulties[?]" In January 1808, however, Tucker backed down, endorsing Cabell's efforts to transform Corotoman.[18]

Bad luck and summer droughts had undercut Gresham. After a poor crop in 1806 the next year proved even worse. On July 22, 1807, a prolonged drought suddenly gave way to a succession of thunderstorms through August that, in Tucker's words, "drown'd nearly the whole Crop of Tobacco & all the Corn that was in the lower parts of the fields." In early September a driving rain and wind tore the remaining "Corn all to pieces." The dank conditions spread disease among the slaves, so Gresham lightened his demands for their labor, to Cabell's disgust. That year Corotoman yielded only 7,000 pounds of tobacco, less than a third of the anticipated crop. Unforgiving, Cabell blasted Gresham as a selfish obstacle to needed reforms: "That the Corotoman estate should bring itself in debt for nearly two years in succession is irreconcilable with anything like tolerable management." Instead of the weather, Cabell blamed Gresham as a "scoundrel" and his subordinate overseers as "plunderers" who had embezzled their way to prosperity at the owners' expense.[19]

In January 1808, Cabell fired Gresham and promptly removed twenty-three slaves, which he claimed as his wife's share, deploying them in Nelson County on his own plantation and those of his brothers. Their removal disrupted a previously stable slave community, for he conceded that they consisted "of families taken indiscriminately from many others." He later recognized, "The insular situation of the Corrottoman estate produced an uncommon attachment among the negroes belonging to them." The removed slaves also suffered severely from exposure during their long journey in the dead of winter. Their doctor reported, "They were bought up by water in extreme cold & snowy weather & in the course of the Winter I believe every grown one & several of the smaller ones had the Pleuresy." At Corotoman, Cabell divided the remaining slaves, compelling half to create a separate quarter in the back lands of the estate: a division that further disrupted family ties.[20]

As the new manager Cabell hired George Robertson, who came recommended by Colonel Taylor as an improver who would get the most out of slaves, but his arrival and the removal of the "surplus" slaves, provoked, in Tucker's words, "a rebellious spirit." Writing to Tucker, Robertson reported that the remaining slaves complained that Cabell had left too few "hands on the plantation to work it and the work would be so hard on them they would not be able to do it and they would not stand it. They would go to you and complain." Cabell hastened to Corotoman "to prevent the negros from disobeying the manager. They refuse to be ruled by him & wish to get the upper hand."[21]

After apparently restoring order, Cabell left Corotoman on February 1, but the next day, Robertson reported to Tucker that the slaves refused to submit to "correction," a euphemism for whipping:

> They are determined not to be corrected in any other way but by being overpowerd and when this is the case Tis nothing to be done with them until they are brought to order. Mr. Cabell left Corotoman yesterday and had not been gone more than three hours before one of the men cald tom night went of[f] without being tuched and says he will not be corrected by me. . . . I have been many years in this lin[e] of business but never was so treated by negros before and I do not think they ever [will] be brought to a true sense of their duty until they are severely corrected.

Rallying to the tough new regime, Tucker said of Tom Night, "We must make an example of him, by sending him off the plantation as soon as it can be done with convenience." By *sending*, Tucker meant selling, the usual means to get rid of a troublesome slave, particularly one named Tom Night, perhaps for nocturnal adventures of the sort that so troubled masters and so thrilled fellow slaves.[22]

Ten days later, Tucker reported information apparently derived from a runaway who had fled to Williamsburg to seek redress. One of Robertson's young and brutal overseers had beaten (and perhaps killed) a young woman as a punishment for lingering too long while visiting her child on another estate: "To *strip* a poor woman for over-staying her time with her Child a few minutes was a piece of bar-barianism perfectly of a Tissue with his subsequent Conduct to her. The story is even worse than I thought it [at first]. I verily believe overseers [are] the greatest Brutes in the Creation." Tucker likened the beating at Corotoman to a recent murder near Williamsburg of an overseer by infuriated slaves: "Lightfoot, who had been murder-ing the negroes under his orders was himself murdered last week. So much for there being no person to prosecute him for killing the negroes. And if this young Brute at Corrotoman is not check'd I shall not wonder if he meets with the same fate. I had almost said that I should not lament it, in such abhorrence do I hold a Conduct of the Kind." But Tucker lacked the backbone to overrule Cabell and overturn the Robertson regime, for he wanted an income from Corotoman without taking responsibility for its management. He assured Cabell, "As to every thing that relates to Robertson, & the arrangements to be made with him, &c., I leave it wholly to yourself. I am no judge of any thing relative to overseers, or plantations & shall be content with whatever you think best."[23]

The next big flare-up came a month later and involved Billy, who had been Cabell's manservant. In February 1808, Cabell caught Billy pilfering, so Tucker advised, "Bring Billy down with you as I am determined to send him back with a memento against thiev-ing." The "memento" probably entailed whipping. Then Cabell and

Tucker exiled Billy to Corotoman as a field hand: a harsh fall for a manservant. On March 12, 1808, however, Robertson reported that Billy refused to work. When Robertson prepared to "correct" him, Billy picked up a brick as a weapon and ran away, swearing that "he would di[e] before he would be corrected and gave me a great deal of impertinent language." His defiance induced three other "very insolent" slaves to run away, and Robertson predicted that they would head to Williamsburg to complain to Tucker. "I never had so disorderly [a] set of people to manage in my life," Robertson concluded.[24]

Staying in Williamsburg, Tucker expected Cabell to fix the latest blowup at Corotoman. Meanwhile, more slaves fled into the forest. On June 20, Cabell reported, "I found no less than fourteen crop hands in the woods when I got to Corotoman. I got them all in, had some of them corrected, sent two to Lancaster Prison to be sold (one of whom is my man Billy) and I turned off the assistant overseer, whose cruelty I could no longer bear." Playing both good and bad cop, Cabell sacked Robertson's brutal young assistant but only after rounding up the runaways and flogging or jailing the ringleaders, pending their sale. In late August a woman and her child left the Lancaster jail by sale to a slave trader, who took them far away to Georgia or South Carolina to pick cotton. Apparently Billy played the penitent and got a reprieve, for he remained at Corotoman during the next decade.[25]

Despite Cabell's latest intervention, resistance persisted, and the restive slaves got support from the nearby common whites, who also hated the strict new regime at Corotoman. Former tenants resented losing their lands, and debtors disliked being pressed suddenly to pay their arrears. Both the slaves and the common whites pined for the good old days of Gresham's laxer regime. To spite Robertson and Cabell, slaves and common whites colluded in stealing from the estate. Cabell suspected that the malcontents got encouragement from Gresham, who lived on a nearby farm. In November 1809,

Cabell again had to return to Corotoman to restore order: "On my arrival, ten of the most able and likely young negros were in the woods. The banditti who live in the fork of Carter's Creek, were plundering & insulting the estate in the most abominable manner. The people thereabouts [were] generally railing at & threatening Robertson, the manager. . . . The stocks of sheep & hogs [were] constantly thinned by the depredations of runaways and lawless white freebooters." And one of Robertson's assistants was "holding an illicit intercourse with the young women on the estate," which may have sparked the latest flight to the woods.[26]

Cabell recovered the latest runaways, and he claimed victory in 1810 by exulting in the labor that Robertson had goaded from the reduced workforce. Every winter, the men cleared more of the forest in the rear of the plantation: "The land is under a system of good tillage & the soil gradually improving & the estate assuming constantly a more agreeable & spacious aspect as the forest farms become more open." In a good year, the estate produced 3,000 bushels of wheat for the market, and 2,500 barrels of corn, of which 1,000 had to be retained to feed the slaves, leaving a surplus of 1,500. Cabell had terminated the cultivation of tobacco, which he detested as a soil killer. Due to several good harvests, the new regime proved profitable during the five years of 1808–1812.[27]

But the troubled plantation began to wear down Cabell, who lamented, "I never open a letter from that quarter, but with a sure conviction on my mind, that I am to hear something disagreeable— something to create inquietude & distress." Rather than endure further "painful assaults upon my peace of mind," Cabell longed to "retire to the hollow of a mountain to live on Indian bread." He wished "extremely for Charles's return that something may be done to put a stop to this never ceasing . . . vexatious correspondence with the managers." But Cabell should have been more careful in his wishes, for Charles Carter was the wild card in the family deck.[28]

Divisions

More idealistic than the rest of the family, Charles became known as "Phylosopher Carter" to their friends. Mercurial and sentimental, Charles struggled as a student at the College of William and Mary, so St. George Tucker sent the boy away to Winchester to study with his older stepbrother, Henry St. George Tucker, who soon complained, "He is so fanciful that it is difficult to meet his wishes; & so irritable that he regards every failure in the attempt to please him as clearly demonstrative of a desire to vex him." In 1806 St. George Tucker gave up on training Charles for the law and instead sent him away first to Paris and later to Edinburgh to study medicine.[29]

From Europe, Charles wrote dutiful and affectionate letters to his parents, but his idealism unnerved them. In December 1806 he reminded Tucker, "I informed you some time since that it was my intention to emancipate all the Slaves which fell to my share. Be assured that I am still resolved on doing so. I am sure that you will aid me in my endeavours to carry into effect this first wish of my Heart." In November 1807, Charles explained, "Many reasons, my dear Father Tucker, incline me to make this determination, the principal one of which is that I don't feel myself authorized to deprive another of his Liberty. What man is there who can justify the making another labour for his support or who should be willing to trust to the humanity of his Temper in the exercise of that right which a Master possesses over his Slave?" Unlike his peers back in Virginia, Charles could imagine blacks as his equal in rights.[30]

Tucker, however, had made his peace with slavery and wanted to preserve his annual income from Corotoman. He tried to discourage Charles by citing the financial inconvenience to the family of losing their slave labor. Yet, Charles remained resolute: "Unfortunate as it is, that in relinquishing this property, I must injure those I would least wish to injure, but I know them too well not to feel assured that they will pardon me for doing so." This only proved how little he really knew of the Tuckers, who did not share his abolitionist dream.[31]

During the spring of 1812, Carter returned from Europe with, in Cabell's words, "some opinions very adverse to the interests of Virginia estates." He proposed to free his share of the slaves, provided that his mother, sister, Tucker, and Cabell would consent. But they balked, lest their own slaves become restive. In May, family friend Dr. Philip Barraud (who was John Hartwell Cocke's father-in-law) advised Tucker on how to dissuade Charles. "I think it may be proved to him that he can do much more for those people than they can do for themselves. John Cocke . . . talked romantically after marriage on this very topic. His best Judgment is now against the Doctrine from sound Experience." Charles backed away from freeing the Corotoman field hands, but he pressed his mother to commit to manumit, after her death and Tucker's, the Williamsburg household slaves, whom Charles stood to inherit.[32]

Tucker abruptly rejected even that limited and delayed proposal, for he expected complete control over his household. Fearing that the house slaves might hasten his death with poison, Tucker instructed Lelia to inform Charles that any prospective emancipation

> would probably, if known to them, be the source of misconduct on their parts and possibly of consequences as fatal as have in more than one Instance flowed from Servants knowing that the period of their Emancipation depended upon the *Death of a person* whom they might possess the means of secretly destroying. Such a Temptation ought in no case to be held out to poor ignorant Creatures who might be misled by the Councils of others.

Tucker also reminded Charles that under Virginia's revised manumission law of 1806, any emancipated slaves had to leave the state within a year, which would send them into perpetual Banishment from their friends & Connexions, poor, ignorant, and friendless. Those in the decline of Life would perish miserably, & those who were not would be obliged to encounter every hardship that poverty, ignorance, want of friends, and a complexion indicative of a State of Slavery would expose them to—perhaps to be taken up & sold as runaway Slaves, &c. In the latter case . . . they might be sold to cruel masters and experience a Lot an hundred times harder than that to which them have been for more than twenty years accustomed & in which they probably are, and will continue as happy, as they are capable of being.

During the sixteen years after his failed emancipation plan, Tucker had learned all of the lines of a pro-slavery paternalist, persuaded that slavery protected "poor, ignorant Creatures" who had to be kept so forever.[33]

In early 1812, Charles Carter settled at Corotoman, where he tried to introduce a milder management that undermined and irritated Robertson. Supporting their manager, Tucker and Cabell regretted Carter's meddling as naive and dangerous. The tensions came to a head in August 1812, when two young enslaved men ran away from Corotoman to Williamsburg. Appealing to Tucker's paternalism, they sought protection against Robertson's abuse. One had been severely whipped, and the other was about to be flogged, when both broke free of their ropes and escaped. One had offended by leaving the plantation overnight to visit his wife, and the other had been caught "resting a few minutes in the heat of the day." They reported that five other slaves had fled into the nearby woods. Lelia added that Robertson had pursued and caught one of the other runaways, John Chub: "In the contest he received a blow—came home that night & died the next morning."[34]

The abrupt appearance of runaways with fresh scars and grim stories troubled Tucker, who preferred to keep a denying distance from his plantation and its field hands. After putting them to work on a nearby farm, Tucker unburdened himself in a letter to Cabell: "This is an abominable state of things & I almost wish I was dead that I might neither hear nor see any more such [runaways]." Eloquent in his self-pity, Tucker felt victimized by the turmoil that he expected Robertson to keep confined to Corotoman.[35]

The Tuckers and Cabells blamed Carter for sympathizing with, and perhaps even encouraging, the slave protest against Robertson. In a pained letter to Polly, Lelia disavowed her son.

> Could a Mother inspire a Child with her own opinions & feelings, how different would the conduct of mine be—but alas! We have only the power of wishing . . . but in Charles's case I indulge the hope that a personal experience of difficulties will make a change. . . . He promised me, & he tells me that he has fulfilled his promise, to say to the Negroes that he would not give countenance to their running away, or to their disobedience—that his right after a division would extend but to a third of them & in the mean time that he enjoined them all to pay the fullest attention to Mr. Robertson's orders.

But Robertson's power was already too compromised. In September, Cabell sought a new estate manager because, he explained, "Robertson's authority over the negroes seems to be entirely destroyed and a great clamor has been raised about his cruelty."[36]

On behalf of their community, the runaways had won an important concession by compelling Tucker and Cabell to sack Robertson. Slaves, however, could achieve only a partial and temporary victory given the superior power of the masters. Indeed, the new manager, John Richeson, was another improver recommended by Colonel Taylor, and Robertson lingered until the end of the year to help Richeson restore order. In December, Cabell reported renewed "uncertainty and difficulties & embarrassments" at Corotoman. Ten slaves had fled in the night "under the pretext . . . that Mr. Robertson would beat them." Cabell added, "Richeson was very uneasy least Charles's indulgence to his people might interfere seriously with his authority on the adjacent plantation." Cabell ordered five of the recently retrieved runaways sold "for incorrigible ill conduct."[37]

Meanwhile, Cabell and Carter struggled over how to divide the land and slaves of Corotoman. It was no easy matter to split up a large and complex estate that included 200 human beings with the differential values dictated by age, gender, health, and skill. Cabell and Carter relied on three distinguished arbiters experienced at managing Virginia estates: John Hartwell Cocke, Richard Corbin, and Colonel Henry Skipwith. In December 1812 they met at Corotoman to divide the land and sort the diverse slaves into two lots of equal value. Carter received 3,250 acres of fertile lowlands along Taylor's Creek and another 1,200 acres of forested hinterland. Cabell and Tucker retained the western lowlands: 3,195 acres along Carter's Creek. Carter probably got the extra forest land to settle charges owed by Cabell and Tucker for the period during Carter's absence in Europe.[38]

After dividing the slaves by lot, Cabell complained bitterly that Carter had obtained the best carpenters, but Cabell's friend Cocke defended the award and revealed the complexity of valuing and dividing human beings: "The other carpenter of equal value to Joe Brown was put into one lot & the [black]smith into the other lot and Charles drew that which had the Carpenter in it. The other rough carpenters of inferior value, we equally divided between the two lots—with the exception of one, which Charles selected call'd Sam." There was the further complication that Cabell had unilaterally sold five recovered runaways without Carter's permission. Rather than a cash settlement, he wanted three more slaves as his share from the estate.[39]

Dissatisfied with Cocke's explanation, Cabell threw a dramatic fit: "I am lost in astonishment & my soul already torn by affliction is almost crushed by this new catalogue of unprovoked injuries. . . . Sometimes I feel as if I should become deranged." Used to dominating others, slaveholders rarely took disappointment well. Once again, Tucker took Cabell's side, advising him, in regard to Carter, "that you should never see each other again—nor even write. . . . My wife is wretched; & I am not far from it, from this Cause." Lelia agreed, denouncing her son for manifesting "unbridled passion, prejudice, pride, & obstinacy," although that description better fits Cabell's conduct given Cocke's explanation of the dispute. But Carter had become the black sheep of his family for advocating better treatment of their slaves.[40]

Cabell's petulance over the carpenters would cost him dearly, for he could not sell his share of the slaves and the lands until he had completed the legal division by entering into formal deeds of partition and mutual release with Carter. Nothing could be done so long as Cabell refused to write or speak to him. That delay bought time for the slaves to make other plans.

During February 1813, the same month that Cabell fell out with Carter, British warships appeared in Chesapeake Bay. Because Corotoman lay along a navigable river near the bay, Cabell worried, "Our situation in that quarter is truly distressing. I expect every day to hear that the British Tenders will take that course, as all our force is gone to Norfolk & Hampton." Given the recent unrest at Corotoman, Cabell expected the slaves to seek out the British as liberators: "The negroes will probably not wait for them to come in pursuit of them."[41]

In November, Cabell returned to Corotoman to find the enemy pressing their raids along the nearby Potomac: "burning vessels, plundering along the Maryland shore & receiving refugee slaves from both shores in great numbers." In one week, the enemy liberated 200 slaves, and Cabell despaired of repelling any British raid on Corotoman: "Great Passiveness appeared . . . among the militia. No signals had been agreed on—no plan for rendezvousing with quickness & vigor. In short the feeble & scattered militia in Lancaster [County] act as if they had no other reliance but on the mercy of the enemy, or on providence, or on the wilderness around their farms."[42]

To reduce the danger from a raid, Cabell had Richeson relocate most of the Tucker-Cabell slaves away from their riverside community to a new quarter in the woods at the head of Carter's Creek, placing them beyond sight of any British vessels. "The settlement at the sloop landing is to be entirely broken up," Cabell explained, save for "some few old ones . . . & one family to watch the granary." The elderly seemed the least likely to escape. Ominously named "Deadman's Bones," the new quarter was an unhealthy location. Rather than risk losing many slaves to the British, Cabell preferred to risk a few more deaths by malaria.[43]

The move apparently backfired, disgusting many slaves and preparing them to try their luck with the British. If so, they were not about to share this decision with Cabell, who returned from visiting Corotoman to gush, "I found Richeson managing the property & particularly the negroes remarkably well. All were satisfied & not a murmur to be heard. . . . I talked freely with some of the negros relative to the British & from all I could discover they seemed to have no intention of going away." Given what would happen five months later, Cabell was played by his canny slaves in November 1813.[44]

Families

The liberation of the Corotoman slaves followed a classic pattern: three young men initially fled and then led the British back in force to liberate their brothers, sisters, children, parents, cousins, uncles, and aunts. On April 18, 1814, four British barges entered Carter's Creek in pursuit of two merchant sloops. The raiders faced no resistance from the militia because, a local man reported, "it being not only court, but election day for Lancaster County, of which the enemy, by some means not yet discovered, must have been apprized." The militiamen had gone to the courthouse to drink and vote, leaving the rest of the county undefended. When British barges probed into the creek, Richeson drove "all the stock of every kind" into the forest "and directed all the Negroes to get up to the new settlement, and from thence into the woods." But three defiant young men—Canada Baton, Tom Saunders, and Ezekiel Loney—bolted to join the raiders. An agitated Richeson reported, "I have been more distress[ed] this time than all the rest together. If these times should last, I *mean to go home next year*." He predicted that more slaves would flee if the British returned, which they soon did.[45]

At about midnight on April 21–22, the British came back to retrieve the relatives and friends of Baton, Loney, and Saunders. Expecting the enemy to repeat the route of the first raid, Richeson and Carter's manager, James J. White, stood guard at night near the mouth of Carter's Creek. Instead, the three young men shrewdly guided the raiders around Richeson and White by ascending the adjoining and unguarded Taylor's Creek. The raiders then marched across the neck of land to the new slave quarters at Deadman's Bones. In his distraught report, Richeson observed, "Canada, Tom Sanders & Zekel made their elopement 2 days Sooner than the rest, without the least cause, and I believe was the cause of bringing the British up to the new Settlement."[46]

In this second raid, the British took away thirty-nine slaves from Deadman's Bones and another twenty-seven from Carter's adjoining estate. Carter's slaves may have preferred his ownership to Cabell's, but they favored freedom most of all. This flight by sixty-nine slaves (including the original three) represented the greatest number to leave one Chesapeake plantation during the war. Speaking for himself and Tucker, Cabell lamented, "The 43 negroes we lost are the flower of our people. By this plunder . . . I lose one half the personal property I acquired by my wife." Cabell overstated his loss by one slave, but perhaps he knew of the determined young pregnant woman who delivered her child on board the *Jasseur* within a few hours of leaving Corotoman. She took a great risk to ensure that her child would be born free. As assessed by their owners, the runaways included the highest-value slaves: relatively young, healthy, active, and resourceful—the usual sort who fled to the British. Richeson set their aggregate value at $11,080: a great fortune for that time. Carter set his loss for twenty-seven slaves at $7,210.[47]

About half of Cabell's and a third of Carter's slaves fled to the British—which meant that most of the Corotoman slaves did *not* escape. What explains those who remained behind? Suddenly awakened and forced to choose, many groggy people must have been confused and torn by the agitation. On the one hand, they longed for freedom and disliked Richeson's management. On the other hand, they also cherished the familiarity of their homes, friends, and connections. By Virginia standards, Corotoman had an especially isolated, insular, and parochial slave community. Those who ran away would probably never again see anyone left behind. At midnight not everyone could immediately give up all that he or she had known—however laced with exploitation. And they could not know how they would fare with the British. What would freedom mean in the context of a crowded warship? And at the end of the raid, some militia appeared and opened fire, apparently killing one Briton. Some of the slaves may have been blocked from getting away.[48]

Age helped to differentiate those who left from those who stayed. The oldest and sickest people found staying easier than going, while the youngest children generally followed the choices of their parents. Among the runaways, ten were men and fourteen were women. They brought along forty-five children but left behind the old people, for the oldest runaway was the last to go: forty-five-year-old Dick Carter. Some in the adult middle probably stayed because they could not bear to forsake their elderly parents. Those who remained may have regretted their lost opportunity, for two weeks later a Carter friend reported that he had visited Corotoman and "found the rest of the negroes on the estate in a perfect state of rebellion."[49]

Married adults in their twenties and thirties led the flight and drew from their marriage and kin connections to recruit others, primarily their own children, but sometimes nieces and nephews. The oldest of the initial three runaways, Tom Saunders, helped to organize the mass escape, which was at its core a Saunders family reunion. Half of the adults (12 of 24) were a Saunders or married to one, and nearly half of the children (21 of 45) had a Saunders for a parent. Family relationships largely determined who fled and who stayed.

Many choices pivoted on the early decision of a key person in the family, with the influence to persuade or dissuade others. One of the "deciders" was Sukey Saunders Carter, the thirty-two-year-old sister of Tom Saunders. By joining her brother and taking her four children, she compelled her reluctant husband, Dick Carter, to leave too, while waving his hat and telling Richeson, "I do not wish sir to leave my master, but I will follow my wife and children to death."[50]

Sisters apparently led the decision to go, for nine of the fourteen departing siblings were women, and they were the oldest in five of the seven lines. It is also revealing that they left behind two relatively elderly brothers, "Old Sam Loney" and the millwright Charles Saunders, who seem to have been disqualified by their age, as was "Old John Brown," aged sixty, the husband of the much-younger Sukey Saunders Brown (twenty-three), who did leave. Given more trust and lighter work by the masters, older men may have been loath to leave, so their younger sisters and wives took charge.

At age forty-two, Fanny Loney Saunders was the apparent matriarch among the sisters. She seems to have bestowed prestige on her younger brother Ezekiel Loney, one of the original three runaways, for he became an especially influential uncle, drawing away his nieces Betsy Bush, Nancy Loney, and Gabriel Loney, who left their parents behind. And the sisters Nelly Marx Loney and Hannah Marx Saunders united two of the early refugees and leaders: their husbands Ezekiel Loney and Tom Saunders.

Some families had been ruptured by the recent partition of the

estate between Charles Carter, on the one hand, and Tucker and
Cabell, on the other. The British raid enabled such families to reunite
by fleeing together. For example, the division had separated Hostler Joe Cox (forty-two) from his wife Franky Cox (thirty-eight).
He retained three of their children, but seven others went with their
mother. On April 22 the couple reunited by escaping with the British, taking along eight of their ten children.

Not all marriages and families were happy ones, however, so the
midnight decision may have enabled some members to escape from
others. For example, Fanny Saunders took away seven of her children, two of them retrieved from the Carter side, but two other young
children, James (six) and Elizabeth (eight), remained behind, as did
Fanny's husband, Charles Saunders. Fifty years old and respected as
"the millwright," Charles may have been relatively well treated and
perhaps felt too old to go. In the gap in the evidence, we can imagine
a heated argument, in which Fanny defied Charles and wrested away
seven of their nine children. But we can equally well imagine a hob-
bled but noble Charles sacrificing himself to stay behind with two sick
children, while urging his wife and the others to risk the escape.

The runaways included a few loners, usually adolescent males
who lacked any evident kinship ties to the others. The departure of
thirteen-year-old Charles James mystified because he left his parents and apparently had no relatives among the other runaways.
One of the original three, twenty-one-year-old Canada Baton (or
Kennedy Beaton, as he became known among the British), was
an especially intriguing outlier. He not only lacked apparent kin
among the refugees but also left behind an especially large and
influential family.

His mother was "Great Jenny," the premier matriarch among
the Corotoman slaves. Evidently great in proportions, personality,
and influence, she bore many children by her husband, Smith Peter
(probably a blacksmith). Tucker's wife Lelia had a long and senti-

mental attachment to Jenny, for they had grown up together on her father's plantation. Sir Peyton Skipwith had given Jenny as a present to his daughter during her first marriage to George Carter (who died in 1788). After Lelia married Tucker in 1791, Jenny and her family went to Williamsburg to serve as house slaves. They later returned to Corotoman and became the only plantation slaves that Tucker took a continuing interest in. When Cabell later hired them out, Tucker urged that they be assigned only "to respectable farmers who would treat them with *kindness* as well as bare humanity. I would rather they should remain near you & their friends and connections among the other negroes than remove them . . . for the sake of a better hire." Great Jenny had her reasons to stay behind: age and a relatively privileged position with the ownership. In leaving such a matriarch, Canada Baton was very much on his own.[51]

Inevitably, the confusion of the raid produced separations. Tom Saunders returned to retrieve his wife, Hannah Marx (twenty-eight), and two of their children, Jo (six months) and Delia (six years), but they left without Delia's twin brother, Thomas Jr. Another community leader, Jim Bully Cook, and his wife, Betty Saunders Cook, got away with three of their children but left behind two others, only six and eight years old.

Cabell demonized the British for disrupting enslaved families, whom he insisted had enjoyed his paternal protection. Cabell asserted that the slaves were "carried forcibly from our shores, accompanied by circumstances of enormity, such as the separation of husband from wife, brother from sister, [and] parents from their infant children" contrary "to the laws of civilized warfare." Cabell probably wrote the propaganda account of the raid published as "The Inhuman Enemy," in the *Richmond Enquirer*: "Visit the Northern Neck—behold . . . negro cabins pilfered—& Slaves dragged on board their ships—infants torn from their parents, and parents torn from their children. On Corotoman estate, a woman hurried off in the pangs of child-birth—the foreman forced away at the point of the bayonet, . . . the whole plantation rung with the shrieks of the sufferers." Cabell, however, forgot that he had sold slaves and divided their families. Slavery exercised distorting power over the minds of masters, who rarely could recognize the moral evasions driven by their self-interest and prickly honor.[52]

Priding themselves on their paternal superiority, the masters felt unjustly disgraced by the runaways. To clear their own consciences, Tucker and Cabell blamed foolish slaves, deceptive Britons, and an uncooperative Carter. Refusing to believe that the runaways could fare better with the British, Tucker castigated them as "unhappy wretches who have been deluded to their ruin." Cabell cast himself as the chief victim and Carter as his prime tormenter, assuring a friend, "The storm that has long been gathering has at length burst upon me. . . . But Polly this morning . . . with uplifted hands acquitted me of all blame & acknowledged that all my counsels & efforts had been over-ruled by the family. Mrs [Lelia] Tucker in her letter, on the subject, expresses the deepest regret at having opposed the plan (often suggested by myself) of removing the property." Reinventing his relationship to Carter, Cabell confessed that he had "sacrificed about half my wife's estate to the desire of conciliating her connections." In his view, Carter's obduracy had left the slaves in harm's way, frustrating Cabell's sage plan to sell or remove them.[53]

Removal

After the great escape of April 1814, the Corotoman owners wondered what to do with the slaves left behind. Once again, Tucker dithered, "Situated as we are I really am at a loss to know what to advise." Washing his hands of the cruel business, Tucker expected Cabell to take charge: "I cannot manage such property. I never could. They are yours at my wife's death—take care of them in the meanwhile. . . . Whatever they may earn I wish you to have it as some compensation for your trouble and Expense." And he deftly appealed to Cabell's filial loyalty: "Have I ever behaved to you otherwise than as to the husband of her choice & of mine & her mother's approbation?" Although Tucker could not manage slaves, he could manipulate his family.[54]

His other son-in-law, John Coalter, dished out harsh advice, proposing that Tucker and Cabell retain only the elderly slaves and some young children, who "would be no object with the Enemy." They would suffice to tend the livestock and raise enough corn to feed themselves. "As to the able bodied slaves—males & females," Coalter would "sell all above 14 [years], as they will now be so broken in upon & deranged that it will not be easy again to get them in proper training." The children Coalter "would keep as a stock to begin on after the war." Of course, this plan had to be kept from the slaves, who would resist the dispersion of their families: "All this I would keep profoundly to myself until you have them at least on board ship or indeed until they were up the Country at the place of sale . . . least the slaves should take the alarm & abscond." Coalter considered slaves a tricky form of livestock meant for breeding and working. He dismissed their family ties as irritating inconveniences best ignored by their masters. Across the bottom of the letter, Tucker penned an endorsement that it contained "better advice than I was probably able to give." He then forwarded the letter to Cabell. Tucker had completed his retreat from his earlier rhetoric about the injustice of slavery.[55]

Loath to sell the mature slaves at a loss on the war-disordered market, Cabell decided to remove them into the interior. In early May he headed to Corotoman in a schooner with five armed guards. "What a scene of trouble, difficulty & loss lies before me!" Cabell anticipated. Dodging British warships, he reached the estate and forced the able-bodied slaves on board and sailed away to Hobbes Hole. Disembarking, they marched over land to Richmond, where Cabell hired boats to take them up the James River. To keep them moving, he relied on food and whiskey, augmented by prodding from the guards. Cabell took some slaves to work at his Nelson County plantation. He hired another sixteen, primarily Great Jenny and her children and grandchildren, to farmers near Lynchburg. "The estate is now broken up—as it ought to have been at the beginning of the war," Cabell concluded.[56]

8

FLIGHT

───◦◦◦───

Our poor Negroes, I wish they were al[l] happy some where.
A grate many went of[f] last night from Richmond County.
—MRS. T. B. GLASSCOCK, DECEMBER 4, 1814[1]

D R. WALTER JONES was the leading man of Kinsale in Westmoreland County on Virginia's Northern Neck. Trained in medicine
at the University of Edinburgh, Jones was a cosmopolitan man of
the Enlightenment, an avid Patriot, and a friend of Thomas Jefferson
and James Madison. Lauded by the *Richmond Enquirer* as "sternly
republican," Jones served five terms in Congress before retiring to
his plantation in 1811. Jones considered himself a benevolent master,
but his slaves voted otherwise with their feet during the war.[2]

Jones felt shocked that the runaways included his most trusted
slaves. He extolled Ben as "a hale man, uncommonly large & strong,
trusted and trust-worthy in every Business of a farm"; Rachael as "a
healthy woman, very trusty & an excellent house servant"; and Presley
as "a very likely lad & good body servant." Fleeing first, in November
1813, Presley represented the greatest blow, for a body servant was a
master's favorite and confidante: no one knew Jones better than Pres-

In this caricature from 1831, Thomas McLean, a British engraver, depicts a white sailor
and a black cook on a British warship. Note the graffiti of a warship on the cookstove.
(Courtesy of the National Maritime Museum, Greenwich, England)

ley did. Presley, however, preferred to serve a Royal Navy captain. In 1815 a visitor to HMS *Havannah* recognized Presley, whom he praised as "uncommonly likely & trained as a House Servant." The visitor noted that Presley had renamed himself "Washington," evidently after the great revolutionary leader who had won liberty and independence for the Americans.[3]

As a black Washington, Presley returned to free his friends and family left behind. In October 1814, Presley guided a British raiding party to Kinsale, liberating the rest of the slaves and casting Jones out. Presley's return represents a common pattern in the slave escapes during the war. Runaways tended to bolt in two stages: in the first, a pioneer runaway made initial contact with the British, and then in the second stage, he returned home to liberate kin and friends.

Presley left behind an embittered and homeless master. In early December, Jones wrote, "I have dated this [letter] from no place as I am still an unsettled vagabond & am not sure where I shall spend the winter." Blaming the inept militia for his losses, Jones concluded, "The disaffection of the blacks is daily gaining extent & boldness. . . . The same heedless Imbecillity that destroys our efforts against the external Enemy paralyzes every thing like vigilance & Police in respect to the more dangerous internal population." No longer seeing Presley as a trusted dependent, Jones had to recast him as part of the menacing internal enemy.[4]

Stages

The first runaways tended to escape on a calm night after spotting a British ship during the day in nearby waters. Sight and sound drew them to the warships, which were loud as well as large. The Royal Marine officer Major Wybourn noted that Rear Admiral Cockburn sailed in his flagship with "the band playing almost the whole day, while the fleet glided along with a rapid tide." Mary K. Hall dwelled beside Chesapeake Bay in Lancaster County on May 11, 1813, when the British fleet "anchored in full view" of the shore "and the drum was distinctly heard to beat,—and on the following night" two slaves escaped in a stolen canoe. At night the British kept lanterns lit at their mast heads "for the purpose of shewing the negroes the position of the ship for better facility in getting to her." The runaways sought British attention by waving pieces of white cloth from the shore or from the prows of canoes. Captain Robert Barrie recalled that slaves "were constantly escaping from the shore & joining our Ships. On these occasions their general practice was to shew something to represent the white Flag."[5]

Masters and militia officers scrambled to lock down and guard the boats and canoes, but resourceful slaves exploited the many lapses by negligent owners. In July 1813 a dozen slaves escaped from three different owners by uniting to steal the six-oared mail boat that served Hampton, Virginia. A month later some careless American naval officers left a large boat at a landing on the Potomac. Exploiting the windfall, seven slaves from two farms came together to escape by stealing the naval boat. In September 1813 the overseer John Parrott on Gwynn Island had his slaves haul the farm's heavy boat up from the river into the yard of his home. Somehow, during the next night, the sly slaves proved both quiet and strong enough to lug the boat away without awakening Parrott.[6]

When a lone man escaped, he often returned to retrieve his wife and children. In August 1813, Golden fled to a British warship in the Patuxent River. In September, he came back to his master, claiming that the British had treated him poorly. But a few nights later, Golden bolted back to the British, taking away his wife, Cate, and their three children.[7]

Masters expected an initial runaway to return for his family. After Samuel Roots escaped to a warship, his master "did watch on the Bank of the Potowmack river for nights with his Gun," for he "expected the said Sam Roots would return from the Brittish for his wife & Cloaths." Apparently, the master prevailed, for he later sought compensation for a man but not for a woman.[8]

To retain black men, the British needed to help the initial runaways recover their families. During a raid in southern Maryland, an officer asked William Dare, a runaway who had become a sergeant of marines, "if he was not preparing to march." Dare replied, "No that he had been promised the priviledge of staying that he might get his wife and that he would have her that night at the risk of his life." He succeeded. Lieutenant James Scott recalled another "shrewd fellow, who had been extremely ill used by his master," so he bolted to a warship, leaving behind his wife and children. "The ties of paternal and marital affection, however, rendered the poor fellow restless and unhappy," so he obtained Cockburn's leave to rescue them. Expecting such a return, the owner compelled the slave family to sleep with him in his locked bedroom. But the "shrewd fellow" broke in and brought off his wife and children in "the boat which the Admiral had kindly sent to facilitate his object."[9]

Often the second stage of an escape assumed a larger scale, as the pioneers returned to recruit entire slave quarters or neighborhoods to follow them back to a warship. The British assisted such large-scale escapes by secretly landing black men at night and arranging to pick them up again, along with their kin and friends, a few nights later at a particular point or beach. A free black, Charles Ball, recalled such a two-stage escape from Calvert County, Maryland, in October 1814:

> The slaves of Mrs. Wilson effected their escape in the following manner. Two or three of the men having agreed . . . [to] run away and go to the fleet, they stole a canoe one night, and went off to the ship that lay nearest the shore. When on board, they

informed the officer of the ship that their mistress owned more
than a hundred other slaves, whom they had left behind them.
They were then advised to return home, and remain there until
the next night, and then bring with them to the beach, all the
slaves on the plantation—the officer promising that he would
send a detachment of boats to the shore, to bring them off.

As planned, the pioneers came home the next night "about midnight,
and partly by persuasion, partly by compulsion, carried off all the
slaves on the plantation" with one exception. When they reached the
beach, the runaways kindled a fire as a signal, and the British boats
rowed ashore to take them off. In the morning the overseer found
nothing but empty cabins and one forlorn slave: probably too old or
sick to leave. In his elderly reminiscence, Ball exaggerated the numbers, for legal documents reveal that Martha Wilson lost fourteen
slaves: two men, five women, and seven children.[10]

These group escapes required considerable planning to unite
people from disparate farms and to secure enough canoes or a big
enough boat. The plotters carefully gathered up prized possessions
including clothes and Bibles. In June 1814 in Princess Anne County,
William Boush awoke one morning to discover that thirteen of his
slaves had stolen his fishing boat and escaped. His neighbor reported
that the runaways "had emptied the feathers out of their beds and
took the ticks and all their cloaths out of their chests and carried off
every thing they could conveniently carry."[11]

The escapes could turn perilous when too many slaves crowded
into a dugout canoe or small boat. The danger grew as they pulled
out into a river with a powerful current or onto the choppy waters
of a windy bay. Sometimes the warships had shifted away, requiring
the fugitives to row through the night to catch up. One midshipman
recalled "the mournful picture they exhibited, as parties of six or
eight ascended the ship's side, stepping from the frail canoe which

they sometimes paddled in the night a distance of several miles, whilst the gunnel of their little bark sunk nearly to the surface of the water with the burden it contained." Near the mouth of the bay, the tide swept some canoes into the even more dangerous waves of the Atlantic. Writing about the spring of 1813, Lieutenant Scott recalled, "Canoes full of the runaways now constantly sought the protection of some of the squadron, and it is to be feared that many perished during the dark nights by drifting out to sea."[12]

Sometimes the runaways looked back to see armed white men in a pursuing boat as the fugitives struggled to stay afloat and pull away to the safety of a distant warship. An Eastern Shore man recalled joining a posse in pursuit. Descending a creek and turning a bend, they spotted the refugees, who had landed to rest, but "so soon as the said slaves discovered the deponent and his associates, they immediately launched their craft and put off into the Chesapeake Bay." Although these runaways consisted of two men, one young woman, and two young children (an infant and a four-year-old), they rowed with a desperation that increased their lead, so the pursuers turned back. Other runaways were less fortunate. Near Hampton in July 1813, armed fishermen pursued, intercepted, and fired on an over-loaded dugout canoe. After wounding one man, they captured all twenty-two of the runaways, a mix of men, women, and children.[13]

The dangers diminished when the British sent ashore armed parties to help retrieve family and friends. Guided by a pioneer runaway, these raids served a dual purpose by enabling more slaves to escape and by taking the food needed in ever larger quantities for the swelling numbers on board the warships. In Calvert County, twenty-year-old Rachael Bannister ran away from her master, who recalled that "a short time afterwards [she] returned home in company with British soldiers in arms & demanded her clothes & went off again with the said British soldiers & several times passed & repassed with other British soldiers & pillaged fruit & other things."[14]

In August 1813, Jack and his wife, Jenny escaped from the farm of Caleb Jones in St. Mary's County, Maryland, to a British brig. The *National Intelligencer* reported,

> But on Sunday night last, to the great surprise and terror of the neighborhood, Mr. Jones received a visit from his fellow, accompanied with about twelve or fifteen British. They took from him every negro he had (six or seven in number) except one, who happened to be from home at the time. They robbed him of many of his sheep and hogs, of his poultry, and much of the contents of his house. They also took several other negroes belonging to different persons in the neighborhood; and his fellow, who was their conductor, was armed with a brace of pistols and a sword and treated his master very insolently.

Jack broke into Jones's bedroom to retrieve an eight-year-old slave boy hidden there: probably his son. At dawn the raiders withdrew with their plunder and people. The raid suggests a deal had been struck between Jack and the British. He would lead them to a prime supply of foodstuffs in return for the chance to retrieve friends and kin, while taking a delicious revenge on his master with rebuking words and plundering deeds.[15]

In June 1814 on Maryland's Patuxent River, four young men escaped from the Sotterley Plantation of John Rousby Plater. The master especially valued Peregrine Young, "a most valuable [house] servant" appraised at $700, and Ignatius Seale, "a black smith" assessed at $800. A month later, all four returned to Plater's plantation, bearing arms and wearing the red jackets of Colonial Marines. They guided a raid that liberated forty-four more slaves: nine men, twelve women, and twenty-three children. They included eight Youngs, nine Seales, and three Woods, who must have been related to the pioneers. Spotting the initial runaways in uniforms, Plater

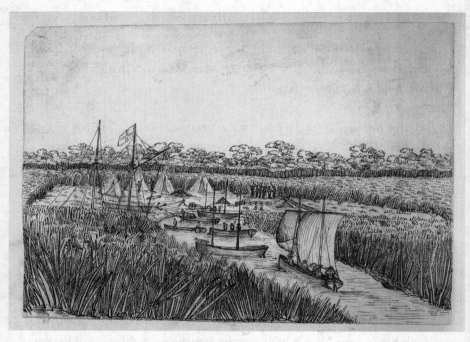

British Boats Landing at the Mouth of Lake Borne, *1815, pen and ink drawing by Rear Admiral Sir Pulteney Malcolm. Although an image from the Gulf Coast at the end of the war, this drawing represents the sort of boats and temporary encampments that the British also deployed in the Chesapeake. (Courtesy of the William L. Clements Library, University of Michigan)*

rebuked the British captain: "It is improper, sir, to take slaves; and to put arms in their hands is more so." The captain pointedly replied, "Who began the war?"[16]

Kin

The British incursion enabled many Tidewater slaves to reconstitute families that had been divided by sale, inheritance, and rental. In July 1813 a twenty-one-year-old slave named Benjamin escaped from his master in Calvert County. A few days later the runaway guided a British attachment to a different farm, to retrieve his wife,

Cecelia, so that they could reunite in freedom. Similarly, Joe Lane fled from his master in Northumberland County, Virginia, and went to the British, who then helped him retrieve his wife, Barbara, and their three children, from another owner in the county. In October 1814 in the same county, Sall escaped with three of her children from the farm of Robert Forester. Then she led a British officer to another farm forcibly to retrieve her two daughters who had been sold to a different owner.[17]

By traveling at night, slaves had maintained ties with spouses and children on other farms in their neighborhood, constituting a community across multiple white-owned properties. That community suddenly became apparent to white folk when a network of enslaved kin and friends came together one night to flee. In Warwick County, Virginia, in 1813, masters explained the flight of Watt and Maria from Robert Dunn's farm in terms of their relationship with blacks on another farm: "At the same time [that] the said negros went off, the negros of John Skinner in the same neighbourhood went away . . . and it is believed they all went together. The said Watt had one of the said Skinner's negro women Nan for his wife and Maria was the wife of negro Bill belonging to Skinner." Similarly, in December 1814 in Northampton County, Lucy, her husband, Paul, and their children Caleb and Mary lived apart on the farms of three different owners until they reunited by escaping in two stolen canoes with other fugitives. Indeed, it became compelling legal evidence that the runaways had gone to the British if many had left diverse farms during the same night when several watercraft went missing. For example, Levin Winder attested that his father's three slaves fled, and "many crafts & other slaves were missing on the same night from the same neighborhood."[18]

Family ties could keep slaves rooted in familiar neighborhoods, or it could uproot them together to seek the new possibilities of a British warship. In Essex County on the Rappahannock River, Samuel Jackson ran away to join a British raiding party, but he soon reconsidered and returned home to "his wife & children, saying he could not feel comfortable or satisfied without them." In appeals to runaways to return, masters dwelled on the family left behind as their ace card. Visiting a British warship, Thomas Primrose asked his runaway "Jerry if he did not wish to go home to see his mother and sisters." Much depended on the initial decision of a family leader, who could persuade others to follow. Jim Bruce got his master's permission to visit his family on the Virginia shore of the Potomac, but "to his extreme anguish, he found his wife and child or children had gone to the British." His wife's owner told Bruce to go back to his master in Maryland. Instead, Bruce followed her down the river to seek a British warship. By escaping first, his wife induced her husband to take her lead.[19]

At least one same-sex couple ran away to reunite. In Calvert County a witness recalled that a slave woman named Unity had been married to Joe Gurny, but "a short time after their marriage they fell out and parted. She then formed an intimacy with a negro woman the property of David Avis by the name of Philis Caden. They both joined the Methodist Church, claimed a Sisterhood," and Unity changed her name to Minty Caden. Until they ran away together to the British, each had belonged to a different owner.[20]

Slaves had an extra incentive to flee when they belonged to estates facing disruption by the master's death and debts. In 1814 the Charles B. Carter executors rented his slaves to four different farmers in two different counties, yet they all managed to escape together to the British. In early 1814 in Westmoreland County, executors prepared to divvy up the thirty-four slaves of the late John Turberville. Taking matters into their own hands, the slaves frustrated that division by fleeing together to the British. In the morning, the overseer checked on their quarters to find "that every Negroe was gone" and "that all the women took their children with them."[21]

An escape was always a gamble, for some relatives might fail to evade masters and patrollers during the confusion of the fateful night. Instead of uniting families, the risky attempt might increase and perpetuate their divisions. Lieutenant Scott recalled, "One negress who came down with an infant in her arms, suddenly recollecting she had forgotten" something, left her child with the British sailors while she ran back to her cabin. When she failed to return in good time, the anxious raiders had to shove off without her. Captain Charles B. H. Ross of HMS *Albion* adopted her baby, but the mother's lost bid for freedom had cost her a child.[22]

While reuniting slave families who had been divided by sale and inheritance, many escapes ruptured relationships with free white relatives left behind. Although rarely acknowledged publicly, many masters and overseers had fathered children by enslaved women. In Richmond County, the county clerk, Bartholomew McCarty, recorded the skin color for most of the local slaves who escaped to the British. A rural county on the Rappahannock River, Richmond County should not be confused with the city of Richmond to the south on the James River. Of the 106 runaways with a specified skin color, McCarty reported that 48 (45 percent) had the "tawny," "yellow," or "mulatto" tones of mixed race.[23]

Masters and overseers lost relatives as well as property when mixed-race slaves escaped. In 1813 in Northampton County, Virginia, fifteen interrelated slaves fled from two different owners, John K. Floyd and John Eyre. An appraiser described nine of them as "black" and six as "yellow." The runaways included the aptly named Chocolate, "a dark coloured woman," and her daughters Elisha, Mira, and Betty, all described as "yellow," which suggests that their father was a white man. John K. Floyd called one of the runaways "Southey," but the latter claimed the name of "John Floyd." Given his "yellow" complexion and preferred name, he was probably the master's son.[24]

In the same county, Arthur Jacob, an overseer, had inside information of an impending escape, because a slave, Violet, was his mistress. Jacob had quarreled with the master and chose not to tip him off to the escape. He later stated that "he didn't care if all the negroes in the county went. Other people might as well work for themselves as him." But maybe Jacob also wanted Violet to become free.[25]

Mixed-race house servants were especially familiar, important, and valuable to their masters. It pained Richard Ross to concede that his "mulatto" slave Thomas Perks had left "voluntarily" with the British troops. Aged thirty-four, Perks "was a handsome waiter . . . fond of music and played well upon the violin." Such a genteel slave had great value in elite circles. Ruing his loss, Ross recalled that he "had been frequently offered one thousand dollars by traveling Gentlemen for Thomas Perks."[26]

Thomas Archer of Yorktown recalled the anguish expressed by his neighbor Major Thomas Griffin in November 1813, when his five "mulatto slaves," four of them house servants, fled to the British: "Thomas Griffin having reared these Negroes was strongly attached to them and used every effort in his power (without success) to repossess them." Unable to recover his cherished mulattoes from the British, Griffin sought enhanced compensation from his own government: "the highest value ought to be set in consequence of their complexion & their being house Servants."[27]

Virginians denied their relatives on the other side of an arbitrary racial line. Defined by material interest, the property line between freedom and slavery exaggerated difference and called it race. That tragic polarity drove some enslaved people to seek freedom far from the white relatives who would own them as property but disown them as kin.

Names

Slaves ran away literally to make names for themselves. During the eighteenth century, the Virginians had renamed newly arrived slaves, rejecting African names in favor of either English or, among the most whimsical masters, classical names like Cato and Caesar. By 1800, the Chesapeake slaves had lost the battle to retain African names, but they had resisted the mocking classical names, which became rare. Instead, in the lists of runaways from the War of 1812, we find almost all bore the same English first names found among their masters but with a diminutive twist: Tom (rather than Thomas), Dick (rather than Richard), Harry (instead of Harold), Sam (instead of Samuel), Nat (instead of Nathaniel), Sally (instead of Sarah), and Polly (instead of Mary).[28]

Historians have been so keen to find African cultural traits surviving among the enslaved in the Chesapeake that we can miss the bigger story: how they claimed and reworked Euro-American culture for their own ends. The Chesapeake refugees read or heard the Bible and longed to earn and keep wages, own homes, and wear high-quality clothing, especially in church. They emulated the gendered order of the dominant culture, aspiring for men to protect and provide for women and children, who would work in and around the house rather than in the fields or in a master's house. And slaves wanted surnames as tokens of personal respect and markers of familial ties. Seeking equality, many slaves claimed the dominant culture's markers of respectability for themselves.[29]

By refusing to recognize the last names claimed by slaves, masters treated them as perpetual children and dependents. By obscuring their family relationships, the denial of surnames also facilitated treating every slave as a commodity without honor. In public, white men insisted on being addressed by their surnames, reserving their first names for their closest friends. When addressing a black, however, whites asserted superiority by using her or his first (or "Christian") name. Consequently, a white man bristled when so addressed (unless by a close friend). In a confrontation with an unruly stonemason, the very genteel Joseph C. Cabell took particular offense at his "calling me by my Christian name, as tho he had been speaking to a negro."[30]

Slaves claimed and used surnames among themselves to assert their honor and identify their family ties. In the presence of a master or overseer, the slaves usually had to keep mum about surnames, but once free and with the British they could proudly announce their full names. John Cowper explained to Cabell, "Our slaves, as you know, have a way of nomenclature of their own, sometimes taking the surnames of their owners, sometimes of the Families from whence they were derived, after their Fathers if white or Free."[31]

By claiming the master's name, mixed-race slaves sought to remember what the master meant to keep hidden: a blood tie as a daughter, son, niece, nephew, or cousin. Or by claiming the surname of a previous master, a slave could subtly challenge the legitimacy of his sale to a new master. A white man from Norfolk belatedly discovered that "it is most common for negroes to adopt the sirname of their first owner and to retain it." The persistence of that original surname entered a protest against the accelerating sales that disrupted enslaved families.[32]

In the Chesapeake, the master sought to reserve his surname, denying the efforts by slaves to claim it. A Virginian explained, "Slaves in Virginia have not been much in the habit of assuming Sirnames especially in an open & publick manner. Their masters generally dislike it. They have done it, however, in many instances and the practice is becoming common. In this case it is believed the slaves adopted the name of their master after going to the British, though it is not known that they did so before." By claiming the master's surname, the enslaved Dick Carter asserted a humanity and manhood on a par with Charles Carter at Corotoman. After the war, Augustine Neale closely investigated the names on British lists and concluded, "These negroes were fond of their masters' names, they being highly respectable people." No act of submission, taking a master's surname was instead as defiant as taking his pig at night.[33]

After the war ended, masters belatedly scrambled to learn the surnames of their runaways in order to identify them on British lists: the surnames provided valuable evidence to support a legal claim for compensation from the government. Masters questioned their remaining slaves to learn the surnames that the masters had previously sought to deny. A token of freedom for the runaway, the surname might later become the master's ticket to track his former slave down.[34]

Persuasion

Masters tried to dissuade slaves from escaping by denouncing the British as cunning deceivers who meant to sell them into the harsher slavery of the West Indies. The *Richmond Enquirer* claimed that Virginia slaves enjoyed "perfect freedom" when compared to the grim conditions of the West Indies. Another writer imagined that the British kept the deluded runaways "constantly at hard labor, in doing all the drudgery and dirty work on the ships; that they are whipped about like dogs, and that if any of them should be taken sick, they are immediately thrown overboard, lest their disease should infect the ship's crew." In May 1813 a Norfolk correspondent marveled at the recent surge in runaways from nearby Princess Anne County:

> One would have thought, from the treatment which the fathers of these deluded wretches met with, by deserting to the British [during the] last war, that they would have been deterred from such a course; but it seems [that] they have forgot how the great Lord Dunmore enticed the Princess Anne negroes away from their masters, with fine promises, and afterwards shipped them off to Jamaica, where they were sold to masters, whose cruelty, added to the effects of a sickly climate, soon put an end to their lives. The negroes of Princess Anne, with very few exceptions, fare better than a great many poor white families; they are treated with humanity and even with indulgence, and yet, such is the discontentedness of their nature, that we see them flying away from certain good, to encounter that, which from the foul example of Lord Dunmore, they must consider a certain evil.

By insisting that deluded slaves fled from true happiness into sure destruction, masters avoided questioning their own conduct or the slave system.[35]

Determined to believe their own story, masters claimed that indiscreet British officers had confessed to their profits from selling the runaways in the West Indies. Widely circulated, this scuttlebutt became mistaken for evidence. Governor Barbour officially endorsed the story in a speech to the state legislature in December 1813, when he declared it "now satisfactorily ascertained that they are consigned to the West Indies, sold to the planters at enormous prices and exposed to accumulated hardships." Virginians convinced themselves that they had to protect their gullible slaves from exploitation by the devious Britons.[36]

In fact, the Virginians proved especially credulous, believing returning and supposedly repentant runaways who reaffirmed the cherished story of brutish Britons. On January 21, 1814, in Mathews County, a militia officer "was not a little pleased this morning to find two stout Black Fellows in camp." They had deserted during the night before from a British watering party. When the "Black Fellows" explained that they had grown "heartily tired and anxious to return to their masters," the officer exulted, "I consider this desertion a valuable occurrence for us, as they will give our negroes a correct account of their situation on board and make them better satisfied at home." Instead, the number of escapes accelerated from Mathews County, for the "Black Fellows" only pretended to be alienated so that they could return to help their kin escape.[37]

The masters' tale won support from Ben George, a free black from Accomack County on Virginia's Eastern Shore. Convicted of stealing brandy by the county court and sentenced to three years in the state prison, in July 1813 he was sent across Chesapeake Bay in a boat bound to Richmond. Capturing that boat, the British offered to liberate George, but he preferred to proceed on to serve his prison term rather than lose the chance eventually to return to his family and friends in Accomack. Captain John G. Joynes of that county insisted that George had reacted against "the extreme cruelties which he saw practiced while on the board [of] the enemy's ship." George played his role perfectly, for the whites of Accomack petitioned for his pardon "not only as a reward for his conduct, but as it is believed he will be the means of preventing many negroes from deserting to the enemy." A delighted Council of State promptly pardoned George and sent him home. By capturing George, the British did him a great favor, for he could play out a pleasing story that liberated him from jail. But the Accomack slaves continued to run away to the British, for they faced life sentences rather than the three years given to Ben George.[38]

Masters preached their story of betraying Britons to gathered slaves, with poor results. John Shaw recalled that his master had disingenuously offered to help his slaves join the British if they disliked his ownership. The slaves wisely declined the insincere offer, but a few weeks later Shaw and his compatriots escaped in a stolen canoe. Similarly, a Lancaster County slave named Davy recalled "that his said Master called them all together and asked them if they intended leaving him and going off to the British." They all professed loyalty, but shortly after midnight three slaves bolted in a stolen dugout canoe. Apparently the master's speech had backfired by alerting slaves to the nearby warship.[39]

Runaways mocked owners who pretended to feel a concern for their slaves by warning of British tricksters. A British officer noted that the runaways "possessed infinitely more sense and judgment than their late owners give them credit for." Upon reaching a warship, a runaway told that officer, "S'pose you sell me to West Indee planter to-day, what difference 'tween dat an' Yankee sell me to Carolina planter to-morrow?" Chesapeake slaves knew that sale by their masters to the Deep South was a far more real and imminent threat

than any British conveyance to the West Indies. The runaways preferred to take their chances with the British as their best chance for
freedom rather than their worst threat of sale faraway. [40]

Unwilling to admit that their slaves sought freedom, masters
claimed that the British forced them to go away. Any ambiguous
evidence became signs of force to their owners. In Calvert County,
Thomas M. Harris recalled that the slaves of George Wilkinson
"appear'd to be compell'd to go by the Brittish forces, as they were
crying so as to be heard . . . at the distance of about one Hundred
yards." But were they mourning the departure from their master or
the abandonment of some relatives on another nearby farm? Perhaps
they sought loudly to alert other slaves to the chance to get away. We
cannot know with the certainty that Harris asserted. [41]

On the night of June 16–17, 1814, British marines, including
black recruits, raided the farm of Elizabeth Ballard on the Patuxent
River in Maryland. Alerted that Ballard had hidden a slave girl, Eliza
aged ten, in her second-floor bedroom, the British commander sent
a black marine named Charles to retrieve her. Ballard's son insisted
that Eliza "had requested to be concealed thro' fear of being carried
off by them" and that she went "against her will and by force." That
seems unlikely, for Charles was Eliza's father. [42]

Many masters regarded as force any persuasion by British officers and their guides. In 1814, the British enticed runaways by
offering future land as well as immediate freedom and pay for their
work. In August in Prince George's County, a planter found Captain
Joseph Nourse of the Royal Navy in his detached "kitchen where
the negroes were and . . . distinctly heard Capt. Nourse persuade
his negroes to go off and offered them money and told them that
they should have land to work and should be free and as well off as
any white people." In St. Mary's County, a slave named Anthony
visited his wife at another farm, where he spoke with British raiders who promised that "he should be free & have land of his own."
Anthony balked until, two days later, he learned "that as his wife had

gone with the British, he had better to go, which he did." Land and freedom were enticing, but the ties of family proved clinching for Anthony. [43]

In July 1814 in St. Mary's County, Nathaniel Washington confronted a group of slaves, including five of his own, preparing to depart with a British raiding party. He "advised them to return to their respective homes, that if they went with the British, they would be either carried to the West Indies or to the Spaniards & sold." A British officer intervened "and told the Negroes not to mind" Washington. Turning to the master, the officer declared loudly, "They are as free as you are and receive ten Dollars per month for their services." The officer's superior, Captain Nourse, then added, "Sir, they are as free as you are. Be gone immediately."[44]

On July 20, 1814, Nourse led a raid into that county to plunder the farm and burn the tobacco barn of William Kilgour. "Under the direction of a negro of Mr. Kilgour's who had gone to them," the raiders "patiently selected the bacon and other things belonging to him." They then withdrew with their plunder and two slave boys. Following the retreating British, Kilgour accosted the boys, one of whom agreed to return home: "He was immediately surrounded by a parcel of soldiers & officers, who said he was a fool to go with me. Stay with them, they would set him free & pay him for his services. He, the boy, then said he would remain with them if they would do that for him. They said he was a fine boy & should not be whipped & should be as free as they were."[45]

Kilgour recognized two marines as former slaves: "I mentioned to them [that] they would be sorry for their conduct. I was immediately surrounded by the soldiers & officers. They said I must go away, I had nothing to do with them negroes, they were as free as I was & at that time under pay for their services." Then a runaway "turned around to me & said, yes, he was not going to work for white men for nothing. He was then under pay & slapt his pocket, which appeared to have two or three Dollars in the same." The

British appealed to the pride of young men, their determination to escape the pain and humiliation of the whip, and their aspiration to get paid for their work.[46]

Masters dismissed "persuasion" as a form of force because slaves had no legal right to leave their owner. In Kent County, Maryland, in September 1814, during a parlay under a flag of truce, a militia officer, Ezekiel Chambers, rebuked a British officer for taking away slaves. Chambers recalled,

> He said they had not been carried but had gone at their own request. I told him that it was scarcely necessary to state to him the nature of our slave-laws in this country—that negro slaves were considered as mere articles or property, as much so as a horse or a cow; and [I] asked him if one of Mr. Jones's horses or cows should have walked into the water and have manifested a disposition to get into his boat whether he would have felt himself authorized to take it off.

Impressed with his own logic, Chambers did not record the Briton's response, which may have been that a human being could reason as no cow or horse ever could. The officer probably also did not feel bound to obey the laws of Maryland that defined some people as property on a par with livestock.[47]

In a few cases the raiders did take some slaves by force, scooping up some of the reluctant along with many of the eager. In Calvert County in July 1814, a British raiding party took twenty slaves from a master who reported that "two of which were tied by" the British "and a negro Woman, while endeavouring to make her escape, was fired on and made to return & Join them." The other seventeen apparently left willingly.[48]

The best assessment came from Walter Jones, an unusually frank master despite losing twelve runaways. Brushing aside the usual

planter rhetoric, Jones admitted that it was "a matter of perfect noto-
riety here . . . that for one Slave that was forcibly captured, hundreds
fled voluntarily to the British forces under the temptations set forth
to invite their desertion." Of course, he denounced those temptations as seductive lies, but Jones recognized their allure to those who
chose to join the British.[49]

The initially reluctant fugitives usually warmed to freedom on
a warship once they were paid, fed, and clothed by the British. The
newcomers also heeded British warnings that masters whipped and
sold away or executed any refugees who returned. A master who
visited a warship to cajole a runaway to return reported that he
simply "replied that he was in better hands." Joseph C. Cabell concluded, "Nor is it [a] matter of astonishment that when the lapse of
nearly twelve months had weakened the ties of kindred, the dread of
punishment if they returned, [and] the prospect of freedom abroad,
should have induced the slaves to leave the U. States." A free black,
Charles Ball, visited a warship to try to persuade runaways to return
home, but he "found that their heads were full of notions of liberty and happiness" in a Crown colony "where they would have
lands given to them, and where they were to be free." Few runaways
fled homeward again except to trick their masters and recruit more
runaways.[50]

Ships

The British insisted that slaves became free by taking refuge under
the protecting flag of the empire. As extensions of British sovereignty, the warships brought the liberating *Somerset* doctrine within
tempting sight and sound of the Tidewater slaves. A naval officer
assured a master that his runaway "was under the protection of his
Majesty's flag, that by the British Laws there were no slaves and
that those laws prevailed on Board his ship; and that as the negro

was unwilling to go with him." The officer "could not compel him to go." The British stuck to that principle despite offers of ransom money from the planters.[51]

To refute charges that they took slaves by force, the British encouraged masters to visit the warships, under a flag of truce, to speak to the runaways. The admirals and captains treated these visitors with exquisite politeness. Thomas R. Yeatman of Mathews County reported, "My reception was kind, familiar and elegant." The captains promised to release any runaways who consented to return with their masters. But they could meet with the runaways only in the presence of British officers, who refuted any charge that the refugees would be sold in the West Indies.[52]

After assembling the fugitives on deck, the captain announced, "Your masters come for you, you are at liberty to follow them, but recollect that you are as free as themselves," which hardly helped the visitors' cause. The masters then had to persuade the runaways as free people able to decide for themselves: an embarrassing turnabout for planters who had so long commanded and punished them as slaves. An amused Lieutenant Scott described the solicitous speech by some Virginians: "The heroes questioned their late negroes in softened accents respecting the cause of their desertion; some quaint and home[ly] replies to these queries convinced the envoys of their loss of time in the attempt, and they took their departure."[53]

The visiting master almost always returned home empty-handed and with an earful from his defiant runaways. Cabell noted that the runaways "were produced, but on being enquired of whether they were willing to return, they declined & some of them very impertinently." Captain Joseph Nourse reported, "I have never found the smallest disposition in any that have fled from their masters to return. On the contrary, I believe no temptation would induce them to it, nor has any one been carried off by Force."[54]

Frustrated masters blamed meddling British sailors or marines, who pointedly reminded the slaves of their risks in returning. In November 1813 on board a British brig, Thomas Archer of York-town assured the fugitives "that if they would return with their master they would not be punished. A marine who was stationed at the cabin Door with arms in his hands exclaimed if you return you will all be killed. They were then asked if they would return to their homes with their master. They were much agitated and at last replyed that they could not—weeping at the same moment." According to Cabell, the British told the runaways "that they w[oul]d be hung immediately on getting ashore, and even pretended that from the tops of their masts, they could see negros hanging on trees along the shore."⁵⁵

Fellow runaways also bolstered the resolve of anyone who wavered. Reverend Armistead Smith claimed that one runaway would have returned to his master "had he not been overpersuaded by his Brother, Brook's fellow [Humphrey], to the contrary. He repeatedly insinuated to him 'how hard his Fare had been at home, only 1 peck of corn pr. Week & no time even allowed to grind it & never a mouthful of meat to eat with it, whereas on the contrary here we have a plenty of meat & Bread 3 times a day.'" In disgust, Smith concluded, "Thus these poor wretches are & will be deluded." Hardly deluded, Humphrey knew full well that he ate better on a British warship than he had as a Virginia slave.⁵⁶

In July 1814, John J. Brooke sent his trusted slave, Benjamin Mason, to a British warship to try to persuade his son and two other runaways to return. None would leave the British, for Mason dis-covered that they "had been treated very well & that his said Son had new clothes & a plenty to eat & drink." Mason concluded "that the negroes who had gone to the British lived well & that the British officers had told him . . . that all the negroes who went to the British would certainly be free." An honorable man, Mason returned home as he had promised, but after making his report to his Master, Mason ran away to join his son on the warship.[57]

Suppression

The escapes threatened to impoverish white families who had invested most of their net worth in black bodies. The five slaves of Rebecca Cooper—two men, two women, and a girl—comprised "almost the entire means of support left for a widow and large family of helpless children," until the five eloped to the British. In Mathews County, after losing ten runaways to the British, Houlder Hudgins dreaded losing the rest of his slaves lest "he should be left in his old age destitute of that support which his declining years and the helpless state of his family demanded." Cabell insisted that the runaways threatened "to reduce thousands of families to beggary & wretchedness." By relying on the income from enslaved labor, Virginians suffered when slaves escaped to seek their own security.[58]

To reduce their losses, masters moved slaves away from the shores frequented by British raiders. After warships appeared near Mathews County, Reverend Smith hired away Bob and Robin to inland Richmond so "that they wd. be out of the way of the Enemy." During the summer and fall of 1814, the shore raids intensified, so many masters began to pack up and move their furniture, livestock, and slaves into the interior. They delayed as long as possible because such moves were expensive and disruptive, and an abandoned farm would languish without labor to raise the crops: a dead loss to the owner. In Surry County in July 1814, Nicholas Faulcon dithered: "I am at a loss to know what to decide upon. To break up at this season of the year, or at any time indeed before my crop is secured, would be ruinous to us; and by waiting until it is secured, I run the risk of losing the greater part, perhaps the whole, of my moveable property," which meant his slaves.[59]

To suppress runaways, county magistrates greatly increased the nocturnal slave patrols. In June 1812, before the British warships came into Chesapeake Bay, Lancaster County paid just four men to patrol during the month, and each man performed an average of just thirty hours, or about one hour per night. A year later, during the surge in escapes, the county paid thirty patrollers, and their man-hours grew from the 121 in June 1812 to 1,008 in June 1813. A month later, the patrols increased to 1,544 hours by thirty-seven men: a major commitment for a rural county during the prime months for farm labor.[60]

In 1813, Princess Anne County had a particularly vigilant and active volunteer company devoted to suppressing escapes by "patrolling the desert that skirts the southern boundary of Lynn-haven Bay." In the sand dunes, "runaways and outliers" had set up hidden camps while awaiting a chance to contact and escape to a warship. A rough interrogation of one captured woman induced her to lead the volunteers to a camp of twenty refugees. Shooting first and asking questions later, the volunteers wounded and captured six runaways while the rest escaped deeper into the "Sand Hills." But the correspondent added, "One, who was only wounded, compromised for his life by giving such information as must inevitably lead to the detection of the whole gang."[61]

The Princess Anne volunteers nearly scored their greatest triumph on August 29, 1813, when they lured a British boat into an ambush by posting two of their men, with blackened hands and faces, on the beach, where they waved white handkerchiefs in the air. Another seventeen volunteers hid behind the dunes with their guns loaded and cocked. The fake blacks attracted a boat, rowed by six British sailors, from HMS *Plantagenet*. Just before reaching shore, the officer in the boat noticed that the two waving men on the beach had white ankles. He yelled out, "White men in disguise by God! Let us push off." As his men struggled to turn about and row away, the militia opened fire, hitting two of the British, but the other four pulled away out of range and back to their ship.[62]

The British insisted that masters promptly hanged recaptured or returned runaways, but such summary executions seem unlikely, for slaves were too valuable to sacrifice without assurance of state compensation. During the war, Virginia compensated no masters for the execution of intercepted runaways. Some suffered gunshot wounds while resisting recapture, as in the Hampton and Princess Anne County episodes of 1813. In Lancaster County in September 1814, Timothy McNamara sued James Brent, a veteran slave patroller, for shooting his "negro man slave," who apparently was fleeing to the British. Upon considering "the circumstances of the case," the county court dismissed the lawsuit. After the war, McNamara received federal compensation for a slave named Adam, the probable victim of Brent's bullet.[63]

The county authorities struggled with how to handle cases of intercepted runaways. In July 1814 in Westmoreland County, General John P. Hungerford pressed the Council of State for guidance: "What should be done with those slaves who have joined the enemy and are afterwards apprehended in counseling other negroes to go off? Or with those who are apprehended in attempting to go?" Embarrassed by the query, the Council punted, insisting that the county justices had to decide. Disliking any publicity about the execution of slaves, the state leaders wanted local magistrates to handle the recaptured as discreetly as possible.[64]

Instead of executing recaptured runaways, the captors whipped and then jailed them until the masters could reclaim their slaves. British raiders captured two county jails and liberated slaves held there "for endeavouring to escape to us." At the end of the war, a county clerk reported that the Mathews County jail held nine runaways recently captured in a British schooner. The clerk warned their owners to pay the jailor's fees and a reward to the militiamen promptly or the slaves would be auctioned. The jails, however, often proved flimsy and the guards negligent. In July 1813 the Northampton County militia captured and jailed a runaway named George, but he soon escaped with "many others who were in jail with him." Stealing several canoes, they safely reached a British warship.[65]

Upon recovering a runaway, the master tended to sell him to a new owner far away from the coast, where escape would be more difficult, rather than permit his example and expertise to influence others. In April 1814 two runaways returned to Mathews County on a mission from Admiral Cockburn to assure slaves of the British "readiness to receive, protect, and assist them and put Arms in their Hands." But the local militia captured the two agents in a stolen canoe. On April 19, 1814, Reverend Armistead Smith reported, "A court martial has been sitting for 4 or 5 days on the Trial of 2 Black fellows, one belonging to Capt. Blake, the other to a Mr. Hope of Hampton, as Spies from the Enemy." In early May, Cockburn noted that his agents had been captured and prosecuted; "they managed, however, to tell so good a Tale & their Comrades kept so faithfully their Secret, that they escaped condemnation, & have only been sold for the back Settlements, and it is supposed by those who have since come off that they will . . . contrive to elude the Vigilance of those who have charge of them, & that we shall probably see them again *here* [before] very long." Cockburn was too optimistic, for few if any slaves escaped from the interior to the warships.[66]

Patterns

During the war, about 3,400 slaves escaped from the shores of the Cheseapeake to join the British. Almost all came from the shores of a navigable river or bay, where the slaves could see or hear a warship or where British raiders came ashore. Virtually no slaves escaped to the British from the Piedmont counties, owing to the dangerous distance to the coast along roads patrolled by armed militiamen. "By far, the greater number, if not the whole, were taken from proprietors who inhabit the Country bordering on the Bays and Rivers," James Monroe noted. In 1822 a Virginia enumeration of the wartime runaways indicated that all came from a Tidewater county, primarily from the Northern Neck, which the British targeted for most of their raids. Among the masters who received postwar compensation, the average owner lost just 3.2 slaves, for slave ownership was highly dispersed in the Tidewater counties by 1813. Most of the runaways came from modest farms rather than great plantations, for the latter were few and far between in the Tidewater.[67]

There were two types of escapes: first, by a few hardy young men, and second, by larger groups that also included women and children. Two-thirds of the wartime runaways were male, usually adolescents and young men, who could best endure the physical challenges of dodging patrollers, hiding in the woods, stealing a boat, and paddling for hours. As the slaves most exposed to whipping and long-distance market sales, young men also had the most to gain by seeking the freedom offered by the British. But the wartime escapes included more females, at least a third of the fugitives, when compared to the 12 percent of prewar runaways. Few children ran away before the war, but they accounted for at least a fifth of the wartime runaways. The prewar fugitives had lacked the military assistance of a powerful ally that dominated the waterways within sight of their farms. The wartime runaways could exploit that ally to escape in larger, family groups, but only from the Tidewater.[68]

The distinctive nature of the wartime group escapes becomes evident when compared to the runaways advertised in the Virginia newspapers during 1813 and 1814. A separate pool of fugitives, the advertised slaves included none of the runaways who went to the British. By offering a reward, an advertiser sought to interest readers in recovering the runaway, so it was pointless to advertise for slaves assumed to have reached the enemy. Instead, the advertised runaways continued the prewar pattern of individualized and localized escapes. Most advertised fugitives fled from the interior rather than from the Tidewater counties closest to the warships. No advertised escape involved more than three people. The great majority (81 of 129, or 63 percent) of the advertised runaways were young men fleeing alone without a wife or child or friend. Women comprised only a fifth (25 of 129) of the advertised runaways, and they also usually escaped alone (15 of 25) or, occasionally, with a child or two or with a husband. Children accounted for only 4 percent (5 of 129) of the advertised runaways.[69]

Most of the advertised runaways were lonely people fleeing on their own, usually to seek out family members elsewhere in Virginia or Maryland. Rarely did masters expect the runaways to head north to a free state, and in only three wartime advertisements did the masters speculate that the fugitives might seek the British warships. Even in those three cases, the runaways apparently did not reach the British, for their masters received none of the postwar compensation reserved for those who lost slaves to the enemy.[70]

Unlike the advertised runaways from the Piedmont, the Tidewater slaves could seize a new and rare opportunity to escape together to nearby warships. The powerful bonds of marriage and kinship shaped the decisions by slaves to stay or go. Few would bolt without a good prospect of retrieving their closest kin, particularly wives and children. Despite a longing for freedom, even in the Tidewater most slaves stayed put through the war rather than leave behind spouses, parents, children, and grandparents. Where escapes as groups became possible, however, runaways could reunite families sundered or threatened by the rental or sale of relatives. In parts of the Tidewater, the British helped the slaves to reverse the threat posed to their families by the triumph of market relations in the wake of the American Revolution.

9

FIGHT

*Our negroes are flocking to the enemy from all quarters,
which they convert into troops, vindictive and rapacious—with
a most minute knowledge of every bye path. They leave us
as spies upon our posts and our strength, and they return
upon us as guides and soldiers and incendiaries.*
—GENERAL JOHN P. HUNGERFORD, AUGUST 5, 1814[1]

LIEUTENANT JAMES SCOTT and Captain John G. Joynes were ambitious young officers at military odds. Devoted to the empire, Scott became Rear Admiral Sir George Cockburn's protégé on his flagship HMS *Albion*, while Joynes was a planter in the Accomack County militia on Virginia's Eastern Shore. Where Scott meant to rise through the ranks of a hierarchical and professional military service, Joynes was a fiery Republican who defied the dominant Federalists of his county in both elections and the militia. Scott and Joynes developed a fierce rivalry during the British raids on the exposed farms and militia batteries of Accomack County. Visiting HMS *Albion*, under a flag of

Admiral Sir George Cockburn, *an oil painting by John James Halls, 1817. Made in London, the portrait depicts Cockburn with Washington, D.C., ablaze in the background, the episode from a long career in which Cockburn took the greatest pride and most wanted to memorialize in his portrait. (Courtesy of the National Maritime Museum, Greenwich, England)* truce, Joynes confronted Scott to denounce his nocturnal raiding: "tarnation seize me in the bramble-bush of damnation if I don't blow you to hell if you put your foot within a mile of my command. . . . I would give you such a whipping as would cure you from rambling a-night, like a particular G[o]d d[amne]d tom-cat."[2]

Fired up by the challenge, Scott secured Cockburn's permission to attack Joynes's battery at Chesconessex Creek in a raid guided by one of his former slaves and conducted by other runaways who had become Colonial Marines in the British service. At dawn on June 25, 1814, the raiders captured the battery as Joynes fled, leaving behind his cherished sword, feathered hat, and uniform coat. Scott kept the sword but gave the clothing to "a serjeant of the Black Marines." In an angry letter to Scott, Joynes denounced "the dishonor I had put upon him by making over his military attire, cocked-hat, sky-scraper feathers and all, and allowing them to be worn by a 'G[o]d d[amne]d black nigger.'" Serving as guides and marines, the runaways enabled the British to wage a war intended to embarrass as well as to defeat the Virginians.[3]

As they recruited more runaways, the British had to increase their shore raids to obtain more livestock and provisions to feed the fugitives. Thanks to the local expertise of the former slaves, those raids could push deeper into the forested countryside. Black guides and fighters steered the raiding parties around militia ambushes to find hidden herds and secluded farms. The runaways naturally led the raids to the places they knew best: their former neighborhoods, where they could retrieve kin and plunder their former masters.[4]

By aggressively recruiting runaways, the British could escalate their war in the Chesapeake during the campaign of 1814. The naval officers sought to punish their foes for deploying torpedoes and snipers and for looting and burning villages in Canada, where the British commander called for revenge on the American coast. Vice Admiral Sir Alexander Cochrane agreed: "Their Sea Port Towns laid in Ashes & the Country wasted will be some sort of retaliation for their savage Conduct in Canada."[5]

In 1814 the British also felt invincible thanks to their great victories in Europe over Napoléon's collapsing empire. During the spring and summer, that triumph freed up dozens of British warships and thousands of troops to cross the Atlantic to fight the Americans. Bitter over the American declaration of war in 1812, when the British had faced Napoléon at his peak, they sought payback in 1814 at his nadir. Lord Eglinton declared, "The only thing now is those cursed Americans. I hope a sufficient force will be sent to crush them at once, to attack their strongholds, arsenals, shipping, and naval yards, and destroy them." Sir John Beresford insisted, "The Power of the Southern States ought if possible to be broken down, & they richly deserve it." He reasoned that an invasion of the South "might be rendered infinitely more formidable by the emancipation of the Slaves, & purposes of humanity might be answered by it, for they are cruelly oppressed."[6]

Tangier

In April 1814, to accommodate the refugees, Cockburn occupied and fortified Tangier Island, within Chesapeake Bay and a dozen miles from Virginia's Eastern Shore. He recommended the island as "surrounded by the districts from which the negroes always come." Although low, marshy, and sandy, Tangier offered an adequate anchorage for big ships and fresh water from newly dug wells. On the southern end of the island, where sea breezes kept the mosquitoes at bay, the British built Fort Albion, bristling with cannon and featuring a hospital, church, and barracks for troops and cabins for refugees. They also laid out large gardens and grazed livestock on the broad meadows. Owing to the might of the British squadron, the Virginians could do nothing to oust the dangerous new base in their midst. "However deplorable, . . . we have nothing to do but acquiesce," lamented Governor Barbour.[7]

Unable to resist, the islanders made the best of the occupation by

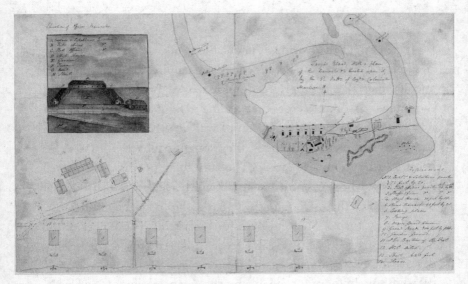

Tangier Island, with a plan of the Barracks, &c erected upon it by the 3d. Battalion of Regular & Colonial Marines, *1814. From the papers of Vice Admiral Sir Alexander F. I. Cochrane. (Courtesy of the National Library of Scotland, Edinburgh)*

Colonial Marines Drilling at Tangier Island in 1814, *a modern painting of Gerry Embleton originally published in Ralph E. Eshelman and Burton K. Kummerow,* In Full Glory Reflected: Discovering the War of 1812 in the Chesapeake *(Baltimore: Maryland Historical Society Press, 2012). (Courtesy of Gerry Embleton, Ralph Eshelman, and Burton Kummerow)*

supplying their guests with fish, oysters, wood, and cattle. In return, the British paid generously and promised to protect the local property, which was not much, for Cockburn described the inhabitants as "very poor and living in much wretchedness." The local Methodist preacher described "his acquaintance with the admiral and high officers of the ships" as "intimate and pleasant." On the Eastern Shore, Virginia's militia officers distrusted visitors from Tangier as smugglers and spies for the British. One officer complained that "very little patriotism or love of Country can be calculated upon or expected from the inhabitants."[8]

But the British also kept a close eye on the islanders, registering their boats and compelling them to obtain passports before visiting the Eastern Shore. Cockburn's paternalism could dissolve into rage when he suspected the islanders of harboring a deserter or helping spies from Virginia. In July 1814 he had a subordinate "inform the Inhabitants of the Islands that if I hear of another Instance of any Canoe or persons belonging to the Main[land] fishing in Company with them or being near the Islands without its being immediately reported, I shall direct everything on the Islands to be destroyed & the Inhabitants sent as Prisoners to Bermuda." Within his velvet glove, Cockburn kept an iron fist.[9]

Colonial Marines

The British government wanted to enlist the male runaways into one of the black army regiments for the West Indies, but its recruiting officer, Lieutenant Colonel Thomas Brown, did not reach Tangier Island until July. By then it was too late, for Cockburn had already organized the runaways as a special unit of Colonial Marines under the command of a white drill sergeant, William Hammond, who received a temporary officer's rank of ensign. As marines (rather than soldiers), the recruits fell under naval command, which Cockburn preferred for he meant to control their operations. The runaways

also wanted their own unit committed to serving in familiar territory, for they dreaded being ordered away to the West Indies. Despite
Cochrane's support, Brown could entice none of the runaways to
join his army regiment.[10]

Adult male refugees had the choice of enlisting in the Colonial
Marines, entering the Royal Navy, or joining the "work party,"
which built the barracks and fortifications on Tangier. Relatively few
refugees became sailors, and usually at the lowest-paid, least-skilled
rank of "landsmen," neophytes who literally had to learn the ropes.
Some former house slaves entered the paid service of British officers. The British categorized as "supernumeraries" those refugees
who could not, or would not, provide military service. Women, children, the sick, and a few elderly comprised the majority of these, but
some able-bodied men also balked at combat. They received rations
and "slop clothing" (but no wages) in return for some labor on the
ships or in a shore camp. Women worked as laundresses, nurses, and
cooks. Some also accompanied the shore raids to help recruit more
runaways. The British tended quickly to move the other supernumeraries on to Bermuda or Halifax, Nova Scotia.[11]

Pay, uniforms, food, and alcohol enticed runaways to enlist as
Colonial Marines. The British offered an $8 bounty, plus regu-
lar monthly pay of $6 from which was deducted the cost of the
uniform. For men who had been kept in rags, a snappy uniform
added to the appeal of enlisting. Cockburn reported that "*all*,
without exception of those who come off to us have only the
few dirty Rags of covering in which they escape." A prisoner on
HMS *Dragon* recognized a runaway on board and recalled "that
the British [did] give Jim a Red Coat, with which he was much
pleased." Cochrane also noted that, when deployed on shore raids,
the smartly dressed Colonial Marines acted "as an inducement to
others to come off." The daily military ration of meat and wheat
bread also improved on the slave diet, which relied on corn meal.
In addition, the recruits received a daily ration of rum, in contrast

to slaves, who usually got alcohol only during a few days of harvest and the Christmas holiday.[12]

In August 1814 the British raided the St. Mary's County farm of Jesse Edwards, taking away his cattle, a cart, and a nineteen-year-old slave named Phil. When Edwards protested, a British captain cursed him as "a damned old democratical rascal and that he should neither have boy or cattle again." The next day, the persistent Edwards visited the British camp at Benedict, where a soldier announced, "Well old man you have lost your Boy, you will never get him again, he has this day enlisted in the King's service; he is as free as you are." Edwards then found Phil "very drunk laying across a Soldier, in soldier's dress, so drunk that he did not know his master." Playing his best card, Edwards persuaded Phil's enslaved mother to appeal to General Robert Ross to release her boy to return to her in slavery. The general demurred and then told Edwards, "Sir, you need not be disturbed at the freedom of this Boy only, for in a few days they will all be free."[13]

The British also offered recruits the chance to fight and plunder their masters. When Harry Butler enlisted, an officer "ask'd the said Negro man if he would Kill his Master. . . . The Negro man Answered yes." Lieutenant Scott remembered a "pugnacious" runaway from Norfolk who sought "to wipe off old scores with his master." Some vengeful runaways became instant marines. In July 1814, Samuel Turner noticed "Jim armed with a Cutlass" after "having seen him but a few Hours before in the employment of his Mistress on the Farm." In Richmond County in December 1814, under a flag of truce, Dr. Horace Welford visited the Colonial Marines. He recognized two who "asked some questions after their mistress and said they should be very glad to see her but as to their master, they wished not to see him as they were then as free as he was or words to that effect."[14]

To avoid alienating the black recruits, the British also practiced restraint in punishing them for misdeeds. A captain caught some new Colonial Marines asleep while on guard duty: an offense that military justice punished with the whip. Cockburn, however, wisely worried that flogging would offend the blacks as a violation of their promised freedom, so he advised the captain to "begin by trying the Effects of the milder Punishments of turning their Jackets [inside out] & stopping their Grog."[15]

Although barred from acting as commissioned officers, blacks did serve as corporals and sergeants. Given the paucity of white officers for the Colonial Marines, the black corporals and sergeants exercised more authority than did their white counterparts in other battalions. As a consequence, their former masters mistook the corporals and sergeants for officers. One Marylander recalled a talented runaway named Frisby: "A slave of so useful abilities was not likely to want employment under his new masters and . . . he was known & reported to have been an officer among their troops." On July 19, 1814, another witness saw Frisby "acting as an officer with the said Troops and assisted in setting fire to the Court House and Jail" during the raid on Prince Frederick Town in Calvert County. Although only a corporal, Frisby acted with the authority of an officer in the eyes of Americans, who unwittingly cast a damning light on slavery for suppressing talented people who found greater opportunities by joining the British.[16]

Possessing his own racial prejudices, Cockburn initially doubted that former slaves would amount to much as marines: "Blacky hereabouts is naturally neither very valorous nor very active." On April 13 he rather dismissively reported, "They pretend to be very bold and very ready to join us in any expedition against their old Masters." A month later, however, Cockburn began to sing a different tune as he noticed how well the new recruits responded to their training on Tangier. They were "getting on astonishingly and are really very fine Fellows. . . . They have induced me to alter the bad opinion I had of the whole of their Race & I now really believe these we are training, will neither shew want of Zeal or Courage when employed by us in attacking *their old Masters*." With glee, he noted that the black troops excited "the most general & undisguised alarm" among the Virginians: "they expect Blacky will have no mercy on them and they know that he understands bush fighting and the *locality* of the *Woods* as well as themselves, and can perhaps play at hide & seek in them even better."[17]

Combat

In early 1814 the Virginians made escape more difficult by locking up their boats at night. On May 10, 1814, Cockburn reported to Cochrane, "Great pains are taken along the Shores of the Chesapeake to prevent the escape of the Negroes, by securing all the Boats & Canoes and placing strong guards over them and on the different Points along the Shore, in spite however of all this we are continually getting a few, but not the Quantities you would do were you once fairly landed on the Main." Cockburn responded by increasing British shore raids to drive away the guards and liberate slaves directly from their farms and plantations. In adopting this riskier strategy, the British felt emboldened by the reinforcement offered by the black recruits.[18]

On May 29, 1814, Cockburn first sent the Colonial Marines into combat, attacking a militia battery at the mouth of Pungoteague Creek in Accomack County, near Tangier Island. While British barge crews fired small cannon and rockets from the front, about 130 men, including 30 Colonial Marines, landed and charged the rear of the battery. The commander of the raid, Captain Charles B. H. Ross, reported that the marines "dashed thro' the woods with three hearty cheers and drove everything before them," routing the militiamen, who fled deeper into the forest. The raiders pursued for three-quarters of a mile, nearly falling into an ambush set by the Virginians. A militiaman spoiled the surprise by firing prematurely in anger upon spotting an advancing black trooper. Michael Harding fell, the first Colonial Marine to die in battle, but his sacrifice saved many others, as the British hastily withdrew from the trap and retreated to their barges, hauling away a captured cannon as a trophy. In addition to Harding's death, the marines suffered one wounded: Kennedy Beaton (or Canada Baton), Great Jenny's son who had escaped from Corotoman Plantation just five weeks before this skirmish. Praising the black marines, Captain Ross concluded, "Their Conduct was marked by great Spirit and Vivacity and perfect obedience."[19]

During the next month, the British repeatedly tested the Colonial Marines in combat. On June 1, 1814, they assisted Captain Robert Barrie's attack on American gunboats in Maryland's Patuxent River. Barrie reported, "I was highly pleased with the conduct of the Colonial Marines, under Ensign Hammond, every Individual of which Evinced the greatest eagerness, to come to Action with their former masters." In mid-June, they helped raids along the shores of the Patuxent, burning tobacco barns and liberating slaves. According to Barrie, the marines "conducted themselves with the utmost Order, Forbearance, and Regularity." On June 25 they captured a militia battery and burned the barracks at Chesconessex in Accomack County. Cockburn praised "how uncommonly and unexpectedly well the Blacks have behaved in the several Engagements . . . & though one of them was shot & died instantly in the front of the others at Pungoteake it did not daunt or check the others in the least, but on the contrary animated them to seek revenge."[20]

Cockburn especially admired Sergeant Johnson. Eager to retrieve his family, Johnson persuaded Cockburn to send him back to Westmoreland County as an agent to promote escapes. Returning to his master on June 1, Johnson told the usual cover story that he had been "badly treated" by the British. The county militia commander, Richard E. Parker, remarked, "His tale was credited, but hearing of it myself on Friday, I had him arrested and examined on Oath." Johnson proved "so plausible and artful" that Parker released him to his master, who "promised to keep him under guard." On Sunday, June 5, however, an elderly, free black woman revealed to Parker that Johnson "planned to return to the enemy with many others by meeting up with the Barges to be in Yeocomico that night." Parker called out the militia, posting them along the Potomac at Yeocomico, and he had Johnson arrested. After "a very long and minute investigation," which probably involved flogging, Johnson confessed that "he was sent to spirit away as many slaves as possible, who were to be taken off in their barges."[21]

When Johnson failed to show at the rendezvous, Cockburn anxiously wondered what had become of his favorite. On June 8 the admiral hung on to a slim hope that a boatload of runaways recently seen in the distance would "prove to be my Friend Johnson with his Family for I shall be very sorry if we do not get him again." Johnson must have been an impressive man, for Cockburn called no other sergeant, of whatever color, "my Friend." But Johnson never did come back.[22]

Despite the loss of Sergeant Johnson, the Colonial Marines continued to grow in numbers, the esteem of their officers, and the dread of Virginians. The Colonial Marines served as light infantry skirmishers who led the advance and guarded the flanks of British operations in the woods, giving the British a tactical edge in their shore operations. Lieutenant James Scott recalled, "The enemy, who prided himself on his skill in bush-fighting, was completely foiled. . . . In all our excursions, flanking parties were thrown into the woods, which disconcerted their ambushing schemes and rendered their rifles of little avail." By July 17 the number of Colonial Marines had grown to 120, and Cockburn praised them as "the best skirmishers possible for the thick Woods of this Country." Captain Robert Rowley agreed: "Our skirmishers are fine light troops. 'Tis astonishing with what rapidity & precision they advance."[23]

Pleased by their performance, the British admirals sought more

Colonial Marines, expanding their structure to three companies on July 22. Crediting Hammond for training the new marines so well, Cockburn and Cochrane secured his promotion to lieutenant: a rare step for a former enlisted man in the class-conscious British forces. By late September the unit had grown to 300 men, which led to a further reorganization. In combination with 200 white marines, they formed the Third Battalion of Royal and Colonial Marines. Praising their "steadiness and bravery," Cochrane urged the government to reward each man with a supplemental bonus of $8. Crediting "their hatred to the citizens of the United States," Cochrane considered the blacks the most effective and intimidating troops for fighting the Americans.[24]

At first, the American newspapers had mocked the black marines as cowardly blunderers, but militia officers soon sounded a tale of growing alarm. On August 5, 1814, Brigadier General John P. Hungerford reported grim news from Westmoreland County, Virginia:

> Our negroes are flocking to the enemy from all quarters, which they convert into troops, vindictive and rapacious—with a most minute knowledge of every bye path. They leave us as spies upon our posts and our strength, and they return upon us as guides and soldiers and incendiaries. It was by the aid of these guides that ambushes were formed every where in the woods. . . . From this cause alone the enemy have a great advantage over us in a country where the passes and by-ways through our innumerable necks and swamps are so little known to but very few of our officers and men, and through which [the enemy] can penetrate and be conducted with so much ease by these refugee blacks.

While their masters were sleeping, the slaves had mastered the nocturnal landscape of forests and swamps: an expertise that enabled the British to outfight Virginians on what they had once considered their own terrain.[25]

Pacification

During July and August, Cockburn escalated his shore raids, targeting both shores of the Potomac and Patuxent Rivers. In twenty-five days he mounted nine major raids against Westmoreland and Northumberland Counties on Virginia's Northern Neck or the nearby southern Maryland counties of St. Mary's and Calvert. A British officer vividly recalled the nightly barge raids: "Numbers of boats filled with armed men gliding in silence over the smooth water, arms glittering in the moonshine, oars just breaking the stillness of night, the dark shade of the woods we are pushing for, combining with expectation of danger to affect the mind." After two or three miles of open water, the barges struck the shore and the marines jumped into the waves to wade ashore, often under fire.[26]

Exploiting the superior mobility provided by naval supremacy, Cockburn sought to weary the militia, destroy or seize valuable resources, and deplete the republic's treasury. And he meant to enrich his naval officers with plundered tobacco, which fetched a high price on the European market. The admiral also wanted to flush out and destroy a flotilla of American gunboats, commanded by Joshua Barney, which had taken shelter up the Patuxent River. In addition, Cockburn sought more runaways, observing that "the Black Population inclined to join us is more numerous on the Shores of the Potowmac than any where else within the Chesapeake."[27]

Attentive to the political context of war, Cockburn meant to discredit the Madison administration as incompetent to defend even the national capital. The admiral boasted that the Chesapeake region remained in such a "horrible State" for defense that "it only requires a little firm & Steady Conduct to have it completely at our Mercy." If the Americans failed to bolster the Chesapeake's flimsy defenses, Cockburn planned to burst through them to seize Washington, D.C., and Baltimore. To attack either city, however, he needed reinforcements from Europe. While waiting for their arrival, he kept his

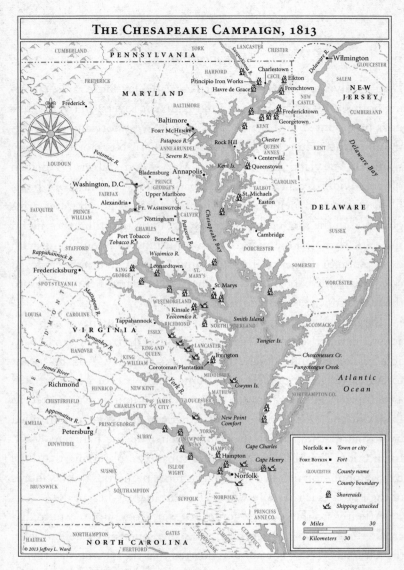

THE CHESAPEAKE CAMPAIGN, 1813

The Chesapeake Campaign, 1813. Map by Jeffrey L. Ward after an original by Robert Pratt, published in Ralph Eshelman and Burton K. Kummerow, In Full Glory Reflected: Discovering the War of 1812 in the Chesapeake (Baltimore: Maryland Historical Society Press, 2012). Note the broad distribution of raids throughout Chesapeake Bay and the priority given to attacks on American shipping by the British during their first campaign.

THE CHESAPEAKE CAMPAIGN, 1814

The Chesapeake Campaign, 1814. Map by Jeffrey L. Ward after an original map by Robert Pratt, published in Ralph Eshelman and Burton K. Kummerow, In Full Glory Reflected: Discovering the War of 1812 in the Chesapeake (Baltimore: Maryland Historical Society Press, 2012). Note the greater number of shore raids and their concentration along the Potomac and Patuxent Rivers in northern Virginia and southern Maryland, in comparison to the previous year. This new pattern reflected the greater aggressiveness of the British and the priority given to preparations for an attack on Washington, D.C.

men busy and the enemy guessing by mixing and matching raids on the Potomac and Patuxent shores. After one raid, he announced, "I shall again move elsewhere, so as to distract Jonathan, . . . and yet not allow him to suspect that a serious & permanent Landing is intended any Where."[28]

Cockburn sought to neutralize southern Maryland, converting its people and resources into British assets. He promised to protect civilians who wisely submitted but to plunder those who stubbornly resisted. To qualify for protection, the locals had to stay in their homes rather than rally as a militia to attack the raiders. The inhabitants also had to show trust in his protection, by keeping nearby their livestock, goods, and slaves. The British bought provisions and animals at the Baltimore market rate, but the owners had no choice but to sell to the raiders. Admiral Edward Codrington explained that his superior, Cockburn, meant "to do fair justice and to give due encouragement to such inhabitants as remain on their property & have shewn no disposition to act hostile towards us." To prove that point, the British officers whipped a few sailors caught pillaging the properties of submissive civilians, who were compensated in money and invitations to watch the floggings. Some of the worst offenders were the camp women who lodged in the transport ships. In August 1814, Codrington ordered, "None of the women are to be permitted to leave their ships."[29]

All bets were off, however, when inhabitants shot at the raiders or fled and hid away their animals, slaves, and valuables. Captain Rowley noted, "If they run away & stock driven off—then we hunt for [that] stock, drive it down to the boats & take it off as plunder & fire their houses." Runaways often led the British to the hiding places of cattle and militiamen. On July 11, Cockburn reported, "The other day two Heroes on Horseback fired at one of my Lieut[enant]s when on Shore and then rode off as hard as they could." A black informant identified the suspects and their homes, which lay about three miles inland. That night, a runaway guided Lieutenant James

Scott's raiding party, which surprised and captured the men and took
away their livestock. After smashing the furniture, Scott desisted
from burning the house only because of plaintive appeals from "the
distressed mother and sister for mercy." Cockburn predicted that
this punitive raid would "induce Jonathan to be more guarded in his
behavior towards us & to treat us in future with due Respect."[30]

To intimidate resistance, the British also took away militiamen
for imprisonment in distant and frosty Nova Scotia. When the raiders seized men at night from beds in their homes, American officials
protested that the rules of civilized warfare exempted militiamen
from capture when not on active duty. The officials also complained
that the raiders seized some men too old for militia service, including one ninety-five-year-old Virginian. Codrington retorted that
because President Madison had begun the war and sent troops to
ravage Canada, "terror & suffering" had to "be brought home to
the doors of his own fellow citizens" as "the one way to shorten this
Yankee war."[31]

The raiders found plenty of cooperation in southern Maryland,
where antiwar Federalists prevailed. They despised the Republicans
for declaring war and sending the regular troops away to invade
Canada, leaving them defenseless. In June the Madison administration briefly posted a new regiment of regulars to defend the mouth
of the Patuxent, but they proved worse than useless, for the indolent
officers allowed their raw recruits to roam, "committing depredations, on the person & property of the Inhabitants," in the words of
Joshua Barney. Quickly withdrawn, the regulars left the local defense
to the militiamen, who balked at risking their lives in a lost cause.
After more than a year of frequent alarms and prolonged exposure
to harsh weather, the militiamen were fed up. In St. Mary's County,
their commander found "a thinly scattered population dispirited by
a destruction of their property, worn out by fatigue & militia duty."
Given the apparent folly of resisting the raids, most men felt that
discretion would best protect their property.[32]

Preferring British to American protection, many Maryland farmers barred militiamen from their premises. The owners reasoned that the militia would flee in a panic once they had attracted British raiders, who would then punish the farmers by looting and burning their premises. The compromised planters included Colonel Michael Taney, a Federalist who commanded the Calvert County militia. By covertly selling his cattle to the British and by immobilizing his militia, Taney secured his mansion and plantation from raids. Despite this passivity, Maryland's antiwar governor, Levin Winder, kept his fellow Federalists in charge of the militia in the southern counties.[33]

If the militiamen bothered to turn out, they usually stayed at a safe distance from the raiders. Barney described the militia as "here and there, but never where the enemy was." After several forays deep into southern Maryland, the British Captain Joseph Nourse reported, "I have never, at any time when landed, seen more than one or two armed people of the Militia." Cockburn exulted that the passive militia left "the whole of the fine Country in this Neighbourhood completely at our disposal and Mercy." After just 120 British raiders marched unopposed seven miles inland and back, Barney declared, "The people are all frightened out of their senses, running about the country like so many mad people." In mid-August, a planter complained that the British felt so secure that after marching through St. Mary's County, the officers "amused themselves at nine pins for an hour or two" before returning to their ships."[34]

Disgusted by the local passivity, Barney charged the Federalists with sabotage and treason. He insisted that more inhabitants gathered to loot a beached American gunboat than to repel the British raiders. Rather than defend his flotilla, some locals fed information and supplies to the British and sabotaged a cannon at Benedict by spiking it. Barney dared not send an officer to scout the lower reaches of the river "for he would be *betrayed* by our internal foes, such is my situation." He arrested one militia officer as an avid Federalist and suspected spy, but the secretary of the navy ordered the man's release, deeming it virtually impossible to prove treason in a civil court.[35]

The local Federalists blamed Barney for provoking the British raids, and they saw no reason to risk their lives and farms to defend his gunboats. After losing property to a British raid, Thomas B. King denounced Barney as driven by Republican politics rather than military duty when he shifted his gunboats into the Patuxent: "as he knew Calvert, St. Mary's, Charles, and Prince George's Count[ies] were all Federalist, he thought it would be the means of making them all advocates of old Jim Madison, but ... I think when I tell you the mischief the British have done it will be enough to make you and every man abuse Jim Madison and old Barney in Hell." King ascribed every runaway, stolen cow, and burned barn to Barney's attempt to force the southern Marylanders to fight the British.[36]

But submission to the British often failed to buy the promised protection, for Cockburn's discrimination between the passive and the resistant broke down in practice. On July 30 at Chaptico in St. Mary's County, the inhabitants did not resist, and Cockburn later boasted that he had protected their property. One of his captains reported, "The men all fled but the Ladies remained to see the wonderful Admiral Cockburn and the British folks." If so, they saw Cockburn's men ransack the village, breaking windows and wrenching off doors to steal their metal hinges. They even trashed the Episcopal church, shattering the windows, breaking the pipe organ and communion table, and ransacking the tombs in search of buried jewelry. One plundered tomb belonged to the family of Francis Scott Key, who would soon write the defiant "Star-Spangled Banner."[37]

Driven to free and recruit as many runaways as possible, the raiders also took slaves away from any owner, no matter how submissive. John Rousby Plater surrendered his Sotterley Plantation to British power and obtained Cockburn's pledge of protection, but forty-eight of the colonel's slaves still left with the raiders. Colonel Taney's tacit cooperation saved his buildings but not his slaves, whom the British welcomed as runaways. Barns and warehouses filled with tobacco also attracted indiscriminate looting because that commodity promised such rich profits to the naval officers.[38]

Many officers tolerated rampant plundering because they felt contempt for submissive Americans as dishonorable money-grubbers. One naval officer recalled a cooperative farmer on the Potomac: "He had two daughters, rather homely, and as uncouth as himself. They . . . seemed to know and care very little about what was going on; offered us a glass of peach brandy, and hoped the Britishers would not carry off their negroes, which appeared to be their only apprehension." Lieutenant Scott disdained another farmer who offered to prostitute his comely daughters to the British officers if they would not take his cattle. In fact, the Britons came to buy them, to the man's delight: "The farmer fairly gloated over his dollars as he counted them by tens into his bag, and offered, with the most cringing servility, to supply us with whatever quantity of cattle we might want."[39]

British officers also promoted looting as an antidote to desertion. After one raid, a Marylander noted, "Their Men did not desert here nor will they so long as they can plunder unmolested. Plunder secures their fidelity." After robbing Americans, the British sailors and marines became less inclined to join them. Previously rampant, British desertion dwindled during the profitable summer raids of 1814.[40]

Despite their broken promises, the British pacified southern Maryland as far north as the village of Benedict on the Patuxent. If the locals could not abide British domination, they fled with their livestock, slaves, and furniture. A Baltimore newspaper lamented that a tract fifty miles long by twenty wide had been "conquered" with "many families moving up north, literally choking the roads with hungry fugitives of all colours and ages." In August, Cockburn boasted that the inhabitants had "learnt that it is wiser for them to submit entirely to our Mercy than to attempt to oppose us in Arms. They very readily complied with whatever Directions I gave for the line of Conduct they were to adopt, and the Supplies they were to furnish to our Forces." He felt amused when people begged for his permission to leave home to visit a relative or deliver a few geese to another farm: "In short, it is quite ridiculous the perfect Dominion we have from the Entrance of this River to Benedict."[41]

Northern Neck

Cockburn alternated raids on southern Maryland with attacks on the Northern Neck of Virginia, primarily the counties of Westmoreland and Northumberland, which stretched for about 100 miles along the lower Potomac River. Prosperous in the colonial era, the Northern Neck had stagnated after the revolution as decades of cropping and erosion had depleted the fertility of the soil. Relatively poor and very rural, the region was a low priority for defense compared to the more populous and prosperous cities of Norfolk, Richmond, and Washington, D.C. A Northern Neck writer denounced the federal and state governments' "false principle of economy and a cruel indifference" for abandoning the Northern Neck to "an exasperated foe and rebellious slaves." Owing to "that fallacious and miserable argument which has caused all our evils—the calculating [of] dollars and cents," both governments treated the region as too vulnerable to defend and too poor to bother with.[42]

The Northern Neck enticed the British as an especially vulnerable target with many slaves for liberation. The dispersed militia struggled to assemble before the mobile raiders could strike and withdraw to their ships. Westmoreland County had only 580 militiamen, and many were sick with the summer malaria. The militia grew weaker still as more farmers gave up and fled, removing their livestock and slaves. Colonel Richard E. Parker reported, "In many places corn fields are deserted and turned out, and every appearance of insecurity and wretchedness exhibited." While guarding the many waterways to resist the British, the hard-pressed militiamen also had to watch a restive local majority of slaves.[43]

As in southern Maryland, the British promised to protect the passive and threatened to punish resistance. A Northern Neck man recognized "that they intended to lay the country waste—that *those who remained at home*, would be treated well and their property respected, but all who fled, or *joined the militia*, should become the peculiar objects of their vengeance." Despite this threat, the Northern Neck Federalists as well as Republicans united against the raiders, unlike the Marylanders on the other side of the Potomac. In response, the raiders destroyed nearly all of the houses on their marches into the Northern Neck. During 1814, Westmoreland and Northumberland suffered far more raids, destruction, and lost slaves than the rest of Virginia's Tidewater counties combined.[44]

On July 20, about 1,000 British marines and armed sailors landed to seize and ransack the village at Nomini Ferry. "Everything in this neighbourhood was . . . destroyed or brought off, and after Visiting the Country in several other Directions, covering the Escape of the Negroes who were anxious to join us, we quitted the River at dark and returned to the Ships carrying with us 135 Refugee Negroes," Cockburn reported.[45]

At dawn on August 3, five hundred raiders landed at the mouth of Yeocomico River, where the militia commander, Captain William Henderson, had only one cannon and forty men. A British captain reported, "The boats grounded, the troops were out in an instant, though up to their hips in the water and [exposed to] galling fire, away we dashed." The militia "fled in all directions," and the British captured another prize cannon. Pushing inland, the victors plundered and burned fifteen homes along the six-mile route to Henderson's home and store, which they also looted and torched. A nearby resident, Walter Jones, reported that the raiders "were joined by far the greater number of negroes, who were near their path."[46]

During the afternoon, the British barges ascended the river to the village of Kinsale, where the raiders found a large militia force occupying a ridge. Colonial Marines led the British charge that took

the ridge, killing eight militiamen and scattering the rest. After plundering and burning the village and three old schooners, the raiders
withdrew with their plunder loaded on five other captured vessels.
"The Buccaneers spared nothing at Kinsale but the hovel of a poor
old negro woman," complained one militia officer.[47]

By mid-August the British had devastated the Northern Neck. A
resident lamented, "We are all here in the utmost confusion; houses
and farms deserted, women and children living in tents in the woods.
Every one has either deserted his neighborhood of the water or is
in the militia." General Hungerford complained, "Unless the Government will give this quarter more effectual aid, the ruffian system
of warfare carried on by the enemy . . . will light up one universal
conflagration throughout these counties."[48]

Poison

By dominating southern Maryland and ravaging the Northern
Neck, the British bred desperation among their foes. Angered by
the destruction and frustrated by their weakness, some Americans
concluded that the British deserved destruction by any means. At
Benedict on June 17 and Nomini Ferry on July 20, the raiders found
poisoned liquors left behind by retreating militiamen. At Benedict,
the plot appalled a leading man, Clement Dorsey, who warned the
British commander that at least one, and up to four, casks of whiskey
had been tainted. Dorsey sought to prevent the British from burning the village in retaliation, but the naval officers had already staved
the whiskey casks to keep their men from getting drunk. Thereafter, a British officer recalled, when his men found food or drink left
behind, "we used to force the natives to eat a part first, that, in the
event of its being poisoned, they might die with the Britishers."[49]

A month later at Nomini Ferry, after routing the local militia,
the British found glasses and a liquor bottle left on the porch of a
house. Recalling the Benedict episode, Lieutenant Scott grew sus-

picious when he noticed that the glasses had not been used and that the bottle was full. A runaway slave confirmed that a militiaman had poisoned the alcohol, so the British burned the house and put up a nearby placard declaring their reason. Retreating to their barges, the British burned every house en route. Years later Scott claimed that a naval surgeon had examined the bottle and found "a very large quantity of arsenic," but in 1814 Cockburn regretted that the suspected bottle had been smashed before it could be tested.[50]

Probably the act of a rogue individual, the poisoning embarrassed the militia Commanders Hungerford and Parker, who convened an investigation by a panel of their officers, who cleared their superiors by denying that the liquor had been tainted. Parker claimed that he had taken a parting drink and had suffered no ill effects. Hungerford's aide, John Taylor Lomax, also derided any reliance on the word of a black man: "That it was very probable that a slave in the moment of his liberation, might wish to excite as angry and vindictive a spirit as possible, in the bosoms of the enemies to his former masters." More inclined to believe a slave than a Virginian, Cockburn dismissed the investigation's report with contempt.[51]

The poisoning episodes compounded the British disdain for their foes as devious and dishonorable. The naval officers vowed to take a fuller revenge in their next and biggest attack: on the national capital of the despised republic. Captain Nourse longed "to burn Washington, and I hope soon to put the first torch to it myself." With southern Maryland pacified and the Northern Neck devastated, the route to Washington lay open.[52]

Fire

During the spring, Cochrane had expected reinforcement by 20,000 veteran troops from Europe, but instead he got only 3,700 and not until mid-August. The modest numbers argued for restraint as did the caution of the newly arrived army general, Robert Ross, who cited his orders from Earl Bathurst to avoid risky battles and heavy casualties from "extended operations at a distance from the coast." As a newcomer, Ross also lacked the burning contempt for Americans that Cockburn and Cochrane had developed during their operations in the Chesapeake.[53]

Cockburn had long wanted to attack the American capital. Lieutenant Scott recalled that the admiral "always fixed an eye of peculiar interest upon Washington," for "every measure he adopted was more or less remotely connected, conceived, and carried into execution, as affording preliminary steps" to capturing the capital. By pacifying the Patuxent Valley, Cockburn had eliminated resistance and ensured fodder and provisions along his preferred route of attack. He promised that the invaders could advance to the head of that river "without meeting with the slightest opposition or requiring any Sacrifice from us whatever." By also ravaging the Potomac Valley, the admiral had diverted American attention away from the Patuxent. In mid-August he persuaded Cochrane and Ross to adopt his aggressive plan to attack the republic's capital.[54]

On August 19–20 the British troops landed without resistance at Benedict, midway up the Patuxent. The barges and tenders of the fleet then ascended the river in parallel with the troops marching north along the west bank. A midshipman later recalled, "Never, in the whole course of my life, have I since witnessed a more imposing spectacle than the numerous tenders, launches, barges, and cutters of the fleet presented, with their colours gaily streaming, whilst the sun glistened on their various fancy sails and the uniforms of the Royal Marines." Unable to resist, Joshua Barney blew up his gunboats just before the British advance could capture them on August 22. A day later Cochrane remained on the river with the fleet and most of the white marines, while Ross marched inland with his soldiers, the Colonial Marines, and armed sailors led by Cockburn. There was no way that he would miss the attack or trust that Ross could remain resolute without a steady stream of aggressive advice.[55]

Ill prepared for the Chesapeake in summer, the troops endured a miserably hot and dusty march along sandy roads. One officer had never "suffered more severely from heat and fatigue." Dozens collapsed from heat prostration beside the road. Ross's chief aide, Captain Falls, became "deranged" by heat stroke. Cochrane concluded, "The Worst Enemy we have to contend with is the climate."[56]

On August 24 the Britons faced their first resistance at Bladensburg, just east of Washington. To block their advance Brigadier General William H. Winder, posted his troops on the high ground along the western bank of the Anacostia River. A professional politician but an amateur soldier, Winder's only previous military experience involved getting captured in Canada, but he was the nephew of Maryland's Federalist governor, which Madison hoped might assure a little more cooperation from the state militia. Although Winder had superior numbers, 7,000 men versus the 4,500 Britons, the American force consisted primarily of raw militia who had never seen combat. Only Barney's 400 armed seamen could be relied on to fight. By contrast, the well-trained Britons had been hardened by years of victories under Lord Wellington in Spain.[57]

Under heavy fire, the British pushed across a bridge over the river and through the American lines on the other side. The militiamen panicked, throwing down their guns to flee. One witness recalled that "the militia ran like sheep chased by dogs." Only Barney's flotilla men fought on until overwhelmed. A British army officer reported that the American defeat thrilled the nearby slaves: "On ascending a rise of the turnpike-road, from which we had just driven the enemy, we were greeted by a group of negroes, to whom our victory gave freedom. They were of course, rejoiced beyond measure at the happy change in their circumstances, and manifested their joy, in a thousand extravagant ways. Their description of the swagger and blustering of the Americans, previous to the action was highly amusing."[58]

Slavery had contributed to the American defeat, for just before the battle began, the militia became spooked by an insistent rumor that a slave revolt had erupted in the District of Columbia and the adjoining counties in Maryland. General Walter Smith of the militia recalled "that *each man more feared the enemy he had left behind, in the shape of a slave in his own house or plantation, than he did anything else.*" So they fled and dispersed to protect their homes. In fact, there was no such plot, but the imagined internal enemy had won the battle.[59]

Chaos reigned in Washington, where many of the militiamen had fled. A resident, Margaret Bayard Smith, pitied "our poor broken militia. . . . Every hour the poor wearied and terrified creatures are passing by the door. . . . Our men look pale and feeble but more with affright than fatigue,—they had thrown away their muskets and blankets." The president and his cabinet packed up their records and fled into the Maryland and Virginia countryside. Exploiting the confusion, local looters spread through the city before the British troops arrived. Madison's body servant recalled, "A rabble, taking advantage of the confusion, ran all over the White House, and stole lots of silver and whatever they could lay their hands on."[60]

At dusk the British troops marched into the city. Aside from a few snipers, the invaders faced no resistance, merely suffering the loss of one horse shot out from under Ross. Later in life, Michael Shiner recalled his boyhood as a slave in the capital; nothing made a more vivid impression than the spectacle of the entering Britons: "they looked like flames of fier all red coats and the stocks of the[i]r guns pain[t]ed with red ver Milon and the iron work shin[e]d like a spanish dollar." Then nine years old, Shiner started to run but "ole Mrs. Reid caught hold of" him and demanded, "Wher are you runig to you niger you[?] What do you recon the Br[i]tish Wants With such a niger as you[?]" Feeling more terrified than liberated, Shiner hid from the British instead of joining them.[61]

The departing American officers had set fire to the navy yard and its ships, which lit up the sky with an immense red fireball. A

British colonel recalled, "I think this was one of the finest, and at the same time, the most awful sights I ever witnessed—the Columns of fire issuing from the houses, and Dock Yard, the explosions of [gunpowder] Magazines at intervals, the sky illuminated from the blazes, the Troops all under Arms." Breaking into the White House, and scattering the looters, the delighted British officers devoured the meal left behind by the fleeing Madisons. Later that night, Cockburn ordered the mansion torched by fifty sailors and Colonial Marines, who broke the windows with long poles and hurled in incendiary devices, "so that an instantaneous conflagration took place and the whole building was wrapt in flames and smoke."[62]

Giddy with triumph, Cockburn next led his burning party to the printing office of Joseph Gales, who edited and published the *National Intelligencer*, the official newspaper of the Madison administration. As a British immigrant to the United States, Gales offended Cockburn as a traitor, which the editor had compounded with blistering denunciations of the admiral's raids. "I am really afraid my friend Josey will be affronted with me, if after burning Jemmy's palace, I do not pay him the same compliment,—so my lads, take your axes, pull down the house, and burn the papers in the street," Cockburn ordered.[63]

Rather than torch the entire city, the British selectively burned buildings with military or political import. Applying Cockburn's doctrine of discrimination, Ross assured civilians that their homes remained safe so long as they stayed peaceably in them. Only a couple of private homes burned as punishment for hosting snipers. In addition to the White House and the *National Intelligencer* shop, the British torched the Capitol, the War Office, the Treasury, and three rope walks rich in naval stores. Ross ordered the public flogging of a few soldiers who did abuse civilians, and the British carefully paid for their provisions.[64]

Cockburn would never have burned the entire city, for he longed for applause from the ladies of Washington. The admiral appealed to a young lady, "Were you not prepared to see a savage, a ferocious creature, such as Josey represented me? But you see I am quite harmless, don't be afraid, I will take better care of you than Jemmy did!" Cockburn sought to prove that the British were true gentlemen and to shame American men as cowards. He eagerly solicited validation from those women, who complimented the British on their gallantry and mercy. "He, and all his officers and soldiers were perfectly polite to the citizens," Margaret Bayard Smith conceded. Lieutenant Scott exulted, "The Admiral was surrounded by a host of lovely women, who certainly outshone their countrymen in generalship. . . . The kind affable manner in which he calmed their fears, his lively conversation and gentlemanly demeanour, soon won over their better feelings." A gifted ham actor, Cockburn regarded the capture of Washington, D.C., as his finest moment on stage.[65]

On August 25 the British completed their destruction of military stores, a process interrupted by a ferocious windstorm that ripped off the roofs from some houses and drenched the troops with gales of rain. For nearly two hours the sky turned as dark as night, save for when vivid flashes of lightning lit up everything brighter than day. At sunset, after twenty-four destructive hours in the city, the British marched away, covering fifty miles unopposed to reach the Patuxent late on August 26.[66]

Despite American dread, no slave uprising erupted in Washington during the British occupation. According to the 1810 census, the city had 8,208 residents, of whom 1,437 were enslaved. Like Michael Shiner, most hunkered down and stayed put. After the war, residents received compensation for only three runaway slaves. Like their masters, the Washington slaves were not prepared for the whirlwind British visit to their city. On August 26, during the British retreat through Montgomery and Prince George's Counties, rural slaves did throng to the British as liberators. A British officer recalled, "We were joined by numbers of negro slaves, who implored us to take them along with us, offering to serve either as soldiers or sailors, if we would but give them their liberty; but as General Ross persisted in protecting private property of every description, few of them were fortunate enough to obtain their wishes." A newcomer to the Chesapeake campaign, Ross did not share the admirals' zeal to liberate slaves. The general also worried about slowing his retreat lest the Americans rally and counterattack. But some persistent runaways did tag along, making good their escape with the British.[67]

During the British retreat, their only trouble came in passing through Upper Marlboro, near the head of the Patuxent, where a few soldiers straggled behind to loot, and some locals worked up the courage to seize six of them. Informed of this loss, General Ross sent back armed horsemen to arrest a ringleader, Dr. William Beanes, rousted from his sleep at midnight. When the British threatened to burn Upper Marlboro, the other villagers released the captive soldiers. The British kept Beanes, whom they despised as a traitor and backstabber, for he was an immigrant from Scotland who had treated British officers to tea when they had first passed through town.[68]

Meanwhile, another British naval expedition ascended the Potomac under the command of Captain James Gordon. Rather than stand and fight, the American commander blew up Fort Washington (which commanded the river) and fled, opening a safe passage for Gordon to bring his warships up to Alexandria on August 29. Defenseless, the Federalist town fathers surrendered to the British, who exacted a massive ransom, loading twenty-one prize ships with plunder from the warehouses. En route down river, the retreating British dodged cannon fire from the bluffs, escaping with only minimal damage. While the British celebrated another victory, the Republicans blasted the Federalists of Alexandria as craven defeatists.[69]

The British exulted in their triumphant campaign. From the pacified banks of the Patuxent, Captain Robert Rowley noted the "perfect unanimity . . . between Army & Navy. General good humour pervades, and some of the military officers having brought their wives, the battle being ended we have regular Balls, dinner parties, Pick Nicks on shore . . . the bands serenading in the woods." The Britons celebrated their victorious march of fifty miles and back through an enemy country to destroy a gunboat flotilla, defeat a larger army at Bladensburg, and ravage Washington, D.C., which Codrington described as "the capital & pride of the Virginians and all other supporters of the Jefferson & Maddison party and the haters of everything English."[70]

While boasting of their prowess, the British also dwelled on the folly of their foes, who, in the words of Colonel Arthur Brooke, "would tamely allow a handful of British Soldiers to advance thro' the heart of their Country, and burn, & destroy the Capitol of the United States." Above all, the British delighted in striking a blow at American presumption. Bermuda's governor (and Cockburn's brother) cherished the victory "as wounding to the pride as destructive to the resources of the enemy" and likely "to put an end to the unequal & unnecessary contest in which they have so rashly embarked." Addressing Parliament, the ruling Prince Regent praised the operation as "most brilliant" for having given the Americans a rancid taste of the "calamities of a war in which they have been so wantonly involved."[71]

Meanwhile, Americans felt shock, shame, and gloom. Thomas Tudor Tucker, the treasurer of the United States, wrote to his brother St. George Tucker, "I feel myself humbled & degraded. I have no longer a country or a Government that I can speak of with pride." Tucker had hoped that the war would secure "the lasting respect of all Nations. What an Illusion!" Instead of resigning in disgrace, the president made a scapegoat of the secretary of war, John Armstrong, a self-promoting bungler who had slighted Washington's defense. Madison replaced Armstrong with James Monroe, who also remained secretary of state.[72]

After the sack of Washington, many Marylanders despaired of resisting the apparently invincible Britons. Anticipating an attack on

Baltimore, Charles Carroll, one of Maryland's wealthiest men, urged a peaceful surrender, reasoning that "resistance will be fruitless and if made will only cost the lives of some valuable citizens." Governor Levin Winder considered his state capital, Annapolis, indefensible and assured his nephew, General William Winder, that it "wou'd be worse than useless to make an unavailing sacrifice of lives, and by that means bring on the destruction of the city." The Annapolis magistrates met and agreed to surrender if the British appeared in force, and they privately urged Lieutenant H. A. Fay, the commander of the little American garrison, to withdraw for fear that any "firing from the forts would only exasperate the Enemy & cause the distruction of the City." With only forty-two soldiers, ten of them too sick to fight, and the rest "confirmed drunkards," Fay privately agreed with the magistrates. Twice he had ventured at night to one of the forts and surprised the garrison, "by scaling the walls & entering the Fort undiscovered," because the men had passed out from too much liquor. By September in the Chesapeake region, the Americans desperately needed a victory to reverse their downward spiral.[73]

Anthem

After embarking from the Patuxent on August 29, Ross and his troops withdrew to Tangier Island to recuperate and prepare for the next attack. Meanwhile, the navy raided Maryland's Eastern Shore to keep the militia distracted. On August 31 an especially promising young naval officer, Captain Sir Peter Parker, led a daring night raid meant to surprise an encampment of 200 militiamen at Caulk's Field near Chestertown. Although guided by an "intelligent black man" to the camp's location, Parker found the militia awake and prepared. Rendered overly confident by the recent victories, Parker attacked despite having only 124 men. After suffering heavy casualties, including a mortally wounded Parker, the British withdrew to their ships.

First View of the Battle of Patapsco Neck, *1814. In this 1814 engraving, Andrew Duluc represents the British attack on North Point, near Baltimore on September 12. At the top center, indicated by the letter O, Major General Ross dies. At M, to the right, British light infantrymen, who included the Colonial Marines, flush out the American riflemen who shot Ross. The main body of British troops appears at L. (Courtesy of the Maryland Historical Society).*

This surprising militia victory thrilled the Americans and served as a dark omen for the impending British attack on Baltimore.[74]

The British officers hated Baltimore as a Republican hotbed notorious for riots against Federalists and for sending privateers to prey on British commerce. Admiral Codrington assured his wife, "I do not like to contemplate scenes of blood & destruction, but my heart is deeply interested in the coercion of these Baltimore heroes, who are perhaps the most inveterate against us of all the Yankees and I hope they will be chastised even until they excite my pity." This time Cochrane wanted no selective burning, seeking instead the city's total destruction.[75]

On September 10 and 11, led by Cochrane, Cockburn, and Ross, the British ascended the Patapsco River in overwhelming naval force. Their fifty warships included ten massive ships of the line, twenty frigates, five bomb-vessels, and a boat equipped to fire Congreve rockets. But they could land only 4,200 troops to attack the 15,000 defenders. Although primarily militia, the defenders had the shelter of strong earthworks; an able and active commander in General Samuel Smith; and the motivation of fighting to save their homes and shops.[76]

On September 12, Ross landed his troops, including the Colonial Marines, at North Point to probe Baltimore's eastern defenses. When the militia advanced beyond their earthworks, the British drove them back but suffered heavy casualties, including Ross, an inspirational leader popular with his men. His death deflated their morale, for they lacked confidence in his replacement, Colonel Brooke. Still the people of Baltimore expected the worst. John Moore reported, "I was surrounded with crowds clapping their hands together, writhing with agony, and uttering in loud exclamations their despair and grief."[77]

Brooke decided that his men were too few, the defenders too many, and their earthworks too strong, so he halted his advance and called on the navy to push into the harbor and destroy its waterfront defenses, principally Fort McHenry. On the night of September 13–14, Cochrane's ships bombarded the fort with rockets, mortars, and cannon. "The portals of hell appeared to have been thrown open," Moore wrote from the terror-stricken city. But the fort held, suffering surprisingly little damage as most of the enemy shots proved loud but errant. In the morning the admirals dismissed further bombardment as futile, so they withdrew their ships down the river after evacuating Brooke's troops from North Point. The British losses included four Colonial Marines. As they sailed away, the naval officers sought to restore shaken discipline by hanging two white sailors convicted of trying to desert to the enemy.[78]

For another day the city remained on edge as rumors insisted that the British intended a renewed attack. On September 15,

Moore reported, "A most laughable tragi-comedy took place nearly opposite to our door. A black-boy coming up the street with his wagon, the horses took fright & set off at full trot so that the poor fellow . . . could not stop them, until he met the advance of the first brigade opposite Mrs. Glendy's. This threw the [militia] men (who were . . . pretty well charged with whiskey) into the utmost confusion & perhaps mistaking the black with his waggon & horses for British soldiers, as the officer commanding the Brigade called out with all his might, kill him, kill him." In the crowded confusion on the stone bridge, the pushing and shoving troopers "precipitated Horses & men headlong" into the creek, crushing "one poor Pig! who was discovered this morning among epaulets, hats, caps, muskets & bayonets &c., &c., laying on the field of battle!" The "poor negro lad" survived but with a nasty sword wound inflicted by the militia officer. When in a panic, the militiamen associated any black man with the enemy.[79]

Desperate for a victory to wipe away the disgrace of Washington, Americans made the most of their survival at Baltimore. Dr. Philip Barraud exulted, "The Charm is broken, Wellington's veterans can be cut down like ordinary Militia—nay they can be dismayed by them and made to retire before them. The display of this truth is worth Legions to our Country and will add to our means of defence." Americans longed to vindicate their cherished reliance on the militia amateurs.[80]

Patriotism also got a boost from a stirring song written by Francis Scott Key, who had watched the bombardment of Fort McHenry. Although a Federalist lawyer who had opposed the declaration of war, Key wanted to see the British defeated, for they had plundered his family's tomb at Chaptico and arrested his friend Dr. William Beanes. On September 17 a friend published Key's lyrics in a handbill with the suggestion that people sing it to the tune of a British drinking song, "To Anacreon in Heaven." Widely reprinted by American newspapers, the song became known as "The Star-Spangled Banner," which Congress proclaimed as the national anthem in 1931. Today people sing only the first verse, neglecting the rest, which includes (in the third verse) Key's dig at the British for employing Colonial Marines to liberate slaves:

> *No refuge could save the hireling and slave*
> *From the terror of flight or the gloom of the grave.*
> *And the star-spangled banner—O! Long may it wave,*
> *O'er the land of the free and the home of the brave.*

Key regarded the land of the free and the home of the brave as properly a white man's republic. In this sentiment, he expressed the consensus of his contemporaries.[81]

Nothing irritated British officers more than Americans claiming victory. Avid readers of their coverage in the American press, the British howled that, in the words of Sir Pulteney Malcolm, the Americans "published lies without end." In the British version of the battle, they had suffered no defeat, for they had merely probed the defenses, wisely withdrawing once they found the enemy numerous and entrenched, rather than suffer the heavy casualties necessary to take the city. Tetchy Britons insisted that the defenders had done nothing but cower within their fortifications. In this highly political war, however, the spin of newspapers mattered as much as the spin of bullets. Baltimore gave the Americans something to celebrate, which they made the most of, stiffening their resolve to repel the Britons and suppress their black allies.[82]

Shooting Parties

During the fall, the British soldiers left the Chesapeake, reducing the operations once again to modest shore raids conducted by the navy. Seeking slaves and provisions, the raiders targeted both shores of the Potomac River, where resistance remained weak. Many British officers soured on the petty raiding once it lacked some larger strategic purpose, in contrast to the summer raids that had prepared for the offensive against Washington. The setback at Baltimore also deflated the British hopes for a quick and triumphant end to the war. In August, Captain Robert Rowley had thrilled in the raiding and delighted in his share of the plunder: "We are here very happy, the Captains more like brothers than anything else, our minds well employ'd by the Energetic movements of our Admiral." By November, he felt very differently: "It is horrible here. . . . I must tell you I am heartily tired of the Chesapeake and of the mode of Warfare we are obliged to carry on."[83]

Captain Robert Barrie, however, did sustain his enthusiasm for shore raids, which he called "shooting parties." During the fall, Cockburn and Cochrane sailed away for operations farther south, leaving Barrie in command of a small squadron in the Chesapeake. In his primary raid, Barrie ascended the Rappahannock River with 500 men, 150 of them Colonial Marines, in fifteen barges accompanied by eight schooners and one sloop. On December 2 they seized the village of Tappahannock. Fleeing in a panic, the local militia abandoned their arms and flag, which displayed an American eagle over the motto "Death or victory." Preferring life and defeat, the militia hid in the forested hills, even when Barrie sought to draw them out by torching the courthouse and jail. The raiders then ransacked the village, smashing windows and furniture and looting the family tomb of Thomas Ritchie, the publisher of the *Richmond Enquirer*, which compounded his well-advanced case of Anglophobia.[84]

On December 3 the British evacuated Tappahannock, moving slowly down the Rappahannock to attract and assist the escape of as many slaves as possible. Masters reported "that the said negroes became uncommonly sullen and obstinate and could scarcely be made to do any work after they heard the British were up the said Rappahannock River." An overseer noted that a slave named Jack "did declare that he never would serve his master . . . again—and that he refused repeatedly to do the work of the plantation when ordered." In short order, Jack ran off: one of the 200 to escape to Barrie's barges.[85]

On December 6 a tip from the runaways persuaded Barrie to send 360 men, including 90 Colonial Marines, to attack a militia camp at Farnham Church, an Anglican ruin about seven miles from the river. After firing once, the 100 militiamen scattered, forsaking their badly wounded captain. Walter Jones assured James Monroe, "It was but a *quasi* battle for not one of the Enemy were hurt (this is true, tho you will see a very different account in Print)." Lieutenant Hammond and the Colonial Marines scoured the nearby countryside, "releasing about Twenty Negroes, several of whom he found in the Woods handcuffed round the Trees." Barrie ordered a store filled with liquor burned, but the damage to his white marines had already been done. About a dozen got "beastly Drunk" and lost in the woods, so Barrie had to leave them behind. Here was a swap all too characteristic of the Chesapeake campaign for the British: to liberate twenty slaves while losing a dozen Britons to drink and desertion.[86]

Great Advantage

During the campaign of 1814, black recruits enabled the British to intimidate the Tidewater Virginians and Marylanders. Lieutenant Scott boasted that "the inhabitants within ten miles of the shore, with the assistance of the negroes, were completely within our power." Of the Eastern Shore, Scott remembered, "So completely were the inhabitants aware of the power lodged in our hands by means of this body" that several "young ladies on the main land" sent bouquets and letters begging the British not to deploy black troops against their neighborhood.[87]

In St. Mary's County in June, Lieutenant George C. Urmstone went ashore with a flag of truce to demand that the locals sell their livestock to the British, but Captain James Jaboe of the militia refused and threatened to hang Urmstone if he ever returned. Irritated by Jaboe's impertinence, Urmstone returned to HMS *Albion* and "inquired among the runaway slaves, who knew Captain Jabo?" One of his former slaves came forward to guide Urmstone's raiding party of Colonial Marines eight miles inland through gusting winds and torrents of rain to the captain's house. Breaking in, Urmstone rousted a shocked Jaboe from his bed and hauled him away, shivering in his nightshirt, to captivity on the warship. Nothing pleased Urmstone's friend, Lieutenant Scott, more than the humiliation of a proud American: "The haughty individual, with his blustering swagger and insulting language, delivered in the full pride of regimentals topped by a towering hat and sweeping feather, could not be recognized in the ludicrous, passive figure that now met our views." [88]

Americans feared the critical assistance that the armed runaways provided to the British raiders. In southern Maryland in July, General Philip Stuart urged removing all of the slaves into the interior so "that the Enemy may not be strengthened by a species of force, by us the most to be dreaded of any within his means." In Westmoreland County, General Hungerford rued "the great advantage the Enemy have over us in being informed by our Blacks of all our movements." His aide, John Taylor Lomax, added that the slaves were "constantly going to the enemy—informing them of our posts & . . . acting as the best guides when required. In short the country is infested, in the persons of these blacks, with the most dangerous spies & traitors (if the name can be so applied) that can well be conceived." In these alarmed tributes to black military prowess, the slaveholders forgot their standard line that blacks were cowards unsuited for equality with whites. [89]

During 1814, black guides, sailors, and marines sapped the resistance in southern Maryland and Virginia's Northern Neck. For over a year, Admiral Cockburn had longed to attack Washington, D.C., but he dared not try until August 1814. The recent reinforcements from Europe helped, but their numbers were disappointing: too few to risk on a deep strike into the interior unless Cockburn felt assured of little resistance. His infectious confidence in the attack derived from the domination he had secured over the Patuxent and Potomac Valleys by aggressive raids during the spring and summer, and that success depended on the local knowledge and combat performance of his black guides and marines. No mere by-product of the British operations in the Chesapeake, the runaways transformed that offensive by becoming essential to its success.

10

CRISIS

Yet the hour of emancipation is advancing, in the march of time.
It will come; and whether brought on by the generous energy of
our own minds; or by the bloody process of St. Domingo, excited
and conducted by the power of our present enemy, if once stationed
permanently within our Country, and offering asylum & arms
to the oppressed, is a leaf of our history not yet turned over.
—THOMAS JEFFERSON, AUGUST 25, 1814[1]

D URING 1814 miseries of war grew for the Virginians. A shifting,
mobile threat, the amphibious raids drew out thousands of militiamen. A Virginian said of the mobile enemy, "10,000 of his troops can
employ 100,000 of our militia; and the cost and the waste are heavier
upon us in nearly the same proportion." Virginia farms sprouted weeds
instead of crops as militia service called away farmers during the critical
weeks for planting in the spring and harvesting in the summer. "To suffer or beg must be the lot of many if they are taken from home 2 or 3
months in the summer," explained Lieutenant Colonel Basset Burwell.[2]

View of the Capitol of the United States after the Conflagration, *an engraving by Jesse*
Torrey, 1817. Note the trader with a coffle of chained slaves in the right foreground. Torrey
regarded the destruction of the Capitol as a divine judgment against the nation for allowing
the domestic slave trade. From Torrey's Portraiture of Domestic Slavery *(1817). (Courtesy*
of the American Antiquarian Society)

Virginia failed adequately to equip, provision, or pay the militiamen. In the Northern Neck, General Alexander Parker denounced
the hardships of the militia as "shockingly disgraceful" to the state.
For want of medical supplies, Parker felt that in any skirmish "my
wounded will be more unfortunate than the dead," as their misery
would "be protracted through all the pangs of want and suffering."
And most of the Tidewater people were too poor to provide any
surplus food to the troops. Thomas Jefferson Randolph lamented
serving in "a wretched country. . . . We have nothing in abundance,
but ticks and musketoes. . . . We very often see large establishments
apparently the abode of wealthy persons, [but] upon approaching
them we find them occupied by squalid, indigent wretches who cannot give a meal of any kind to two persons."[3]

At Norfolk the militia encampments were especially large, chaotic, and filthy. In October 1814 a militiaman, James Bendall, wrote
home to his wife: "My Bed is mity hard on one thick plank," and he
often had to stand guard for twenty-four hours "and neaver Eate in
the time." Bendall could scrounge enough firewood to cook his food
only three days a week. Debilitated by disease, he concluded, "I am
porer than Ever you see me in your life."[4]

The militiamen suffered from the malaria borne by mosquitoes
and the dysentery and typhus that bred in the filth of military camps.
A Norfolk doctor reported that the exhausted victims of dysentery
became confined to dirty straw beds with "eyes sunk, cheeks hol-
lowed" and tormented by a fiery thirst. Lacking fresh fruit and vegetables, some soldiers suffered from scurvy, which yellowed their
teeth and rotted their gums. "Instead of a force . . . in the garrison, it
may be, with more truth said, that we have an army in the Hospital,"
lamented Thomas Newton of Norfolk.[5]

During the fall of 1814 a third of the soldiers at Norfolk were too
sick to perform duty, and many died. An officer recalled, "What was
much more to be dreaded . . . than the sword, was the climate which

doomed to eternity in numbers Incredable the hale and blooming youth of our country." Dr. Philip Barraud blamed their deaths on "the Effects of the Militia System—*bad* Discipline, *bad* Cloathing, *bad* Tents, *bad* Cooking, and all the *bad* consequence of *bad* officers." Burials became so common that the commander ordered them conducted quietly at night "in order to avoid depressing the spirits of the survivors." One militia general, Charles Fenton Mercer, estimated that 3,000 men perished of disease at Norfolk during the war. While the British killed few Virginians in combat, the Royal Navy forced them to mass in Norfolk, where mosquitoes and filth did the job.[6]

When discharged from service, the sick, weary, and unpaid men often struggled to travel homeward to a distant county. Lacking public funds, the new governor of Virginia (chosen in December to replace the termed-out James Barbour), Wilson Cary Nicholas, could only pity the poor militiamen "turned adrift at Norfolk 600 miles from home after a six months tour with only three dollars of the public money." Many did not make it. Another state official lamented, "Worn down with fatigue & disease, destitute of money or friends, neglected by the public, some have sunk down in death on the street *in Richmond* unassisted & unheeded." On January 3, 1815, the *Richmond Enquirer* reported, "The roads are strung from Norfolk to the Upper Country with diseased & dying militia."[7]

The returning militiamen spread their diseases to neighbors in the countryside. At Richmond, John Campbell reported, "The whole Country around us here has been diseased by our poor, ragged, dirty militia armies." From the Northern Neck in November, an inhabitant reported an epidemic of "a putrid sore-throat, which . . . has baffled the skill of physicians, and terminated fatally in less than twenty four hours," rendering the district "now more than ever exposed to successful ravages of the enemy." The victims suffocated from a swollen windpipe. In King George County, the disease wiped out a family of ten (save one little boy), and the alarmed neighbors sought to contain their risk by setting "fire to the house and burn them up; which was done." The practice of burning the houses and bodies of victims spread throughout the Northern Neck.[8]

The sick and discharged men returned to farms ravaged by neglect, a volatile climate, and crop pests. The wheat languished after the hard winter of 1813–1814, followed by a spring infestation of the Hessian fly and a fungus known as "the rust." In late July, Edward Ross reported that an ominous earthquake shook the region "with a report like 10 thousand Cannons." On July 28–29, severe thunderstorms swamped low grounds and battered crops with rain, hail, and gale-force winds. The swollen rivers and streams carried away crops, fences, livestock, and mills. Managing a plantation beside the James River, Ross noted that the raging waters were "sweaping away everything with an indescribable force & velocity. . . . Tobacco Houses, Canoes, Carts, Oxen, Horses and Negroes are floating down the River, coming from above, without we are able to save any thing." Writing to her husband away in a militia camp, Sarah Kemp observed, "We have had very high waters, higher than it has ever been since we have lived here." Their forge, iron house, dam, and fences were all gone. "Thus you see our prospects are gloomy in the extreme," another woman assured her brother in the militia. When it rained at the wrong time, misery poured in rural Virginia. And then a drought settled in for the rest of the summer, scorching the corn and tobacco plants that had survived the flood.[9]

Discharged without full pay, the militiamen struggled to meet heavy new war taxes levied by both the state and the federal government. "The same man whose crop was ruined by his absence . . . is not able to pay his taxes. He has no money and nothing to sell," noted Nathaniel Beverley Tucker. And the British blockade prevented the export of crops to market while driving up the cost of imports, including the salt needed to sustain livestock. Thomas Jefferson asked, "How can a people who cannot get 50 cents a bushel for their wheat, while they pay 12 D[ollars] a bushel for their salt, pay five times the amount of taxes they ever paid before?" John Randolph declared that "the searching miseries of war penetrate even into the hovel of the shivering negro, whose tattered blanket and short allowance of salt" attested to the economic distress of his master.[10]

Hard times on the farm and in the militia sapped the willing-ness to serve. In August, Randolph reported that "a late requisition of militia for Norfolk carries dismay and grief into the bosoms of many families in this country. . . . This is our court day, when the conscripts are to report themselves, and I purposely abstain from the sight of wretchedness that I cannot relieve." A rural veteran of the revolution declared, "I never saw men brought to this extremity before." He concluded, "Men thinks hard of their government and are not willing to serve their Cuntrey." One officer wryly noted the rampant ailments cited by men to seek exemption from serving: "I had not the most distant idea that there was half as many dislocated limbs, broken bones, sore shins, ruptures, pulmonary complaints, asthmatic, and rheumatic afflictions as are made known when men are called to the list." Some men simply refused to appear at the mus-ters convened for a draft. Governor Nicholas lamented, "More patri-otism or public spirit I fear are not to be counted upon."[11]

Defeatism spread among the militia officers and state officials. Unless the men received tax relief, St. George Tucker expected "*Sedi-tion* or *Revolt*." In September the commander in Accomack County warned that without pay and food for the suffering militiamen, "we must give up the show of resistance and submit to the mercy of a merciless Enemy." In late November the commander in Middlesex County told the governor that without increased aid, "I will agree to become a *Vassal*" to the British. Another militia officer, Henry St. George Tucker, urged his father to remove into the interior because neither the state nor the nation could protect the Tidewater from a British invasion during the next year: "The prospects of the Coun-try are melancholy beyond all former Example—a divided people—a feeble Congress—and an administration of very little efficiency! . . .

If the war should not speedily be terminated, the Vandals of Great Britain will next Summer burn our seaports and ravage our coasts with almost unresisted fury." In December, John Campbell of the Council of State predicted, "If the war continues . . . we shall be *beaten, disgraced, massacred*, and *burnt* up again."[12]

The Republicans had declared the war to vindicate the republican form of government by proving that it could rally the people to defeat the empire. Instead, repeated defeats, mounting taxes, and internal discontent cast doubt on the republic and its union of states. Campbell confessed to his brother, "I begin to think James that the national character of this Republic is to be sunk, *woefully sunk*, by this war instead of being elevated." After listening to the "babbling fools" in Congress, his brother David despaired: "I can literally say that the nation is ruled by fools and the administration opposed by knaves." In late August the loss and partial burning of Washington and the capitulation of Alexandria deepened the widespread gloom in Virginia. "You, no doubt, have heard of the disgraceful disasters that have overwhelmed our Country," John Minor wrote to Jefferson. Decrying "the vanity & short-sightedness that forms our American Character & fashions all our Councils," Walter Jones insisted that the conflict had delivered "many damning proofs of the Imbecillity of our form of Government & its peculiar unfitness for war."[13]

In late 1814 the federal government teetered on the brink of bankruptcy. In December the new secretary of the Treasury, Alexander J. Dallas, grimly reported that to fund the war for another year the government needed $56 million: three times the national revenue. Only loans could bridge the gap, but investors had lost confidence in the administration because the war seemed futile and endless. Deprived of cash, the nation's banking system verged on collapse, and a belated effort to create a new national bank crumbled as the administration bickered with Congress. Without funds the government could not offer the bounties needed to recruit soldiers for a renewed military campaign in the spring. In early January, despair gripped the Madison administration when a gloomy rumor insisted that peace negotiations with the British had broken down. Visiting the capital, Edward Ross reported that "disappointment was visible in every face present. . . . Mr. Dallas declared, at the impulse of the moment, to all present, that he had flattered himself with a peace . . . but that now he gave up the Country for utterly lost."[14]

The Union seemed on the verge of collapse as the Federalists in New England flirted with secession, which would then provoke a civil war. In late 1814 delegates from most of the New England states held a convention in Hartford to discuss secession, alarming the Virginians as the "climax [to] a ruinous & disastrous war." In November, Samuel Hopkins wrote from Washington, *Something must be done & quickly, or the ship will Sink.* At the start of 1815 the *Richmond Enquirer* described a nation dissolving under the pressures of war:

> In the Northern and Eastern states, rebellion and civil war stare you in the face. The people generally are losing confidence in the energy of the government. They are suffering, they are bleeding under the pressure and calamities of war. The militia dragged suddenly into service, without preparation; unaccustomed to the hardships of the camp, pining after their homes and their families, are *dying* by hundreds with disease. On the Atlantic frontier, the enemy are making inroads into our country, conflagrating our towns, villages and hamlets—plundering our people.

The Virginia adjutant general, Claiborne W. Gooch, predicted that without a miracle, *"This union is inevitably dissolved."*[15]

Desperate Measures

In January 1815, in an act of desperation, the Virginia state legislature revived the state regular defense corps that it had considered, but rejected, two years before. The legislators proposed to conscript

10,000 men to serve within the state. In 1813 the federal government had nixed proposed state armies on constitutional grounds, and the government of Virginia had given way. In early 1815, however, the hard-pressed Madison administration set aside its scruples and invited the coastal states to recruit their own regulars for local defense. Madison and Monroe could hardly say no to Virginia, which had advanced loans, derived from state banks, to save the nation from bankruptcy.[16]

In a second measure of desperation, in late 1814 some Virginians broached the previously unthinkable: the enlistment of black troops. During the similar crisis of the American Revolution, Virginians had armed and freed five hundred blacks for their able service. Thereafter, however, the state's leaders denied that blacks had fought for American independence and insisted that white men would never serve beside them. Masters argued that blacks were too cowardly to fight, although they also dreaded their slaves as a formidable internal enemy: living with slavery required such contradictions of belief. George Tucker (St. George's cousin) owned slaves but knew better than to question their courage. He recalled "a thousand instances" where slaves "stormed dangers and difficulties, while their cowardly masters have fallen back, or fainted before the breach."[17]

During the war alarm of 1807, the Federalist former governor Henry Lee had urged a Republican successor, William H. Cabell, to enlist free blacks. Appealing to fear rather than empathy, Lee reasoned that sending free blacks to fight the British in Canada would reduce the danger of insurrection at home: "You deprive the slaves of intelligence, of advisers, and of leaders. You kill the blacks as well as the white in battle, and thus hold up in a degree the present proportion between the two classes." But Governor Cabell rejected Lee's proposal. A newspaper essayist frankly explained, "We are conscious of treating them with injustice, and we dread the consequences of letting them acquire any knowledge or power whereby they might be enabled to retaliate for the wrongs with which we oppress them."[18]

During the War of 1812, that fear of armed blacks hampered an American army that desperately needed more troops. In 1810 the republic had about 240,000 enslaved and 36,000 free black men of military age, but the Madison administration barred them all from serving. Some desperate recruiting officers overlooked the restriction to enlist a few mixed-race men. One of them, William Williams, died defending Fort McHenry at Baltimore, and his officers belatedly discovered that he was, in fact, a runaway slave.[19]

Because so many merchant marine sailors were black, the government did accept them into the navy but never as officers. At Norfolk, men of color dominated the gunboat crews, and the best American force in the Chesapeake, Joshua Barney's flotilla men, included many free blacks and some hired slaves. Just before the battle at Bladensburg, President Madison asked Barney if the "negroes would not run at the approach of the British." Barney replied, "No sir, they don't know how to run; they will die by their guns." And so they did, while Madison and the white militia fled for their lives. To deny the military ability of blacks, Virginians had to overlook those who fought so ably in the naval units posted in the Chesapeake.[20]

During the war, Irish American leaders in Philadelphia and New York challenged the restriction on black troops. These leaders sought reinforcements to ease the burden borne by the many Irish immigrants serving in the beleaguered American army. The secretary of war, John Armstrong, also denounced the restriction on black troops: "We must get over this nonsense . . . if we mean to be what we ought to be." Armstrong, however, faced formidable opposition from southern Republicans, including Madison, who blanched at the idea of arming free blacks, considering it the slippery slope to slave revolts. And in September 1814, Madison sacked Armstrong in favor of his great rival in the cabinet, James Monroe of Virginia.[21]

Monroe reconsidered the ban on black troops in late 1814, after Congress rejected his proposal to conscript white men. Without enough troops to carry on the war, Monroe accepted New York's plan to raise two regiments of blacks for service within that state. In November 1814 the official newspaper of the administration, the *National Intelligencer*, published two essays promoting free black troops, in an apparent bid to soften southern opposition in Congress. Committed to Monroe's political fortunes, that newspaper would never have promoted black troops without his tacit support.[22]

Published on November 11, the first essay proposed a radical plan to hire slaves as troops by giving their bounty and pay to their masters, with freedom and land awarded to the recruits who honorably served and survived the war. The author insisted that by enlisting a quarter of their slaves, Americans could repel the British attempt to free them all. "Experience has proven that blacks thus organized make as good soldiers as European troops," he declared. While floating this essay as a trial balloon, the paper's editor also expressed doubts: "Such a project would be very obnoxious to the Southern states, and we may safely venture to say will never be put in execution." Then why print it?[23]

The editor probably sought to prepare public opinion to accept a more moderate proposal to recruit free blacks. Two weeks later an anonymous Virginian wrote: "It is a fact, well ascertained, that no men make better sailors than the blacks, and that they would make equally good soldiers, can hardly be doubted." While praising their strength, hardiness, and courage, the author also emphasized "their habits of submission, [and] the ease with which they can be made to submit to any kind of discipline." In a further appeal to white prejudices, the author insisted that most free blacks were lazy "wretches" who set bad examples to the slaves and bred faster than whites. Unfit for civilian life, they belonged in the army, and once enlisted "a very small proportion of them would ever return to the places of their original residence. Many would be destroyed by the casualties of war," while the survivors would settle, at war's end, on western bounty lands. Although the war ended before anything came of this proposal, it attested to the dire state of the white man's republic in late 1814.[24]

Cumberland Island

By year's end, the Virginians got a respite when the British withdrew most of their warships from the Chesapeake. In mid-September, Admirals Cochrane and Cockburn departed for the West Indies and Bermuda to prepare for a winter campaign against New Orleans and Georgia. A month later, more ships left with Sir Pulteney Malcolm and still more in mid-December, after Captain Robert Barrie wrapped up his "shooting party" on the Rappahannock. One of Barrie's transports, the *Regulus*, carried away most of the Colonial Marines, and some of their women and children, for service in the Deep South. The British left behind a small squadron of five frigates and three lesser vessels under the command of Captain John Clavell. Preoccupied with blockading the mouth of Chesapeake Bay, Clavell rarely raided the shores of Virginia and Maryland. At last, most of the drafted militia could go home, but they expected the British to return in greater numbers and with a vengeance in the spring.[25]

Meanwhile, at Jamaica in the West Indies, Cochrane assembled the primary fleet, reinforced by troops from Europe, for an attack against New Orleans. Near the mouth of the Mississippi River, New Orleans controlled the trade of the great American heartland: the vast watershed between the Appalachian Mountains, on the east, and the Rocky Mountains, to the west. By capturing New Orleans, the British could deepen the economic chaos in the United States and either provoke western secession or dictate harsh peace terms to the American government. Cochrane predicted, "The capture of New Orleans will be the severest blow America can meet with."[26]

As a diversion to preoccupy American forces in the Southeast, Cochrane directed Cockburn to lead a smaller force from Bermuda to attack and occupy the Sea Islands of Georgia. For this operation, Cockburn had two battalions of marines, including 365 Colonial Marines, and two companies from the Second West India Regiment, a black corps based in the Bahamas. In a great nightmare for the Georgia planters, black troops comprised most of Cockburn's land force. He hoped also to draw reinforcements from nearby Florida; Creek Indian allies and a black marine corps led by Major Edward Nicolls. In August 1814, Cochrane had sent Nicolls to the Gulf Coast to rally the Creeks and entice runaway slaves from the Georgia frontier.[27]

On January 10, Captain Philip Somerville led the advance squadron of the British expedition to Cumberland Island, a Sea Island near the border with Spanish East Florida. Landing without opposition, the British made their base at the island's southern tip, which offered a good anchorage for many ships. They commandeered "Dungeness," a plantation where a four-story mansion overlooked groves of lemon and orange trees, fields of cotton and corn, herds of cattle, and scores of slaves.[28]

At dawn on January 13, Captain Barrie commanded when the British crossed over to the mainland to strike the American fort at Point Peter on the St. Marys River. Marching through a dense forest to the fort, the black troops fell into an ambush, but they quickly routed the American riflemen. A British officer reported, "Blacky, on the impulse of the moment, left the ranks and pursued them into the woods, fighting like *heroes*." He added, "Blacky had *no idea of giving quarters*, and it was with difficulty the officers prevented their putting *the prisoners to death*." After capturing the abandoned fort, the invaders pressed into the undefended town of St. Marys, where they plundered homes and stores, taking away their loot in captured merchant ships. On January 23, after the arrival of Cockburn to assume command, the British evacuated the town and blew up the fort.[29]

Panic spread among the coastal planters, who feared a bloody slave rebellion and a British advance to attack Savannah, the state's premier city and seaport. According to Governor Peter Early, Georgia faced "insurrection on one side, and Indian massacre on the other," for he especially dreaded that the "*enemy have black troops with them.*" Hastening to the coast with 800 militiamen, General David Blackshear was slowed "by the multitude of wagons flying from the horrors of invasion and insurrection."[30]

Cockburn longed to attack Savannah, but he had to wait for the arrival of Major Nicolls from Florida. Nicolls, however, had gone westward to support the British attack on New Orleans, where the redcoats suffered a crushing defeat that also put a damper on Cockburn's ambitions. From his headquarters on Cumberland Island, Cockburn settled for raiding the other Sea Islands, seeking cotton to plunder and slaves to liberate. Because few whites lived on the islands, they offered little resistance to the British raids.[31]

Some runaways came away in stolen boats and canoes, while many more joined raiding parties that reached their plantations. Often, as in the Chesapeake, the British first induced the slaves to help them kill the master's cattle and plunder his larder for a feast. Then the officers warned that they had better leave rather than risk the whip or the gallows from masters angered over the loss of their livestock and liquor. The British also painted a bright future of freedom and land for those who came with them. Most persuasive of all was the conspicuous appearance of the uniformed and armed Colonial Marines, who displayed the trust and good treatment afforded by the British.[32]

Rather than fault slavery or themselves, the Sea Island masters blamed the flight on seductive lies allegedly told by the British. According to Roswell King, the British assured slaves that they would go to hell if they died in bondage, so they had better save their souls by seeking freedom. Another Georgian implausibly reported that the British assured female slaves "that the Queen of England was a Negro Woman" and that British gentlemen preferred "Negro Women as wives," so they "would for the rest of their lives, be maintained in affluence, without labor, having servants, horses & carriages kept for their use."[33]

On St. Simons Island, King managed Pierce Butler's plantation which lost 138 slaves to the British. He warned the slaves not "to leave their comfortable homes and go into a strange country where they would be separated, and probably not half live the year out." But he noted the power of family ties and the influence of the boldest who first cast their lot with the British: "some said they must follow their daughters, others their wives." Far from being separated, they sought to remain united by leaving together. King angrily concluded, "I found my reasoning had no effect on a set of stupid negroes, half intoxicated with liquor and nothing to do but think [that] their happy days had come." However, he conceded that "they appeared sorry, solemn, and often crying" as they weighed a decision that would shape the rest of their lives.[34]

Embarrassed by his failure to preserve his employer's property, King denounced the runaways in angry letters to Butler. On February 12, King declared, "God cursed the Negroe by making him Black. I Curse the Man that brot the first from Africa, and the Curse of God is still on them, to send them away to die a miserable death." Four days later, he worked himself into a further rage: "I have these twelve years past taken all means to make these ungrateful wretches comfortable but it is all nonsense and folly. To treat Negroes with humanity is like giving Pearls to swine, it is . . . giting insult and ingratitude in return." Then to culminate his outrage, on March 4 he indulged in a vengeful fantasy of recapturing the runaways: "How will it please me to have the pleasure to git your Negroes back and pick out one husband, one wife, one fellow, one wench and sell them—leaving their children or parents behind, as it may happen, to reflect on their wanton, impudent folly." Recognizing the value of family ties to the slaves, King knew the ultimate way to punish them. His rant revealed an addiction to domination over others, his illusion of doing right by them, and his rage at losing that power over 138 people who called his paternalism a lie.[35]

By mid-March, Cockburn had drawn 1,700 refugees to Cumberland Island. The women, children, elderly, and lame he enrolled as supernumeraries, who received food and clothing and did some work until the British could ship them on transports to Bermuda. The young men he recruited as Marines. By early March, Cockburn had organized two additional companies of Colonial Marines, increasing their overall strength to 450 men. One terrified planter recalled "the magical transformation of his own negroes, whom he left in the field but a few hours before, into regular soldiers, of good discipline and appearance." He saw a mortal threat to the South in the growing numbers of black troops trained by the British.[36]

Some of the runaways came from nearby East Florida, a Spanish colony. Because Spain allied with the British in Europe and remained neutral in the war with America, Florida's governor, Sebastián Kindelán, expected Cockburn to respect the property of the colonists. In the course of the war, however, Cockburn had become committed to freeing any slaves who sought haven under the British flag, whether from a weak ally or the despised enemy. Cockburn defined Cumberland Island and every British warship as extensions of British territory subject to British law, including the *Somerset* decision. Therefore, "every Idea of the People in Question being considered as Private Property is at an End."[37]

Cockburn assured Kindelán that masters could visit their former slaves and retrieve those who consented to return, but no British officer would force anyone back into slavery. Cockburn explained that no Spanish subject could "have the slightest claim to *my* Services to drive back for them the People in question." Kindelán retorted, "Where is the Slave who will voluntarily return to Slavery if left to his own election?" Cochrane was uneasy with Cockburn's emancipation of an ally's slaves but agreed that "they should not, for humanity's sake, be sent back to their former Masters, who would not fail to inflict upon them the greatest cruelties." After the war a Florida colonist (but British subject), John Forbes, sued Cockburn for damages from the loss of runaway slaves. In 1824 the Court of King's Bench ruled in favor of Cockburn that "the plaintiff ceased to have any right or title to the slaves the moment they threw themselves upon the protection of the British flag."[38]

News

On February 8, Cockburn received disturbing news: "an ugly account of peace being signed." At Ghent on December 24, 1814, British diplomats had concluded a peace treaty with American negotiators. Worried about a renewed blowup in Europe, the imperial government sought to get out of the American war by offering generous terms. "It was fortunate for us that London is not as near to Washington as to Paris," St. George Tucker noted. The peace treaty restored the prewar boundaries in North America: a great gain for the United States given that victorious British forces had occupied eastern Maine, northern Michigan, a corner of western New York, Tangier Island in the Chesapeake, and Cumberland Island on the coast of Georgia. Although British impressment of American sailors had been a major cause of the war, the treaty ignored that issue, which seemed moot to both sides after Napoléon's defeat had reduced the Royal Navy's demand for hands.[39]

Eager to press their military advantage over the Americans, British officers felt frustrated by the sudden peace on terms so favorable to their enemy. Cockburn complained, "This Peace . . . has knocked all my Schemes on the Head." He insisted that a proper treaty would have made the enemy "pay dearer for their unjust and unprincipled Aggression." Using a British nickname for Americans, Captain Barrie declared, "This Peace is a sad Damper to many of us who most sincerely wished to have fought [Jo]nathan into complete humiliation." Barrie had sought "a disunion of the states, which would most certainly have taken place had the war been kept up for eight months longer."[40]

While depressing to British officers, the news thrilled Americans, for it saved their nation from collapse. On February 13 in Baltimore, a man reported, "We have just received information of peace. Peace is in every one's mouth, and, altho the streets are full of People whose mouths are wide open like snuff boxes, yet they cannot hold their peace, but run about grinning and chattering like so many monkies." In Richmond, William H. Cabell assured his brother Joseph that the "glorious peace for America ... has come exactly when we least expected but when we most wanted it. . . . You cannot form too extravagant an idea of the real joy which it has diffused through every circle here."[41]

On February 15, 1815, the news came to Williamsburg, triggering a giddy celebration driven by a profound relief at escaping a national disaster. St. George Tucker reported, "It set us all in tip top spirits." Just two months before, Tucker had noted the nation's "horrid prospects" as he prepared to move his family and slaves into the interior, away from the danger of a British raid. He had then noted, "A happy new year to us all. We are all sadly in need of it." That happiness came to Williamsburg in mid-February. Tucker "could hardly persuade myself [that] the news of peace was true, so unlooked for was it by us all." Exulting in "the blessed news of Peace," Tucker expressed a patriarch's relief: "Heaven be prais'd for it! I hope henceforth to feel as if my house was my own & my wife & my children not in danger of being taken from me." Peace would "not only put an end to the horrors of a foreign war, but postpone those of a civil war, the flames of which I think were preparing." Anticipating New England's secession to ally with the British, Tucker had expected a war between the states.[42]

A few minutes after the news arrived, the public celebration began. A drummer played on "the old palace ground" and the inhabitants placed candles in their windows as an "illumination." Tucker noted, "The Detachment of Militia paraded the streets, every Man with a lighted Candle at the End of his Musket. The sight was the most picturesque I ever saw. When performing their Evolutions, it appeared a perfect Galaxy of Stars as bright as Venus herself, revolving round one Center." The militiamen stopped in front of Tucker's door to give three cheers, so he treated them to "Antique Spirits to drink the health of General [Andrew] Jackson & his army." A month before, Jackson's army had a won a sensational victory, crushing a British force near New Orleans.[43]

As Tucker saw it, liberty had been saved by sparing the republic from destruction, but slaves must have felt differently. In early January in Williamsburg, a militiaman named Pleasants Murphy had recorded, "Hundreds of People [had] Collected at the Raleigh [Tavern] at a negro hanging." Murphy concluded, "At Night we Borrowed a fiddle and had a dance in Our Barracks." One man's freedom was another's slavery in Virginia, so the peace that saved the republic also shut down a war that had freed thousands of slaves. While Virginians loudly celebrated, many of their slaves privately mourned the passing of an opportunity.[44]

The official copy of the treaty reached Washington, D.C., on February 16. A day later, the Senate unanimously consented to the treaty and the president hastily ratified it. The attending British diplomat, Anthony St. John Baker, marveled, "The impatience of the Govt. to ratify it was so great" that the American document "consisted only of a few Sheets of Paper blotted and in many places ill spelt which were corrected on Mr. Monroe & myself comparing our copies."[45]

Luck rather than genius had saved the administration from disaster. Colonel John Taylor assured Monroe, "A succession of lucky accidents enabled the administration to get the nation out of the war, for which no one rejoices more than myself. Had it lasted two years longer, the republican party and our form of government itself would have been blown up." General Charles Fenton Mercer of the Virginia militia agreed that the peace had saved the United States from "bankruptcy, disunion, and civil war, combined with foreign invasion; in fine, from national dishonor and ruin."[46]

But the Republicans quickly spun the peace treaty as culminating a glorious war that had exalted the United States. After failing to conquer Canada or compel British maritime concessions, the Republicans redefined national survival as victory. Monroe assured the Senate that "our Union has gained strength, our troops honor, and the nation character, by the contest." The *Richmond Enquirer* agreed: "We have waged a War which has covered us with *glory*." Americans had displayed "as much public spirit, as much heroic courage, as much devotion to country as ever distinguished any people." Talk of desertions, disunion, national bankruptcy, and the failure of republicanism suddenly vanished beneath a crescendo of celebration.[47]

Along the Atlantic seaboard, the myth of the glorious war got a boost when the peace news arrived at the same time that Americans learned of the sensational American victory near New Orleans. On January 8, in the war's most lopsided battle, Jackson's army had routed 6,000 British regulars. At a cost of only thirty minutes and seventy-one casualties, the Americans killed 290 Britons, wounded 1,262, and captured 484. Before dying in the battle, the overconfident British commander had marched his men across open ground in a frontal assault on entrenched Americans who could readily blast away at the exposed attackers. The Battle of New Orleans nicely fit the cherished stereotype of bungling Britons unsuited for war in North America, so it became celebrated in American story and song. The Americans quickly repressed from memory their many earlier defeats suffered while invading Canada.[48]

Withdrawal

Contrary to a popular myth, the Treaty of Ghent did *not* end the war on December 24, 1814; instead, per the terms of that treaty, war persisted until the United States ratified the treaty on February 17, 1815. Upon learning of the peace treaty in early February, Cockburn suspended his raids, but he continued to welcome runaways from the coasts of Florida and Georgia. He delayed evacuating his force from Cumberland Island until he was officially notified that the United States had ratified the treaty. That notification did not reach the admiral until early March, allowing three more weeks for exporting plunder and liberating slaves.[49]

On March 6, 1815, two American officials, Captain Thomas M. Newell of the army and Thomas Spalding, a Sea Island planter, visited Cumberland Island to press Cockburn for an immediate transfer of control to the Georgians. Newell and Spalding insisted that the first article of the peace treaty barred the British from taking away any American slaves, who, instead, should be restored to their owners. Cockburn offered a much narrower reading of the article and a far broader mandate for the liberating power of the British flag. He argued that the treaty obligated him only to restore slaves who had been captured at Dungeness on Cumberland Island: a mere 81 of the 1,700 refugees from Georgia and Florida. On March 8, Cochrane arrived at Cumberland Island and endorsed Cockburn's position.[50]

The admirals did allow Newell, Spalding, and other planters to visit the warships to address the runaways in hopes of persuading them to return to slavery. Instead, the visitors got an earful, for Newell complained that the British officers "permitted the Slaves to be insulting, without ever checking them." The most "insolent" runaways came from the Chesapeake and served as Colonial Marines. Despite the admirals' orders, many British captains refused to cooperate and made excuses to keep the American officials away from their warships. Only thirteen runaways, all Georgians, agreed to go back. Bound by his interpretation of the treaty, Cockburn also forcibly returned the eighty-one slaves who had been captured at Dungeness, which the British had fortified. Meanwhile, Cockburn sent transports, heavily laden with refugees, away to Bermuda. On March 13, Cockburn completed his withdrawal from the island, but several warships remained in the harbor for another five days, before the admiral sailed away on the last one. Until their departure, the British captains continued to take on board runaways, further infuriating the Georgians. The last-minute refugees included at least two of the eighty-one that Cockburn had forced back to their owner at Dungeness.[51]

In the Chesapeake the Royal Navy officers also sought to preserve the freedom of the runaways. On February 20, 1815, three days after the ratification of peace, the British staged one last raid. A barge with a lieutenant and ten armed men visited the plantation of George Loker in St. Mary's County, Maryland. They came to liberate four enslaved children, and three women, including the "wife of a negro man" who guided the raid. When Loker protested that the war was over, the British lieutenant replied "that he would take all that would come to him until he received an official account" of ratification.[52]

On February 27, Loker and another master visited HMS *Havannah* to demand the return of their slaves. Captain William Hamilton responded "that having once been received on board a British Ship, [the fugitives] could no longer bear the Character of Slave, and that I could not be justified in using force to make them return, but that they might . . . endeavor to persuade them to do so." Hamilton assembled the slaves, assured them that "they were as free as any people," and asked if any wished to return to slavery, but none did.[53]

Despite the peace, Hamilton would do no more for Americans so long as they continued to entice and harbor British deserters, including two sailors and two marines, all of them white, who had escaped during the last raid. Loker's companion reported that Hamilton declared, "No Negros would be restored unless we caused the Seamen to be given up who had recently deserted from his Ship." Once again, the desertion of white sailors from British ships promoted the liberation of slaves by naval officers.[54]

Meanwhile, on February 23, three American commissioners had contacted Hamilton's commander, Captain John Clavell, with an official notice of the peace. They demanded the return of all of the runaways in British hands within American territorial waters, which included Chesapeake Bay. Clavell refused to relinquish any runaways "now serving on board His Brittanic Majesty's ships, as by entering into the service, they made themselves free men." One of the commissioners, Thomas M. Bayly of Virginia, retorted that Americans would "never believe that their Slaves can make themselves free by entering into His Britannic Majesty's Sea or Land Service." Clavell soon received Cockburn's orders to withdraw from Tangier Island, but "On no account [is] a Single Negro [to] be left, except by his own request, if he joined you prior to the Ratification of the Treaty" at 11:00 p.m. on February 17.[55]

In early March, Bayly went to Tangier with Clavell's permission to take a list of the runaways there. During that month, many slaveholders, including Charles Carter of Corotoman, flocked to the island to cajole the refugees to return home. The masters discovered, however, that most of the runaways had already sailed away, and the few who remained clung to freedom. On March 21, Clavell completed the evacuation of the island, burning the fort and barracks and taking away the last refugees. Replenishing their water supply from wells on St. George's Island in the Potomac, Clavell and his ships lingered in the bay until April 14, when they sailed away bound for Bermuda. To pressure the British to return the runaways, the Madison administration refused, in the postwar prisoner exchanges, to include about sixty British-owned slaves captured by American privateers from British merchant ships. But the British officers and their government stood firm in protecting the refugees.[56]

Many British officers had developed an empathy for the runaways and a conviction that naval honor required strict adherence to the protection offered by the British flag. Captain Hamilton reported that his officers so opposed returning Loker's runaways to his "cruel punishment," that they offered to spend their own funds to compensate the master. Instead, Clavell ordered Hamilton to sail for Bermuda, saving the runaways and the officers' money. But Hamilton's offer revealed the surprising ties that had emerged between naval officers and runaways during the war.[57]

Initially reluctant and grudging, many British officers had grown into their role as liberators. The transition appears in the words of an officer who recalled, "The 'niggers' soon made themselves prime favourites amongst our soldiers and sailors, whom they amused every evening with their songs and dances, of which they performed a regular 'round,' beginning with

> *Who 'tole de pigeon pie*
> *An' hid 'im in de bag o'rye?"*

A song of defying the master by stealing and hiding a pie helped the soldiers and sailors to see the runaways in a new light as fellow people engaged in a common struggle against the Americans. Some officers formed friendships with blacks, such as Cockburn's affection for Sergeant Johnson. In September 1814, Lieutenant G. R. Gleig went on shore to visit "an old negro couple," in the Patuxent Valley: "We carried as a present for our old friends, the Negroes, a bottle of rum and some dose of salts for which they were very grateful." Although many local whites had also helped the British, Gleig never referred to them as "old friends" or gave presents to them.[58]

National honor and naval duty had become invested in promises made to the runaways. By defying masters' invitations to break those promises, the British claimed moral superiority over the crass Americans. The contrast vindicated the British insistence that they practiced and protected a more authentic and consistent brand of freedom. After the peace, Lieutenant John Fraser of the Royal Marines explained, "No British officer ever entertained the most distant opinion that those Negroes, who had come in under the Commander in Chief's Proclamation, could under any circumstances be ever given up." Cockburn urged his government scrupulously to honor the pledges made to the refugees, in order to preserve, among American slaves, a reputation "highly favourable to the British char-

acter & interest." Exulting in their own rectitude, the naval officers
sought to do right by the refugees.[59]

Major Edward Nicolls of the Royal Marines stood out as an
especially zealous abolitionist. In a long and distinguished military
career, he suffered 107 wounds, attesting to his reckless courage and
many combat assignments. In 1814 Cochrane sent Nicolls to West
Florida to rally the Creek Indians and recruit runaways. Bold and
resourceful, Nicolls raised and trained about 300 black marines while
providing a haven for their women and children.[60]

Committed to liberating slaves, in Spanish Florida as well as the
United States, Nicolls exhorted his white marines to be patient with
the new black recruits: "Remember they have been oppressed by
cruel taskmasters and, under slavery, man's best faculties are kept
dormant. What a glorious prospect for British soldiers to set them
free. How grateful will they be to you, how ready to mix their Blood
with yours in so good a cause." Turning to the runaways, he promised to help them save their families by smashing slavery: "never
again will you have to undergo the heartrending misery of seeing the
partner of your love or the children of your affection cruelly dragged
from your [side], sold to a foreign oppression and carried beyond
your reach for ever." Nicolls understood that runaways sought to
defend their imperiled families.[61]

On a bluff beside the Apalachicola River, about fifteen miles
above its mouth on the Gulf of Mexico, Nicolls's marines erected a
strong rectangular fort, 120 feet per side, with earthen walls eighteen
feet thick rising fifteen feet high and topped by a thick palisade of
pine logs. The fort mounted eight cannon and one howitzer. At the
end of the war, Cochrane ordered the fort surrendered to the Spanish, but Nicolls and his officers refused, "having espoused the cause
of the Slaves," according to Thomas Spalding. In June 1815, Nicolls
did withdraw with his white marines, and he sent 123 blacks to
Trinidad as free settlers. About 450 Florida refugees, however, preferred to stay on the Apalachicola as maroons rather than retreat as

A View of the Town of St. George, Bermuda, *an 1815 aquatint by I. J. C. Stadler. The capital of the colony of Bermuda was crowded with soldiers and sailors and the harbor filled with ships. Note the two black women in the right foreground. (Courtesy of the New York Public Library)*

marines, so Nicolls entrusted the fort and its armament to the blacks, who continued to fly the Union Jack. The British government subsequently disavowed the major's actions as driven by an "ill-judged zeal." Meanwhile, Georgians denounced the "Negro Fort" as a great menace, which continued to attract runaways and send out raiding parties. Spalding warned that the Negro Fort would "become a nucleus around which a dangerous Population will concenter."[62]

On August 27, 1816, American gunboats ascended the river and opened fire on the Negro Fort. A cannon shot penetrated the main powder magazine, which erupted in a massive explosion, destroying the fort and killing most of the defenders. The American commander, Colonel Duncan Clinch, credited God for "chastising the blood-thirsty and murderous wretches that defended the fort." Some survivors escaped deeper into Florida, joining the Seminole Indians, who continued to resist American expansion. Two years later, many of the maroons crossed Florida to the east coast, built large dug-out canoes, and sailed to the Bahamas, a British colony where they founded a distinctive and enduring settlement.[63]

Bermuda

At the end of the war, the British evacuated the refugees from Georgia and the Chesapeake to Bermuda, where they became the responsibility of Commodore Andrew Fitzherbert Evans, who commanded the naval dockyard. Reluctant to feed and clothe those too old, too young, or too sick to work, Evans complained to Cockburn that the dockyard could employ only "young, healthy & active Men unencumbered with Women & Children or aged, diseased & infirm objects." Evans derided even the able-bodied men, deeming "their Sloth so invincible, even when there is no Compulsion used . . . that I despair of deriving any material advantage from their exertions."[64]

Evans's rant offended Cockburn because the black marines had earned his respect, and he knew that the British needed to provide a haven for their women and children. In reply, Cockburn directed Evans to recognize "the injury done the Enemy in taking these People from his power, the gratification of having relieved so many Fellow Creatures from Slavery, and in our having established from amongst them at little or no expense a most efficient and useful Corps now above 400 strong, which is constantly and actively employed with us here and giving daily proofs of its gallantry and grateful attachment to us." Per Cochrane's April 1814 proclamation, the British officers had to assist all refugees without any "discrimination whatever . . . as to the Age, Sex and Abilities of the Persons." With "the faith of our Country" so pledged it became Evans's duty to provide "a ready Asylum with all reasonable protection from us."[65]

During the spring and summer of 1815, the Royal Navy moved

most of the refugees on to Nova Scotia, but the Colonial Marines and their families remained on Bermuda. Anticipating another war with the United States, sooner rather than later, Cochrane advised that the Colonial Marines would provide "a corps of guides and pilots ready to attend any expedition sent upon the Coast of America. . . . They are a very fine body of men; perfectly orderly and sober." Praising them as "fine, brave, active fellows, worth all the West India Regiments united," Cochrane considered the Colonial Marines the best force to deploy against the United States: "They were infinitely more dreaded by the Americans than the British Troops."[66]

Imperial bureaucrats, however, disliked retaining a unique unit of marines when the West Indian regiments remained undermanned. Thinking that all black men were alike, distant officials insisted that the Chesapeake and Georgia blacks should join the African-born men of the West Indian regiments.

In August 1815 the naval and colonial officials of Bermuda received orders to transfer the Colonial Marines to the army. In polite but firm protest, the officials described the Colonial Marines as especially intelligent and able troops but sticklers for their rights. Their commander, Major Andrew Kinsman, warned, "They are particularly tenacious of promises made to them. . . . Nothing in the form of bad faith should be observed towards them." The black marines cited British pledges that they would always remain together in a special unit under the officers who had trained and led them, to whom they felt fiercely loyal. Possessing "strong & determined prejudices," the Colonial Marines also held "high ideas of superiority . . . over the African Negroes" of the West India Regiments.[67]

Bermuda's governor, James Cockburn, reiterated the importance of the Colonial Marines in the event of a new war with the Americans. Treating them fairly, he reasoned, was essential to "retaining our influence over a large portion of the population of the United States, where our conduct towards these Negroes is strictly watched (though for different ends) both by Whites & Blacks." A forced

Philanthropie Moderne. *By a French pro-slavery artist, this cartoon was widely reproduced in the United States. It depicts a British abolitionist and Royal Navy officer seducing brutish blacks from their duty and employing them to burn Washington, D.C. Note the farm tools smoldering in the foreground. (Courtesy of the American Antiquarian Society)*

transfer would bolster the American propaganda that the British had mistreated the runaways, which would then dampen the enthusiasm of American slaves for the British as potential liberators. Cockburn cherished that enthusiasm as a valuable military resource for the future. Apparently impressed by that argument, the imperial government postponed the transfer.[68]

About 450 Colonial Marines remained at Ireland Island (part of Bermuda) in June 1816, when John Patterson of Mathews County, Virginia, sailed to Bermuda on the *Maid of the Isles*, a schooner with a cargo of corn. Most of his sailors were enslaved: a common phenomenon in Tidewater Virginia as well as Bermuda. On arrival, Patterson recognized at least fifteen Colonial Marines as former slaves from Mathews. They included one of his own, named Hull, who had become a drummer. Two other Colonial Marines—Sci Gillett and Ned—had also escaped from Patterson and served at Ireland Island, but their former master never saw them.[69]

Sci Gillett probably dreaded reviving painful memories. In February 1813, at the age of sixteen, he had joined the band of defiant slaves who declared themselves "Englishmen" and robbed a store. Under pressure from Patterson, Sci had testified against his eight older friends, saving his own life but sending two to the gallows and six to sale and transportation. In March 1814 he had escaped from Patterson and joined the British, enlisting as a Colonial Marine. He had a tangled tale to tell, but did not want to.[70]

The other marines from Mathews County did visit the *Maid of the Isles* to reminisce with the crew, for, as Patterson noted, they had been "raised together in the same neighbourhood." Resplendent in "Red Coats, white Jackets & pantaloons, black gaiters & stocks, black hats with narrow brims bound with white and white feathers," the marines made a vivid impression as they told war stories of Baltimore and Cumberland Island. The enslaved crew and free marines could see how each of their wartime choices—to stay or to go—had played out. The schooner's captain, William Dixon, recalled that Hull came on board to offer his own peace to his former master. Hull "saluted the said Patterson . . . by presenting his hand" and declaring "that he did not elope from him in consequence [of] ill treatment, that he had always treated him well but that he preferred having his freedom."[71]

Memory

In 1815 the British withdrew from American shores but not from American nightmares, for a dread of Britons, blacks, and Indians merged in postwar nationalism. Americans remembered the war in racial terms: as a nefarious cabal by the British with Indians and blacks to destroy the white man's republic. In February 1815 a Maryland state senator castigated the "vindictive enemy, who has asso-

ciated to himself as fit allies, savage Indians and ferocious blacks."
American orators and writers insisted that a truly civilized nation
would never deploy Indians or blacks in war against white people.
Some reform-minded Americans, primarily in the Northeast, did
admire the British measures to suppress the slave trade and ameliorate slavery, but Anglophiles were a small minority in the United
States. Most Americans regarded the British Empire as their great
and enduring enemy who allied with Indians along the frontier and
stirred up southern slaves.[72]

American newspapers claimed that the peace treaty had come in
the nick of time to spare the United States from a racial bloodbath.
Lurid stories insisted that the British had prepared a massive force
of West Indian black troops to invade the South during the spring of
1815 "to excite insurrection among the negroes of the United States,
and to involve a civilized people in all the horrors of a St. Domingo
revolution." With the supposed motto of "beauty and booty," the
black troops would pillage and rape their way across the South.
One writer concluded that anyone "whose blood does not boil with
indignation and his sinews stiffen to revenge is not worthy to be an
American citizen."[73]

During the spring of 1816 the American press took a grim interest in the Easter Rebellion by slaves on the British West Indian colony of Barbados. The rebels believed that their masters had blocked
a parliamentary plan to emancipate them, so hundreds rallied to burn
seventy plantations and their cane fields, before British troops suppressed the revolt with great bloodshed. Planted on posts, the heads
of dead rebels decorated the crossroads of the island. Of course, the
American press reported the usual story: that the rebels had meant to
kill all the white men and take their women and children. In fact, the
rebels showed remarkable restraint, killing only one white civilian,
but facts rarely got in the way of shoving every black protest into the
fantasy stereotype of the Saint-Domingue massacre.[74]

The *Richmond Enquirer* and *National Intelligencer* cast the Barbados revolt as the just deserts for Britons who had attacked slavery in America during the recent war. By playing with deadly fire in America, they had been burned in the West Indies: "It was they who would have taught our slaves to rebel, to desert, and to massacre their masters; it was they who wove them into regiments, landed them upon our shores and taught them to lure away their fellows. The British nation ought to have recollected, that the day of visitation might come upon them, when the dagger which they pointed at our throats, might be aimed at their own." The very real (but carefully limited) British use of black troops during the war became multiplied to monstrous proportions in the American imagination. By treating blacks as British dupes and pawns, the writer also erased their initiative in escaping and fighting slavery.[75]

Americans regarded the British as the manipulating hand behind every resistance by darker-skinned peoples — Mexicans, Indians, and maroons — to the south in Florida and to the west in Texas. In 1816 such fears led to the American raid into west Florida to destroy the Negro Fort. Two years later, Andrew Jackson led a larger invasion to burn the towns of black maroons and Seminole Indians. To cap his victory, Jackson executed a British trader, Alexander Arbuthnot, and a former Royal Marine officer, Robert Ambrister. Holding abolitionist principles, Ambrister had returned on his own to Florida to help train and lead the Indians and runaways in resisting the Americans. But Jackson treated Arbuthnot and Ambrister as British covert agents and traitors to the white race. Although the new American president, James Monroe, and most of his cabinet regretted the invasion and executions, Jackson won even greater popularity in a nation that especially hated the British for aiding Indians and slaves. Fortunately for the republic, the British government did nothing but protest the executions, balking at a renewed war because chastened by their military debacle at New Orleans in 1815.[76]

American leaders justified expansion and white supremacy as defensive measures needed to protect freedom from a British plot to deploy savages and maroons against the republic. That dread helped to push American expansion southward and westward across the continent to consolidate an ever larger, and presumably more secure, republican union. While the confidence of Manifest Destiny was one side of the nationalism coin, a pervasive and defensive racial anxiety lay on the underside.[77]

American nationalists reacted against British writers who sympathized with slaves as victims of the republic's hypocrisy. The cultural critic Sydney Smith outraged Americans by puncturing their superior pretensions to liberty: "under which of the old tyrannical governments of Europe is every sixth man a slave whom his fellow-creatures may buy and sell and torture?" The southern animus against the British grew during the 1830s, when the empire compelled the West Indian colonists to emancipate their slaves. Southerners feared that the precedent would inspire slave revolts and abolition within the United States. In response to British gibes and West Indian emancipation, southerners again accused the British of cynically promoting slave discontent to threaten the republic. Anglophobes also cited the empire's exploitation of Ireland and India to discredit the British guise of humanitarianism.[78]

British leaders further alarmed Americans by announcing that slavery rendered the southern states especially vulnerable to attack and subversion. In every war scare with the United States, the British threatened once again to raid the coast and rally the slaves with a promise of freedom. During a diplomatic crisis in 1830, the British government appointed Sir George Cockburn to command the North American station: a not very subtle reminder to the Americans of their risk. In 1841 a Royal Navy veteran of the Chesapeake campaign boasted of Britain's abolition of slavery in the West Indies "whilst, to the United States of America, it will ever prove the source of weakness and disunion, and may ultimately prove their ruin." In 1855 Lord Palmerston, the British foreign secretary, warned the Americans that "a British Force landed in the southern part of the Union, proclaiming freedom to the Blacks, would shake many of the stars from their banner." Taking these threats seriously, the United States expended great sums and ingenuity constructing massive new coastal forts, particularly to defend southern ports and, above all, to secure Norfolk and the mouth of the Chesapeake.[79]

Slaves overheard their masters denounce the British as a menace to the republic through their black proxies and abolitionist pawns. That alarm confirmed the slaves' devotion to the legend of the king who would return to free them. In South Carolina's Denmark Vesey plot of 1822, a leader insisted "that the English were to come & help them—that the Americans could do nothing against the English & that the English would carry them off to St. Domingo." In 1829 the radical black abolitionist David Walker promoted slave revolt in America and declared that the British "have been for many years, and are now our greatest earthly friends and benefactors." American talk unwittingly had confirmed to listening blacks that the British offered their best chance to win freedom for all. Then, in the endless feedback of rhetorical dread, Americans regarded the Anglophilia of slaves as a special menace to the republic of white men.[80]

11

AGENTS

*[The British] have professed to afford [the runaways] an asylum
as freemen. They are admitted of course to be voluntary Agents,
and as such must have a right to go where they think fit.*
—JAMES MONROE, APRIL 7, 1815[1]

H EADING HOME to Yorktown in November 1813, Major Thomas
Griffin stewed in frustration after visiting a British warship in
a vain bid to recover five runaways. At Hampton, Griffin fell in
with Patrick Williams, a mariner from New York who recently had
been released from a British captivity. At Nassau in the Bahamas,
Williams claimed that he saw the British sell a runaway slave carpenter from Norfolk for $1,000. The story confirmed what Virgin-
ians wanted to believe, so Griffin took Williams before a magistrate,
John Tabb Smith, to make a deposition under oath. At last the Virginians claimed legal proof to their deeply held suspicion, and the
newspapers rushed it into print. Securing a copy of the deposition
from Griffin, Joseph C. Cabell passed it on to St. George Tucker,
who eagerly forwarded it to President Madison. Keen to expose the

Gabriel Hall. *Enslaved in Maryland, Gabriel Hall escaped to the British during the war.
He arrived in Halifax in 1815 and prospered as a farmer. Taken in 1892, when he was
ninety-two years old, this is the only known photograph of a black refugee from the war.
(George H. Craig photograph, courtesy of the Nova Scotia Archives)*

British as fraudulent liberators Cabell and Tucker endorsed a shaky witness with a suspect story, which they conveyed to the highest level of American power.[2]

Despite Williams's obscurity, President Madison and Secretary of State Monroe eagerly embraced the deposition as proving British perfidy. On January 28, 1814, Monroe informed the American peace negotiators in Europe: "It is known that a shameful traffic has been carried on in the West Indies, by the sale of these persons there, by those who professed to be their deliverers. Of this fact, the proof which has reached this Department shall be furnished you." Although Monroe failed to send the deposition to the commissioners, they hurled the sensational charge at their British counterparts. In Parliament, members of the opposition demanded an explanation from the government. In response, the foreign secretary, Viscount Castlereagh, denied that the naval officers had sold any runaways. An official investigation cleared the Royal Navy of the charge to the satisfaction of the opposition in Parliament.[3]

The secretary of state's confident accusation also caught the attention of American senators who sought his evidence. The request proved embarrassing because Monroe had lost his copy of the Williams deposition. In October 1814, his undersecretary urgently wrote to St. George Tucker, seeking the original. The comedy of errors deepened as Tucker turned for help to Cabell, who sought out Griffin and Smith, but none could find the original or the elusive Williams, who had vanished. Along every step in the chain of credibility, gentlemen had invested their reputations on a copy that rested on a flimsy story from a shaky witness who had gone missing. Madison and Monroe had relied on Tucker, a federal district judge renowned for integrity, who trusted his son-in-law Cabell, a state senator. And Cabell believed what Griffin and Smith had told him about William's story because it echoed what Virginians wrote and read in their newspapers about the slave-stealing Britons. That left

Monroe in the lame position of sending to the Senate letters from
Cabell, Tucker, Griffin, and Smith, conveying that they remembered
such a deposition although none could produce it or the witness.[4]

Vice Admiral Sir Alexander Cochrane seethed at the attack on
his reputation, which a personal enemy in Britain exploited in a
scandalous pamphlet, charging that the admiral had diverted 200
runaways to work as slaves on his plantation in Trinidad. Cochrane
dismissed Monroe's charge as "a story trumped up among the People on the [American] coast to prevent their Negroes [from] deserting: a thousand such having been related by the refugees coming off
from the Shore." In March 1815, Cochrane sent a warship, at great
official cost, on a special mission to Norfolk with a letter demanding proof of the charge from the secretary of state.[5]

In Washington, D.C., the lead British diplomat, Anthony
St. John Baker, also sought to vindicate "the officers of a Nation
whose exertions for the total abolition of the slave trade have been
so conspicuous." By refuting the American charge, Baker and
Cochrane defended the humanitarian guise that the British Empire
had assumed. Discovering the flimsiness of the American evidence,
Baker reported to Cochrane, "The proof consists of the copy of an
affidavit of a single obscure individual, the original of which cannot
be found. This Government is extremely embarrassed by the notice
which has been taken of a charge which they had lightly made without proper foundation under the feelings of animosity created by
the measures which were adopted [by the Royal Navy] with respect
to the Negroes." Put on the defensive, Monroe fell back on Tucker's
reputation as "a Gentleman of distinguished respectability" as lend-
ing credibility to the incredible claims. Meanwhile, Monroe sent a
special agent, William Shaler, to Williamsburg, to help search for the
original, but he too came up empty.[6]

By proving that the Britons had sold the runaways, Monroe
hoped to discredit them as liberators among American slaves:

The exposure will produce a good effect in any future war, for if it is made to appear that the slaves have been sold in the West Indies, and their condition, under new masters, separated from their connections and friends, become worse than it was before, it will be more difficult to impose on them in any future war with whatever power it may be. These slaves . . . have been raised by our own Citizens, who take an interest in their welfare, not as property only but as persons. Much interest and sympathy are felt by the parties for each other. Their condition is, in general, as favorable as that of the Peasantry of Europe and much better than it is in some Countries.

Monroe's wishful thinking reveals that the war had promoted a pro-slavery defense framed to refute the British appeal as potential emancipators.[7]

To substantiate his charge against the British, Monroe pursued other leads found in newspaper stories about returning American prisoners who claimed to have seen the British sell runaways as slaves. Captain Perrin Willis insisted that an unnamed Virginian had told him that the British sold American runaways in Jamaica by order of the vice admiralty court. Captain James Jaboe returned from his Halifax captivity to assert that he had heard of slave sales there. Another former captive, Thomas L. Hall, added that he had seen a Halifax newspaper advertising thirteen Chesapeake slaves for sale. Edward Ironmonger told friends that he had witnessed such sales in Bermuda, but when deposed under oath, he merely claimed to have heard of the slave sales from others. A Philadelphia newspaper story claimed that a mariner "had heard it said that American Negroes had sold at Bermuda & elsewhere at an advanced price but knew not from what authority the report proceeded." Upon closer examination, all of these reports dissipated into vague rumors based on hearsay.[8]

At the direction of Earl Bathurst, British colonial officials investigated the supposed leads and found no evidence for any of them. In Norfolk the British consul "made particular Enquiry" but could find no master who had lost a slave carpenter during the war, which undercut Williams's claim. In Nassau the registrar of the vice admiralty court, agent for prisoners, collector of customs, and royal governor attested that no American slaves had been sold in the Bahamas during the war. The customs collector added that the few blacks who had arrived there were "enjoying that freedom which was held out to them by the officers commanding his Majesty's Forces on the American Coast." Jamaica's vice admiralty court never ordered the sale of any slaves captured on American ships, but instead freed them to serve in the army or navy. After a "most minute investigation," Governor James Cockburn of Bermuda felt "astonishment that the American government should have deemed a story as that trumped up by [Edward] Ironmonger worthy of a moment's attention." The governor of Nova Scotia investigated Hall's dubious charge that a Halifax newspaper had advertised slaves for sale in a colony that no longer sustained slavery. After every printer denied it under oath, the governor concluded that "there never was a more impudent and unfounded statement made upon Oath by any Man."[9]

The negative evidence did not daunt Monroe and other true believers in a British plot to seduce and sell American slaves. As with any conspiracy theory, the believers wove a tautology where the lack of substantial evidence became their proof for a cunning cover-up: that the Britons were deft tricksters who had expertly covered their tracks. General Thomas Pinckney of South Carolina assured Monroe that despite all of the evidence to the contrary, the slaves were "carried to the West India Islands, where they are by fraudulent contrivances, difficult to be detected, substantially sold as Slaves."[10]

The believers operated from the premise that the British were a wicked people responsible for American slavery; incapable of liberating slaves, they must have taken them for sale as plunder. Asserting that the British "were not men who might be expected to under-

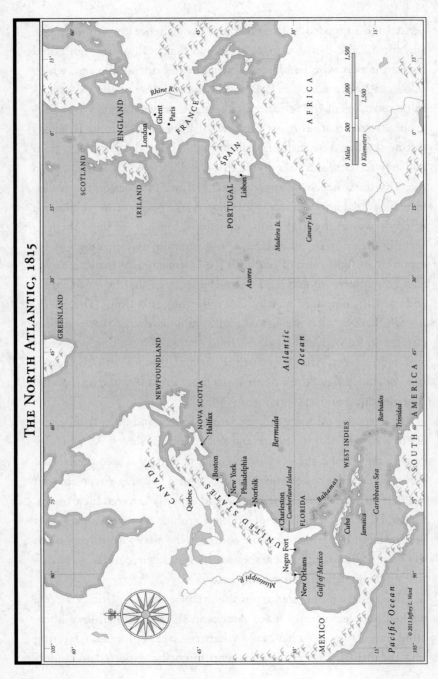

THE NORTH ATLANTIC, 1815

GREENLAND

CANADA

NEWFOUNDLAND

Quebec

NOVA SCOTIA
Halifax

Boston

UNITED STATES
New York
Philadelphia
Norfolk

Charleston
Cumberland Island

FLORIDA
Negro Fort

New Orleans
Mississippi R.
Gulf of Mexico

MEXICO

Pacific Ocean

Bermuda

Atlantic
Ocean

WEST INDIES
Bahamas
Cuba
Jamaica
Caribbean Sea

Barbados
Trinidad

SOUTH AMERICA

SCOTLAND

ENGLAND
London

IRELAND

Rhine R.
Ghent
Paris
FRANCE

SPAIN
PORTUGAL
Lisbon

Azores

Madeira Is.

Canary Is.

AFRICA

0 Miles   500   1,000   1,500
0 Kilometers   1,500

© 2013 Jeffrey L. Ward

The North Atlantic, 1815, a map by Jeffrey L. Ward.

take a crusade to abolish slavery," the *National Intelligencer* concluded that the slaves "were first stolen or cajoled away, and then frequently, but secretly, sold into a slavery ten-fold more severe than that which they had escaped." Insisting that "no liberal, enlightened, or honorable man" could doubt "the patriotic Monroe," the paper next developed the ingenious argument that by publicizing the accusation in 1814, the secretary of state had compelled the British to hide or relinquish their perfidy: "May it not have *prevented* the sale of many of our slaves, and thus have lessened the motive for stealing them?" Knowing what they wanted to believe, the conspiracy theorists bent the Britons to fit the absence of evidence.[11]

Judicious Americans eventually recognized that the British had freed, rather than sold, the runaways. In 1814 as a negotiator at Ghent, John Quincy Adams had pressed the charge of slave sales, from a conviction that Monroe held the proof. Two years later, as the minister to Great Britain, Adams had to disabuse Monroe of his fantasy, which relied on the discredited depositions of Hall and Williams. Adams wondered "how declarations, so utterly destitute of foundation should have been given." The last word should belong to Joseph C. Cabell, who had done so much in 1813 to promote the Williams deposition. Fourteen years later, Cabell conceded, "It is but candid, however, to admit that the statement of Williams was never sustained by other evidence and is [in] no way countenanced by the evidence since disclosed on the subject. We have *since* heard of the negroes at various points—at Halifax, Bermuda, Trinidad—and, wherever heard from, they were free."[12]

Returns

Deft at defending illusion against reality, masters still insisted that predatory Britons had seduced slaves away from their true patrons and protectors. If not sold into a worse slavery in the West Indies, the refugees were "wretches" marooned "on the barren Beach of

Tangier" or exiled to frigid Nova Scotia: a Virginian's notion of hell.
"It is said they are badly treated at Bermuda and dying very fast,"
Roswell King declared. Surely, the repentant runaways had discovered their mistake and, if provided with the means, would return
home to beg forgiveness from their masters.[13]

James Spilman of Virginia put that theory to the test by visiting
Bermuda on a mercantile voyage in the spring of 1815. Spilman
believed that the runaways were "generally disposed to return,
but are subject to the continual persuasion & intimidation urged
by the whites of every description." But he could persuade only
four men to return to slavery in Virginia. Anthony Champ, Isaac
Smith, John Hall, and Joseph Webster came from the Rappahannock Valley, and all had escaped at the end of the war during Captain Barrie's "shooting party" of December 1814. By the following
spring, they evidently felt the pull of family left behind. In Essex
and Lancaster Counties, they became proverbial as the only runaways to come home again. They later became star witnesses for
masters seeking compensation for other slaves lost to the British
during the war.[14]

Five other runaways can be documented as returning to slavery
in Virginia after the war: Lewis Jackson, Simon Willis, James Steward, Raleigh W. Downman's Nassau, and Thomas McClanahan's
Sam. Nassau, Jackson, and Willis also had fled from the Rappahannock in December 1814. In July 1815, Nassau's master in Lancaster
County reported that the runaway had "Returned, having escaped
from Bermuda." Jackson fled homeward from a British watering
party at St. George's Island, in the Potomac, in March 1815. Simon
Willis had a longer odyssey after enlisting in the Royal Navy as a
ship's carpenter on HMS *Devastation*. Sent to the coast of Georgia
in January 1815, Willis deserted from a shore party and made his
way overland back to Essex County. McClanahan's Sam apparently
left with the raiders under duress and promptly returned at the end

of the war, finding passage from Havana on a merchant ship to Philadelphia, and then walked back to his master in Northumberland County.[15]

On September 20, 1814, in Anne Arundel County, Maryland, James Steward had escaped with three other men by rowing away in a stolen boat to a warship. A young "mulatto" with "small eyes" but "remarkably large feet," he enlisted in the Royal Navy as a sailor. At the end of the war, he fought in the British assault on Fort Bowyer, Alabama, where his best friend died. Perhaps in shock at his loss, Steward deserted and tried to pass as a free black named Tom. Attempting that dodge in Alabama showed far more imagination than realism, for that territory had virtually no free blacks, and the whites meant to keep it that way. The fort's commander, Colonel Gilbert C. Russell, owned a nearby plantation and decided that "Tom" had best work as his slave pending the discovery of his true identity and owner. Russell described Tom in a newspaper ad eventually reprinted in Baltimore, where Frederick Grammar recognized the fugitive as his slave. Grammar wrote to seek Steward's return, but Russell replied, "Tom has married one of my *virgins* and expresses much anxiety to remain where he is." To strengthen his bargaining position, the colonel also noted that, otherwise Tom "might take to the woods and our County affords no jails to hold him." Ultimately, Russell paid $550 so that Tom could remain his married slave in Alabama.[16]

What explains the nine runaways who apparently preferred slavery in the Chesapeake over freedom with the British? All were young men who evidently escaped without other close kin. Fleeing during the last five months of the war, they had less time to adjust to their new circumstances. One of them, Sam, had been taken by force. The others had found their freedom circumscribed by the demands and hardships of military service. These nine were exceptions that proved the rule, for almost all of the 3,400 Chesapeake runaways preferred British freedom over American slavery.[17]

Special Agents

During the spring of 1815, Monroe sent three special agents—
Thomas Spalding, Eli Magruder, and Augustine Neale—to visit Bermuda and Halifax to seek the repatriation of the runaways. If the
British would not compel the refugees to return, the agents were
supposed to persuade them to come home to slavery. Monroe sought
to exploit the British pose as liberators: "They have professed to
afford them an asylum as freemen. They are admitted of course to
be voluntary Agents, and as such must have a right to go where they
think fit." Monroe felt no contradiction in persuading "voluntary
Agents" to renounce their freedom, for he believed them incapable
of liberty and longing for the protection of their old masters.[18]

A rich and erudite planter from the Sea Islands of Georgia, Spalding had visited Cumberland Island in early March in a failed bid
to dissuade Rear Admiral Cockburn from removing the runaways.
Reaching Bermuda on May 19, Spalding requested their forcible
repatriation by Governor James Cockburn, but the admiral's brother
was not about to compel the refugees to return as slaves to America. Spalding reported that the governor "instantly lost his temper,"
declaring "that he would rather Bermuda, and every man, woman,
and child in it, were sunk under the sea, than surrender one slave that
had sought protection under the flag of England." By protecting the
refugees, the governor defended the honor of his brother and their
empire.[19]

Governor Cockburn did let Spalding speak to the former slaves,
but none agreed to return to slavery in Georgia. Unwilling to believe
blacks capable of free choice, Spalding blamed meddling by British
officials: "Every means are employed to instill into the minds of the
Slaves by the officers of the Colonial Regiment, and those that direct
their labours at Ireland [Island], the most deadly hatred to their
ancient masters, as well as to the U. States generally." The British
kept the runaways "as important means to be employed against [the

United States] in the event of another war, as well from their knowledge of the country as from the stimulus which that hatred will give
to their actions." In fact, the refugees had their own reasons to stay,
for Spalding noted that dockyard workers were "paid high wages."
They also remembered their hardships as slaves in Dixie, the land of
cotton where old times were not forgotten. James Spilman reported
that they bristled upon learning that Spalding "came from Georgia
and to which country the Negroes have a great aversion."[20]

Spalding also worked at cross purposes with a second special
agent, Eli Magruder, who had arrived on May 6 with a chartered
merchant ship from New York. A former merchant from Barbados,
Magruder could better perform as an agent under cover. Rather too
proud of his new authority, Magruder expected to dictate to Spalding, but Georgia planters did not take well to the orders of others, so
Spalding sailed home in a huff at the end of the month. Magruder then
consulted the best Bermudian lawyer, Francis Forbes, on whether
the runaways could be reclaimed as property through the courts.
Unfortunately that best lawyer was the Crown's attorney general, so
the consultation blew Magruder's cover to no good end, for Forbes
insisted that British law forbade the departure of any black without
the governor's license.[21]

The third special agent, Augustine Neale, sailed to Halifax instead
of Bermuda. Monroe entrusted Neale's instructions to Walter Jones,
who worried that young Virginia gentlemen made lousy covert
agents. High strung and obsessed with honor, they had short fuses
and scant capacity for keeping secrets. Anticipating that Neale
would erupt upon hearing some Briton slur the American character,
Jones warned, "I know that with most young men, especially our
Virginians, irritability of passion is apt to be confounded with firm-
ness of Spirit." To succeed in his mission for the public, Neale had
to set aside his "individual Character for a time." Taking the advice
to heart, Neale became the most discreet of the three government
agents, but Spalding and Magruder had set that bar pretty low.[22]

Jones directed Neale first to seek proof that the British had sold runaways: "This is an affair of no light concern as it respects the perfidy of those who seduced our Slaves or the future conduct in peace or war of the Slaves themselves." In supplementary instructions, Monroe assured Neale that he could prevent a future race war in America by discrediting the British as slave liberators. Monroe and Jones sought to break the attachment of southern slaves to the British.[23]

But the instructions proved contradictory. While seeking proof that the British kept the runaways as slaves, Neale was also supposed to treat them as free to decide their future by persuading them to return to bondage in America. Jones explained,

> The dread of punishment, on their return, which has been so industriously impressed upon the fugitives by their new protectors, has no foundation. It is within our knowledge that those who have returned have been gladly received & not punished at all. Some have been sent to parts of the Country remote from the Coast, where it is well known that they live in greater Comfort & Equality with the whites than in the older and more populous settlements of the State.

This misguided sales pitch undercut the prime reason for a runaway to return: a nostalgia for home and family left behind. If truly welcomed back, why would they face the distrust of sale into the interior? And why return at the risk of sale to a strange place "remote from the Coast" and so from their homes and kin, which probably meant to the dreaded Deep South?[24]

To impress the refugees, Neale hired and brought along Joseph Webster, "quite an intelligent and smart negroe" and one of the four slaves who had returned from Bermuda to Virginia with Spilman. Neale expected Webster to "give positive evidence of the humanity & forgiveness with which their former masters hailed their return."[25]

Monroe sent Neale to Nova Scotia in a naval schooner with the unfortunate name of *Nonsuch*, which helped to confirm that Neale's mission was no such thing as a private venture. Indeed, the British in Nova Scotia learned from an indiscreet New York newspaper that the *Nonsuch* would sail to Halifax "to bring home the blacks taken from the southern states by the British naval commanders during the late war, and who are to be delivered back to their owners." In another misstep, the crew consisted primarily of free blacks, who were not exactly on board with Neale's mission.[26]

Arriving in Halifax on August 25, Neale hoped to rally the white Nova Scotians in support of his mission. "The white Labourers complain that their wages are now less and employment rendered uncertain by the introduction of coloured people," he noted. For this reason, however, the merchants welcomed the black influx, and they had more clout with the government than did the common white laborers. Moreover, even the poor whites turned against Neale's mission once their dislike for "the despised Americans" trumped their distaste for black competitors. Foiling the Americans became more popular than ousting the refugees.[27]

A scrupulous investigator, Neale had to inform Monroe that the runaways were neither enslaved nor discontented in Nova Scotia: "But, sir, from a candid investigation into the condition of the Fugitives in this province, it is fair to conclude, upon the evidence I have heretofore had, that the *far greater portion* of them are in situations much easier & have prospects far better than I could have supposed." He cautioned Monroe to cease claiming that the Britons had deceived and sold the runaways, for even if "a *few* solitary slaves have been sold, it will be equally notorious that thousands of the Slaves taken from the U.S. have been emancipated. The latter fact being so much the stronger case, will so entirely do away the first" that it was pointless to pursue a few stray leads.[28]

Despite the odds against him, Neale tried to persuade the refugees to return to Virginia. He played up "the winter's frost of this climate" and appealed to their "customary attachment" to homes in old Virginia. But even the nostalgic balked at returning to "the horrors of anticipated punishment," so Neale found it "extremely difficult to soothe their feelings into a contrary temper." Above all, family ties kept them from returning: "For example, a Parent or wife wishes to return, but the child or husband does not—and vice versa." Having escaped to live together in freedom, they were not about to separate again in slavery.[29]

Neale's soothing message soured in mid-September, when Captain Trant of the *Nonsuch* cracked down on his black sailors. Deeming them "mutinous," he imprisoned two in the hold of the ship, but another shipmate freed them, and all three "escaped to the shore, where they confirmed the terrors & prejudices of the Negroes to the vessel—that she had come most certainly to force them away & Joe [Webster] was sent on shore to decoy them on board." Two more black sailors soon deserted to join the mutineers. Thereafter the five "were daily seen, sometimes on the wharf, waving defiance & insult to the vessel." Aided by a white constable, Trant tried forcibly to retrieve the deserters, but they were defended by "a Mob of white persons" who struck down and kicked the beleaguered captain. Worse still, Webster "was all most murdered by the Blacks set on by the British." The Halifax magistrates dismissed Neale's protests, telling him to stay on board his ship and depart as soon as possible.[30]

In the end, Neale found one old woman, Harriot Johnson, who agreed to return to her home near Baltimore. Nova Scotia's government, however, refused to issue a passport for her departure, and the admiral of the squadron ordered the *Nonsuch* to sail away on September 19 without Johnson. Indeed, Neale's voyage suffered a net loss, for he left behind five deserters without a single refugee to compensate. Deprived of half of her able seamen, the *Nonsuch* had a difficult passage home. A frustrated Neale denounced Halifax as "the most unfriendly port & inhospitable clime I believe in the world." All but one of the refugees disagreed, and they had the support of five deserters from the *Nonsuch*.[31]

Halifax, from Dartmouth Point, *an 1817 aquatint by G. I. Parkyns. (Courtesy of the Archives of Nova Scotia)*

None of the special agents retrieved a single refugee, which led all three to decline as futile the additional missions to the West Indies proposed by Monroe. Some Georgia planters did enlist a Halifax mercantile firm to help them woo the refugees to return, but the Nova Scotian merchants reported "that they can find none that wish to return except some old ones that are not worth sending." Any refugees who disliked Nova Scotia had a better alternative than returning to slavery: moving on to Boston and New York to find paying work "remote from their former Masters," as Neale put it. Soon Monroe lost interest in further missions that could only discredit the consoling fictions he wanted to believe as a slaveholder.[32]

Refugees

As the chief naval base for the North American squadron, Halifax was the easiest place for the Royal Navy to send hundreds of runaways. And the government of Nova Scotia would take them in—

albeit grudgingly—in contrast to Bermuda, which restricted black newcomers to Ireland Island. Admiral Cockburn noted that "the laws at Halifax do not oppose any difficulty on account of [the] Colour of People landing there and endeavoring by honest labor to earn their own Maintenance." Never particularly significant in Nova Scotia, slavery had withered away during the decade before 1812 as the Crown judges refused to assist the few masters in recovering their runaways. In effect, the judges applied the *Somerset* decision: that slavery lacked the sanction of either natural or positive law in Nova Scotia.[33]

Nova Scotia was a cold, northern colony on a long peninsula jutting between the Atlantic, to the east, and the Bay of Fundy, to the west. Fertile soil appeared only in modest pockets between gray rocky ridges and amid many bogs and lakes. Farmers struggled to push their plows through the rocky soils and to raise crops during the short growing season between the last frost of May and the first frost of September. They grew mixed crops of grains and the hay to feed a few livestock. The great port of Halifax hosted merchant ships, a fishing fleet, the North American squadron of the Royal Navy, and the province's capital. A lieutenant governor and a council—both appointed by the Crown—administered the colony along with an assembly elected by the men who owned at least a farm or a shop.[34]

During the summer of 1813 the first refugees from the Chesapeake reached Halifax. On arrival, they took an oath of allegiance to the king. Poor and often sick, the refugees strained Governor Sherbrooke's budget to provide rations, clothing, and medical care. The imperial government promised compensation, but in the short term the burden fell on the government and taxpayers of Nova Scotia.[35]

Most Nova Scotians assumed this responsibility with a sour grace, disdaining blacks as dirty, lazy, and larcenous. After the American Revolution the colony had reluctantly taken in about 3,000 black refugees, but the inhabitants treated them so badly that

most left during the 1790s, for either the northern American seaports or the new British colony of Sierra Leone, on the west coast
of Africa. In 1815 the Nova Scotians similarly responded to the new
surge of black refugees from America. Whenever any refugee trans-
gressed, the press and public cast the culprit as the face of an entire
race. In 1817, when a house caught fire, the authorities blamed a
young black servant, so a Halifax newspaper warned against employing any refugees: "no kindness, comfort, or hospitality, can insure
their integrity," for they comprised "a race whose principles are so
repugnant to the dictates of gratitude and morality." Dismayed by
that prejudice, the colony's surveyor general lamented, "The common Sentiment has been—let them that encouraged their coming
among us maintain them or answer for the consequences. We *want
none of the Seed of Cain among us.*"[36]

Americans often misunderstood the British Empire as a mono-
lith moved by a centralized power with a coherent vision for all the
parts. In fact, that empire (like every empire) presented a complex set
of disparate interests and scattered officials often working at cross
purposes with one another and frequently opposed by their colonists. The Royal Navy's admirals had promised freedom and land to
black refugees only to deliver them to Nova Scotia, where the governor had to make good on those promises. That governor shared
many of the prejudices held by legislators who balked at spending
tax money on black newcomers or rewarding them with land grants.
Deriding the refugees as "miserable wretches," Sherbrooke asserted
that "the generality of them are so unwilling to work that several
of them are absolutely starving owing to their own idleness." Six
months later, however, Sherbrooke had to admit that "the greatest
part of these People have since been able to support themselves by
their labour & industry so that a very small proportion of them now
remain chargeable to Government."[37]

During 1813–1814 about 1,200 black refugees reached Halifax,
and the end of the war in early 1815 promised a further surge from

Bermuda. For short-term funding, the governor turned to the assembly, but the members resented taking in "a separate & marked Class of people unfitted by nature to this Climate or to an association with the rest of His Majesty's Colonists." In addition to the public cost, the legislators worried about their competition in the labor market to the "discouragement of white labourers & servants."[38]

After conveying the assembly's protest to his superiors in London, Sherbrooke did provide for the new refugees from the Crown's customs revenue for the port of Halifax. The surge of fugitives began to arrive in late April and continued through the summer and fall. The Halifax poorhouse could not cope with their numbers, so Sherbrooke sent the sick, disabled, and elderly to the former prison on Melville Island, about three miles from the harbor. During the summer the island housed 727 refugees, although their number declined in the fall as their health improved and they left to find paying work. More refugees arrived, but in diminishing numbers, during 1816 and 1817. According to an official list kept in Halifax, 1,611 refugees entered the port between April 27, 1815, and October 24, 1818. Adding the previous 1,200 yields a total of 2,811 war refugees sent to Nova Scotia: comparable to the 3,000 runaways who arrived there after the revolution.[39]

That total does not include another 381 refugees who had been sent on to the neighboring colony of New Brunswick. To reduce Nova Scotia's burden, Sherbrooke diverted one large transport, the *Regulus*, to New Brunswick, with the reluctant consent of that colonial government. Arriving at the port of St. John on May 25, 1815, the transport unloaded 168 men, 112 women, and 100 children. That was the first and the last shipment of the refugees to New Brunswick, where the officials followed the Nova Scotia practice of feeding and clothing the newcomers until they found work as common laborers in the port or countryside.[40]

In the preindustrial economy of the Maritime colonies, most of the wage work was seasonal. During the warmer months, ships, docks, and farms needed extra hands, but that work diminished in the winter, casting most laborers adrift without pay. Worse still, the refugees arrived during a recession that sharply reversed the wartime boom artificially stimulated by military expenditures, smuggling, and privateering. During the hard postwar years, 1816–1819, even the summer failed to provide enough work for Nova Scotia's newly swollen laboring class.[41]

Rather than remain laborers most of the refugees wanted to become land-owning farmers, so they expected the government to keep the promise made in Admiral Cochrane's April 1814 proclamation. In June 1815, Earl Bathurst chided Sherbrooke for failing to grant the promised lands to the refugees, but the governor preferred to retain the refugees as a pool of cheap wage labor to benefit the merchants and farmers of the colony. The governor blamed his own delay on black reluctance, assuring Bathurst in July that "the negroes on their first arrival seem to dread so arduous an undertaking as the tilling of ground." If "instead dispersed through the province as farmers' servants, labourers, &c," they could serve a prolonged apprenticeship in northern agriculture before receiving their own lands.[42]

When Bathurst remained insistent, Sherbrooke promised to seek "the most favorable situations now unappropriated for the purpose of locating such of the free Negroes as are willing to become Settlers." But Nova Scotia's limited stock of good land had long been granted, leaving only barren pockets "unappropriated" in 1815. Sherbrooke also defined a "favorable situation" as near Halifax, where the settlers could continue to work for wages during the warm season. The colony's surveyor general placed most of the refugees at Preston, ten miles east of Halifax, or at Hammonds Plains, about twenty miles west of the port. Both townships previously had been granted to disbanded British soldiers and Irish immigrants, who had quickly abandoned their new lands as too difficult to farm. During the late 1780s and early 1790s, some revolutionary refugees had lived there until they left for Sierra Leone. Thereafter, the lands lay unsettled for fifteen years, attesting to their poor quality.[43]

During the fall of 1815, Sherbrooke's government provided provisions and boards, nails, axes, and saws to enable the refugees to build huts at Preston, where about 151 men, 117 women, and 200 children spent the winter. Another 180 black men began to cut trees and build huts at Hammonds Plains. While given hand tools by the government, the settlers got none of the oxen and horses needed to haul logs or plow the land. Sherbrooke's measures sufficed to satisfy Bathurst as fulfilling the letter of Cochrane's wartime promises to the refugees.[44]

Growing steadily, Preston had 924 black settlers and Hammonds Plains had 504 by the end of 1816. Former Chesapeake slaves tended to settle at Preston, while former Georgians prevailed at Hammonds Plains, although each township had a minority of refugees from the other region of origin. Smaller black settlements developed at Windsor Road, Refugee Hill, Beech Hill, Porters Lake, and Fletchers Lake, all on the periphery of Halifax. Other refugees persisted in Halifax as urban laborers and artisans, or they scattered around the colony to work for wages on farms and as loggers.[45]

The black settlers received only ten acres per family: a tenth of the land needed for a proper farm in Nova Scotia. Seeking mutual support and security in a white-dominated colony, the refugees wanted to cluster together, but none of the townships near Halifax had enough ungranted land to enable both clustering and substantial farms, so they had to settle for paltry lots. Sherbrooke also saw no reason to help the refugees prosper as independent farmers, for he wanted to retain them as a reserve of cheap labor for the port. His government granted them just enough land to sustain a family on potatoes during the cold season, when the refugees could not find paying work. As seasonal retreats from unemployment, the little farms promised to reduce the government's expenditures for poor relief during the winter. To discourage the black settlers from selling out to move away, the government denied them legal title to the land, instead merely giving them permission to occupy. Such paltry farms and scanty tenure fell far short of the 100-acre lots and free-hold titles routinely granted to white settlers in Nova Scotia.[46]

Despite their daunting hardships, the refugees worked their new lands with a zeal that impressed the whites who knew them best. Each township had a supervisor, a locally prominent man who issued tools and rations to the settlers. The Preston supervisor, Theophilus Chamberlain, characterized the newcomers as "able" and "industri-ous." With mere hand tools, they built "snug houses" and cleared garden plots to grow potatoes and vegetables between the rocks. In 1816 at Lake Porter, Rufus Fairbanks reported that "they raised upwards of three hundred Bushels of Potatoes beside other Vegeta-bles upon Lands which the year before was covered with a Forest." In 1817, John Rule extolled two black farmers as "very ingenious and industrious men," who had "erected a very Comfortable House, cleared several acres of Land now in Cultivation . . . cut a road and Errected a very considerable Bridge."[47]

A Quaker doctor, Seth Coleman, often visited the refugees. In March 1815, Coleman noted "a disposition in them to labour, and to help themselves, but the fact is they have nothing to do" during the long winter when they could neither farm nor find paying work in Halifax. Coleman then "found many of them subsisting on what we should think literally nothing." Often the men watched the children, while the women walked several miles to the white-owned farms "to seek a day's work at Washing or Sewing." He deemed the refugees "a Virtuous People" despite their lack of education. Indeed, Coleman never saw any of the refugees intoxicated, which could be said of very few white folk in the colony.[48]

The well-informed Nova Scotians regretted the racial prejudice expressed by most colonists and officials. Coleman declared, "My feelings have been often hurt at the expressions of People who are ignorant of their Situations, they say Thievish Black Dogs, they

deserve this or they deserve that. . . . Place the same number of White
People in the Same Situation under all the disadvantages that those
have had to incounter, what would have been the report of them[?]"
Chamberlain urged the black settlers to "laugh at the Squibs that
ignorance or ill nature and contempt has induced some silly Body to
throw out against them." Unfortunately, such silly bodies included
Governor Sherbrooke, who continued to deride the refugees as lazy.
No one, however, ever tested *his* ability to clear land to subsist a
family amid the rocks of Preston.[49]

Despite their hard work, the refugees soon faced the limits of
their craggy and swampy lands. Usually austere, the Nova Scotia climate became menacing in 1816: the notorious year without a
summer thanks to a volcanic explosion in the East Indies that cast
enough dust into the upper atmosphere to deflect the sun's warmth
across the Northern Hemisphere. Unable to raise sufficient crops,
the refugees needed government rations. In December, Sherbrooke's
newly arrived successor, Lord Dalhousie, reported, "I find the
Negroe families that settled, in a state of starvation, their crops having totally failed."[50]

Afflicted by hunger on their little lots of poor land during an
especially harsh year, the refugees soon confronted another plague:
the words of Lord Dalhousie. Eager to reduce the government's
expenditures on food relief, he sought to send blacks back to their
masters in the United States or deport them to Sierra Leone or Trinidad. Indeed, he blamed the refugees for their poverty and hunger:
"Slaves by habit & education, no longer working under the dread of
the lash, their idea of freedom is idleness, and they are therefore quite
incapable of Industry." Dalhousie also derided Admiral Cochrane's
wartime promise of freedom to American slaves as "a silly thing."
A diverse lot, British imperialists did not agree on issues of race and
freedom.[51]

In 1817, Dalhousie belatedly toured the black settlements, which
revealed the refugees in a very different light. He conceded that

"almost every man had one or more Acres cleared and ready for seed & working with an industry that astonished against difficulties of nature almost insurmountable & opposed, abused & cheated by the old Settlers near whom they had been placed." Sadly, two years later Dalhousie revived his former canard: "the habits of their life and constitutional laziness will continue & these miserable creatures will for years be a burden upon the Government." Here we see the power of prejudice to overcome the reality briefly revealed to Dalhousie by visiting the refugees on their little farms, surrounded by neighbors who wanted them to fail.[52]

Despite their hardships, the refugees preferred freedom in Nova Scotia over a return to slavery in America. They cherished their new ability to earn their own money and their freedom from domination by an owner. Maria Fuller explained, "We are not now in the U. States, and we can do as we like here." Another refugee preferred Nova Scotia because "what I works for here, I gets." An elderly woman agreed, "Oh! de difference is, dat when I work here, I work for myself, and when I was working at home [in Maryland], I was working for other people."[53]

The imperial government also balked at breaking the promises of freedom made to people who had helped to fight the Americans. But Earl Bathurst would pay to ship the refugees to Trinidad, where they could join the thriving community founded after the war by former Colonial Marines and their families. Given the refugees' poor treatment in Nova Scotia, their relocation to Trinidad had merit, but a mere ninety-five agreed to depart in a single vessel in January 1821. Most were former Georgians from Beech Hill or Hammonds Plains, while almost none left the largest Chesapeake black community at Preston. After that one shipment in 1821, no more Nova Scotia blacks accepted the government's repeated invitations to relocate.[54]

The refugees dreaded getting on any ship bound for the West Indies via the American coast. Given that Dalhousie had proposed restoring them to slavery, most did not trust any British captain taking his orders from the governor or his successor, James Kempt. In 1823 Governor Kempt explained, "These people entertain so great a fear to slavery that no persuasion can induce them to remove to any place where Slavery exists." In 1825 he complained that "fanatical preachers" had persuaded most "that it would not be intended to send them to Trinidad, but to sell them to their former Masters in the United States."[55]

Despite their hardships, the refugees had made homes and communities, and they wanted to stick together in Nova Scotia. One puzzled official marveled, "They seem to have some attachment to the soil they have cultivated, poor and barren as it is." In addition to deriving a basic subsistence from their small farms, the inhabitants earned cash by marketing berries, wreaths, shingles, brooms, oars, chairs, flower boxes, and baskets in Halifax. During the 1820s and 1830s, many moved into the port, working for wages on the docks, aboard ships, and as domestics in prosperous homes. Others became urban blacksmiths, chimney sweeps, glaziers, shoemakers, and carpenters.[56]

Although most remained poor, they were still better off free in Nova Scotia than as slaves in America. In their new homes, they had restored the family ties that had been their prime goal in escaping from slavery. In a careful study of the refugee families, historian Harvey Amani Whitfield found that when enslaved in the United States, only 44 percent of the married couples had lived on the same farm. In stark contrast, over 90 percent of the couples lived together in Hammonds Plains and Preston in 1820. Despite their mistreatment in Nova Scotia, they could live without fear that a master's death, debt, or whim would sell someone precious far away never to be seen again. Their poverty was hard, but slavery had been far worse.[57]

Slavery had deepened rather than dampened the determination by blacks to defend their families. In 1815 Rufus Fairbanks employed black loggers outside Halifax. To save money, Fairbanks had left their wives and children behind to subsist in the poorhouse of the port. But a defiant woman declared that "she had rather go into the woods and perish with her Husband than to be left in the Poor House with her Children to be devoured by Vermin and die there." After she arrived with her four children, another man went to the poorhouse, Fairbanks explained, "without my consent" and carried his three children back to the logging camp. Soon the other workers followed suit. And then a "Poor old Man and Woman . . . come and begged I would allow them to go with them as the women were their Daughters." Unable to retain the workers without their families, Fairbanks reluctantly took them all in.[58]

Merikens

Despite their previous dread of the West Indies as the worst den of slavery, the most fortunate refugees settled on the island of Trinidad. Conquered by the British from the Spanish during the 1790s, Trinidad was especially large, fertile, and underdeveloped. While preserving the slave-worked plantation sector on Trinidad, the British government distrusted its expansion as a security risk. In the spring of 1815 a colonial official lamented that seven-eighths of Trinidad was "lying waste and unproductive" for want of labor. He urged the introduction of a new group "healthy & free, with habits and science ready formed and sufficiently numerous to stand unsupported and distinct from our present Population on its immediate arrival." Some imperial officials hoped to fill that bill with some of the black refugees from America.[59]

During the war the British sent a few refugees to Trinidad, but the significant arrivals began in May 1815, primarily coming from the Gulf Coast of Florida and Louisiana. By the end of 1815 at least 210 had disembarked at the capital and chief harbor, Port of Spain, where the governor, Sir Ralph Woodford, welcomed them as "mostly creoles, intelligent and apparently well disposed." Woodford settled most of them in the densely forested lands in the Naparima region, about forty miles south of Port of Spain.[60]

As a conservative imperialist, Woodford had complex views on race and slavery in Trinidad. On the one hand, he cherished the rights of property and upheld the racial supremacy of white men. He regretted the abolition of the slave trade for undermining the profitability of plantations and the security of the planters, and he denounced Methodist missionaries for preaching to the slaves and allowing some to become preachers. On the other hand, the governor was also a dutiful imperial servant who obeyed the orders of his superiors, who favored Christianizing the slaves and restricting the slave trade. When reminded by Earl Bathurst of his duty, Woodford vowed "to promote the benevolent Views of His Royal Highness the Prince Regent and the Imperial Parliament towards the Slaves of this Colony." The governor also bristled when planters lobbied for their own assembly or criticized his administration. An authoritarian, Woodford spoke up for the planters' interests in part because he did not want them to speak directly to London. Finally, to defend the colony against foreign invasion and internal revolt, the governor relied on a garrison where two-thirds of the soldiers were black. Both a slave society and an imperial colony, Trinidad was rife with contradictions that Woodford had learned to live with.[61]

Woodford dreaded the revolutionary ferment in the Spanish colonies along the nearby shores of South America. Early and often (but in vain), he tried to dissuade his government from its policy of neutrality, which, in fact, favored the revolutionaries at the expense of the Spanish royalists. The British government hoped for increased commerce with the independent new republics, but Woodford feared that the revolutions would lead to "Ruin and Desolation and the eventual Dominion of the Sambos." He gasped when a leading revolutionary, Simon Bolivar, recruited soldiers among the slaves by promising them freedom. And Woodford became apoplectic when Bolivar welcomed naval support from the black republic of Haiti. The governor worried that either his colony's slaves would escape to South America to enlist with Bolivar or they would import his revolution into Trinidad. In the spring of 1816, Woodford's alarm grew upon learning of the Easter Revolt by the slaves on the nearby British West Indian island of Barbados. Woodford noted "an Attempt to fire a Liquor Store" in Port of Spain "and the Rapidity with which the News of the Insurrection was spread by the Negroes" of Trinidad despite his efforts to suppress that information.[62]

In sum, the American refugees landed in a colony roiled by news of the slave unrest in Barbados and agitated by the revolutions in South America. At such a tense moment, the advent of hundreds of former slaves from America, most with military training, proved controversial. The planters feared that the newcomers would share their military expertise with slaves, but the governor expected them to bolster the colony's defenses against internal as well as external threats.[63]

The biggest surge of refugees to Trinidad came in August 1816, when the former Colonial Marines arrived from Bermuda: 404 men along with 83 women and 87 children. Unlike the previous American black refugees to Trinidad, most of the Colonial Marines came from the Chesapeake, with about a quarter hailing from the Sea Islands of Georgia. In August 1815 the imperial government had proposed transferring the Colonial Marines to a West Indian army regiment. Protests by the marines, their officers, and Bermuda's governor stalled the transfer, but the government became insistent in November 1815. After several days of discussion, the Colonial Marines embraced an alternative offered by the government: discharge from the service and settlement on their own farms in Trinidad.[64]

During the summer of 1816, their commanding major, Andrew Kinsman, accompanied the former Colonial Marines to Port of Spain and on to the Naparima region, where Woodford sought to satisfy "the strong disposition manifested by these People to keep together & form a separate Community." He also calculated that Naparima's coast and river would enable the settlers to subsist by catching fish and sea turtles. To supplement the wild bounty, the government provided each man with a weekly ration of four pounds of salted fish and six pounds of flour or plantains and yams. The government delivered hammers, nails, and saws to enable them to construct houses, as well as machetes, hatchets, axes, and hoes to facilitate clearing and cultivating their lands. To maintain order and cohesion, each of the Colonial Marine companies received a distinct village, where the former sergeants and corporals governed as constables. And Woodford appointed a white magistrate, Robert Mitchell, to supervise the constables. Proud of their distinctive origins in America, the black settlers called themselves "the Merikens."[65]

Initially granted sixteen acres, each former marine got more and better land than did the black refugees in Nova Scotia, and a Meriken received additional acreage once he demonstrated an ability to cultivate more. For eight months the settlers relied on government rations, but thereafter they subsisted on their own crops of potatoes, yams, cassava, rice, maize, pumpkins, and plantains. They also kept chickens and pigs and became renowned hunters. In November, just three months after their first settlement, Woodford reported, "They are far advanced in their Plantations and they are reported to behave well in general." Unlike the governors of Nova Scotia, Woodford consistently praised his black settlers as industrious, "orderly and peaceable."[66]

Woodford, Mitchell, and Kinsman expected gratitude and loyalty to the government from the settlers. In his parting address, Kinsman exhorted his former men "cheerfully [to] take up Arms against any Enemy who may attempt to disturb the peace of the Colony." He added, "They must not receive any [enslaved] Negroes in their Houses, or Plantations, and must apprehend all Runaways." To keep their land, the newcomers had to defend the slave society around them.[67]

But separating the Merikens from the slaves proved harder than expected. Although relatively underdeveloped, Naparima had about 400 free whites who owned 3,300 slaves, some of whom soon discovered that they had relatives among the newcomers (apparently those from Georgia). This discovery deeply alarmed the local planters, who suspected that the former marines would help the slaves to escape or fight for their freedom. In a protest petition to the governor, the planters dreaded "the intercourse, particularly by night, between the American Negroes and the slaves of your Petitioners." Contact with free and propertied blacks would promote "impatience and discontent in the Minds of their Slaves," ultimately ripening into revolt. The planters wanted the Company Towns broken up and the settlers dispersed as wage laborers throughout the slave districts. In effect the planters sought to impose the Nova Scotia plan on the newcomers.[68]

Unlike the Nova Scotians, however, the Trinidad planters lacked an elected assembly to press their views, and Woodford brooked no opposition to his government. By defending the Company Towns, Woodford sustained the former marines as a military reserve should either the island's planters or their slaves become troublesome. Woodford insisted that the Merikens provided "additional Security from having thereby doubled the number of free Men in a District where, as the Petitioners Complain, the slaves so dangerously preponderate." For Woodford, class trumped race, for he expected free black farmers to defend the colony against a slave revolt. The governor also charged the protesting planters with racial hypocrisy, for some were free people of color: "Many of the present Petitioners were Slaves a few years ago, and now possess some of the finest Estates in the Island." Race and class did not break along identical fault lines in the social complexity of Trinidad.[69]

A strong group identity, hard work, good land, experienced leaders, a warm climate, and a supportive government promoted the success of the Company Towns. In 1817, Woodford visited and praised the settlers' progress in felling trees, planting gardens, and building homes. By May 1818 the Merikens had cleared 1,200 acres and planted most of them. Seven years later they raised 2,000 barrels of corn and 400 barrels of rice. In 1825, Woodford reported that their houses were "much more spacious, comfortable, and cleaner than the houses of slaves." But the Merikens had one big problem: a shortage of women. The British government helped by sending to Naparima some African women taken from intercepted slave ships.[70]

Among the diverse peoples of Trinidad, the Merikens sustained an enduring and distinctive identity. Mid-nineteenth-century missionaries described the people as "self-reliant and sensitive of control," "independent of the outer world," and "unwilling to submit." Proud of their freedom, the Merikens felt superior to the enslaved and indentured peoples elsewhere on Trinidad. Their culture synthesized the Christianity of the Chesapeake with the more African beliefs borne by the refugees from the Georgia Sea Islands. Primarily Baptists, the Merikens became noted for their loud, ecstatic, and physical worship, rich in jumps, shakes, shouts, and spiritual songs. Expressed in biblical analogy, their "Memory Spirituals" recalled overcoming slavery through migration and resettlement. In one they sang of their relocation across the sea to a better country known as "Ninevah land":

> We're gwine, w'ere gwine to Ninevah land
> Praise ye the Lord
> Captain sailing to Ninevah land
> Praise ye the Lord
> Ninevah land is a beautiful land
> Praise ye the Lord
> Ninevah land will soon overflow
> Praise ye the Lord.

Through courage and hard work, and with the help of a paternalistic colonial regime, the Merikens had found their Ninevah land in Trinidad after enduring a long captivity in America.[71]

Letters

Sometimes a runaway fled from slavery in the Chesapeake to experience the wider world. Shortly before escaping from Yorktown, a slave named Tom declared "most positively that he would go when and where he pleased." In 1814 William "Rolla" Ross escaped from Anne Arundel County (Maryland). When his master visited HMS *Menelaus*, Ross refused to return home, "expressing a desire at the same time to travel." And travel he would, later writing to his mother "that he had shipped himself on board of one of his Majesty's Ships and was on the India Station." From the deck of a British ship he saw far more of the world than he ever had when working a hoe on his master's fields.[72]

Voyages carried the refugees around the Atlantic and beyond, sometimes to reap a surprising prosperity. Jacob G. Parker learned that his former house servant Jacob, "a bright mulatto," was "retained by some officer of the British Navy as his servant during the war" and subsequently moved to Cadiz, Spain, as the servant "of an English Gentleman." From Halifax in 1827, Lewis Smith wrote to his former master, "I must inform you *Sir* that since I have left you that I have Travelled through, or over the Four parts of the globe and I am happy to have it in my power to State to you, that I have been, and still am in Such a Capacity of life, that I have hitherto and still am able to Save my Hundred pounds a yea[r]."[73]

Sailors and ships linked the Chesapeake to Trinidad, Bermuda, Nova Scotia, England, and Scotland: places that provided havens to runaways. With the postwar revival of trade, Chesapeake mariners ran into familiar former slaves on distant streets and docks. Many mariners agreed to take letters from the refugees back to relatives retained in slavery. In 1827, at Corotoman Plantation, Joseph C. Cabell reported, "The remaining slaves frequently receive messages of kindness and affection from their relatives in the British Colonies."[74]

In 1820 John Massey captained a vessel carrying corn to Halifax, where he recognized many blacks as former slaves who had visited his store in King George County, Virginia. Massey reported that these refugees "were particularly earnest & anxious in making enquiries after persons & affairs in King George." He returned home with "several letters from runaway negroes in Nova Scotia to their Masters & Black relatives," but he accepted only letters that conformed to his rules: "that they must be particular in their style of writing & not be insulting to their Masters." To make sure, Massey read their letters before sealing them.[75]

In writing to former masters, some refugees sought to buy their freedom in Virginia or Maryland so that they could return home as free people to relatives trapped in slavery. Judging from the surviving documents, these bids failed. In 1813 Peter Charles escaped from Northampton County, settling after the war in Nova Scotia. Three years later, his former master received "a letter from the said negro Peter in Cannada, proposing to return, provided he could do so without being reduced to slavery." The refugee longed to reunite with his enslaved wife and children in Virginia, but evidently the master refused, for he later received compensation from the government for Peter Charles.[76]

Seven precious letters from Chesapeake refugees survive because a master filed them to support his case for government compensation. The refugees wrote six of the letters, with the seventh drafted by the daughter of an employer. In three cases, the writer directly addressed a master. Even in the other four, meant primarily for a relative, the author usually had to send it through the master, who first read the letter. Often the writers asked the master to read the letter to an illiterate relative and to write a reply. Addressing his mother, Archibald Clark appended a postscript meant for his former master: "Mr. W[illia]m Berry, I would be very Happy to hear from you that you are all well and write her answer to this Letter."[77]

The letters ask after relatives left behind. In July 1816, from Leith in Scotland, Archibald Clark wrote to his enslaved mother, seeking news of his son, who remained trapped in Maryland, and from his wife, who had escaped separately and gone to parts unknown. However, he had to trust that his former master would read the letter to his illiterate mother and write her reply. If he did, we cannot know, for any reply had no value for a master seeking money for a runaway, so it would never end up in the compensation file that alone preserves Clark's words.[78]

Toby Forester wrote to update his parents on his escape after departing from them on August 27, 1814, in Prince George's County, Maryland. Then aged sixteen, Forester left with two other young men by following the British army retreating from Washington, D.C., to the Patuxent River. On January 5, 1819, Forester wrote from London, "When I left Home I st[ee]red my corse to molbro {Marlborough] from molbro to nottingham not knowing whear I was goin. My brother sandy was the last I saw at molbro. I took leave of him telling him whear I expected I should go but not noing for a sertenty . . . and we resided at Nottingham two days, from Nottingham we porseded for benedick. At benedick we took [British] shipping." Becoming a servant for a naval officer, Forester participated in the attacks on Baltimore and the Northern Neck. His ship then sailed to Jamaica to join the fleet that assailed New Orleans in early 1815. At war's end, he visited Havana, Cuba, before proceeding to Portsmouth in England. Thrown out of work, he initially struggled "in a strang contry" but eventually found a patron: "a gentleman in London that behaved remarkable well to me."[79]

While regretting separation from loved ones, the writers delighted in their new freedom. From Halifax in December 1816, William Whiddington assured his mother, "Thanks be to God, I arriv'd in this place safe and have had no cause to repent coming away—though I was very sorry to leave you, and all my relations." He counted on an eternal reunion in heaven: "though I may never see any of you again, my dear Mother, yet I shall always think of you and love you and I hope I shall act so honestly and soberly in this World that when I die I may meet all my Friends in a happy state of Eternity." Two years later from Halifax, Jeremiah West wrote to his former master: "Thank God i can enjoy all comforts under the flag of old England and Here i Shall Remain til [it] please god to call me out of the world."[80]

The writers also dwelled on the material benefits of freedom, reporting good wages or thriving businesses, money saved, and the respect of gentlemen earned. Clark assured his mother, "I have been very well off these two years last past. I have had 20 Guineas and all my Cloth[e]s," working as a gentleman's servant in Scotland. Whiddington assisted a Halifax doctor and assured his mother, "I am a sober, well behaved Lad. I get six dollars a month and am now comfortably cloathed and live well." From Halifax, Jeremiah West wrote to his former master: "i am a doing well at my Trade. i am well furnished with tools and the Gentlemen gives me great encouragement in my Trade." From London, Toby Forester reported, "I ham in the ocapation of a dentist and as my busones is so urgent that I ham often out of London you will Direct [your reply] to Wm Johnaston being my assistant." Able to employ another man, Forester had excellent prospects: "as soon as I make my fortune I intend to com home for I ham in a very fare way."[81]

Although vetted by the mariner John Massey, the letter from Bartlet Shanklyn expressed the most defiant tone. Addressing Abraham B. Hooe, his former master in Virginia, Shanklyn contrasted his prosperity in freedom with his suffering in slavery. Thriving as a blacksmith at Preston, he felt that Hooe should know, "I have [a] Shop & Set of Tools of my own and am doing very well. When i was with you [you] treated me very ill and for that reason i take the liberty of informing you that I am doin as well as you if not beter. When I was with you I worked very had and you neither g[ave] me money nor any satisfaction but sin[ce] I have been hear I am able to make Gold and Silver as well as you." By writing so bluntly, Shanklyn claimed equality with Hooe—if not superiority—as measured by making and saving money. No slave could safely say so to a master, but Shanklyn was no man's slave any longer.[82]

The other refugees made a similar point more discreetly by writing to former masters as if they were equals in friendship. Jeremiah West addressed David P. Davenport as "My Dear Friend," while "Hopeing that these lines may find you enjoying all [the] comforts of life." After earnestly soliciting a reply, West concluded, "i Rema[i]n your Friend." But West also made clear that he would never return to slavery in Virginia, so any reunion in this world had to be on his terms: "If in case you Should ever come to Halifax I shall see you, if not we will not see each outher till we meet Either in Heaven or Hell." By including Hell as an option, West subtly warned Davenport to pay heed to his soul's future by doing right by others.[83]

The letters reveal the great emotional complexity to the master-slave experience. While proud of their accomplishments in freedom, some writers missed their personal relationship with a former master. William Whiddington assured his mother, "I wish also to hear how my Master and Mistress and my Young Masters are—particularly Master Clement and I beg you will remember me to them all—and to all enquiring Friends. I wish to know where Mr. Clement is and how he does for I feel a great love for him." The master's son, Clement, had grown up beside the enslaved Whiddington in Maryland.[84]

The letters often seek an equality of friendship never truly possible so long as one remained the slave and the other a master. If so, the masters handled the letters with far less sentiment and respect than the writers expected and deserved. In Halifax in 1827, Lewis Smith felt pleasantly surprised suddenly to receive a letter from his former master, Thomas Griffin of Yorktown: the same master who had solicited Patrick Williams's deposition alleging that the British had sold the runaways. In November 1813, at the age of twenty-one, Smith had escaped with four younger Griffin slaves: Bob, Billy, James, and Jack, aged fourteen to seventeen. They last saw Griffin a few days later when he visited HMS *Dragon* to plead with them to return.

A witness reported, "They were then asked if they would return to their homes with their master. They were much agitated and at last replyed that they could not—weeping at the same moment." Evidently, the runaways felt mixed feelings in forsaking their master: pulled back by familiarity but ultimately pushed away by slavery.[85]

Fourteen years later, Smith welcomed Griffin's letter as a potential happy ending, that the runaways could enjoy both freedom and their former master's good wishes and respect. In reply, Smith addressed "My Dearest friend" to report, "My happiness would be greatly increas'd to see you once more, and the Boys [feel] likewise." But any reunion would have to be in Halifax, where they could remain free. Referring to Bob, Billy, Jim, and Jack as "the Boys," Smith added, "You mention to me that you wish to hear from the Boys. *They are all here* and doing well." But why, Smith wondered, in a friendly letter did Griffin fail to update him on "the State of your Family" or on whether any of Smith's "Family were living with you or not"? And why did Griffin ask Smith to have his reply notarized by a magistrate?[86]

Perhaps Smith guessed Griffin's real purpose in writing: fishing for evidence to strengthen his legal case for compensation for the five runaways. Although Smith refused to have his reply notarized, Griffin submitted it to the compensation commissioners after coldly inscribing, "The above named Lewis Smith is one of the slaves seduced from my Service by the British during the last war." By replying, Smith had tried to claim the mutuality of friends, but Griffin cashed that letter in as a commodity worth $280 for each of the five runaways. He did not really care that Smith and the boys were prospering and healthy—just that he could prove that they had left with the British and gone to Halifax.[87]

At least Griffin's greed assured that readers today know the success story that Smith so longed to tell: "I have Dropt Anchor and have Five Children who can eat their allowance and attend their School regular. . . . I have purchas'd a Town lot, and Built two Houses thereon, one of which I make my own Residence, keeping a Grocery shop therein, and the other commands me a handsome Rent." The "Boys" had prospered as men with surnames — their first acquisition in freedom. Bob had become Robert Griffin and Jim was James Goosley: "Robert Griffin has Buil[t] a Very fine House, directly opposite to Me, and is doing Well, following the Occupation of a Truckman, and [James] Goosley has done the Same."[88]

Christian and bourgeois in their values, these seven letters resemble those of middle-class white folk proud of material success but attentive to their eternal souls. We do not expect to find runaways building and owning houses and thriving as dentists, blacksmiths, and truckmen. Their accomplishments refute the misunderstanding, which persists in some histories, that the refugees were ruined by slavery and so ill suited for freedom that they could find only poverty and misery in Nova Scotia.[89]

But how representative were these seven writers of the many refugees? Former house slaves and artisans, the writers were the best prepared to become literate and succeed in the broader world. In one delicious irony, Archibald Clark could write a letter, but his former master, James Pumphrey, could not even sign his own name. Most of the refugees were poorer and less literate than the writers, but the letters warn of what we lose when we seek the typical at the lowest common denominator. The writers revealed the broad range of consequences for the runaways, with more of them experiencing material success than depicted in the records of officials who fixated on complaining about the poor. From Halifax in 1815, Augustine Neale assured Monroe that the refugees were doing surprisingly well: "But, sir, from a candid investigation into the condition of the Fugitives in this province [Nova Scotia], it is fair to conclude, . . . that the *far greater portion* of them are in situations much easier & have prospects far better than I could have supposed." Just as slavery was diverse and complex, so too were the experiences of runaways who visited the four corners of the globe.[90]

12

FIRE BELL

*[The Richmond Fire Bell] always produces a very great alarm
in this Country . . . on account of the apprehension that it may be
the Signal for, or Commencement of, a rising of the Negroes.*
—ALEXANDER DICK, MAY 21, 1808[1]

*But this momentous question [of Missouri], like a fire bell in the night,
awakened and filled me with terror. I considered it at once as the
knell of the Union. . . . But as it is, we have the wolf by the ears,
and we can neither hold him, nor safely let him go.
Justice is in one scale, and self-preservation in the other.*
—THOMAS JEFFERSON, APRIL 22, 1820[2]

DURING THE WAR of 1812, Virginians asserted their patriotic
superiority over the New England Federalists, who had soured
on the national government as they continued to lose elections and
shrank into political insignificance except in the Northeast. When
James Madison succeeded Jefferson to the presidency in 1809, the
"Virginia Dynasty" seemed alarmingly perpetual to the Federalists

Horrid Massacre in Virginia. *In this woodcut published in 1831, a Virginian condemns the
rebels of Southampton County and celebrates the white men who fought them. The rebels
appear as brutes killing white women and children and as cowards in flight from the militia.
(Courtesy of the Library of Congress)*

of New England. Despairing of national power, they tried to consolidate their regional base by persuading local voters that the powerful Virginians meant to ruin New England's mercantile economy, by imposing Jefferson's embargo and Madison's war.[3]

The Federalists denounced the Virginians as arrogant bullies corrupted by their power over abject slaves. In a letter to President Madison, a New Englander blasted, "[You] daily complain of G. Britain for pressing and enslaving a few thousands of your seamen, & yet you southern Nabobs, to glut your av[a]rise for sorded gain, make no scruple of enslaving some millions of the sons and daughters of Africa." Trained to dominate, the slaveholders allegedly also sought to master the people of New England. In Congress, Josiah Quincy of Massachusetts hyperbolically warned that the next generation of New Englanders were "destined to be slaves, and yoked in with negroes, chained to the car of a Southern master." The Federalists developed this critique to score political points in New England rather than to free slaves in Virginia. Quincy conceded, "My heart has always been much more affected by the slavery to which the Free States have been subjected, than that of the Negro." By applying the term *slavery* to the political marginalization of New England, Quincy cast the leading Virginians as the indiscriminate tyrants of white as well as black people.[4]

During the war, northern Federalists predicted military disaster for a South weakened by the need to guard slaves as well as a long coast. In Connecticut, a Federalist newspaper warned southerners, "We do not know what you would do, between an external invasion on the one hand, and the internal dread of your slaves on the other." Federalists insisted that the southern states needed the protection of northern troops, which they threatened to withhold to punish the Republicans for declaring an unjust war. In Massachusetts a minister preached, "Let the southern Heroes fight their own battles, and guard their slumbering pillows against the just vengeance of their lacerated slaves."[5]

Honor

Prickly about their honor, southerners resented attacks on their character and hated the insinuation that they depended on northern protection. They also claimed an exclusive right to discuss the internal enemy—and only among themselves. The *Richmond Enquirer* warned that northerners gave slaves "false ideas of their strength and prompts them to an attempt, which, with whatever horrors its progress might be attended, must inevitably terminate in their ruin."[6]

Virginians privately obsessed about their danger from the "internal enemy," but they wrote very differently when publicly refuting their northern critics. In April 1813, the *National Intelligencer* denied that the South risked a serious slave revolt: "The slaves in general are well-disposed. . . . We believe the negroes themselves, on the approach of an invading force, would, if permitted, gladly advance to repel it. The slaves in the South are, in general, a peaceable, inoffensive race content to do the duty to which they were born, and attached to the families from whom they respectively receive protection and support." During the war and under the pressure of northern criticism, the South's spokesmen developed the pro-slavery case that would blossom in future decades. Deemphasizing the threat of an internal enemy, the emerging pro-slavery ideology dwelled instead on the alleged stupidity, docility, and happiness of slaves protected by their paternalistic and superior owners. But the war did not allow the southern press to stay on that slippery message, for the next day the same newspaper warned that the British had just landed on Kent Island, Maryland, where "Several negroes had deserted to them and become pilots for them in plundering."[7]

Proud of their sacrifices in fighting the empire, the Virginians despised the many New Englanders who sympathized and traded with the enemy. Making much of their own honor, the Virginians denounced the Yankees as corrupted by greed. A Virginian boasted that the war would "prove to our Yankee brethren that Southern patriotism is not to be estimated by Dollars and Cents." Rigorously blockaded by the British, the Virginians seethed when the enemy initially exempted the New Englanders, who profited by trading with the foe. Compelled to rally thousands of militiamen for service, the Virginians also resented that New England's Federalist governors refused to mobilize their militia for federal service. Virginians blamed the American defeats in Canada on New England's failure to assist the war effort. "If the New England men wou'd now do their duty, Canada to the works of Quebec wou'd be ours," insisted Wilson Cary Nicholas. While the British spared New England from raids and invasion until 1814, when they seized eastern Maine, Virginia bore the brunt of British animus. Governor James Barbour claimed that the British targeted Virginia for destruction from "a deadly and implacable hate, the result of the magnanimous and distinguished part acted by Virginia in resisting at all times British aggressions."[8]

The Virginians regarded the New England Federalists as insidious traitors. St. George Tucker concluded that the Yankees were "determined to *rule* or to *dissolve* the union." Britain "is promised civil war by our Northern Traitors," agreed Dr. Philip Barraud. A Virginia veteran of the revolution, Colonel John Minor, recalled, "It was my lot . . . in the last war to see in the Southern States the Horrors of a Civil War, at the recollection of which I now shudder and feel an indignation against those bad men, who by attempting to divide the nation, threaten us with a Civil War."[9]

By fighting the British, the Virginians meant to vindicate their military prowess and save the republic. Barbour vowed to defend "the ark of our political salvation—the Union of these States" from "all the horrors of civil war." John Campbell assured the Yankees, "If you raise the standard of rebellion, your green fields will be wash'd with the blood of your people and your country laid desolate by the flames of civil discord! If you attempt to pull down the pillars of the Republic, you shall be crush'd into atoms." In late 1814,

Thomas Jefferson predicted that Virginians would rather fight New Englanders than the British: "we can get ten men to go to Massachusetts for one who will go to Canada." During the War of 1812, Virginians opposed secession, in contrast to the stand they would take fifty years later.[10]

The Virginia officers in the national army worked up a great dislike for their northern colleagues as inept, corrupt, and sorely lacking in southern honor. Colonel S. B. Archer declared, "I have my doubts whether even now the Northern and Eastern section of this Country are not too far gone in depravity ever by themselves to be regenerated." After denouncing one cowardly scoundrel, Colonel Isaac A. Coles noted, "I need not tell you that this man was not a Virginian." Returning home from national service, Nathaniel Beverley Tucker assured his father, "I have come back into old Virginia, more of a Virginian than ever, and as to Messrs. the Yankees, I love them not."[11]

In early 1813, James Madison appointed an ambitious New Yorker, John Armstrong, as the secretary of war. Armstrong quickly offended the army's southern officers, who felt slighted and passed over for promotion in favor of northern men. Southerners suspected that Armstrong used patronage to build a political following that could elevate him to the presidency in 1816 at the expense of his great rival, James Monroe of Virginia. Southern officers felt especially miffed when the northern politicians William Duane and Jacob Brown gained powerful roles in Armstrong's army. Several Virginia officers resigned in a huff, denouncing Armstrong as "an unfeeling & unprincipled Scoundrel." Brigadier General Thomas Parker explained that he would never "Submit to the degradation of being Commanded by Mr. Brown."[12]

Armstrong also offended Virginia's leaders by failing to repair and garrison Fort Powhatan, which guarded the approach to Richmond via the James River. Located at Hood's Point on a high bluff thirty-five miles south of the city, the fort could block the ascent of British barges. But the secretary of war delayed for months any reply to Governor Barbour's urgent request to rebuild the fort. Then Armstrong unwittingly added insult to injury by forwarding a discouraging report by Colonel John Swift, a military engineer, who declared the fort "worthless" for "any other purpose than that of affording a point of security to the inhabitants in the vicinity of the Fort in case of the *insurrection of negroes.*"[13]

In private appeals to their state government, Virginians obsessed about an impending slave revolt. Indeed, Armstrong and Swift were far less explicit than the Richmond Committee of Vigilance, chaired by the mayor, which privately warned the state government that if the British captured the fort, "A Saint Domingo Scene will be exhibited." But Virginians felt insulted when a northerner made the same point in a public and official statement, for they had grown especially sensitive to northern charges that slavery weakened the South's capacity for self-defense. When the nation failed to protect Virginia against British raids during the war, the state leaders felt doubly offended by any suggestion of southern weakness and dependence on the North. Worse still, the legislators considered Armstrong's letter and Swift's report at the same time that they heard, in February 1814, that the War Department balked at compensating the state for the heavy costs of the militia force posted at Norfolk.[14]

In a pointed retort, the House of Delegates insisted that Virginia had long defended the nation and "has never found it necessary to call on the U[nited] States to secure her repose against *an interior enemy* nor does she at present urge any such claim for protection." Joseph C. Cabell, a state senator, explained, "The style of Genl. Armstrong's & Col. Swift's letters have given offence to all parties here . . . and that, as they had not been consulted as to the utility of Fort Powhatan as a position of defence against an insurrection of slaves, they might have abstained from any intimations of a nature calculated to wound the feelings & degrade the character of the state." The episode shook the confidence of Virginia's leaders in the president for retaining the despised Armstrong as a counterweight to Monroe in the cabinet. Cabell attested that Barbour felt "treated with great neglect if not contempt by the Secretary of War."[15]

Nationalisms

During the crisis of 1814, Virginia's leaders rallied men to defend the state rather than the nation, appealing to their pride as Virginians rather than to their patriotism as Americans. Noting the nation's failure to defend the state, the *Richmond Enquirer* exhorted:

> Virginians! Brave Virginians! You have every motive to rouse you. Remember Hampton! Remember the Northern Neck! Call to mind the wrongs you have suffered, the slanders which have been heaped upon you by the mercenary prints of the enemy! . . . Virginia is now thrown upon her own resources. Her sons must show that they are equal to her defence. The eyes of the Union are upon us: shall we draw upon us their scorn? The bones of our fathers sleep in our soil; shall we suffer a foreign enemy to trample on them?

Knowing his readers well, the author cited only atrocities and insults directed against Virginians, and he invoked the Union only as an external audience eager to scorn them.[16]

In 1788 Virginia had narrowly and reluctantly ratified the Federal Constitution in response to Madison's hopeful promise that a stronger union would amplify the state's power on a continental scale. The War of 1812 put that promise to the test, and Virginians concluded that the nation had failed them by neglecting their defense and insulting them with Armstrong's response regarding Fort Powhatan. The nation also proved impotent to compel cooperation from the New England states, which escaped the brunt of a war borne by Virginia. In addition, the Madison administration sought to buy northern support by reserving key positions in the War Department and the army for men of suspect principles and abilities.

If the Union could not fulfill Madison's promise to Virginia with Madison as president, what could the state expect from a northern leader in the future? The hated Armstrong crashed and burned politically in August 1814, when he became the scapegoat for the British capture of the capital, but perhaps some other New Yorker—DeWitt Clinton or Daniel D. Tompkins—might succeed in building a national coalition to govern the nation without Virginia. While Virginians began the war as champions of the Union, they ended it with powerful new doubts. Feeling betrayed for their wartime nationalism, the Virginians sought support from the other southern states against the distrusted northerners, who seemed poised to seize control of the Union. The South began to become Virginia's nation during the War of 1812, but this was a slow process that did not fully mature until the secession of 1861.[17]

Historians often note the surge in American nationalism that immediately followed the War of 1812. As never before, newspapers and orators celebrated patriotism, while displays of the flag and the eagle proliferated in engravings, paintings, and taverns. But that effusive nationalism was, ironically, highly sectional: strongest in the Middle Atlantic and western states and weaker in Virginia and other southern states. In fact, the war generated competing nationalisms, for the southern states developed a far stronger bond and shared identity with one another. As a consequence of the war, southerners felt suspicious of the Middle Atlantic version of patriotism, which we often mistake for the sentiment of the entire nation. Rather than promoting a unifying nationalism, the experiences of war bred distinct regional variants.[18]

At war's end in early 1815, Virginians exulted in Andrew Jackson's great victory at New Orleans as a vindication of the South rather than of the nation. As a Tennessee slaveholder and Anglophobe, Jackson appealed to the South far more than did any northern-born

commander. The Norfolk doctor Philip Barraud assured St. George
Tucker that Jackson's triumph

> established the claims & reputation of the Southern portion of
> this Empire. The people of the East shall hence forth no longer
> dare to charge on this section of the States the foul calumny of
> seeking wars without the spirit to maintain them with valor or
> with their Blood. . . . It fixes the power & ability of these states
> to protect their Firesides & to punish their Enemies without
> Yankee aid. . . . It teaches England that we are not weak, altho
> we have Slaves & rich Lands. It establishes beyond all doubt that
> the South is the soil for Generous, Loyal & valorous men.

By contrast, Barraud recalled "the never-to-be-forgotten turpitude
& traitorous conduct of the Eastern portion of our Nation." Tucker
agreed that the "Explosion of Joy for Jackson's Victory" exceeded
anything he had ever experienced in Virginia.[19]

To celebrate the peace, Richmond staged a grand illumination
with candles in the windows, bonfires on the hills, rockets in the
air, and patriotic paintings on the public buildings. Everywhere
Jackson's image stole the show. "The favorite figures of the evening
were 'Jackson' and 'Peace,'" reported the *Richmond Enquirer*. The
"Wax-work Museum" displayed "a transparent scroll with the name
of *Jackson*," while the state capitol presented "a large transparent
painting" featuring "a triumphal crown surrounded by Cornuco-
pias and encircling the name of 'Jackson' with that never-dying day,
'The 8th of January 1815.'" Next to Jackson, the displays honored
the leading Virginians, Madison and Monroe, with a couple of naval
heroes thrown in—but it was revealing that no generals from the
North appeared. Of course, northerners also claimed Jackson for
their nationalism, but they linked him with their own heroes in a
bigger cast, while Virginians detached and elevated Jackson as the
one great champion of southern nationalism.[20]

In addition to its geopolitical significance in discouraging the British from again waging war in North America, the Battle of New Orleans reshaped America's political culture. Southerners interpreted the battle as proof of their superior honor and fighting ability in stark contrast to the selfish and corrupt northerners. By claiming martial superiority, southerners refuted northerners who charged that slavery rendered their region weak and dependent on the North. After the war, when some Virginians proposed establishing a national committee to raise subscriptions to aid the families of dead or disabled militiamen, St. George Tucker responded, "We are not enough *one nation* for such a plan to succeed." He expected that only state initiatives could raise the funds.[21]

Colonization

The War of 1812 gave Virginians a great scare, revealing the military potential of black troops deployed against them. Long a specter, the internal enemy had become real in the red coats of British troops rather than as the anticipated murderous massacre at midnight. But the Virginians persuaded themselves that the black troops had brought their state to the verge of a "Saint Domingo Scene."

Fears of insurrection surged in February 1816, when the magistrates in the Piedmont counties of Spotsylvania and Louisa discovered a plot organized by George Boxley. A storekeeper, farmer, and militia officer, Boxley owned a few slaves, which made him an unusual leader for a slave uprising. But he became embittered after the leading men of Spotsylvania blocked his ambitions to gain promotion in the militia and win a seat in the legislature. Frustrated by his wartime militia service at Norfolk, Boxley longed to smite Virginia's leaders on behalf of a just and vengeful God. Addressing slaves at his store, Boxley declared that God had charged him "with the holy purpose of *delivering* his fellow creatures from bondage; that a little *white bird* had perched upon his shoulder and revealed it to him." He recruited about thirty young men for a plot to steal arms and horses for a mass escape (after robbing the Fredericksburg banks) northward to a free state. A local writer noted, "The negroes were mostly actuated by an irresistible idea of freedom."[22]

In late February, however, an anxious female slave tipped off the magistrates, who began to make arrests and increase slave patrols. Driven to act prematurely, Boxley could rally only about a dozen followers, and they quickly lost confidence in the scheme and slipped home to resume their slavery. Although the plot collapsed far short of any violent acts, the terrified magistrates arrested, tried, and convicted eleven slaves, sending five to the gallows and six into exile by sale and transportation. Convicting Boxley proved harder because all of the witnesses to his treason were black and therefore barred by Virginia law from testifying against a white man. Uncertain what to do with Boxley, the authorities kept him in jail until May 14, when he escaped after breaking his irons and cutting a passage through the ceiling of his cell. His visiting wife had smuggled in a file, perhaps with the complicity of the jailer. Suspicions arose that some powerful local people wanted Boxley gone rather than risk an embarrassing trial that would acquit for lack of evidence. He fled north, eventually settling in Indiana, where he became a prominent preacher and radical abolitionist. He left behind a Virginia more troubled than ever by its growing black population.[23]

Once again, Virginians blamed free blacks for resistance among the slaves. In an 1817 petition to the state legislature, the citizens in Isle of Wight County argued that free blacks tended "to promote insubordination & a spirit of disobedience among the slaves, & finally to lead to insurrection & blood." In fact, during the war, while hundreds of slaves fled to the British, almost all the free blacks had remained loyal to Virginia. But they made tempting scapegoats because getting rid of them would deprive no white man of his property. By reiterating that their greatest danger came from free blacks, Virginians ensured that they would lament but never end slavery.[24]

Although still modest in number (30,570 in 1810), the state's free black population was growing at a faster rate (22 percent from 1810 to 1820) than either the free white (9 percent over that decade) or the slave populations (11 percent). Because the state barred the import of slaves or the advent of free blacks, the growth in the black population derived entirely from their natural increase. By comparison, Virginia's white population grew more slowly because diminished by outmigration to the southern and western frontiers during the 1810s. Poor whites without slaves dominated that free migration, so their departure tended to reduce the white proportion of Virginia's population. At the same time, masters did sell thousands of slaves to the Deep South. During the 1810s, that coerced migration cut the growth in the slave population to half that of the free blacks in Virginia. Reluctant to move elsewhere because other family members remained enslaved nearby, free blacks proved the most loyal to Virginia as measured by persistence. White Virginians, however, felt threatened by that persistence.[25]

To reduce the black population, many Virginians promoted the postwar African colonization movement. A prominent Virginia politician, Charles Fenton Mercer, took the lead after finding inspiration in his discovery of the previous effort, in the wake of Gabriel's rebellion, by the state government to seek a foreign colony for free blacks and perhaps emancipated slaves. In 1801–1802, Governor Monroe and President Jefferson had tried but failed to find an overseas haven. In 1816, however, Mercer felt a new urgency and sensed a new opportunity. The urgency came from the threats of violent upheaval demonstrated by the British invasion, the Colonial Marines, and Boxley's plot. The opportunity came from the postwar burst of enthusiasm for ambitious new measures to improve the republic. In December 1816 in Washington, D.C., Mercer assembled elite men to organize a national society to promote African colonization. Drawn from both the North and the upper South, and from both political parties, the founders included such prominent Virginians as James

Madison, John Marshall, James Monroe, John Randolph, John Tyler, and Bushrod Washington (a Supreme Court justice and the nephew of the late president).[26]

Disdaining blacks as well as slavery, the colonizationists wanted to whiten America. Madison sought to remove "from our country the calamity of its black population." Mercer deemed slavery "the blackest of all blots, and foulest of all deformities" on American society, but he regarded free blacks as even worse: a motley set of prostitutes and thieves. An opponent, William Branch Giles, charged the colonizationists with exaggerating the immorality of free blacks for popular effect: "It would be unjust to put down the whole colored population as dissolute and burdensome, but the free people of colour are despised, and there is a rage about getting rid of them. . . . This being the most seductive inducement, it is accordingly the most used by the friends of the project, and to produce its greatest effect, it is greatly exaggerated." Giles described most of the free blacks as "honest labourers, whose labour adds to the wealth of the State."[27]

Protective of private property, the colonizationists insisted that slaves could be freed only with the consent of their masters; that whites could not coexist peacefully with any large number of free blacks; and that white prejudice was so deep and immutable that free blacks would never escape from poverty and degradation within America. Therefore, the colonizationists reasoned, everyone would benefit from shipping free blacks away to Africa—perhaps to be followed later by the more numerous slaves. Claiming that the republic needed a purely white population, the colonizationists refused to consider the alternative of a multiracial republic of equal citizens. John Randolph declared that the races could never "occupy the same territory, under one government, but in the relation of master and vassal."[28]

The colonizationists spoke and wrote softly about slavery lest they alarm the southern majority averse to any public discussion. One member conceded "that Slavery must be touched with great delicacy and that any attempt to unsettle the state of the Slaves would be considered as kindling a fire of destruction." Although dread of the internal enemy motivated the colonizationists, that dread also starkly limited what they could say or do, for slaveholders in the Deep South distrusted colonization as a covert abolitionist plot against their property.[29]

Most members vaguely hoped that an African colony would encourage more masters to manumit and deport their slaves, but many southern members, including Randolph, supported colonization only as a means to protect slavery by deporting free blacks. And many members continued to own, buy, and sell slaves. In 1821 the president of the national society, Bushrod Washington, sold fifty-four slaves to the Deep South, for he needed the money to pay his debts more than his conscience needed consistency. This younger Washington showed far less principle than his late, great uncle, who had emancipated all of his slaves while providing funds to care for the elderly and train the young. But George Washington had lived and died before the great decay of Virginia's economy, a downturn that accelerated after 1816, compounding the debts and sapping the scruples of his heirs.[30]

The more daring colonizationists sought a government program, either federal or by the states, to emancipate the slaves gradually by compensating their masters and deporting the freed. The reverence for private property ruled out any immediate and uncompensated abolition of slavery. But that solicitude for property also meant that few Americans would tax themselves to raise the massive compensation required to free and transport over a million slaves. And most slaveowners preferred to retain the labor of their slaves and profit from selling their offspring rather than accept any compensation.

Given the prohibitive cost of deporting the most expensive slaves—those in the prime of their working lives—the gradual emancipation proposals focused on buying infants, particularly girls, as the most cost-effective way to shrink the slave population. The chief proponent of this scheme, Thomas Jefferson, dismissed the suffering that losing children would cause to black families as inconsequential compared to the good of the republic and the superior "happiness" of their children once free in Africa.[31]

In fact, Virginia could never afford to purchase and export enough slave children to make a difference. In early 1820, Thomas Mann Randolph Jr., Jefferson's son-in-law and the governor of Virginia, urged the legislature to appropriate a third of the state's revenues to buy and deport slave children, but the legislators balked at spending the taxpayers' money to get rid of their valuable property. While far too expensive for the legislators, the governor's program would have bought a mere tenth of the annual increase in the state's slave population. Even if dedicated entirely to buying and deporting slaves, Virginia's annual budget could not stop the increase in slave numbers—much less fulfill the fantasy of eliminating black people in America while respecting the property of whites.[32]

In addition, very few free blacks wanted to go to Africa: a distant continent that they had never known, for most were third- or fourth-generation Americans. Seeking equal rights in America, they preferred to stay and tough it out rather than take a dangerous leap into the unknown of West Africa. Indeed, the new American colony there, Liberia, was a malarial deathtrap and war zone for the 12,000 who did emigrate. Madison conceded that his slaves had a "horror of going to Liberia."[33]

Mercer and Monroe overplayed their hand by obtaining financial and naval assistance from the federal government to subsidize and protect the shipment of blacks to Liberia. The federal involvement horrified southern conservatives, such as Randolph, who dreaded any intervention by the United States in slavery as setting a precedent dangerous to the South. They feared any expansion of federal power as a slippery slope that could lead to enforced emancipation by the Union. Consequently, the conservatives bolted from the colonization movement during the mid-1820s. Randolph explained, "I am against all colonization, etc. societies—[I] am for the good old plan of making the negroes *work*, and thereby enabling the master to feed and clothe them well, and take care of them in sickness and old age." The defection by the states' rights men reduced the colonization movement to a hollow, pointless shell even before the northern abolitionists renounced it as a fraud during the next decade. There could be, and would be, no consensus solution to the problem of slavery in America.[34]

Diffusion

In 1819 Virginia remained the preeminent slave state, home to nearly a third of the nation's one and a half million slaves. Virginia's leaders believed they had too many slaves for their own safety and more than their economy demanded. Rather than free slaves and deport them, Virginians preferred to sell them or to move away with them. By "diffusing" slaves to the new states of the Deep South and the West, Virginians could reduce the annual increase in the number enslaved more effectively and profitably than could any program of overseas colonization. Diffusion cost taxpayers nothing and precluded any role for the federal government. And the proponents could still claim that they opposed slavery in principle because diffusion allegedly benefited the enslaved. They would leave a crowded and depleted country for the western land of milk and honey, where they could be better fed, clothed, and housed by more prosperous owners. In the West, slaves supposedly could live with fewer constraints because the whites there felt more secure in their great majority. Some Virginians even argued that diffusion might prepare white people to embrace emancipation once slaves became small minorities spread evenly across a vast land. "An uncontrouled dispersion of the slaves now in the U.S. was not only best for the nation, but most favorable for the slaves," concluded Madison.[35]

After the War of 1812, southern settlers and their slaves surged westward into the vast and fertile watershed of the Mississippi River. By 1820, the enslaved population west of the Appalachians had doubled during the preceding decade. In 1818, Randolph lamented: "Alabama is at present the loadstone of attraction: Cotton, Money, Whiskey & as the means of obtaining all those blessings, *Slaves*—the road is thronged with droves of these wretches & the human carcase-butchers, who drive them on the hoof to market." A romantic traditionalist, Randolph rued the outmigration of slaves as a failure of paternalism in Virginia. He wanted Virginians and their slaves to stay put, but Randolph fiercely opposed any government interference with the rights of masters to buy, sell, or move their human property at will. If the alternative was restriction by federal power, Randolph preferred diffusion.[36]

The Virginians in Congress got a rude shock on February 13, 1819, when James Tallmadge Jr. of New York proposed amendments to a bill to admit Missouri as a new state in the Union. Tallmadge wanted to require Missouri to adopt a constitution barring further slave imports and committed gradually to emancipate slaves born after 1819. Most northern congressmen, Republicans as well as Federalists, supported Tallmadge's amendments, for they believed that slavery contradicted and, therefore, threatened free government. Jonathan Roberts of Pennsylvania insisted that slave states were "marred as if the finger of Lucifer had been drawn over them." By restricting the expansion of slavery, the "retrictionists" sought to preserve the West for free white settlers, who alone could sustain a true republic (so they argued).[37]

Restrictionists denounced diffusion as a fraud. John Sergeant of Pennsylvania demanded, "Has any one seriously considered the scope of this doctrine? It leads directly to the establishment of slavery throughout the world." Restrictionists argued that diffusion thrust slaves into the greater hardships of the frontier and ruptured their families. And far from promoting antislavery sentiment, expansion swelled the western demand for slaves, inflating their value in the

Chesapeake states. An abolitionist, Robert J. Evans, asked, "Should this *odious* privilege of enslaving fellow creatures be extended to the immense region beyond the Mississippi, will there not be a never failing market open for the commerce in human flesh[?]" If so, Virginia would "furnish to this great mart of men, a never ending supply." If diffused, slaveholding would become predominant and perpetual in the nation.[38]

In response, southern congressmen denied that Congress had any legitimate authority to impose restrictions on a new state. Southerners claimed to defend the Federal Constitution and the rights of the states, rather than slavery, by opposing restriction. They denounced restriction as a cunning ploy meant to reduce the South to poverty and dependence within a nation dominated by the North. Rather than any sympathy for slaves or solicitude for free government, the restrictionists manifested, in the words of Spencer Roane (Virginia's leading judge), "their lust of dominion and power." Roane insisted that the controversy was "forced upon us by the cruelty and injustice of northern intriguers." Opposing any restriction on slavery's expansion, Nathaniel Beverley Tucker declared, "Let this precedent be once established and the power of the southern states is gone forever." Southern congressmen feared the political implications of the more rapid population growth in the North, which already had 20 percent more free people than the South.[39]

The South could ill afford to become a minority region defined by slavery and confined within a geographic line. Restriction would dishonor the South as insufficiently republican because tainted by slavery. National power would accrue to the region that gave shape to western expansion. "It is indeed not a question of freedom or slavery, but a question [of] who shall inherit our rich possession to the west," Isaac A. Coles explained. The North could claim the nation's future by preempting that vast and promising region for its own people and institutions. Dabney Carr warned that once empowered by the West, the national North could "draw a *cordon* round us & when they had cooped us up on every side . . . then should we feel the full weight of their tender mercies!" If restricted, the South would become a claustrophobic corner of growing poverty and weakness in the Union.[40]

Virginia already was reeling from a great economic decline. In 1819 the entire nation endured its first massive economic depression, and no state suffered more than Virginia. The depression derived from a sharp downturn in foreign demand for America's agricultural exports, especially Virginia's tobacco, flour, and wheat. From 1818 to 1821, Virginia's exports fell by 56 percent, compared to 42 percent for the nation as a whole. As foreign demand dried up, the price paid for farm produce in Richmond declined by 48 percent between November 1818 and February 1821. Virginians struggled to pay their debts when they could no longer sell their crops for a decent price. Bankruptcies and land sales surged. From Richmond in early 1820, Francis Walker Gilmer mourned, "Things here grow worse & worse—the merchants all failed—the town ruined— the banks broke—the Treasury empty—commerce gone, confidence gone, character gone."[41]

The Missouri crisis erupted when the Virginians already feared for their diminished place in the nation. Restriction threatened to limit the western market for slaves and the West as a haven for slaveholders just when Virginians most needed that outlet. Governor William Branch Giles wanted the West to remain "an almost boundless reservoir for the reception of slaves."[42]

Nothing terrified Virginians more than the prospect of being trapped within a state with a growing black majority in the Tidewater and Piedmont regions. Spencer Roane bluntly explained that Virginians were "averse to be dammed up in a land of Slaves, by the Eastern people." Dreading a massive slave revolt, Roane declared that northerners regarded restriction as "an abstract question; but it is, as to us, a question of life or death." Similarly, John Tyler warned that restriction would increase the "dark cloud" of slavery "over a particular portion of this land until its horrors shall burst." Only with a vibrant interstate slave trade, and an untrammeled western expansion by slaveholders, could Virginians vent enough slaves annually to release the demographic pressure that, to their minds, threatened an inevitable race war. It was telling that Thomas Jefferson bitterly opposed restriction and declared that the Missouri crisis, "like a fire bell in the night, awakened and filled me with terror"— for Virginians associated a fire bell's alarm with a slave revolt.[43]

During the Missouri debates, congressmen from all regions threatened disunion and civil war, but the southerners showed greater unity and passion, for they felt more imperiled in their property and security. Randolph declared, "God has given us the Missouri and the devil shall not take it from us." In February 1820, alarmed moderates saved the union by crafting a compromise. Maine (previously part of Massachusetts) became a free state, while Missouri joined without any restriction on slavery, thereby maintaining the balance in the Union, and so in the Senate, of eleven free states and eleven slave states. Congress also imposed a line west of Missouri to the Pacific along the 36°30' latitude (an extension of Missouri's southern boundary), barring slavery to the north, where most of the remaining federal territory lay. While the South got Missouri, it faced a future of many more free states entering the Union.[44]

President Monroe and Senator James Barbour (the former governor) supported the compromise as essential to save the Union, but most of Virginia's congressmen and state leaders angrily opposed any western restriction on slavery. The state legislators voted 142 to 38 to instruct their U.S. senators to reject the compromise. Nineteen of the twenty-two Virginia congressmen voted against the 36°30' restriction line; no state delegation provided more negative votes or more fiercely opposed any compromise.[45]

Despite their disgust with the Missouri Compromise, most Virginians were not prepared for secession and civil war as the alternative. In the *Richmond Enquirer*, Thomas Ritchie grumbled, "We submit. . . . We bow to it, though on no occasion with so poor a grace and so bitter a spirit. The South and the West are wronged, they must bear up patiently." After 1820, Virginians adopted a selective and conditional nationalism. They supported the nation when it served their interests, as it usually did, for the South enjoyed a political clout disproportionate to the region's declining share of the nation's population. That power derived from the greater cohesion of the southern congressmen when compared to their northern counterparts. The defense of slavery and its expansion provided a far tighter bond for southern leaders than antislavery did for the more numerous northern congressmen. Southerners cherished a robust national government that enforced the fugitive slave law in northern states, compensated masters for wartime runaways, and pushed expansion southwestward into Texas. Southerners cheered when the nation acted on the racial dread of an alliance by the British with Indians and blacks. But southern leaders scuttled back to a states' rights sectionalism at the slightest hint that northerners might deploy federal power to tax slaves or limit slavery. By loudly threatening secession, the southerners could alarm enough northerners, solicitous of the Union, into retreating in Congress.[46]

Fear

While fending off northerners, Virginia's leaders also faced unrest within the state. Based in the Piedmont and Tidewater, Virginia's elite confronted discontent from the people living west of the Blue Ridge in the Shenandoah Valley and Allegheny Mountains. The westerners felt trapped in underdevelopment because neglected by a state government dominated by easterners who enjoyed disproportionate power under Virginia's antiquated state constitution. The old constitution also imposed a property requirement that disenfranchised the poorer half of the state's white men.[47]

The westerners demanded a convention to draft a new state constitution. In October 1829 in Richmond, they got such a convention, but most of the delegates came from the Piedmont and Tidewater, so it produced only modest changes in the new constitution. The delegates slightly widened the electorate, reducing the disenfranchised to a third of white men. Legislative representation, however, remained skewed in favor of the eastern elites, who insisted that they could not trust the westerners to protect slavery. Appalled by the prospect of majority rule, John Randolph declared, "I would not live under King Numbers." Thanks to the power of property in Virginia, he did not have to.[48]

A recent insurrection alarm had hardened the convictions of the eastern conservatives during the run-up to the convention. In mid-July 1829, panic had rippled through the Tidewater counties, filling the jails with slaves suspected of plotting a bloody rebellion. Once again, the alarm began with the overheard talk of blacks, who had responded to what they heard from whites. During that summer the white folk buzzed with speculation about the fate of slavery under the new state constitution anticipated from the convention scheduled to meet in the fall. In turn, hopeful slaves spoke of gaining freedom from the new order. Then alarmed whites interpreted that wishful thinking as, instead, a plot to seize freedom by bloodshed.[49]

The scare began in Mathews County, a Tidewater county that had suffered from British raids during the War of 1812. On July 18, 1829, Christopher Tompkins, who figured so prominently in the war, reported to Governor Giles, "About ten days ago information was communicated confidentially by a negro to a widow woman that it was expected generally among the slaves that they were to be free in a few weeks." Two white apprentices overheard and reported similar chatter by slaves gathered at a blacksmith's shop. Arrests and interrogations revealed "the general belief among the blacks . . . that the late convention election had exclusively for its object the liberation of the blacks & that the question had been decided by the result of the convention election & that it had been kept secret from them

& that their free papers had been withheld improperly but were to be delivered at August court." The slaves had updated the old myth of emancipation by a liberator king who had been frustrated by selfish masters. In the new version, "King Numbers"—the Virginia voters—had promised freedom. In fact, this American monarch had less substance as a liberator than had the old British king.[50]

The alarm in Mathews County became contagious, echoing through anxious letters carried across the Tidewater, into the Piedmont, and on to the state government in Richmond. Following the usual script, fearful whites sought to share the news without tipping off the slaves to the panic, but the enslaved could hardly miss the frantic conduct of masters and patrollers. In Hanover County on July 26, Colonel Bowling Starke reported, "The alarms have been of such a character that they could *not* be concealed from the negroes. They all know it and know our situation," by which he meant the militia's lack of guns. The agitation among the whites bred more slave talk, which escalated the alarm. A member of the Council of State noted, "These rumours have been much talk'd of by the slaves themselves & have probably increas'd the spirit of insubordination."[51]

The alarm was especially great in Hanover County, where the county court had tried and convicted three slaves of conspiring and killing their master. On June 29, they had ambushed and shot William Boyers after discovering his intent to have "dispersed them over the world by sale or removal." Virginia slaves did not want to be diffused.[52]

The more things changed in Virginia, the more they remained the same. After an interlude of security and laxity, Virginians again sprung into agitated alarm and action. In every county, the militia officers rediscovered that their men had neglected, lost, or sold most of their weapons since the last crisis. One colonel observed, "Should this alarm be well founded, we are in a helpless situation for want of arms." So the local commanders plaintively begged the governor to send new arms and ammunition to their counties.[53]

The great fear of 1829 derived from the echo chamber of rumors, either wishful or terrifying, exchanged anxiously across the color line. One militia general regarded the talk in Northampton County as the very best proof of an impending race war: "I feel & see; every man here feels and sees that it is absolutely important to place the militia in a state to suppress Insurrection. It is heard from the lips of all. . . . Believe me, sir, the People of this shore are not easily agitated by danger & the present state of the public mind proves that we are in the midst of it."[54]

In Virginia, nothing seemed more real and motivating than the fear of an internal enemy, for that dread shaped how delegates spoke and voted in the state convention as well as what militia officers and the governor wrote to one another. The pervasive alarm expressed a fundamental truth: that the exploitation of the slaves made them potential enemies. In Warwick County, Captain William Presson lamented "our Continual exposure to the hatred of those unfortunate & infatuated beings, a hatred existing from & consequent upon their relative situations in society." Captain Presson did not suffer from the illusion that the slaves loved their masters. After the War of 1812, Virginians did indulge in new notions of happy and docile slaves, but the internal enemy never entirely vanished. Whenever trouble loomed, that haunting fear returned to grip the minds and words of Virginians.[55]

August 1 passed without the expected revolt, but the nagging dread lingered. In early September, Oliver Cross warned the Council of State, "That Virginia has an internal enemy none will deny I am sure. We have lately been seriously alarmed. We are always more or less alarmed & yet we are without the means of defence. . . . It behooves us all to be on the watch — to put ourselves in a situation to sustain that dreadful calamity. Come it will sooner or later." The Virginians had woven themselves into a total system of beliefs and behavior enforced by their cultural convictions and material interests. That system sentenced them to a terrible and recurrent fear.

Visiting Virginia, the English traveler Morris Birkbeck found that slavery was the "evil uppermost in every man's thoughts; which all deplore, many were anxious to flee, but for which no man can devise a remedy." Trapped within a system of their own making, they coped with its terrors by insisting that their greatest danger came from free blacks rather than from slaves.[56]

Where possible, slaves did conspire, but to escape rather than to murder. And they found their inspiration in the precedents set during the last war, rather than in some fantasy of Saint-Domingue. On the Atlantic side of the Eastern Shore counties of Accomack and Northampton, runaways revived the lessons of the war as learned in the slave quarters. Once again, they organized nocturnal escapes, obtained arms and boats, arranged leadership and sentinels, and fled to freedom. But this time they escaped to the northern states rather than to British warships. Northampton's leading magistrate, John Eyre, reported that the white people were "much excited by the many evidences of discontent exhibited by our slaves & particularly by the elopement of several boat loads of them well provided with arms for their defence."[57]

In adjoining Accomack County, the alarm revived another key player from the war: John G. Joynes. In 1813 and 1814 as a militia captain, Joynes had opposed slave escapes and battled British raiders, with Lieutenant James Scott as his great foil. Fifteen years later, Colonel Joynes commanded the Accomack militia. On August 10, 1829, he reported the "alarming extent to which the elopement of Slaves from this County to the states of New York and Pennsylvania has recently taken place, and the fact of their going off in gangs and armed, bidding defiance to the citizens." Although a mass slave revolt did not erupt on August 1, there was a big escape from the Eastern Shore: "A boat's crew eloped from the sea side in this County (which is now the usual mode adopted by them) and after proceeding some distance up the coast, they landed on an Island in the upper part of this county and established a regular camp and

THE NOBLE VIRGINIANS GOING TO BATTLE.

Cæsar, Sancho, Congo, fight you dogs!

The Noble Virginians Going to Battle. *In this crude engraving from 1820, a New England antislavery writer, William Hillhouse, mocks the Virginians as boastful cowards who forced their slaves to fight for them during the recent war. Produced during the peak of the Missouri crisis, the image conveys the New England Federalist attack on Virginia as weakened by slavery—a criticism that especially enraged Virginians. From* Pocahontas: A Proclamation *(1820). (Courtesy of the American Antiquarian Society)*

placed armed centinels out with orders to shoot down any white man who should approach within 15 yards of them. . . . This is only one of several cases that have taken place." Seeking new arms from the state, Joynes implied that the runaways were better armed than the local militia, which suggests the destination for some of the lost, stolen, and sold guns from the last war.[58]

Nat Turner

In 1829, Oliver Cross had warned that a bloody slave revolt would come "sooner or later." It came sooner, on the night of August 21–22, 1831, in Southampton County. A messianic preacher, Nat Turner, finally fulfilled a measure of the great Virginia nightmare: a midnight massacre of men, women, and children in their beds and cribs. The revolt fell short of the fantasy only in its small scale: Turner began with merely six men, and his force grew to sixty as they visited more farms to slaughter families, steal guns, and rally slaves. The rebels killed about sixty whites, most of them women and children. Turner sought to break through to the county seat, then known aptly enough as Jerusalem, to procure more arms before seeking a maroon haven in the Great Dismal Swamp. But his men were too few, their cohesion too weak, and their training with firearms too limited to resist the militia counterattacks during the next day.[59]

After routing the rebels, the patrollers massacred them, sometimes after inflicting brutal tortures. In the chaotic aftermath, spooked Virginians killed suspects who, in fact, had never had anything to do with Turner. In all, the Virginians butchered about 100 slaves, more than the total of sixty rebels. Indeed, most of the true rebels survived to stand trial. Turner and twenty-two others died on the gallows and the state sold and transported another twenty-one convicts. In retrospect, Turner's exceptional revolt has served as a distorting prism for interpreting slave resistance in Virginia, for on no other occasion did that resistance involve indiscriminate murder.[60]

From Southampton County, the terror spread throughout the Tidewater and Piedmont and lingered into the fall. On October 4 in Nelson County, Joseph C. Cabell noted that "the white females in this neighbourhood can scarcely sleep at all in the night," owing to the rampant rumors of slave uprisings. Three days later in Fluvanna County, John Hartwell Cocke marveled, "We hear of insurrections in every quarter of the State." In the Northern Neck, a resident reported, "The blowing of a horn or the sight of a few unknown persons in company was quite sufficient to cause a neighborhood panic and call its undisciplined militia to arms."[61]

In January 1832 in Virginia's House of Delegates, the uprising shocked the representatives into breaking the public code of silence on slavery. Dismayed by the debate, William Goode insisted that violating the code courted disaster, for he deemed slaves "an active and intelligent class, watching and weighing every movement of the Legislature." Discussion would raise their hopes, which when dashed would produce a massive revolt to "the destruction of the country." Most of the legislators, however agreed to discuss Thomas Jefferson Randolph's plan for a very gradual emancipation and deportation of Virginia's slaves.[62]

Thirty-nine years old in 1832, Randolph was the son of Thomas Mann Randolph Jr., and the grandson of Thomas Jefferson. Radical only by Virginia standards, Randolph's plan would free no living slave and, indeed, none save those born after July 3, 1840. Becoming state property, those children would be worked for Virginia's profit until adulthood and then either sold farther south or shipped to Africa. Fearing for whites rather than feeling for blacks, Randolph primarily sought to whiten Virginia rather than to free slaves.[63]

After a long and frank debate, the legislators voted 73 to 58 against adopting any plan, no matter how slow, to abolish slavery. While the western delegates favored emancipation, virtually all of the Tidewater and Piedmont delegates wanted no further discussion of the troubling issue. Although "an evil, and a transcendent evil," slavery had become inextricably woven into their society, economy, and culture. John Thompson Brown urged his fellow legislators to put up and shut up about slavery, which he deemed "our lot, our destiny—and whether, in truth, it be right or wrong—whether it be a blessing or a curse, the moment has never yet been, when it was possible to free ourselves from it." Instead of acting against slavery, the legislators tightened their restrictions on slaves, making it illegal to teach any to read and write.[64]

In defeat, Thomas Jefferson Randolph anticipated a grim future for Virginia. Without emancipation, he expected that disunion and civil war "must come, sooner or later; and when it does come, border war follows it, as certain as the night follows the day." Northern invaders would then rally "black troops, speaking the same language, of the same nation, burning with enthusiasm for the liberation of their race." In that event, he warned Virginians that nothing could "save your wives and your children from destruction."[65]

A veteran of the War of 1812 in Virginia, Randolph recognized the prowess of black troops when trained and organized by an invader with a professional military. A better prophet than a legislator, Randolph aptly predicted that during the next generation, the internal enemy would help to shatter slavery in Virginia, but they would wear the blue coats of the Union rather than the red coats of the British. During the War of 1812 in the Chesapeake, the British had never invested more than 4,000 troops, supplemented by 400 armed runaways, and that for only a few months in 1814. Such a limited force and brief incursion could rattle, but never topple, slavery. During the Civil War, however, the Union would invade the South for more than four years with more than a million men, over 180,000 of them African Americans who helped to destroy the slave system.[66]

EPILOGUE

———⬦———

*Never did a finer set of negroes leave an estate
than those that left Corrotoman.*
—JOSEPH C. CABELL, JANUARY 27, 1824[1]

Ⅰ N APRIL 1815, St. George Tucker opened a letter from his nephew
Henry Tucker, a merchant on Bermuda who announced plans to
send a brig to buy provisions in Virginia by drawing on his uncle's
credit. Still reeling from his wartime losses, Tucker was in no mood
to advance money for his nephew after discovering the name of his
brig: *James Cockburn.* The name honored the governor of Bermuda
and the brother of the admiral, Sir George Cockburn. Mistaking the
brig's name as a tribute to the admiral hated by Virginians, Tucker set
his nephew straight: he had no money to spare "in consequence of
the depredations committed upon the [Corotoman] Estate in which
my wife held her Dower, by the naval force under the command of
the person whose name your Vessel bears, by which an Estate which
yielded from $1500 to $2,000 per annum to me, has become only a
dead weight and expense; (the negroes thereon to the number of sev-

George R. Roberts, *an undated photograph. A free black from Baltimore, Roberts served
on American privateers during the War of 1812. Slaves sought freedom by escaping to, and
fighting for, the British, but free blacks often served the United States by enlisting in the
navy or on privateers. (Courtesy of the Maryland Historical Society)*

419

enty of the best hands having been shamefully carried off in the night from a defenceless private property)." Virginians nurtured bitter memories of a destructive war that had threatened the slave system.[2]

Tucker preferred to blame ungrateful slaves and larcenous Britons, rather than larger market and climatic forces, for the financial woes of his old age. In January 1821 he lamented. "My own private affairs are thrown into a state of uncertainty, and unproductiveness infinitely beyond anything that I had ever calculated upon as possible." With Corotoman yielding losses and his bank stock nearly worthless, Tucker regarded his judge's salary as his "last plank in a storm." The depression and a run of bad crops primarily undercut Tucker's estate, but he became implausibly fixated on the runaways of 1814 as the fundamental blow to his prosperity.[3]

Vexation

After the mass escape from Corotoman in April 1814, Joseph C. Cabell had moved almost all of the remaining slaves into the interior. Despite the news of peace in February 1815, Cabell delayed returning them to Corotoman because a deadly epidemic then afflicted the Tidewater. At last, at year's end, he hired guards to take the slaves by boat down the James River to Richmond and then by schooner to Corotoman. Apparently they proved restive, for Cabell paid the lead guard an extra $4 "for his trouble in starting the negroes from Richmond."[4]

In late 1815, Cabell also made peace with his brother-in-law, Charles Carter, resolving their acrimonious dispute over the division of the estate and its slaves. Initiated in 1812, the division had been postponed by Cabell's dissatisfaction with his share of the enslaved carpenters and by Carter's demand for compensation for the death of one slave whom Cabell had unilaterally removed to his Nelson County property before the war. Despite the overt agreement in 1815, Cabell remained privately contemptuous of "the Doctor's mismanagement of his affairs, his entire ignorance of the proper mode of conducting business, [and] his strange notions—especially as to his own claims & duties."[5]

In December 1815, Cabell estimated his debts at $3,000. Disrupted by the war, Corotoman had produced no marketable crops for two years, 1814 and 1815, rendering the estate "a dead weight and expense," in Tucker's words. Like any great Virginia planter, however, Cabell had a relentless optimism that the next year would produce a bumper crop to wipe away his losses: "I have a well founded hope that the crops of 1816 & 1817 will deliver me from that worst of evils—a heavy debt." By restoring the plantation to profitability, Cabell hoped to improve his prospects of finding a buyer for Corotoman: "If I could but get that load from my mind, how well a man I should be!"[6]

But he picked the wrong years to expect profits. During 1816, the notorious cold year without a summer, the harvests fell short throughout Virginia. The estate manager, John Richeson, lamented that he had "more trouble" with that year's corn crop "than any 10 crops in my life." The next year brought better weather but an infestation of the Hessian fly, which afflicted wheat, the major crop harvested at Corotoman. That spring, Richeson also deemed the slaves "more sickley than I ever new them." The year 1818 brought little improvement: "a very good crop of corn, & a very sorry crop of wheat." The harvest would, Cabell concluded, "scarcely bear the expences of the place." And for want of sufficient carpenters, "every thing has been going out of repair." Unable to sell the estate, except at a great loss, Cabell felt "compelled to keep it."[7]

Conflict persisted between the slaves and Richeson. When pushed too hard, the slaves refused to work. When Richeson resorted to the whip, some slaves fled into the woods, further disrupting work. Apparently they also felt stinted in their food, for Richeson informed Cabell that the corn crop would fall short in 1816 because "the negroes had stolen a good deal from the field." If so, they must have been hungry, for there was no local market for loose corn.[8]

Richeson blamed the unrest on the family of Great Jenny, the large, resourceful, and influential matriarch of the slave community at Corotoman and the mother of Canada Baton, who had escaped in April 1814 to become a Colonial Marine. Richeson regarded Great Jenny's daughter Nancy as an especially saucy truant. In April 1817, after Nancy's latest escape, Richeson assured Tucker, "She has not forgot her . . . tricks. Her mother says she has never seen her since she went off, but she lies." Her brother Mathew soon joined Nancy in flight, apparently into the nearby woods, where they got food and clothing secretly from their clever mother on the plantation. In late September, Nancy and Mathew remained on the lam, so Richeson advised Tucker, "I think you had better get clear of great Ginney & her set or at least a part of them." Tucker balked because of the long and close (albeit unequal) ties of his wife, Lelia, with Great Jenny and her clan. Despite Richeson's complaints, Cabell retained Great Jenny and her many children and grandchildren (including Nancy), for they remained at Corotoman in 1834.[9]

In January 1818, John's son and assistant, Henry Richeson, punched and tried to flog a slave named Billy, who struck back with a stick, then "drew his knife and immediately took his leave of the plantation." Stealing a canoe that night, Billy made his way to Williamsburg, seeking out Tucker, just as that slave had done after a similar confrontation at Corotoman ten years earlier. Agitated when confronted by the harsh truth of plantation slavery, Tucker blamed both Billy and the Richesons for the invasion of his illusions. Tucker hired a man to flog the runaway, but it distressed the owner when the flogger reported that Billy's already scarred back attested to previous, brutal whippings. Tucker promptly wrote to rebuke the Richesons for their cruelty. During the following summer, he sent Billy away to Cabell's plantation in Nelson County rather than return him to Corotoman.[10]

Of course, the Richesons felt undercut when a runaway could, at the price of a bloody back, get the master's attention to the detriment of their management. A defensive John Richeson replied that Billy had received only "2 or 3 lite flogings in the course of his stay at Corotoman." Deeming him "the worst negro for deception that I ever had to do with in my life," Richeson insisted, "Billy has not had a flogging since Mr. Cabell gave it to him himself when he was at Corotoman." It is hard to imagine the slight and genteel Cabell wielding a whip, so presumably he had ordered the Richesons to flog Billy.[11]

In 1818, Corotoman belatedly produced a profit of about $1,000, but that remained too small for Cabell's needs and plans. He blamed John Richeson, who had become depressed and drunken after his wife died in late 1816. Defending Richeson, Tucker urged forbearance: "I can heartily forgive & sincerely pity him . . . he seems to be a good hearted man, and as his removal to Corrotoman may have been the primary cause of his misfortune, I think we should regard his situation accordingly."[12]

Richeson kept his job in 1818 but lost his life on October 30, 1820. Cabell reported, "Poor Richeson, he could not resist his propensity to drink. He drank very hard after I left him in May & alcohol carried him out of the world. . . . Richeson, poor man, had not a mind big enough for the business and the little he had, he almost totally destroyed by drink in the last years of his life. He has brought both the estate & his own name into disgrace." At Corotoman, Cabell "found the estate in the hands of boys & almost in a state of ruin. It has been going down for several years, but this year it has sunk rapidly" and would produce no profit.[13]

To restore order, Cabell turned to George Robertson, the hard-driving manager who had run Corotoman until 1812, when he was sacked in favor of Richeson. Although sixty-eight years old, Robertson impressed Cabell with his zeal and energy: "The old man will produce a great change in the course of the year, if the negroes will but act well." During the following spring, Cabell reported impressive improvements, which "keep me almost constantly & agreeably excited." Superb on "the capital point of the economy of labour,"

Robertson seemed to have broken the slave resistance, which had roiled the estate for more than a decade. Cabell exulted, "The negroes were all at home, working with a brisk, lively step & a cheerful & contented countenance. Under Richeson 1/3 of the labour was lost, because he was afraid to put the negroes up to the proper point of labour, & they were constantly discontented & often running away. Robertson did not hesitate a moment to insist on a full day's work. Here is a striking proof of the necessity & propriety of discipline."[14]

Within a year, however, the illusion of happy slaves and a progressing estate dissolved. In March 1822, Cabell again rued owning "that ill-fated place Corrottoman," after learning that "one of the Barns containing about 200 barrels of corn & nearly all the corn for the support of the place, was set fire to by some incendiary & reduced to ashes. . . . It is a cutting stroke to my present circumstances, the more so as it opens such a horrible prospect for the future." Cabell deemed Robertson "the innocent cause of this fiendlike act," which suggests that some slave had furtively sought revenge on the hard-driving manager.[15]

In the fall of 1822, upon discovering that Corotoman was losing money faster than ever, Cabell lost faith in Robertson. During Richeson's last, allegedly ruinous year, the plantation had yielded a profit of $160.63, while Robertson's following two years produced a combined loss of $1,655. In 1821 a fierce summer drought had withered the crops before a fierce gale pummeled them in September. The next year proved little better. "What with the worm in the corn, & the garlic in the wheat, our crops have sunk almost to nothing," Cabell mourned. Never one to fault the climate or pests when there was a manager to blame, he concluded, "Robertson, I fear, has worn out . . . he is old & obstinate, & bigoted to the accursed mania of enclosing to the destruction of livestock." Although Cabell had pushed the enclosing program, Robertson became the scapegoat when the fenced-in cattle developed a herd disease.[16]

To cap off Cabell's travails, he lamented that the "infernal Yankees are carrying off our negroes from time to time," which he deemed "a growing & alarming evil on that estate." Fleeing in boats, the latest fugitives sought freedom in a northern state. Cabell blamed the influence of "the colonization society [and] the Missouri question" for keeping alive the dream of freedom among the slaves. And yet, he too sometimes longed to escape into the more dynamic economy of the free states. In 1819, Cabell shared with his friend John Hartwell Cocke a secret dream of buying western land in Illinois: "*Between you & myself*, I should like to hold a large tract of land *in a free state*, and the time to make the acquisition is flying rapidly by. . . . This hint is confidential." But Cabell could never extricate himself from slavery in Virginia to buy any land in Illinois, for he remained tethered to his debts and to his Tucker and Carter connections.[17]

Fed up with his losses, in December 1822 Cabell concluded, "To hold so fine an estate merely to make fortunes for overseers & to bring the owners in debt is a disgrace I cannot much longer submit to." He resolved to move to Corotoman to set things straight through close supervision: "Nothing but the presence of an active owner for half the year will stop the tide of ill fortune which besets that place." Once again, however, friends persuaded Cabell that his shaky health would never survive six months of exposure to the Tidewater malaria. Instead, he renewed his quest for a buyer, but Cabell still refused to sell at a loss despite the marked decline in property values throughout Virginia during the early 1820s. Although the Lancaster County assessors appraised his half of Corotoman at $26,550, Cabell hoped to sell it for a delusional $50,000. Cabell also felt constrained by his paternalism, for he preferred to sell the slaves with the land rather than separately: "Otherwise, what should we do with the old slaves who are numerous[?]" To abandon the elderly to starve would ruin Cabell's reputation as a Virginia gentleman.[18]

After Robertson's death, Cabell hired a Mr. Crittenden to manage Corotoman. Of course, he too disappointed the absentee owner and died prematurely in December 1826. Once again, the sickly Cabell dragged himself back to Corotoman to restore order. Finding "the estate in very bad condition," he "spent the holidays in trouble & vexation, & intense suffering from the cold." Cabell considered the slaves three to six weeks behind in their plowing, wood-cutting, and hauling, so he pressed them hard to catch up. Becoming desperate, Cabell lowered his asking price for the land to $30,000, but he still could not find a buyer. Instead, he became responsible for Carter's half of Corotoman as well.[19]

Death And Debt

On November 30, 1825, Charles Carter abruptly died, leaving an orphan daughter, Rebecca Parke Farley Carter, known as "Parke" to the family. Her mother was already dead. About forty years old, Charles suffered an early and sad end for a once idealistic youth who had vowed to free his slaves. Instead, in 1812 he had buckled to family pressure, moving to Corotoman to live among the slaves he had never wanted to own. It must have been a lonely existence, especially after his wife died. But this is just a guess, for the partial survival of documents has played a cruel trick on Carter. Surprisingly few of his letters survive in the thick dossiers of St. George Tucker and Joseph C. Cabell. Their many words loom large in this story, while Carter remains in the shadows. His obscurity allows only speculation about how he reconciled himself to isolation and slaveholding after a vibrant youth spent dreaming of freedom in Paris and Edinburgh. He had studied medicine at the finest universities in the world, but Carter found his practice limited to a Virginia plantation. Ultimately, he seems the passive victim of his own resignation to fate—and we can only imagine him through the words of men who neither liked nor understood him, particularly Cabell.[20]

Parke was away at a boarding school in Fredericksburg, so Charles died in the company of just two men, Ellison Currie, a leading local planter, and Cabell. Carter's last wish was to revive entail and primogeniture, which had preserved properties and slave communities through the colonial generations. When told he could not, Carter became resigned and "remarked that the law had made as good a will as he could make for himself": his last recorded words. That passivity assured that his slaves would not be manumitted. Under Virginia law, no one could manumit them without also providing for their ouster from the state. Carter probably considered expulsion even crueler than slavery, for many of his slaves had family and friends on nearby farms and plantations, especially the Cabell half of Corotoman.[21]

The county court appointed Carter's old enemy, Cabell, to administer the estate. Cabell reported that Carter "left his affairs in a bad state," with at least $10,000 in debts. Reuniting Corotoman under his management, Cabell applied his improving principles. First, he ousted Henry Corbin, the brother of Carter's late wife and allegedly "a corrupter of the slaves, a disorganizer among the overseers" and "the incessant fomenter of discord between my brother-in-law & myself." Apparently, Corbin had tried to block Cabell's takeover as a betrayal of Carter's best interests. At the end of the year, Cabell also evicted the white tenants on Carter's lands and demanded a payment of all their arrears in rent. Eventually, he would even forbid the harvesting of oysters from the creeks and coves of the estate.[22]

Cabell and his wife, Polly (who was Carter's sister), adopted Parke—a nice solution because the Cabells had no children of their own. In January 1826, Cabell exulted, "That little innocent has awakened in my bosom feelings which I did not think it capable of feeling. We think of her by day, & dream of her by night."[23]

While adding Parke to his family, Cabell soon had to subtract St. George Tucker. After retiring from his judicial post in 1824, Tucker and his wife, Lelia, spent every summer and fall in a small cottage on Cabell's Edgewood plantation in Nelson County, returning home to Williamsburg for the winter and spring. At Edgewood on the morning of September 15, 1827, while dressing himself, Tucker suffered a

stroke, falling to the ground paralyzed on his right side and unable
to speak or write. "Our peaceful little family has been thrown into
great commotion & distress," Cabell reported. Formerly so strong,
vigorous, and eloquent, Tucker became a bed-ridden, silent shell. On
November 10, 1827, he died at the age of seventy-five and was buried at Edgewood, far from his beloved Williamsburg. Lelia remained
with the Cabells until her own death in 1837, at the age of sixty-nine.
With the deaths of Carter and Tucker, Cabell became solely responsible for all of Corotoman, but the mounting interest on Cabell's
debts threatened to consume the entire estate.[24]

During the troubled 1820s, Virginia's great planters continued to
live beyond their increasingly limited means. Few could curtail their
spending or liquidate their assets, for the appearance of wealth and
ease mattered enormously to them. No Virginia gentleman could
abide the idea of living like some damned Yankee trader, by skimping
on fine wines or new clothes, or by denying hospitality to a broad
circle of family and friends. What would other gentlemen and ladies
say? Worse still, a new and conspicuous frugality might seem desperate, alarming long indulgent creditors into suing to wrest something
from an evidently collapsing estate. And despite all the past evidence
of floods, blights, and droughts, planters remained convinced that a
few years of good crops and better prices would restore their wealth,
saving them from distasteful sacrifices.

Cabell and his older brother, William H. Cabell, faced ruin
because they had cosigned for much of the massive debt left at death
by their friend, Wilson Cary Nicholas. The Cabells felt betrayed
that Nicholas had continued to live grandly while compounding his
debts to the end. Expecting to lose $15,000 because of the Nicholas
entanglement, Joseph C. Cabell assured a friend, "I cannot depict to
you the misfortunes & afflictions brought on my family by a man
whom I once revered as one of the greatest & best of mankind. Alas!
what poor blind creatures we are."[25]

In fact, Cabell was no better than Nicholas, for every Virginia gentleman fooled others by first deceiving himself. Surely, he reasoned, another loan or investment would restore his fortune. In 1822 Cabell confessed, "I am getting deeper into debt and feel restless & unhappy to think how I am going on. My wife is more disturbed than I am—more so than is requisite & proper." And yet, a year later, over his family's protests, he borrowed more money to buy another plantation, "Midway," in Amherst County. Cabell kept throwing good money after bad, gambling on an implausible run of better crops and more dutiful slaves on additional lands. In 1824 he boasted, "The best thing I ever did was to buy Midway. . . . In a little time all my friends will see & applaud the wisdom of this measure." Two years later, after another round of crop failures and mounting interest on his debts, he faced ruin: "These dreadful seasons are . . . truly distressing." In 1828, his already ruined brother William begged Joseph to sell Midway at a loss to reduce his burden of debt: "But the misfortune is that you do not want to sell, & blind yourself to the dangers of your situation." Cabell, however, had one last desperate hope of saving his estates: government compensation for the slaves who had escaped from Corotoman during the war.[26]

Commission

In the December 1814 Treaty of Ghent, the first article required the British to withdraw promptly from their American posts and territorial waters and to leave behind any private property still there on the day of ratification:

> All territory, places, and possessions whatsoever taken by either party from the other during the war, or which may be taken after the signing of this Treaty . . . shall be restored without delay and without causing any destruction or carrying away any of

the Artillery or other public property originally captured in the said forts or places, and which shall remain therein upon the Exchange of the Ratifications of this Treaty, or any Slaves or other private property.

Americans insisted that the British had to relinquish any runaways who were still on American soil or on warships within American waters on February 17, 1815. The British interpreted the article far more narrowly: as applying only to those slaves captured within the delimited areas fortified by the British. Under that reading, the British returned no Chesapeake runaways because they had fortified only Tangier Island, where they had captured no slaves. Similarly, on Cumberland Island in Georgia, Admiral Cockburn did restore eighty-one slaves who had belonged to the plantation that they fortified, but the British sailed away with another 1,600 runaways from other plantations in early March, three weeks after ratification.[27]

Their owners demanded their return, but preferred compensation in cash from the British, for they expected trouble from any restored runaways. William Prentiss explained, "For my part, I do not wish to see these unfortunate black people brought back, but a property worth perhaps a million dollars, if it could be recovered, would afford great relief to the sufferers."[28]

The British had never compensated masters for the slaves removed during the revolution, and southerners had blamed the Federalist administrations of the 1790s for dropping the issue in favor of improving relations with the empire. That was a political mistake that the secretary of state in 1815, James Monroe, would never repeat: "A vigorous effort of the Government to obtain justice is claimed, and expected." Attentive to the interests of his fellow slaveholders, Monroe directed the American minister to Great Britain, John Quincy Adams, to demand compensation from the British for the slaves removed by the Royal Navy in early 1815.[29]

The British countered that Royal Navy warships were their sovereign territory even when within American waters. They also insisted that the runaways had become free, and ceased to be property, by fleeing to those warships. Lord Liverpool assured Adams that fugitives "could not be considered precisely" as "private property; a table or a chair, for instance might be taken and restored without changing its condition, but a living and human being was entitled to other considerations." Rejecting a discussion of human rights, Adams insisted on the legal letter of the first article in the Treaty of Ghent. Although privately opposed to slavery, Adams nurtured a powerful ambition for higher office in America, which meant that he could not appear soft on an important issue to southerners.[30]

Backing down, the British and American diplomats agreed to submit the dispute to the Russian czar, Alexander I, for binding arbitration. In the privacy of his diary, Adams found it "whimsical . . . that the United States and Great Britain, both speaking English," should resort to a Russian to parse the meaning of their words in a treaty. Apparently the czar understood the American idiom better than the British, ruling for the republic and against the empire in April 1822. Relying on "the literal and grammatical sense of the first article of the Treaty of Ghent," the czar insisted that the British had to compensate the Americans for the runaways who were on board their ships (if within American territorial waters) as well as in their occupied forts on February 17, 1815.[31]

To determine the compensation, the American and British diplomats established a joint commission composed of two commissioners assisted by two arbitrators—with Britain and the United States providing one of each. Convening in Washington, D.C., in August 1823, the commissioners required masters to submit documents attesting that the British had taken away their particular slaves at the end of the war. Whenever the two commissioners disagreed on the evidence, they assigned the case to one of the arbitrators chosen by lot. Because the British and American commissioners almost always disagreed, the process proved tedious and slow, with the nationality of the chosen arbitrator usually determining each decision.[32]

Rather than wrangle over the value of each slave, the commissioners agreed to set an average value per slave on a regional basis. Because slaves were more expensive in the Deep South, the board fixed the average value of a Louisiana slave at $580; an Alabama, Georgia, or South Carolina slave at $390; and a Chesapeake claimant could collect only $280 per slave. This average value applied regardless of the age, gender, or skill of the particular slave. With claims submitted for 3,601 runaways, the British faced a total liability of $2,693,120 if they had to pay interest from February 17, 1815.[33]

The British balked at the cost, particularly the interest, and the Americans wearied of the delay. Consequently, in November 1826 the United States accepted the British offer to settle the claims with a lump sum of $1,204,960, which the American government would then distribute through a new set of commissioners. Newly elected president, Adams appointed Langdon Cheves of South Carolina, Henry Seawell of North Carolina, and James Pleasants of Virginia. Thorough, able, logical, and tireless, Cheves became the leader.[34]

The lump sum became an apple of discord, pitting the Chesapeake claimants against their Deep South rivals for larger slices of a finite pie. "We always expected some resistance from the British Government, but never from our fellow-citizens," lamented a Chesapeake spokesman. In fact, nothing could better ignite squabbling among Americans than a scramble for $1,204,960 cast into their midst.[35]

If the new commissioners adhered to the convention signed with the British in 1822, the fund would not compensate every master who lost any slave at any time during the war. On the contrary, the claimant would have to prove that the lost slave remained on an American island or aboard a British ship still within American waters on February 17, 1815. This strict definition would preclude compensation for the many slaves removed to Bermuda or Halifax during 1813 and 1814—or even January and early February 1815. Because those earlier runaways came from the Chesapeake, the tight definition satisfied the Deep South claimants, for almost all of their slaves had gone away after ratification on February 17. By excluding the many Chesapeake claimants, the Deep South claimants hoped to secure virtually the whole fund: interest as well as principal. If, however, the commission loosened the rules, the Chesapeake claimants would get more money, depriving the Georgians and Louisianans of interest on their losses. Citing their longer and greater sufferings during the war, the Chesapeake claimants insisted that they deserved much of the compensation fund.[36]

To support their cases, the Chesapeake claimants enlisted testimony from a few runaways who had returned to Virginia after the war. Defending black witnesses as reliable, Pleasants insisted, "[They] are intelligent, far more so than they are generally supposed by those whose opportunities have not led them to examine their characters closely. They are in general as moral as most other persons. They are strongly religious, as much so generally, I incline to think, as the white people. . . . They have their preachers, many of them quite respectable as teachers of religion & morals." When in their own interest, Virginians could belatedly acknowledge what they usually denied: the ability, piety, and morality of their slaves.[37]

Of course, the Deep South claimants protested that no colored person should ever testify against the interest of a white man. Insistent that only a consistent assertion of racial inequality could preserve slavery, Cheves demanded, "Ought we not to beware lest we be stirring a volcanic fire?" But Henry Seawell sided with Pleasants to permit the black testimony. Then in May 1828, Congress intervened, directing the commissioners to compensate widely, to the relief of the Chesapeake claimants, rather than to concentrate the funds to reward their rivals in the Deep South.[38]

Compensation

Among the Chesapeake claimants, Joseph C. Cabell had the most to lose—or gain—for he sought compensation for all sixty-nine slaves from Corotoman: his own forty-two as well as the twenty-seven belonging to the late Charles Carter. Deeply in debt, Cabell was desperate. "God grant that it may succeed," he assured William Wirt, "for the Vast increase of my difficulties by miscalculations . . . has placed me on the edge of a fearful precipice. . . . I acknowledge that, in my peculiar situation at this time, the claim is of vital importance." To serve as his agent Cabell hired Wirt, an old friend who had become the attorney general of the United States. Unable to pay a retainer, Cabell promised Wirt 5 percent of any compensation.[39]

Leaving no stone unturned, Cabell investigated the diaspora of the Corotoman runaways, tracking down leads from Trinidad to Nova Scotia with the help of two free black sailors, Holland Wood and Thomas Wood. In May 1821 in Halifax, Holland Wood had spotted six former friends from the Corotoman estate. They reported that the refugee women worked as servants in the hotels, while the men repaired the road between Halifax and Windsor. Five years later in Trinidad, Thomas Wood recognized another six Corotoman runaways, including Dick Carter, who had vowed "I will follow my wife and children to death." Happily in 1826, Dick Carter was with his wife, Sukey, the probable organizer of the escape. Cabell also hired Addison Hall and James Kelley, two leading men in Lancaster County, to question the slaves still at Corotoman to reconstitute their family ties and identify the surnames on British lists of runaways.[40]

Cabell won a sweet victory on May 21, 1828, when the commissioners approved $20,640 in compensation for the sixty-nine Corotoman slaves. After deducting expenses, including Wirt's commission, Cabell reaped $18,000: a substantial fortune for that time. Writing to thank Wirt, Cabell exulted:

The recovery of the Corrottoman claims is in regard to Doctor Carter's estate & my own, one of those strokes of good fortune, which are decisive in their consequences. Our estates were on the brink of ruin. . . . You can imagine the effect of $18,000 suddenly brought to the aid of two estates in Virginia pressed to the utmost & on the verge of putting up all the slaves to the highest bidder to be scattered to the four winds of heaven—lands rented out to be ploughed to be barren or sold for a song—the improvements of 20 years all lost to the owners—the graves of ancestors trodden under the hoof of the herds of speculators. Then, look at the revenue—creditors paid off or satisfied—credit restored—owners looking up—improvements advancing—prospects brightening—the heart ache relieved.

Cabell's windfall saved the Corotoman slaves from an auction that would have divided and scattered families. By rescuing Cabell, the award spared the Corotoman slaves from paying for the financial sins of their master. The sixty-nine runaways of 1814 made possible the infusion of cash fourteen years later that rescued Cabell from his many blunders. Instead of cursing the runaways, Cabell should have thanked them for providing the basis for his financial bailout in 1828. Virginia's slave system generated an endless series of such ironies.[41]

APPENDIX A

———— ⌘ ————

Corotoman Enslaved Families, 1814

After the war, in a bid for compensation, Joseph Cabell gathered information on the family relationships of the Corotoman runaways. At his behest, two local notables, Addison Hall and James Kelley, "diligently enquired among the slaves" who remained behind to reconstitute "the names, surnames, nick-names & connections of the negroes" who had left. Their report revealed family dynamics and structures ordinarily opaque to uninterested masters. The following table documents the thick interweaving of connections among the runaways and illuminates the patterns of who chose to go or to stay. The record has gaps and oddities, including a surprising number of children by the same parent with the same age. Rather than indicating a spate of twins in the community, the matching ages represent guesswork by Hall and Kelley, for they had no plantation register to pin down birth dates.[1]

In the following table, an asterisk indicates an adult with a sibling among the escapees; the person's age appears within parentheses; a name within brackets was a relative left behind; and an italicized name identifies a person who came from the Carter side of the estate's partition.

Family Relationships among the Corotoman Refugees, April 1814

Husband	Wife	Children
*Tom Saunders (29)	*Hannah Marx Saunders (28)	1. Delia Saunders (6) 2. [Tom Saunders Jr. (6)] 3. Jo Saunders (6 months)
Hostler Joe Cox (42)	*Franky Cox (38)	1. [Hearty Cox (15)] 2. Dean Bundy Cox (13) 3. Talbot Cox (11) 4. Nelley Cox (11) 5. Joe Cox Jr. (8) 6. [Nick Cox (7)] 7. Edinburgh Cox (4) 8. Peyton Cox (4) 9. Hollis Cox (2) 10. James Cox (10 months)
[*Charles Saunders (50)]	*Fanny Loney Saunders (42)	1. Dinah Saunders (16) 2. Fanny Saunders (15) 3. Henry Saunders (13) 4. Nancy Saunders (12) 5. [Elizabeth Saunders (8)] 6. [James Saunders (6)] 7. Charles Saunders (6) 8. Alfred Saunders (4) 9. Lucinda Saunders (1)
Jim Bully Cook (30)	*Betty Saunders Cook (31)	1. [James Cook (8)] 2. [Mary Anne Cook (6)] 3. Sarah Cook (6) 4. Sukey Cook (4) 5. Cordelia Cook (3)
*Dick Carter (45)	*Sukey Saunders Carter (32)	1. Morrow Carter (8) 2. George Carter (6) 3. James Carter (4) 4. Solomon Carter (2)
[Joe Brown]	*Aggy Brown (37)	1. Joseph Brown Jr. (8) 2. Edinburgh Brown (4) 3. Hollis Brown (3)

Husband	Wife	Children
George Brown (35)	*Amy Saunders Brown (29)	1. Young Brown (8) 2. James Brown (6) 3. George Brown Jr. (3) 4. unknown infant (3 weeks)
*Ezekiel Loney (27)	*Nelly Marx Loney (23)	1. China Loney (2)
Spencer Philips Wood (26)	Betty Stevens Wood (27)	1. Willoughby Wood (6) 2. Radnor Wood (4) 3. Nancy Wood (1)
[unknown]	[*Nancy Cain]	1. Betsey Bush (13)
*Peter Craney (33)	[unknown and deceased]	1. [James (6)]
[Smith Peter Baton]	[Great Jenny]	1. Canada Baton (21) 2. [Letty] 3. [Jenny] 4. [Polly] 5. [Nancy] 6. [Julia] 7. [Rocksy] 8. [Nelson] 9. [Patty]
Henry Lee (33)	*Unity Lee (34)*	1. *Criss Lee (15)* 2. *Henry Lee Jr. (12)* 3. *Emily Lee (8)* 4. *Nelly Lee (6)* 5. *Robert Lee (4)*
[*Old John Brown (60)*]	**Sukey Saunders Brown* (23)	1. *Joe Brown Jr. (6)*
[*Israel Brown*]	[*Rachel Brown*]	1. *Charity Brown (15)* 2. *Tom Brown (11)*
[unknown]	**Sarah Anne Saunders Moore* (20)	1. [Eliza (unknown)]

Husband	Wife	Children
[unknown]	*Sukey Cook* (38)	
[unknown]	*Merinda Saunders* (16)	
[*Old Sam Loney]	[Jenny Cook]	1. *Nancy Loney* (6) 2. *Gabriel Loney* (6)
[unknown]	[unknown]	1. *Dinah Dennis* (14)
[unknown]	[unknown]	1. *Charles James* (13)

SIBLING RELATIONSHIPS BETWEEN ADULTS AMONG THE COROTOMAN REFUGEES, APRIL 1814

Fanny Loney Saunders (42)—Ezekiel Loney (27)—[Old Sam Loney]
Betty Saunders Cook (31)—Amy Saunders Brown (29)—*Sarah Anne Saunders Moore* (20)
Sukey Saunders Carter (32)—Tom Saunders (29)—[Nancy Cain]
[Charles Saunders (50)]—*Sukey Saunders Brown* (23)
Hannah Marx Saunders (28)—Nelly Marx Loney (23)
Dick Carter (45)—Peter Craney (33)
Franky Cox (38)—*Aggy Brown* (37)

Note: Names in brackets were those who stayed behind; those in italics came from the Carter side; names underlined were women.

Sources: Joseph C. Cabell to William Wirt, Oct. 8, 1827, JCC&CFP (38-111), box 19, SSCL-UVA; Addison Hall and James Kelley, deposition, Feb. 21, 1828, and Joseph C. Cabell, *Argument in Support of the Claims of Joseph C. Cabell, St. George Tucker, Charles Carter and Others* (n.p., n.d.), in RG 76, entry 185, box 3, folder 6, USNA-CP. For Great Jenny's other children, see Cabell, "Account of Expences of the Removal of the Corotoman Negroes," May 6–20, 1814, and "List of Negroes Hired in Lynchburg," RABC, box 48, folder 5, HL.

APPENDIX B

Numbers

How many slaves escaped from the shores of the Chesapeake during the War of 1812? Historians usually rely on the "definitive list" compiled by the postwar commission established to compensate masters. That list records 3 from the District of Columbia, 714 from Maryland, and 1,721 from Virginia, for a total of 2,438. The Chesapeake region accounted for two-thirds (2,438 of the 3,580 total) of the wartime runaways as determined by the claims commission, with Georgia generating the next largest number of runaways: 833. The balance (319) fled in smaller numbers from Louisiana, Delaware, South Carolina, and the territories of Mississippi and Alabama.[2]

The 3,580 total for the United States understates the true number of runaways, particularly in the Chesapeake, because the commission required claimants to submit complex documentation formally notarized by county magistrates. Owing to the dispersed settlement pattern, poor access to information, and shaky literacy of common whites, many Chesapeake masters failed to submit claims or had them rejected. Some "sufferers" had moved out of state, and others had died leaving tangled estates. In May 1815 from the Northern Neck, Walter Jones lamented, "The sufferers in this quarter have been careless in verifying their losses, as a late Law of the State directs." In March 1828 on the Eastern Shore of Virginia, Thomas Badger stated "that he knows a great many slaves went from this shore, some of which have never been claimed at all."[3]

In fact, about 5,000 (rather than 3,580) slaves probably escaped from the United States during the war. British records indicate that from 1813 through 1816, they relocated at least 4,192 American runaways to three colonies: Nova Scotia (2,811), Trinidad (1,000), and New Brunswick (381). An additional number, probably 300, became scattered throughout the British Empire, primarily as sailors, dock-workers, and the servants of military officers, raising the total to about 4,492. Moreover, that total does not include those who died during the war: some from combat and more from disease. And the 4,492 excludes the runaway Georgians who remained in Florida as maroons. Including the dead and the maroons raises the probable total to at least 5,000, a number suggested by Thomas Spalding in 1815 and recently confirmed by historian Thomas Malcomson from his careful research in British naval records. If we accept the claims commission's calculation that the Chesapeake region accounted for 68 percent of the wartime runaways (and Virginia's share was 48 percent of the total), and apply those percentages to the 5,000, we derive a revised estimate of 3,405 for the Chesapeake, including 2,400 from Virginia (rather than just 1,721 per the official list).[4]

On the one hand, the flight of 2,400 slaves caused a sensation as the greatest number to escape from Virginia in any two-year period between the end of the American Revolution and the start of the Civil War. On the other hand, their escape made little dent in Virginia's total slave population, which continued to grow through natural increase. Indeed, many more slaves left the state by sale to the Deep South during the 1810s: at least 90,000, or nearly thirty-eight times the number who escaped from Virginia to the British. Despite the numbers of wartime runaways and of export sales, in 1820 Virginia had more slaves than ever before: 425,153, up from 392,518 in 1810. During the troubled 1810 the increase in the state's slave population was about fourteen times the number of wartime runaways from Virginia. In sum, the importance of the wartime escapes lay primarily in the psychological and political over-reactions provoked among the Virginians, who felt shocked by any surge in runaways as a dangerously slippery slope toward slave revolt. Despite their modest numbers, the wartime runaways terrified Virginians who dreaded slaves as their "internal enemy."[5]

NOTES

Abbreviations

Collections

AC	*Annals of Congress*
APA-GMR	Auditor of Public Accounts, General Militia Records: List of Furloughs & Discharges (Library of Virginia, Richmond)
ASP-FR	*American State Papers: Class 1, Foreign Relations*, 38 vols. (Buffalo: William S. Hein, 1998; reprint of Washington, DC, 1832–61)
ASP-MA	*American State Papers: Class 5, Military Affairs* (Washington, D.C.: Gates Seaton, 1860)
BFP	Bryan Family Papers (Small Special Collections Library, University of Virginia, Charlottesville)
CFP	Campbell Family Papers (Special Collections, Rubinstein Library, Duke University, Durham, NC)
CO	Colonial Office (National Archives of the United Kingdom, London)
CVSP	*Calendar of Virginia State Papers and Other Manuscripts from January 1, 1808, to December 1, 1835*, 12 vols. ed. H. W. Flournoy (New York: Kraus Reprint, 1968; reprint of Richmond, 1890)
FO	Foreign Office (National Archives of the United Kingdom, London)
JBEP	James Barber Executive Papers (Library of Virginia, Richmond)
JCCFP (38-111-c)	Joseph C. Cabell Family Papers (Small Special Collections Library, University of Virginia, Charlottesville)

JCC&CFP (38-111)	Joseph C. Cabell and Cabell Family Papers (Small Special Collections Library, University of Virginia, Charlottesville)
JHCFP	John Hartwell Cocke Family Papers (Small Special Collections Library, University of Virginia, Charlottesville)
JMP	James Monroe Papers (Library of Congress, Washington, D.C., and New York Public Library, New York City)
JTEP	John Tyler Executive Papers (Library of Virginia, Richmond)
LWP	Levin Winder Papers (Maryland Historical Society, Baltimore)
MSP	Maryland State Papers (Maryland State Archives, Annapolis)
PJM-PS	*Papers of James Madison, Presidential Series*, ed. J. C. A. Stagg, 5 vols. to date (Charlottesville: University Press of Virginia, 1984–)
PTJ-RS	*Papers of Thomas Jefferson, Retirement Series,* ed. J. Jefferson Looney, 9 vols. to date (Princeton, N.J.: Princeton University Press, 2005–)
RABC	Robert Alonzo Brock Collection (Huntington Library, San Marino, CA)
SACP	Sir Alexander Cockburn Papers (Library of Congress microfilm edition of originals at the National Archives of Scotland, Edinburgh)
SGCP	Sir George Cockburn Papers (Library of Congress, Washington, DC)
SPMP	Sir Pulteney Malcolm Papers (William L. Clements Library, University of Michigan, Ann Arbor, MI)
TCP	Tucker-Coleman Papers (College of William and Mary, Williamsburg, VA)
TFP	Tompkins Family Papers (Virginia Historical Society, Richmond)
WBGEP	William Branch Giles Executive Papers (Library of Virginia, Richmond)
WCNEP	Wilson Cary Nicholas Executive Papers (Library of Virginia, Richmond)
WHWP	William H. Winder Papers (Maryland Historical Society, Baltimore)
WPSP	William Patterson Smith Papers (Rubinstein Library, Duke University, Durham, NC)

Archives and Libraries

HL	Huntington Library, San Marino, CA
LAC	Library and Archives Canada, Ottawa, Ontario
LC	Library of Congress, Washington, DC

LV   Library of Virginia, Richmond
MdHS   Maryland Historical Society, Baltimore
MdSA   Maryland State Archives, Annapolis
NSA   Nova Scotia Archives, Halifax
NAUK   National Archives of the United Kingdom, London
SC-DUL   Special Collections, Rubinstein Library, Duke University, Durham, NC
SCSL-CWM   Special Collections, Swem Library, College of William and Mary, Williamsburg, VA
SSCL-UVA   Small Special Collections Library, University of Virginia, Charlottesville
USNA-CP   United States National Archives, College Park, MD
USNA-DC   United States National Archives, Washington, DC
VHS   Virginia Historical Society, Richmond
WLCL-UM   William L. Clements Library, University of Michigan, Ann Arbor, MI

Introduction

1   Robert Greenhow to Charles K. Mallory, Sep. 8, 2013, JBEP, reel 5516, LV.
2   Depositions of Charles Massey Jr., July 6, 1815, and Abraham B. Hooe, July 6, 1815, APA-GMR, entry 258, box 779, King George County folder, LV; deposition of George N. Grymes, Jan. 6, 1825 ("had taken"), RG 76, entry 190, box 3, case 177 (Abraham B. Hooe), USNA-CP.
3   For the nature of slave neighborhoods, see Kaye, *Joining Places*, 4–12, 22–50.
4   Bartlet Shanklyn to Abraham B. Hooe, May 21, 1820, RG 76, entry 190, box 3, case 177 (Abraham B. Hooe), USNA-CP. For the adaptation of market values by the enslaved, see Schermerhorn, *Money over Mastery*, 18–19.
5   For the Chesapeake side of the story, see Bartlett and Smith, "'Species of Milito-Nautico-Guerilla Warfare,'" 173–204; Cassell, "Slaves of the Chesapeake," 144–55; George, "Mirage of Freedom," 427–50. For the experience of refugees in Nova Scotia, see Grant, "Black Immigrants," 253–70; Whitfield, *Blacks on the Border*; Whitfield, *From American Slaves*. For the earlier, revolutionary escapes, see Frey, *Water from the Rock*; Pybus, *Epic Journeys*; Pybus, "Jefferson's Faulty Math," 243–64; Schama, *Rough Crossings*; J. W. St. G. Walker, *Black Loyalists*.
6   Sir George Cockburn to Sir Alexander Cochrane, May 10, 1814, in Dudley, *Naval War of 1812*, vol. 3:64–65.
7   Morgan, "Ending the Slave Trade," 116–91.

8   P. Hamilton, *Making and Unmaking*, 81; L. K. Ford, *Deliver Us from Evil*, 26; Hickey, "America's Response," 361–79; A. Rothman, *Slave Country*, 21; Sidbury, "Saint Domingue in Virginia," 531–52; Birkbeck, *Notes on a Journey*, 17; W. D. Jordan, *White over Black*, 394; Sutton, "Nostalgia, Pessimism, and Malaise," 51.

9   Birkbeck, *Notes on a Journey*, 21; John Randolph quoted in J. Quincy, *Figures of the Past*, 178.

10   D. B. Davis, *Problem of Slavery*, 173–79; L. K. Ford, *Deliver Us from Evil*, 46–47; Wolf, *Race and Liberty*, 87, 102–3; Patrick Henry quoted in W. D. Jordan, *White over Black*, 544; J. Taylor, *Arator*, 127; Jefferson, *Notes on the State of Virginia*, 128.

11   Thomas Jefferson to John Holmes, Apr. 22, 1820, in P. L. Ford, *Works of Thomas Jefferson*, vol. 12:158–59.

12   William Duane to Thomas Jefferson, Aug. 11, 1814, in Looney, *PTJ-RS*, vol. 7:533.

13   Oakes, *Freedom National*, 17–99.

Chapter One: Revolution

1   St. G. Tucker, *Dissertation on Slavery*, 1.

2   Henry Tucker to St. George Tucker, July 31, 1774, quoted in P. Hamilton, *Making and Unmaking*, 30–31. For Richard Henry Lee's parade, see Van Cleve, *Slaveholders' Union*, 38.

3   Drescher, *Abolition*, 124; Pearson, *Remaking Custom*, 113.

4   St. George Tucker to Richard Rush, Oct. 27, 1813, in Coleman, "Randolph and Tucker Letters," 212–13; Coleman, *St. George Tucker*, 28–29; Cullen, *St. George Tucker*, 3–8; P. Hamilton, "Revolutionary Principles," 533.

5   McColley, *Slavery and Jeffersonian Virginia*, 9–10; R. B. Davis, *Jeffersonian America*, 128–32; Morgan, *Slave Counterpoint*, 29–33; Schermerhorn, *Money over Mastery*, 6–7.

6   Darrell, "Diary," 144 ("its disk"); Morgan, *Slave Counterpoint*, 32; Roberts and Roberts, *Moreau de St. Mery's American Journey*, 52; Sobel, *World They Made Together*, 131; John Randolph to James M. Garnett, Aug. 21, 1812, John Randolph Papers, box 3, SSCL-UVA. For the story of Colonel Randolph, see Fedric, *Slave Life*, 9 ("Bring in").

7   Carter, *Virginia Journals*, vol. 1:78; Roberts and Roberts, *Moreau de St. Mery's American Journey*, 47–53; Janson, *Stranger in America*, 333–34; [G. Tucker], *Letters from Virginia*, 18–19.

8   Morgan, *Slave Counterpoint*, 34; Sobel, *World They Made Together*, 100–104.

9   Kulikoff, *Tobacco and Slaves*, 131; Carter, *Virginia Journals*, vol. 1:127

("the shabbiness"); Ball, *Fifty Years in Chains*, 47, 51; D. P. Jordan, *Political Leadership*, 6-7; Morgan, *Slave Counterpoint*, 39, 45; Samuel Mordecai to R. Mordecai, Sep. 11, 1814 ("miserably poor"), Mss, 2, M 8114, a2, VHS.

10   D. P. Jordan, *Political Leadership*, 8; Kulikoff, *Tobacco and Slaves*, 141–53; Morgan, *Slave Counterpoint*, 30–33.

11   Birkbeck, *Notes on a Journey*, 19–21; Wyllie, "Observations," 393–96; Darrell, "Diary," 147; R. B. Davis, *Jeffersonian America*, 133–34, 152; D. P. Jordan, *Political Leadership*, 9; Lowrey, *James Barbour*, 63–64; McColley, *Slavery and Jeffersonian Virginia*, 12–18; Morgan, *Slave Counterpoint*, 34.

12   W. C. Bruce, *John Randolph*, vol. 2:158; Carter, *Virginia Journals*, vol. 1:5, 85; Darrell, "Diary," 144 ("Now & then"); Roberts and Roberts, *Moreau de St. Mery's American Journey*, 69; Jefferson quoted in Sobel, *World They Made Together*, 117; Schermerhorn, *Money over Mastery*, 37.

13   Carter, *Virginia Journals*, vol. 1:102, 127, 140; Wyllie, "Observations," 391; Darrell, "Diary," 146; Edward Ross to David Parish, Oct. 10, 1813 ("the very worst"), Parish-Rosseel Papers, St. Lawrence University Archives, Owen D. Young Library, Canton, NY; Augustus Foster in R. B. Davis, *Jeffersonian America*, 131, 135; McColley, *Slavery and Jeffersonian Virginia*, 37–38.

14   Carter, *Virginia Journals*, vol. 1:127 ("I felt"); R. B. Davis, *Jeffersonian America*, 134; John Randolph to Josiah Quincy, Mar. 22, 1814, in E. Quincy, *Life of Josiah Quincy*, 352.

15   Kulikoff, *Tobacco and Slaves*, 128–30 (Jefferson quote on 129); Holton, *Forced Founders*, 46–47, 66; George Washington to Bryan Fairfax, Aug. 24, 1774, quoted in Chernow, *Washington*, 111.

16   Dunn, "After Tobacco," 344–45; Morgan, *Slave Counterpoint*, 59–62, 81, 90–95. For the vetoed legislation, see Holton, *Forced Founders*, xix–xx, 66–73; Wolf, *Race and Liberty*, 23–24.

17   D. B. Davis, *Problem of Slavery*, 471–501; C. L. Brown, *Moral Capital*, 96–100; Drescher, *Abolition*, 98–105; Schama, *Rough Crossings*, 427n16; Van Cleve, *Slaveholders Union*, 17, 31–36.

18   Drescher, *Abolition*, 103–5; Van Cleve, *Slaveholders' Union*, 31–38; C. L. Brown, *Moral Capital*, 118–26 (Ambrose Serle quote on 120), 134; Blumrosen and Blumrosen, *Slave Nation*, 15, 20, 30–38; Waldstreicher, *Slavery's Constitution*, 39–42.

19   Schama, *Rough Crossings*, 16–18 (*Virginia Gazette* advertisement quote on 18); Morgan, *Slave Counterpoint*, 461.

20   C. L. Brown, *Moral Capital*, 134–43; Drescher, *Abolition*, 109; R. G. Parkinson, "'Manifest Signs of Passion,'" 53–55, 57 (Jefferson quote); Van Cleve, "Founding a Slaveholders' Union," 120–21.

21   Schwarz, *Twice Condemned*, 175; James Madison to William Bradford, Nov. 26, 1774, quoted in Frey, "Between Slavery and Freedom," 376; Madison to Bradford, June 19, 1775, quoted in Pybus, *Epic Journeys*, 8; Holton, *Forced Founders*, 137–40, 151; McDonell, *Politics of War*, 22–23, 47–49. For the Virginia code of silence regarding slave plots, see Aptheker, *American Negro Slave Revolts*, 67; Wolf, *Race and Liberty*, 115.

22   Lord Dunmore quoted in Mullin, *Flight and Rebellion*, 131; Frey, "Between Slavery and Freedom," 377; Holton, *Forced Founders*, 141–48; McDonell, *Politics of War*, 49–65; Schama, *Rough Crossings*, 70; Schwarz, *Twice Condemned*,181–83.

23   Frey, "Between Slavery and Freedom," 378; Holton, *Forced Founders*, 157–89; McDonell, *Politics of War*, 134–39; Schama, *Rough Crossings*, 67–69; R. G. Parkinson, "'Manifest Signs of Passion,'" 57.

24   Holton, *Forced Founders*, 153–56; McDonell, *Politics of War*, 140–44, 152–59; Pybus, *Epic Journeys*, 10–11; *Pennsylvania Gazette*, July 17, 1776, quoted in Schama, *Rough Crossings*, 8, see also 77.

25   Aptheker, *American Negro Slave Revolts*, 79–80; Schama, *Rough Crossings*, 5, 69 ("alter the World"); McConville, *King's Three Faces*, 175–82. For peasant revolts in the name of an idealized king, see Emmanuel LeRoy Ladurie, *The Peasants of Languedoc*, John Day, trans. (Urbana: University of Illinois Press, 1974), 265–86.

26   *Virginia Gazette*, Nov. 24, 1775, quoted in R. G. Parkinson, "'Manifest Signs of Passion,'" 57; Lund Washington to George Washington, Dec. 3, 1775, quoted in Pybus, *Epic Journeys*, 19–20.

27   Frey, "Between Slavery and Freedom," 394–95; McDonell, *Politics of War*, 139–40n7; Mullin, *Flight and Rebellion*, 136; Pybus, *Epic Journeys*, 11; Pybus, "Jefferson's Faulty Math," 249; Robert Carter quoted in Morton, *Robert Carter*, 55–56.

28   Frey, "Between Slavery and Freedom," 383–85; Hoffman, *Spirit of Dissension*, 185; McDonell, *Politics of War*, 176, 438; Morgan, *Slave Counterpoint*, 342; Mullin, *Flight and Rebellion*, 134–35.

29   *Virginia Gazette*, Nov. 24, 1775, quoted in R. G. Parkinson, "'Manifest Signs of Passion,'" 57; Pybus, *Epic Journeys*, 30–31.

30   Drescher, *Abolition*, 120; Frey, "Between Slavery and Freedeom," 387–89.

31   Frey, "Between Slavery and Freedom," 376, 396–98; Fenn, *Pox Americana*, 55–62; McDonell, *Politics of War*, 161–62, 249; Pybus, *Epic Journeys*, 11–12, 17–19; Pybus, "Jefferson's Faulty Math," 249–50.

32   Frey, "Between Slavery and Freedom," 379–82, 389 (Col. George Corbin to Col. William Davies, Aug. 1781, quote); McDonell, *Politics of War*, 292–94, 343–44, 398–400, 438–39.

33 Frey, "Between Slavery and Freedom," 382; McDonell, *Politics of War*, 439; Pybus, *Epic Journeys*, 45–46; Pybus, "Jefferson's Faulty Math," 243–46.

34 Feltman, *Journal*, 6 ("numbers"); St. George Tucker quoted in Coleman, *St. George Tucker*, 74; McDonell, *Politics of War*, 440–43, 476–89; R. G. Parkinson, "'Manifest Signs of Passion,'" 60; Pybus, "Jefferson's Faulty Math," 256–57; Carter, ed., *Virginia Journals*, vol. 1:83.

35 Kulikoff, "Uprooted Peoples," 144; McDonell, *Politics of War*, 476–89; R. G. Parkinson, "'Manifest Signs of Passion,'" 60. After the war, Jefferson claimed that 30,000 slaves fled to Cornwallis but 27,000 of them died—enormous exaggerations that have long misled many historians. For the best analysis of the actual numbers, see Pybus, "Jefferson's Faulty Math," 243–64.

36 Pybus, "Jefferson's Faulty Math," 246; James Madison to (his father) James Madison, Sep. 8, 1783, quoted in Hunt, *Writings of James Madison*, vol. 2:15; P. Hamilton, *Making and Unmaking*, 62.

37 Drescher, *Abolition*, 126; McColley, *Slavery and Jeffersonian Virginia*, 85–87; Pybus, *Epic Journeys*, 66–70.

38 Berlin, *Many Thousands Gone*, 263–64; Frey, *Water from the Rock*, 218; Kulikoff, "Uprooted Peoples," 144–45; McDonell, *Politics of War*, 490–91; Morgan, *Slave Counterpoint*, 384.

39 Evans, *"Topping People,"* 177–94; J. Lewis, *Pursuit of Happiness*, 1; Morton, *Robert Carter*, 51–53; Schama, *Rough Crossings*, 71.

40 Kulikoff, *Tobacco and Slaves*, 300–11; J. Lewis, *Pursuit of Happiness*, 48–50.

41 McDonell, *Politics of War*, 261–62, 338–39, 388–94, 486–87; Evans *"Topping People,"* 198; Shalhope, *John Taylor*, 38; Coleman, *St. George Tucker*, 63; D. B. Davis, *Problem of Slavery*, 78–80; St. G. Tucker, *Dissertation on Slavery*, 8.

42 Mullin, *Flight and Rebellion*, 134; R. G. Parkinson, "'Manifest Signs of Passion,'" 59–65; A. Rothman, *Slave Country*, 8; Roberts and Roberts, *Moreau de St. Mery's American Journey*, 310 ("the American people"); Furstenberg, "Beyond Freedom and Slavery," 1295–97; Thomas Jefferson to Marquis de Chastellux, Sep. 2, 1785 ("zealous"), quoted in Waldstreicher, *Slavery's Constitution*, 64.

43 St. George Tucker to Richard Rush, Oct. 27, 1813, in Coleman, "Randolph and Tucker Letters," 213–15; Coleman, *St. George Tucker*, 33–36, 49–78; Cullen, *St. George Tucker*, 15–23; P. Hamilton, *Making and Unmaking*, 44–48.

44 St. George Tucker to Richard Rush, Oct. 27, 1813, in Coleman, "Randolph and Tucker Letters," 215–16; Coleman, *St. George Tucker*, 37–47;

Cullen, *St. George Tucker*, 21–22; P. Hamilton, *Making and Unmaking*, 40–44, 51; P. Hamilton, "Revolutionary Principles," 533.

45   William Allison (merchant) quoted in P. Hamilton, *Making and Unmaking*, 74–75; St. George Tucker quoted in Evans, *"Topping People,"* 196.

46   Brugger, *Beverley Tucker*, 5; Cullen, *St. George Tucker*, 38–49, 55, 63–64. P. Hamilton, *Making and Unmaking*, 51–59, 75.

47   Coleman, *St. George Tucker*, 83–94 (Frances B. R. Tucker to St. George Tucker quotes on 90 and 91); P. Hamilton, *Making and Unmaking*, 51–52, 68.

48   St. George Tucker to Richard Rush, Oct. 27, 1813, in Coleman, "Randolph and Tucker Letters," 218–19; Coleman, *St. George Tucker*, 96–98; [G. Tucker], *Letters from Virginia*, 122 ("have something").

49   Cullen, *St. George Tucker*, 75; P. Hamilton, *Making and Unmaking*, 78–80, 93 (St. George Tucker quote), 108.

50   Brugger, *Beverley Tucker*, 11; Coleman, *St. George Tucker*, 104–8; P. Hamilton, *Making and Unmaking*, 93.

51   Beeman, *Old Dominion*, 28–35; 42–44; Ely, *Israel on the Appomattox*, 73; D. P. Jordan, *Political Leadership*, 9–16, 66, 209–10; Wolf, *Race and Liberty*, 126–27.

52   Beeman, *Old Dominion*, xi, 39–41; D. P. Jordan, *Political Leadership*, 13–14, 23; McDonell, *Politics of War*, 524; Wolf, *Race and Liberty*, 126–27.

53   Beeman, *Old Dominion*, 28, 53; Evans, *"Topping People,"* 192; Thomas Mann Randolph (governor) quoted in D. P. Jordan, *Political Leadership*, 14; McDonell, *Politics of War*, 519 (Jefferson quote), 524–26; Wolf, *Race and Liberty*, 126–27.

54   Einhorn, "Patrick Henry's Case," 549–73; McCoy, "James Madison and Visions," 244; Patrick Henry quoted in Shalhope, *John Taylor*, 33 ("unbounded power"), in Waldstreicher, *Slavery's Constitution*, 144 ("might lay"), and in Beeman, *Old Dominion*, 7–8 ("This government"); Morton, *Robert Carter*, 60; Cullen, *St. George Tucker*, 60; S. Dunn, *Dominion of Memories*, 134–45.

55   D.B. Davis, *Problem of Slavery*, 125–26; Shalhope, *John Taylor*, 50–57; McCoy, "James Madison and Visions," 226–32, 244–47; A. Rothman, *Slave Country*, 4–5; Van Cleve, "Founding a Slaveholders' Union," 122, 129–131; Beeman, *Old Dominion*, 3–13; S. Dunn, *Dominion of Memories*, 135–37; Waldstreicher, *Slavery's Constitution*, 3–19, 141–45.

56   S. G. Tucker, *Dissertation on Slavery*, 1–2; M. Mason, "Necessary but Not Sufficient," 11–31; Patrick Henry quoted in L. K. Ford, *Deliver Us from Evil*, 23 ("as repugnant") and in Deyle, *Carry Me Back*, 26 ("the general inconveniency").

57 Allen, "David Barrow's *Circular Letter*," 446–47 ("The holding"), 450 (*"doing"*); L. K. Ford, *Deliver Us from Evil*, 25–26.

58 Morgan, *Slave Counterpoint*, 428–34 (William Spencer, Methodist, quote on 428); Aptheker, *American Negro Slave Revolts*, 103; R. Parkinson, *Tour in America*, vol. 2:433.

59 Weems quoted in J. Davis, *Travels*, 335–36; Roberts and Roberts, *Moreau de St. Mery's American Journey*, 306; W. D. Jordan, *White over Black*, 418–19.

60 L. K. Ford, *Deliver Us from Evil*, 35; Wolf, *Race and Liberty*, 21–27.

61 Wolf, *Race and Liberty*, xi–xii, 6.

62 Ely, *Israel on the Appomattox*, 71; Wolf, *Race and Liberty*, 143; Morgan, *Slave Counterpoint*, 489–90; Nicholls, "Passing through This Troublesome World," 65–68.

63 Wolf, *Race and Liberty*, xi–xii, 6; Berlin, *Many Thousands Gone*, 279–80.

64 R. S. Dunn, "Black Society," 74; Morton, *Robert Carter*, 251, 260–65, 266–67 (Carter and anonymous angry neighbor quote). For similar criticism of Warner Mifflin for freeing his slaves, see McColley, *Slavery and Jeffersonian Virginia*, 156. For Carter's Morattico Baptist church, see Sobel, *World They Made Together*, 191.

65 Robert Pleasants, "Memorial," to the governor and Council of State, ca. 1790, Pleasants Family Papers, RABC, box 13, folder 18, HL.

66 John Randolph to Tudor Randolph, Dec. 13, 1813, Grinnan Family Papers, box 3, SSCL-UVA; Ely, *Israel on the Appomattox*, 22–27; P. Hamilton, *Making and Unmaking*, 99–103; Kierner, *Scandal at Bizarre*, 5–7, 28–32, 37–42, 49–61.

67 Richard Randolph's will quoted and analyzed in Dawidoff, *Education of John Randolph*, 49; Ely, *Israel on the Appomattox*, 27, 35–36; Kierner, *Scandal at Bizarre*, 72, 85–89.

68 Old Dick quoted in J. Davis, *Travels*, 425. See also, McColley, *Slavery and Jeffersonian Virginia*, 118.

69 Critic of manumission quoted in W. D. Jordan, *White over Black*, 580–81; Birkbeck, *Notes on a Journey*, 14; Ely, *Israel on the Appomattox*, 9; Kulikoff, *Tobacco and Slaves*, 432; W. C. Bruce, *John Randolph*, vol. 2:129; R. Parkinson, *Tour in America*, vol. 2:446; St. George Tucker to Jeremy Belknap, June 29, 1795, in Belknap, "Queries," 407; James Madison to Edward Coles, Sep. 3, 1819, in Hunt, *Writings of James Madison*, vol. 8:455.

70 Ely, *Israel on the Appomattox*, 8–11; L. K. Ford, *Deliver Us from Evil*, 68; Nicholls, "Passing through This Troublesome World," 59–68; Roberts and Roberts, *Moreau de St. Mery's American Journey*, 60; St. G. Tucker, *Dissertation on Slavery*, 9.

71   Petitions from Mecklenberg, Amelia, and Pittsylvania Counties quoted in Schmidt and Wilhelm, "Early Proslavery Petitions," 139 ("We risked," "the Enemies," and "the Horrors"); McDonell, *Politics of War*, 490–92; McColley, *Slavery and Jeffersonian Virginia*, 142; Wolf, *Race and Liberty*, 93–95; D. B. Davis, *Problem of Slavery*, 303–4.

72   Schmidt and Wilhelm, "Early Proslavery Petitions," 135–36; R. S. Dunn, "Black Society," 80–81; Wolf, *Race and Liberty*, 94–95, 129 (Francis Asbury quote); Sobel, *World They Made Together*, 207–9; Raboteau, "Slave Church," 198–200; J. Lewis, "Problem of Slavery," 285–86; Scully, *Religion*, 8. For a radical Baptist who felt marginalized and obliged to leave Virginia, see Allen, "David Barrow's *Circular Letter*," 440–51.

73   Drescher, *Abolition*, 147–49, 160–62; Hickey, "America's Response," 362–64; Roberts and Roberts, *Moreau de St. Mery's American Journey*, 49; Sidbury, "Saint Domingue in Virginia," 531–52.

74   L. K. Ford, *Deliver Us from Evil*, 26, 547n40; Chernow, *Washington*, 710; Thomas Jefferson to St. George Tucker, Aug. 28, 1797, quoted Egerton, *Gabriel's Rebellion*, 14.

75   Thomas Evans to John Cropper, Dec. 6, 1796 ("the revolutionary storm"), quoted in D. P. Jordan, *Political Leadership*, 122; D. P. Jordan, "John Randolph of Roanoke," 399.

76   St. George Tucker quoted in Brewer, "Entailing Aristocracy," 307; Jefferson quoted in Grossberg, "Citizens and Families," 14.

77   Historians used to argue that entail had become an anachronism that applied to few estates; but in the most recent and careful study, Holly Brewer demonstrates that three-fourths of the Tidewater Virginia lands were subject to entail in 1776. See Brewer, "Entailing Aristocracy," 307–46; Grossberg, "Citizens and Families," 3–27; McGarvie, "Transforming Society," 1393–1425.

78   Brewer, "Entailing Aristocracy," 327–28, 341; St. George Tucker quoted in McGarvie, "Transforming Society," 1397.

79   Stanton and Bear, *Jefferson's Memorandum Books*, vol. 1:354n90.

80   Grossberg, "Citizens and Families," 3–5; Brewer, "Entailing Aristocracy," 315, 341–45. For the bourgeois nature of the revolution, see also G. S. Wood, *Radicalism of the American Revolution*.

81   St. George Tucker to Jeremy Belknap, Nov. 27, 1795, in Belknap, "Queries," 421; R. B. Davis, *Jeffersonian America*, 142–43 (quoted words of Sir Augustus John Foster, visiting diplomat), 163; Ball, *Fifty Years in Chains*, 45–52; Torrey, *Portraiture of Domestic Slavery*, 15. A quantitative study of nine Tidewater and Piedmont counties reveals that the number of elite planters who held more than 100 slaves peaked in 1776 and declined thereafter. See R. S. Dunn, "Black Society," 67.

82 John Randolph to Josiah Quincy, Mar. 22 and July 1, 1814, in E. Quincy, *Life of Josiah Quincy*, 351 ("Nothing"), 354 ("They whose fathers"); Randolph quoted in Dawidoff, *Education of John Randolph*, 88–89 ("The old families"); Kirk, *John Randolph*, 80.

83 Kirk, *John Randolph*, 27–28. For Jefferson's sale of his wife's entailed property see Stanton and Bear, eds., *Jefferson's Memorandum Book*, vol. 1:354n90.

84 Jefferson, *Notes on the State of Virginia*, 125–27; Brewer, "Entailing Aristocracy," 339–40; Deyle, *Carry Me Back*, 35–36; Morgan, *Slave Counterpoint*, 522; McColley, *Slavery and Jeffersonian Virginia*, 27–30.

85 Stanton, "'Those Who Labor for My Happiness,'" 150; Deyle, *Carry Me Back*, 28; Richard Blow to George Blow, Feb. 5, 1819, quoted in J. Lewis, *Pursuit of Happiness*, 142–43; R. Parkinson, *Tour in America*, vol. 2:431–32; Jefferson quoted in, Norton, Gutman, and Berlin, "Afro-American Family," 185; Randolph, *Speech*, 17 ("grand menagerie").

86 Deyle, *Carry Me Back*, 31–33; R.S. Dunn, "After Tobacco," 346; R.S, Dunn, "Black Society," 67; Walsh, "Rural African Americans," 327, 339, where Walsh observes, "After the war [slaves] had a great deal more to fear . . . as slaveowners became more preoccupied with short-term returns" and so sold more slaves "and the new owner was less often a relative or neighbor of their former master." In Mathews County, Virginia, in 1812, exactly half of the taxpayers (361 of 722) owned slaves, but 289 (80 percent) of the masters owned no more than five slaves. See Mathews County personal tax return, 1812, LV.

87 Armistead Smith to William Patterson Smith, Feb. 12, 1814, WPSP, box 1, SC-DUL.

88 Hughes, "Slaves for Hire," 260–86.

89 Hughes, "Slaves for Hire," 265; Zaborney, "Slave Hiring," 85–102.

90 This analysis relies on the close and careful study of the John Tayloe III estate (especially the home plantation known as Mount Airy) conducted by Richard S. Dunn. See R.S. Dunn, "Tale of Two Plantations," 43–51. See also Bailor, "John Taylor of Caroline," 300; Walsh, "Rural African Americans," 329–31. For the slave expression ("put you"), see Wiencek, *Master of the Mountain*, 10.

91 J. B. Lee, *Price of Nationhood*, 258–61.

92 Kulikoff, "Uprooted Peoples," 149; Kulikoff, *Tobacco and Slaves*, 429–30; R.S. Dunn, "Black Society," 59; Steward, *Twenty-Two Years a Slave*, 47; Fedric, *Slave Life in Virginia and Kentucky*, ix. For the advertisements for runaways, see Sidbury, *Ploughshares into Swords*, 29, 31.

93 Deyle, "'Abominable' New Trade," 833–34; Deyle, *Carry Me Back*, 16–21, 38; Kulikoff, "Uprooted Peoples," 149–51; Jordan, *White over*

Black, 321; John Campbell to Maria Campbell, Dec. 12, 1812, CFP, box 2, DUL-SC.

94   John Randolph quoted in Kirk, *John Randolph*, 169. L. K. Ford, *Deliver Us from Evil*, 4; Deyle, *Carry Me Back*, 24–26; John Randolph to James Lloyd, Dec. 15, 1814, in Kirk, *John Randolph*, 258; Richard D. Bayly to John Cropper, Jan. 6, 1805 ("I am"), John Cropper Papers, Section 1, VHS.

95   Deyle, *Carry Me Back*, 34–35; Grimes, *Life of William Grimes*, 33 ("It grieved me"), 43 ("It is not uncommon"); Old Dick quoted in J. Davis, *Travels*, vol. 2:154; Gudmestad, *Troublesome Commerce*, 8 ("destroyed"). Schermerhorn, *Money over Mastery*, 65.

96   Torrey, *Portraiture of Domestic Slavery*, 42–43 ("Thus her family"); Gudmestad, *Troublesome Commerce*, 35–36.

97   St. George Tucker to Jeremy Belknap, Nov. 27, 1795, in Belknap, "Queries," 421, James Madison to Robert Walsh, Mar. 2, 1819, in Hunt, *Writings of James Madison*, vol. 8:426–27; Thomas Jefferson to Thomas Cooper, Sep. 10, 1814, in *PTJ-RS*, vol. 7:651; Wyllie, ed., "Observations," 398–99; Herndon, *William Tatham*, 105; Torrey, *Portraiture of Domestic Slavery*, 17–18.

98   Gov. Henry Lee to Robert Goode, May 17, 1792, quoted in Sidbury, "Saint Domingue in Virginia," 539. For marital disruption by sales, see also Schermerhorn, *Money over Mastery*, 14–15.

99   Berlin, *Many Thousands Gone*, 265–66; Morgan, *Slave Counterpoint*, 503–8; Schermerhorn, *Money over Mastery*, 11–15. Sobel, *World They Made Together*, 108.

Chapter Two: Night and Day

1   Benjamin Faulkner's Phil, quoted by Griff, a fellow slave, in the trial of Phil, King and Queen County, July 21, 1813, JBEP, reel 5514, LV.

2   Stanley, "James Carter's Account," 337–38.

3   ibid.

4   ibid., 337.

5   Jefferson quoted and explained in Stanton, "'Those Who Labor for My Happiness,'" 148–50, 159–60. For efforts by other planters to unite couples, see Chernow, *Washington*, 112; Egerton, *Gabriel's Rebellion*, 16; Morgan, *Slave Counterpoint*, 527; Walsh, "Work and Resistance," 112–13; R. S. Dunn, "Tale of Two Plantations," 43–46; William Munford to Sarah Munford, Dec. 29, 1809, Munford-Ellis Family Papers, box 1, SC-DUL.

6   Grimes, *Life of William Grimes*, 50; John Randolph quoted in W. C.

Bruce, *John Randolph*, vol. 2:693; Morton, *Robert Carter*, 113; Chernow, *Washington*, 117; Gudmestad, *Troublesome Commerce*, 42–44.

7 Lobb, *Uncle Tom's Story*, 15 ("threats"); John Peterkin, journal, July 5, 1818 ("an invincible repugnance" and "Going away"), WLCL-UM; [G. Tucker], *Letters from Virginia*, 33.

8 Henry St. George Tucker to St. George Tucker, Feb. 17 ("Poor little fellow") and Mar. 1, 1804, in Coleman, *Virginia Silhouettes*, 9–10; P. Hamilton, *Making and Unmaking*, 109, 153–54.

9 D. C. Barraud, deposition, Nov. 2, 1827, RG 76, entry 190, box 3, case 194 (Elizabeth J. Nimmo), USNA-CP; Jefferson, *Notes on the State of Virginia*, 129; Fithian, *Journal and Letters*, 184–85 ("List" and "Thank you"), 199; Morgan, *Slave Counterpoint*, 530–32, 558.

10 Unnamed slave woman quoted in Fedric, *Slave Life in Virginia*, 15; Ball, *Fifty Years in Chains*, 39.

11 Ely, *Israel on the Appomattox*, 105; McColley, *Slavery and Jeffersonian Virginia*, 67–70; Morgan, *Slave Counterpoint*, 512–5; A. Rothman, *Slave Country*, 4; Stanton, "'Those Who Labor for My Happiness,'" 149, 169 (visitor quoted: "they were almost sure"); Pybus, "Thomas Jefferson and Slavery," 270–71 (includes Peter Fossett quotation).

12 Dew, "David Ross," 189–209 (Ross quote on 201, "less understanding"); Morgan, *Slave Counterpoint*, 347–48.

13 Dew, "David Ross," 220–23; Thomas P. Bouldin, "Account of Sales of the Slaves of David Ross," July 21–23, 1817, RG 76, entry 85, box 5, folder 42, USNA-CP.

14 Widow McCroskey to St. George Tucker, Nov. 23 ("Every day") and Dec. 3, 1803 ("What a scene"), in Coleman, *Virginia Silhouettes*, 11–13, 14.

15 Chernow, *Washington*, 802–3; Walsh, "Rural African Americans," 328, 331–32; Whitman, *Price of Freedom*, 75; Steward, *Twenty-Two Years a Slave*, 49; Lobb, *Uncle Tom's Story*, 18–20 ("a great calamity" and "the frantic terror").

16 John H. Cocke to Joseph C. Cabell, Apr. 29, 1814, JCC&CFP (38-111), box 10, SSCL-UVA; R. S. Dunn, "After Tobacco," 346–53, 362; R. S. Dunn, "Tale of Two Plantations," 55–57; Federic, *Slave Life*, 13; Morgan, *Slave Counterpoint*, 171–74; Shalhope, *John Taylor*, 108–11, 141–42; Stanton, "'Those Who Labor for My Happiness,'" 150–55; Walsh, "Work and Resistance," 106–10; Walsh, "Rural African Americans," 337; Morton, *Robert Carter*, 110–13; J. Taylor, *Arator*, 132 ("Slaves are"), 139–40 ("an object of terror").

17 R. S. Dunn, "Tale of Two Plantations," 51n23; Kulikoff, *Tobacco and Slaves*, 409–10; Morgan, *Slave Counterpoint*, 218–19, 326; Morton, *Rob-*

ert Carter, 93–94; Roberts and Roberts, *Moreau de St. Mery's American Journey*, 305.

18 Loux, "John Hartwell Cocke, Jr.," 330–31; John H. Cocke, "Standing Rules for the Government of Slaves on a Virginia Plantation," JCC&CFP (38-111), box 11, SSCL-UVA.

19 John H. Cocke, "Standing Rules for the Government of Slaves on a Virginia Plantation," JCC&CFP (38-111), box 11, SSCL-UVA; J. Taylor, *Arator*, 138–40.

20 John H. Cocke to Joseph C. Cabell, Apr. 29, 1814 ("on one of my River hills"), and Cocke, "Standing Rules for the Government of Slaves on a Virginia Plantation" ("Arrangement"), JCC&CFP (38-111), boxes 10 and 11, SSCL-UVA: Cocke to Cabell, July 5 and Sep. 18, 1815 ("Overseers"), JCCFP (38-111-c), box 4, SSCL-UVA.

21 Joseph C. Cabell to John H. Cocke, July 24, 1812 ("conceited"), and Cocke to Cabell, July 24, 1812, JCCFP (38-111-c), box 8, SSCL-UVA; Cabell to Cocke, July 5, 1813, and July 11, 1816, JCCFP (38-111-c), boxes 9 and 11, SSCL-UVA; Thomas Jefferson to Thomas Mann Randolph, Apr. 19, 1772, quoted in Stanton, "'Those Who Labor for My Happiness,'" 160; Shalhope, *John Taylor*, 140–41; Sobel, *World They Made Together*, 60; Grimes, *Life of William Grimes*, 36–37; Kulikoff, *Tobacco and Slaves*, 409–10; Morgan, *Slave Counterpoint*, 326–28, 333; Morton, *Robert Carter*, 93–95, 112.

22 John Randolph quoted in W. C. Bruce, *John Randolph*, vol. 2:702–5.

23 Walsh, "Work and Resistance," 109–10, 118 (overseer James Eagle quote on 118); Kulikoff, *Tobacco and Slaves*, 389–92; Morgan, *Slave Counterpoint*, 329; Sidbury, *Ploughshares into Swords*, 25. R. Parkinson, *Tour in America*, vol. 2:419–22.

24 R. Parkinson, *Tour in America*, vol. 2:419–22; Joseph C. Cabell to St. George Tucker, July 31, 1810, TCP, reel M-25, SCSL-CWM. For disincentives to slave enterprise, see W. C. Bruce, *John Randolph*, vol. 2:118–19; R. B. Davis, *Jeffersonian America*, 149; R. S. Dunn, "Tale of Two Plantations," 65; Kulikoff, *Tobacco and Slaves*, 411; McColley, *Slavery and Jeffersonian Virginia*, 23–24, 70–71, 138–40.

25 Steward, *Twenty-Two Years a Slave*, 14–17, 24; Ball, *Fifty Years in Chains*, 59; Roberts and Roberts, *Moreau de St. Mery's American Journey*, 59; trial of Isaac, Sep. 1, 1812, JBEP, reel 5505, LV; [G. Tucker], *Letters from Virginia*, 100–101. A few overseers devised still more sadistic modes of torture. See Fithian, *Journal and Letters*, 51.

26 Thomas Chrystie to Philip Croxton, May 19, 1811, Thomas Chrystie Papers, box 1, VHS.

27 Frey, *Water from the Rock*, 236; McColley, *Slavery and Jeffersonian Vir-*

ginia, 64–65; J. D. Rothman, *Notorious in the Neighborhood*, 141; Lobb, *Uncle Tom's Story*, 14–15; St. George Tucker to Jeremy Belknap, June 29, 1795, in Belknap, "Queries," 409; St. G. Tucker, *Dissertation on Slavery*, 8–9, 32–35; Morton, *Robert Carter*, 113–14; Wyllie, "Observations," 400–401; Saunders, "Crime and Punishment," 42–43.

28   Zachary Shackleford et al. to James Barbour, Oct. 12, 1813, JBEP, reel 5516, LV; Frances Baylor to Barbour, Nov. 23, 1814, John Baylor to Barbour, Nov. 26, 1814, and F. Baylor to Barbour, Dec. 7, 1814, in JBEP, reel 5524, LV; McColley, *Slavery and Jeffersonian Virginia*, 65–66; Morgan, *Slave Counterpoint*, 289, 314–15; J. D. Rothman, *Notorious in the Neighborhood*, 135; Schwarz, *Twice Condemned*, 210–11, 216.

29   Schwarz, *Twice Condemned*, 215–16, 231–40; Morgan, *Slave Counterpoint*, 394–95; Saunders, "Crime and Punishment," 35–41; St. George Tucker to Jeremy Belknap, June 29, 1795, in Belknap, "Queries," 405.

30   Miles King to Christopher Tompkins, June 30, 1809 (all quotations), TFP (Mss 1 T5996 d 13), VHS; Mathews County Court of Oyer and Terminer trial transcript, June 15, 1809, JTEP, reel 6008, LV. For Miles King's pious correspondence, see King to Thomas Jefferson, Aug. 20, 1814, in *PTJ-RS*, vol. 7:573–89.

31   Miles King to Christopher Tompkins, June 30, 1809 (all quotations), TFP (Mss 1 T5996 d 13), VHS; Mathews County Court trial transcript, June 15, 1809, JTEP, reel 6008, LV.

32   Miles King to Christopher Tompkins, June 30, 1809, TFP (Mss 1 T5996 d 13), VHS.

33   George Washington, quoted in Chernow, *Washington*, 115; Fithian, *Journal and Letters*, 51; Ball, *Fifty Years in Chains*, 44.

34   Darrell, "Diary," 146; Morgan, *Slave Counterpoint*, 102, 136–39, 358–59; Lobb, *Uncle Tom's Story*, 22; Steward, *Twenty-Two Years a Slave*, 14; Walsh, "Work and Resistance," 98–105, Chernow, *Washington*, 115–16; Herndon, *William Tatham*, 104.

35   Grimes, *Life of William Grimes*, 40; Fedric, *Slave Life in Virginia*, 17; Lobb, *Uncle Tom's Story*, 25 ("driving a pig"), 49; Schwarz, "Gabriel's Challenge," 296–97; Schwarz, *Twice Condemned*, 222–27; Walsh, "Work and Resistance," 102; [G. Tucker], *Letters from Virginia*, 115–18.

36   R. Parkinson, *Tour in America*, vol. 2:432; Ball, *Fifty Years in Chains*, ix; Steward, *Twenty-Two Years a Slave*, 29. For masters who understood the morality of slaves stealing from their exploiters, see Jefferson, *Notes on the State of Virginia*, 132; John Randolph to Harmanus Bleeker, July 26, 1814, in Kirk, *John Randolph*, 247.

37   R. Parkinson, *Tour in America*, vol. 2:420; Sobel, *World They Made*

Together, 33 ("Nigger day-time"), 253n12 ("uncurbed liberty"); Egerton, *Gabriel's Rebellion*, 17; Morgan, *Slave Counterpoint*, 509, 525; Stanton, "'Those Who Labor for My Happiness,'" 165; Steward, *Twenty-Two Years a Slave*, 30; Old Dick quoted in J. Davis, *Travels*, 415; [G. Tucker], *Letters from Virginia*, 79.

38   Lobb, *Uncle Tom's Story*, 24–25 ("Slavery did"); Grimes, *Life of William Grimes*, 39; Morgan, *Slave Counterpoint*, 121–22; Frederick Douglass quoted in Aptheker, *American Negro Slave Revolts*, 64.

39   Sobel, *World They Made Together*, 96–98; Morgan, *Slave Counterpoint*, 521–24; Nicholls, *Whispers of Rebellion*, 13–18. For a sophisticated interpretation of slave neighborhoods elsewhere in the South, see Kaye, *Joining Places*, esp. 4–12, 21–50.

40   Birkbeck, *Notes on a Journey*, 14–5; Fithian, *Journal and Letters*, 245; Torrey, *Portraiture of Domestic Slavery*, 12–13; Steward, *Twenty-Two Years a Slave*, 32; Schwarz, *Twice Condemned*, 211–14. Schwarz found that the prosecution of arson surged between 1785 and 1831 but that it was a difficult crime to prove and so to convict.

41   Trial of Daniel, Aug. 11, 1815, trial of John Fox and Nelson, May 21, 1816, and trial of Delphy, June 10, 1816, in WCNEP, boxes 2 and 4, LV; Schwarz, *Twice Condemned*, 203–5, 210–11; Birkbeck, *Notes on a Journey*, 17; Wyatt-Brown, *Southern Honor*, 424 ("palma-christal").

42   John F. D. Smyth quoted in Sobel, *World They Made Together*, 32–34 ("in which he performs"); Jefferson, *Notes on the State of Virginia*, 129; Benjamin Faulkner's Phil, quoted by Griff, a fellow slave, in trial of Phil, King and Queen County, July 21, 1813 ("that black people"), JBEP, reel 5514, LV. [G. Tucker], *Letters from Virginia*, 80.

43   Ely, *Israel on the Appomattox*, 236–44; McColley, *Slavery and Jeffersonian Virginia*, 63, 103; Morgan, *Slave Counterpoint*, 388–90; J. D. Rothman, *Notorious in the Neighborhood*, 95–98; Sheldon, "Black-White Relations," 30–41; Steward, *Twenty-Two Years a Slave*, 27; Alexander Dick, travel journal, 167 (Mar. 10, 1808: "began to box & kick"), reel 2370, SSCL-UVA.

44   Hunt, *First Forty Years*, 89–90; Bowers, *Diary of Elbridge Gerry, Jr.*, 193–99; John Minor to James Barbour, Aug. 11, 1812, JBEP, reel 5504, LV; Peter Francisco to James Barbour, June 21, 1813, JBEP, reel 5513, LV; Richard Cranch Norton, "Notebooks & Diaries," Aug. 2, 1812 ("We were somewhat alarmed"), Massachusetts Historical Society, Boston.

45   Janson, *Stranger in America*, 404–5.

46   McColley, *Slavery and Jeffersonian Virginia*, 92–94; Morgan, *Slave Counterpoint*, 340–41, 464–65; Mullin, *Flight and Rebellion*, 89–91, 103; Whitman, *Price of Freedom*, 69–71; J. Davis, *Travels*, 400. In an investigation of the 648 slaves who belonged to John Tayloe III between 1809

and 1828, Richard Dunn found only a few runaways—and all of them eventually were caught. See R. S. Dunn, "After Tobacco," 359–63.

47   Mullin, *Flight and Rebellion*, 103–23; Ann L. Meredith, "Twenty Dollars Reward," [*Richmond*] *Enquirer*, June 4, 1813; Morgan, *Slave Counterpoint*, 526–30; Whitman, *Price of Freedom*, 71–74.

48   Thomas Mann Randolph Jr. to Nicholas P. Trist, Nov. 22, 1822, Trist Family Papers (10487), SSCL-UVA.

49   McColley, *Slavery and Jeffersonian Virginia*, 95–96; Morgan, *Slave Counterpoint*, 525; Mullin, *Flight and Rebellion*, vii; Sidbury, *Ploughshares into Swords*, 24; Sterling Seawell, testimony, Gloucester County trial of Lewis Williams's Sam, Apr. 20, 1813 (all quotations), JBEP, reel 5511, LV.

50   William H. Cabell to Joseph C. Cabell, Dec. 31, 1810, JCCFP (38-111-c), box 2, SSCL-UVA.

51   Morgan, *Slave Counterpoint*, 398–401; Sobel, *World They Made Together*, 150; Roberts and Roberts, *Moreau de St. Mery's American Journey*, 305; Nicholls, "Passing through This Troublesome World," 54; Jefferson, *Notes on the State of Virginia*, 133; Morgan, "Interracial Sex," 77; Stanton, " 'Those Who Labor for My Happiness,' " 152–53; Cocke quoted in J. D. Rothman, "James Callender," 108, 113n67; Onuf, *Mind of Thomas Jefferson*, 227; [G. Tucker], *Letters from Virginia*, 75. For the definitive account of Jefferson and Hemings, see Gordon-Reed, *Hemingses of Monticello*. For the implications of miscegenation in Virginia, see C. E. Walker, *Mongrel Nation*, 13–55.

52   J. D. Rothman, *Notorious in the Neighborhood*, 4–10, 105–6, 134, 153; Morgan, "Interracial Sex," 62–63, 67–68, 77. For enslaved women seeking to become concubines, see J. Davis, *Travels*, 400.

53   Grimes, *Life of William Grimes*, 29–30, 33.

54   Comte de Volney quoted in J. D. Rothman, "James Callender," 87 ("as white"); Alexander Dick, travel journal, 167 (Feb. 17, 1808: "mostly his own"), reel 2370, SSCL-UVA; Torrey, *Portraiture of Domestic Slavery*, 14–15; Morgan, *Slave Counterpoint*, 433.

55   W. D. Jordan, *White over Black*, 549–54, 580 (legislator quoted); Thomas Jefferson to Joseph C. Cabell, Nov. 28, 1820 ("in danger"), in P. L. Ford, *Works of Thomas Jefferson*, vol. 12:170; John Taylor quoted in Bailor, "John Taylor of Caroline," 297; Onuf, *Mind of Thomas Jefferson*, 217–18.

56   Morgan, *Slave Counterpoint*, 253, 354–58; Sobel, *World They Made Together*, 128–36; W. C. Bruce, *John Randolph*, vol. 2:130; John Peterkin, "Journal," Nov. 8, 1817 ("During the warm"), WLCL-UM.

57   Henry St. George Tucker to St. George Tucker, Nov. 11, 1802, to Frances Coalter, Feb. 16, 1803, and to St. George Tucker, Oct. 10, 1803 ("Today"), in Coleman, *Virginia Silhouettes*, 7–8.

58   John Randolph quoted in Dawidoff, *Education of John Randolph*, 52–53 ("People may say" and "I know not"); Randolph quoted in W. C. Bruce, *John Randolph*, vol. 2:244.

59   W. C. Bruce, *John Randolph*, vol. 2:696–99.

60   John Faulcon to John Hartwell Cocke, Dec. 26, 1828, quoted in J. Lewis, *Pursuit of Happiness*, 140.

61   J. D. Rothman, *Notorious in the Neighborhood*, 6–7; Ely, *Israel on the Appomattox*, ix–x, 13–14, 218–21, 236, 240; Morgan, *Slave Counterpoint*, 257–61, 269, 273, 437; Wolf, *Race and Liberty*, 128.

62   Mullin, *Flight and Rebellion*, 102.

63   John W. Tomlin to Benjamin Brand, Jan. 6, 1809, Elkanah Talley to Brand, Sep. 10, 1809, and Benjamin Lipscomb to Brand, May 7, 1810, in Benjamin Brand Papers, sec. 4, VHS.

64   Powhatan County testimony quoted in James Clarke et al. to Wilson Cary Nicholas, Mar. 1, 1816, WCNEP, box 4, LV.

65   Thomas Mann Randolph Jr. to Nicholas P. Trist, Nov. 22, 1818 (all quotations), Trist Family Papers (10487), SSCL-UVA; Gaines, *Thomas Mann Randolph*, 76; Stanton, "*'Those Who Labor for My Happiness,'*" 83; Wiencek, *Master of the Mountain*, 101–2. My thanks to Laura Voisin George for her help with the Randolph letter.

66   Thomas Mann Randolph Jr. to Nicholas P. Trist, Nov. 22, 1818, Trist Family Papers (10487), SSCL-UVA; Stanton, "*'Those Who Labor for My Happiness,'*" 83; Wiencek, *Master of the Mountain*, 102.

67   [G. Tucker], *Letters from Virginia*, 34–35.

CHAPTER THREE: BLOOD

1   Sutcliff, *Travels in Some Parts*, 50.

2   "St. George Tucker Notes," June 2 and July 25, 1798, TCP, box 63, SCSL-CWM.

3   For St. George Tucker's rationalism and deism, see Brugger, *Beverley Tucker*, 6; P. Hamilton, *Making and Unmaking*, 55.

4   P. Hamilton, *Making and Unmaking*, 81; Drescher, *Abolition*, 147–52; L. K. Ford, *Deliver Us from Evil*, 26; Thomas Jefferson quoted in Chernow, *Washington*, 710; Hickey, "America's Response," 361–79; A Rothman, *Slave Country*, 21; Sidbury, "Saint Domingue in Virginia," 531–52; Birkbeck, *Notes on a Journey*, 17; W. D. Jordan, *White over Black*, 394; Sutton, "Nostalgia, Pessimism, and Malaise," 51.

5   George Mason quoted in Kirk, *John Randolph*, 155; Jefferson, *Notes on the State of Virginia*, 128 ("convulsions"), 151 ("Indeed, I tremble"). For

slavery as a state of war, see D. B. Davis, *Problem of Slavery*, 45; Onuf, *Mind of Thomas Jefferson*, 209–11.

6   W. D. Jordan, *White over Black*, 542–67; St. G. Tucker, *Dissertation on Slavery*, 49–51.

7   P. Hamilton, "Revolutionary Principles," 533–35; St. G. Tucker, *Dissertation on Slavery*, 2, 27–28, 56–57.

8   St. G. Tucker, *Dissertation on Slavery*, v, 54–60 (59: "middle course"; 60: "without").

9   St. George Tucker to Jeremy Belknap, June 29, 1795 ("a large majority"), and Apr. 3 and Aug. 13, 1797, in Belknap, "Queries," 407, 426, 427–28; Ludwell Lee to Tucker, Dec. 5, 1796, in Coleman, *Virginia Silhouettes*, 4–5; Tucker to Robert Pleasants, June 29, 1797, in "St. George Tucker Notes," 38, TCP, box 63, SCSL-CWM; P. Hamilton, "Revolutionary Principles," 535–37; P. Hamilton, *Making and Unmaking*, 81–82; David Meade to Joseph Prentiss, Sep. 4, 1799 ("In truth"), quoted in Egerton, *Gabriel's Rebellion*, 15.

10   *Virginia Independent Chronicle and General Advertiser*, June 2, 1790, quoted in Wolf, *Race and Liberty*, 115; W. D. Jordan, *White over Black*, 384; McColley, *Slavery and Jeffersonian Virginia*, 118–19; Aptheker, *American Negro Slave Revolts*, 158; St. George Tucker to Jeremy Belknap, Aug. 13, 1797, in Belknap, "Queries," 427–28.

11   *Boston Gazette*, June 18, 1792 ("blow up"), quoted in Aptheker, *American Negro Slave Revolts*, 211; Barnes, *Pungoteague to Petersburg*, vol. 1:36–38; Col. H. Guy to Thomas Newton Jr., May 9, 1792, Willis Wilson to Gov. Henry Lee, May 10, 1792, Littleton Savage to Lee, May 17, 1792, Miles King to Robert Goode, May 17, 1792, Thomas Newton Jr. to Lee, and James Baytop to Lee, June 9, 1792 ("defenceless"), in Flournoy, CVSP, vol. 5:541, 542, 546, 547, 552, 585.

12   Barnes, *Pungoteague to Petersburg*, vol. 1:36–38; Miles King to Robert Goode, May 17, 1792, Thomas Newton Jr. to Lee, and Col. Smith Snead to Lee, May 21 ("only a few") and July 9, 1792, in Flournoy, CVSP, vol. 5:547, 552, 555, 625.

13   Col. Smith Snead to Gov. Henry Lee, July 9, 1792, in Flournoy, CVSP, vol. 5:547, 552, 625.

14   John Wood, editor of the *Petersburg Daily Courier*, quoted in *Federal Gazette & Baltimore Daily Advertiser*, Nov. 16, 1814; John Randolph to Joseph Scott, Dec. 29, 1806, Randolph-Tucker Papers, Brock Collection, box 7, HL; Hadden, *Slave Patrols*, 143; Morgan, *Slave Counterpoint*, 385–88, 398; Wyatt–Brown, *Southern Honor*, 405–6.

15   Morgan, *Slave Counterpoint*, 387–88; Hadden, *Slave Patrols*, 143; Col.

Smith Snead to Gov. Henry Lee, May 5, 1792, Thomas Newton Jr. to Lee, May 10, 1792, and Willis Wilson to Gov. Henry Lee, May 19, 1792, in *CVSP*, vol. 5:534, 540, 551; Wyatt-Brown, *Southern Honor*, 411, 418–20.

16   Frank Carr to William Wirt, Jan. 19, 1802, quoted in Wyatt-Brown, *Southern Honor*, 409, see also 413–15.

17   Janson, *Stranger in America*, 402–4; Wyatt-Brown, *Southern Honor*, 411–12, 425; Nicholls, *Whispers of Rebellion*, 19.

18   Wyatt–Brown, *Southern Honor*, 406–8, 421–22; James Rush to John Mason, Nov. 10, 1800 ("power"), quoted in Nicholls, *Whispers of Rebellion*, 68; Col. Smith Snead to Gov. Henry Lee, May 21, 1792, in Flournoy, *CVSP*, vol. 5:555.

19   Wyatt-Brown, *Southern Honor*, 421–22, 427, 427–34 (John Cowper quoted on 431).

20   Morgan, *Slave Counterpoint*, 387–88; Wyatt-Brown, *Southern Honor*, 404, 418–20; James Maud to Col. Robert Carter, Nov. 9, 1793, quoted in Aptheker, *American Negro Slave Revolts*, 154.

21   Wyatt-Brown, *Southern Honor*, 432–33; Nicholls, *Whispers of Rebellion*, 9. For skepticism about slave revolts, see Johnson, "Denmark Vesey," 915–76; Morgan, "Conspiracy Scares," 159–66.

22   Egerton, *Gabriel's Rebellion*, 20–33, 48–49, 52–53; Schwartz, "Gabriel's Challenge," 287–94; Mullin, *Flight and Rebellion*, 141; Nicholls, *Whispers of Rebellion*, 25–26.

23   Egerton, *Gabriel's Rebellion*, 52–67; L. K. Ford, *Deliver Us from Evil*, 49–50; Mullin, *Flight and Rebellion*, 141–43; Sidbury, *Ploughshares into Swords*, 7; Shalhope, *John Taylor*, 101–2.

24   Egerton, *Gabriel's Rebellion*, 30–31, 34–49 (Jack Ditcher quote on 40); Mullin, *Flight and Rebellion*, 156–57.

25   Egerton, *Gabriel's Rebellion*, 55–57; Mullin, *Flight and Rebellion*, 145–46 (all quotes), 156–57; Morgan, *Slave Counterpoint*, 533; Nicholls, *Whispers of Rebellion*, 32–38.

26   Egerton, *Gabriel's Rebellion*, 49 ("all poor"); Mullin, *Flight and Rebellion*, 147 (Gilbert quote), 158; Schwarz, "Gabriel's Challenge," 295; Nicholls, *Whispers of Rebellion*, 38.

27   Egerton, *Gabriel's Rebellion*, 50–51, 64–65; Sidbury, *Ploughshares into Swords*, 6–7; Nicholls, *Whispers of Rebellion*, 28–29; John Randolph to Joseph H. Nicholson, Sep. 26, 1800, in W. C. Bruce, *John Randolph*, vol. 2:250.

28   Egerton, *Gabriel's Rebellion*, 69–79; L. K. Ford, *Deliver Us from Evil*, 52; Mullin, *Flight and Rebellion*, 151; Nicholls, *Whispers of Rebellion*, 57–70.

29   Egerton, *Gabriel's Rebellion*, 83–112; Nicholls, *Whispers of Rebellion*, 72–92; John Randolph to Joseph H. Nicholson, Sep. 26, 1800, in W. C.

Bruce, *John Randolph*, vol. 2:250; John Minor quoted in L. K. Ford, *Deliver Us from Evil*, 53; Sidbury, *Ploughshares into Swords*, 7.

30   Thomas Jefferson to James Monroe, Sep. 20, 1800, in Egerton, *Gabriel's Rebellion*, 92–93; John Randolph to Joseph H. Nicholson, Sep. 26, 1800, in W. C. Bruce, *John Randolph*, vol. 2:250; L. K. Ford, *Deliver Us from Evil*, 53–54; Nicholls, *Whispers of Rebellion*, 87–88.

31   Egerton, *Gabriel's Rebellion*, 147.

32   [G. Tucker], *Letter to a Member*, 3–4 ("the danger" and "has waked"), 7 ("they sought freedom"), 14 ("hold out the lure," "have," and "convert"), 22 ("see our folly"). For the pamphlet's author, see W. D. Jordan, *White over Black*, 561–62. It remains a common mistake to equate George Tucker with St. George Tucker. For example, see Mullin, *Flight and Rebellion*, viii, 157.

33   [G. Tucker], *Letter to a Member*, 16 ("a foreign enemy"), 18–21; Egerton, *Gabriel's Rebellion*, 151–53.

34   James Monroe to Thomas Jefferson, June 15, 1801, in Oberg, *Papers of Thomas Jefferson*, vol. 34:345–47; Egerton, *Gabriel's Rebellion*, 151–52.

35   James Monroe to Thomas Jefferson, June 15, 1801 ("a subject" and "involves the future peace"), Jefferson to Monroe, July 21, 1801, Monroe to Jefferson, Nov. 17, 1801, Jefferson to Monroe, Nov. 22 and Nov. 24, 1801 ("either blot or mixture"), in Oberg, *Papers of Thomas Jefferson*, vol. 34:345–47, 614, and vol. 35:683, 712, 718–20; Egerton, *Gabriel's Rebellion*, 153–60; L. K. Ford, *Deliver Us from Evil*, 61; Monroe quoted in McColley, *Slavery and Jeffersonian Virginia*, 135 ("without expense").

36   James Monroe to John Drayton, Oct. 21, 1800, quoted in Mullin, *Flight and Rebellion*, 141; Egerton, *Gabriel's Rebellion*, 164–74; L. K. Ford, *Deliver Us from Evil*, 55–58; McColley, *Slavery and Jeffersonian Virginia*, 113; Schwarz, "Gabriel's Challenge," 302–3; anonymous Virginian published in the *New York Commercial Advertiser*, Sep. 30, 1800 ("If we will"), and quoted in Aptheker, *American Negro Slave Revolts*, 65; Alexander Dick, travel journal, 180 (May 15, 1808), reel 2370, SSCL-UVA.

37   Egerton, *Gabriel's Rebellion*, 173–75.

38   L. K. Ford, *Deliver Us from Evil*, 65; McColley, *Slavery and Jeffersonian Virginia*, 103–4; Jordan, *White over Black*, 356, 400 (quote from member in Alexandria).

39   Aptheker, *American Negro Slave Revolts*, 76; L. K. Ford, *Deliver Us from Evil*, 65; Thomas B. Robertson quoted in W. D. Jordan, *White over Black*, 580; Shalhope, *John Taylor*, 146–49; Robson, "'Important Question Answered,'" 651.

40   Richard D. Bayly to John Cropper, Jan. 6, 1805, John Cropper Papers,

sec. 1, VHS; John Minor quoted in W. D. Jordan, *White over Black*, 576; Wolf, *Race and Liberty*, 124–26; L. K. Ford, *Deliver Us from Evil*, 65.

41   Thomas Robertson in the *Virginia Argus*, Jan. 17, 1806, quoted in Wolf, *Race and Liberty*, 124; *Richmond Enquirer*, Jan. 5, 1805 ("the melancholy race"), quoted in Sheldon, "Black-White Relations," 35.

42   W. D. Jordan, *White over Black*, 575–76; L. K. Ford, *Deliver Us from Evil*, 65; Wolf, *Race and Liberty*, 121–23.

43   John Winston, petition, Dec. 11, 1820, quoted in Nicholls, *Whispers of Rebellion*, 146.

44   Jeter, *Recollections of a Long Life*, 67–69 (all quotations); W. D. Jordan, *White over Black*, 552.

45   J. Taylor, *Arator*, 131 ("incapable of removal"); Shalhope, *John Taylor*, 142–48; Thomas Jefferson quoted in Stanton, "'Those Who Labor for My Happiness,'" 163; W. C. Bruce, *John Randolph*, vol. 2:130.

46   Hickey, "America's Response," 365–68; Beeman, *Old Dominion*, xii–xiii.

47   Riley, "Slavery and the Problem of Democracy," 230–31; D. P. Jordan, *Political Leadership*, 3; Onuf, *Mind of Thomas Jefferson*, 252–55; McColley, *Slavery and Jeffersonian Virginia*, 130–31; Deyle, *Carry Me Back*, 23; Jefferson to Walter Jones, Mar. 31, 1801, quoted in Leichtle and Carveth, *Crusade against Slavery*, 47 ("that no more good"); Jefferson to William Burwell, Jan. 28, 1805 ("long since"), quoted in A. Rothman, *Slave Country*, 34; Jefferson quoted in Blackburn, *Overthrow of Colonial Slavery*, 285 ("The existence").

48   Gideon Granger to James Jackson, Mar. 23, 1802, quoted in Blackburn, *Overthrow of Colonial Slavery*, 280; John, *Spreading the News*, 140–41.

49   Blackburn, *Overthrow of Colonial Slavery*, 286; Drescher, *Abolition*, 137; Ericson, "Slave Smugglers," 185; M. Mason, "Necessary but Not Sufficient," 18; Fehrenbacher and McAfee, *Slaveholding Republic*, 136–47; Deyle, *Carry Me Back*, 24.

50   Boyd and Hemphill, *Murder of George Wythe*, 17, 37, 44, 53.

51   Kirtland, "George Wythe," 92–94; Boyd and Hemphill, *Murder of George Wythe*, 4–8,93 (John Randolph quote); Ely, *Israel on the Appomattox*, 22–24, 478n28.

52   McColley, *Slavery and Jeffersonian Virginia*, 136; Kirtland, "George Wythe," 92–94; Morgan, "Interracial Sex," 58–59. Some historians have accepted the canard that Wythe fathered Brown, but Morgan makes a persuasive case against that misunderstanding.

53   Boyd and Hemphill, *Murder of George Wythe*, 9–27, 37–44, 50, 53.

54   Boyd and Hemphill, *Murder of George Wythe*, 29, 31n10, 58–59; McColley, *Slavery and Jeffersonian Virginia*, 136.

55   Catterall, *Judicial Cases concerning Slavery*, vol. 1:112 ("freedom");

Morgan, "Interracial Sex," 56; Wolf, *Race and Liberty*, 147–48; McColley, *Slavery and Jeffersonian Virginia*, 136; J. D. Rothman, *Notorious in the Neighborhood*, 221–22. For the public uproar against Wythe's ruling, see St. George Tucker's comment, in Hening and Munford, *Reports of Cases*, 137.

56   St. George Tucker to Robert Pleasants, June 29, 1797 ("my name") in "St. George Tucker Notes," 38, TCP, box 63, SCSL-CWM; Tucker quoted in P. Hamilton, "Revolutionary Principles," 543–44 ("Utopian idea").

57   Henry Lee to St. George Tucker, Jan. 18, 1796, in Coleman, *Virginia Silhouettes*, 5; Tucker, Williamsburg appraisal, Apr. 1, 1815, TCP, box 34, SCSL-CWM; P. Hamilton, "Revolutionary Principles," 531–36, 545–46; P. Hamilton, *Making and Unmaking*, 83. For the premium placed on providing genteel sons with a substantial inheritance, see also Shalhope, *John Taylor*, 113–14.

58   St. George Tucker to Jeremy Belknap, June 29, 1795, in Belknap, "Queries," 409; P. Hamilton, "Revolutionary Principles," 549; Nathaniel Beverley Tucker quoted in P. Hamilton, *Making and Unmaking*, 151–52.

59   Berlin, *Many Thousands Gone*, 281; Cullen, *St. George Tucker*, 67; Doyle, "Judge St. George Tucker," 428–31; Sidbury, *Ploughshares into Swords*, 35.

60   St. George Tucker ruling in *Hudgins v. Wrights*, in Hening and Munford, *Reports of Cases*, 141; Wolf, *Race and Liberty*, 149.

61   St. George Tucker ruling in *Hudgins v. Wrights*, in Hening and Munford, *Reports of Cases*, 138; Catterall, *Judicial Cases concerning Slavery*, vol. 1:112–13; P. Hamilton, "Revolutionary Principles," 543–44; J.D. Rothman, *Notorious in the Neighborhood*, 222–23; Hening and Munford, *Reports of Cases*, 135. For Tucker's deference to statutory law, see McGarvie, "Transforming Society," 1423.

62   St. George Tucker and Spencer Roane rulings in *Hudgins v. Wrights*, in Hening and Munford, *Reports of Cases*, 139–41.

63   St. G. Tucker, *Dissertation on Slavery*, 48. For an example of the persistent myth of Tucker as a life-long foe of slavery, see Nicholls, *Whispers of Rebellion*, 148.

64   [G. Tucker], *Letters from Virginia*, 73.

Chapter Four: Warships

1   Thomas M. Bayly to James Barbour, June 5, 1812, JBEP, reel 5502, LV.

2   John Floyd and Henry Edmondson to James Barbour, Apr. 2, 1812, in Flournoy, *CVSP*, vol. 10:120–22.

3   John Floyd and Henry Edmondson to James Barbour, Apr. 2, 1812, in Flournoy, *CVSP*, vol. 10:120–21.

4   John Floyd and Henry Edmondson to Gov. James Barbour, Apr. 2, 1812, in Flournoy, *CVSP*, vol. 10:120–23. For Tom's fate and price, see Auditor of Public Accounts, entry 756 (Condemned Slaves); Henry County Court, Apr. 14, 1812, trial of Tom, reel 2551, LV.

5   The governor and Council of State applauded Floyd and Edmonson: "your Country is indebted to you for the vigilance with which you have discharged your official duties." See Barbour to Floyd and Edmondson, Apr. 20, 1812, Executive Letter Book, p. 250, RG 3, reel 3009, LV.

6   Drescher, *Abolition*, 223–28, 233–35; D. B. Davis, *Problem of Slavery*, 366–68; Blackburn, *Overthrow of Colonial Slavery*, 310–15 (Lord Grenville quote on 313); Richardson, *Moral Imperium*, 154–64; Drescher, "Emperors of the World," 133–35; Morgan, "Ending the Slave Trade," 101–5; Hilton, "1807 and All That," 73–74.

7   C. L. Brown, *Moral Capital*, 341–89; Hilton, "1807 and All That," 69–70.

8   Richardson, *Moral Imperium*, 141–43, 150–51; Drescher, *Abolition*, 212–22; D.B. Davis, *Problem of Slavery*, 102–3, 343–85; Morgan, "Ending the Slave Trade," 116–17; Jenkins, *Henry Goulburn*, 41–42.

9   Blackburn, *Overthrow of Colonial Slavery*, 300–305 (Henry Brougham quote on 301); Richardson, *Moral Imperium*, 143–47, 152–54; Stephen, *Crisis of the Sugar Colonies*, 151–57; Morgan, "Ending the Slave Trade," 119; Jenkins, *Henry Goulburn*, 43–44.

10   Drescher, *Abolition*, 117–18; D. B. Davis, *Problem of Slavery*, 117–19, 381–82; Buckley, *Slaves in Red Coats*, 41; Richardson, *Moral Imperium*, 97–98, 164–66; Blackburn, *Overthrow of Colonial Slavery*, 307–8. For the population figures, see Duffy, *Soldiers, Sugar, and Seapower*, 18. For the black regiments, see Buckley, *Slaves in Red Coats*, 2–24, 65, 78–84.

11   Fergus, "'Dread of Insurrection,'" 766; Buckley, *Slaves in Red Coats*, vii, 16, 22, 33 (George Pinckard quote: "Compared to slavery"), 38, 67–79, 96, 124–25, 130–33.

12   Buckley, *Slaves in Red Coats*, 79–109.

13   Fergus, "'Dread of Insurrection,'" 767–75; Drescher, *Abolition*, 224–25; Brereton, *History of Modern Trinidad*, 38–40, 52–54; Epstein, "Politics of Colonial Sensation," 716; Stephen, *Crisis of the Sugar Colonies*, 157.

14   Morgan, "Ending the Slave Trade," 108–9; Jenkins, *Henry Goulburn*, 67, 72–73.

15   Brereton, *History of Modern Trinidad*, 63–64; George Canning quoted in Richardson, *Moral Imperium*, 179; Stephen, *Crisis of the Sugar Colonies*, 187–88.

16   D. B. Davis, *Problem of Slavery*, 159–60; Epstein, "Politics of Colonial Sensation," 739; Stephen, *Crisis of the Sugar Colonies*, 189 ("the fatal error"), 202 ("free, strong"); Jenkins, *Henry Goulburn*, 72–74.

17 Richardson, *Moral Imperium*, 99–100, 103–26.

18 Epstein, "Politics of Colonial Sensation," 712–41 (William Garrow quotations on 719–20).

19 John Lewis to Stapleton Crutchfield, May 23, 1813, MG 24, F 132, reel A-2076, LAC.

20 Tucker and Reuter, *Injured Honor*, 1–17, 70–76; Lambert, *Challenge*, 7–9.

21 George Berkeley to William Marsden, July 4, 1807, MG 12 (Admiralty 1), vol.497:213, reel B-1445, LAC; Kettner, *Development of American Citizenship*, 50, 55; M. Lewis, *Social History of the Navy*, 435; Zimmerman, *Impressment*, 21.

22 Colley, *Captives*, 4–12; Zimmerman, *Impressment*, 23–24.

23 Bickham, *Weight of Vengeance*, 58–60; Tucker and Reuter, *Injured Honor*, 33, 47; Perkins, *Prologue to War*, 28–29, 86, 90n41, 93–95; Gwynn, *Frigates and Foremasts*, 130–31; Lambert, *Challenge*, 18–19; M. Lewis, *Social History of the Navy*, 436–37; Zimmerman, *Impressment*, 18.

24 Tucker and Reuter, *Injured Honor*, 62; Lavery, *Nelson's Navy*, 125–26.

25 Hinderaker, *Elusive Empires*, 260–61; Kettner, *Development of American Citizenship*, 173.

26 M. Lewis, *Social History of the Navy*, 434–35; Zimmerman, *Impressment*, 19–20; Horsman, *Causes of the War*, 30; Perkins, *Prologue to War*, 192.

27 Lambert, *Challenge*, 13, 34–35; Tucker and Reuter, *Injured Honor*, 208; David M. Erskine to George Canning, Oct. 5, 1807, and Phineas Bond to Canning, Dec. 1, 1807, MG 16 (FO 5), vol. 52:297, and vol. 53:151, reel B-1872, LAC.

28 Perkins, *Prologue to War*, 7–10, 74–75,107; Tucker and Reuter, *Injured Honor*, 52, 65, 72; Horsman, *Causes of the War*, 84–87.

29 Gwynn, *Frigates and Foremasts*, 132; Francis Jackson ("I came to treat") quoted in Bartlett, "Gentlemen versus Democrats," 145.

30 Tucker and Reuter, *Injured Honor*, 65, 72; David M. Erskine to George Canning, Oct. 5, 1807 ("highly grating"), MG 16 (FO 5), vol. 52:297, reel B-1872, LAC; Perkins, *Prologue to War*, 75.

31 Richard Blow to Buchanan and Pollack, June 24, 1807 ("a General Panack"), Richard Blow Letterbook (Mss 5:2, B6235:2), VHS; John E. Douglass to George Berkeley, June 27, 1807, MG 12 (Admiralty 1), vol. 497:221, reel B-1445, LAC; John Hamilton to George Canning, June 27, 1807 ("an Atonement"), MG 16 (FO 5), vol. 53:262, reel B-1872, LAC.

32 Tucker and Reuter, *Injured Honor*, 101–5.

33 Tucker and Reuter, *Injured Honor*, 105–6; Thomas Mathews to Gov. Cabell, June 29, 1807, J. E. Douglas to Mayor Richard E. Lee, July 3, 1807, in Flournoy, *CVSP*, vol. 9:521, 525–26.

34   Mayor Richard E. Lee to Gov. William Cabell, July 4, 1807 ("The mili-
      tia"), Lee to J. E. Douglas, July 4, 1807 ("The day"), Thomas Mathews to
      Cabell, July 8, 1807, Lee to Mathews, July 15, 1807 ("to cast sarcasms"),
      and Mathews to Cabell, July 29, 1807, in Flournoy, *CVSP*, vol. 9:525, 526,
      533–34, 542, 560–61; William Tatham to Thomas Jefferson, July 15, July
      18 ("I wish"), and July 26, 1807, in Peterson, *Defence of Norfolk*, 39, 53.

35   Thomas Mathews to Cabell, July 17, 1807, in Flournoy, *CVSP*, vol.9:541–
      42; Sir George Cranfield Berkeley to David M. Erskine, July 28, 1807,
      Thomas M. Hardy to Mathews, July 27, 1807, and Mathews to Hardy,
      Aug. 1, 1807, MG 12 (Admiralty 1), vol. 497:235, 300, 301, reel B-1445,
      LAC; Tucker and Reuter, *Injured Honor*, 109–16.

36   William Tatham to Thomas Jefferson, July 14 and July 20, 1807, in
      Peterson, *Defence of Norfolk*, 38, 59; Thomas Mathews to Gov. William
      Cabell, July 30, 1807, in Flournoy, *CVSP*, vol. 9:545–46.

37   Thomas M. Hardy to John Hamilton, July 15, 1807 ("Now, Sir"), Hardy
      to Sir George Cranfield Berkeley, Aug. 11, 1807 ("Black Pilot"), MG 12
      (Admiralty 1), vol. 497:292, 295, reel B-1445, LAC.

38   John Hamilton to Thomas M. Hardy, July 30, 1807, MG 12 (Admiralty
      1), vol. 497:297, reel B-1445, LAC.

39   Thomas Jefferson to William H. Cabell, July 24, 1807, in Peterson,
      Defence of Norfolk, 50n55; Thomas M. Hardy to Littleton W. Tazewell,
      Aug. 2, 1807, Tazewell Family Papers, box 3, LV; Thomas Mathews to
      William H. Cabell, Aug. 3, 1807, Tazewell to Mathews, Aug. 3, 1807,
      Mathews to Cabell, Aug. 7, 1807, and Thomas Newton Jr. to Cabell, Aug.
      31, 1807, in Flournoy, *CVSP*, vol.9:570–72, 575, 576–77, 594; Hardy to
      Mathews, Aug. 3, 1807, and Mathews to Hardy, Aug. 5, 1807, MG 12
      (Admiralty 1), vol. 497:301, 302, reel B-1445, LAC; John Hamilton to
      George Canning, Aug. 2, 1807, MG 16 (FO 5), vol. 53:281, reel B-1872,
      LAC; Robert B. Taylor quoted in James Barbour to the Council of State,
      May 12, 1812, in Flournoy, *CVSP*, vol. 10:137.

40   David M. Erskine to George Canning, July 2, 1807, and Phineas Bond to
      Canning, July 14, 1807("Indecent Tunes"), MG 16 (FO 5), vol. 52:232,
      and vol. 53:99, reel B-1872, LAC; R. B. Davis, *Jeffersonian America*, 293;
      Perkins, *Prologue to War*, 39–41, 50–51, 142–43.

41   Horsman, *Causes of the War*, 103–8; Tucker and Reuter, *Injured Honor*,
      101–8, 114; Albert Gallatin to Thomas Jefferson, July 25, 1807 ("none"),
      in Adams, *Writings of Albert Gallatin*, vol. 1: 345–48.

42   Tucker and Reuter, *Injured Honor*, 126–27; Lambert, *Challenge*, 10–13;
      James Monroe to James Madison, Oct. 10, 1807, in S. M. Hamilton, *Writ-
      ings of James Monroe*, 10.

43   James Monroe to James Madison, Oct. 10, 1807, in S. M. Hamilton, *Writ-*

ings of James Monroe, 14; Tucker and Reuter, *Injured Honor*, 114–15, 129–37; Horsman, *Causes of the War*, 99, 109–10, 117–22; Perkins, *Prologue to War*, 24, 148–56, 184–204; Stagg, *Mr. Madison's War*, 20–22; Tucker and Hendrickson, *Empire of Liberty*, 19, 204–11; Lambert, *Challenge*, 24–27.

44   Perkins, *Prologue to War*, 26–30, 157–59, 166–70, 204–5; Horsman, *Causes of the War*, 125–38; Tucker and Reuter, *Injured Honor*, 119–22; Lambert, *Challenge*, 28–29.

45   Nevins, *Diary of John Quincy Adams*, 56; Malone, *Jefferson, the President*, 563–65, 571–74, 594–97; Stagg, *Mr. Madison's War*, 22–28.

46   Malone, *Jefferson the President*, 613–15; Tucker and Hendrickson, *Empire of Liberty*, 179, 212; Schoen, "Calculating the Price," 191–92.

47   James Madison, Message to Congress, Nov. 5, 1811 ("trampling"), in Stagg, *PJM-PS*, vol. 4:1–5; Stagg, *Mr. Madison's War*, 71–79, 84, 110–11; Horsman, *Causes of the War*, 179–82; Perkins, *Prologue to War*, 46–49, 223, 241, 249–59, 266–67, 343–47, 350–51, 367, 435; Roger H. Brown, *Republic in Peril*, 88; Hickey, *War of 1812*, 26–30; Watts, *Republic Reborn*, 263–74.

48   Hickey, *Don't Give Up the Ship*, 42; Perkins, *Prologue to War*, 403–15; Roger H. Brown, *Republic in Peril*, 44–47, 131, 143–45; Stagg, *Mr. Madison's War*, 110–14; Horsman, *Causes of the War*, 224.

49   Roger H. Brown, *Republic in Peril*, 76–82; Hickey, *War of 1812*, 27, 47; James Monroe to John Taylor, June 13, 1812, in S. M. Hamilton, *Writings of Monroe*, vol. 1:205–6.

50   John Randolph to the Freeholders, May 30, 1812, in *Richmond Enquirer*, June 12, 1812; Kirk, *John Randolph*, 132–34, 140–51, 167–68 (Randolph speech in Congress, Dec. 9, 1811: all quotations); John Randolph to James M. Garnett, Jan. 12, 1812, John Randolph Papers, box 3, SSCL-UVA; Risjord, *Old Republicans*, 134–35.

51   William Sharp to Thomas Mathews, Nov. 14, 1808 ("the negro houses" and "Unfortunately"), Mathews to Gov. William H. Cabell, Nov. 18, 1808, Gov. William H. Cabell Executive Papers, ser. 1: Chronological Files, LV; L. K. Ford, *Deliver Us from Evil*, 26; Alexander Dick, travel journal, 182 (May 21, 1808: "always produces"), reel 2370, SSCL-UVA,

52   Peggy Nicholas to Wilson Cary Nicholas, Dec. 21, 1808, Papers of the Randolph Family of Edgehill and Wilson Cary Nicholas (no. 5533), box 2, SSCL-UVA.

53   William Dame to Gov. John Tyler, June 19, 1809 ("satisfactory evidence"), and J. B. to Gen. T. R., n.d., in Flournoy, *CVSP*, vol. 10:62–63, 97. For skepticism of black conspiracy letters, see Wyatt-Brown, *Southern Honor*, 425. For a more accepting view of such letters, see Sidbury, "Saint Domingue in Virginia," 540.

54   Richard W. Byrd to James Monroe, May 30, 1810 (all quotations), and William Sharp to Monroe, June 6, 1810, in Flournoy, *CVSP*, vol. 10:82, 83; for the conviction and transportation, see Aptheker, *American Negro Slave Revolts*, 247.

55   Elizabeth Kennon to Lady Skipwith, June 9, 1810, Mss. 1, SK 366a, 12–15, VHS.

56   John Campbell to David Campbell, Dec. 27, 1811, CFP, box 1, SC-DUL; John Coalter to St. George Tucker, Dec. 29, 1811 ("the wretched"), and Philip Barraud to St. George Tucker, Dec. 31, 1811, TCP, box 31, SSCL-CWM; Robert Gamble to James Breckenridge, Dec. 27, 1811, and Jan. 5, 1812, Breckinridge Family Papers, sec. 2 (Mss 1 B 7427 a 2-213), VHS; Lowery, *James Barbour*, 61.

57   Joynes, "Burning of the Richmond Theatre," 297–300 (witness Thomas R. Joynes's words on 298).

58   Peggy Nicholas to Wilson Cary Nicholas, Dec. 21, 1808, Papers of the Randolph Family of Edgehill and Wilson Cary Nicholas (no. 5533), box 2, SSCL-UVA.

59   Jonathan Russell to James Monroe, Sep. 17, 1812, in Madison, *Message from the President*, 11–12.

60   Bickham, *Weight of Vengeance*, 18.

61   "Report on Relations with Great Britain," Nov. 29, 1811, in Meriwether, *Papers of Calhoun*, vol. 1:67; orator Cornelius P. Van Ness quoted in M. Mason, "Battle of the Slaveholding Liberators," 669; Waterhouse, *Journal*, 78 ("muster the crew"), 93; "Honor Calls for War" and "Impressed Seamen," *Philadelphia Aurora*, June 19, 1812, and Mar. 26, 1813; Chamier, *Life of a Sailor*, 201 ("Why, I declare"). For the black proportion of American sailors, see Bolster, *Black Jacks*, 6.

62   M. Mason, "Battle of the Slaveholding Liberators," 668–69; "The Goal" and "Honor Calls for War," *Philadelphia Aurora*, Apr. 28 and June 19, 1812; Waterhouse, *Journal*, 188 ("were stripped"); Richard M. Johnson, speech, Dec. 11, 1811, *AC*, 12th Congress, 1st session, 465; *Richmond Enquirer*, Nov. 24, 1812.

63   Charlotte County citizens to President Madison, July 15, 1812, in Stagg, *PJM-PS*, vol. 5:34; John Campbell to David Campbell, Aug. 10, 1812, CFP, box 2, SC-DUL; *Norfolk & Portsmouth Herald*, June 19, 1812; Philip Barraud to St. George Tucker, Apr. 2, 1813, TCP, box 32, SCSL-CWM; John Connell to James Barbour, July 1, 1812, and Gideon Spencer to Barbour, Dec. 19, 1812, JBEP, reels 5503 and 5507, LV.

64   *Philadelphia Aurora*, May 17, 1813; [Baptist Irvine], "Extract of a Letter," *Baltimore Whig*, June 10, 1813; *Richmond Enquirer*, June 25, 1814.

65   Baker, "'Slave' Writes Thomas Jefferson," 140 ("tyrants," "Britain has

got," and "almost naked"); Reverend Lemuel Haynes quoted in Eustace, *1812*, 190–91. Baker makes a persuasive case that the author of this anonymous letter had been a slave.

66   George Chalmers to Viscount Melville, Aug. 3, 1812, Viscount Melville Papers, HL; Bartlett, "Gentlemen versus Democrats," 148; M. Mason, "Battle of Slaveholding Liberators," 678–81.

67   Perkins, *Prologue to War*, 2–5, 73; Horsman, *Causes of the War*, 30–39; Tucker and Reuter, *Injured Honor*, 49; Stagg, *Mr. Madison's War*, 18–19; John Borlase Warren, "Proclamation," Oct. 5, 1812 ("the Noblest Cause"), MG 12 (Admiralty 1), vol. 502:321, reel B-1448, LAC; Thomas Barclay to Richard Barclay, Mar. 10, 1807, MG 16 (FO 5), vol. 53:186, reel B-1872, LAC; Lovell, *Personal Narrative*, 10 ("declaring war").

68   M. Mason, "Battle of the Slaveholding Liberators," 66–69; Sir Pulteney Malcolm to Miss Malcolm, Sep. 1, 1814, SPMP, box 1, WLCL; Lovell, *Personal Narrative*, 153; Bullard, *Black Liberation*, 97; [R.J. Barrett], "Naval Recollections," 466 ("forth").

69   Sir David Milne to George Home, Feb. 5, 1812, and Apr. 26, 1814, in Hume, "Letters Written during the War of 1812," 285, 293; Edward Codrington, journal, Oct. 27 and Nov. 6, 1814, MG 24, F 131 (Codrington correspondence), reel A-2076, LAC; Bartlett and Smith, "'Species of Milito–Nautico–Guerilla Warfare,'" 187.

70   Gould, "Making of an Atlantic State System," 253–54; R. B. Davis, *Jeffersonian America*, 57, 149 ("the black race").

71   McColley, *Slavery and Jeffersonian Virginia*, 116–17: Wyllie, "Observations," 398; M. Mason, "Battle of the Slaveholding Liberators," 682–84; Fehrenbacher and McAfee, *Slaveholding Republic*, 25, 93.

72   William Tatham to James Barbour, Dec. 27, 1812, JBEP, reel 5507, LV; Robert B. Taylor quoted in James Barbour to the Council of State, May 12, 1812, in Flournoy, *CVSP*, vol. 10:137; Kendall Addison to Barbour, June 10, 1812, JBEP, reel 5502, LV; Robert Greenhow to Charles K. Mallory, Sep. 8, 1813, JBEP, reel 5516, LV. See also Thomas R. Joynes to Barbour, Jan. 13, 1812, N. Cargill to Barbour, Feb. 8, 1812, and Griffin Sith to Barbour, Feb. 8, 1812, JBEP, reel 5499, LV; Barbour to James Monroe, June 23, 1812, Executive Letter Book, p. 349, RG 3, reel 3009, LV; Charles K. Mallory to Robert Greenhow, Sep. 10, 1813, Executive Letter Book, 366, RG 3, reel 3010, LV. For a very shaky report of a British-assisted slave plot in Richmond, see William Neal, deposition, July 19, 1813, in Flournoy, *CVSP*, vol. 10:264.

73   Sir George Cranfield Berkeley, "Thoughts upon a War between America and Great Britain," Sep. n.d., 1807, MG 24 A 8 (Henry Bathurst Papers), reel H-2961, LAC; Sir Alexander Cochrane, "Thoughts on American

War," Apr. 27, 1812, Henry Dundas, Viscount Melville, Papers, HL; Lambert, *Challenge*, 25.

CHAPTER FIVE: INVASION

1   Walter Jones to Thomas Jefferson, Feb. 16, 1814, in Looney *PTJ-RS*, vol. 7:201.

2   Norma Taylor Mitchell, "John Campbell," in Sara B. Bearss et al., eds., *Dictionary of Virginia Biography* (Richmond: Library of Virginia, 2001), vol. 3:572–73; John Campbell to David Campbell, June 12 ("We wait") and June 21, 1812 ("The Cannon"), CFP, box 2, SC-DUL.

3   "The Fourth of July," *Richmond Enquirer*, July 7, 1812 (all quotations except Campbell's); Thrift, "Thomas Ritchie," 170–73, 186–87; Ambler, *Thomas Ritchie*, 57–60; John Campbell to David Campbell, July 5, 1812, CFP, box 2, SC-DUL.

4   For Barbour's nickname, see D. P. Jordan, *Political Leadership*, 111; Lowrey, *James Barbour*, 62; James Barbour to James Singleton, May 26, 1812, Executive Letter Book, p. 286, RG 3 (Office of the Governor), reel 30009, LV; John Campbell to David Campbell, July 5, 1812, CFP, box 2, SC-DUL.

5   Lowrey, *James Barbour*, 41, 51–59.

6   John Campbell to David Campbell, Sep. 7 and Oct. 17, 1812 ("Barbour takes it"), CFP, box 2, SC-DUL; William Wirt to Dabney Carr, Mar. 31, 1813, William Wirt Papers, LV.

7   James Barbour to the Council of State, May 12, 1812 ("literally nothing"), in Flournoy, *CVSP*, vol. 10:133; Barbour to William Eustis, Apr. 17 and May 19, 1812, Barbour to William Sharp, July 15, 1812, Executive Letter Book, pp. 237, 277, 399, RG 3 (Office of the Governor), reel 3009, LV; Lowrey, *James Barbour*, 62–69.

8   Walter Jones to James Monroe, May 30, 1813, JMP, ser. 1, reel 5, LC; Thomas Cooper to Thomas Jefferson, Aug. 17, 1814, in Looney, *PTJ-RS*, vol. 7:558; A. Taylor, *Civil War of 1812*, 325–29.

9   James Barbour to William Eustis, Apr. 17 and May 19, 1812, Barbour to James Monroe, June 23, 1812, Barbour to William Sharp, July 15, 1812 ("the great dangers"), and Barbour to James Madison, July 18, 1812, Executive Letter Book, pp. 237, 277, 349, 399, 414, RG 3 (Office of the Governor), reel 3009, LV; Charles K. Mallory to Barbour, July 22, 1812, JBEP, reel 5503, LV; "To the Virginia Legislature," *Richmond Enquirer*, Dec. 15, 1812.

10 Walter Jones to James Monroe, May 30, 1813 ("very badly equipped," "in driblets," and "a few muskets"), JMP, ser. 1, reel 5, LC; court mar-

tial of Lt. Horatio Woodard, Apr. 15, 1813, JBEP, reel 5511, LV; Jones to Thomas Jefferson, Feb. 16, 1814, in Looney, *PTJ-RS*, vol. 7:201.

11   William Tatham to James Barbour, May 11, 1812, JBEP, reel 5501, LV; Thomas Wells to Court of Nottaway County, Nov. 5, 1812 ("Were all"), JBEP, reel 5508, LV; John Campbell to David Campbell, July 31, 1812, and June 27, 1813 ("Nine-tenths"), CFP, box 2, SC-DUL; John Stokely to James Barbour, June 26, 1814 ("was often compelled"), JBEP, reel 5521, LV; Walter Jones to James Madison, Nov. 8, 1813, James Madison papers, American Memory Series, LC.

12   William Sharp to James Barbour, Apr. 18, 1812, in Flournoy, CVSP, vol. 10:125–6; Henry Howard to Charles K. Mallory, Dec. 1, 1812 ("not more"), JBEP, reel 5507, LV; John C. Pryor to Barbour, May 2, 1812 ("Many of the pistols"), and William Bolling to Barbour, May 30, 1812 ("The Swords"), JBEP, reel 5501, LV. For similar laments, see Mann Page to Barbour, Apr. 18, 1812, JBEP, reel 5500, LV; Kendall Addison to Barbour, July 2, 1812, JBEP, reel 5503, LV; Barbour to William Boyd, July 9, 1812, and to James Machin, July 14, 1812, Executive Letter Book, pp. 383, 392, RG 3 (Office of the Governor), reel 3009, LV; Charles K. Mallory to Kendall Addison, Aug. 21, 1812, Executive Letter Book, p. 22, RG 3 (Office of the Governor), reel 3009, LV; Enoch Renno to Barbour, Apr. 21, 1813, and John Dangerfield to Barbour, July 16, 1812, JBEP, reel 5503, LV.

13   James Barbour to Henry E. Coleman, May 28, 1812, Executive Letter Book, p. 292, RG 3, reel 3009, LV. See also Archer Hankins to Charles K. Mallory and Robert Quarles, Apr. 13, 1813, JBEP, reel 5511, LV. For the decision in late 1800 to withhold arms from county arsenals, see Nicholls, *Whispers of Rebellion*, 85.

14   Isaac A. Coles to Joseph C. Cabell, June 6, 1812, J.C. Cabell to Coles, June 8, 1812 ("not to kill"), J.C. Cabell to John Hartwell Cocke, June 17, 1812 ("Do this"), Cocke to J.C. Cabell, June 22, 1812, J.C. Cabell to Cocke, June 26, 1812, JCCFP (38-111-c), box 8, SSCL-UVA; William H. Cabell to J.C. Cabell, June 15 ("Hire a substitute") and June 22, 1812, JCCFP (38-111-c), box 2, SSCL-UVA.

15   Thomas Wells to James Barbour, Aug. 19, 1812, JBEP, reel 5504, LV; Miles Selden to Barbour, June 27 and July 7, 1813, and William Chamberlain to Barbour, July 8, 1813, in Flournoy, *CVSP*, vol. 10:235, 248, 249; Dempsey Veale et al to Barbour, Apr. 3, 1813 ("The cries" and "when they reflect"), JBEP, reel 5511, LV; Thomas Jefferson to James Monroe, May 30, 1813, JMP, ser. 1, reel 5, LC. For the plight of artisans, see George Leslie et al to Barbour, Feb. 19, 1813, JBEP, reel 5509, LV.

16   Princess Anne County memorial, Apr. 3, 1813 ("entirely repugnant"),

JBEP, reel 551, LV; William Lambert to James Barbour, Apr. 15, 1814, in Flournoy, *CVSP*, vol. 10:321.

17 John Stokely to James Barbour, July 31, 1812, JBEP, reel 5504, LV.

18 William Haskins to James Barbour, June 6, 1812, and Noah Zane and John Richardson quoted in Richard McClure to Barbour, June 10, 1812, JBEP, reel 5502, LV.

19 James Barbour to Richard McClure, June 22, 1812, Executive Letter Book, pp. 345–46, RG 3 (Office of the Governor), reel 3009, LV.

20 James Barbour to Richard Mason, June 27, 1812, Executive Letter Book, p. 429, RG 3 (Office of the Governor), reel 3009, LV.

21 James Barbour, "To the Patriotic Citizens of Richmond," *Richmond Enquirer*, Sep. 4, 1812; "Spirit of the People," *Richmond Enquirer*, Sep. 8, 1812; B.W. Leigh to Littleton Waller Tazewell, Jan. 7, 1813, Tazewell Family Papers, box 3, LV; John Taylor to James Monroe, Mar. 18, 1813, JMP, ser. 1, reel 5, LC.

22 William Sharp to James Barbour, Feb. 4 and Feb. 6, 1813, and Andrew J. McConnico to Barbour, Mar. 6, 1813, in Flournoy, *CVSP*, vol. 10:184–86, 195; *Richmond Enquirer*, Feb. 9, 1813; Charles Stewart to William Jones, Mar. 17, 1813, in Dudley, *Naval War of 1812*, vol.2:315–6.

23 Nathaniel Burwell to James Barbour, Mar. 30, 1813, and Robert B. Taylor to Barbour, Apr. 24, 1813, in Flournoy, *CVSP*, vol. 10:217, 227; John Campbell to David Campbell, Feb. 5, 1813, CFP, box 2, SC-DUL; Thomas Wilson to the Council of State, Feb. 12, 1813 (*"our worst enemy"*), JBEP, reel 5509, LV.

24 Testimony by John Patterson's Sci, Mathews County trial of Harry et al., Mar. 18, 1813 JBEP, reel 5511, LV.

25 Testimony by John Ripley (all quotations), and John Patterson's Sci, Mathews County trial of Harry et al., Mar. 18, 1813, JBEP, reel 5511, LV.

26 John Patterson, testimony, Matthews County trial of Harry et al., Mar. 18, 1813, JBEP, reel 5511, LV.

27 Matthews County trial of Harry et al., Mar. 18, 1813, JBEP, reel 5511, LV.

28 William Jennings testimony, James City County trial of Anthony, Tassy, and Kit, Mar. 31, 1813 (all quotations), JBEP, reel 5511, LV; "Important Information," *National Intelligencer*, Apr. 6, 1813. For another apparent reference to this episode (or one very much like it), see Maria Carter Beverley to Robert Beverley, Apr. 4, 1813, Beverley Family Papers, sec. 1, VHS.

29 James City County trial of Anthony, Tassy, and Kit, Mar. 31, 1813 ("to rebel"), JBEP, reel 5511, LV; "Important Information," *National Intelligencer*, Apr. 6, 1813 ("that 2000 negroes"); Shepperson, *John Paradise and Lucy Ludwell*, 445–46.

30 Council of State Record Book, pp. 159 (Apr. 10), 172 (Apr. 17), 175 (Apr. 19), and 224 (Apr. 10, 1813, letter of William Robertson), RG 75, reel 2990, LV.

31 For Mathews County, see Christopher Tompkins et al. petition, Apr. n.d., 1813, and John Patterson to William Robertson, Apr. 12, 1813, JBEP, reel 5511, LV; Council of State Record Book, 172 (Apr. 17, 1813), RG 75, reel 2990, LV. For James City County, see William Walker et al. petition, Apr. n.d., 1813, JBEP, reel 5511, LV.

32 William Walker et al. petition, Apr. n.d., 1813, JBEP, reel 5511, LV.

33 William Wardlaw to St. George Tucker, Apr. 13, 1813, TCP, box 32, SCSL-CWM; Council of State Record Book, p. 172 (Apr. 17, 1823), RG 75, reel 2990, LV; Mathews County, Mar. 18, 1813, trial of Harry et al., Auditor of Public Accounts, entry 756 (Condemned Slaves, 1783–1865), reel 2551, LV; James Barbour to the sheriff of James City County, Apr. 19, 1813, Barbour to the sheriff of Mathews County, Apr. 19, 1813, and Barbour to Thomas W. Alley, Apr. 19, 1813, Executive Letter Book, pp. 228–29, RG 3, reel 3010, LV. For the prices paid, see, Council of State Record Book, p. 251 (June 5, 1813), RG 75, reel 2990, LV.

34 James Barbour to the sheriff of Mathews County, Apr. 19, 1813, Executive Letter Book, p. 228, RG 3, reel 3010, LV.

35 Spencer George to James Barbour, Apr. 9, 1813, in Flournoy, CVSP, vol. 10:223; Lancaster County Court papers, Apr. 8, ("having consulted") Apr. 20, and Nov. 12, 1813, reel 197, LV.

36 "The Little Plot," National Intelligencer, Aug. 24, 1814 ("talk" and "perfectly contemptible"); "Fredericktown," Federal Gazette & Baltimore Daily Advertiser, Sep. 26, 1814 ("whipped"); Levin Winder, order, Aug. 20, 1814, and Frederick County grand jury, indictment, Sep. 13, 1814, Winder Papers, 1 folder, SC-DUL; Robert Cumming to Levin Winder, Aug. 20, 1814, MSP, ser. A, box S1004-129, doc. 36, MdSA.

37 Powhatan County Court, trial of Thomas Harris's Peter, Sep. 21, 1814, JBEP, reel 5523, LV. For Sci's escape with seven other slaves, see Thomas R. Yeatman, deposition, Mar. 16, 1814, APA-GMR, entry 258, box 779, Mathews County folder, LV. For the paucity of wartime executions and transportations for conspiracy, see Schwarz, Twice Condemned, 329.

38 Joseph C. Cabell to St. George Tucker, Feb. 6, 1813, TCP, box 32, SCSL-CWM; Lowrey, James Barbour, 71–72; "Virginia Legislature," Richmond Enquirer, Jan. 28, 1813; Robert Quarles to James Barbour, Feb. 11, 1813, and Charles K. Mallory to Barbour, Feb. 13 and Feb. 15, 1813, and Quarles to Barbour, Feb. 17, 1813, in Flournoy, CVSP, vol. 10:191–93; Francis Preston to Barbour, Feb. 19, 1813, JBEP, reel 5509, LV; "Self Defence," Federal Gazette & Baltimore Daily Advertiser, Feb. 20, 1813.

39   John Campbell to David Campbell, Mar. 7, 1813, CFP, box 2, SC-DUL;
      James Barbour to James Monroe, Mar. 17, 1813, Executive Letter Book,
      p. 198, RG 3 (Office of the Governor), reel 3010, LV; Monroe to Bar-
      bour, Mar. 21, 1813, in Flournoy, *CVSP*, vol. 10:212; Barbour to Robert
      B. Taylor, Mar. 9, 1813, and Barbour to Monroe, Mar. 24, 1813, Executive
      Letter Book, pp. 184, 208, RG 3 (Office of the Governor), reel 3010, LV;
      James Barbour, statement, Mar. 31, 1813, Council of State Record Book
      for 1812–1813, p. 139, RG 75, reel 2990, LV. For a previous flirtation with
      the idea of a state regular force, see Barbour to Monroe, June 23, 1812,
      Executive Letter Book, p. 349, RG 3 (Office of the Governor), reel 3009,
      LV; "To the Virginia Legislature," *Richmond Enquirer*, Dec. 15, 1812.

40   Charles Fenton Mercer to James Mercer Garnett, Apr. 29, 1813, in Mercer
      Papers, LV; James Barbour to State Senate and House of Delegates, May
      17, 1813, Executive Letter Book, p. 252, RG 3 (Office of the Governor),
      reel 3010, LV; Nathaniel H. Claiborne, dissent, Mar. 24 ("insurrection")
      and Mar. 31, 1813 ("the spirit"), and Peter V. Daniel, dissent, Mar. 31,
      1813, Council of State Record Book for 1812–1813, pp. 123, 142, RG 75,
      reel 2990, LV.

41   Council of State Record Book for 1812–1813, pp. 174, 202, 229, RG 75,
      reel 2990, LV; James Barbour to Robert B. Taylor, Mar. 23, 1813 ("The
      inattention"), Executive Letter Book, p. 202, RG 3 (Office of the Gover-
      nor), reel 3010, LV; John Campbell to David Campbell, July 14 and July
      16, 1813 ("The *General Government*"), CFP, box 2, SC-DUL; "Proposi-
      tions!" *Richmond Enquirer*, July 30, 1812.

42   Edward Colston to Benjamin Watkins Leigh, Apr. 19, 1813, Leigh Papers,
      SC-DUL; John Campbell to David Campbell, June 18, 1813, CFP, box 2,
      SC-DUL.

43   For the British strategy, see Walter Jones to James Monroe, May 30, 1813,
      JMP, ser. 1, reel 5, LC; William Jones to Manuel Eyre, May 12, 1813, in
      Dudley, *Naval War of 1812*, vol. 2:119; Sir John B. Warren to Lord Mel-
      ville, July 22, 1813, MG 24, F 132 (Warren correspondence), reel A-2076,
      LAC; "Defence of the Sea-Board," *Richmond Enquirer*, Oct. 13, 1814
      ("They have *wings*"). For American recognition of the British caution,
      see James Maurice to Robert B. Taylor, Mar. 18, 1813, JBEP, reel 5510, LV;
      William Wirt to St. George Tucker, Mar. 26, 1813, TCP, box 32, SCSL-
      CWM; Wirt to Dabney Carr, Mar. 31, 1813, Wirt Papers, LV; William
      Chamberlayne to James Barbour, July 1, 1813, JBEP, reel 5514, LV; *Rich-
      mond Enquirer*, July 2, 1813; Henry St. George Tucker to St. George
      Tucker, Aug. 14, 1813, TCP, box 33, SCSL-CWM.

44   George Cockburn to John B. Warren, Mar. 23, 1813, and William
      Jones to Manuel Eyre, May 12, 1813, in Dudley, *Naval War of 1812*,

vol. 2:118, 326; Kendall Addison to James Barbour, Apr. 9, 1813 ("In that case"), JBEP, reel 5511, LV; William R. Custis to Barbour, June 3, 1813, JBEP, reel 5513, LV. For the Princess Anne County raid, see John Myers to Barbour, June 17, 1813, and Major Nimmo to Robert B. Taylor, June 15, 1813, in Flournoy, *CVSP*, vol. 10:230. In 1812, Virginia spent $104,881 on the following categories: militia officers ($5,602); militia fine fund ($5,633); manufactory of arms ($69,200); rifles ($6,493); lead and gunpowder ($3,119); gun carriages ($4,292); and "public arms" ($10,542). In 1813, Virginia spent $433,363 on the following categories: militia officers ($6,069); militia fine fund ($3,463); manufactory of arms ($59,853); rifles ($4,345); lead and gunpowder ($18,526); gun carriages ($8,272); public arms ($955); and "Defense of the State" ($331,880). The last category, new in 1813, represented expenditures to feed and pay the militiamen in active service, and it accounts for the entire increase over the 1812 level of defense funding. In 1812, before the war came to Virginia, the state's total expenditures equaled $453,047. A year later the British invaded Chesapeake Bay, and the state spent $829,445, with defense expenditures accounting for almost all of the increase. For these figures, see Commonwealth of Virginia, *Journal of the State Senate, 1812*, 61–62; Commonwealth of Virginia, *Journal of the State Senate, 1813*, 29–30. Note: for all categories I rounded off to the nearest dollar, omitting all cents.

45   Thomas Jefferson to James Madison, June 21, 1813, Jefferson to Nathaniel H. Hooe, July 21, 1813, and Jefferson to Jeremiah A. Goodman, July 26, 1813, in Looney *PTJ-RS*, vol. 6:217, 314, 331; John M. Garnett to Archibald R. S. Hunter, Nov. 29, 1813, War of 1812 Collection, box 3, WLCL-UM; Thomas Mann Randolph Jr. to Joseph C. Cabell, Dec. 29, 1813, Randolph Papers, folder 1, SC-DUL.

46   Francis Preston to James Barbour, Feb. 19, 1813 ("more dreadful"), JBEP, reel 5509, LV; Peter V. Daniel, dissent, Mar. 31, 1813 ("From the pure atmosphere"), in Council of State Record Book for 1812–1813, p. 142, RG 75, reel 2990, LV; Barbour to the Senate and House of Delegates, Nov. 30, 1812, in *Richmond Enquirer*, Dec. 3, 1812; John Randolph to Josiah Quincy, July 4, 1813, in W. C. Bruce, *John Randolph*, vol. 1:394.

47   Robert Hines and James Chalmers to James Barbour, Mar. 6, 1813, JBEP, reel 5509, LV; James Semple to Barbour, Mar. 22, 1813, JBEP, reel 5510, LV; James Singleton to Barbour, Apr. 10, 1813 ("midnight murder"), and Archer Hankins to Charles K. Mallory and Robert Quarles, Apr. 13, 1813, JBEP, reel 5511, LV; Barbour to the citizens of Williamsburg, Mar. 9, 1813, and Barbour to Robert B. Taylor, Mar. 24, 1813, Executive Letter Book, pp. 186, 205, RG 3, reel 3010, LV; John C. Cohoon et al. to

Barbour, June 28, 1813, JBEP, reel 5513, LV; "Important Information," *National Intelligencer*, Apr. 6, 1813; Bowers, *Diary of Elbridge Gerry, Jr.*, 198–99 ("the blacks"); Hunt, *First Forty Years*, 89–90; "An Inhabitant of Amelia" to James Barbour, July 29, 1813 ("a great number"), JBEP, reel 5515, LV. See also Maria Corbin to Elizabeth Meade, June 30, 1812, Patrick Crawford Hoy Papers, sec. 1, VHS; Richard Ligon to Barbour, n.d. [ca. Dec. 1813], JBEP, reel 5517, LV; "The Enemy in York River," *Richmond Enquirer*, Nov. 26, 1813.

48   "Female Heroism," from the *Richmond Enquirer* ("with such tremendous effect") and Robert Greenhow to James Barbour, Dec. 15, 1813 ("the rescue"), both reprinted in *Niles' Weekly Register*, vol. 5:279 (Dec. 25, 1813).

49   Hugh Mercer to James Barbour, July 19, 1814, and Daniel Coleman et al. to Barbour, Aug. 3, 1814 ("uttered threats" and "in one instance"), JBEP, reel 5522, LV; Charles Johnston to Benjamin Hatcher, Sep. 16, 1814 ("a general rising" and "a plot"), in Flournoy, *CVSP*, vol. 10:387–88.

50   James Barbour to Daniel Coleman et al., Aug. 5, 1814 ("never manifest" and "sufficient number"), and Barbour to Alexander Parker, Aug. 26, 1814, Executive Letter Book, pp. 80, 89, RG 3 (Office of the Governor), reel 3011, LV.

51   Lowrey, *James Barbour*, 75; John Stokely to James Monroe, Jan. 30, 1813, JMP, ser. 1, reel 5, LC; Philip Barraud to St. George Tucker, Feb. 16, Feb. 24 ("to reclaim"), Mar. 15, and May 6, 1813, TCP, box 32, SCSL-CWM; Elizabeth Trist to Thomas Jefferson, July 7, 1813, in Looney, *PTJ-RS*, vol. 6:265; James McDowell to James Barbour, Aug. 10, 1813, in Flournoy, *CVSP*, vol. 10:276; William Bowling to Barbour, Sep. 11, 1813, JBEP, reel 5516, LV; Robert B. Taylor to John Armstrong, June 18 and July 13 ("become"), 1813, RG 107, M 221, reel 57, USNA-DC.

52   Archibald Stuart et al. to James Barbour, Aug. 10, 1813, and Edward Jones et al. to Barbour, Nov. 29, 1813, in Flournoy, *CVSP*, vol. 10:276–77, 291–92; Barbour to Richard E. Parker, Aug. 27, 1813, and Barbour to Francis Preston, Nov. 26, 1813, Executive Letter Book, pp. 358, 382, RG 3, reel 3010, LV; Robert Quarles to John Hartwell Cocke, Sep. 16, 1813, JHCFP, box 15, SSCL-UVA; Peter Fulkerson et al. to Barbour, Oct. 20, 1813, JBEP, reel 5516, LV; Lowery, *James Barbour*, 76; Robert Quarles to Cocke, Dec. 11, 1813, Wilson J. Cary to Cocke, Dec. 21, 1813, and Robert B. Taylor to Cocke, Dec. n.d., 1813, JHCFP, box 15, SSCL-UVA; Taylor to John Armstrong, Dec. 20, 1813 ("that the hope"), RG 107, M 221, reel 57, USNA-DC; Taylor to the adjutant general, Dec. 13 and Dec. 20, 1813, in *Richmond Enquirer*, Dec. 30, 1813, Joseph C. Cabell to Cocke, Dec. 13, 1813, JCCFP (38-111-c), box 10, SSCL-UVA.

53 James Barbour to Leaven Gayle, Mar. 17, 1814, Executive Letter Book, p. 42, RG 3, reel 3011, LV.

54 Leaven Gayle to James Barbour, Feb. 14, 1813 ("After"), JBEP, reel 5509, LV; Gayle to Barbour, Mar. 13, 1813, JBEP, reel 5510, LV; Council of State Record Book, p. 234 (May 25, 1813), RG 75, reel 2990, LV; Christopher Tompkins to Barbour, May 25, 1813, JBEP, reel 5512, LV; Gayle to Barbour, Dec. 11, 1813, JBEP, reel 5517, LV.

55 Council of State Record Book, p. 113 (Mar. 19, 1813), 288 (July 10, 1813), RG 75, reel 2990, VHS; William Robertson to Leaven Gayle, Mar. 21, 1813, Executive Letter Book, p. 200, RG 3, reel 3010, LV; John Patterson to James Barbour, Feb. 5, 1814 ("the most uninformed" and "no military talent"), JBEP, reel 5518, LV.

56 "Seventy-Six" to James Barbour, May 11, 1814, JBEP, reel 5520, LV.

57 Mathews County personal property tax list for 1812 and the Mathews County land tax list for 1814, LV.

58 John Patterson to James Barbour, June 14, 1813, and Christopher Tompkins to Barbour, June 15, 1813 (all quotes including Hudgins's words), and Patterson to Barbour, June 18, 1813, JBEP, reel 5513, LV; Barbour to Thomas Hudgins, Aug. 12, 1813, Executive Letter Book, p. 351, RG 3, reel 3010, LV.

59 Christopher Tompkins, order, Aug. 25, 1813 ("& said"), TFP (Mss 2 T5994 b), VHS; Tompkins to James Barbour, Aug. 26, 1813 ("that they"), JBEP, reel 5515, LV; Armistead Smith to William Patterson Smith, Apr. 19, 1814, WPSP, box 1, SC-DUL.

60 Eshelman, Sheads, and Hickey, *War of 1812 in the Chesapeake*, 247; Scott, *Recollections*, vol. 3:181–83; John Patterson to James Barbour, Feb. 5, 1815, JBEP, reel 5518, LV; Christopher Tompkins to Barbour, Feb. 11, 1814, and Leaven Gayle to Barbour, Mar. 12, 1814, JBEP, reel 5519, LV; Tompkins to Barbour, Mar. 3, 1814, in Flournoy, *CVSP*, vol. 10:305; [R. J. Barrett], "Naval Recollections," 20–21; "Letter to a Member of the House of Delegates from His Friend in Mathews County," Jan. 8, 1814, in *Virginia Argus*, Jan. 22, 1814 ("Buckskins"). For the water demands of a large warship, see Shomette, *Flotilla*, 167.

61 Christopher Tompkins to James Barbour, May 25, 1813, JBEP, reel 5512, LV; Leaven Gayle to Tompkins, Apr. 18, 1813, Tompkins, orders, Apr. 18 and Aug. 26, 1813, and Thomas Hudgins to Tompkins, Sep. 1, 1813, TFP (Mss 2 T5994 b), VHS; Scott, *Recollections*, vol. 3:116, 181, Gayle to Barbour, Feb. 4, 1814, JBEP, reel 5518, LV; Tompkins to Barbour, Mar. 12, 1814 ("affords us"), in Flournoy, *CVSP*, vol. 10:309.

62 Council of State Record Book, p. 59 (Jan. 29, 1814), RG 75, reel 2990, LV; James H. Roy to James Barbour, Jan. 29, 1814, Christopher Tompkins

to Barbour, Jan. 29, 1814, Leaven Gayle to Barbour, Feb. 4, 1814, and John Patterson to Barbour, Feb. 5, 1814, JBEP, reel 5518, LV; Tompkins to Barbour, Feb. 14, 1814, JBEP, reel 5519, LV; Roy to Tompkins, Feb. 4, 1814, TFP (Mss 1 T5996 c 92), VHS; Armistead Smith to Dr. Lee, Feb. 5, 1814 ("Our poor Militia" and "cowed"), and Smith to William Patterson Smith, Apr. 19 and June 24, 1814, WPSP, box 1, SC-DUL; Tompkins to Barbour, Mar. 3, 1814, in Flournoy, *CVSP*, vol. 10:305.

63   Armistead Smith to William Patterson Smith, Feb. 12, 1814, WPSP, box 1, SC-DUL; John Tabb to Christopher Tompkins, Jan. 17, 1814, TFP (Mss 1 T5996 c 101), VHS; John Patterson to James Barbour, Feb. 5, 1814, JBEP, reel 5518, LV; Leaven Gayle to Barbour, Mar. 12, 1814, JBEP, reel 5519, LV; Barbour to Gayle, Mar. 17, 1814, Executive Letter Book, p. 42, RG 3, reel 3011, LV.

64   Leaven Gayle to Robert Barrie, Jan. 24, Mar. 9, and Mar. 10, 1814, Barrie Papers, box 1, WLCL; Christopher Tompkins to James Barbour, Mar. 8, 1814, and Gayle to Barbour, Mar. 12, 1814 ("The desertion"), JBEP, reel 5519, LV; "Baltimore, March 25," *Richmond Enquirer*, Mar. 30, 1814; William Lambert to William Jones, Apr. 1, 1814, RG 45, M 124, reel 62, USNA-DC; Armistead Smith to William Patterson Smith, Feb. 12, 1814, WPSP, box 1, SC-DUL.

65   Christopher Tompkins to James Barbour, Mar. 12, 1814 ("that they knew"), in Flournoy, *CVSP*, vol. 10:308; John Patterson to Tompkins, May 4, 1814, and Tompkins to Barbour, May 8, 1814 ("that some Negro"), JBEP, reel 5520, LV; Armistead Smith to William Patterson Smith, May 17, 1814, WPSP, box 1, SC-DUL; Leaven Gayle to the adjutant general, May 26, 1814, in *National Intelligencer*, June 8, 1814.

66   Christopher Tompkins to James Barbour, Mar. 12, 1814 ("Tis a curious fact"), in Flournoy, *CVSP*, vol. 10:309; Christopher Tompkins, Battalion/Regimental Order Book, 61st Regiment, Virginia militia, Mar. 12 and Sep. 27, 1814 VHS; Thomas Tabb et al. to the legislature, Nov. 23, 1814, Virginia General Assembly, Legislative Petitions, box 159, folder 14, reel 122, LV. For the law, see "Chap. IX, An Act to Perpetuate Evidence of the Desertion of Slaves, to the Enemy, and for Other Purposes," Jan. 10, 1814, in [Virginia State Legislature], *Acts Passed at a General Assembly of the Commonwealth of Virginia* (Richmond: Samuel Pleasants, 1814), 34–35.

67   James Banks et al. to the legislature, Oct. 22, 1814 (all quotations), Finley Dixon et al. to the legislature, Oct. 22, 1814, and W. H. Ashbury et al. to the legislature, Oct. 22, 1814, Virginia General Assembly, Legislative Petitions, box 159, folder 13, reel 122, LV.

68   Thomas Tabb et al. to the legislature, Nov. 23, 1814, Virginia General Assembly, Legislative Petitions, box 159, folder 14, reel 122, LV. For

Tompkins's marriage to Smith's daughter, see Armistead Smith to William Patterson Smith, Apr. 19, 1814, WPSP, box 1, SC-DUL.

69   MATHEWS COUNTY PROPONENTS AND
OPPONENTS OF BOAT RESTRICTION, 1814

	No. of Signers on the Tax List	No. With No Slaves	No. with 1–5 Slaves	No. with 6+ Slaves	Total No. of Slaves Owned	No. of Slaves per Signer	No. of Runaways Lost
Proponents	67	12 (18%)	24 (36%)	31 (46%)	484	7.2	33
Opponents	239	135 (56%)	90 (38%)	14 (6%)	357	1.5	18

Sources: For the opponents, see the signatures on James Banks et al. to the legislature, Oct. 22, 1814, Finley Dixon et al. to the legislature, Oct. 22, 1814, and W. H. Ashbury et al. to the legislature, Oct. 22, 1814, Virginia General Assembly, Legislative Petitions, box 159, folder 13, reel 122, LV. For the proponents, see the signatures on Thomas Tabb et al. to the legislature, Nov. 23, 1814, Virginia General Assembly, Legislative Petitions, box 159, folder 14, reel 122, LV. For the slaveholdings, see Mathews County personal property tax list for 1812, LV. Only slaves aged twelve and older were taxable.

70   Mathews County personal property tax list for 1812, LV; Houlder Hudgins petition to the legislature, Dec. 5, 1815, Virginia General Assembly, Legislative Petitions, box 159, folder 11, reel 122, LV.

71   Thomas Tabb et al. to the legislature, Nov. 23, 1814, Virginia General Assembly, Legislative Petitions, box 159, folder 14, reel 122, LV.

72   John Morrison to Littleton W. Tazewell, Mar. 18, 1813, Tazewell Family Papers, box 3, LV.

CHAPTER SIX: LESSONS

1   Scott, *Recollections*, vol. 3:115.

2   Depositions of Cornelius Matthias, May 5, 1823, and David Shirley, May 5, 1823 (all quotations), APA-GMR, entry 258, box 779, LV. Willis's wife probably never escaped to the British, for her owner received no postwar compensation for a runaway slave. For the claim by William Mathias (misnamed as William Matthews) for Willis and the absence of a postwar claim by Daniel Shirley, who owned Willis's wife, see *ASP-FR*, vol. 5:814, 816.

3   Testimony by John Ripley ("Englishmen"), and John Paterson's Sci, Mathews County trial of Harry et al., Mar. 18, 1813, JBEP, reel 5511, LV; Benjamin Fowlee, deposition, Dec. 21, 1827 ("the negroes"), RG 76, entry 190, box 6, case 513 (John J. Brooke), USNA-CP; Frederick Douglass quoted in Bolster, *Black Jacks*, 1.

4   Lester, "Sir John Borlase Warren," 485–88 (Thomas Grenville quote on
     487); Gwynn, *Frigates and Foremasts*, 125–26.
5   Gwynn, *Frigates and Foremasts*, 134–42; Sir David Milne to George
     Home, Apr. 9, 1812, in Hume, "Letters Written during the War of 1812,"
     286; Herbert Sawyer to Andrew Allen, Aug. 5, 1812, Sir Robert Barrie
     Papers, box 5, SC-DUL; Petrides and Downs, *Sea Soldier*, 168–69, 177;
     Scott, *Recollections*, vol. 3:62–63; John W. Croker to Sir John Borlase
     Warren, Jan. 9, 1813, in Dudley, *Naval War of 1812*, vol. 2:14.
6   John W. Croker to Sir John Borlase Warren, Jan. 9, 1813, and Warren to
     Croker, Mar. 28, 1813, in Dudley, *Naval War of 1812*, vol. 2:14, 80–81;
     Lambert, *Challenge*, 64, 109–12, 243.
7   Dudley, *Naval War of 1812*, vol. 2:309; Morriss, *Cockburn*, 8; Pack, *Man
     Who Burned the White House*, 24–64.
8   Morris, *Cockburn*, 7–8, 34, 36, 38–39, 43–46. For the praise of subor-
     dinates, see Rowley, "Captain Robert Rowley," 244–47; Scott, *Recollec-
     tions*, vol. 3:63; Petrides and Downs, *Sea Soldier*, 157 ("very fond"), 160,
     185–87; Gleig, *Narrative of the Campaigns*, 82; [R. J. Barrett], "Naval
     Recollections," 456 ("that undaunted seaman").
9   Gwynn, *Frigates and Foremasts*, 131–32; Morris, *Cockburn*, 144; Pack,
     Man Who Burned the White House, 103–8; [Anonymous], *Personal Narra-
     tive*, 10 ("snarled"); Bartlett, "Gentlemen versus Democrats," 142–46, 149–
     50; Jenkins, *Henry Goulburn*, 77; Bickham, *Weight of Vengeance*, 64–65.
10   John W. Croker to Sir John Borlase Warren, Feb. 10 and Mar. 20, 1813, in
     Dudley, *Naval War of 1812*, vol. 2:17–19, 76; Admiralty to Warren, May
     26, 1813, MG 12, Admiralty 2, vol. 933:263, reel B-3434, LAC; Bartlett,
     "Gentlemen versus Democrats," 151–54; Henry Bathurst to Sir Sidney
     Beckwith, Mar. 20, 1813, George Cockburn to Sir John Borlase Warren,
     Mar. 13 and Mar. 23, 1813, in Dudley, ed., *Naval War of 1812*, vol. 2:325–
     26; Gleig, *Narrative of the Campaigns*, 207 ("To penetrate"); Warren to
     Lord Melville, July 22, 1813, MG 24, F 132, reel A-2076, LAC.
11   Gleig, *Narrative of the Campaigns*, 48; [Anonymous] *Personal Narra-
     tive*, 3 ("we saw"), 48 ("the boundless"); G. C. M. Smith, *Autobiography
     of Lieutenant-General Sir Harry Smith*, vol. 1:197; Edward Codrington,
     journal, July 7, Aug. 13 ("Low, flat" and "This Chesapeake"), Aug. 21
     and Aug. 22, 1814, MG 24, F131 (Codrington letters), reel A-2076, LAC;
     Scott, *Recollections*, 160–61 ("bloated"); [R. J. Barrett], "Naval Recollec-
     tions," 20, 460.
12   George Cockburn to Sir Alexander Cochrane, May 10, 1814, in Dud-
     ley, *Naval War of 1812*, vol. 3:65; Sir Sidney Beckwith to Sir John Bor-
     lase Warren, Aug. 13, 1813 ("moving thro'"), MG 12, Admiralty 1, vol.
     504:48, 73, reel B-1449, LAC: Sir Charles Napier quoted in W. N. Bruce,

Life of General Sir Charles Napier, 60 ("We have [a] nasty sort"); Scott, *Recollections*, vol. 3:109; Chaptico letter to the postmaster general, July 22, 1813 ("The enemy"), in *Richmond Enquirer*, July 30, 1813.

13   William Jones to Manuel Eyre, May 12, 1813 ("our extensive"), in Dudley, *Naval War of 1812*, vol. 2:119; Sir John Borlase Warren to Lord Melville, July 22, 1813 ("sudden & secret"), MG 24, F 132, reel A-2076, LAC.

14   Petrides and Downs, *Sea Soldier*, 175–76 ("Never"); Scott, *Recollections*, vol. 3:96 ("searching out"), 122.

15   John Cropper to James Barbour, Mar. 20, 1813, in Flournoy, *CVSP*, vol. 10:208; Charles Stewart to William Jones, Mar. 22, 1813, in Dudley, *Naval War of 1812*, vol. 2:316–17; Scott, *Recollections*, vol. 3:131; William H. Broadnax to James Barbour, Oct. 1, 1813, JBEP, reel 5516, LV; Nicholas Faulcon to John Hartwell Cocke, Jan. 18, 1814, JHCFP, box 15, SSCL-UVA; Sir Harry Smith quoted in Bartlett, "Gentlemen versus Democrats," 150 ("species").

16   William Lambert to James Monroe, Apr. 18, 1813, RG 59, M588 (Department of State, War of 1812 Papers), reel 6, USNA-DC; *Niles' Weekly Register*, vol. 4:159 (May 8, 1813), and vol. 5:13 (Sep. 4, 1813: "newspapers"); John S. Skinner to William Jones, Dec. 6, 1813, in Dudley, *Naval War of 1812*, vol. 2:396.

17   George Cockburn, Secret Orders, Mar. 7, June 17, and Sep. 2, 1813, SGCP, reel 10, LC; James Barbour to Robert B. Taylor, Mar. 27, 1813, Executive Letter Book, p. 210, RG 3 (Office of the Governor), reel 3010, LV; Mann Page to Barbour, Mar. 14, 1813, in Flournoy, *CVSP*, vol. 10:202; Cockburn to Sir John Borlase Warren, Mar. 23, 1813, in Dudley, *Naval War of 1812*, vol. 2:326; *Federal Gazette & Baltimore Daily Advertiser*, Apr. 29 and May 4, 1813; *Richmond Enquirer*, June 1, 1813; *Niles' Weekly Register*, vol. 4:14 (Sep. 4, 1813: "to shew"); Robert Steed to Taylor, Aug. 30, 1813, RG 107, M221, reel 57, USNA-DC; Gideon Granger to James Monroe, Apr. 1, 1813, in Hecht, "Post Office Department," 147–48.

18   Petrides and Downs, *Sea Soldier*, 181 ("desired effect"); William H. Nicholson to Thomas Wright, Aug. 16, 1813 ("was so great"), War of 1812 Collection, box 1, MdHS; Scott, *Recollections*, vol. 3:76, 117, 189, 196; Levin Winder to James Madison, Apr. 26, 1813, MSP, ser. A, box S 1004-129, doc. 288, MdSA; Thomas Digges to Winder, July 14, 1814, MSP, ser. A, box S 1004-132, doc. 183, MdSA. Major Wybourn called the island "Portsouci," by which he meant Spesutie. See Eshelman, Sheads, and Hickey, *War of 1812 in the Chesapeake*, 201.

19   Lovell, *Personal Narrative*, 168 ("The plan"); Scott, *Recollections*, vol. 3:190.

20   Scott, *Recollections*, vol. 3:117; "Barbarity of the Enemy," *National Intelligencer*, Dec. 8, 1813; Sir John Borlase Warren to the Admiralty, May 28, 1813, MG 12, Admiralty 1, vol. 503:557, reel B-1448, LAC.

21   *Niles' Weekly Register*, vol. 4:209 (May 29, 1813: "Certainly"); George Cockburn to Sir John Borlase Warren, Mar. 13 and Mar. 23, 1813, in Dudley, *Naval War of 1812*, vol. 2:321–23, 326; Robert B. Taylor to James Barbour, Mar. 13, 1813, in Flournoy, *CVSP*, vol. 10:201; Edward S. Waddy to Ben James Harris, Mar. 25, 1813, Harris Papers, box 1, SC-DUL.

22   Sir John Warren to Lord Melville, Mar. 29, 1813, MG 24, F 132, reel A-2076, LAC; Gleig, *Narrative*, 374–77 ("experience").

23   Petrides and Downs, *Sea Soldier*, 170.

24   Sir John Borlase Warren to the Admiralty, Nov. 30, 1812, MG 12, Admiralty 1, vol. 503:74, reel B-1448, LAC; "British Wit!" *Richmond Enquirer*, Dec. 10, 1814.

25   W. N. Bruce, *Life of General Sir Charles Napier*, 61–62 ("It is quite shocking"). For Beckwith's cousins, see P. Napier, *Black Charlie*, 21. For the Americans as "rebels," see William Lambert to James Barbour, Aug. 12, 1814, in Flournoy, *CVSP*, vol. 10:372.

26   John G. P. Tucker to St. George Tucker, Aug. 1, 1814, and Thomas T. Tucker to St. G. Tucker, Aug. 6, 1814, TCP, box 33, SCSL-CWM; P. Hamilton, *Making and Unmaking*, 113; Brugger, *Beverley Tucker*, 12; Lambert, *Challenge*, 293–94, 297, 300.

27   A. Taylor, *Civil War of 1812*, 102–6, 354–58; Petrides and Downs, *Sea Soldier*, 193 ("traitors").

28   John O'Neill to Thomas Leiper et al., June 8, 1813 ("the oppressors"), in Binns, *Recollections*, 220–21; "The Case of O'Neale," *Philadelphia Aurora*, May 11 and May 17, 1813; Henry Miller to John Borlase Warren, May 8, 1813, and Warren to Miller, May 10, 1813, in *New York City Shamrock*, May 22, 1813; Eshelman, Sheads, and Hickey, *War of 1812 in the Chesapeake*, 132–33; John O'Neill to John Mason, Aug. 30, 1813, RG 45, ser. RE 1812–1815, box 590, USNA-DC; Scott, *Recollections*, vol.3:102–5.

29   *Baltimore American*, July 16, 1812; Hickey, *War of 1812*, 55; Thomas Jefferson to James Madison, June 29, 1812, in Stagg, *PJM-PS*, vol. 4:519; *Norfolk & Portsmouth Herald*, Aug. 29, 1812; *Norfolk Gazette & Public Ledger*, Aug. 24, 1812; Wehjte, "Opposition in Virginia," 84; *Richmond Enquirer*, May 20, 1813.

30   Gilje, *Rioting in America*, 60–63; Hickey, *War of 1812*, 56–71 (all quotations); Pasley, *"Tyranny of Printers,"* 246–47; Bickham, *Weight of Vengeance*, 187–88.

31   Sir John Borlase Warren to Lord Melville, July 22, 1813, MG 24, F 132, reel A-2076, LAC: Scott, *Recollections*, vol. 3:114.

32   George Cockburn to Sir John Borlase Warren, Mar. 13, 1813, in Dudley, *Naval War of 1812*, vol. 2:321; Scott, *Recollections*, vol. 3:207–8. For the officer's note, see *Niles' Weekly Register*, vol. 5:85 (Oct. 2, 1813: "for the use").

33   Robert Rowley to Owsley Rowley, Nov. 8, 1814 ("They will do"), in Rowley, "Captain Robert Rowley," 240–50; Gleig, *Narrative of the Campaigns*, 207; Edward Codrington, journal, Sep. 2, 1814,. MG 24, F131 (Codrington letters), reel A-2076, LAC; Lambert, *Challenge*, 51.

34   Scott, *Recollections*, vol. 3:90, 122; George Cockburn to Sir John Borlase Warren, May 3, 1813, in Dudley, *Naval War of 1812*, vol. 2:342; Petrides and Downs, *Sea Soldier*, 194 ("a country"); W. N. Napier, *Life of General Sir Charles Napier*, 60 ("They fight").

35   Bartlett, "Gentlemen versus Democrats," 150–1; Lovell, *Personal Narrative*, 169–71 ("dastardly"); Morriss, *Cockburn*, 94; Scott, *Recollections*, vol. 3:68–72; Lambert, *Challenge*, 246–47.

36   Morriss, *Cockburn*, 95–96; *Niles' Weekly Register*, vol. 4:159 (May 8, 1813: "appears"); Major Wyborn quoted in Delia Pennington deposition, June 12, 1813, in *National Intelligencer*, Sep. 18, 1813; George Cockburn and Charles Napier, orders, July 12, 1813, SGCP, reel 10, LC.

37   Eshelman, Shead, and Hickey, *War of 1812 in the Chesapeake*, 126–28, 132–36; Scott, *Recollections*, vol. 3:100–101 ("hoisted"), 13–14 ("teach a salutary lesson"); George, *Terror*, 27–36; *Niles' Weekly Register*, vol. 4:164 (May 8, 1813); *Federal Gazette & Baltimore Daily Advertiser*, June 2, 1813; George Cockburn to Sir John Borlase Warren, May 3, 1813, in Dudley, *Naval War of 1812*, vol. 2:342.

38   George Cockburn to Sir John Borlase Warren, May 6, 1813, in Dudley, *Naval War of 1812*, vol. 2:344–45; Scott, *Recollections*, vol. 3: 110–12 ("offered any useless"); Petrides and Downs, *Sea Soldier*, 185; Eshelman, Sheads, and Hickey, *War of 1812 in the Chesapeake*, 125–26, 128; *Niles' Weekly Register*, vol. 4:182 (May 15, 1813), 196 (May 22, 1813); James Pillar Boyd to James McHenry, May 23, 1813 ("imprudent"), War of 1812 Collection, box 1, MdHS.

39   Francis B. Chandler, deposition, in *Niles' Weekly Register*, vol. 5:92 (Oct. 9, 1813); James Pillar Boyd to James McHenry, May 23, 1813 ("buried their cannon"), War of 1812 Collection, box 1, MdHS; Scott, *Recollections*, Vol. 3:110–12.

40   George Cockburn quoted in *Federal Gazette & Baltimore Daily Advertiser*, June 2, 1813; Scott, *Recollections*, vol. 3:158–59. For the coal shipment, see Cockburn, order, June 19, 1813 ("from Motives" and "New York Hospital"), SGCP, reel 10, LC.

41   "Latest from Bermuda," *Federal Gazette & Baltimore Daily Advertiser*,

Apr. 28, 1813 ("treated"); Captain Goodall quoted in Lelia Tucker to Mary W. Cabell, May 16, 1814 ("every eating"), JCCFP (38-111-c), box 10, SSCL-UVA; Major Wybourn quoted in Petrides and Downs, *Sea Soldier*, 188.

42   *Niles' Weekly Register*, vol. 4:164 (May 8, 1813: "It is justice"); Scott, *Recollections*, vol. 3:102; Petrides and Downs, *Sea Soldier*, 178, 183, 185 ("a train of boarding school misses").

43   Scott, *Recollections*, vol. 3:165 (all quotations).

44   Shomette, *Flotilla*, 10; Morriss, *Cockburn*, 93; Dudley, *Naval War of 1812*, 309; Sir John Borlase Warren to Lord Melville, Feb. 19 and June 1, 1813, MG 24, F 132, reel A-2076, LAC.

45   Eshelman, Sheads, and Hickey, *War of 1812 in the Chesapeake*, 225–28; Morriss, *Cockburn*, 94–95; Petrides and Downs, *Sea Soldier*, 190–93; Scott, *Recollections*, vol. 3:142–43, 147–48; Charles Napier quoted in W. F. Butler, *Sir Charles Napier*, 58; George Cockburn to Sir Alexander Cochrane, Apr. 2, 1814, in Dudley, *Naval War of 1812*, vol. 3:43.

46   Eshelman, Sheads, and Hickey, *War of 1812 in the Chesapeake*, 236–38; Stapleton Crutchfield to James Barbour, June 25, 1813, and Robert G. Scott to Barbour, June 25, 1813, in Flournoy, *CVSP*, vol. 10:232, 234; Sir Sidney Beckwith to Sir John Borlase Warren, June 28, 1813, in Dudley, *Naval War of 1812*, vol. 2:362.

47   Eshelman, Sheads, and Hickey, *War of 1812 in the Chesapeake*, 237–38; Sir Sidney Beckwith to Sir John Borlase Warren, July 5, 1813, in Dudley, *Naval War of 1812*, vol. 2:364; "To the Editor of the Enquirer," *Richmond Enquirer*, July 16, 1813 ("women"); Capt. Cooper to Charles K. Mallory, July 10, 1813, in *Richmond Enquirer*, July 13, 1813.

48   Council of State Journal for 1812–1813, p. 278 (June 30, 1813: "that many of the Females"), RG 75, reel 2990, LV; Stapleton Crutchfield to James Barbour, June 28, 1813, in *Richmond Enquirer*, July 2, 1813.

49   "Anniversary of Independence," "Enormities at Hampton," and "To the Editor of the Enquirer," *Richmond Enquirer*, July 6 ("That barbarity"), July 9 and July 16, 1813 ("Men of Virginia!"); *Niles' Weekly Register*, vol. 4:291 (July 3, 1813); James Pleasants Jr. to William Bolling, July 3, 1813, Bolling Papers, box 1, SC-DUL; Barbour to Calvin Jones, July 15, 1813, in Flournoy, *CVSP*, vol. 10:260; G. A. Smith, *Slaves' Gamble*, 94.

50   Sir Sidney Beckwith to Sir John Borlase Warren, July 5, 1813 ("a desperate Banditti"), in Dudley, *Naval War of 1812*, vol. 2:364; Beckwith to Robert B. Taylor, June 30, 1813, in *Richmond Enquirer*, Oct. 1, 1813; Warren to Lord Melville, July 6, 1813, MG 24, F 132, reel A-2076, LAC; John C. Sherbrooke to Henry Bathurst, July 13, 1813, MG 11, CO 217 (Nova Scotia), vol. 91:143–47, reel B-1054, LAC. For Virginians' wel-

come for the deserters, see John Campbell to David Campbell, July 14, 1813, CFP, box 2, SC-DUL.

51 Bartlett, "Gentlemen versus Democrats," 143; *Boston Gazette* quoted in Hoge, "British Are Coming," 1271 ("that there breathes not"); *Niles' Weekly Register*, vol 4:164 (May 8, 1813), 196 (May 22, 1813: "Cockburn stood"), 402 (Aug. 21, 1813: reward for head and ears), vol. 8:103 (Apr. 8, 1815: "He should be lashed naked"), 284 (June 24, 1815: chamber pots).

52 George Cockburn to Robert Barrie, Dec. 22, 1813 ("The Book"), Robert Barrie Papers, box 1, WLCL-UM; George Cockburn to Sir Alexander Cochrane, May 10, 1814 ("My Ideas"), in Dudley, *Naval War of 1812*, vol. 3:65; Morriss, *Cockburn*, 293n42.

53 Morriss, *Cockburn*, 96.

54 Robert B. Taylor to John Armstrong, June 29, 1813, RG 107, M221, reel 57, USNA-DC; Scott, *Recollections*, vol. 3:152, 155; Capt. Cooper to Charles K. Mallory, July 10, 1813, in *Richmond Enquirer*, July 13, 1813; John Campbell to David Campbell, July 16, 1813, CFP, box 2, SC-DUL. For the reversion to petty raiding, see William Allen to James Barbour, July 1, 1813, William Tazewell to Barbour, July 2, 1813, and George French to Barbour, July 29, 1813, in Flournoy, *CVSP*, vol. 10:239, 240, 265–66; Shomette, *Flotilla*, 19–20; Sir John Borlase Warren to John Wilson Croker, July 16, 1813, MG 12, Admiralty 1, vol. 503:408, reel B-1449, LAC; Robert Barrie to Dolly Gardner Clayton, Sep. 4, 1813, Barrie to Warren, Nov. 14, 1813, and Barrie to Clayton, Feb. 4, 1814, in Dudley, *Naval War of 1812*, vol. 2:385, 395, and vol. 3:15n, 17; Warren to Sir George Prevost, Sep. 21, 1813, RG 8, vol. 680:97, reel C-3173, LAC.

55 Dudley, *Naval War of 1812*, vol. 2:311; Robert Barrie to Sir John Borlase Warren, Sep. 22 ("we were extremely ignorant") and Nov. 14, 1813, MG 12, Admiralty 1, vol. 505:66, 68, reel B-1449, LAC; Barrie to George Cockburn, Oct. 12, 1813 ("a sad annoyance" and "complain bitterly"), SGCP, reel 9, LC; Eshelman, Sheads, and Hickey, *War of 1812 in the Chesapeake*, 244; Cockburn to Barrie, Dec. 22, 1813 ("keeping my Yankee Friends"), Robert Barrie Papers box 1, WLCL-UM.

56 Robert Barrie to Dolly Gardner Clayton, Sep. 4, 1813, in Dudley, *Naval War of 1812*, vol. 2:386; Petrides and Downs, *Sea Soldier*, 195; Rouse, "British Invasion," 319.

57 Shomette, *Flotilla*, 20; Dudley, *Naval War of 1812*, vol. 2:311; Scott, *Recollections*, vol. 3:187.

58 *Niles' Weekly Register*, vol. 4:159 (May 8, 1813), 406 (Aug. 21, 1813), 422 (Aug. 28, 1813), and vol. 5:13 (Sep. 4, 1813: "took"); "Retreat of the Enemy's Fleet," *Richmond Enquirer*, Aug. 31, 1813. For the Kent Island deserters, see Sir John Borlase Warren to John Wilson Croker, July 29

and Aug. 23, 1813, in Dudley, *Naval War of 1812*, vol. 2:369, 382; *Federal Gazette & Baltimore Daily Advertiser*, Aug. 9, Aug. 16, and Aug. 20, 1813; Maj. Meredith to Gen. Smith, Aug. 23, 1813, in *Federal Gazette & Baltimore Daily Advertiser*, Aug. 24, 1813; Scott, *Recollections*, vol. 3:160–61; *Niles' Weekly Register*, vol. 4:391 (Aug. 14, 1813); "Kent Island," *Richmond Enquirer*, Aug. 31, 1813; Warren to Lord Melville, Sep. 27, 1813, MG 24, F 132, reel A-2076, LAC. For a close study of desertion and punishment on twenty-seven ships of the North American Station, see Malcomson, "Creating Order and 'Disorder.'" Malcomson finds that 601 men deserted from these ships during the years 1813–1814.

59   Philip Barraud to St. George Tucker, Mar. 30 and Apr. 2, 1813, TCP, box 32, SCSL-CWM; "Retreat of the Enemy's Fleet," *Richmond Enquirer*, Aug. 31, 1813 (both quotes); Andrew Moore to Thomas Jefferson, Oct. 8, 1813, in Looney, *PTJ-RS*, vol. 6:545.

60   St. George Tucker to Joseph C. Cabell, Mar. 31, 1813, BFP, box 2, SSCL-UVA; Sir John Borlase Warren to John Wilson Croker, Aug. 14, 1813, MG 12, Admiralty 1, vol. 504:47, reel B-1449, LAC; Petrides and Downs, *Sea Soldier*, 181–82 ("the four villains").

61   Scott, *Recollections*, vol. 2:14; George Cockburn, orders, Mar. 7, 1813, SGCP, reel 10, LC.

62   Admiralty to Sir John Borlase Warren, Mar. 8 and June 15, 1813, MG 12, Admiralty 2, vol. 932:239, 271, reel B-3434, LAC; Warren to John Wilson Croker, June 8, 1813, MG 12, Admiralty 1, vol. 504:78, reel B-1449, LAC; George Cockburn to Capt. Lawrence, June 12, 1813, and Cockburn, order, Nov. 12, 1813, SGCP, reel 10, LC; Henry Hotham to John Talbot, May 14 and 15, 1813, John Talbot, Order Book, reel A-1632, LAC. For raids designed to recover deserters, see Petrides and Downs, *Sea Soldier*, 182–83; Scott, *Recollections*, vol. 3:216–20. For the fate of Patrick Hallidan, see Warren to Cockburn, Aug. 28, 1813, SGCP, reel 9, LC.

63   Henry Hotham, "Statement of the Number of Men Short of Complement," Sep. 2, 1813, SGCP, reel 9, LC. The return provides numbers of men on duty per ship broken down into these categories: petty officers, able seamen, ordinary seamen, landsmen, boys, and marines. The reported shortfalls appear only in the categories of seamen (apparently both able and ordinary), boys, and marines. The shortfall in boys was negligible. The percentage of seamen missing is as a proportion of the reported numbers of able and ordinary seamen plus the shortfall. For the duties and treatment of marines, see Petrides and Downs, *Sea Soldier*, 202–6.

64   Bartlett and Smith, "'Species of Milito-Nautico-Guerilla Warfare,'" 179; Shomette, *Flotilla*, 14; George Cockburn to Sir Alexander Cochrane, June 25, 1814 ("They are stronger men"), in Dudley, *Naval War of 1812*,

vol. 3:116; Cockburn to Cochrane, Aug. 15, 1814, SGCP, reel 6, LC. For the use of black guides to track British deserters, see Scott, *Recollections*, vol. 3:216.

65   Edward Codrington, journal, Oct. 27, 1814, MG 24, F 131 (Codrington letters), reel A-2076, LAC; Captain Forrest letter to unknown, July 27, 1813, *Niles' Weekly Register*, vol. 4:356 (July 31, 1813).

66   M. Mason, "Battle of Slaveholding Liberators," 677; Sir David Milne to George Home, Apr. 26, 1814, in Hume, "Letters Written during the War of 1812," 293. For Warren's assurances, see Robert B. Taylor to James Barbour, July 1, 1813, in Flournoy, *CVSP*, vol. 10:239.

67   Henry Bathurst to Sir Sidney Beckwith, Mar. 20, 1813, in Dudley, *Naval War of 1812*, vol. 2:325–26; Bartlett and Smith, " 'Species of Milito-Nautico-Guerilla Warfare,' " 187; George Cockburn, orders, Mar. 7, 1813, SGCP, reel 10, LC; G. A. Smith, *Slaves' Gamble*, 88.

68   Sobel, *World They Made Together*, 51–52; Walsh, "Work and Resistance," 100–104, 113.

69   Edmund Baily, deposition, Nov. 8, 1824, RG 76, entry 190, box 10, case 1020 (Thomas Primrose), USNA-CP; William Camp to James Barbour, July 7, 1813, JBEP, reel 5514, LV. For the story of Anthony, see the depositions of Dixon Brown, May 12, 1814, John Hughes, May 12, 1814, and John Young (July 12, 1821), RG 76, entry 185, box 4, folder 15, USNA-CP. For Sam, see Walker Luken and Levin Scott, deposition, May 9, 1814 ("was fishing"), RG 3, depositions, 1814–1821, Northampton County folder, LV.

70   William Jennings, testimony, Mar. 31, 1813, James City County trial of Anthony, Tassy, and Kit, JBEP, reel 5511, LV. For Charles's escape, see Joseph Gatewood, Samuel Hoskins, William Taylor, and John Prewett, deposition, Mar. 1, 1823, RG 76, entry 190, box 8, case 760, USNA-CP.

71   Depositions of Levin G. Winder, Feb. 13, 1815, and Peggy Collins, Dec. 27, 1827 (all quotations), RG 76, entry 190, box 6, case 542 (John H. Winder), USNA-CP. Collins dated both escapes as in 1814 and two weeks apart, which is implausible. In a deposition taken closer to the time of the escapes, Levin G. Winder dated them as July 10, 1813, and May 12, 1814.

72   Kendall Addison to Sir John Borlase Warren, May 14, 1813, and Warren to Addison, May 16, 1813, CO 37 (Bermuda), vol. 71:93, 94.

73   Sir John Borlase Warren to John Wilson, May 28, 1813, MG 12, Admiralty 1, vol. 503:279, reel B-1448, LAC; Admiralty to Warren, July 9, 1813, MG 12, Admiralty 2, vol. 933:4, reel B-3434, LAC. For the 18 runaways to Cockburn early in May, see Malcomson, "Freedom by Reaching the Wooden World," 2, which relies on Cockburn's journal, May 4, 1813, National Maritime Museum, Greenwich, England.

74   *National Intelligencer*, May 1 and 12, 1813; Kendall Addison to George
      Cockburn, June 7, 1813 ("avail"), SGCP, reel 9, LC; Addison to James
      Barbour, July 19, 1813 ("The Negroes"), JBEP, reel 5514, LV. For collab-
      orative escapes from the Eastern Shore, see Lewis Roberts and Nathan-
      iel Smith, deposition, Nov. 26, 1827, RG 76, entry 185, box 4, folder 14,
      USNA-CP.

75   John Turberville to William Hening, Nov. 8, 1813, in Flournoy, *CVSP*,
      vol. 10:283; Walter Jones to James Madison, Nov. 8, 1813, James Madison
      Papers, American Memory Series, LC.

76   William H. Nicholson to Levin Winder, Sep. 1, 1813, MSP, ser. A, box
      S1004-129, doc. 4, MdSA; Sir John Borlase Warren to Lord Melville, Sep.
      6, 1813, MG 24, F 132, reel A-2076, LAC.

77   Robert Barrie to Sir John Borlase Warren, Nov. 14, 1813 ("The Slaves"),
      in Dudley, *Naval War of 1812*, vol. 2:396; Barrie quoted in Joseph C.
      Cabell to St. George Tucker, Nov. 24, 1813 ("the poor devils"), TCP, box
      33, SCSL-CWM. For an estimate of 600 blacks sent on to Bermuda in
      1813, see Shomette, *Flotilla*, 21.

78   G. A. Smith, *British Eyewitness*, 43, 117; Scott, *Recollections*, vol. 3:61–
      62; Gleig, *Narrative of the Campaigns*, 38–41; Petrides and Downs, *Sea
      Soldier*, 163–64; Edward Codrington to his wife, July 14 and 17, 1814,
      MG 24, F 13 (Codrington Letters), reel A-2076, LAC; [Anonymous],
      "Recollections of the Expedition," 448; Jarvis, "Maritime Masters and
      Seafaring Slaves," 586–87, 594; David Milne to George Home, Apr. 26,
      1814, in Hume, "Letters Written during the War of 1812," 291; Robert
      Rowley to Owsley Rowley, June 18, 1814, in Rowley, "Captain Rob-
      ert Rowley," 242–43; P. Hamilton, *Making and Unmaking*, 10; George
      Cockburn to Robert Barrie, Oct. 21, 1814, Robert Barrie Papers, box 1,
      WLCL-UM; Sir Pulteney Malcolm to unknown, Aug 3, 1814, SPMP,
      box 1, WLCL.

79   Jarvis, "Maritime Masters and Seafaring Slaves," 590, 591n7; William
      Smith and John Noble Harvey to George Horsford, Aug. 14, 1813 (all
      quotations), SACP, file 2326, reel 1, LC; Sir Alexander Cochrane to Sir
      John Borlase Warren, Mar. 8, 1814, SACP, file 2326, reel 1, LC.

80   Sir John Borlase Warren to Lord Melville, Mar. 13, 1813, MG 24, F 132,
      reel A-2076, LAC; George Cockburn, order; Sep. 25, 1813, SGCP, reel
      10, LC; Andrew Fitzherbert Evans to Cockburn, Oct. 1, 1813, SGCP,
      reel 9, LC. For the numbers of dockyard workers, see Evans to the Lords
      of the Admiralty, Oct. 12, 1813, Admiralty 359:34A, National Maritime
      Museum, Greenwich, England. My thanks to Thomas Malcomson for
      providing a copy of this document.

81 Lovell, *Personal Narrative*, 152 ("they considered"); George Cockburn to Andrew Fitzherbert Evans, Oct. 2, 1813, SGCP, reel 6, LC; Weiss, *Merikens*, 5.

82 Andrew Fitzherbert Evans to George Cockburn, Oct. 1, 1813 ("I am sorry"), SGCP, reel 9, LC; Cockburn to Evans, Oct. 2, 1813 ("riotous"), SGCP, reel 6, LC; Sir Alexander Cochrane to Cockburn, Apr. 28, 1814, in Dudley, *Naval War of 1812*, vol. 3:51–52; Evans to the Admiralty, Oct. 12, 1813, Admiralty 359:34A, National Maritime Museum, Greenwich, England. For the compromise, see Sir Alexander Cochrane to Francis Forbes, May 8, 1814, SACP, file 2349, reel 8, LC.

83 W. N. Bruce, *Life of General Sir Charles Napier*, 60; Scott, *Recollections*, vol. 3:77; Surry County gentleman's letter, July 2, 1813, in *Richmond Enquirer*, July 6, 1813; "Invaders Retired," *Federal Gazette & Baltimore Daily Advertiser*, Sep. 1, 1813; "The Enemy in York River!" *National Intelligencer*, Nov. 29, 1813; Petrides and Downs, *Sea Soldier*, 185.

84 Scott, *Recollections*, vol. 3:120–21.

85 Sir John Borlase Warren to Lord Melville, June 23, 1813, MG 24, F 132, reel A-2076, LAC; "The Enemy in the York River," *Richmond Enquirer*, Nov. 26, 1813; Thomas Brown to George Cockburn, June 23, 1814, in Dudley, *Naval War of 1812*, vol. 3:122; William Boush, deposition, Feb. 12, 1824, RG 76, entry 190, box 4, case 282 (William Boush), USNA-CP; Thomas Bridges and James Wrightson, deposition, May 19, 1821, RG 76, entry 190, box 8, case 785 (Francis Wrightson), USNA-CP; J.P. Ferguson to William Bolling, Sep. 24, 1813, Bolling Papers, box 1, SC-DUL; Capt. A.R. Kerr to George Cockburn, June 22, 1814, SGCP, reel 9, LC; E.F. Chambers, deposition, July 3, 1828 ("into an intricate position"), RG 76, entry 190, box 9, case 862 (Richard Frisby), USNA-CP; Shomette, *Flotilla*, 141. For the slave who misled the militiamen, see Marine, *British Invasion of Maryland*, 150 ("for some gentleman").

86 Sir John Borlase Warren to Lord Melville, Feb. 25 ("The Black force") and Apr. 19, 1813 ("penetrate"), and [Thomas Barclay], "Intercepted Letter from Baltimore, dated Good Friday [1813]," MG 24, F 132, reel A-2076, LAC.

87 Sir Charles Napier quoted in W. N. Bruce, *Life of General Sir Charles Napier*, 62–63; P. Napier, *Henry at Sea*, 175.

88 John Barrow to Henry Goulburn, Sep. 30, 1813, with undated memorandum affixed apparently by Goulburn ("into"), Colonial Office 37 (Bermuda), vol. 71:89, NAUK; Sir John Borlase Warren to Lord Melville, Feb. 14, 1814, MG 24, F 132, reel A-2076, LAC; *Federal Gazette & Baltimore Daily Advertiser*, July 10, 1813; Edward Codrington, journal,

July 16, 1814, MG 24, F 131 (Codrington Letters), reel A-2076, LAC; Sir Alexander Cochrane, "Thoughts on American War," Apr. 27, 1812, Henry Dundas, Viscount Melville, Papers, HL; Morris, *Cockburn*, 98; Lambert, *Challenge*, 268.

89   Bartlett and Smith. "'Species of Milito-Nautico-Guerilla Warfare'" 176–77; Morriss, *Cockburn*, 96–47; Sir Alexander Cochrane quoted in Shomette, *Flotilla*, 71 ("I have it"); Bartlett, "Gentlemen versus Democrats," 152–53; Cochrane to the Admiralty, Mar. 25, 1814 ("They are a whining"), SACP, file 2345, reel 7, LC. For the escalation, see also Sir David Milne to George Home, Jan. 2 and 30, 1814, in Hume, "Letters Written during the War of 1812," 290, 291; Lambert, *Challenge*, 305.

90   Sir Alexander Cochrane to the Admiralty, Mar. 10 ("A little money") and Mar. 25, 1814, SACP, file 2345, reel 7, LC; George Cockburn to Sir Alexander Cochrane, Apr. 2, 1814 ("I do not think"), and Cochrane to Cockburn, Apr. 28, 1814, in Dudley, *Naval War of 1812*, vol. 3:43, 52; Sir Pulteney Malcolm to unknown, Oct. 3, 1814 ("Cochrane"), and Jan. 29, 1815, SPMP, box 1, WLCL-UM. For the shortfall in troops, see Bartlett, "Gentlemen versus Democrats," 152–54.

91   Sir Alexander Cochrane, proclamation, Apr. 2, 1814, in Dudley, *Naval War of 1812*, vol. 3:60; Cochrane to Lord Melville, Mar. 25, 1814 ("and bring the consequences"), SACP, file 2345, reel 7, LC.

92   Sir Alexander Cochrane to George Cockburn, Apr. 8, 1814, in Dudley, *Naval War of 1812*, 61; Cassel, "Slaves of the Chesapeake," 150; "Cochrane's Proclamation," *National Intelligencer*, May 19, 1814; Shomette, *Flotilla*, 72; G. A. Smith, *Slaves' Gamble*, 101–2.

93   Sir Alexander Cochrane, proclamation, Apr. 2, 1814, in Dudley, *Naval War of 1812*, vol. 3:60; Cochrane to Lord Melville, Mar. 25, 1814 ("in it I keep"), SACP, file 2345, reel 7, LC; Henry Goulburn to John Wilson Croker, Jan. 19, 1814, quoted in Weiss, "Cochrane and His Proclamation," 2–3.

94   Sir Alexander Cochrane to Lords of the Admiralty, Mar. 25, 1814, and Cochrane to John W. Croker, Feb. 26, 1815, SACP, file 2345, reel 7, and file 2348, reel 8, LC; Henry Bathurst to Edward Barnes, May 20, 1814, and Cochrane to Bathurst, July 14, 1814 ("I entirely Agree"), in Dudley, *Naval War of 1812*, vol. 3:73, 132; Weiss, "Corps of Colonial Marines," 89n5.

95   Henry Goulburn to John W. Croker, Jan. 19, 1814 ("receive on board"), quoted in Weiss, "Corps of Colonial Marines," 89n5; Joseph Nourse to George Cockburn, July 23, 1814, in Dudley, *Naval War of 1812*, vol. 3:159; Henry Bathurst to Robert Ross, Aug. 10, 1814, and Bathurst to Sir Alexander Cochrane, Oct. 26, 1814, SACP, file 2326, reel 1, LC.

96   Sir Alexander Cochrane to George Cockburn, May 27 and July 1, 1814

("Let the Landings"), in Dudley, *Naval War of 1812*, vol. 3:130; Cockburn to Lt. Boyd, May 5, 1814, and to Joseph Nourse, July 15, 1814 ("You are to encourage"), SGCP, reel 10, LC.

97 Sir Alexander Cochrane to George Prevost, Mar. 11, 1814, in Dudley, *Naval War of 1812*, vol. 3:40; Bartlett and Smith, "'Species of Milito-Nautico-Guerilla Warfare,'" 188–89; Whitfield, *Blacks on the Border*, 32–36.

CHAPTER SEVEN: PLANTATION

1 St. George Tucker to Joseph C. Cabell, Oct. 11, 1807, BFP, box 1, SSCL-UVA.

2 Dick Carter quoted in Joseph C. Cabell to the commissioners, Dec. 4, 1827, RG 76, entry 185, box 3, folder 6, USNA-CP. John Richeson served as Cabell's source for the incident. For Dick Carter's age, see [Cabell], *Argument in Support of the Claims of Joseph C. Cabell, St. George Tucker, Charles Carter and Others* (n.p., n.d.), in RG 76, entry 185, box 3, folder 6, USNA-CP.

3 Morton, *Robert Carter*, 7–31; Brewer, "Entailing Aristocracy," 330; P. Hamilton, *Making and Unmaking*, 93; Wharton, *Corotoman*, 8–13. For the size of the estate when owned by George Carter, see the Lancaster County land tax lists for 1786–1789, LV. For George Carter's death in 1788, see [John Coalter], "Legal Opinion re Title to a Slave Named Jenny," Randolph-Tucker Papers, RABC, box 7, item 2, HL.

4 St. George Tucker to Joseph C. Cabell, July 30 and Oct. 11, 1807 ("I never did" and "the complaints"), BFP, box 1, SSCL-UVA; P. Hamilton, *Making and Unmaking*, 93

5 George Gresham to St. George Tucker, Apr. 12 and Apr. 30, 1805 ("the best of any"), TCP, reel M-22, SCSL-CWM.

6 Lynn A. Nelson, "Joseph Carrington Cabell," in Sara B. Bearss et al. eds., *Dictionary of Virginia Biography* (Richmond: Library of Virginia, 2001), vol. 2:488–89; St. George Tucker to Joseph C. Cabell, Jan. 23, 1804, BFP, box 1, SSCL-UVA; William H. Cabell to J. C. Cabell, May 28, 1806, JCCFP (38-111-c), box 2, SSCL-UVA; J. C. Cabell to W. H. Cabell, Oct. 23, 1806, JCC&CFP (38-111), box 4, SSCL-UVA.

7 Joseph C. Cabell to William H. Cabell, Oct. 23, 1806, JCC&CFP (38-111), box 4, SSCL-UVA.

8 Joseph C. Cabell to William H. Cabell, Oct. 26, 1806, and St. George Tucker to J. C. Cabell, Oct. 28 and Nov. 3, 1806 (all quotations), JCC&CFP (38–111), box 4, SSCL-UVA; P. Hamilton, *Making and Unmaking*, 122.

9 Joseph C. Cabell to St. George Tucker, Oct. 31 ("the feelings," "unbounded," "the appearance," and "change the nature"), and Nov. 7, 1806, and J. C.

Cabell to William H. Cabell, Nov. 1, 1806 ("resist"), JCC&CFP (38-111), box 4, SSCL-UVA.

10   Joseph C. Cabell to St. George Tucker, Nov. 7, 1806, JCC&CFP (38-111), box 4, SSCL-UVA.

11   William H. Cabell to Joseph C. Cabell, Nov. 4 ("I am opposed") and Nov. 6, 1806, JCC&CFP (38-111), box 4, SSCL-UVA.

12   St. George Tucker to Joseph C. Cabell, Nov. 9, 1806, Cabell to Tucker, Nov. 9, 1806, Tucker to Cabell, Nov. 10, 1806 ("as well Slaves"), Cabell to Tucker, Nov. 10, 1806, and John Hartwell Cocke to Cabell, Nov. 17, 1806, JCC&CFP (38-111), box 4, SSCL-UVA.

13   L. A. Nelson, "Joseph Carrington Cabell," 488; P. Hamilton, *Making and Unmaking*, 130, 140; Cabell quoted in Wharton, *Corotoman*, 9.

14   Joseph C. Cabell to Isaac A. Coles, May 31, 1807 ("I fear"), JCC&CFP (38-111), box 4, SSCL-UVA; J. C. Cabell to Coles, Nov.16,1807, and Nov. 17, 1808, JCC&CFP (38–111), box 5, SSCL–UVA; J. C. Cabell to Coles, Nov. 29, 1809 ("The theater" and "I fear"), and John Hartwell Cocke to J. C. Cabell, Dec. 26, 1809, JCC&CFP (38-111), box 7, SSCL-UVA; William H. Cabell to J. C. Cabell, Nov. 21, 1807 ("I am certain"), JCCFP (38-111-c), box 2, SSCL-UVA; John Hartwell Cocke to Ann Barraud Cocke, Dec. 13, 1812 ("This place"), JCCFP (38-111-c), box 9, SSCL-UVA.

15   St. George Tucker to Joseph C. Cabell, Aug. 13, 1807, BFP, box 1, SSCL-UVA; Tucker to Cabell, Oct. 28, 1806, and Cabell to Isaac A. Coles, May 31, 1807, JCC&CFP (38-111), box 4, SSCL-UVA; Cabell to Coles, Nov. 29, 1809, and John Hartwell Cocke to Cabell, Dec. 26, 1809, JCC&CFP (38-111), box 7, SSCL-UVA; E. Brookes to Cabell, Jan. 16, 1809, TCP, reel M-24, SCSL-CWM; Tucker to Cabell, Sep. 20, 1807 ("It is utterly impossible"), BFP, box 1, SSCL-UVA.

16   Joseph C. Cabell to St. George Tucker, Oct. 14 and Oct. 19, 1807 ("The removal"), JCCFP (38-111-c), box 2, SSCL-UVA; Cabell to Nicholas Cabell, Nov. 6, 1807, JCC&CFP (38-111), box 5, SSCL-UVA; Wharton, *Corotoman*, 9; George Gresham to Tucker, Apr. 30, 1805, and Mar. 10, 1808, TCP, reels M-22 and M-24, SCSL-CWM.

17   St. George Tucker to Joseph C. Cabell, Aug. 13 and Oct. 11, 1807 ("not so well" and "Would it not"), BFP, box 1, SSCL-UVA.

18   Joseph C. Cabell to Isaac A. Coles, Nov. 16, 1807 ("I have met"), J. C. Cabell to Nicholas Cabell, Nov. 20, 1807, and J. C. Cabell to Coles, Jan. 8, 1808, JCC&CFP (38-111), box 5, SSCL-UVA; Charles Carter to St. George Tucker, Apr. 12, 1808, TCP, reel M-24, SCSL-CWM.

19   St. George Tucker to Joseph C. Cabell, Sep. 20 ("drown'd") and Oct. 11, 1807, BFP, box 1, SSCL-UVA; J. C. Cabell to Tucker, Oct. 19, 1807 ("That the Corotoman estate"), JCCCFP (38-111-c), box 2, SSSL-UVA;

J. C. Cabell to Nicholas Cabell, Nov. 6, 1807 ("plunderers"), and J. C. Cabell to Isaac A. Coles, Nov. 6, 1807 ("scoundrel"), JCC&CFP (38-111), box 5, SSCL-UVA; George Gresham to Tucker, Mar. 10, 1808, TCP, reel M-24, SCSL-CWM.

20   Joseph C. Cabell to Nicholas Cabell, Nov. 6, 1807 ("of families"), and J. C. Cabell to Isaac A. Coles, Jan. 8, 1808, JCC&CFP (38-111), box 5, SSCL-UVA; J. C. Cabell to N. Cabell, Jan. 7 and Jan. 27, 1808, JCC&CFP (38-111), box 6, SSCL-UVA; George Cabell to J. C. Cabell, Nov. 5, 1815 ("They were brought"), JCCFP (38-111-c), box 5, SSCL-UVA; J. C. Cabell to Langdon Cheves, Henry Sewall, and James Pleasants, Dec. 4, 1827 ("The insular situation"), RG 76, entry 185, box 3, folder 6, USNA-CP.

21   Joseph C. Cabell to Isaac A. Coles, Nov. 16, 1807, JCC&CFP (38-111), box 5, SSCL-UVA; Cabell to Coles, Jan. 27, 1808 ("to prevent"), JCC&CFP (38-111), box 6, SSCL-UVA; George Robertson to St. George Tucker, Feb. 2 and Mar. 12, 1808 ("hands on the plantation") TCP, reel M-24, SCSL-CWM; Tucker to Cabell, Feb. 8, 1808 ("a rebellious spirit"), BFP, box 1, SSCL-UVA.

22   George Robertson to St. George Tucker, Feb. 2 ("They are determined") and Mar. 12, 1808, TCP, reel M-24, SCSL-CWM; Joseph C. Cabell, "Note Relative to the Claim for Compensation for Slaves Carried Away from Corotoman," May 1823, in RG 76, entry 185, box 3, folder 6, USNA-CP; Tucker to Cabell, Feb. 8 and Feb. 12, 1808, BFP, box 1, SSCL-UVA.

23   St. George Tucker to Joseph C. Cabell, Feb. 12, 1808 ("To *strip*" and "Lightfoot"), BFP, box 1, SSCL-UVA; Tucker to Cabell, Oct. 8, 1808 ("As to every thing"), BFP, box 1, SSCL-UVA.

24   St. George Tucker to Joseph C. Cabell, May 27, 1807, Feb. 12, 1808 ("Bring Billy"), and Apr. 8, 1808, BFP, box 1, SSCL-UVA; George Robertson to Tucker, Mar. 12, 1808 ("he would"), TCP, reel M-24, SCSL-CWM.

25   Joseph C. Cabell to Nicholas Cabell, June 20, 1808 ("I found"), JCC&CFP (38-111), box 6, SSCL-UVA. For the sale of the slaves, see Ellison Currie to St. George Tucker, Aug. 25, 1808, TCP, reel M-24, SCSL-CWM. Currie reported that initially the buyer could offer only "Georgia & South Carolina notes," which indicates that he came from there to buy Virginia slaves. For Billy's subsequent presence at Corotoman, see Henry Richeson to St. George Tucker, Jan. 23, 1817 [*sic*: 1818], and John Richeson to Tucker, Feb. 22, 1818, TCP, reel M-28, SCSL-CWM.

26   Joseph C. Cabell to Isaac A. Coles, Dec. 1, 1808, JCC&CFP (38-111), box 5, SSCL-UVA; George Robertson to St. George Tucker, Dec. 18, 1808, TCP, reel M-24, SCSL-CWM; Cabell to Coles, Nov. 29, 1809 ("On

my arrival"), JCC&CFP (38-111), box 7, SSCL-UVA; Cabell to Tucker, July 31, 1810, TCP, reel M-25, SCSL-CWM.

27   Joseph C. Cabell to Isaac A. Coles, Nov. 29, 1809, and Cabell to John H. Cocke, Nov. 31, [*sic*] 1809, JCC&CFP (38-111), box 7, SSCL-UVA; Cabell to St. George Tucker, July 31, 1810 ("The Land"), TCP, reel M-25, SCSL-CWM. For the profits, see St. George Tucker to Charles Carter, May 25, 1812, TCP, box 31, SCSL-CWM.

28   Joseph C. Cabell to St. George Tucker, Jan. 29, 1811, Ms. 6038, SSCL-UVA.

29   Henry Skipwith to St. George Tucker, Sep. 9, 1804 ("Phylosopher Carter"), and Henry St. George Tucker to St. G. Tucker, Sep. 30, 1804 ("He is so fanciful"), TCP, reel M-21, SCSL-CWM; St. G. Tucker to Cabell, Feb. 8, 1808, BFP, box 1, SSCL-UVA. For Charles Carter in Europe, see St. G. Tucker to Joseph C. Cabell, June 19, 1806; John Rennolds to St. G. Tucker, Aug. 16, 1811, Carter to St. G. Tucker, Sep. 3, Nov. 8, and Dec. 11, 1811, TCP, box 31, SCSL-CWM.

30   Charles Carter to St. George Tucker, Dec. 5, 1806 ("I informed"), and Nov. 21, 1807 ("Many reasons"), TCP, reels M-23 and M-24, SCSL.

31   Charles Carter to St. George Tucker, Nov. 21, 1807, TCP, reels M-23 and M-24, SCSL. Although Tucker's letters to Carter do not survive, their content can be estimated from Carter's responses.

32   Joseph C. Cabell, June 8, 1812, JCCFP (38-111-c), box 8, SSCL-UVA; Dr. Philip Barraud to St. George Tucker, May n.d., 1812, and Charles Carter to Lelia Carter Tucker, Jan. 18, 1813, TCP, boxes 31 and 32, SCSL-CWM.

33   St. George Tucker to Lelia Tucker, Jan. 19, 1813, TCP, box 32, SCSL-CWM.

34   Joseph C. Cabell, "Notes Relative to the Claim for Compensation for Slaves Carried Away from Corotoman by the British Forces in the Late War," RG 76, entry 185, box 3, folder 6, USNA-CP; Wharton, *Corotoman*, 8–10; J. C. Cabell to Isaac A. Coles, June 8, 1812, JCCFP (38-111-c), box 8, SSCL-UVA; St. George Tucker to J. C. Cabell, Aug. 5, 1812, BFP, box 2, SSCL-UVA; St. G. Tucker to Charles Carter, Aug. 18, 1812, TCP, box 32, SCSL-CWM; St. G. Tucker to J. C. Cabell, Aug. 12, 1812 ("resting"), and Lelia Carter Tucker to Polly Cabell, Aug. 25, 1812, BFP, box 2, SSCL-UVA.

35   St. George Tucker to Joseph C. Cabell, Aug. 12, 1812, BFP, box 2, SSCL-UVA.

36   Lelia Carter Tucker to Polly Cabell, Aug. 25, 1812, BFP, box 2, SSCL-UVA; Joseph C. Cabell to John Hartwell Cocke, Sep. 15, 1812, JCCFP (38-111-c), box 9, SSCL-UVA.

37   Joseph C. Cabell, "Notes Relative to the Claim for Compensation for Slaves Carried Away from Corotoman by the British Forces in the Late War," RG 76, entry 185, box 3, folder 6, USNA-CP; John Richeson and Cabell, memorandum of agreement, Sep. 12, 1812, JCCFP (38-111-c), box 9, SSCL-UVA; Cabell to St. George Tucker, Dec. 26, 1812 ("uncertainty," "under the pretext," and "Richeson"), JCCFP (38-111-c), box 2, SSCL-UVA; Cabell to John Hartwell Cocke, Jan. 5, 1813 ("for incorrigible"), JCCFP (38-111-c), box 1, SSCL-UVA.

38   Joseph C. Cabell to John Hartwell Cocke, Sep. 20, 1812, JCCFP (38-111-c), box 1, SSCL-UVA; Charles Carter to St. George Tucker, Oct. 1, 1812, and J. H. Cocke to Tucker, Dec. 18, 1812, TCP, box 32, SCSL-CWM; J. H. Cocke to Ann Barraud Cocke, Dec. 13, 1812, JCCFP (38-111-c), box 9, SSCL-UVA; Lancaster County land tax list, 1814, LV.

39   Joseph C. Cabell to John Hartwell Cocke, Jan. 5, 1813, JCCFP (38-111-c), box 1, SSCL-UVA; Cabell to St. George Tucker, Jan. 12, 1812, JCCFP (38-111-c), box 2, NSCL-UVA; Cocke to Tucker, Jan. 22, 1812 [sic: a misdate for 1813 and misfiled by that misdate], TCP, box 31, SCSL-CWM.

40   Joseph C. Cabell to St. George Tucker, Feb. 4, 1813 ("I am lost"), TCP, box 32, SCSL-CWM; S. G. Tucker to J. C. Cabell, Feb. 8, 1813, and Lelia Tucker to Polly Cabell, Feb. 12, 1813, BFP, box 2, SSCL-UVA; J. C. Cabell to John Hartwell Cocke, May 25, 1813, JCCFP (38-111-c), box 1, SSCL-UVA.

41   Joseph C. Cabell to St. George Tucker, Feb. 13, 1813 ("Our situation" and "The negroes"), TCP, box 32, SCSL-CWM; Tucker to Cabell, Feb. 15, 1813, BFP, box 2, SSCL-UVA; Cabell to Isaac A. Coles, May 21, 1813, JCCFP (38-111-c), box 9, SSCL-UVA.

42   Joseph C. Cabell to John Hartwell Cocke, Nov. 16, 1813, JCCFP (38-111-c), box 10, SSCL-UVA.

43   Joseph C. Cabell to John Hartwell Cocke, Nov. 16, 1813, and Cocke to Cabell, Dec. 12, 1813, JCCFP (38-111-c), box 10, SSCL-UVA.

44   Joseph C. Cabell to John Hartwell Cocke, Nov. 16, 1813, JCCFP (38-111-c), box 10, SSCL-UVA.

45   William Lambert to William Jones, Apr. 22, 1814 ("it being"), RG 45, M 124, reel 62, USNA-DC; Joseph C. Cabell, "Notes Relative to the Claim for Compensation for Slaves Carried Away from Corotoman by the British Forces in the Late War," RG 76, entry 185, box 3, folder 6, USNA-CP; John Richeson to St. George Tucker, Apr. 20, 1814, JCCFP (38-111-c), box 10, SSCL-UVA. Richeson's letter sets the first escape as on the morning of April 20, but Cabell subsequently insisted that Richeson was mistaken and that it occurred on April 18. For the ages of the first three runaways, see Richeson, "List of Negroes," RG 76, entry 185, box 3, folder 5, USNA-CP.

46   John Richeson to St. George Tucker, Apr. 22, 1814, RG 76, entry 185, box
      3, folder 5, USNA-CP; Joseph C. Cabell, "Notes Relative to the Claim
      for Compensation for Slaves Carried Away from Corotoman by the Brit-
      ish Forces in the Late War," RG 76, entry 185, box 3, folder 6, USNA-CP;
      William Lambert to William Jones, Apr. 22 and Apr. 29, 1814, RG 45, M
      124, reel 62, USNA-DC.

47   Joseph C. Cabell to John Hartwell Cocke, Apr. 28, 1814 ("The 43"),
      JCCFP (38-111-c), box 10, SSCL-UVA; John Richeson, "List of
      Negroes," and William H. Richardson, "List of Negroes of Dr. Charles
      Carter," RG 76, entry 185, box 3, folder 5, USNA-CP; Joseph C. Cabell,
      "Notes Relative to the Claim for Compensation for Slaves Carried Away
      from Corotoman by the British Forces in the Late War," and Joseph C.
      Cabell to the Board of Commissioners, Dec. 4, 1827, RG 76, entry 185,
      box 3, folder 6, USNA-CP. Cabell's quotation overstates the number of
      slaves lost from his and Tucker's portion by 1; rather than 43 the true
      number was 42. For the pregnant runaway from Corotoman, see "Mr.
      Crawford's Statement," *National Intelligencer*, May 16, 1814.

48   For the firefight at the end of the raid, see William Lambert to James Bar-
      bour, Apr. 22, 1814, in *Richmond Enquirer*, Apr. 30, 1814.

49   Carter friend's report conveyed in Sally Skipwith Kennon Sinclair to
      Ellen Mordecai, May 1, 1814 ("the rest"), in [Anonymous], "Kennon
      Letters," 366; John Richeson, "List of Negroes," and William H. Rich-
      ardson, "List of Negroes of Dr. Charles Carter," RG 76, entry 185, box
      3, folder 5, USNA-CP; George Robertson, deposition, May 22, 1821,
      APA-GMR, 1811–1812, entry 258, box 779, LV. After the war, Cabell
      gathered information on the family relationships of the Corotoman run-
      aways. At his behest, two local notables, Addison Hall and James Kelley,
      "diligently enquired among the slaves" who remained behind to recon-
      stitute "the names, surnames, nicknames & connections of the negroes"
      who had left. Their report revealed family dynamics and structures ordi-
      narily opaque to the uninterested masters. See Addison Hall and James
      Kelley, deposition, Feb. 21, 1828, and Joseph C. Cabell, *Argument in
      Support of the Claims of Joseph C. Cabell, St. George Tucker, Charles
      Carter and Others* (n.p., n.d.), in RG 76, entry 185, box 3, folder 6,
      USNA-CP. For a fuller discussion of the family relationships, see appen-
      dix A at the end of this book.

50   Joseph C. Cabell, "Notes Relative to the Claim for Compensation for
      Slaves Carried Away from Corotoman by the British Forces in the Late
      War," and Richard Carter quoted in Cabell to the Board of Commission-
      ers, Dec. 4, 1827, RG 76, entry 185, box 3, folder 6, USNA-CP.

51   St. George Tucker to Charles Carter, May 25, 1812, and Tucker to John Hartwell Cocke and Henry Skipwith, Nov. 13, 1812, TCP, boxes 31 and 32, SCSL-UVA; Tucker to Joseph C. Cabell, May 16, June 1, and June 8, 1814 ("to respectable farmers"), JCCFP (38-111-c), box 10, SSCL-UVA. For Sir Peyton Skipwith's gift of Jenny to Lelia, see [John Coalter], "Legal Opinion re Title to a Slave Named Jenny," Randolph-Tucker Papers, Brock Collection, box 7, item 2, HL.

52   Joseph C. Cabell, "Explanatory Notes Touching the Claim for Slaves Carried Off by the British Forces from Corrottoman on Rappahannock River in Virginia," July 3, 1824 ("carried forcibly"), and [Cabell], *Argument in Support of the Claims of Joseph C. Cabell, St. George Tucker, Charles Carter and Others* (n.p., n.d.), in RG 76, entry 185, box 3, folder 6, USNA-CP; "The Inhuman Enemy," *Richmond Enquirer,* May 11, 1814.

53   St. George Tucker to Joseph C. Cabell, Apr. 24, 1814 ("unhappy wretches"), Tucker to John Richeson, Apr. 24, 1814, and Cabell to John Hartwell Cocke, Apr. 28, 1814, JCCFP (38-111-c), box 10, SSCL-UVA.

54   St. George Tucker to John Richeson, Apr. 24, 1814, and Tucker to Joseph C. Cabell, Apr. 24 ("Situated"), Apr. 27, May 6, and June 8, 1814 ("I cannot" and "Have I ever"), JCCFP (38-111-c), box 10, SSCL-UVA.

55   St. George Tucker to Joseph C. Cabell, Apr. 27, 1814, and John Coalter to Cabell, Apr. 28, 1814 (all quotations), JCCFP (38-111-c), box 10, SSCL-UVA. Coalter sent his letter to Tucker to forward to Cabell.

56   Joseph C. Cabell to John Hartwell Cocke, Apr. 30 ("What a scene") and May 14, 1814 ("The estate"), JHCFP, box 16, SSCL-UVA; Cabell, "Account of Expences of the Removal of the Corotoman Negroes That Arrived at Warminster," May 6–20, 1814, and Richard Powell to Cabell, July 9, 1814, RABC, box 48, folders 5 and 7, HL; Lelia Tucker to Polly Cabell, May 16, 1814, JCCFP (38-111-c), box 10, SSCL-UVA; "List of Negroes Hired in Lynchburg, Summer 1814 till 1 Jan. 1815," Cabell Family Papers, RABC, box 48, folder 5, HL.

Chapter Eight: Flight

1   Mrs. T. B. Glasscock to Sarah Barryman, Dec. 4, 1814, Mss 2 G4616 b, VHS.

2   T. A. Mason, "Luminary of the Northern Neck," 3978–82 (includes the quotation from the *Richmond Enquirer*).

3   Joseph C. Cabell to John Hartwell Cocke, Nov. 16, 1813, JCCFP (38-111-c), box 10, SSCL-UVA; depositions of Walter Jones, May 8, 1815, and John C. Hudson, May 8, 1815, APA-GMR, entry 247, box 778, Northumberland County folder, LV; John Tapscott, deposition, Dec.

6, 1827, RG 76, entry 190, box 5, case 373 (Walter Jones), USNA-CP; Robert Murphy, deposition, May 28, 1821 ("uncommonly likely" and "Washington"), APA-GMA, entry 258, box 779, Westmoreland County folder, LV.

4   Robert Murphy, deposition, May 28, 1821, APA-GMA, entry 258, box 779, Westmoreland County folder, LV; Walter Jones to James Monroe, Dec. 10, 1814, JMP, ser. 1, reel 5, LC; Hadden, *Slave Patrols*, 162.

5   "From Below," *Federal Gazette & Baltimore Daily Advertiser*, Sep. 3, 1813 ("for the purpose"); Petrides and Downs, *Sea Soldier*, 174 ("band playing"); Basil Halton, deposition, Nov. 25, 1824, RG 76, entry 190, box 7, case 630 (Walter Edelen), USNA-CP; depositions of John Hunt, June 19, 1815, and Mary K. Hall, Nov. 22, 1827, RG 76, entry 190, box 5, case 340 (William Gibson), USNA-CP; Robert Barrie to John Wilson Croker, Oct. 1, 1815, MG 16 (FO 5), vol. 111:298, reel B-2006, LAC.

6   For the Hampton mail boat, see the depositions of Charles M. Collier, May 26, 1814, and John Bully, Aug. 23, 1827, and Feb. 20, 1828, RG 76, entry 190, box 3, case 129 (John Skinner), USNA-CP; "Norfolk, July 9," *Federal Gazette & Baltimore Daily Advertiser*, July 13, 1813. For the navy boat, see John Chandler, deposition, May 13, 1824, RG 76, entry 190, box 5, case 349 (Thomas Chandler), USNA-CP; Chandler to James Madison, Sep. 13, 1813, RG 76, entry 190, box 5, case 409 (John Chandler), USNA-CP. For Parrott's boat, see John Parrott, deposition, Feb. 19, 1828, RG 76, entry 190, case 584 (Susanna Mayo), USNA-CP. For the Potomac boat, see Ephraim Brown, deposition, Apr. 25, 1823, RG 76, entry 190, box 4, case 206 (Ann Thompson), USNA-CP.

7   For Golden's story, see depositions of Dr. Isaac Rawlings, May 4, 1821, and Ellen Clark and John Ireland, Apr. 3, 1828, RG 76, entry 190, box 6, case 562, USNA-CP. For the similar retrievals by Joshua Cormick and Jacob Silence in June 1813, see Malcomson, "Freedom by Reaching the Wooden World," 2.

8   For the Roots case, see the depositions of William Sebastian, Jan. 25 and Apr. 3, 1828 ("did watch"), RG 76, entry 190, box 7, case 645 (Jesse McKenny), USNA-CP; *ASP-FR*, vol. 5:814. Between 25 and 30 years old, Roots had belonged to Jesse McKenny.

9   Zachariah Southoron, deposition, Apr. 5, 1815 ("if he was not preparing" and "No that he had been promised"), RG 76, entry 190, box 7, case 606 (John Dare), USNA-CP; Scott, *Recollections*, vol. 3:118–19.

10   John Stoddert to Alexander Greer, Apr. 20, 1823, and depositions of Greer, May 5, 1823, and Walter Mitchell, Feb. 12, 1828, RG 76, entry 190, box 7, case 632 (Alexander Greer), USNA-CP; Scott, *Recollections*, vol. 3:118; John Mercer to Levin Winder, Aug. 30, 1814, LWP, box 1, MdHS; George

Cockburn to Robert Barrie, Mar. 26, 1814, Robert Barrie Papers, box 1, WLCL-UM; Cockburn to Capt. Watts, Apr. 27, 1814, SGCP, reel 10, LC; John Crawford, statement, in *Richmond Enquirer*, May 11, 1814; David Hardgrave, deposition, May 30, 1814, in Flournoy, *CVSP*, vol. 10:333; Littleton W. Tazewell to James Monroe, Oct. 12, 1814, JMP, ser. 1, reel 7, LC; Ball, *Fifty Years in Chains*, 470–71. For eyewitness accounts closer in time to the escape described by Ball, see the depositions of Samuel Cranford, June 6, 1823, and James Hollingshead, June 12, 1823, RG 76, entry 190, box 8, case 786 (Martha Wilson), USNA-CP; *ASP-FR*, vol. 5:806.

11   Depositions of William Boush, Feb. 12, 1824, and James Collins, Nov. 3, 1827 ("had emptied"), RG 76, entry 190, box 4, case 282 (William Boush), USNA-CP. For Bibles, see the depositions of Thomas Oldham, Sep. 10, 1827, and Henry H. Travers, Sep. 10, 1827, RG 76, entry 190, box 5, case 426 (B. M. Leland), USNA-CP.

12   Mordecai A. Jones, depositions, Aug. 25, 1821, and June 26, 1828, RG 76, entry 190, box 7, case 639 (Mordecai Jones), and box 5, case 347 (Robert Dunkinson), USNA-CP; John Price, deposition, June 12, 1821, RG 76, entry 190, box 7, case 628 (William Dixon), USNA-CP; [R. J. Barrett], "Naval Recollections," 467 ("the mournful picture"); Scott, *Recollections*, vol. 3:119.

13   Levin J. Thomas, deposition, Feb. 21, 1825 ("so soon"), RG 76, entry 190, box 4, case 315 (Thomas Badger), USNA-CP; William S. Williams, Jan. 14, 1828, RG 76, entry 190, box 6, case 523 (William Nottingham Jr.), USNA-CP. For the Hampton capture, see "Propositions!" *Richmond Enquirer*, July 30, 1813.

14   James and George Denton, deposition, Jan. 22, 1828 ("a short time"), RG 76, entry 190, box 6, case 556 (James D. Denton), USNA-CP; *ASP-FR*, vol. 5:803.

15   "Private Correspondence," *National Intelligencer*, Aug. 30, 1813; Caleb Jones, deposition, Apr. 5, 1815, RG 76, entry 190, box 7, case 638 (Caleb Jones), USNA-CP. The raid yielded six more slaves: Job (24 years old), Lucy (24), Peter (20), Suckey (19), Abraham (8), and James (7). For Point Lookout, see Eshelman, Sheads, and Hickey, *War of 1812 in the Chesapeake*, 173–75.

16   John Rousby Plater to John Quincy Adams, June 30, 1821, and the depositions of Plater, June 23, 1821 ("a most valuable" and "a black smith"), and Joseph Brewer, June 23, 1821, RG 76, entry 190, box 4, case 310 (John Rousby Plater), USNA-CP; Eshelman, Sheads, and Hickey, *War of 1812 in the Chesapeake*, 201; Joseph Nourse to George Cockburn, July 23, 1814, in Dudley, *Naval War of 1812*, vol. 3:159. I have categorized those 16 and older as women or men and those younger as children. For the

newspaper account of Plater's discussion with the British captain, see "Extract of a Letter from a Gentleman of St. Mary's to the Editor," *Federal Gazette & Baltimore Daily Advertiser*, June 24, 1814.

17   For the story of Benjamin and Cecelia, see Bennet Sollers, deposition, Aug. 26, 1823, RG 76, entry 190, box 8, case 797 (Walter Helen), USNA-CP. For Joe Lane's family, see the depositions of William Ball, June 13, 1815, and John Grinstead, Apr. 18, 1828, RG 76, entry 190, box 9, case 801 (Mottram Ball), USNA-CP. For the story of Sall and her children, see Mary G. Wilkins, deposition, Jan 26, 1828, RG 76, entry 185, box 3, folder 7, USNA-CP. For other cases of divided slave couples reunited by escape, see Charles Brown, deposition, Dec. 29, 1827, RG 76, entry 190, box 6, case 503 (Trueman Taylor), USNA-CP; depositions of William Boush, Aug. 30, 1827, and D. C. Barraud, Nov. 2, 1827, RG 76,, entry 190, box 3, case 194 (Elisabeth J. Nimmo), USNA-CP.

18   Edward Lee, William Hawkins, and James Burke, deposition, Sep. 24, 1827 ("At the same time"), RG 76, entry 190, box 3, case 198 (Robert Dunn), USNA-CP. For Lucy and Paul, see Edward Richman, deposition, Dec. 7, 1827, RG 76, entry 185, box 4, folder 14, USNA-CP. Northampton County produced 34 surviving depositions about runaway slaves during 1813. In 6 of them, the witnesses merely report visiting warships where they saw runaways. In the rest of the depositions (28) the witnesses say something about the conditions of escape. In 21 of the 28, the witnesses report slaves escaping in a cluster from multiple farms on the same night. For the depositions, see Northampton County folder, RG 3 (Office of the Governor), depositions, 1814–1821 (accession no. 1151894), LV. See especially the deposition of Levin Winder, Feb. 13, 1814.

19   Samuel Jackson, deposition, Apr. 7, 1828, RG 76, entry 190, box 4, case 224 (John Jones), USNA-CP; Thomas Peterkin, deposition, Nov. 8, 1824 (Thomas Primrose), RG 76, entry 190, box 10, case 1020 (Thomas Primrose), USNA-CP; Thomas Griffin, deposition, Nov. 19, 1822, RG 76, entry 190, case 734 (Thomas Griffin), USNA-CP. For Jim Bruce, see Henry A. Callis, deposition, Nov. 15, 1824, RG 76, entry 190, box 7, case 701 (Anthony Addison), USNA-CP. For the role of family ties as either inhibiting or enabling flight, see Schermerhorn, *Money over Mastery*, 50–51.

20   Mrs. Alletha Smith, deposition, Mar. 1, 1828, RG 76, entry 190, box 6, case 569 (Susanna Rawlings), USNA-CP; *ASP-FR*, vol. 5:802, 805.

21   For the Carter estate slaves, see the depositions of Richard Clarke, Apr. 9, 1828, Old Tom, Apr. 9, 1828, and Simon Willis, Apr. 17, 1828, RG 76, entry 190, box 9, case 811 (Charles B. Carter estate), USNA-CP. For the Turberville estate slaves, see the depositions of Vincent T. Branson, Apr.

29, 1823 ("that every Negroe" and "that all the women"), and John Murphy, May 2, 1823, RG 76, entry 190, box 8, case 720 (John Turberville Sr.), USNA-CP. For their gender as indicated by their names (and in a few cases their age), see *ASP-FR*, vol. 5:817. A Virginia state accounting for 1,198 runaways claimed by 400 owners finds that 105 of the latter were widows or estates, and they lost a total of 363 slaves, or 3.5 per owner (compared to 2.8 per owner for the rest). See "List of Depositions Related to Slaves and Other Property Plundered by the Enemy during the Late War, 1812," B 1054672, Auditor of Public Accounts (RG 48), LV.

22   Scott, *Recollections*, vol. 3:119-20. For a husband separated from his wife during an escape, see W. Settle, deposition, Mar. 4, 1828, RG 76, entry 190, box 7, case 696 (William B. Tomlin), USNA-CP.

23   The data come from many depositions, primarily taken by Bartholomew McCarty as county clerk, in which the deponent often (but not always) provides information about skin color and occupation and age. No other county clerk recorded skin color as frequently as McCarty did. It is possible that McCarty and the deponents tended to record skin color more often for the lighter-skinned, but there are depositions in which only a few of the slaves receive a skin designation and that designation is "black." Does that suggest that the others listed on that deposition without a recorded skin color were *not* "black"? If so, McCarty's data underestimates the proportion of the light-skinned. In 66 of the 106 cases, he also reports a primary occupation for the runaway. As expected, mixed-race people prevailed among the county's escaped house servants: 8 (80 percent) of 10. But they were surprisingly numerous among the runaway artisans—6 (43 percent) of 14—and even the field hands: 17 (40 percent) of 42. In 40 of the 106 cases, where McCarty noted color, he either neglected to record occupation (n = 9) *or* listed the children as "houseboy" or "housegirl" (n = 31), which means they did light chores and were not proper "house servants," who were adults. In the case of the children, 11 (35 percent) of 31 were light-skinned. See APA-GMR, entry 258 (List of Furloughs and Discharges), box 779, Richmond County folder, LV.

24   Depositions of William S. Teackle and Thomas H. Floyd, Oct. 20, 1827 (all quotations), and Southey Goffigan, Nov. 5, 1824, RG 76, entry 190, box 4, case 257 (John K. Floyd), USNA-CP.

25   Depositions of Levin G. Winder, Feb. 13, 1815, and Peggy Collins, Dec. 27, 1827 (includes Arthur Jacob quote), RG 76, case 542 (John H. Winder), USNA-CP. Ownership of the 16 was divided between John H. Winder and his father, John. See *ASP-FR*, vol. 5:817.

26   Richard Ross, deposition, Sep. 24, 1821 (Thomas Perks), RG 76, entry 190, box 8, case 789 (Richard Ross), USNA-CP; William Sudler, deposi-

tion, Apr. 28, 1823, RG 76, entry 190, box 8, case 776 (Thomas K. Carroll), USNA-CP; Richard Frisby to John Quincy Adams, May 26, 1821, RG 76, entry 190, box 9, case 862 (Richard Frisby), USNA-CP.

27   Depositions of Thomas Archer, June 21, 1814, and Samuel S. Griffin, Aug. 15, 1814 ("the highest value"), APA-GMR, entry 258, box 779, York County folder, LV.

28   Greenberg, "Name, Face, Body," 4.

29   For works that emphasize African survivals late into the eighteenth century, see Rucker, *River Flows On*; Sidbury, "Saint Domingue in Virginia," 531–52; Sobel, *World They Made Together*.

30   Joseph C. Cabell, "Narrative of the Arrest of Michael Gleason," Aug. 6, 1821 ("calling me"), and Cabell to William Wirt, Feb. 18, 1828, JCC&CFP (38-111), box 14, SSCL-UVA.

31   John Cowper to Joseph C. Cabell, Oct. 5, 1827, JCC&CFP (38-111), box 19, SSCL-UVA; Greenberg, "Name, Face, Body," 4–5; [Wirt], *Argument in Support of the Chesapeake Claims*, 25–26, in RG 76, entry 185, box 3, folder 6, USNA-CP.

32   D. C. Barraud, deposition, Nov. 2, 1827 ("it is most common"), RG 76, entry 190, box 3, case 194 (Elizabeth J. Nimmo), USNA-CP; W. Williams Jr. and Thomas James, deposition, Nov. 17, 1827, RG 76, entry 190, box 8, case 784 (Samuel Beauchamp), USNA-CP; Gideon White, deposition, Mar. 15, 1828, RG 76, entry 190, box 8, case 737 (Arthur T. Jones), USNA-CP.

33   Swenson Whitehead, statement, n.d. ("Slaves in Virginia"), RG 76, entry 190, box 3, case 193 (John Johnston), USNA-CP; Augustine Neale, statement, n.d. ("These negroes"), RG 76, entry 190, box 5, case 440 (Warren Hudnall), USNA-CP; Neale, memorandum, Mar. 14, 1828, RG 76, entry 190, box 6, case 475 (Pemberton Claughton), USNA-CP.

34   C. C. Lee memorandum, May 19, 1828, RG 76, Entry 190, box 6, case 502 (Ann and Elizabeth McCarty), USNA-CP.

35   "Norfolk, May 7," "Advices from Point Look-Out," and "From Below," *National Intelligencer*, May 12, 1813 ("One would" and "constantly at hard labor"), Aug. 25 and Aug. 26, 1813; "Interesting," and "Our Slaves," *Richmond Enquirer*, Sep. 14 and Dec. 16, 1813 ("perfect freedom"); M. Mason, "Battle of the Slaveholding Liberators," 673-74; G A. Smith, *Slaves' Gamble*, 92, 97.

36   James Barbour, speech to the House of Delegates, Dec. 22, 1813, Executive Letter Book, 14, RG 3 (Office of the Governor), reel 3011 LV. For alleged cases of British officers boasting of their income from selling runaways, see Joseph C. Cabell to St. George Tucker, Nov. 24, 1813, TCP, box 33, SCSL-CWM; John Hamilton Brown, deposition, Apr. 4, 1815, RG 76, entry 185,

box 4, folder 13, USNA-CP; Michael Taney, deposition, Aug. 11, 1815, RG 76, entry 190, box 6, case 514 (Michael Taney Sr.), USNA-CP.

37 "To a Member of the House of Delegates," *Virginia Argus,* Jan. 29, 1814.

38 John G. Joynes to James Barbour, July 29, 1813, JBEP, reel 5515, LV; Council of State Record Book, p. 308 (July 29, 1813), RG 75, reel 2990, LV. For other examples of free blacks preferring to stay home rather than go away with the British, see Toby Richards, deposition, Nov. 4, 1823, RG 76, entry 190, box 10, case 986 (Morton A. Waring), USNA-CP.

39 John Shaw reminiscence in Whitfield, *Blacks on the Border,* 37; Caroline Shearman's Davy, deposition, July 4, 1828, RG 76, entry 190, case 962 (Joseph Shearman estate), USNA-CP.

40 [Anonymous], "Recollections of the Expedition," 28.

41 Jesse Baker, deposition, May 31, 1821, RG 76, entry 190, box 7, case 641 (Joshua King), USNA-CP; Thomas M. Harris, deposition, Oct. 12, 1821, RG 76, entry 190, box 7, case 608 (George Wilkinson), USNA-CP.

42 Depostions of Levin W. Ballard, Apr. 7, 1815 ("had requested" and "against her will"), and May 15, 1821, and of Mary W. Hodgkin, Dec. 7, 1827, RG 76, entry 190, box 8, case 718 (Elizabeth Ballard), USNA-CP.

43 John C. Crump, deposition, Oct. 18, 1823, RG 76, entry 190, box 6, case 573 (John C. Crump), USNA-CP; Caleb Jones, deposition, Apr. 5, 1815, RG 76, entry 190, box 7, case 638 (Caleb Jones), USNA-CP; John Hamilton Brown, deposition, Apr. 4, 1815 ("kitchen"), RG 76, entry 185, box 4, folder 13, USNA-CP; Anthony quoted in Jesse Baker, deposition, May 31, 1821, RG 7, entry 190, box 7, case 641 (Joshua King), USNA-CP.

44 Nathaniel Washington, deposition, Apr. 7, 1815, RG 76, entry 190, box 7, case 652 (Nathaniel Washington), USNA-CP; Arthur Tilghman Jones, deposition, Oct. 9, 1823, RG 76, entry 190, box 8, case 737 (Arthur Tilghman Jones), USNA-CP.

45 "Movements of the Enemy," *Federal Gazette & Baltimore Daily Advertiser,* July 28, 1814 ("Under the direction"); depositions of William Kilgour, Sep. 7, 1815, and H. S. Boteler, May 15, 1821, RG 76, entry 190, box 7, case 622 (H. S. Boteler), USNA-CP.

46 Depositions of William Kilgour, Sep. 7, 1815 and H. S. Boteler, May 15, 1821, RG 76, entry 190, box 7, case 622 (H. S. Boteler), USNA-CP.

47 B. Contee to James Monroe, Oct. 7, 1814, RG 59, M 179, reel 30, USNA-CP; Ezekiel Chambers, deposition, May 21, 1821, RG 76, entry 190, box 8, case 737 (Arthur T. Jones), USNA-CP.

48 Vincent Bramham, deposition, Nov. 8, 1827, RG 76, entry 185, box 3, folder 4, USNA-CP; Dr. Benjamin Williams, deposition, Apr. 7, 1815, RG 76, entry 190, box 6, case 490 (Dr. Benjamin Williams), USNA-CP. For other cases of apparent force, see Mary L. Saunders, deposition, Oct.

29, 1827, RG 76, entry 190, box 5, case 391 (George Yerby), USNA-CP; Michael Taney, deposition, Aug. 11, 1815, RG 76, entry 190, box 6, case 514, USNA-CP.

49 Walter Jones to Augustine Neale, June 8, 1815, RG 76, entry 185, box 4, folder 13, USNA-CP.

50 John T. Keeling, deposition, Nov. 4, 1822, RG 76, entry 190, box 4, case 241 (Lemuel Cornick), USNA-CP; Hezekiah Smoot, deposition, June 16, 1818, RG 76, entry 190, box 9, case 185 (Thomas Smith), USNA-CP; deposition of Nicholas Cook, May 16, 1821 ("the artifices"), and James Roney, Dec. 16, 1822 ("replied"), RG 76, entry 190, box 4, case 235 (Nicholas Cook), USNA-CP; John Chandler, deposition, May 13, 1824, RG 76, entry 190, box 5, case 349 (Thomas Chandler), USNA-CP; Joseph C. Cabell, "Explanatory Notes Touching the Claim for Slaves Carried off by the British Forces from Corrottoman on Rappahannock River in Virginia," July 3, 1824, RG 76, entry 185, box 3, folder 6, USNA-CP; Ball, *Fifty Years in Chains*, 472.

51 George Scherer, deposition, May 26, 1820, RG 76, entry 190, box 7, case 709 (Mathew Beard), USNA-CP; Thomas Whittington, deposition, Oct. 18, 1823, RG 76, entry 190, box 9, case 818 (Thomas Whittington), USNA-CP; Ball, *Fifty Years in Chains*, 469; Commodore Beresford quoted in Thomas Peterkin, deposition, Nov. 8, 1824 ("was under the protection"), RG 76, entry 190, box 10, case 1020 (Thomas Primrose), USNA-CP; Kendall Addison to John Borlase Warren, May 14, 1813, and Warren to Addison, May 16, 1813, MG 12, Admiralty 1, vol. 503:283, 284, reel B-1448, LAC.

52 Thomas Holmes, deposition, Mar. 12, 1828, RG 76, entry 190, box 8, case 791 (Ann Gaines, widow of Ambrose Gaines), USNA-CP. For reports of politeness, see John Turberville to George Cockburn, Nov. 4, 1813, William Middleton to Turberville, Nov. 6, 1813, and Thomas R. Yeatman to Christopher Tompkins, Mar. 11, 1814, in Flournoy, *CVSP*, vol. 10:283, 284, 307; Ball, *Fifty Years in Chains*, 470-72; Lelia Tucker to Mary W. Cabell, May 16, 1814, JCCFP (38-111), box 10, SSCL-CWM.

53 British captain quoted in Hugues Lavergne, deposition, Nov. 26, 1824, RG 76, entry 190, box 8, case 763 (Louis Dolives), USNA-CP; Arthur Smith, deposition, Aug. 5, 1822, APC-GMR, entry 258, box 779, Isle of Wight County folder, LV; depositions of John C. Crump, Oct. 18, 1823, and Arthur Smith, May 3, 1826, RG 76, entry 190, box 6, case 573 (John C. Crump), USNA-CP; Scott, *Recollections*, vol. 3:129-30.

54 John Goodall, deposition, Feb. 25, 1824, APA-GMR, entry 258, box 779, Elizabeth City County folder, LV; John G. Joynes, deposition, Dec. 2, 1827, RG 76, entry 190, box 5, case 345, USNA-CP; Ball, *Fifty Years in*

Chains, 472; Joseph C. Cabell to John Hartwell Cocke, Nov. 16, 1813, JCCFP (38-111-C), box 10, SSCL-UVA. Joseph Nourse to George Cockburn, Aug. 12, 1814, SGCP, reel 9, LC. The one conspicuous exception came in the last month of the war, when a group of slaves captured on a mail boat near Hampton chose to return to their masters, to the amazement of the Virginia newspapers. See "Norfolk, Jan. 6," *Richmond Enquirer*, Jan. 11, 1815, *Niles' Weekly Register,* vol. 7:319 (Jan. 14, 1815).

55   Thomas Archer, deposition, Apr. 1, 1815, RG 76, entry 190, box 8, case 734 (Thomas Griffin), USNA-CP; Hezekiah Smoot, deposition, Feb. 5, 1828, RG 76, entry 185, box 3, folder 8, USNA-CP; William A. Christian, deposition, Feb. 18, 1825, RG 76, entry 190, box 4, case 296 (Thomas Parramour), USNA-CP; Joseph C. Cabell to St. George Tucker, Nov. 24, 1813 ("that they"), TCP, box 33, SCSL-CWM; Cabell, "Explanatory Notes Touching the Claim for Slaves Carried Off by the British Forces from Corrottoman on Rappahannock River in Virginia," July 3, 1824, RG 76, entry 185, box 3, folder 6, USNA-CP.

56   Armistead Smith to William Patterson Smith, Feb. 5 (the quotations) and Feb. 12, 1814, WPSP, box 1, SC-DUL. For Humphrey as the name of "Brooks's fellow," see the postwar compensation claim of John Brooks in *ASP-FR*, vol. 5:809.

57   Benjamin Mason quoted in the depositions of Benjamin W. Hushaw, Jan. 18, 1828 ("had been treated"), and John G. Mackell, Jan. 19, 1828 ("that the negroes"), RG 76, entry 185, box 4, folder 15, USNA-CP.

58   Charles M. Collier, deposition, Dec. 29, 1822 ("almost the entire"), APA-GMR, entry 258, box 779, LV; Martha Dilson, deposition, Mar. 20, 1828, RG 76, entry 190, box 8, case 753 (Mary Blake, widow of Thomas Blake), USNA-CP; depositions of Benjamin Hewitt, Mar. 6, 1824, and James Hughes, Mar. 4, 1823, RG 76, entry 190, box 9, case 842 (Elizabeth Barnhouse), USNA-CP; Houlder Hudgins, petition to the state legislature, Dec. 5, 1815, Virginia General Assembly Legislative Petitions, box 159, folder 15 (Mathews County) reel 122, LV; Milia Palmer to unknown, n.d., RG 76, entry 190, box 5, case 435 (William Palmer), USNA-CP; *ASP-FR*, vol. 5:815; Ann Massey, deposition, June 11, 1823, RG 76, entry 190, box 6, case 563 (Lee Massey), USNA-CP; John C. Cabell to John Hartwell Cocke, Nov. 16, 1813, JCCFP (38-111-c), box 10, SSCL-UVA; James Barbour, speech to the House of Delegates, Dec. 22, 1813, Executive Letter Book, p. 14, RG 3 (Office of the Governor), reel 3011, LV.

59   Armistead Smith to William Patterson Smith, Feb. 12, 1814, WPSP, box 1, SC-DUL; Himmelheber, "Sotterley Plantation," 92; Walter Jones to John Tayloe, Aug. 12, 1814, WHWP, box 2, MdHS; Mrs. T. B. Glasscock to Sarah Barryman, Nov. 11, 1814, Mss 2 G4616 b, VHS; St. George Tucker

to John Coalter, Dec. 26, 1814, Mss 1 G8855 e 28-52, VHS; Philip Barraud to Tucker, Aug. 16 and 30, 1814, TCP, box 33, SCSL-CWM; Nicholas Faulcon to John Hartwell Cocke, July 25, 1814 ("I am at a loss"), and Sep. 13, 1814, JHCFP, boxes 16 and 17, SSCL-UVA; Landon Carter to Robert Wormely Carter, July 30, 1814, Carter and Wellford Family of Sabine Hall Papers, box 3, SSCL-UVA.

60   Lancaster County Court papers, court orders, vol. 24:91 (June 16, 1812), 157 (July 21, 1813), 159 (July 19, 1813), reel 39, LV; Council of State Record Book, p. 116 (Mar. 20, 1813), RG 75, reel 2990, LV. For a similar wartime increase in the number of slave patrols in Accomack County, see Hadden, *Slave Patrols*, 163, 300n160.

61   "Runaway Negroes," *Richmond Enquirer*, Oct. 8, 1813 (with quotations). For a reminiscence of the "Sand Hills" raid that includes the story of the forced guide, see William Whitehurst, deposition, Oct. 20, 1827, RG 76, entry 190, box 4, case 239 (Edward Seymour), USNA-CP. For similar orders in Maryland, see Cassell, "Slaves of the Chesapeake," 147.

62   *National Intelligencer*, Sep. 7, 1813; "Norfolk, Sep. 3," *Federal Gazette & Baltimore Daily Advertiser*, Sep. 7, 1813; Henry Keeling, deposition, Apr. 9, 1823 ("White men in disguise"), APA-GMR, entry 258, LV. For rumors of a later attempt to use whites in black face as decoys, see Joseph Nourse to George Cockburn, Aug. 12, 1814, in Dudley, *Naval War of 1812*, vol. 3:161.

63   For the British insistence on summary executions, see Joseph C. Cabell to St. George Tucker, Nov. 24, 1813, TCP, box 33, SCSL-CWM. For the Lancaster case, see Lancaster County Court papers, vol. 24:198, reel 39, LV. For Brent's activity and payment as a slave patroller, see vol. 24:196. For McNamara's compensation, see *ASP-FR*, vol. 5:814.

64   John Taylor Lomax (on behalf of John P. Hungerford) to the adjutant general, July 31, 1814 ("What should"), JBEP, reel 5522, LV; Council of State Record Book, p. 287 (Aug. 2, 1814), RG 75, reel 2990, LV. For the paucity of wartime convictions for conspiracy or revolts, see Schwarz, *Twice Condemned*, 236–37.

65   St. G. Tucker, *Dissertation on Slavery*, 32. For slaves liberated from jails in Calvert County (Maryland) and Northumberland County (Virginia), see Joseph Nourse to George Cockburn, July 23, 1814 ("for endeavouring"), in Dudley, *Naval War of 1812*, vol. 3:157; Joseph Rogers, deposition, June 12, 1815, RG 76, entry 190, box 5, case 440 (Warren Hudnall), USNA-CP. For the Mathews County nine, see John Patterson to Levin Winder, Feb. 25, 1815, MSP, ser. A, box S1004-134, document 212, MdSA. For the jail break by George, see William W. Wilson, deposition, May 9, 1814 ("many others") in the Northampton County folder.

66   George Cockburn to Capt. Watts, Apr. 6, 1814, SGCP, reel 10, LC;
      Cockburn to Sir John Borlase Warren, Apr. 13, 1814 and Cockburn to Sir
      Alexander Cochrane, May 10, 1814 ("they managed"), in Dudley, *Naval
      War of 1812*, vol. 3:47, 65; Armistead Smith to William Patterson Smith,
      Apr. 19, 1814, WPSP, box 1, SC-DUL; John Crawford, statement, in
      Richmond Enquirer, May 11, 1814; Burwell Bassett to the adjutant gen-
      eral, May 4, 1814, *Virginia Argus*, May 11, 1814: "About six weeks ago
      two negroes were sent on shore near Gwynn's Island, with twenty dollars
      each, to entice the negroes off." Gwynn Island lies in Mathews County.

67   James Monroe to Anthony St. John Baker, Apr. 1, 1815, MG 16 (FO 5),
      vol. 106:173, reel B-2005, LAC; "List of Depositions Related to Slaves and
      Other Property Plundered by the Enemy during the Late War, 1812," 1822,
      Auditor of Public Accounts (RG 48): B 1054672, LV. A partial account-
      ing, this register identifies 394 owners of 1,186 runaways—none of whom
      came from a Piedmont county. This register requires many judgment calls
      as most names appear at least twice, for the second half repeats much of
      the first half of the volume but with variations to spellings of names. The
      fuller federal list compiled after the war to compensate masters who lost
      runaways concluded that 762 Maryland and Virginia masters lost 2,435
      runaways, an average of 3.2 slaves per owner. See *ASP-FR*, vol. 5: 801–18.

68   For the Virginia peacetime runaways of the late eighteenth century, see
      Morgan, *Slave Counterpoint*, 525–30. For the proportions of male and
      female runaways from Virginia to the British during the War of 1812,
      see the names listed by the postwar claims commission in *ASP-FR*, vol.
      5:808–18. I sorted the names by apparent gender. For example, I counted
      every Bob and Toby as male and placed Milley, Sukey, and Maria on
      the female side of the count. This method yielded 1,091 probable males
      (66 percent) and 565 (34 percent) probable females. The calculations
      exclude 65 slaves either unnamed or of uncertain gender, for the over-
      all total of 1,721 wartime runaways from Virginia. My sorting probably
      undercounts females, whose names were less well known to many of the
      masters seeking compensation. Among the Virginia owners, 34 of 540
      claimed to have lost 10 or more slaves; their claims named 633 slaves, 334
      (53 percent) males and 299 (47 percent) females. The former record rarely
      categorizes the children among the runaways. A bit better but still erratic
      is the accounting of 1,198 Virginia runaways claimed by 400 owners in
      the "List of Depositions Related to Slaves and Other Property Plundered
      by the Enemy during the Late War, 1812," B 1054672, Auditor of Pub-
      lic Accounts (RG 48), LV. For most entries, the clerk merely character-
      ized a runaway as "male" or "female" but occasionally identified one as
      a "boy," "girl," or "child." Such specification was most complete in the

record for Northumberland County, which lost more slaves (288) than any other county. In Northumberland, at least 43 (15 percent) of the 288 were children, meaning people under the age of 12. For owners who lost 10 or more slaves, the percentage of female runaways rose to nearly 47 percent, indicating that they especially benefited from group escapes. See also "Mr. Crawford's Statement," *National Intelligencer*, May 16, 1814.

A British list of 1,611 "American Refugee Negroes," who reached Halifax, Nova Scotia, between April 27, 1815, and October 24, 1818, reveals similar proportions of women and adult men. Among the refugees to Halifax, females comprised 37 percent of all the adults (those 16 years and older) and accounted for a bit more, 39 percent, of those in the prime of life (16 to 45); the proportion of males was greatest for those over 45. Children (those under 16 years old) accounted for 23 percent of the refugees.

HALIFAX REFUGEES, BY AGE AND GENDER, 1815–1818

Age Group	Male	Female	Total	Percentage
0–15 years	—	—	367	23
16–45 years	622	406	1028	64
46+ years	158	58	216	13
Totals	780	464	1611	100

Source: "Halifax List: Return of American Refugee Negroes Who Have Been Received into the Province of Nova Scotia from the United States of America," Apr. 27, 1815, to Oct. 24, 1818, http://www.gov.ca/nsarm/virtual/Africanns/1812.

Note: The Halifax list is often imprecise about the gender of children, so that has not been calculated in the table.

69   The data come from the advertisements for 1813 and 1814 as reprinted in Meaders, *Advertisements*, 189–227.

70   Meaders, *Advertisements*, 189–227. The advertisements specify an anticipated destination for 92 runaways, and in 85 percent of such cases the master suspected that the fugitive remained within the Chesapeake region. In only 15 percent of the cases did the master suspect that the runaway meant to flee from the region, either by heading north to a free state (8 of 92 cases, 9 percent) or by seeking out a British warship (6 of 92 cases, 6 percent). The six runaways assumed to be warship-bound appeared in the three advertisements posted by Thomas Wilson of Henrico County, William Robinson Howard of Fairfax County, and Elizabeth Mims of Goochland County. For their lack of postwar compensation, see *ASP-FR*, vol. 5:808–18.

CHAPTER NINE: FIGHT

1   John P. Hungerford to the adjutant general, Aug. 5, 1814, in Flournoy, *CVSP*, vol. 10:368.

2   John G. Joynes to Thomas M. Bayly, Apr. 13, 1814, in Flournoy, *CVSP*, vol. 10:319; Scott, *Recollections*, vol. 3:131–36.

3   Scott, *Recollections*, vol. 3:131–36 (quotations); Eshelman, Sheads, and Hickey, *War of 1812 in the Chesapeake*, 224–25.

4   George Cockburn to Sir Alexander Cochrane, Apr. 2, 1814, in Dudley, *Naval War of 1812*, vol. 3:43–45; Joseph Nourse to George Cockburn, Aug. 12, 1814, SGCP, reel 9, LC; Shomette, *Flotilla*, 167–68.

5   Sir Alexander Cochrane to George Cockburn, Apr. 28, 1814, and Cockburn to Cochrane, May 10 and June 25, 1814, in Dudley, *Naval War of 1812*, vol. 3:51, 64–65, 116; Bartlett, "Gentlemen versus Democrats," 147–49.

6   Lord Eglinton to Sir Thomas Brisbane, May 1, 1814, Brisbane Papers, folder 1, WLCL-UM; Sir John Beresford to Viscount Melville, Dec. [n.d.], 1813, Viscount Melville Papers, HL; Robert Barrie to Dolly Gardner Clayton, Feb. 4, 1814, in Dudley, *Naval War of 1812*, vol. 3:17; Sir David Milne to George Home, May 30, 1814, in Hume, "Letters Written during the War of 1812," 293; Edward Codrington, journal, July 31, 1814, MG 24, F 131 (Codrington letters), reel A-2076, LAC; Shomette, *Flotilla*, 229; Capt. Robert Rowley to Owsley Rowley, Apr. 8, 1814, June 24 and Aug. n.d., 1814, in Rowley, "Captain Robert Rowley," 241, 243, 244. See also the letters of George Hanger, originally in the *London Morning Post* of Nov. 14, 1814 and reprinted in *National Intelligencer*, May 20, 1815.

7   George Cockburn to Sir Alexander Cockburn, Apr. 2 ("surrounded") and April 13, 1814, in Dudley, *Naval War of 1812*, vol. 3:43, 47; Cockburn to Cochrane, May 9, 1814, SGCP, reel 6, LC; Shomette, *Flotilla*, 73–74; Thomas M. Bayly to James Barbour, Apr. 14, 1814, JBEP, reel 5520, LV; John G. Joynes to Bayly, Apr. 13, 1814, Thomas R. Joynes to Bayly, June 10, 1814, and Bayly to Barbour, June 23, 1814, in Flournoy, *CVSP*, vol. 10:319, 342; Barbour to Bayly, Apr. 25, 1814, Executive Letter Book, p. 57 RG 3 (Office of the Governor), reel 3011, LV; *Niles' Weekly Register*, vol. 6:344 (July 16, 1814); Edward Herbert, deposition, May 25, 1814, RG 76, entry 185, box 3, folder 5, USNA-CP.

8   Wallace, *Parson of the Islands*, 40–44, 128–31, 138–39 ("his acquaintance"); Leaven Gayle to James Barbour, Mar. 13, 1813 ("very little"), JBEP, reel 5510, LV; George Cockburn to Sir John Borlase Warren, June 17, 1813 ("very poor"), SGCP, reel 6, LC; Cockburn to Sir Alexander Cochrane, Apr. 2, 1814, in Dudley, *Naval War of 1812*, vol. 3:43; Cock-

burn, orders, Apr. 16, and June 30, 1814, SGCP, reel 10, LC; Thomas M. Bayly to Barbour, Apr. 14, 1814, JBEP, reel 5520, LV; Bayly to Barbour, June 16 and June 23, 1814, in Flournoy, *CVSP*, vol. 10:343, 346; Bayly to Barbour, June 29, 1814, JBEP, reel 5521, LV.

9   Thomas M. Bayly to James Barbour, Apr. 14, 1814, in *Richmond Enquirer*, Apr. 30, 1814; George Cockburn to unknown, June 2, 1814, SGCP, reel 7, LC; George Cockburn, orders, June 30, 1814, SGCP, reel 10, LC; Cockburn to Capt. Watts, July 27, 1814 ("inform"), SGCP, reel 7, LC.

10 Sir Alexander Cochrane to Sir George Prevost, Mar. 11, 1814, and George Cockburn to Sir John Borlase Warren, Apr. 13, 1814, in Dudley, *Naval War of 1812*, vol. 3:40, 47; Cochrane to Thomas Brown, July 20, 1814, and Cochrane to Cockburn, July 21, 1814, SACP, file 2349, reel 8, LC; Cockburn to Cochrane, Aug. 15, 1814, SGCP, reel 6, LC; Cockburn to William Hammond, May 19, 1814, SGCP, reel 10, LC; Weiss, *Merikens*, 7; Weiss, "Corps of Colonial Marines," 83.

11 Paul Bable, deposition, Feb. 5, 1828, RG 76, entry 185, box 4, folder 14, USNA-CP; depositions of John G. Joynes, Feb. 16, 1828, and Zachariah Crocket and Job Parker, Feb. 23, 1828, RG 76, entry 185, box 4, folder 16, USNA-CP; George Cockburn to Sir Alexander Cochrane, Apr. 29, 1814, SGCP, reel 6, LC; R. E. Parker to James Barbour, June 11, 1814, in Flournoy, *CVSP*, vol. 10:338; Cockburn to Cochrane, May 9, 1814, in Dudley, *Naval War of 1812*, vol. 3:62; Cockburn to Capt. Watts, July 27, 1814, and Cockburn to Edward Griffiths, Aug. 10, 1814, SGCP, reel 7, LC; Cockburn to Watts, June 30, 1814, SGCP, reel 10, LC; Lovell, *Personal Narrative*, 153. For runaways who became sailors, see Arthur Smith, deposition, Aug. 5, 1822, APA-GMR, entry 258, box 779, Isle of Wight County folder, LV; Lewis Neth Jr., deposition, July 21, 1821, RG 76, entry 190, box 8, case 764 (Lewis Neth), USNA-CP; Malcomson, "Freedom by Reaching the Wooden World," 5. For the personal servants of British officers, see Jacob G. Parker, deposition, Nov. 10, 1823, RG 76, entry 190, box 4, case 258 (Jacob G. Parker), USNA-CP; Robert Murphy, deposition, May 28, 1821, APA-GMA, entry 258, box 779, Westmoreland County folder, LV. For supernumeraries see George Cockburn to Andrew Fitzherbert Evans, Oct. 2, 1813, SGCP, reel 6, LC; Sir Alexander Cochrane to Cockburn, Apr. 28, 1814, in Dudley, *Naval War of 1812*, vol. 3:51–52. For the rations provided to supernumeraries, see Cockburn to Cochrane, Apr. 29 and June 26, 1814, SGCP, reel 6, LC; Cochrane to Cockburn, May 26, 1814, in Dudley, *Naval War of 1812*, vol. 3:67. For the slops, see Cockburn, order, Apr. 17, 1814, SGCP, reel 10, LC. For women as cooks and laundresses, see Isaac Smith, deposition, Jan. 31, 1828, RG 76, entry 190, box 7, case 607 (William C. Daw-

kins), USNA-CP; William Miles, deposition, June 7, 1828, RG 76, entry 190, box 9, case 898 (William Williams), USNA-CP; Mr. Rennolds, deposition, Apr. 15, 1828, RG 76, entry 190, box 8, case 775 (William Sudler), USNA-CP. For women as recruiters, see Augustine Neal, memorandum, Mar. 31, 1828, RG 76, entry 190, box 5, case 417 (Kenner W. Cralle), USNA-CP.

12   Bartlett and Smith, "'Species of Milito-Nautico-Guerilla Warfare,'" 188; George Cockburn to Sir Alexander Cochrane, Apr. 29 (*"all*, without exception") and June 26, 1814, SGCP, reel 6, LC; Cockburn to Capt. Watts, June 30, 1814, SGCP, reel 10, LC; James Jaboe, deposition, Apr. 30, 1821 ("that the British"), RG 76, entry 190, box 7, case 650 (Dr. Hezekiah Dent estate), USNA-CP; Cockburn, order, Apr. 17, 1814, SGCP, reel 10, LC; Cochrane to Cockburn, May 26, 1814 ("as an inducement"), in Dudley, *Naval War of 1812*, vol. 3:67; Meschack Hammons, deposition, July 9, 1821, RG 76, entry 190, box 6, case 555 (Eliza J. Hungerford), USNA-CP; Peter Wilson, deposition, Apr. 5, 1828, RG 76, entry 190, box 6, case 559 (James M. Sollers), USNA-CP. For bounties, rations, and alcohol, see also Cochrane to Cockburn, Apr. 28 and May 26, 1814, in Dudley, *Naval War of 1812*, vol. 3:51–52, 67.

13   Nathaniel Washington, deposition, Apr. 7, 1815 (all quotations), RG 76, entry 190, box 7, case 652 (Nathaniel Washington), USNA-CP; Jesse Edwards, deposition, Apr. 4, 1815, RG 76, entry 190, box 7 case 631 (Jesse Edwards), USNA-CP.

14   John King, deposition, Feb. 25, 1828 ("ask'd"), RG 76, entry 190, box 9, case 910 (Thomas Beacham), USNA-CP; Scott, *Recollections*, vol. 3:143; Lovell, *Personal Narrative*, 150; Samuel Turner, deposition, Apr. 28, 1828, RG 76, entry 190, box 7, case 700 (Jane Parran), USNA-CP; Dr. Horace Welford, deposition, May 5, 1823, RG 76, entry 190, box 4, case 293 (Eliza C. and John Darby), USNA-CP.

15   George Cockburn to Capt. Watts, July 7, 1814, SGCP, reel 7, LC.

16   Depositions of D. A. Hall, undated ("A slave of so useful"), and Thomas R. King, Apr. 22, 1828 ("acting as") in RG 76, entry 190, box 8, case 773 (William Harris), USNA-CP. For a similar case, see Thomas B. Hungerford to Robert P. Dunlop, Mar. 27, 1828, RG 76, entry 190, box 8, case 745 (Thomas B. Hungerford), USNA-CP. For the raid on Prince Frederick, Maryland, see Eshelman, Sheads, and Hickey, *War of 1812 in the Chesapeake*, 177.

17   George Cockburn to Sir Alexander Cochrane, Apr. 2, 1814 ("Blacky"), Cockburn to Sir John Borlase Warren, Apr. 13, 1814 ("They pretend") and Cockburn to Cochrane, May 10, 1814 in Dudley, *Naval War of 1812*, vol. 3:43–44, 47, 65–66.

18   George Cockburn to Sir Alexander Cochrane, May 10, 1814, in Dudley, *Naval War of 1812*, vol. 3:65.

19   Scott, *Recollections*, vol. 3:199–204; Capt. Charles B. H. Ross to George Cockburn, May 29, 1814, SGCP, reel 9, LC; Thomas M. Bayly to James Barbour, May 31, 1814, JBEP, reel 5521, LV. For the premature sniper, see "Skirmish at Accomack," *Richmond Enquirer*, June 15, 1814.

20   Robert Barrie to George Cockburn, June 1, 1814 ("I was highly pleased"), Cockburn to Barrie, June 3, 1814, Barrie to Cockburn, June 19,1814 ("conducted"), and Cockburn to Sir Alexander Cochrane, June 25, 1814 ("how uncommonly"), in Dudley, *Naval War of 1812*, vol. 3:79, 83, 111–14, 116; [R. J. Barrett], "Naval Recollections," 467. For the attack on Chesconessex, see Thomas R. Joynes to Thomas M. Bayley, June 25, 1814, in Flournoy, *CVSP*, vol. 10:351; Eshelman, Sheads, and Hickey, *War of 1812 in the Chesapeake* 224–25; Shomette, *Flotilla*, 128. The muster tables for the Colonial Marines reveal that only 3 deserted: less than 1 percent of their total by the end of December 1814. See Malcomson, "Freedom by Reaching the Wooden World," 71, citing Muster Tables, 3rd Battalion of Royal and Colonial Marines, Apr. 4–Dec. 31, 1813, Admiralty 96:341, NAUK.

21   Richard E. Parker to James Barbour, June 11, 1814 (all quotations), in Flournoy, *CVSP*, vol. 10:338; George Cockburn to Robert Barrie, June 3 and June 8, 1814, in Robert Barrie Papers, box 1, WLCL-UM; Parker never names the black spy, but it must have been Johnson given the county and the dates, which coincide with Cockburn's references to his mission.

22   George Cockburn to Robert Barrie, June 3 and June 8, 1814 ("prove to be my Friend"), in Robert Barrie Papers, box 1, WLCL-UM. Historian John Weiss assumes that Johnson was hung in late June. Although that fate is possible, there is no evidence for his execution in the surviving records from Westmoreland County or the state of Virginia. See Weiss, *Merikens*, 7.

23   Scott, *Recollections*, vol. 3:269; George Cockburn to Sir Alexander Cochrane, July 17, 1814 ("the best skirmishers") in Dudley, *Naval War of 1812*, vol. 3:154; Cockburn to Cochrane, Aug. 15, 1814, SGCP, reel 6, LC; Rowley, "Captain Robert Rowley," 245.

24   George Cockburn to Sir Alexander Cochrane, June 23, 1814, SGCP, reel 6, LC; Cockburn to Capt. Watts, July 22, 1814, SGCP, reel 7, LC; Cochrane to John Wilson Croker, Sep. 2, 1814, SACP, file 2348, reel 8, LC; Admiralty to Cochrane, Sep. 30, 1814, MG 12, Admiralty 2, vol. 933:233, reel B-3435, LAC; Cochrane to Croker, Sep. 28, 1814 ("steadiness"), SACP, file 2348, reel 8, LC; Cochrane to Earl Bathurst, July 14, 1814 ("their hatred"), quoted in Cassel, "Slaves of the Chesapeake," 151–52.

25   "Norfolk, June 3," *National Intelligencer*, June 6, 1814; Charles Bagwell to James Barbour, June 9, 1814, and John P. Hungerford to the adjutant general, Aug. 5, 1814 ("Our negroes"), in Flournoy, *CVSP*, vol. 10:337, 368.

26   Morriss, *Cockburn*, 99–102; Charles Napier quoted in W. N. Bruce, *Life of General Sir Charles Napier*, 61 ("Numbers").

27   George Cockburn to Sir Alexander Cochrane, July 17, 1814, in Dudley, *Naval War of 1812*, vol. 3:136; Bartlett and Smith, "'Species of Milito-Nautico-Guerilla Warfare,'" 174–75; Shomette, *Flotilla*, 102–38, 166–67.

28   George Cockburn to Sir Alexander Cochrane, May 9 and June 25, 1814 ("horrible State"), Cochrane to Lord Melville, July 17, 1814, Cockburn to Cochrane, July 17, 1814, Cockburn to Robert Barrie, July 16, 1814 ("I shall"), and Cockburn to Cochrane, July 31, 1814, in Dudley, *Naval War of 1812*, vol. 3:62, 116, 134, 136, 153, 168; Morriss, *Cockburn*, 100–102; Shomette, *Flotilla*, 174–78.

29   "From the Enemy in Our Waters," *National Intelligencer*, Apr. 30, 1814; "Most Glorious and Blessed War," "Progress of the Enemy," and "Movements of the Enemy," *Federal Gazette & Baltimore Daily Advertiser*, June 22, July 27, and July 28, 1814; Joshua Barney to William Jones, June 13, 1814, George Cockburn to Sir Alexander Cochrane, July 19, July 31, and Aug. 15, 1814, in Dudley, *Naval War of 1812*, vol. 3:99, 163, 168, 190; Edward Codrington to the captains of the squadron, Aug. 22 and Aug. 24, 1814 ("to do fair justice"), MG 24, F 131, reel A-2075, LAC; Scott, *Recollections*, vol. 3:220, 247–48; Shomette, *Flotilla*, 168. For the punishment of looters, especially camp women, see Edward Codrington, general order, Aug. 25, 1814, Cochrane, general order, Aug. 25, 1814, and Codrington, general order, Sep. 3, 1814 ("None of"), in Dudley, *Naval War of 1812*, vol. 3:230–31.

30   Robert Rowley to Owsley Rowley, ca. July 23, 1814, in Rowley, "Captain Robert Rowley," 245; Sir Pulteney Malcolm to Miss Malcolm, Sep. 1, 1814, SPMP, box 1, WLCL-UM; George Cockburn to Robert Barrie, July 11, 1814 ("The other day" and "induce"), and Cockburn to Sir Alexander Cochrane, July 24, 1814, in Dudley, *Naval War of 1812*, vol. 3:151, 166; Scott, *Recollections*, vol. 3:223–26, 241; Shomette, *Flotilla*, 105–7, 170–1.

31   George Cockburn to Robert Barrie, June 8, 1814, SGCP, reel 7, LC; John Mason to Cockburn, June 15, 1815, SGCP, reel 9, LC; Cockburn to Mason, June 24, 1814, SGCP, reel 6, LC; Sir Alexander Cochrane to Thomas Barclay, July 21, 1814, RG 94, entry 127, box 17, folder 1, USNA-DC; Cochrane, standing order, July 27, 1814, MG 24, F 131, reel A-2075, LAC; Cochrane to Barclay, July 31, 1814, SACP, file 2349, reel

8, LC; Edward Codrington to his wife, July 31, 1814, MG 24, F 13, reel A-2076, LAC; John Mitchell to John Mason, Oct. 8, 1814, RG 94, entry 127, box 7, folder 3, USNA-DC. For the elderly Virginian (Elijah Williams), see John P. Hungerford to Cockburn, Aug. 8, 1814, SGCP, reel 9, LC; Cockburn to Hungerford, Aug. 11, 1814, SGCP, reel 6, LC.

32   Philip Stuart to James Madison, Aug. 1, 1814 ("a thinly scattered"), WHWP, box 2, MdHS; "The Enemy in the Potomac," *Federal Gazette & Baltimore Daily Advertiser*, May 7, 1814; "From Below," *Richmond Enquirer*, July 23, 1814; Joshua Barney to William Jones, June 16, 1814, in Dudley, *Naval War of 1812*, vol. 3:102; Marine, *British Invasion of Maryland*, 65; St. Mary's County petition to Congress, Dec. 14, 1813, War of 1812 Collection, box 1, MdHS; Philip Stuart to Levin Winder, June 23, 1814, LWP, box 1, MdHS; Stuart to Winder, Aug. 29, 1814, MSP, ser. A, box S1004-131, doc. 145, MdSA; Shomette, *Flotilla*, 113–18, 141–42, 165, 172–73. In the 1813 state elections, the St. Mary's citizens voted 300 to 0 for the Federalist candidate, while Calvert County voted Federalist by a 405 to 375 margin. The adjoining two counties of Prince George (874 Federalist versus 640 Republican) and Charles (550 Federalist versus 0 Republican) were also heavily Federalist. For the election returns by Maryland county, see *Niles' Weekly Register*, vol. 5:111 (Oct. 16, 1813).

33   Shomette, *Flotilla*, 132–33, 180–88.

34   "Private Correspondence" and "Movements of the Enemy," *Federal Gazette & Baltimore Daily Advertiser*, July 28, 1814; Philip Key to James Monroe, July 25, 1814, RG 59, M179, reel 30, USNA-CP; Scott, *Recollections*, vol. 3:229; Robert Barrie to George Cockburn, June 19, 1814, Joshua Barney to William Jones, July 21, 1814 ("The people"), Cockburn to Sir Alexander Cochrane, July 17, 1814, and Joseph Nourse to Cockburn, July 23, 1814, in Dudley, *Naval War of 1812*, vol. 3:111–13, 147, 154, 159; Shomette, *Flotilla*, 132–33, 165 (Barney quote: "here and there"); Gleig, *Narrative of the Campaigns*, 88, 102; Edward Codrington to his wife, Aug. 21, 1814, MG 24, F 13, reel A-2076, LAC; John Rousby Plater to Levin Winder, Aug. 15, 1815 ("amused themselves"), MSP, ser. A, box S1004-130, doc. 3, MdSA.

35   Joshua Barney to William Jones, June 13, June 21, July 8, July 21 ("for he would be *betrayed*"), July 24, and Aug. 1, 1814, in Dudley, *Naval War of 1812*, vol. 3:99–101, 108, 145, 147, 148, 182; Philip Stuart to Levin Winder, June 23, 1814, LWP, box 1, MdHS; Shomette, *Flotilla*, 117–18, 135, 163. See also *National Intelligencer*, July 20, 1814.

36   Thomas B. King to unknown, July 14, 1814, quoted in Eshelman, Sheads, and Hickey, *War of 1812 in the Chesapeake*, 177; Shomette, *Flotilla*, 165, 194.

37   Robert Rowley to Owsley Rowley, ca. August 1814 ("The men"), in Rowley, "Captain Robert Rowley," 245–46; Philip Key to James Madison, Aug. 1, 1814, JMP, ser. 1, reel 5, LC; Eshelman, Sheads, and Hickey, *War of 1812 in the Chesapeake*, 100–101; Shomette, *Flotilla*, 206–7.

38   Shomette, *Flotilla*, 110–11, 133, 186, 437n6; William Wood, deposition, Aug. 1, 1822, RG 76, entry 190, box 6, case 514 (Michael Taney), USNA-CP; Eshelman, Sheads, and Hickey, *War of 1812 in the Chesapeake*, 201.

39   [R. J. Barrett], "Naval Recollections," 455–57; [C. Napier], "Narrative of the Naval Operations," 475 ("He had two daughters"); E. H. D. E. Napier, *Life and Correspondence of Admiral Sir Charles Napier*, vol. 1:78; Scott, *Recollections*, vol. 3:185–86, Michael Taney, deposition, Aug. 11, 1815, RG 76, entry 190, box 6, case 514 (Michael Taney, USNA-CP.

40   Scott, *Recollections*, vol. 3:227, 269; Joshua Barney to William Jones, July 24 and Aug. 4, 1814, in Dudley, *Naval War of 1812*, vol. 3:148, 184; Clement Dorsey to Philip Stuart, June 17, 1814, *Federal Gazette & Baltimore Daily Advertiser*, June 21, 1814; Philip Key to James Monroe, July 25, 1814 ("Their Men"), RG 59, M 179, reel 30, USNA-CP; Shomette, *Flotilla*, 110, 212. For the decline in desertion, see George Cockburn to Cochrane, Aug. 15, 1814, SGCP, reel 6, LC.

41   George Cockburn to Robert Barrie, July 16, 1814 ("In short"), and Cockburn to Sir Alexander Cochrane, July 17 and Aug. 13, 1814 ("learnt"), in Dudley, *Naval War of 1812*, vol. 3:153, 154, 173; Cockburn to Cochrane, Aug. 15, 1814, SGCP, reel 6, LC; Clement Dorsey to Levin Winder, Aug. 15, 1814, MSP, Scharf ser., box S1005-51, doc. 89, MdSA; Shomette, *Flotilla*, 113, 188–89. For the massive flight, see "The Enemy Below," *National Intelligencer*, Aug. 4, 1814; "Extract of a Letter from Charles County," and "Distresses of War," *Federal Gazette & Baltimore Daily Advertiser*, Aug. 6, 1814 ("conquered"); *Baltimore Federal Republican*, Aug. 26, 1814.

42   Walter Jones to James Madison, Nov. 8, 1813, James Madison Papers, American Memory Series, LC; William Brent Jr. et al. to James Barbour, Aug. 1, 1814, in Flournoy, *CVSP*, vol. 10:366; "To the Editor of the Enquirer," *Richmond Enquirer*, Dec. 24, 1814 ("false principle"); Wilson Cary Nicholas to James Monroe, Dec. 29, 1814, Executive Letter Book, p. 154, RG 3 (Office of the Governor), reel 3011, LV.

43   Richard Brent to James Barbour, Feb. 11, 1814, in Flournoy, *CVSP*, vol. 10:300; Augustine Neale et al., memorial, Mar. 10, 1828, in *ASP-FR*, vol. 6:856; James Barbour to the Northumberland County militia officers, Apr. 25, 1814, Executive Letter Book, 59, RG 3 (Office of the Governor), reel 3011, LV; "Letter from a Correspondent in Northumberland

County," *National Intelligencer*, May 6, 1814; Richard E. Parker to Barbour, June 11, 1814, in Flournoy, *CVSP*, vol. 10:338; John Taylor Lomax to Barbour, July 31, 1814, JBEP, reel 5522, LV; Walter Jones to John Tayloe, Aug. 12, 1814, WHWP, box 2, MdHS. For the militia strength in Westmoreland County, see John P. Hungerford to the adjutant general, Aug. 5, 1814, in Flournoy, *CVSP*, vol. 10:368.

44   Richard E. Parker to James Barbour, July 24, 1814 ("that they intended"), in *Richmond Enquirer*, July 30, 1814; "To the Editor of the Enquirer," *Richmond Enquirer*, Dec. 24, 1814.

45   George Cockburn to Sir Alexander Cochrane, July 21, 1814, in Dudley, *Naval War of 1812*, vol. 3:163–66; Richard E. Parker to the adjutant general, July 23, 1814, in *Richmond Enquirer*, July 27, 1814; John P. Hungerford to James Barbour, July 21, 1814, in Flournoy, *CVSP*, vol. 10:362; Scott, *Recollections*, vol. 3:246–47; Field, *Britain's Sea-Soldiers*, vol. 1:298–99; Eshelman, Sheads, and Hickey, *War of 1812 in the Chesapeake*, 247–48; Shomette, *Flotilla*, 197–200.

46   Walter Jones to John Tayloe, Aug. 12, 1814 ("were joined"), WHWP, box 2, MdHS; George Cockburn to Sir Alexander Cochrane, Aug. 4, 1814, in Dudley, *Naval War of 1812*, vol. 3:169; Field, *Britain's Sea-Soldiers*, vol. 1:299; Scott, *Recollections*, vol. 3:254; Peter Rowley to Owsley Rowley, Aug. n.d., 1814 ("The boats"), in Rowley, "Captain Robert Rowley," 244; Eshelman, Sheads, and Hickey, *War of 1812 in the Chesapeake*, 268–69; Shomette, *Flotilla*, 208–9.

47   Walter Jones to John Tayloe, Aug. 12, 1814, WHWP, box 2, MdHS; "The Enemy in the Potomac," *Richmond Enquirer*, Aug. 10, 1814; John P. Hungerford to the adjutant general, Aug. 5, 1814, in Flournoy, *CVSP*, vol. 10:367; unnamed militia officer to unknown, Aug. 5, 1814 ("The Buccaneers"), in Norris, *Westmoreland County*, 359; Eshelman, Sheads, and Hickey, *War of 1812 in the Chesapeake*, 268–69; Shomette, *Flotilla*, 210.

48   George Cockburn to Edward Griffiths, Aug. 10, 1814, SGCP, reel 7, LC; "Kinsale," in *Federal Gazette & Baltimore Daily Advertiser*, Aug. 13, 1814 ("We are all"); John P. Hungerford to the adjutant general, Aug. 5, 1814, in Flournoy, *CVSP*, vol. 10:368.

49   Clement Dorsey to Philip Stuart, June 17, 1814, in *Richmond Enquirer*, June 25, 1814; Robert Barrie to George Cockburn, June 21, 1814, SGCP, reel 9, LC; Eshelman, Sheads, and Hickey, *War of 1812 in the Chesapeake*, 78–79; Scott, *Recollections*, vol. 3:210–11; Lovell, *Personal Narrative*, 167–68 ("we used to force"); Shomette, *Flotilla*, 120–22.

50   George Cockburn to Sir Alexander Cochrane, July 21, 1814, in Dudley, *Naval War of 1812*, vol. 3:165; Scott, *Recollections*, vol. 3:242–44; Richard E. Parker to James Barbour, July 24, 1814, in *Richmond Enquirer*,

July 30, 1814; Field, *Britain's Sea-Soldiers*, vol. 1:299; Eshelman, Sheads, and Hickey, *War of 1812 in the Chesapeake*, 248; Shomette, *Flotilla*, 212.

51 John P. Hungerford to James Barbour, July 27, 1814, in Flournoy, *CVSP*, vol. 10:363; Hungerford to George Cockburn, Aug. 5, 1814, SGCP, reel 9, LC; John Taylor Lomax to Richard E. Parker, ca. July 24, 1814, in *Richmond Enquirer*, July 30, 1814; Cockburn to Parker, July 24, 1814, and Cockburn to Hungerford, Aug. 11, 1814, SGCP, reel 6, LC.

52 Robert Rowley to Owsley Rowley, August n.d., 1814, in Rowley, "Captain Robert Rowley," 244–45; Scott, *Recollections*, vol. 3:210–11; Joseph Nourse to George Cockburn, July 23, 1814, in Dudley, *Naval War of 1812*, vol. 3:159. For a later accusation of poisoning during the attack on Baltimore, see Christopher Claxton to Thomas M. Hardy, Sep. 16, 1814, SACP, file 2329, reel 2, LC.

53 Earl Bathurst to Edward Barnes, May 20, 1814 ("extended operations"), in Dudley, *Naval War of 1812*, vol. 3:73; Morriss, *Cockburn*, 100–103.

54 Scott, *Recollections*, vol. 3:239; George Cockburn to Sir Alexander Cochrane, July 17, 1814 ("without meeting"), SGCP, reel 10, LC; Morriss, *Cockburn*, 103–4; Shomette, *Flotilla*, 237–38.

55 Morriss, *Cockburn*, 104–8; Edward Codrington to his wife, Aug. 26, 1814, MG 24, F 13, reel A-2076, LAC; [R. J. Barrett], "Naval Recollections," 458 ("Never").

56 Gleig, *Narrative of the Campaigns*, 61 ("suffered"); Edward Codrington to his wife, Aug. 31, 1814, MG 24, F 13, reel A-2076, LAC; Sir Alexander Cochrane to Earl Bathurst, Sep. 2, 1814, War Office 1, vol. 141:29, NAUK.

57 Eshelman, Sheads, and Hickey, *War of 1812 in the Chesapeake*, 83–85; Gleig, *Narrative of the Campaigns*, 67–68; [Anonymous], "Recollections of the Expedition," 454–56.

58 Eshelman, Sheads, and Hickey, *War of 1812 in the Chesapeake*, 83–85; Ball, *Fifty Years in Chains*, 468 ("the militia"); Arthur Brooke, diary, Aug. 24, 1814, in George, "Family Papers," 303; [Anonymous], "Recollections of the Expedition," 455 ("On ascending"); Weiss, "Corps of Colonial Marines," 83.

59 Walter Smith quoted in Lossing, *Pictoral Field Book*, 938; Tobias E. Stansbury to Richard M. Johnson, Nov. 15, 1814, in *ASP-MA*, vol. 1:562. Stansbury identified Smith as especially insistent that a slave revolt menaced the white women of Washington.

60 Mordecai Booth to Thomas Tingey, Aug. 24, 1814, in Dudley, *Naval War of 1812*, vol. 3:209–10; Margaret Bayard Smith to Mrs. Kirkpatrick, Aug. n.d., 1814, in Hunt, *First Forty Years*, 100; Jennings, *Colored Man's Reminiscences*, 11–12 ("A rabble"); Thomas Tingey to William Jones, Aug. 27, 1814, in Dudley, *Naval War of 1812*, vol. 3:219.

61   Arthur Brooke, diary, Aug. 24, 1814, in George, "Family Papers," 303; Eshelman, Sheads, and Hickey, *War of 1812 in the Chesapeake*, 270; John G. Sharp, ed., "Michael Shiner Diary," available online through "The Navy Department Library." The original is in LC.

62   Arthur Brooke, diary, Aug. 24, 1814 ("I think"), in George, "Family Papers," 303; Gleig, *Narrative of the Campaigns*, 70; Scott, *Recollections*, vol. 3:304; Margaret Bayard Smith to Mrs. Kirkpatrick, Aug. n.d., 1814 ("so that an instantaneous"), in Hunt, *First Forty Years*, 111; Eshelman, Sheads, and Hickey, *War of 1812 in the Chesapeake*, 270–72.

63   George Cockburn quoted in Margaret Bayard Smith to Mrs. Kirkpatrick, Aug. n.d., 1814, in Hunt, *First Forty Years*, 111; Scott, *Recollections*, vol. 3:306; [Anonymous] "Recollections of the Expedition," 25.

64   Scott, *Recollections*, vol. 3:311; Arthur Brooke, diary, Aug. 24, 1814, in George, "Family Papers," 303; Eshelman, Sheads, and Hickey, *War of 1812 in the Chesapeake*, 270–72; Morriss, *Cockburn*, 108.

65   Margaret Bayard Smith to Mrs. Kirkpatrick, Aug. n.d., 1814 ("He, and all his officers," and Cockburn quoted "Were you not"), in Hunt, *First Forty Years*, 112; Scott, *Recollections*, vol. 3:307 ("the admiral"); Edward Codrington to his wife, Aug. 31, 1814, MG 24, F 13, reel A-2076, LAC; Eustace, *1812*, 208–9.

66   Gleig, *Narrative of the Campaigns*, 75–78; [Anonymous], "Recollections of the Expedition," 27; John G. Sharp, ed., "Michael Shiner Diary," available online through "The Navy Department Library"; Arthur Brooke, diary, Aug. 25, 1814, and Robert Ross to Elizabeth Ross, Sep. 1, 1814, in George, "Family Papers," 305, 308; George Cockburn to Sir Alexander Cochrane, Aug. 27, 1814, in Dudley, *Naval War of 1812*, vol. 3:222; Morriss, *Cockburn*, 108.

67   For the city's population, see Pitch, *Burning of Washington*, 29. For the postwar compensation claims, see *ASP-FR*, vol. 5:801. For fear of slave revolt in Washington, see George, "Mirage of Freedom," 439–40; Cassel, "Slaves of the Chesapeake," 153; Tobias E. Stansbury to Richard M. Johnson, Nov. 15, 1814, in *ASP-MA*, vol. 1:562. For the passivity of the Washington slaves, see Margaret Bayard Smith to Mrs. Kirkpatrick, Aug. n.d., 1814, in Hunt, *First Forty Years*, 113. For the slaves rebuffed, see Gleig, *Narrative of the Campaigns*, 80 ("We were joined"). For some Montgomery County slaves who did leave with the British, see Thomas Bowie, deposition, Sep. 11, 1821, RG 76, entry 190, box 1, case 1 (Thomas Bowie), USNA-CP; John Read Magruder, deposition, Oct. 18, 1823, RG 76, entry 190, box 7, case 712 (John Read Magruder), USNA-CP; [Anonymous], "Recollections of the Expedition," 27.

68   Eshelman, Sheads, and Hickey, *War of 1812 in the Chesapeake*, 12, 207;

"The Enemy," *Federal Gazette & Baltimore Daily Advertiser*, Aug. 30, 1814; Pitch, *Burning of Washington*, 54, 146; Gleig, *Narrative of the Campaigns*, 81.

69 John W. Green to Alexander Parker, Aug. 28, 1814, and Thomas Prosser to James Barbour, Aug. 29, 1814, in Flournoy, *CVSP*, vol. 10:378, 379; Charles Simms to Nancy Douglas Simms, Sep. 3, 1814, in Dudley, *Naval War of 1812*, vol. 3:246; [C. Napier], "Narrative of the Naval Operations," 478–80; Eshelman, Sheads, and Hickey, *War of 1812 in the Chesapeake*, 11.

70 Robert Rowley to Owsley Rowley, Sep. 3, 1814, in Rowley, "Captain Robert Rowley," 250; Edward Codrington to his wife, Aug. 28, 1814, MG 24, F 13, reel A-2076, LAC.

71 Arthur Brooke, diary, Aug. 30, 1814, in George, "Family Papers," 305; Bartlett, "Gentlemen versus Democrats," 155; Lords of the Admiralty to Sir Alexander Cochrane, Sep. 28, 1814, MG 12, Admiralty 2, vol. 933:230, reel B-3435, LAC; George Cockburn to Cochrane, Nov. 3, 1814, SGCP, reel 7, LC; Morriss, *Cockburn*, 109–10; James Cockburn to Earl Bathurst, Sep. 26, 1814 ("as wounding"), CO 37 (Bermuda), vol. 72:66, NAUK; Prince Regent quoted in Bickham, *Weight of Vengeance*, 169.

72 Thomas T. Tucker to St. George Tucker, Sep. 9, 1814, TCP, box 33, SCSL-CWM; James Monroe to George Hay, Sep. 7, 1814, in [Anonymous], "Letters of James Monroe," 218.

73 Charles Carroll to Charles Carroll Jr., Aug. 26, 1814, quoted in Horne, *Negro Comrades*, 61; H. A. Fay to the adjutant general, July 4, 1814 ("confirmed drunkards" and "by scaling the walls"), WHWP, box 2, MdHS; Levin Winder to W. H. Winder, Aug. 29, 1814, and Fay to W. H. Winder, Aug. 31, 1814 ("firing from the forts"), WHWP, box 3, MdHS.

74 Henry Crease to Sir Alexander Cochrane, Sep. 1, 1814 ("intelligent"), MG 12, Admiralty 1, vol. 507:12, reel B-1453, LAC; E. F. Chambers, deposition, July 3, 1828, and Richard Frisby, memorial, n.d., RG 76, entry 190, box 9, case 862 (Richard Frisby), USNA-CP; Eshelman, Sheads, and Hickey, *War of 1812 in the Chesapeake*, 11.

75 Edward Codrington to his wife, Sep. 10, 1814, MG 24, F 13, reel A-2076, LAC; Sir Alexander Cochrane to Lord Melville, July 17, 1814, and Cochrane to Arthur Brooke, Sep. 12, 1814, in Dudley, *Naval War of 1812*, vol. 3:134–35, 276; Eshelman, Sheads, and Hickey, *War of 1812 in the Chesapeake*, 11.

76 Eshelman, Sheads, and Hickey, *War of 1812 in the Chesapeake*, 11–12.

77 Gleig, *Narrative of the Campaigns*, 95; [Anonymous], "Recollections of the Expedition," 30–33; George, "Family Papers," 310–11; Morriss, *Cockburn*, 110–11; John Moore to Elizabeth S. Moore, Sep. 13, 1814,

Moore Papers, 1 folder, SC-DUL; Eshelman, Sheads, and Hickey, *War of 1812 in the Chesapeake*, 11–12.

78   John Moore to Elizabeth S. Moore, Sep. 14, 1814, Moore Papers, 1 folder, SC-DUL; Morriss, *Cockburn*, 111–12; Eshelman, Sheads, and Hickey, *War of 1812 in the Chesapeake*, 12. For the deaths of Colonial Marines, see Weiss, "Corps of Colonial Marines," 83. For the executed sailors, see G. R. Gleig, diary, Sep. 20, 1814, in C. R. B. Barrett, *85th King's Light Infantry*, 182; [R. J. Barrett], "Naval Recollections," 466.

79   John Moore to Elizabeth S. Moore, Sep. 15, 1814, Moore Papers, 1 folder, SC-DUL.

80   Philip Barraud to John Hartwell Cocke, Sep. 19, 1814, JHCFP, box 17, SSCL-UVA; Cocke to Joseph C. Cabell, Sep. 21, 1814, JCCFP (38-111-c), box 11, SSCL-UVA.

81   Pitch, *Burning of Washington*, 191–93; Eshelman, Sheads, and Hickey, *War of 1812 in the Chesapeake*, 12. For the full lyrics of the national anthem, see "Defence of Fort McHenry," *Federal Gazette & Baltimore Daily Advertiser*, Oct. 14, 1814.

82   Sir Pulteney Malcolm to unknown, Oct. 3, 1814, SPMP, box 1, WLCL-UM; Gleig, *Narrative of the Campaigns*, 108; [Anonymous], "Recollections of the Expedition," 33–34.

83   Robert Rowley to Owsley Rowley, Aug. n.d. ("We are here very happy") and Nov. 8, 1814 ("It is horrible"), in Rowley, "Captain Robert Rowley," 246–47. For other officers expressing discontent, see Chamier, *Life of a Sailor*, 178; G. C. M. Smith, *Autobiography of Lieutenant-General Sir Harry Smith*, vol. 1:210. For the October raids along the Potomac, see [Anonymous], "Recollections of the Expedition," 182–83; J. Chowning to the adjutant general, Oct. 8, 1814, in Flournoy, *CVSP*, vol. 10:396–97; F. D. Downing to the adjutant general, Oct. 6, 1814, in *Richmond Enquirer*, Oct. 13, 1814; Sir Pulteney Malcolm to Sir Alexander Cochrane, Oct. 7, 1814, and William Lambert to William Jones, Oct. 13, 1814, in Dudley, *Naval War of 1812*, vol. 3:331, 332.

84   Lovell, *Personal Narrative*, 164–67 ("shooting parties" and "Death or victory"); Archibald Ritchie to James Barbour, Dec. 3, 1814, and John Hartwell Cocke to Barbour, Dec. 4, 1814, in Flournoy, *CVSP*, vol. 10:401, 404–5; Robert Barrie to Dolly Gardner Clayton, Nov. 11, 1814, and Barrie to George Cockburn, Dec. 7, 1814, in Dudley, *Naval War of 1812*, vol. 3:339–40, 342; S. L. Butler, "Captain Barrie's Last Raid," 6442–45; *Niles' Weekly Register*, vol. 7:283 (Dec. 31, 1814); Eshelman, Sheads, and Hickey, *War of 1812 in the Chesapeake*, 263–64.

85   Depositions of William Davis, May 21, 1821 ("that the said negroes"), John Harmon, May 21, 1812, and William Games, July 16, 1821, APA-

GMR, entry 247, box 778, Essex County folder, LV; Vincent Bramham, Nov. 8, 1827, RG 76, entry 185, box 3, folder 4, USNA-CP; overseer quoted in William Games, deposition, Apr. 29, 1823 ("did declare"), RG 76, entry 190, box 4, case 223 (Thomas Jones), USNA-CP; Thomas Jones, deposition, Apr. 29, 1823, RG 76, entry 190, box 3, case 159, USNA-CP. For 200 as the number of runaways, see the depositions of Amelia A. Parker and Ann Glasscock, Nov. 6, 1827, RG 76, entry 190, box 4, case 320 (Edward Saunders), USNA-CP.

86 John Hartwell Cocke to Claiborne W. Gooch, Dec. 7, 1814, in *Richmond Enquirer*, Dec. 10, 1814; S. L. Butler, "Captain Barrie's Last Raid," 6447–49; Robert Barrie to George Cockburn, Dec. 7, 1814 ("releasing" and "beastly Drunk"), in Dudley, *Naval War of 1812*, vol. 3:342; Walter Jones to James Monroe, Dec. 10, 1814, JMP, ser. 1, reel 5, LC. For the Colonial Marines at Farnham Church, see Dr. Horace Welford, deposition, Feb. 22, 1814, RG 76, entry 190, box 5, case 403 (John and Eliza C. Darby), USNA-CP.

87 Scott, *Recollections*, vol. 3:188–89 ("So completely"), 229 ("the inhabitants").

88 George C. Urmstone to Robert Barrie, June 3, 1814, SGCP, reel 9, LC; Barrie to George Cockburn, June 5, 1814, MG 12, Admiralty 1, vol. 507:76, reel B-1451, LAC; Scott, *Recollections*, vol. 3:229–35 (all quotations); Barrie to Cockburn, June 19, 1814, in Dudley, *Naval War of 1812*, vol. 3:111–14 (see also 151–52, 152n7).

89 Philip Stuart to James Madison, July 29, 1814, James Madison Papers, American Memory Series, LC; John P. Hungerford to James Barbour, July 21 ("the great advantage") and Aug. 5, 1814, in Flournoy, *CVSP*, vol. 10:362, 368; John Taylor Lomax to the adjutant general, July 31, 1814, JBEP, reel 5522, LV; "Views and Designs of the Enemy," *Richmond Enquirer*, Feb. 11, 1815.

Chapter Ten: Crisis

1 Thomas Jefferson to Edward Coles, Aug. 25, 1814, in Jefferson, *Notes on the State of Virginia*, 258–59.

2 "Defence of the Sea-Board," *Richmond Enquirer*, Oct. 13, 1814 ("10,000"); Basset Burwell to James Barbour, Apr. 10, 1814, JBEP, reel 5520, LV; Robert Porterfield to Barbour, Oct. 11, 1814, JBEP, reel 5524, LV; Robert Nelson to Barbour, Dec. 13, 1814, in Flournoy, *CVSP*, vol. 10:406.

3 Alexander Parker to James Barbour, Aug. 28, 1814, in Flournoy, *CVSP*, vol. 10:377; Thomas Jefferson Randolph to Thomas Jefferson, Sep. 9,

1814, in Looney, *PTJ-RS*, vol. 7:649; John Hartwell Cocke to Joseph C. Cabell, Sep. 21, 1814, JCC&CFP (38-111), box 11, SSCL-CWM.

4   James Bendall to Rebekah Bendall, n.d. ("and neaver Eate"), Sep. 12, Sep. 26, and Oct. 2, 1814 ("My Bed" and "I am porer"), Bendall Family Papers (Mss 1 B4325 a 3-12), VHS. For the troop numbers at Norfolk, see Moses Porter to James Barbour, July 4, 1814, in Flournoy, *CVSP*, vol. 10:353.

5   Philip Barraud to St. George Tucker, Aug. 2 and 16, 1814, TCP, box 33, SCSL-CWM. For the prevailing ailments and their symptoms, see Robert Archer, Memorandum Book, 6–35 (33: "eyes sunk"), LV; "An Account of the Deaths . . . in the 7th Regt, 4th Brigade," Aug. 30, 1814–Feb. 7, 1815, JHCFP, box 16, SSCL-UVA; Thomas Newton to James Madison, Apr. 18, 1814, in Padgett, "Letters from Thomas Newton," 204.

6   David Campbell to Virginia's senators, n.d. [1815], CFP, box 3, SC-DUL; Blair Bolling, commonplace book, 27–33 (32: "What was much more"), VHS; Philip Barraud to John Hartwell Cocke, Dec. 2, 1814, JHCFP, box 18, SSCL-UVA. For the numbers of the sick, see Moses Porter to James Barbour, Sep. 16, 1814, JBEP, reel 5523, LV; James Bankhead to Barbour, Nov. 24, 1814, JBEP, reel 5524, LV; "Contrast!" *Richmond Enquirer*, Jan. 14, 1815. For the estimate of 3,000 deaths and the words of Charles Fenton Mercer ("in order to avoid depressing"), see Egerton, *Charles Fenton Mercer*, 93.

7   Thomas Newton Jr. to James Monroe, Aug. 6, 1814, RG 59, M 179, reel 30, USNA-CP; Wilson Cary Nicholas to Monroe, Jan. 29, 1815, JMP, ser. 1, reel 5, LC; John Preston to James P. Preston, Nov. 6, 1814 ("Worn down"), Preston Family Papers, sec. 4, folder 5 (Mss 1 P9267 d 165–217), VHS; "The Prospect before Us," *Richmond Enquirer*, Jan. 3, 1815.

8   Nicholas Faulcon to John Hartwell Cocke, May 23 and Sep. 13, 1814, and Feb. 15, 1815, JHCFP, boxes 16, 17, 19, SSCL-UVA; William Lambert to William Jones, Nov. 4 ("a putrid sore-throat") and Nov. 11, 1814, RG 45, M 124, reel 66, USNA-DC; "Contagious Distemper," *Richmond Enquirer*, Jan. 11, 1815 ("fire to the house"); John Campbell to David Campbell, Feb. 8, 1815, CFP, box 3, SC-DUL.

9   Thomas Jefferson to James Madison, Mar. 10 and May 10, 1814, Elizabeth Trist to Jefferson, July 29, 1814, and Jefferson to Dabney Carr, Aug. 24, 1814, in Looney, *PTJ-RS*, vol. 7:240, 360, 501, 601; "Hail Storm," *Richmond Enquirer*, June 1, 1814; Mrs. Robertson to Blair Bolling, July 1, 1814 ("Thus you see"), Bolling Family Papers (Mss 1 B6386 a 13-38), VHS; Nicholas Faulcon to John Hartwell Cocke, June 14, 1814, JHCFP, box 16, SSCL-UVA; Cocke to Joseph C. Cabell, Aug. 11, 1814, JCC&CFP (38-111), box 11, SSCL-UVA; John Randolph to Josiah Quincy, July 4, 1814, in E. Quincy, *Life of Josiah Quincy*, 356; Randolph to Harmanus

Bleeker, July 26, 1814, in Kirk, *John Randolph*, 248; John W. Eppes to James Monroe, Aug. 12, 1814, JMP, ser. 1, reel 5, LC; Sarah Kemp to William Kemp, Sep. 25, 1814, William Kemp folder, SC-DUL; Edward Ross to David Parish, July 29 ("with a report" and "sweaping") and Aug. 13, 1814, Parish-Rosseel Papers, St. Lawrence University Archives, Owen D. Young Library, Canton, NY.

10   William H. Fitzhugh to James Barbour, Oct. 12, 1824, in Flournoy, *CVSP*, vol. 10:397; John Turberville to Barbour, Oct. 16, 1814, JBEP, reel 5524, LV; "Defence of the Sea-Board." *Richmond Enquirer*, Oct. 13, 1814; Thomas Jefferson to Archibald Robertson, June 21, 1814, to John Hartwell Cocke, Aug. 5, 1814, and to William Short, Nov. 28, 1814 ("How can"), in Looney, *PTJ-RS*, vol. 7:430–31, 513–14, and vol. 8:109; Jefferson to James Monroe, Oct. 16, 1814, JMP, ser. 1, reel 5, LC; Nathaniel Beverley Tucker to St. George Tucker, Dec. 18, 1814, TCP, box 33, SCSL-CWM; "John Randolph's Letter," Jan. 7, 1815, in *Richmond Enquirer*, Apr. 1, 1815.

11   John Randolph to John Brockenbrough, Aug. 1, 1814, in W. C. Bruce, *John Randolph*, vol. 1:412; William Gray to John Hartwell Cocke, Aug. 1, 1814 ("I had not"), JHCFP, box 16, SSCL-UVA; Francis Browning to Wilson Cary Nicholas, Feb. 10, 1815 ("I never saw"), WCNEP, box 1, LV; Nicholas to Joseph C. Cabell, Jan. 3, 1814 ("More patriotism"), JCC&CFP (38-111), box 10, SSCL-UVA; Nicholas to James Monroe, Dec. 22, 1814, Executive Letter Book, p. 139, RG 3 (Office of the Governor), reel 3011, LV; Joseph Sexton to Nicholas, Nov. 21, 1815 [misfiled in 1816], WCNEP, box 4, LV.

12   William R. Custis to James Barbour, Sep. 19, 1814 ("we must give up"), in Flournoy, *CVSP*, vol. 10:389; Elliott Muse to Barbour, Nov. 30, 1814 ("I will agree"), JBEP, reel 5524, LV; St. George Tucker to Joseph C. Cabell, Dec. 30, 1814, BFP, box 3, SSCL-UVA; John Campbell to David Campbell, Dec. 17, 1814, CFP, box 3, SC-DUL; John Coalter to St. G. Tucker, Dec. 22, 1814, and Henry St. George Tucker to St. G. Tucker, Jan. 23, 1815, TCP, box 33, SCSL-CWM.

13   Wilson J. Cary to John Hartwell Cocke, Jan. 12, 1814, JHCFP, box 15, SSCL-UVA; David Campbell to Edward Campbell, Jan. 30, 1814 and John Campbell to James Campbell, Apr. 6, ("I begin to think") and June 16, 1814, CFP, box 3, SC-DUL; James W. Wallace to Thomas Jefferson, Sep. 7, 1814, and John Minor to Jefferson, Sep. 8, 1814, in Looney, *PTJ-RS*, vol. 7:643, 644; Walter Jones to John Tayloe, Aug. 12, 1814, WHWP, box 2, MdHS.

14   Hickey, *War of 1812*, 222–25, 231, 247–51; Stagg, *Mr. Madison's War*, 426–27; anonymous British spy's report, Feb. 2, 1815, MG 12, Admiralty 1, vol. 508:100–101, reel B-1452, LAC; Thomas P. Grosvenor to John F.

Mercer, Nov. n.d., 1814, Mercer Papers, HL; Edward Ross to David Parish, Jan. 10, 1815, Parish Papers, St. Lawrence University Archives.

15   Mrs. Robertson to Blair Bolling, Sep. 6, 1814, Bolling Family Papers (Mss 1 B6386 a 13-38), VHS; Samuel Hopkins to John Cropper, Nov. 6, 1814, and Richard D. Bayly to John Cropper, Nov. 10, 1814 ("climax"), Cropper Papers, sec. 1 (Mss 1 C8835 a 1-308), VHS; Claiborne W. Gooch to David Campbell, Dec. 6, 1814 (*"This union"*), CFP, box 3, SC-DUL; Rosalie Stier Calvert to H. J. Stier, Oct. 22, 1814, and Mar. 10, 1815, in Callcott, *Mistress of Riversdale*, 273, 278; "The Prospect before Us," *Richmond Enquirer*, Jan. 3, 1815 ("In the Northern").

16   James Barbour to James Monroe, Sep. 13, 1814, Barbour to the state legislature, Oct. 10, 1814, and Wilson Cary Nicholas to Monroe, Dec. 29, 1814, Executive Letter Book, pp. 92, 105, 154, RG 3 (Office of the Governor), reel 3011, LV; Joseph C. Cabell to Thomas Jefferson, in Looney, *PTJ-RS*, vol. 7:669–70; John Stokely to James Monroe, Oct. 18, 1814, JMP, ser. 1, reel 7, LC; Cabell to Isaac A. Coles, Jan. 3, 1815, JCC&CFP (38-111), box 11, SSCL-UVA; "State Defence," *Richmond Enquirer*, Jan. 11, 1815; "General Orders" and "Instructions from the Governor," *Richmond Enquirer*, Feb. 8, 1815; Lowrey, *James Barbour*, 77–79; Egerton, *Charles Fenton Mercer*, 94–95. For the federal endorsement, see James Monroe to Wilson Cary Nicholas, in Flournoy, *CVSP*, vol. 10:417.

17   [G. Tucker], *Letters from Virginia*, 82.

18   Henry Lee to William H. Cabell, Aug. 24, 1807, in Flournoy, *CVSP*, vol. 9:589; "S.C.," *National Intelligencer*, Nov. 26, 1814 ("We are conscious").

19   Berlin, *Many Thousands Gone*, 369–75; Nash and Soderland, *Freedom by Degrees*, 167–93; Foner, *Blacks and the Military*, 3–22. In 1810, census figures indicate 1,200,000 slaves and 180,000 free blacks in total; calculating military-age men as a fifth of those totals yields 240,000 enslaved and 36,000 free black men. For William Williams, see George, "Mirage of Freedom," 442–43.

20   Charles Gordon to William Jones, Sep. 20, 1814, in Dudley, *Naval War of 1812*, vol. 3:308; James Madison and Joshua Barney quoted in Jennings, *Colored Man's Reminiscences*, 9; Shomette, *Flotilla*, 58, 429n29.

21   For the Irish American appeals and Armstrong's endorsement, see William Duane to Thomas Jefferson, Aug. 11, 1813, in Ford, "Letters of William Duane," 373–74; Duane to John Armstrong, July 12 and July 29, 1814, Duane, "Memoir on the Formation of Military Corps of Coloured Men," Aug. 25, 1814, and Nicholas Gray to James Monroe, Oct. 1, 1814, RG 107, M 221, reel 61, USNA-DC; Thomas Lefferts to Armstrong, Sep. 6, 1814, and James Mease to Armstrong, Aug. 2 and Aug. 8, 1814, RG 107, M 221, reels 63 and 64, USNA-DC; Armstrong to Duane, July 15, 1814 ("We

must"), in Duane, "Selections from the Duane Papers," 63. For Armstrong's downfall, see Skeen, *John Armstrong*, 137–43, 161, 198–204.

22   Daniel D. Tompkins to James Monroe, Dec. 12, 1814, RG 107, M 221, reel 66, USNA-DC.

23   "Black Troops Proposed," *National Intelligencer*, Nov. 11, 1814.

24   "S.C.," *National Intelligencer*, Nov. 26, 1814.

25   George Cockburn to John Clavell, Dec. 13, 1814, in Dudley, *Naval War of 1812*, vol. 3:345–46; Cockburn to Clavell, Feb. 7, 1815, SGCP, reel 7, LC; Clavell to Cockburn, Jan. 16 and 19, 1815, SGCP, reel 9, LC; Morriss, *Cockburn*, 114. For the role of the *Regulus* in withdrawing the Colonial Marines, see John Fraser, deposition, n.d., RG 76, entry 185, box 4, folder 16, USNA-CP; Henry Griffin, deposition, May 3, 1828, RG 76, entry 190, box 4, case 260 (William Taliafero), USNA-CP; James Monroe to Wilson Cary Nicholas, Jan. 14, 1815, in Flournoy, *CVSP*, vol. 10:415–16; Weiss, *Merikens*, 8–9.

26   Sir Alexander Cochrane, "Thoughts on American War," Apr. 27, 1812 ("The capture"), Henry Dundas, Viscount Melville, Papers, HL; Morriss, *Cockburn*, 114–16; Lambert, *Challenge*, 341–45.

27   Sir Alexander Cochrane to John Wilson Croker, Oct. 3, 1814, SACP, file 2348, reel 8, LC; Samuel Jackson to Cochrane, Oct. 26, 1814, SACP, file 2326, reel 1, LC; Morriss, *Cockburn*, 114–16; Bullard, *Black Liberation*, 9–11.

28   George Cockburn to Sir Alexander Cochrane, Jan. 27, 1814, SGCP, reel 7, LC; Bullard, *Black Liberation*, 13–14, 27–33, 47; Morriss, *Cockburn*, 116.

29   George Cockburn to Sir Alexander Cochrane, Jan. 27, 1814, SGCP, reel 7, LC; Robert Barrie to Philip Somerville, Jan. 14, 1815, MG 12, Admiralty 1, vol. 509:169, reel B-1453, LAC; Barrie to Mrs. George Clayton, Jan. 22, 1815, Robert Barrie Papers, box 1, WLCL-UM; John Miller to Thomas Miller, Feb. 12, 1815 ("Blacky"), *Niles' Weekly Register*, vol. 8:103 (Apr. 8, 1815); Archibald Clark, deposition, May 1, 1823, RG 76, entry 190, box 8, case 765 (John Boog), USNA-CP; [R. J. Barrett], "Naval Recollections," 21–22; Field, *Britain's Sea-Soldiers*, vol. 1:301–2; Bullard, *Black Liberation*, 50–52; Morriss, *Cockburn*, 116–17; Miller, *Memoir of General David Blackshear*, 457.

30   Peter Early to David Blackshear, Jan. 19 ("insurrection on one side") and Jan. 25, 1815, John Sawyer to Blackshear, Jan. 27, 1815, and Blackshear to John Floyd, Feb. 2, 1815 ("by the multitude"), in Miller, *Memoir of General David Blackshear*, 448, 453, 455–56, 457; James G. Almy to John C. Almy, Feb. 23, 1815, War of 1812 Collection, box 5, WLCL-UM.

31   George Cockburn to Sir Alexander Cochrane, Feb. 11, 1815, SGCP, reel 7, LC; Cockburn to Cochrane, Feb. 17, 1815, and Robert Ramsay to

Cockburn, Feb. 16, 1815, MG 12, Admiralty 1, vol. 509:175, 177, reel B-1453, LAC; John Houston McIntosh to David Blackshear, Apr. 2, 1815, in Miller, *Memoir of General David Blackshear*, 465; Bullard, *Black Liberation*, 52–60, 74; Scott, *Recollections*, vol. 3:360–61.

32 Roswell King to Pierce Butler, Jan. 20, 1815, and Roswell King, deposition, Feb. 14, 1815, in Bell, *Major Butler's Legacy*, 175–76, 182; John Sawyer to David Blackshear, Jan. 27, 1815, and Blackshear to John Floyd, Feb. 13, 1815, in Miller, *Memoir of General David Blackshear*, 455, 462; William F. Kelly, deposition, Apr. 29, 1823, RG 76, entry 190, box 8, case 765 (John Boog), USNA-CP; Bullard, *Black Liberation*, 63.

33 John Dawson, deposition, Jan. 1, 1824, RG 76, entry 190, box 1, case 38 (Edmund Mathews), USNA-CP; George Baillie to William Jones, Nov. 18, 1815 ("the Queen of England"), in Bullard, *Black Liberation*, 65. For Roswell King's charge, see Bell, *Major Butler's Legacy*, 184.

34 Roswell King, deposition, Feb. 14, 1815, in Bell, *Major Butler's Legacy*, 182.

35 Roswell King to Pierce Butler, Feb. 12 ("God cursed"), Feb. 16 ("I have these twelve years"), and Mar. 4, 1815 ("How will it please"), in Bell, *Major Butler's Legacy*, 177–80.

36 George Cockburn, order, Feb. 4, 1815, SGCP, reel 10, LC; Cockburn to Andrew Fitzherbert Evans, Feb. 4, 1815, SGCP, reel 7, LC; Kingsley, *Treatise on the Patriarchal*, 11 ("the magical transformation"); Roswell King to Pierce Butler, Jan. 20, 1815, in Bell, *Major Butler's Legacy*, 176; James Hamilton Couper, deposition, n.d., RG 76, entry 185, box 8, folder 77, USNA-CP; Morriss, *Cockburn*, 117; Weiss, "Corps of Colonial Marines," 84.

37 George Cockburn to Sebastián Kindelán, Feb. 13, 1815, and Cockburn to Sir Alexander Cochrane, Feb. 28, 1815 ("every Idea"), SGCP, reel 7, LC; Morriss, *Cockburn*, 119.

38 Sebastián Kindelán to George Cockburn, Jan. 31, 1815, Cockburn to John Forbes, Feb. 26, 1815, and Cockburn to William Philip Yonge, Mar. 2, 1815, MG 12, Admiralty 1, vol. 509:12, 25, 29, reel B-1453, LAC; Cockburn to Kindelán, Feb. 13, 1815, and Cockburn to Sir Alexander Cochrane, Feb. 28, 1815 ("have the slightest claim"), SGCP, reel 7, LC; Kindelán to Cockburn, Feb. 18, 1815 ("Where is the Slave"), RG 76, entry 190, box 8, case 763 (Louis Dolives), USNA-CP; Cochrane to John Wilson Croker, Mar. 13, 1815 ("they should not"), SACP, file 2348, reel 8, LC. For the Forbes case, see John Forbes to Cockburn, Feb. 26, 1815, MG 12, Admiralty 1, vol. 509:23, reel B-1453, LAC; *Niles' Weekly Register*, vol. 26:52 (Mar. 27, 1824: "the plaintiff"); Bullard, *Black Liberation*, 93.

39 St. George Tucker to John Hartwell Cocke, Mar. 21, 1815, JHCFP, box 19, SSCL-UVA; George Cockburn to Capt. Palmer, Feb. 8, 1815, and

Cockburn to Andrew Fitzherbert Evans, Feb. 10, 1815, SGCP, reel 7, LC; Cockburn to Evans, Feb. 11, 1815 ("an ugly account"), *Niles' Weekly Register*, vol. 8:102 (Apr. 8, 1815); Jenkins, *Henry Goulburn*, 86–88; Lambert, *Challenge*, 390–93, 397–99; Bickham, *Weight of Vengeance*, 251–61.

40 George Cockburn to Capt. Palmer, Feb. 8, 1815, to Andrew Fitzherbert Evans, Feb. 10, 1815 ("This Peace"), and to Lt. Gov. Cameron, Mar. 3, 1815 ("pay dearer"), SGCP, reel 7, LC; Sir Thomas Cochrane to Sir Thomas Troubridge, Feb. 12, 1815, in *Niles' Weekly Register*, vol. 8:102 (Apr. 8, 1815); Edward Codrington to his wife, Feb. 13 and 14, 1815, MG 24, F 13, reel A-2076, LAC; Robert Barrie to Mrs. George Clayton, Mar. 2, 1815 ("This Peace" and "a disunion"), Robert Barrie Papers, box 1, WLCP-UM; Lovell, *Personal Narrative*, 178.

41 Stephen Chase Jr. to Stephen Chase, Feb. 13, 1815 ("We have just received"), Diedrich Collection, box 1, WLCL-UM; William H. Cabell to Joseph C. Cabell, Feb. 22, 1815, JCC&CFP (38-111), box 11, SSCL-UVA; Jennings, *Colored Man's Reminiscences*, 15–16.

42 St. George Tucker to John Coalter, Dec. 26, 1814 ("horrid prospects" and "A happy new year"), and Feb. 17, 1815 ("It set us," "the blessed news," "Heaven be prais'd," and "not only put an end"), Grinnan Family Papers (Mss 1 G8855), VHS; Tucker to John Hartwell Cocke, Mar. 21, 1815 ("could hardly persuade"), JHCFP, box 19, SSCL-UVA.

43 St. George Tucker to John Coalter, Feb. 16, 1815, BFP, box 3, SSCL-UVA.

44 Murphy, "Pleasant Murphy's 'Journal,'" 236 (January 2, 1815).

45 Anthony St. John Baker to John Clavell, Feb. 19, 1815, MG 16 (FO 5), vol. 106:11, reel B-2004, LAC; Bickham, *Weight of Vengeance*, 267–69.

46 Sir Alexander Cochrane to John Wilson Croker, Mar. 13, 1815, CO 37 (Bermuda), vol. 73:117, NAUK; John Taylor to James Monroe, May 26, 1815, JMP, ser. 1, reel 6, LC; Charles Fenton Mercer to Wilson Cary Nicholas, Apr. 14, 1815, quoted in Egerton, *Charles Fenton Mercer*, 99; Hugh Mercer to James P. Preston, May 25, 1815, Preston Family Papers (Mss 1 P9267 d 144-64), sec. 4, folder 5, VHS.

47 James Monroe to Winfield Scott, Feb. 21, 1815, RG 107, M 7, reel 1, USNA-DC; Monroe to the United States Senate, Feb. 22, 1815, in S. M. Hamilton, *Writings of Monroe*, vol. 5:321–22; "Peace!" and "The Elections," *Richmond Enquirer*, Feb. 18 ("We have waged a War" and "as much public spirit") and Mar. 11, 1815; Bickham, *Weight of Vengeance*, 269–70. For the nation's military failure, see Stagg, *Mr. Madison's War*, 502–3; Hickey, *War of 1812*, 299.

48 Hickey, *War of 1812*, 211–13; Quimby, *U.S. Army*, vol. 2:897–919.

49 George Cockburn to Andrew Fitzherbert Evans, Feb. 10, 1815, Cock-

burn to Sir Alexander Cochrane, Feb. 11, 1815, Cockburn to Lt. Col. Scott, Feb. 19, 1815, and Cockburn to Thomas Pinckney, Mar. 2, 1815, SGCP, reel 7, LC; Cockburn, order, Mar. 1, 1815, SGCP, reel 10, LC. In waiting for official notification, Cockburn acted within the letter of the treaty. See Henry Goulburn to Earl Bathurst, Dec. 30, 1814, MG 24, A8 (Bathurst Papers), reel H-2961, LAC.

50   Thomas M. Newell and Thomas Spalding to George Cockburn, Mar. 12, 1815, MG 12, Admiralty 1, vol. 509:99, reel B-1453, LAC; Newell and Spalding to John Floyd, Mar. n.d., 1815, in *ASP-FR*, vol. 4:109–11; Sir Alexander Cochrane to John Wilson Croker, Mar. 13 and Apr. 6, 1815, SACP, file 2348, reel 8, LC; Morriss, *Cockburn*, 119–20; Bullard, *Robert Stafford*, 47–48.

51   George Cockburn to D. C. Barholomew, Mar. 6, 1815, and Cockburn to Thomas Cochrane, Mar. 6, 1815, SGCP, reel 10, LC; Thomas M. Newell and Thomas Spalding to John Floyd, Mar. n.d., 1815, in *ASP-FR*, vol. 4:109–11, 113; Spalding to Cockburn, Mar. 14, 1815, MG 12, Admiralty 1, vol. 509:101, reel B-1453, LAC; Newell, deposition, July n.d., 1827 ("permitted the Slaves" and "insolent"), RG 76, entry 185, box 3, folder 8, USNA-CP; Margaret Storie, deposition, Sep. 7, 1817, RG 76, entry 190, box 3, case 145 (Archibald Clarke), USNA-CP; Cockburn to Sir Alexander Cochrane, Mar. 13, 1815, SGCP, reel 7, LC; Spalding, deposition, Apr. 2, 1825, RG 76, entry 190, box 3, case 142 (Thomas Armstrong), USNA-CP; Bullard, *Robert Stafford*, 47–48; Bell, *Major Butler's Legacy*, 179; Bullard, *Black Liberation*, 58, 83–84, 91, 99.

52   Thomas Swann to James Monroe, Mar. 6 and 27, 1815, RG 59, M 179, reel 31, USNA-CP; Robert Clarke to Monroe, Mar. 9, 1815, RG 76, entry 185, box 3, folder 12, USNA-CP; George Loker to John Quincy Adams, Mar. 29, 1818, and the depositions of Caleb Barnhouse, Feb. 25, 1818, and George Loker, Mar. 20, 1818 ("wife" and "that he would take all"), and Apr. 24, 1821, RG 76, entry 190, box 3, case 121 (George Loker), USNA-CP; William Hamilton to George Cockburn, Feb. 27, 1815, SACP, file 2334, reel 3, LC.

53   George Loker to John Quincy Adams, Mar. 29, 1818, and Loker's depositions of Mar. 20, 1818 ("they were as free"), and Apr. 24, 1821, Caleb Barnhouse, Feb. 25, 1818, and James Richardson, Mar. 20, 1818, RG 76, entry 190, box 3, case 121 (George Loker), USNA-CP; William Hamilton to George Cockburn, Feb. 27, 1815 ("that having once" and "received on board"), SACP, file 2334, reel 3, LC.

54   Robert Clarke to James Monroe, Mar. 9, 1815 ("No Negros"), RG 76, entry 185, box 3, folder 12, USNA-CP; George Loker to John Quincy Adams, Mar. 29, 1818, and the depositions of Loker, Mar. 20, 1818, and Apr. 24, 1821, Caleb Barnhouse, Feb. 25, 1818, and James Richard-

son, Mar. 20, 1818, RG 76, entry 190, box 3, case 121 (George Loker), USNA-CP; William Hamilton to George Cockburn, Feb. 27, 1815, SACP, file 2334, reel 3, LC. For the American position on British deserters, see James Monroe to Anthony St. John Baker, Apr. 6, 1815, MG 16 (FO 5), vol. 106:167, reel B-2005, LAC.

55 John Clavell to George Cockburn, Feb. 23, 1815, and Cockburn to Clavell, Mar. 10, 1815 ("On no account"), in Dudley, *Naval War of 1812*, vol. 3:349, 350; Thomas M. Bayly, George Graham, and John S. Skinner to Clavell, Feb. 23, 1815, and Clavell to Bayly, Graham, and Skinner, Feb. 23 ("now serving on board"), and Feb. 24, 1815, in *ASP-FR*, vol. 4:108–9; Bayly to James Monroe, Mar. 6, 1815 ("never believe"), RG 76, entry 190, box 10, Tangier Island folder, USNA-CP.

56 Thomas M. Bayly to James Monroe, Mar. 22, 1815, and Bayly to John Clavell, Apr. 13, 1815, RG 76, entry 185, box 3, folder 8, USNA-CP; Bayly, deposition, Mar. 25, 1828, RG 76, entry 185, box 4, folder 15, USNA-CP. For the visitors to Tangier, see depositions of John Crocket, Nov. 10, 1827, and Miskell Saunders, Dec. 20, 1827, RG 76, entry 185, box 3, folder 4, USNA-CP; John D. Ficklin, depositions, Dec. 10, 1821, and Aug. 12, 1822, APA-GMR, entry 247, box 778, Northumberland County, folder, LV; Abraham B. Hooe, June 8, 1821, APA-GMR, entry 258, box 779, Westmoreland County folder, LV; John G. Joynes, deposition, Dec. 2, 1827, RG 76, entry 190, box 5, case 345 (Tully Wise), USNA-CP. For the captured British-owned slaves retained by the Americans, see Anthony St. John Baker to Viscount Castlereagh, Aug. 23, 1815, John Mason to Baker, July 18, 1815, and George Barton to the commissioners of the Transport Service, Aug. 15, 1815, MG 16 (FO 5), vol. 107:197, 199, reel B-2005, and vol. 111:293, reel B-2006, LAC.

57 William Hamilton to George Cockburn, Feb. 27, 1815, SACP, file 2334, reel 3, LC; Weiss, *Merikens*, 10.

58 [Anonymous], "Recollections of the Expedition," 28 ("The 'niggers'"); G. R. Gleig, diary, Sep. 21–22, 1814 ("an old negro couple"), in C. R. B. Barrett, *85th King's Light Infantry*, 182.

59 Robert Barrie to John Wilson Croker, Oct. 1, 1815, MG 16 (FO 5), vol. 111:298, reel B-2006, LAC; John Fraser, deposition, n.d., RG 76, entry 185, box 4, folder 16, USNA-CP; George Cockburn to Earl Bathurst, Feb. 10, 1816, quoted in Horne, *Negro Comrades*, 71. For criticism by other naval officers of Cockburn's returning any slaves, see J.B. Moore, *History and Digest*, vol. 1:352n1.

60 Sir Alexander Cochrane to Edward Nicolls, July n.d., 1814, MG 12, Admiralty 1, vol. 506:485, reel B-1451, LAC; Cochrane to Nicolls, Dec. 3, 1814, SACP, file 2346, reel 7, LC; Owsley, *Struggle for the Gulf Bor-*

derlands, 103–7, 120–21, 182; Field, *Britain's Sea-Soldiers*, vol. 1:303–4; Weiss, *Merikens*, 11.

61   Nicolls, orders for the First Battalion of Royal Colonial Marines, n.d., 1814, quoted in Millett, "Britain's 1814 Occupation of Pensacola," 237–40.

62   Sir Alexander Cochrane to General Lambert, Feb. 3, 1815, and Cochrane to Sir Pulteney Malcolm, Feb. 17, 1815, MG 12, Admiralty 1, vol. 508:562, 566, reel B-1453, LAC; Thomas Spalding, memorandum, May 21, 1815 ("having espoused the cause"), RG 76, entry 185, box 3, folder 8, USNA-CP; Spalding to Thomas Pinckney, Aug. 5, 1815 ("become a nucleus"), RG 76, entry 185, box 4, folder 22, USNA-CP; Edmund Gaines to Alexander Dallas, May 22, 1815, and James Monroe to Anthony St. John Baker, July 10, 1815, MG 16 (FO 5), vol. 107:69, 93, reel B-2005, LAC; Earl Bathurst to Baker, Sep. 7, 1815 ("ill-judged zeal"), MG 16 (FO 5), vol. 105:29, reel B-2004, LAC; Owsley, *Struggle for the Gulf Borderlands*, 183–85; Owsley and Smith, *Filibusterers and Expansionists*, 106–11; Porter, "Negroes and the Seminole War," 260–62. For the Florida refugees to Trinidad, see Weiss, *Merikens*, 57–58.

63   Owsley and Smith, *Filibusterers and Expansionists*, 111–13 (Duncan Clinch quote on 112); Porter, "Negroes and the Seminole War," 261–65, 278; Howard, *Black Seminoles*, 30–32.

64   Andrew Fitzherbert Evans to George Cockburn, Nov. 27 ("incumberances"), Nov. 28 ("young" and "Their Sloth"), and Nov. 30, 1814, SGCP, reel 9, LC.

65   George Cockburn to Andrew Fitzherbert Evans, Dec. 12, 1814, SGCP, reel 6, LC.

66   Sir Alexander Cochrane to Lord Melville, Apr. 2, 1815 ("fine, brave"), MG 12, Admiralty 1, vol. 509, reel B-1453, LAC; Cochrane to John Wilson Croker, Apr. 6, 1815 ("a corps," and "They were infinitely"), SACP, file 2348, reel 8, LC. For other Britons who praised the Colonial Marines at Bermuda, see *Niles' Weekly Register*, vol. 8:71 (Apr. 1, 1815); Gwynn, *Frigates and Foremasts*, 183n79.

67   Sir Henry Torrent to Henry Goulburn, May 19 and June 13, 1815, CO 37 (Bermuda), vol. 73:149, 153, NAUK. James Cockburn to Sir Henry Torrent, Aug. 23, 1815 ("strong & determined prejudices" and "high ideas"), Andrew Fitzherbert Evans to Cockburn, Aug. 8, 1815, and Andrew Kinsman to Cockburn, Aug. 10, 1815, CO 37 (Bermuda), vol. 73:52, 56, 58, NAUK.

68   James Cockburn to Sir Henry Torrent, Aug. 23, 1815, CO 37, vol. 73:52, NAUK; Weiss, *Merikens*, 12.

69   John Patterson, deposition, Nov. 13, 1822, RG 76, entry 185, box 3, folder 11, USNA-CP; Patterson, deposition, May 13, 1823, RG 76, entry 190,

box 3, case 182 (John L. Hudgins), USNA-CP; Patterson, deposition, Dec. 6, 1823, RG 76, entry 185, box 3, folder 6, USNA-CP; depositions of Henry Griffin, May 10, 1823, and William Dixon, June 5, 1823 ("Red Coats"), RG 76, entry 190, box 4, case 214 (John Patterson), USNA-CP.

70 Mathews County Trial of Harrys et al., Mar. 18, 1813, JBEP, reel 5511, LV; Thomas R. Yeatman, deposition, Mar. 16, 1814, APA-GRM, entry 258, box 779, Mathews County folder, LV.

71 John Patterson, deposition, May 13, 1823 ("raised"), RG 76, entry 190, box 3, case 192 (John L. Hudgins), USNA-CP; William Dixon, deposition, June 5, 1823 ("Red Coats"), RG 76, entry 190, box 4, case 214 (John Patterson), USNA-CP.

72 "Further Particulars" and "An Exposition of the Causes and Character of the Late War with G. Britain," *Richmond Enquirer*, Aug. 10, 1814, and Apr. 5, 1815; "Senate of Maryland," *National Intelligencer*, Feb. 4, 1815 ("vindictive enemy"). For the racialized elaboration of Anglophobia during the nineteenth century, see Haynes, *Unfinished Revolution*, 8–13; A. Rothman, *Slave Country*, 122–23; Hickey, *War of 1812*, 305–7; Horne, *Negro Comrades*, 4–5, 9–12.

73 "African as Well as Indian Allies," "Enemies in War, in Peace Friends," and "Affairs of America," *National Intelligencer*, Jan. 20 ("whose blood"), Apr. 8 ("to excite insurrection"), and May 20, 1815; Eustace, *1812*, 212–18.

74 Drescher, *Abolition*, 231–32; Rugemer, "Caribbean Slave Revolts," 94–99. For American coverage of the Easter Revolt, see "Insurrection at Barbadoes," and Sir James Leith, "An Address to the Slave Population of the Island of Barbadoes," Apr. 26, 1816, *American Beacon and Commercial Diary* (Norfolk, Va), June 3 and June 8, 1816; "Extract of a Letter, Dated Barbadoes, April 29," *Alexandria Gazette*, June 4, 1816. For the numbers of Colonial Marines at Bermuda, see Andrew Kinsman to John Wilson Croker, Aug. 22 and Dec. 1, 1815, Admiralty 1, vol. 3319:54, 85, NAUK.

75 "The Insurrection of the Slaves at Barbadoes," *National Intelligencer*, May 31, 1816, reprinted from the *Richmond Enquirer*.

76 "New Orleans, May 12," *American Beacon and Commercial Diary* (Norfolk, Va.), June 6, 1818; "Milledgeville, May 26," and "Arbuthnot and Ambrister," *Richmond Enquirer*, June 9 and Dec. 21, 1818; Thomas Jefferson to James Madison, Mar. 3, 1819, in P. L. Ford, *Works of Thomas Jefferson*, vol. 12:116; Porter, "Negroes and the Seminole War," 265–76; Ammon, *James Monroe*, 421–25; Henry St. George Tucker to St. George Tucker, Dec. 22, 1818, TCP, reel M-29, SCSL-CWM; Lambert, *Challenge*, 420–21.

77 Haynes, *Unfinished Revolution*, 1–2, 181, 216–17; Eustace, *1812*, 207.

78   Sydney Smith quoted in Foreman, *World on Fire*, 28; Haynes, *Unfinished Revolution*, 1–2, 8, 182–88; Fehrenbacher and McAfee, *Slaveholding Republic*, 91; McCoy, *Last of the Fathers*, 263–64; Lambert, *Challenge*, 424–25.

79   Morriss, *Cockburn*, 6; [R. J. Barrett], "Naval Recollections," 467 ("whilst"); Lord Palmerston quoted in Bartlett and Smith, "'Species of Milito-Nautico-Guerilla Warfare.'" 198. For the postwar investment in southern coast fortifications, see "The Naval Depot, No. IV," *National Intelligencer*, Sep. 14, 1816; James Madison to Wilson Cary Nicholas, May 29, 1816, WCNEP, box 4, LV; and Bartlett, "Gentlemen versus Democrats," 141.

80   Gullah Jack quoted in Johnson, "Reading Evidence," 199 ("that the English"); D. Walker, *David Walker's Appeal*, 56; Haynes, *Unfinished Revolution*, 181; Virginia slaves quoted in Scully, *Religion*, 101.

Chapter Eleven: Agents

1   James Monroe to Thomas Pinckney, Apr. 7, 1815, RG 59, M 40, reel 14, USNA-CP.

2   Patrick Williams, deposition, Nov. 17, 1813, RG 76, entry 185, box 4, folder 22; depositions of Thomas Archer, June 21, 1814, and Samuel S. Griffin, Aug. 15, 1814, APA-GMR, entry 258, box 779, York County folder, LV; Joseph C. Cabell to St. George Tucker, Nov. 24, 1813, TCP, box 33, SCSL-CWM; Tucker to James Madison, Dec. 1, 1813, James Madison Papers, American Memory Series, LC; "Our Slaves," *Richmond Enquirer*, Dec. 16, 1813.

3   James Monroe to the United States Plenipotentiaries, Jan. 28, 1814, in *ASP-FR*, vol. 3:702; John Quincy Adams to James Monroe, Sep. 5, 1814, in Manning, *Diplomatic Correspondence*, vol. 1:647–52; Henry Goulburn to Earl Bathurst, Dec. 30, 1814, MG 24, A 8 (Bathurst Papers), reel H-2961, LAC; Sir Alexander Cochrane to the Admiralty, Oct. 3, 1814, SACP, file 2345, reel 7, LC; Edward Codrington to his wife, Nov. 13, 1814, MG 24, F 13, reel A-2076, LAC; M. Mason, "Battle of the Slaveholding Liberators," 674–75; Hansard, *Parliamentary Debates from the Year 1803*, vol. 29, col. 511–13 (Nov. 24, 1814), vol. 31, cols. 567–80 (June 1, 1815); House of Commons, *Papers Relating to the Slave Trade*, 3.

4   John Graham to St. George Tucker, Oct. 26, 1814, TCP, box 33, SCSL-CWM; Thomas Griffin to Joseph C. Cabell, Dec. 5, 1814, JCCFP (38-111), box 11, SSCL; Cabell to Tucker, Nov. 22, 1814, John Tabb Smith to Tucker, Nov. 21, 1814, Thomas Griffin to Graham, Feb. 16, 1815, and James Monroe to the United States Senate, Feb. 28, 1815, in *ASP-FR*, vol. 3:750–51.

5 Edward Codrington to his wife, Mar. 2, 1815, MG 24, F13, A-2076, LAC; Sir Alexander Cochrane to James Monroe, Mar. 8, 1815, MG 12, Admiralty 1, vol. 508:497, reel B-1453, LAC; Cochrane to John Wilson Croker, Mar. 13 ("a story") and Apr. 22, 1815, SACP, file 2348, reel 8, LC; James Madison to Monroe, Mar. 26, 1815, and Tucker to Monroe, Apr. 2, 1815, JMP, ser. 1, reel 6, LC.

6 Anthony St. John Baker to Sir Alexander Cochrane, Mar. 25, 1815 ("The proof"), James Monroe to Cochrane, Apr. 5, 1815, and Baker to Monroe, Apr. 9, 1815 ("The officers of a Nation"), SACP, file 2337, reel 5, LC; *Niles' Weekly Register*, vol. 8:114 (Apr. 15, 1814); Monroe to St. George Tucker, Mar. 26, 1815, TCP, box 34, SCSL-CWM; Monroe to Baker, Apr. 5, 1815 ("a Gentleman"), MG 16, FO 5, vol. 106:191, reel B-2005, LAC. For the canard that Cochrane diverted slaves to his plantation in Trinidad, see "Tecumseh," *Richmond Enquirer*, Dec. 23, 1815.

7 James Monroe to St. George Tucker, Mar. 26, 1815, TCP, box 34, SCSL-CWM; Monroe to Thomas Pinckney, Apr. 6, 1815 ("The exposure"), RG 59, M 40, reel 14, USNA-CP.

8 *Niles' Weekly Register*, vol. 7:54 (Oct. 6, 1814); James Monroe to John Steele, Oct. 28, 1814, Steele to Monroe, Nov. 4, 1814 ("had heard"), Perrin Willis to John Graham, Feb. 17, 1815, Robert G. Scott to Monroe, Apr. 10, 1815, Joseph C. Cabell to Monroe, Apr. 19, 1815, and Edward Ironmonger, deposition, May 25, 1815, RG 76, entry 185, box 4, folder 22, USNA-CP; Thomas L. Hall, deposition, Apr. 5, 1815, RG 76, entry 185, box 3, folder 8, USNA-CP; Walter Jones to James Monroe, May 25, 1815, RG 76, entry 185, box 4, folder 13, USNA-CP. For Jaboe's third-hand report, see Athanasius Fenwick to Monroe, Apr. 6, 1815, RG 76, entry 190, box 9, case 860 (Athanasius Fenwick), USNA-CP.

9 Earl Bathurst to Charles Cameron, Feb. 2, 1815, A. Murray to Cameron, May 6, 1815 ("enjoying"), Bahamas Executive Council meeting, May 8, 1815, and Cameron to Sir Alexander Cochrane, May 9, 1815, SACP, file 2338, reel 5, LC; Anthony St. John Baker to Viscount Castlereagh, Apr. 13, 1815 ("made particular Enquiry"), MG 16, FO 5, vol. 106:179, reel B-2005, LAC; *Royal Gazette and Bahama Advertiser*, May 3, 1815, copy in RG 76, entry 185, box 4, folder 22, USNA-CP; James Cockburn to Earl Bathurst, July 7, 1816 ("most minute"), CO 37 (Bermuda), vol. 74:42, NAUK; Castlereagh to John Quincy Adams, Apr. 27, 1816, RG 76, entry 190, box 7, case 667 (James Young), USNA-CP. For the Nova Scotia evidence, see Bathurst to John C. Sherbrooke, May 10, 1816, Sherbrook to Bathurst, June 20, 1816 ("there never was"), Charles Reeves, deposition, June 20, 1816, and John Howe, William Minns, John Howe Jr., and Anthony K. Holland, deposition, June 20, 1816, MG 11, CO 218

(Nova Scotia), vol. 29:69, 89, 91, 93, reel B-1118, LAC. For Monroe's response, see Monroe to Baker, July 20, 1815, and Baker to Castlereagh, Aug. 13, 1815, MG 16, FO 5, vol. 107:163, 169, reel B-2005, LAC.

10   Thomas Pinckney to James Monroe, Mar. 18, 1815, RG 59, M 179, reel 31, USNA-DC; St. George Tucker to Monroe, Apr. 2, 1815, JMP, ser. 1, reel 6, LC; *Richmond Enquirer*, Apr. 1, 1815; "Captured Slaves," *National Intelligencer*, June 21, 1815; James Madison to Monroe, July 26, 1816, in Hunt, *Writings of James Madison*, vol. 8:352–53. For a concession to the lack of evidence, see Henry Ashton to Monroe, Apr. 1, 1815, RG 76, entry 185, box 4, folder 13, USNA-CP.

11   "Captured Slaves" and "Washington," *National Intelligencer*, June 21 ("the patriotic Monroe") and August 1, 1815 ("no liberal," and "May it not have *prevented*"). See also *National Intelligencer*, Mar. 28, Apr. 12, and June 24, 1815.

12   John Quincy Adams to James Monroe, Aug. 24, 1816, in Manning, *Diplomatic Correspondence*, vol. 1:806; Joseph C. Cabell to William Wirt, Dec. 8, 1827, JCC&CFP (38-111), box 19, SSCL-UVA. It is telling that in 1826–1828, the American claims commission set up to compensate slave owners rejected the claim of James Young, whose case relied on a deposition about the hearsay that the Jamaican vice admiralty court had sold slaves. See RG 76, entry 190, box 7, case 667 (James Young), USNA-CP. The myth of the British selling runaway slaves during the War of 1812 will never die, for the same reason that it was created: to have villainous Britons as foils to good Americans. For example, in 1983 the official history of Westmoreland County, Virginia, assures readers, "The British were not completely reliable partners; many slaves were returned to their masters after the Treaty of Ghent or sold into slavery in the West Indies when the British had completed their missions." See Norris, *Westmoreland County, Virginia*, 589.

13   Roswell King to Pierce Butler, Mar. 18, 1815, quoted in Bell, *Major Butler's Legacy*, 180; Walter Jones to [George Graham], Mar. 26, 1815 ("wretches" and "on the barren Beach"), Jones Papers (Mss 2 J7283 b), VHS; "The Mediterranean Squadron," *National Intelligencer*, July 25, 1815; Thomas Spalding to Thomas Pinckney, Apr. 29, 1815, and Spalding to James Monroe, June 12, 1815, RG 76, entry 185, box 4, folder 22, USNA-CP; Cassel, "Slaves of the Chesapeake," 154–55.

14   James Spilman, "notes," June 11, 1815, RG 76, entry 185, box 4, folder 22, USNA-CP; Eli Magruder to James Monroe, May 10, 1815, RG 76, box 4, folder 13, USNA-CP. For the identities of the four who returned with Spilman, see Joseph Webster, deposition, Dec. 20, 1827, RG 76, entry 190, box 5, case 462 (Presley Neale), USNA-CP; depositions of Anthony

Champ, Oct. 13, 1827, and Isaac Smith, Oct. 18, 1827, RG 76, entry 190, box 7, case 616 (William Waring), USNA-CP. For John Hall, see Richard Kemm, deposition, June 1, 1815, APA-GMR, entry 258, box 779, Lancaster County folder, LV.

15 Rawleigh W. Downman, deposition, July 13, 1815 ("Returned"), RG 76, entry 190, box 5, case 325 (Rawleigh W. Downman), USNA-CP; William Waring's Louis, deposition, Aug. 21, 1821, APA-GMR, entry 247, box 778, Essex County folder, LV; Simon Willis, deposition, Apr. 20, 1828, RG 76, entry 190, box 8, case 769 (Lucy Clements), USNA-CP. For Willis's unique status, see Vincent Bramhan, Nov. 8, 1827, RG 76, entry 185, box 3, folder 4, USNA-CP; depositions of Randal R. Kirk, Apr. 25, 1828, and Thomas McClanahan's Sam, Apr. 26, 1828, RG 76, entry 190, box 5, case 418 (John Christopher), USNA-CP.

16 *Baltimore Patriot*, Apr. 8, 1816 ("small eyes" and "remarkably large feet"); Gilbert W. Russell to Francis Newman, Mar. 2, 1818 ("Tom has married"), Russell to Frederick Grammar, June 24, 1818, Grammar to Horatio Ridout, Aug. 13, 1818, and the depositions of John Weedon, May 27, 1828, and John A. Grammar, Henry E. Mayer, and Horatio Ridout, May 27, 1828, RG 76, entry 185, box 3, folder 7, USNA-CP.

17 For testimony that none of the wartime runaways ever returned to Princess Anne County, see John T. Keeling, deposition, Nov. 4, 1822, RG 76, entry 190, box 4, case 241 (Lemuel Cornick), USNA-CP.

18 James Monroe to Thomas Pinckney, Apr. 7, 1815 ("They have professed"), RG 59, M 40, reel 14, USNA-CP; Monroe to Stephen Pleasanton, May 18, 1815, James Monroe Papers in Virginia Repositories, reel 3282, LV; Walter Jones to James Monroe, May 25 and June 11, 1815, RG 76, entry 185, box 4, folder 13, USNA-CP; Monroe to Jones, May 28, 1815, Mss 2M7576 a 9, VHS; Thomas Spalding to Pinckney, Apr. 29, 1815, RG 76, entry 185, box 4, folder 22, USNA-CP.

19 Bell, *Major Butler's Legacy*, 180; Coulter, *Thomas Spalding*, 190–93; James Monroe to Thomas Pinckney, Apr. 7, 1815, RG 59, M 40, reel 14, USNA-CP; Pinckney to Thomas Spalding, Apr. 23, 1815, and Spalding to Pinckney, Apr. 29, 1815, RG 76, entry 185, box 4, folder 22, USNA-CP; Spalding to Monroe, May n.d., 1815 ("instantly" and "that he would rather Bermuda"), and Edward Griffith to Spalding, May 23, 1815, in *ASP-FR*, vol. 4:113, 115.

20 Eli Magruder to James Monroe, May 10, 1815, RG 76, entry 185, box 4, folder 13, USNA-CP; Thomas Spalding, memorandum, May 21, 1815, and Spalding to Monroe, May n.d., 1815 ("Every means," "as important means," and "paid"), RG 76, entry 185, box 3, folder 8, USNA-CP; Bell, *Major Butler's Legacy*, 180; James Spilman, "Notes," June 11, 1815,

RG 76, entry 185, box 4, folder 22, USNA-CP. The federal government printed only the first part of Spalding's undated May letter, omitting the provocative portions about the former slaves as a military threat. See the published version in *ASP-FR*, vol. 4:113.

21   James Monroe to Walter Jones, Apr. 14, 1815, and Eli Magruder to James Monroe, Apr. 29, 1815, RG 59, M 179, reel 31, USNA-CP; Magruder to Monroe, May 10, 24, 26, and 31, 1815, and John F. Dumoulin to Monroe, May 16, 1816, RG 76, entry 185, box 4, folder 13, USNA-CP; Magruder to Monroe, May 17, 1815, RG 76, entry 185, box 4, folder 22, USNA-CP; Francis Forbes to Magruder, May 23, 1815, and Thomas Spalding to Monroe, May 30, 1815, RG 76, entry 185, box 3, folder 8, USNA-CP; Monroe to Thomas Pinckney, July 17, 1815, and Monroe to Spalding, July 18, 1815, RG 59, M 77, vol. 3:294, 299–301, reel 154, USNA-CP.

22   Walter Jones to Augustine Neale, June 8, 1815, RG 76, entry 185, box 4, folder 13, USNA-CP.

23   Augustine Neale, memorandum, n.d., RG 76, entry 190, box 5, case 462 (Presley Neale), USNA-CP; Walter Jones to Neale, June 8, 1815, and James Monroe to Neale, June 17, 1815, RG 76, entry 185, box 4, folder 13, USNA-CP.

24   Walter Jones to Augustine Neale, June 8, 1815, RG 76, entry 185, box 4, folder 13, USNA-CP.

25   Augustine Neale to James Monroe, June 14, 1815 ("give positive evidence"), Monroe to Neale, June 17, 1815, RG 76, and Neale to Monroe, June 28, 1815, entry 185, box 4, folder 13, USNA-CP; Augustine Neale, memorandum, n.d. ("quite an intelligent"), and John Chowning, deposition, Apr. 1, 1828, RG 76, entry 190, box 5, case 462 (Presley Neale), USNA-CP.

26   "The Mediterranean Squadron," reprinted from *New York Columbian* in *National Intelligencer*, July 25, 1815 ("to bring home"); Augustine Neale to James Monroe, Aug. 14 and 27, 1815, RG 76, entry 185, box 4, folder 13, USNA-CP.

27   Augustine Neale to James Monroe, Aug. 27, Sep. 5 ("The white Labourers"), Sep. 25, and Nov. 15, 1815 ("the despised"), RG 76, entry 185, box 4, folder 13, USNA-CP.

28   Augustine Neale to James Monroe, Aug. 27, Sep. 5 ("But, sir,"), and Sep. 25, 1815 ("a *few*"), RG 76, entry 185, box 4, folder 13, USNA-CP.

29   Augustine Neale to James Monroe, Sep. 5, 1815, RG 76, entry 185, box 4, folder 13, USNA-CP.

30   Augustine Neale to James Monroe, Sep. 15 ("escaped to the shore"), Sep.

25 ("a Mob" and "was all most murdered"), and Nov. 15, 1815 ("were daily seen"), RG 76, entry 185, box 4, folder 13, USNA-CP.

31 Augustine Neale to James Monroe, Sep. 15, Sep. 19 ("the most unfriendly"), and Sep. 25, 1815, RG 76, entry 185, box 4, folder 13, USNA-CP.

32 Eli Magruder to James Monroe, May 30, 1815, Thomas Spalding to Thomas Pinckney, Aug. 5, 1815, and Augustine Neale to Monroe, Sep. 5 ("remote") and Sep. 25, 1815, RG 76, entry 185, box 4, folder 13, USNA-CP; Roswell King to Pierce Butler, Aug. 13, 1815 ("that they can find"), quoted in Bell, *Major Butler's Legacy*, 185–86.

33 George Cockburn to Andrew Fitzherbert Evans, Dec. 12, 1814, SGCP, reel 6, LC; Whitfield, *Blacks on the Border*, 47–48; Fergusson, *Documentary Study*, 8.

34 Whitfield, *Blacks on the Border*, 53.

35 *Niles' Weekly Register*, vol. 4:407 (Aug. 21, 1813); John C. Sherbrooke to Capt. Henry Hotham, Sep. 24, 1813, RG 1, vol. 111, reel 15262, NSA; Hotham to Sherbrooke, Oct. 1, 1813, RG 1, vol. 420, reel 15462, NSA; Earl Bathurst to Sherbrooke, Jan. 23 and Oct. 25, 1814, MG 11, CO 218 (Nova Scotia), vol. 29:37, 47, reel B-1118, LAC; Sir Alexander Cochrane to the Admiralty, Oct. 3, 1814, SACP, file 2345, reel 7, LC; Sherbrooke to Cochrane, Oct. 5, 1814, MG 11, CO 217 (Nova Scotia), vol. 95:130, reel B-1055, LAC. For the earliest refugee landings in Halifax, see Malcomson, "Freedom by Reaching the Wooden World," 3. For the neglect by some officers to report refugee arrivals, see Sherbrooke to Cochrane, Oct. 7, 1814, SACP, file 2326, reel 1, LC.

36 Whitfield, *From American Slaves*, 113–16, 119 (*Acadian Recorder*, Jan. 4, 1817 quotes: "no kindness" and "a race"); Charles Morris to Lt. Col. Addison, n.d. ("The common Sentiment"), RG 1, vol. 419, doc. 81, reel 15462, NSA. For a regret that Nova Scotians blamed all blacks for the misdeeds of a few, see Seth Coleman to Richard Tremain, Mar. 5, 1815, RG 1, vol. 420, doc. 132, reel 15463, NSA. For the experience of the post-revolutionary "Black Loyalists," see Grant, "Black Immigrants," 253–58.

37 Earl Bathurst to John C. Sherbrooke, Jan. 23, 1814, MG 11, CO 218 (Nova Scotia), vol. 29:37, reel B-1118, LAC; Sherbrooke to Bathurst, Oct. 5, 1814 ("miserable wretches" and "the generality"), MG 11, CO 217 (Nova Scotia), vol. 93:324, reel B-1055, LAC; Sherbrooke to Bathurst, Apr. 6, 1815 ("the greatest part"), MG 11, CO 217 (Nova Scotia), vol. 96:93, reel B-1056, LAC. For all his complaints and prejudice, Sherbrooke did keep the refugees fed, clothed, and sheltered—albeit in the discomfort of the poorhouse. Seventy-four died there between September 2, 1814, and March 2, 1815. For the deaths, see "Abstract of Sundries

supplied to Blacks in the Poor House at Halifax," Mar. 2, 1815, RG 1, vol. 420, reel 15462, NSA.

38   Grant, "Black Immigrants," 268; Grant, "Chesapeake Blacks," 194; John C. Sherbrooke to the Assembly, Feb. 23, 1815, in Fergusson, *Documentary Study*, 17; Sir Alexander Cochrane to Sherbrooke, Mar. 25, 1815, Nova Scotia Assembly to Sherbrooke, Apr. 1, 1815 ("a separate & marked" and "discouragement"), and Sherbrooke to Earl Bathurst, Apr. 6, 1815, MG 11, CO 217 (Nova Scotia), vol. 96:93, 97, 99, reel B-1056, LAC; Whitfield, *Blacks on the Border*, 35, 47.

39   Whitfield, *Blacks on the Border*, 50–51; Winks, *Blacks in Canada*, 118–19; John C. Sherbrooke to Earl Bathurst, Sep. 23, Oct. 16, and Nov. 21, 1815, MG 11, CO 217 (Nova Scotia), vol. 96:218, 224, 232, reel B-1056, LAC; "Return of American Refugee Negroes," Apr. 27, 1815–Oct. 24, 1818, RG 76, entry 185, box 6, folder 51, USNA-CP.

40   Spray, "Settlement of the Black Refugees," 64–66; Grant, "Chesapeake Blacks," 194–95; John C. Sherbrooke to Earl Bathurst, May 6, 1815, and George Smyth to Sherbrooke, Apr. 13, 1815, MG 11, CO 217 (Nova Scotia), vol. 96:131, 133, reel B-1056, LAC; Smyth to Bathurst, Apr. 17, 1816, and "A List of Black Refugees Furnished by His Majesty's Ship Regulus," n.d., MG 11, CO 188 (New Brunswick), vol. 22:19, 41, reel B-1126, LAC.

41   Whitfield, *Blacks on the Border*, 49–52; Martell, *Immigration*, 18–20.

42   Earl Bathurst to John C. Sherbrooke, May 10 and June 13, 1815, MG 11, CO 218 (Nova Scotia), vol. 29:54, 56, reel B-1118, LAC; Sherbrooke to Bathurst, July 20, 1815, ("the negroes" and "dispersed"), MG 11, CO 217 (Nova Scotia), vol. 96:186, reel B-1056, LAC.

43   John C. Sherbrooke to Earl Bathurst, July 20, 1815, MG 11, CO 217 (Nova Scotia), vol. 96:186, reel B-1056, LAC; Whitfield, *Blacks on the Border*, 52–53; Ferguson, *Documentary Study*, 38, 68; Lawson, *History of the Townships*, 151–76; Theophilus Chamberlain to Charles Morris, Nov. 17, 1815, RG 1, vol. 419, doc. 41, reel 15462, NSA.

44   John C. Sherbrooke to Earl Bathurst, Sep. 23 and Nov. 21, 1815, Executive Council to Sherbrooke, Nov. 17, 1815, MG 11, CO 217 (Nova Scotia), vol. 96:220, 232, 234 reel B-1056, LAC; Bathurst to Sherbrooke, Nov. 10, 1815, and Feb. 5, 1816, MG 11, CO 218 (Nova Scotia), vol. 29:60, 66, LAC; Fergusson, *Documentary Study*, 38, 51–56.

45   Fergusson, *Documentary Study*, 12, 28, 42–43, 51; Whitfield, *Blacks on the Border*, 39, 52, 55.

46   Fergusson, *Documentary Study*, 39–40, 51, 68–69; Whitfield, *Blacks on the Border*, 37–41, 54–55.

47   Theophilus Chamberlain to Charles Morris, Nov. 17, 1815 ("able" "industrious" and "snug houses"), and Jan. 4, 1816, and John Rule, cer-

tificate, Sep. 30, 1817 ("very ingenious"), RG 1, vol. 419, docs. 41, 46, 67, reel 15462, NSA; Rufus Fairbanks to H. H. Cogswell, Mar. 4 ("they raised"), and May 9, 1816, RG 1, vol. 421, docs. 3, 5, reel 15462, NSA; Fergusson, *Documentary Study*, 38–40.

48   Seth Coleman to William Sabatier, Mar. 23, 1815, in Ells and Harvey, *Calendar of Official Correspondence*, 339. For Coleman's reputation for good judgment and accurate information, see Samuel Head to Charles Morris, Feb. 1, 1816, RG 1, vol. 419, doc. 47, reel 15462, NSA; Sabatier to John C. Sherbrooke, Feb. n.d., 1815, RG 1, vol. 305, doc. 6, reel 15386, NSA.

49   Seth Coleman to William Sabatier, Mar. 23, 1815, in Ells and Harvey, *Calendar of Official Correspondence*, 339; Theophilus Chamberlain to Charles Morris, Jan. 4, 1816, RG 1, vol. 419, doc. 46, reel 15462, NSA.

50   John C. Sherbrooke to Earl Bathurst, June 5, 1816, MG 11, CO 217 (Nova Scotia), vol. 98:67, reel B-1056, LAC; Lord Dalhousie to Bathurst, Dec. 2, 1816, in Fergusson, *Documentary Study*, 29; Whitfield, *Blacks on the Border*, 56–59.

51   Lord Dalhousie to Earl Bathurst, Dec. 9, 1816 ("Slaves by habit"), in Fergusson, *Documentary Study*, 30; Dalhousie, journal, July 8, 1827 ("a silly thing"), in Whitelaw, *Dalhousie Journals*, vol. 3:105; Whitfield, *Blacks on the Border*, 42–44, 60.

52   Lord Dalhousie to Earl Bathurst, Aug. 14, 1817 ("almost"), and June 10, 1819 ("the habits"), in Fergusson, *Documentary Study*, 32, 33. For the local prejudice against the blacks, see also Lawson, *History of the Townships*, 192.

53   Whitfield, *Blacks on the Border*, 6 (Maria Fuller quoted), 37 (unnamed male refugee quoted), 60–61; Mrs. Dair (elderly refugee woman quoted in Whitfield, *From American Slaves*, 52.

54   Martell, *Immigration*, 17; Earl Bathurst to John C. Sherbrooke, Nov. 10, 1815, MG 11, CO 218 (Nova Scotia), vol. 29:60, reel B-1118, LAC; Sherbrooke to Bathurst, Apr. 20, 1816, MG 11, CO 217 (Nova Scotia), vol. 98:55, reel B-1056, LAC; Richard Inglis to Robert D. George, Aug. 20, 1821, RG 1, vol. 422, doc. 30, reel 15463, NSA; Winks, *Blacks in Canada*, 122–23; Whitfield, *From American Slaves*, 45–46.

55   Whitfield, *Blacks on the Border*, 61–62; James Kempt to Earl Bathurst, Oct. 16, 1823 ("These people"), in Bell, *Major Butler's Legacy*, 187; Kempt quoted in Whitfield, *From American Slaves*, 47 ("fanatical preachers"); Fergusson, *Documentary Study*, 31–36.

56   Edward H. Lowe quoted in Fergusson, *Documentary Study*, 46 ("They seem"); John Chamberlain et al. to the assembly, June 8, 1838, in Fergusson, *Documentary Study*, 111; Whitfield, *From American Slaves*, 43;

Whitfield, *Blacks on the Border*, 79; Lawson, *History of the Townships*, 188–89.

57   Whitfield, *Blacks on the Border*, 58–61. For the study of refugee families, see Whitfield, *From American Slaves*, 25, 89.

58   Rufus Fairbanks to unknown, Mar. 8, 1815, RG 1, vol. 305, doc. 22, reel 15386, NSA.

59   Carmichael, "Some Notes on Sir Ralph James Woodford," 30–31; Laurence, "Settlement of Free Negroes," 26; William H. Burnley, report, n.d., ca. May 1815 ("lying waste" and "healthy & free"), CO 295 (Trinidad), vol. 37:97, NAUK.

60   Sir Ralph Woodford to Earl Bathurst, June 6, 1815 ("mostly creoles"), Aug. 5, Nov. 9, and Nov. 30, 1815, CO 295 (Trinidad), vol. 37:51, 139, 209, 229, NAUK; Woodford to Bathurst, Feb. 8, 1816, CO 295 (Trinidad), vol. 39:37, NAUK; Weiss, *Merikens*, 12, 55–62; Weiss, "Corps of Colonial Marines," 85.

61   Sir Ralph Woodford to Earl Bathurst, Apr. 23, Aug. 4, Oct. 5, and Nov. 23, 1816 ("to promote the benevolent Views"), CO 295 (Trinidad), vol. 39:109, and vol. 40:17, 151, 283, NAUK.

62   Sir Ralph Woodford to Henry Goulburn, Oct. 15, 1815, and Woodford to Earl Bathurst, Oct. 16, 1815, and Apr. 23, May 10 ("an Attempt to fire"), June 14, June 25, June 29 ("Ruin and Desolation"), July 10, Aug. 4, and Aug. 28, 1816, CO 295 (Trinidad), vol. 37:160, 177, vol. 39:109, 119, 140, 185, 203, and vol. 40:3–5, 17, 125, NAUK.

63   Sir Ralph Woodford to Earl Bathurst, Aug. 28 and Nov. 10, 1816, CO 295 (Trinidad), vol. 40:103, 169, NAUK.

64   John Barrow to Henry Goulburn, Nov. 14 and Nov. 28, 1815, and James Cockburn to Earl Bathurst, Feb. 10, 1816, CO 37 (Bermuda), vol. 73:180, 190, and vol. 74:9, NAUK.

65   Sir Ralph Woodford to Andrew Kinsman, Aug. 15, 1816, Kinsman undated memorandum number 2, and Kinsman to the Colonial Marines, Aug. 15, 1816, Admiralty 1, vol. 3319:159, 161, 163, NAUK; Woodford to Earl Bathurst, Aug. 28, 1816 ("strong disposition"), and Nov. 10, 1816, CO 295 (Trinidad), vol. 40:103, 169, NAUK.

66   Sir Ralph Woodford to Lewis Johnston, Oct. 23, 1816 ("orderly"), and Woodford to Earl Bathurst, Nov. 10, 1816 ("far advanced"), CO 295 (Trinidad), vol. 40:169, 181, NAUK; Laurence, "Settlement of Free Negroes," 27–30; Weiss, *Merikens*, 18; Weiss, "Corps of Colonial Marines," 81, 85.

67   Andrew Kinsman to the Colonial Marines, Aug. 15, 1816, Admiralty 1, vol. 3319:163, NAUK.

68   Sir Ralph Woodford to Earl Bathurst, Aug. 28, 1816, CO 295 (Trinidad),

vol. 40:103, NAUK; Lewis Johnston et al., "Petition of the White and Free Colored Inhabitants of the Quarters of North and South Naparima," Oct. 7, 1816 ("the intercourse" and "impatience"), CO 295 (Trinidad), vol. 40:173, NAUK.

69 Sir Ralph Woodford to Earl Bathurst, Nov. 10, 1816 ("Many"), Lewis Johnston et al. "Petition of the White and Free Colored Inhabitants of the Quarters of North and South Naparima," Oct. 7, 1816, and Woodford to Johnston et al., Oct. 23, 1816 ("additional Security"), CO 295 (Trinidad), vol. 40:169, 173, 181, NAUK; Laurence, "Settlement of Free Negroes," 27–30; Carmichael, "Some Notes on Sir Ralph James Woodford," 29–31; D. Wood, *Trinidad in Transition*, 38; Horne, *Negro Comrades*, 72–73.

70 Sir Ralph Woodford to Earl Bathurst, Nov. 10, 1816, and Lewis Johnston et al., "Petition of the White and Free Colored Inhabitants of the Quarters of North and South Naparima," Oct. 7, 1816, CO 295 (Trinidad), vol. 40:173, NAUK; Laurence, "Settlement of Free Negroes," 31–35 (Woodford quoted on 32); McDaniel, "Memory Spirituals of the Liberated American Soldiers," 43.

71 Weiss, "Corps of Colonial Marines," 80, 85–86; Wood, *Trinidad in Transition*, 38–39; McDaniel, "Memory Spirituals of the Liberated American Soldiers," 38–58 (missionaries quote on 44–45, and see 54 ("Ninevah").

72 Henry Howard Jr., deposition, June 21, 1814 ("most positively"), APA-GMR, entry 258, box 779, York County folder, LV; Lewis Neth Jr., deposition, July 31, 1821 ("expressing" and "that he had shipped"), RG 76, entry 190, box 8, case 764 (Lewis Neth), USNA-CP. For Jacob, see Jacob G. Parker, deposition, Nov. 10, 1823, RG 76, entry 190, box 4, case 258 (Jacob G. Parker), USNA-CP.

73 Jacob G. Parker, deposition, Nov. 10, 1823 ("a bright mulatto"), RG 76, entry 190, box 4, case 258 (Jacob G. Parker), USNA-CP; Lewis Smith to Thomas Griffin, Oct. 11, 1827, RG 76, entry 190, box 8, case 734 (Thomas Griffin), USNA-CP.

74 James McBride, deposition, Apr. 4, 1823, RG 76, entry 190, box 4, case 214 (John Patterson), USNA-CP; Joseph C. Cabell to Langdon Cheves, Henry Sewall, and James Pleasants, Dec. 4, 1827 ("The remaining slaves"), RG 76, entry 185, box 3, folder 6, USNA-CP; depositions of Fielder Cross, July 16, 1821, and Howard Duvall, Mar. 4, 1822, RG 76, entry 190, box 9, case 852 (Howard Duvall), USNA-CP; Edward Ringhold, deposition, Feb. 15, 1828, RG 76, entry 190, box 9, case 817 (Rebecca Beard), USNA-CP; John Massey, deposition, Feb. 9, 1824, RG 76, entry 190, box 9, case 930 (Benjamin Farrow), USNA-CP; Walter L. Dorrell, deposition, Jan. 21, 1824, RG 76, entry 190, box 8, case 796

(Samuel Collard), USNA-CP; John Hebb, deposition, Mar. 24, 1825, RG 76, entry 190, box 7, case 644 (Thomas Lynch Jr.), USNA-CP; Dennis Lewis, deposition, July 16, 1828, RG 76, entry 190, box 9, case 919 (Daniel McCarty), USNA-CP.

75 John Massey, deposition, Sep. 13, 1827, RG 76, entry 190, box 3, case 177 (Abraham B. Hooe), USNA-CP.

76 Jacob G. Parker, deposition, Nov. 10, 1823 ("a letter"), and John K. Floyd, deposition, Oct. 8, 1827, RG 76, entry 190, box 4, case 258 (Jacob G. Parker), USNA-CP. For the compensation paid for Peter Parker, see Jacob G. Parker claim, in *ASP-FR*, vol. 5:815.

77 Archibald Clark to his mother, July 6, 1816, RG 76, entry 190, box 9, case 883 (James Pumphrey), USNA-CP.

78 James Gross to Chany Gross, Nov. 7, 1825, RG 76, entry 190, box 7, case 700 (Jane Parran), USNA-CP; Archibald Clark to his mother, July 6, 1816, RG 76, entry 190, box 9, case 883 (James Pumphrey), USNA-CP.

79 Toby Forester to his parents, Jan. 5, 1819, and depositions of Charles and Ursula Bowie, Sep. 6, 1821, and Ned Wheeler, Dec. 4, 1827, RG 76, entry 190, box 8, case 752 (Charles and Ursula Bowie), USNA-CP.

80 William Whiddington to Judy Hoxton, Dec. 9, 1816, RG 76, entry 190, box 7, case 609 (William Whittington), USNA-CP; Jeremiah West to David F. Davenport, Nov. 13, 1818, RG 76, entry 190, box 5, case 368 (David F. Davenport), USNA-CP.

81 Archibald Clark to his mother, July 6, 1816, RG 76, entry 190, box 9, case 883 (James Pumphrey), USNA-CP; William Whiddington to Judy Hoxton, Dec. 9, 1816, RG 76, entry 190, box 7, case 609 (William Whiddington), USNA-CP; Jeremiah West to David F. Davenport, Nov. 13, 1818, RG 76, entry 190, box 5, case 368 (David F. Davenport), USNA-CP; Toby Forester to his parents, Jan. 5, 1819, RG 76, entry 190, box 8, case 752 (Charles and Ursula Bowie), USNA-CP.

82 Bartlet Shanklyn to Abraham B. Hooe, May 21, 1820, RG 76, entry 190, box 3, case 177 (Abraham B. Hooe), USNA-CP.

83 Jeremiah West to David F. Davenport, Nov. 13, 1818, RG 76, entry 190, box 5, case 368 (David F. Davenport), USNA-CP.

84 William Whiddington to Judy Hoxton, Dec. 9, 1816, RG 76, entry 190, box 7, case 609 (William Whiddington), USNA-CP.

85 Thomas Archer, deposition, Apr. 1, 1815 ("They were then asked"), and Lewis Smith to Thomas Griffin, Oct. 11, 1827, RG 76, entry 190, box 8, case 734 (Thomas Griffin), USNA-CP.

86 Lewis Smith to Thomas Griffin, Oct. 11, 1827, RG 76, entry 190, box 8, case 734 (Thomas Griffin), USNA-CP.

87 Thomas Griffin undated superscription on Lewis Smith to Thomas Grif-

fin, Oct. 11, 1827, RG 76, entry 190, box 8, case 734 (Thomas Griffin), USNA-CP.

88   Lewis Smith to Thomas Griffin, Oct. 11, 1827, RG 76, entry 190, box 8, case 734 (Thomas Griffin), USNA-CP.

89   Late in the twentieth century, a distinguished American historian, Robin Winks, declared that "the Refugee Negroes were a disorganized, pathetic, and intimidated body who seemed unable to recover from their previous condition of servitude." Favoring the harsh views of Lord Dalhousie, Winks added, "So recently escaped from slavery, they at first assumed that freedom involved no responsibilities." See Winks, *Blacks in Canada*, 114 ("Refugee Negroes"), 126 ("So recently escaped"). For a better grounded and more nuanced interpretation of the refugees (with apt attention to success stories), see Whitfield, *From American Slaves*, 28, 59–74.

90   Augustine Neale to James Monroe, Sep. 5, 1815, RG 76, entry 185, box 4, folder 13, USNA-CP. James Pumphrey marked with an X̲ the memorial written for him. See James Pumphrey to the commissioners, Apr. 20, 1824, RG 76, entry 190, box 9, case 883 (James Pumphrey), USNA-CP.

CHAPTER TWELVE: FIRE BELL

1   Alexander Dick, travel journal, p. 182 (May 21, 1808), SSCL-UVA.

2   Thomas Jefferson to John Holmes, Apr. 22, 1820, in P.L. Ford, *Works of Thomas Jefferson*, vol. 12:158–59.

3   Cleves, "Hurtful to the State," 216–18; M. Mason, *Slavery and Politics*, 42–50, 66–74.

4   Josiah Quincy quoted in M. Mason, *Slavery and Politics*, 46 ("destined"), 56–58 ("My heart"); S. Potter to James Madison, Feb. 7, 1813 ("[You] daily complain"), in Stagg, *PJM-PS*, vol. 5:650–51; Bickham, *Weight of Vengeance*, 184–85; Eustace, *1812*, 190–200.

5   *Connecticut Courant*, July 28, 1812, quoted in M. Mason, *Slavery and Politics*, 70 ("We do not know"), see also 116; Rev. Elijah Parish quoted in Cleves, "Hurtful to the State," 217–18 ("Let the southern Heroes"); Rev. Samuel Spring to James Madison, Aug. 26, 1812, in Stagg, *PJM-PS*, vol. 5:208–9.

6   M. Mason, *Slavery and Politics*, 125–26; [Thomas Ritchie], "Franklin," *Richmond Enquirer*, Aug. 3, 1813.

7   "Southern Population" and "An Extra Sheet," *National Intelligencer*, Apr. 30 ("The slaves") and May 1, 1813 ("Several negroes"). During the war, the *National Intelligencer* usually promoted the views of James Monroe, who, indeed, wrote some of their anonymous pieces. At the

very least, "Southern Population" had to be compatible with his views to appear in that newspaper.

8   John M. Garnett to Archibald R.S. Hunter, Nov. 29, 1813 ("prove"), War of 1812 Collection, box 3, WLCL-UM; "Ends and Means," *Richmond Enquirer*, Mar. 2, 1813; John Coalter to St. George Tucker, Jan. 5, 1813, and Wilson Cary Nicholas to Tucker, Sep. 22, 1814, TCP, box 33, SCSL-CWM; James Barbour to the State Senate and House of Delegates, May 19, 1813, Executive Letter Book, p. 261, RG 3 (Office of the Governor), reel 3010, LV; John C. Cabell to John Hartwell Cocke, Feb. 1, 1814, JCCFP (38-111-c), box 10, SSCL-UVA; "Virginia and Massachusetts Compared," *Richmond Enquirer*, Oct. 28, 1814; James Madison to Nicholas, Nov. 6, 1814, in Hunt, *Writings of James Madison*, vol. 8:319–20; Thomas Jefferson to David Bailie Warden, Dec. 29, 1813, and Walter Jones to Jefferson, Feb. 16, 1814, in Looney, *PTJ-RS*, vol. 7:91, 201; St. George Tucker to Frances Coalter, July 27, 1812, Brown, Coalter, Tucker Papers, box 3, SCSL-CWM. For a similar story told of the Deep South, see Schoen, *Fragile Fabric of Union*, 84–92.

9   Philip Barraud to St. George Tucker, Aug. 23, 1813, and Feb. 18, 1814, TCP, box 33, SCSL-CWM; Tucker to Joseph C. Cabell, July 9, 1812, BFP, box 2, SSCL-UVA; John Minor to James Monroe, Oct. 11, 1812, JMP, ser. 1, reel 5, LC.

10 James Barbour to militia colonels, Mar. 31, 1812, Executive Letter Book, p. 230, RG 3 (Office of the Governor), reel 3009, LV; John Campbell to David Campbell, July 12, 1812, CFP, box 2, SC-DUL; "Federal Notions Examined," *National Intelligencer*, May 7, 1813; Thomas Jefferson to William Short, Nov. 28, 1814, in Looney, *PTJ-RS*, vol. 8:110.

11 S. B. Archer to John Hartwell Cocke, July 9, 1814, JHCFP, box 16, SSCL-UVA; Isaac A. Coles to Joseph C. Cabell, Jan. 25, 1813, JCCFP (38-111-c), box 9, SSCL-UVA; Nathaniel B. Tucker to St. George Tucker, Dec. 18, 1814, TCP, box 33, SCSL-CWM.

12 J. U. Upshaw to Joseph C. Cabell, Sep. 16, 1812, JCCFP (38-111-c), box 9, SSCL-UVA; Thomas Parker to David Campbell, Apr. 16 and Apr. 22, 1813, D. Campbell to John Campbell, Feb. 12, 1814, and J. Campbell to D. Campbell, Apr. 17, 1814, Parker to D. Campbell, July 15, 1814 ("an unfeeling"), CFP, box 3, SC-DUL; "Brigadier General Parker," *Norfolk Herald*, Feb. 18, 1814; Parker to William H. Winder, Feb. 4, 1814 ("Submit to"), WHWP, box 2, MdHS.

13 James Barbour to John Armstrong, May 7 and Oct. 4, 1813, Executive Letter Book, 195, 371, RG 3 (Office of the Governor), reel 3010, LV; John Swift to Armstrong, Oct. 20, 1813, in "Fort Powhatan," *Richmond Enquirer*, Mar. 5, 1814.

14   Richmond Committee of Vigilance to James Barbour, Feb. 3, 1814, JBEP, reel 5518, LV.

15   Report of the House of Delegates committee in "Fort Powhatan," *Richmond Enquirer*, Mar. 5, 1814 ("has never found"); Joseph C. Cabell to John Hartwell Cocke, Feb. 17, 1814 ("The style" and "treated"), JCC&CFP (38-111), box 10, SSLC-UVA; [Cabell], "For the Enquirer," *Richmond Enquirer*, Mar. 5, 1814.

16   "To the Freemen of Virginia!" and "To Arms!" *Richmond Enquirer*, June 18, and Aug. 31, 1814 ("Virginians! Brave Virginians!").

17   David Campbell to Edward Campbell, Jan. 30, 1814, CFP, box 3, SC-DUL; Schoen, "Calculating the Price," 177, 184, 194–200.

18   Haynes, *Unfinished Revolution*, 6–7; Borneman, *1812: The War That Forged a Nation*, 294–304; Hickey, *War of 1812*, 308–9. I was also guilty of generalizing from the Middle Atlantic states. See A. Taylor, *Civil War of 1812*, 438.

19   Philip Barraud to St. George Tucker, Feb. 14, 1815 ("established"), and Feb. 22, 1815 ("the never-to-be-forgotten"), TCP, box 34, SCSL-CWM; Barraud to John Hartwell Cocke, Feb. 15, 1815, and Tucker to Cocke, Mar. 21, 1815, JHCFP, box 19, SSCL-UVA; William Fitzhugh Gordon to his wife, Feb. 10, 1815, in Gordon, *William Fitzhugh Gordon*, 84.

20   "The Grand Illumination," *Richmond Enquirer*, Mar. 4, 1815.

21   P. Hamilton, *Making and Unmaking*, 134, 156, 161–63; St. George Tucker to John Coalter, Mar. 8, 1815, Grinnan Family Papers, box 3, SSCL-UVA. During the war, Tucker wrote savage anti–New England satires, but they were never published. See William Wirt to Tucker, Dec. 27, 1814, and Jan. 19, 1815, TCP, box 34, SCSL-CWM.

22   Thomas, "Poor Deluded Wretches!" 57–58; Schwarz, "George Boxley," 164–65; "Fredericksburg, March 9," *Richmond Enquirer*, Mar. 13, 1816 ("with the holy" and "The negroes"); Waller Holladay and James M. Bell to Wilson Cary Nicholas, Mar. 1, 1816, in Flournoy, *CVSP*, vol. 10:433.

23   Waller Holladay and James M. Bell to Wilson Cary Nicholas, Feb. 25, 1816, WCNEP, box 4, LV; Holladay and Bell to Wilson Cary Nicholas, Mar. 1, 1816, in Flournoy, *CVSP*, vol. 10:433; Nicholas, proclamation, May 18, 1814, WCNEP, box 4, LV; Stapleton Crutchfield to Bell, May 14, 1816, Holladay Family Papers, sec. 237, VHS; "Fredericksburg, May 18," *Richmond Enquirer*, May 22, 1816; Thomas, "Poor Deluded Wretches!" 62; Schwarz, *Migrants against Slavery*, 86–89.

24   Isle of Wight County petition, quoted in M. Mason, *Slavery and Politics*, 112; L. K. Ford, *Deliver Us from Evil*, 70.

25   Wolf, *Race and Liberty*, 135–36; Johnston, *Race Relations*, 48–50. For the

population growth rates in Virginia, see Haulman, *Virginia and the Panic of 1819*, 23.

26   L. K. Ford, *Deliver Us from Evil*, 70–72; Egerton, *Charles Fenton Mercer*, 105.

27   Charles Fenton Mercer quoted in Egerton, *Charles Fenton Mercer*, 106; McCoy, *Last of the Fathers*, 281–82, 285 (Madison quote); M. Mason, *Slavery and Politics*, 112–13; William Branch Giles quoted in Johnston, *Race Relations in Virginia*, 125.

28   John Randolph quoted in W. C. Bruce, *John Randolph*, vol. 2:249.

29   Jesse Kersey to St. George Tucker, July 5, 1814, TCP, box 33, SCSL-CWM.

30   Egerton, *Charles Fenton Mercer*, 167–70; McCoy, *Last of the Fathers*, 281–82; W. D. Jordan, *White over Black*, 566; W. C. Bruce, *John Randolph*, vol. 2:247–48; Gudmestad, *Troublesome Commerce*, 6–8.

31   Onuf, "Domesticating the Captive Nation," 45–51; Shade, *Democratizing the Old Dominion*, 194–95.

32   Gaines, *Thomas Mann Randolph*, 124–28; Thomas Jefferson to Thomas Humphreys, Feb. 8, 1817, and Jefferson to Albert Gallatin, Dec. 26, 1820, P. L. Ford, *Works of Thomas Jefferson*, vol. 12:53, 189; Onuf, *Mind of Thomas Jefferson*, 221–26.

33   R. S. Newman, *Transformation of American Abolitionism*, 96–118; Freehling, *Road to Disunion*, 157–58; James Madison quoted in S. Dunn, *Dominion of Memories*, 50.

34   Jesse Kersey to St. George Tucker, Aug. 1, 1824, TCP, box 41, SCSL-CWM; Egerton, *Charles Fenton Mercer*, 168; John Randolph to John Brockenbrough, Jan. 26, 1826, quoted in Kirk, *John Randolph*, 186; Iaccarino, "Virginia and the National Contest," 165–66; McCoy, *Last of the Fathers*, 299–303; Freehling, *Road to Disunion*, 159–61; L. K. Ford, *Deliver Us from Evil*, 304–19.

35   Spencer Roane to James Monroe, Feb. 16, 1820, in [Anonymous], "Letters of Spencer Roane," 174; James Madison to Monroe, Feb. 23, 1820, in Hunt, *Writings of James Madison*, vol. 9:25; Iaccarino, "Virginia and the National Contest," 161–64; McCoy, *Last of the Fathers*, 267–74; L. K. Ford, *Deliver Us from Evil*, 73–74; Forbes, *Missouri Compromise*, 5–6.

36   Gudmestad, *Troublesome Commerce*, 35–36; John Randolph to Harmanus Bleecker, Oct. 10, 1818, quoted in Van Cleve, *Slaveholders Union*, 228.

37   Robert J. Evans to St. George Tucker, Dec. 13, 1819, TCP, reel M-29, SCSL-CWM; M. Mason, *Slavery and Politics*, 177; Hammond, *Slavery, Freedom, and Expansion*, 154–63; Van Cleve, *Slaveholders' Union*, 10–11, 231–33; Jonathan Roberts, speech in the U.S. Senate, Jan. 17, 1820, *AC*, 16th Congress, 127. For the early promotion of diffusion, see Deyle, *Carry Me Back*, 26; L. K. Ford, *Deliver Us from Evil*, 73–74.

38 John Sergeant quoted in M. Mason, *Slavery and Politics*, 180; Robert J. Evans to St. George Tucker, Dec. 13, 1819, TCP, reel M-29, SCSL-CWM; Iaccarino, "Virginia and the National Contest," 161–65; Van Cleve, *Slaveholders' Union*, 235.

39 Ammon, *James Monroe*, 449–51; Ammon, "Richmond Junto," 411–12; Freehling, *Road to Disunion*, 145–46; M. Mason, *Slavery and Politics*, 195; Van Cleve, *Slaveholders' Union*, 229, 241; Nathaniel Beverley Tucker quoted in P. Hamilton, "Revolutionary Principles and Family Loyalties," 554; Spencer Roane to James Monroe, Feb. 16, 1820 ("their lust" and "forced upon"), in [Anonymous], "Letters of Spencer Roane," 174–75; Roane to James Barbour, Dec. 29, 1819, and John W. Eppes to Barbour, May 3, 1820, in [Anonymous], "Missouri Compromise," 7, 23; M. Mason, *Slavery and Politics*, 193, 199; Thomas Jefferson to Joseph C. Cabell, Jan. 22, 1820, and Jefferson to Charles Pinckney, Sep. 30, 1820, in P. L. Ford, *Works of Thomas Jefferson*, vol. 12:155, 165; Onuf, *Mind of Thomas Jefferson*, 214; Lowrey, *James Barbour*, 118; Wolf, *Race and Liberty*, 175–78.

40 Henry St. George Tucker to James Barbour, Feb. 11, 1820, in [Anonymous], "Missouri Compromise," 11; St. George Tucker to Joseph C. Cabell, Feb. 16, 1820, Cabell File, SCSL-CWM; H. S. G. Tucker to S. G. Tucker, Mar. 8, 1820, TCP, reel M-29, SCSL-CWM; Isaac A. Coles to Cabell, Dec. 20, 1820, Wickham Family Papers, box 1, VHS; Dabney Carr to John Coalter, Feb. 18, 1820, Grinnan Family Papers, sec. 4, VHS; Van Cleve, *Slaveholders' Union*, 232–34.

41 Joseph C. Cabell to St. George Tucker, Apr. 30, 1819, TCP, reel M-29, SCSL-CWM; Haulman, *Virginia and the Panic of 1819*, 3–4, 8–11, 18–19, 51, 57–61; Francis Walker Gilmer to Peachy R. Gilmer, Jan. 16, 1820, quoted in Gutzman, *Virginia's American Revolution*, 178; S. Dunn, *Dominion of Memories*, 7–10. Ammon, "Richmond Junto," 410; D. P. Jordan, *Political Leadership*, 32 205–7, 224.

42 Joseph C. Cabell to St. George Tucker, June 29, 1819, TCP, reel M-29, SCSL-CWM; Isaac A. Coles to Cabell, Aug. 8, 1819, JCCFP (38-111-c), SSCL-UVA; Hammond, "'Uncontrollable Necessity,'" 153–54; Branch Giles quoted in S. Dunn, *Dominion of Memories*, 45.

43 Spencer Roane to James Monroe, Feb. 16, 1820, in [Anonymous], "Letters of Spencer Roane," 174–75; John Tyler quoted in Freehling, *Road to Disunion*, 151; Onuf, "Domesticating the Captive Nation," 37–38; S. Dunn, *Dominion of Memories*, 48; Thomas Jefferson to John Holmes, Apr. 22, 1820 ("like a fire bell"), and Jefferson to Albert Gallatin, Dec. 26, 1820 in P. L. Ford, *Works of Thomas Jefferson*, vol. 12:158, 187–88; M. Mason, *Slavery and Politics*, 203; Bailor, "John Taylor of Caroline," 303; Kirk, *John Randolph*, 185–86; Ammon, *James Monroe*, 451–52.

44   [Thomas Ritchie], "Missouri Question—Settled!" *Richmond Enquirer*, Mar. 7, 1820; Ammon, *James Monroe*, 450–54; M. Mason, *Slavery and Politics*, 177; Freehling, *Road to Disunion*, 152–53; John Randolph quoted in Lowrey, *James Barbour*, 115–16; Forbes, *Missouri Compromise*, 6, 94–96.

45   Charles Yancey to John Hartwell Cocke, Jan. 4, 1820, JHCFP, box 30, SSCL-UVA; Joseph C. Cabell to St. George Tucker, Feb. 10, 1820, TCP, reel M-29, SCSL-CWM; Ammon, *James Monroe*, 455–57; Lowery, *James Barbour*, 116–20; M. Mason, *Slavery and Politics*, 198–99; Ammon, "Richmond Junto," 411–14; Iaccarino, "Virginia and the National Contest," 159–60; Forbes, *Missouri Compromise*, 92–93.

46   [Thomas Ritchie], "Missouri Question—Settled!" *Richmond Enquirer*, Mar. 7, 1820; Ammon, "Richmond Junto," 413–14; Iaccarino, "Virginia and the National Contest," 159; Forbes, *Missouri Compromise*, 8–9; Onuf, "Federalism, Republicanism, and the Origins of American Sectionalism," 33–37.

47   Wolf, *Race and Liberty*, 163, 182–86; Freehling, *Road to Disunion*, 169–70; S. Dunn, *Dominion of Memories*, 153–55.

48   Freehling, *Road to Disunion*, 170–77 (John Randolph quote on 174); Gutzman, *Virginia's American Revolution*, 187–97; Wolf, *Race and Liberty*, 186–96; S. Dunn, *Dominion of Memories*, 156–69.

49   Johnston, *Race Relations*, 131–34.

50   Christopher Tompkins to William B. Giles, July 18, 1829, WBGEP, box 7, folder 3, LV.

51   Bowling Starke to William B. Giles, July 26, 1829, WBGEP, box 7, folder 4, LV; John H. Smith, advice, Aug. 4, 1829 ("These rumours"), WBGEP, box 7, folder 5, LV.

52   Trial of Adam, Sandy, Anna, Davy, Jacob, and William, Hanover County court, July 22, 1829, and Richard Morris et al. to William B. Giles, July 30, 1829 ("dispersed"), WBGEP, box 7, folder 5, LV.

53   Warren Roan to William B. Giles, July 13, 1829 ("Should this alarm"), W. H. Perkins to Giles, July 15, 1829, and Catesby Jones to Giles, July 18, 1829, in Flournoy, *CVSP*, vol. 10:567–69; Christopher Tompkins to Giles, July 18, 1829, and R. McCandlish to Giles, July 24 and July 25, 1829, and Thomas H. Botts to Giles, July n.d., 1829, WBGEP, box 7, folder 3, LV; J. Rutherford to Giles, July 27, 1829, William Lambert Jr. to Giles, July 28, 1829, Col. Harwood to Giles, July 30, 1829, and Richard Rousee to Giles, July 31, 1829, WBGEP, box 7, folder 4, LV.

54   S. E. Parker to William B. Giles, Aug. 11, 1829 ("I feel & see"), WBGEP, box 7, folder 5, LV.

55   William Presson to Giles, July 31, 1829, WBGEP, box 7, folder 4, LV.

56   Oliver Cross to Garrett M. Quarles, Sep. 3, 1829, WBGEP, box 7, folder

7, LV; Thomas Jefferson to John Holmes, Apr. 22, 1820, in P. L. Ford, *Works of Thomas Jefferson*, vol. 12:158–59; Morris Birkbeck quoted in S. Dunn, *Dominion of Memories*, 40.

57   S. E. Parker to William B. Giles, Aug. 11, 1829, Northampton County resolution, Aug. 26, 1829, and John Eyre to Giles, Aug. 27, 1829, WBGEP, box 7, folders 5 and 6, LV.

58   John G. Joynes, Levin S. Joynes, and Thomas H. Kellam to William B. Giles, Aug. 13, 1829, WBGEP, box 7, folder 5, LV.

59   Oliver Cross to Garrett M. Quarles, Sep. 3, 1829 ("sooner"), WBGEP, box 7, folder 7, LV; Freehling, *Road to Disunion*, 178–81; Aptheker, "Event," 45–57; Parramore, "Covenant in Jerusalem," 58–76.

60   Aptheker, "Event," 45–57; Parramore, "Covenant in Jerusalem," 58–76; Ely, *Israel on the Appomattox*, 13. For the total number executed, see Schwarz, *Twice Condemned*, 255–59.

61   Joseph C. Cabell to John Hartwell Cocke, Oct. 4 ("the white females") and Oct. 12, 1831, JCC&CFP (38-111), SSCL-UVA; Cocke to Cabell, Oct. 7, 1831, JHCFP, box 23, SSCL-UVA; Jeter, *Recollections of a Long Life*, 175 ("The blowing of a horn").

62   Masur, "Nat Turner and Sectional Crisis," 154–59 (William Goode quote, from speech of Jan. 11, 1832, on 155); Freehling, *Road to Disunion*, 181–85.

63   John Hartwell Cocke to Joseph C. Cabell, Oct. 29, 1831, and Jan. 31 ("the great cause") and Feb. 14, 1832, JCC&CFP (38-111), box 23, SSCL-UVA; Shade, *Democratizing the Old Dominion*, 195–99.

64   Masur, "Nat Turner and Sectional Crisis," 158–61 (William Brodnax quote — "an evil" — and John Thompson Brown quote on 158); Freehling, *Road to Disunion*, 185–90; Shade, *Democratizing the Old Dominion*, 199–203; S. Dunn, *Dominion of Memories*, 54–55.

65   T. J. Randolph, *Speech*, 9 (all quotations); Freehling, *Road to Disunion*, 182; Masur, "Nat Turner and Sectional Crisis," 161.

66   Oakes, *Freedom National*, 208–39.

EPILOGUE

1   Joseph C. Cabell to George Hay, Jan. 27, 1824, JCC&CFP (38-111), box 16, SSCL-UVA.

2   St. George Tucker to Henry Tucker, May 2, 1815 ("in consequence of"), and H. Tucker to St. G. Tucker, June 23, 1815, TCP, box 34, CWM.

3   St. George Tucker to Henry Tucker, Jan. 2, 1820 [*sic*: 1821], TCP, reel M-30, SCSL-CWM.

4   John Hartwell Cocke to St. George Tucker, Mar. 12, 1815, TCP, box 34, SCSL-CWM; Joseph C. Cabell to William Cabell, Mar. 4, 1815, Cabell

Family Papers, ser. 1, box 6 SCSL-CWM; Cabell to Thomas Jefferson, Mar. 5, 1815, in Looney, *PTJ-RS*, vol. 8:317–18; Cabell to Cocke, Sep. 30, 1815, JCC&CFP (38-111), box 11, SSCL-UVA; George Callaway to Cabell, Dec. 27, 1815, Cabell and Bolling Families Papers (38-111-g), box 1, SSCL-UVA; Cabell, "Expences of Lynchburg Negroes," Mar. 9, 1816 ("for his trouble"), RABC, box 48, HL. Unfortunately, Cabell does not indicate the number who persisted, but they must have been at least as numerous as the 69 who departed from both halves of Corotoman.

5   Joseph C. Cabell to William H. Cabell, Oct. 12, 1815, JCCFP (38-111-c), box 2, SSCL-UVA; J. C. Cabell to St. George Tucker, June 7, 1821 ("the Doctor's mismanagement"), TCP, reel M-30, SCSL-CWM.

6   St. George Tucker to Henry Tucker, May 2, 1815, TCP, box 34, SCSL-CWM; Joseph C. Cabell to Isaac A. Coles, Dec. 18, 1815 ("I have"), and Cabell to John Hartwell Cocke, Oct. 7, 1816 ("If I could"), JCC&CFP (38-111), box 11, SSCL-UVA.

7   John Richeson to St. George Tucker, Apr. 25, 1817 ("more trouble") and "more sickley"), Randolph-Tucker Papers, RABC, box 8, folder 4, HL; Joseph C. Cabell to John Hartwell Cocke, Dec. 1, 1817, JCC&CFP (38-111), box 12, SSCL-UVA; Cabell to St. George Tucker, Mar. 9, 1818, RABC, box 48, HL; Cabell to Tucker, Oct. 28, 1818 ("a very good crop," "scarcely bear," and "every thing"), Cabell Family Papers, ser. 1, box 6, SCSL-CWM; Cabell to Tucker, Feb. 13, 1818 ("compelled"), TCP, reel M-28, SCSL-CWM.

8   Joseph C. Cabell to St. George Tucker, Dec. 30, 1816, TCP, reel M-28, SCSL-CWM.

9   John Richeson to St. George Tucker, Apr. 25 ("She has not forgot"), and Sep. 25, 1817 ("I think"), Randolph-Tucker Papers, RABC, box 8, folder 16, HL.

10   Henry Richeson to St. George Tucker, Jan. 23, 1817 [*sic*: 1818] ("drew his knife"), and John Richeson to Tucker, Feb. 22, 1818, TCP, reel M-28, SCSL-CWM. See also the printed versions in Coleman, *Virginia Silhouettes*, 22–23. Although Henry Richeson dated the first letter as 1817, this must have been a slip, common in the first month of the year, for he describes the same incident that his father, John Richeson, discusses in his letter of February 22, 1818. For Billy's redeployment in Nelson County, see Tucker to John Hartwell Cocke, July 4, 1818, JHCFP (38-111-c), box 26, SSCL-UVA. For Billy's subsequent role as a messenger, see Joseph C. Cabell to Tucker, Dec. 5, 1821, TCP, reel M-30, SCSL-CWM.

11   John Richeson to St. George Tucker, Feb. 22, 1818, TCP, reel M-28, SCSL-CWM. See also Coleman, *Virginia Silhouettes*, 22–23.

12   Joseph C. Cabell to St. George Tucker, Oct. 28, 1818 ("improved as fast"),

Cabell Family Papers, ser. 1, box 6, SCSL-CWM; Cabell to Tucker, Dec. 13, 1818, RABC, box 48, HL; Tucker to Cabell, Dec. 16, 1818, BFP, box 2, SSCL-UVA; Cabell to Tucker, Nov. 7, 1819, TCP, reel M-29, SCSL-CWM. For the death of Richeson's wife, see Cabell to Tucker, Dec. 30, 1816, TCP, reel M-28, SCSL-CWM.

13   Joseph C. Cabell to John Hartwell Cocke, Dec. 2, 1820, JCC&CFP (38-111), box 14, SSCL-UVA.

14   Joseph C. Cabell to John Hartwell Cocke, Dec. 2, 1820, JCC&CFP (38-111), box 14, SSCL-UVA; Cabell to St. George Tucker, Jan. 21 ("The old man") and June 7, 1821, TCP, reel M-30, SCSL-CWM; Cabell to Cocke, June 9, 1821 ("keep me," "the capital point," "all at home"), JCCFP (38-111-c), box 1, SSCL-UVA.

15   Joseph C. Cabell to John Hartwell Cocke, Mar. 13, 1822, JCCFP (38-111-c), box 1, SSCL-UVA.

16   Joseph C. Cabell to John Hartwell Cocke, Dec. 2, 1820, and Dec. 11, 1822 ("What with the worm" and "Robertson, I fear"), JCC&CFP (38-111), boxes 14 and 15, SSCL-UVA; Cabell to St. George Tucker, Feb. 10, 1822, TCP, reel M-30, SCSL-CWM.

17   Joseph C. Cabell to John Hartwell Cocke, Dec. 11, 1822 ("infernal Yankees"), JCC&CFP (38-111), box 15, SSCL-UVA; Cabell to St. George Tucker, Dec. 11, 1822 ("a growing" and "the colonization society"), TCP, reel M-30, SCSL-CWM; Cabell to Cocke, July 30, 1819 (*"Between you & myself"*), JCC&CFP (38-111), box 13, SSCL-UVA.

18   Joseph C. Cabell to John Hartwell Cocke, Dec. 11 ("Nothing but") and Dec. 25, 1822 ("To hold so fine"), and Cocke to Cabell, Dec. 23, 1822, JCC&CFP (38-111), box 15, SSCL-UVA. For the renewed effort to sell, see Cabell to William Wirt, Mar. 15, 1823, JCCFP (38–111-c), box 2, SSCL-UVA. For the shrunken value of the estate, see the Lancaster County land tax return, 1822, LV. For the burden of the older slaves, see Cabell to St. George Tucker, Feb. 13, 1818 ("Otherwise"), TCP, reel M-28, SCSL-CWM.

19   Joseph C. Cabell to St. George Tucker, Dec. 19, 1826, TCP, reel M-32, SCSL-CWM; Cabell to John Cowper, Dec. 20, 1826, JCC&CFP (38-111), box 18, SSCL-UVA; Cabell to St. George Tucker, Jan. 7, 1827 (all quotations), Mss 2 C11145 a5, VHS.

20   Joseph C. Cabell to St. George Tucker, Dec. 1, 1825, TCP, box 41, SCSL-CWM; Cabell to William Wirt, Jan. 26, 1826, JCCFP (38-111-c), SSCL-UVA.

21   Joseph C. Cabell to St. George Tucker, Dec. 1, 1825, TCP, box 41, SCSL-CWM.

22   Joseph C. Cabell to St. George Tucker, Dec. 1 ("left his affairs") and Dec.

5, 1825 ("a corrupter" and "the incessant fomenter"), TCP, box 41, SCSL-CWM; Benjamin M. Walker, certificate, July 20, 1826, Cabell, "Notice," Nov. 4, 1826, and Cabell, "To the Public," Jan. 15, 1830, RABC, box 48, HL; Cabell to St. George Tucker, Jan. 7, 1827 (all quotations), Mss 2 C11145 a5, VHS.

23   Joseph C. Cabell to St. George Tucker, Jan. 12, 1826, TCP, reel M-32, SCSL-CWM. Cabell outlived Parke, who died in early 1840. See "Certificate of Appointment by Nelson [Co.] Court of Joseph C. Cabell as Administrator of R.P.F. Carter, Decd.," Feb. 1840, Cabell Family Papers, RABC, box 48, folder 5, HL.

24   Joseph C. Cabell to John Hartwell Cocke, Jan. 7 and Apr. 6, 1826, JCC&CFP (38-111), box 18, SSCL-UVA; Cabell to William Wirt, Jan. 26, 1826, JCCFP (38-111-c), SSCL-UVA; Cabell to Wirt, Sep. 18 and Nov. 25, 1827, JCC&CFP (38-111), box 19, SSCL-UVA; Cabell to Cocke, Sep. 22, 1827 ("Our peaceful little family"), JCCFP (38-111-c), box 1, SSCL-UVA; P. Hamilton, *Making and Unmaking*, 197–200.

25   Joseph C. Cabell to John Hartwell Cocke, Oct. 23, 1820 ("I cannot depict"), and to William Wirt, June 7, 1825, JCC&CFP, boxes 14 and 17, SSCL-UVA.

26   Joseph C. Cabell to John Hartwell Cocke, Mar. 13, 1822 ("I am getting"), June 15, 1824 ("The best thing"), and Sep. 2, 1826 ("These dreadful seasons"), JCCFP (38-111-c), box 1, SSCL-UVA; J. C. Cabell to St. George Tucker, Nov. 9, 1823, TCP, reel M-31, SCSL-CWM; William H. Cabell to J. C. Cabell, July 28, 1828 ("But the misfortune"), JCC&CFP (38-111), box 20, SSCL-UVA.

27   Treaty of Ghent, Article the First, 1814, *The Avalon Project: Documents in Law, History, and Diplomacy* (online), Yale University Law School, New Haven, CT; Thomas M. Bayly to James Monroe, Mar. 6, 1815, RG 76, entry 185, box 3, folder 8, USNA-CP; George Graham to Walter Jones, Mar. 18, 1815, Jones Papers (Mss 2 J7283 b), VHS; Monroe to Anthony St. John Baker, Apr. 1, 1814, and Baker to Monroe, Apr. 3, 1815, in *ASP-FR*, vol. 4:106–7; Lindsay, "Diplomatic Relations," 413; M. Mason, "Battle of Slaveholding Liberators," 676n46.

28   William Prentiss to Adams, Mar. 30, 1818, RG 76, entry 185, box 4, folder 18, USNA-CP; Lindsay, "Diplomatic Relations," 392–406.

29   James Monroe to John Quincy, July 21, 1815, RG 59, M 77, reel 2, p. 407, USNA-CP; Monroe to Adams, Nov. 16, 1815 ("A vigorous effort"), in *ASP-FR*, vol. 4:121.

30   Anthony St. John Baker to Viscount Castlereagh, Apr. 10, 1815, MG 16, FO 5, vol. 106:169, reel B-2005, LAC; John Quincy Adams to James Monroe, Aug. 22 (Lord Liverpool quote) and Sep. 5, 1815, Henry

Bathurst to Adams, Oct. 24, 1815, and Castlereagh to Adams, Apr. 10, 1816, in *ASP-FR*, vol. 4:116, 117, 119, 125–26; Berquist, "Henry Middleton," 28–29; J. B. Moore, *History and Digest*, vol. 1:352, 355.

31 Fehrenbaher and McAfee, *Slaveholding Republic*, 94–95. Adams quote on 95); Berquist, "Henry Middleton," 23–30; Lindsay, "Diplomatic Relations," 30; J. B. Moore, *History and Digest*, vol. 1:358–62 ("the literal and grammatical" on 360).

32 Langdon Cheves to Henry Clay, Apr. 26, 1825, RG 76, entry 185, box 8, folder 82, USNA-CP; Berquist, "Henry Middleton," 23; Lindsay, "Diplomatic Relations," 415; Fehrenbacher and McAfee, *Slaveholding Republic*, 95; J. B. Moore, *History and Digest*, vol. 1:363–70.

33 Langdon Cheves and Henry Sewall to John Quincy Adams, Sep. 13, 1824, RG 76, entry 185, box 7, folder 70, USNA-CP; Berquist, "Henry Middleton," 31; Fehrenbacher and McAfee, *Slaveholding Republic*, 95–96; Lindsay, "Diplomatic Relations," 415–18; J. B. Moore, *History and Digest*, vol. 1:370–78.

34 Joseph C. Cabell to William Wirt, July 28, 1827, JCC&CFP (38-111), box 19, SSCL-UVA; Augustine Neale et al. memorial, Mar. 10, 1828, in *ASP-FR*, vol. 6:855; Fehrenbacher and McAfee, *Slaveholding Republic*, 95–96; Lindsay, "Diplomatic Relations," 415–18; J. B. Moore, *History and Digest*, vol. 1:380–82.

35 Augustine Neale et al. memorial, Mar. 10, 1828, in *ASP-FR*, vol. 6:855.

36 Langdon Cheves to Henry Clay, Apr. 26, 1825, RG 76, entry 185, box 8, folder 82, USNA-CP; Joseph C. Cabell to William Wirt, Jan. 20, 1827, JCC&CFP (38-111), box 19, SSCL-UVA; [Wirt], *Argument in Support of the Chesapeake Claims*, 3, 60, in RG 76, entry 185, box 3, folder 6, USNA-CP; Fehrenbacher and McAfee, *Slaveholding Republic*, 96.

37 C. C. Lee, memorandum, May 19, 1828, RG 76, entry 190, box 6, case 502 (Ann and Elizabeth McCarty), USNA-CP; James Pleasants, memorandum, n.d., RG 76, entry 185, box 4, folder 17, USNA-CP.

38 Joseph C. Cabell to William Wirt, Mar. 15, 1828, Apr. 16 and May 22, 1828, JCC&CFP (38-111), box 20, SSCL-UVA; Langdon Cheves quoted in Fehrenbacher and McAfee, *Slaveholding Republic*, 97; J. B. Moore, *History and Digest*, vol. 1:384–90.

39 Joseph C. Cabell to William Wirt, July 28, Dec. 8 ("God grant"), and Dec. 26, 1827, and Feb. 18, 1828, JCC&CFP (38-111), box 19, SSCL-UVA.

40 Dick Carter quoted in Joseph C. Cabell to the Board of Commissioners, Dec. 4, 1827, RG 76, entry 185, box 3, folder 6, USNA-CP; Cabell to William Wirt, Aug. 26, 1827, JCCFP (38-111), box 19, SSCL-UVA; Thomas Armstrong, deposition, Dec. 1, 1827, Holland Wood, deposition, Dec. 1, 1827, Thomas Wood, deposition, Dec. 3, 1827, Joseph C. Cabell

to Langdon Cheves, Henry Sewall, and James Pleasants, Dec. 4, 1827, and Addison Hall and James Kelley, deposition, Feb. 21, 1828, and [Cabell], *Argument in Support of the Claims of Joseph C. Cabell, St. George Tucker, Charles Carter and Others* (n.p., n.d.), in RG 76, entry 185, box 3, folder 6, USNA-CP; Cabell to Wirt, Dec. 8, 1827, and Feb. 4, 1828, JCC&CFP (38-111), box 20, SSCL-UVA.

41   Joseph C. Cabell to Langdon Cheves, Henry Sewall, and James Pleasants, Dec. 4, 1827 ("uncommon attachment"), RG 76, entry 185, box 3, folder 6, USNA-CP; Cabell to John H. Cocke, May 22, 1828, and Cabell to John Coalter, June 3, 1828, JCC&CFP (38-111), box 20, SSCL-UVA; Cabell to William Wirt, Oct. 22, 1828 ("The recovery"), JCC&CFP (38-111), box 16, SSCL-UVA. The 1828 date on Cabell's letter to Wirt has been misread as 1823, so it has been misfiled under that year. For Great Jenny and her descendants, see "Division of Great Jenney's Family," May 9, 1834, Cabell Family Papers, RABC, box 48, folder 5, HL.

Appendices

1   Addison Hall and James Kelley, deposition, Feb. 21, 1828 (all quotations), and [Cabell], *Argument in Support of the Claims of Joseph C. Cabell, St. George Tucker, Charles Carter and Others* (n.p., n.d.), in RG 76, entry 185, box 3, folder 6, USNA-CP.

2   *ASP-FR*, vol. 5:801–29.

3   Walter Jones to James Monroe, May 25, 1815, RG 76, entry 190, box 4, folder 13, USNA-CP; Thomas W. Badger, deposition, Mar. 31, 1828, RG 76, entry 190, box 5, case 326 (John Winder), USNA-CP.

4   Malcomson, "Freedom by Reaching the Wooden World," 17n117. For an estimate of 3,000 to 5,000 refugees, see Cassel, "Slaves of the Chesapeake," 154. For an estimate of 5,000 made by an American official in 1815, see Thomas Spalding, memorandum, May 28, 1815, RG 76, entry 185, box 3, folder 8, USNA-CP.

5   For Virginia's slave population totals in 1810 and 1820, see Haulman, *Virginia and the Panic of 1819*, 23. John Craig Hammond estimates that 120,000 slaves were exported from Maryland and Virginia during the 1810s, of whom three-fourths came from Virginia. See Hammond, "'Uncontrollable Necessity,'" 153.

BIBLIOGRAPHY

Adams, Henry, ed. *The Writings of Albert Gallatin*, 3 vols. (Philadelphia: J. B. Lippincott, 1879).

Allen, Carlos R., Jr., ed. "David Barrow's *Circular Letter* of 1798." *William and Mary Quarterly*, 3rd ser., 20 (July 1963): 440–51.

Ambler, Charles Henry. *Thomas Ritchie: A Study in Virginia Politics* (Richmond: Bell Book & Stationery, 1913).

American State Papers: Class 1, Foreign Relations, 38 vols. (Buffalo, NY: William S. Hein, 1998; reprint of Washington, D.C., 1832–61).

American State Papers: Class 5, Military Affairs (Washington, DC: Gales & Seaton, 1860).

Ammon, Harry. *James Monroe: The Quest for National Identity* (New York: McGraw-Hill, 1971).

——. "The Richmond Junto, 1800–1824." *Virginia Magazine of History and Biography* 61 (Oct. 1953): 395–418.

[Anonymous], ed. "Kennon Letters." *Virginia Magazine of History and Biography* 31 (1923): 185–206, 296–313; 32 (1924): 76–87, 159–74, 265–80, 344–50; 33 (1925): 65–75, 268–82; 34 (1926): 120–29, 220–31, 322–38; 35 (1927): 13–21, 287–92; 36 (1928): 170–74, 231–38, 363–70; 37 (1929): 46–51, 143–53, 261–68, 335–38; 38 (1930): 157–66, 366–71.

——, ed. "Letters to James Monroe, 1812–1816." *Bulletin of the New York Public Library* 12 (Sep. 1908): 527–30.

——, ed. "Letters of James Monroe, 1812–1817." *Bulletin of the New York Public Library* 6 (June 1902): 210–30.

——, ed. "Letters of John Randolph of Roanoke to General Thomas Marsh Forman [of Rose-hill, Maryland]." *Virginia Magazine of History and Biography* 49 (July 1941): 201–16.

———, ed. "Letters of Spencer Roane, 1788–1822." *Bulletin of the New York Public Library* 10 (Mar. 1906): 167–180

———, ed. "Missouri Compromise: Letters to James Barbour, Senator of Virginia in the Congress of the United States." *William and Mary Quarterly*, 1st ser., 10 (July 1901): 6–24.

———. *Personal Narrative of Events by Sea and by Land, from the Year 1800 to 1815; Concluding with a Narration of Some of the Principal Events in the Chesapeake and S. Carolina in 1814 and 1815; . . . By a Captain of the Navy* (Portsmouth, England: W. Harrison, 1837), reprinted in *Chronicles of St. Mary's* (St. Mary's County Historical Society, MD) 8, no. 1 (Jan. 1960): 1–10.

———. "Recollections of the Expedition to the Chesapeake and against New Orleans, in the Years 1814–15." *Colburn's United Service Journal* (Apr. 1840): 443–56; (May 1840): 25–36; (June 1840): 182–95; (July 1840): 337–52.

Aptheker, Herbert. *American Negro Slave Revolts* (New York: Columbia University Press, 1943).

———. "The Event." In Kenneth S. Greenberg, ed., *Nat Turner: A Slave Rebellion in History and Memory*, 45–57 (New York: Oxford University Press, 2003).

———. "Maroons within the Present Limits of the United States." *Journal of Negro History* 24 (Apr. 1939): 167–84.

Bailey, Robert. *The Life and Adventures of Robert Bailey, from His Infancy up to December, 1821* (Richmond: J. G. Cochran, 1822).

Bailor, Keith M. "John Taylor of Caroline: Continuity, Change, and Discontinuity in Virginia's Sentiments toward Slavery, 1790–1820." *Virginia Magazine of History and Biography* 75 (July 1967): 290–304.

Baker, Thomas N. "'A Slave' Writes Thomas Jefferson." *William and Mary Quarterly*, 3rd ser., 68 (Jan. 2011): 127–54.

Ball, Charles. *Fifty Years in Chains*, ed. Philip S. Foner (New York: Dover, 1970; reprint of) Ball, *Slavery in the United States* (New York, 1837).

Barnes, Alton Brooks Parker. *Pungoteague to Petersburg*, vol. 1: *Eastern Shore Militiamen before the Civil War, 1776–1858* (n.p.: A. Lee Howard, 1988).

Barrett, Charles R. B., ed. *The 85th King's Light Infantry* (London: Spottiswoode, 1913).

[Barrett, Robert J.]. "Naval Recollections of the Late American War." *Colburn's United Service Journal and Naval and Military Magazine*, (Apr. 1841): 455–67; and (May 1841): 13–23.

Bartlett, C. J. "Gentlemen versus Democrats: Cultural Prejudice and Military Strategy in Britain in the War of 1812." *War in History* 1 (1994): 143–54.

Bartlett, C. J., and Gene A. Smith. "'A Species of Milito-Nautico-Guerilla Warfare': Admiral Alexander Cochrane's Naval Campaign against the United States, 1814–1815." In Julie Flavell and Stephen Conway, eds., *Britain and*

America Go to War: The Impact of War and Warfare in Anglo-America, 1754–1815 (Gainesville: University Press of Florida, 2004): 173–204.

Baylor, Orval Walker, and Henry Bedinger Baylor. *Baylor's History of the Baylors* (n.p.: LeRoy Journal Printing, 1914).

Beeman, Richard R. *The Old Dominion and the New Nation, 1788–1801* (Lexington: University Press of Kentucky, 1972).

Beitzell, Edwin W., ed. "Selections from the Coad Papers and Correspondence (part 2): Robbery and Desecration at St. Inigoes, 1814." *Chronicles of St. Mary's* (St. Mary's County Historical Society, MD) 8, no. 3 (Mar. 1960): 4–10.

Belknap, Jeremy, ed. "Queries Relating to Slavery in Massachusetts." Massachusetts Historical Society, *Collections*, 5th ser., vol. 3 (1877): 378–431.

Bell, Malcolm. *Major Butler's Legacy: Five Generations of a Slaveholding Family* (Athens: University of Georgia Press, 1987).

Berkeley, Edmund, Jr. "Prophet without Honor: Christopher McPherson, Free Person of Color." *Virginia Magazine of History and Biography* 77 (Apr. 1969): 180–90.

Berlin, Ira. *Many Thousands Gone: The First Two Centuries of Slavery in North America* (Cambridge, MA: Harvard University Press, 1998).

Berlin, Ira, and Ronald Hoffman, eds. *Slavery and Freedom in the Age of the American Revolution* (Charlottesville: University Press of Virginia, 1983).

Bernstein, Richard B. *Thomas Jefferson* (New York: Oxford University Press, 2003).

Berquist, Harold E., Jr. "Henry Middleton and the Arbitrament of the Anglo-American Slave Controversy by Tsar Alexander I." *South Carolina Historical Magazine* 82 (Jan. 1981): 20–31.

Bickham, Troy. *The Weight of Vengeance: The United States, the British Empire, and the War of 1812* (New York: Oxford University Press, 2012).

Binns, John. *Recollections of the Life of John Binns* (Philadelphia: Parry & McMillan, 1854).

Birkbeck, Morris. *Notes on a Journey in America, from the Coast of Virginia to the Territory of Illinois* (London: Severn, 1818).

Blackburn, Robin. *The Overthrow of Colonial Slavery, 1776–1848* (New York: Verso Press, 1988).

Blumrosen, Alfred W., and Ruth G. Blumrosen. *Slave Nation: How Slavery United the Colonies and Sparked the American Revolution* (Naperville, IL: Sourcebooks, 2005).

Bolster, W. Jeffrey. *Black Jacks: African American Seamen in the Age of Sail* (Cambridge, MA: Harvard University Press, 1997).

Borneman, Walter R. *1812: The War That Forged a Nation* (New York: Harper Perennial, 2005).

Bourchier, Lady, ed. *Memoir of the Life of Admiral Sir Edward Codrington*, 2 vols. (London: Longman, 1873).

Bowers, Claude G., ed. *The Diary of Elbridge Gerry, Jr.* (New York: Brentano's, 1927).

Boyd, Julian P., and W. Edwin Hemphill. *The Murder of George Wythe: Two Essays* (Williamsburg, VA: Institute of Early American History and Culture, 1955).

Brant, Irving. *James Madison: President*, vol. 6: *James Madison: Commander-in-Chief, 1812–1836* (New York: Bobbs-Merrill, 1961).

Brereton, Bridget. *A History of Modern Trinidad, 1783–1962* (Kingston, Jamaica: Heinemann, 1981).

Brewer, Holly. "Entailing Aristocracy in Colonial Virginia: 'Ancient Feudal Restraints' and Revolutionary Reform." *William and Mary Quarterly* 3rd ser., 54 (Apr. 1997): 307–46.

Brown, Christopher Leslie. *Moral Capital: Foundations of British Abolitionism* (Chapel Hill: University of North Carolina Press, 2006).

Brown, Ralph H. "St. George Tucker versus Jedidiah Morse on the Subject of Williamsburg." *William and Mary Quarterly* 2nd ser., 20 (Oct. 1940) 487–91.

Brown, Roger H. *The Republic in Peril: 1812* (New York: W. W. Norton, 1971).

Bruce, William Cabell. *John Randolph of Roanoke, 1773–1833*, 2 vols. (New York: G.P. Putnam's Sons, 1922).

Bruce, William Napier. *The Life of General Sir Charles Napier* (London: John Murray, 1885).

Brugger, Robert J. *Beverley Tucker: Heart over Head in the Old South* (Baltimore: Johns Hopkins University Press, 1978).

———. *Maryland: A Middle Temperament, 1634–1980* (Baltimore: Johns Hopkins University Press, 1988).

Buckley, Roger Norman. *Slaves in Red Coats: The British West India Regiments, 1795–1815* (New Haven, CT: Yale University Press, 1979).

Bullard, Mary R. *Black Liberation on Cumberland Island in 1815* (Delean Springs, FL: E. O. Painter, 1983).

———. *Robert Stafford of Cumberland Island: Growth of a Planter* (Athens: University of Georgia Press, 1995).

Butler, Stuart L. "Captain Barrie's Last Raid." *Northern Neck of Virginia Historical Magazine* 54 (Dec. 2004): 6441–52.

———. *A Guide to Virginia Militia Units in the War of 1812* (Athens, GA: Therian Publishing, 1988).

Butler, William F. *Sir Charles Napier* (New York: Macmillan, 1890).

Byron, Gilbert. *The War of 1812 on the Chesapeake Bay* (Baltimore: Maryland Historical Society, 1964).

[Cabell, Joseph C.]. *Argument in Support of the Claims of Joseph C. Cabell, St. George Tucker, Charles Carter and Others* (n.p.: no pub., 1827).

Callcott, Margaret Law, ed. *Mistress of Riversdale: The Plantation Letters of Rosalie Stier Calvert, 1795–1821* (Baltimore: Johns Hopkins University Press, 1991).

Carmichael, Getrude. "Some Notes on Sir Ralph James Woodford, Bt. (Governor of Trinidad, 1813 to 1828)." *Caribbean Quarterly* 2, no. 3 (1951–1952): 26–38.

Carter, Edward C., II, ed. *The Virginia Journals of Benjamin Henry Latrobe, 1795–1798*, 2 vols. (New Haven, CT: Yale University Press, 1977).

Cassell, Frank A. *Merchant Congressman in the Young Republic: Samuel Smith of Maryland* (Madison: University of Wisconsin Press, 1971).

———. "Slaves of the Chesapeake Bay Area and the War of 1812." *Journal of Negro History* 57 (1972): 144–55.

Catterall, Helen T. *Judicial Cases concerning Slavery and the Negro*, 5 vols. (Washington, DC: Carnegie Institution of Washington, 1926–37).

Chamier, Frederick. *The Life of a Sailor by a Captain in the Navy*, 2 vols. (New York: J. & J. Harper, 1833).

Channing, William Ellery. *Memoir of William Ellery Channing with Extracts from His Correspondence and Manuscripts*, 3 vols. (Boston: W.M. Crosby and H.P. Nichols, 1848).

Chernow, Ron. *Washington: A Life* (New York: Penguin Press, 2010).

Childs, J. Rives. "French Consul Martin Oster Reports on Virginia, 1784–1796," *Virginia Magazine of History and Biography* 76 (Jan. 1968): 27–40.

Clemens, Paul G. E. *The Atlantic Economy and Colonial Maryland's Eastern Shore: From Tobacco to Grain* (Ithaca, NY: Cornell University Press, 1980).

Cleves, Rachel Hope. "'Hurtful to the State': The Political Morality of Federalist Antislavery." In John Craig Hammond and Matthew Mason, eds., *Contesting Slavery: The Politics of Bondage and Freedom in the New American Nation* (Charlottesville: University of Virginia Press, 2011): 207–26.

Coleman, Mary H., ed. "Randolph and Tucker Letters." *Virginia Magazine of History and Biography* 42 (1934): 47–52, 129, 131, 211–23, 317–24.

———. *St. George Tucker, Citizen of No Mean City* (Richmond: Dietz Press, 1938).

———, ed., *Virginia Silhouettes: Contemporary Letters concerning Negro Slavery in the State of Virginia* (Richmond: Dietz Printing, 1934).

Colley, Linda. *Captives* (New York: Pantheon Books, 2002).

Commonwealth of Virginia. *Acts Passed at the General Assembly of the Commonwealth of Virginia, 1811–1812* (Richmond, 1812).

———. *Acts Passed at the General Assembly of the Commonwealth of Virginia, 1812–13* (Richmond, 1813).

———. *Acts of the General Assembly Begun on May 17, 1813* (Richmond, 1813).

———. *Acts Passed at the General Assembly of the Commonwealth of Virginia, 1814–1815* (Richmond, 1815).

———. *Journal of the State Senate . . . 1812* (Richmond: Samuel Pleasants, 1813).

———. *Journal of the State Senate . . . 1813* (Richmond: Samuel Pleasants, 1814).

Coulter, E. Merton. *Thomas Spalding of Sapelo* (Baton Rouge: Louisiana State University Press, 1940).

Covington, James W. "The Negro Fort." *Gulf Coast Historical Review* 5 (Spring 1990): 78–91.

Craton, Michael. *Testing the Chains: Resistance to Slavery in the British West Indies* (Ithaca, NY: Cornell University Press, 1982).

Craton, Michael, James Walvin, and David Wright. *Slavery, Abolition, and Emancipation: Black Slaves and the British Empire* (London: Longman, 1976).

Cullen, Charles T. *St. George Tucker and Law in Virginia, 1772–1804* (New York: Garland, 1987).

Darrell, John Harvey. "Diary of John Harvey Darrell: Voyage to America." *Bermuda Historical Quarterly* 5 (1948): 142–49.

Davis, David Brion. *The Problem of Slavery in the Age of Revolution, 1770–1823* (Ithaca, NY: Cornell University Press, 1975).

Davis, John. *Travels of Four Years and a Half in the United States of America during 1798, 1799, 1800, 1801, and 1802*, 2 vols. (New York: Henry Holt, 1909; reprint of London, 1803).

Davis, Richard Beale, ed. *Jeffersonian America: Notes on the United States of America Collected in the Years 1805–6–7 and 11–12 by Sir Augustus John Foster, Bart* (San Marino, CA: Huntington Library, 1954).

Dawidoff, Robert, Jr. *The Education of John Randolph* (New York: W. W. Norton, 1979).

Dew, Charles B. "David Ross and the Oxford Iron Works: A Study of Industrial Slavery in the Early Nineteenth-Century South." *William and Mary Quarterly* 3rd ser., 31 (Apr. 1974): 189–224.

Deyle, Steven. "An 'Abominable' New Trade: The Closing of the African Slave Trade and the Changing Patterns of U.S. Political Power, 1808–1860." *William and Mary Quarterly*, 3rd ser., 66 (Oct. 2009): 833–50.

——. *Carry Me Back: The Domestic Slave Trade in American Life* (New York: Oxford University Press, 2005).

Documents Furnished by the British Government under the Third Article of the Convention of St. Petersburg and Bayly's List of Slaves and of Public and Private Property Remaining on Tangier Island and on Board H.B.M. Ships of War, after the Ratification of the Treaty of Ghent (Washington, DC: Gales & Seaton, 1827).

Doyle, Christopher. "Judge St. George Tucker and the Case of Tom v. Roberts: Blunting the Revolution's Radicalism from Virginia's District Courts." *Virginia Magazine of History and Biography* 106 (Autumn 1998): 419–42.

Drescher, Seymour. *Abolition: A History of Slavery and Antislavery* (New York: Cambridge University Press, 2009).

———. "Emperors of the World: British Abolitionism and Imperialism." In Derek R. Peterson, ed., *Abolitionism and Imperialism in Britain, Africa, and the Atlantic* (Athens: Ohio University Press, 2010): 129–49.

Duane, William. "Selections from the Duane Papers." *Historical Magazine* 4 (Aug. 1868): 60–75.

Dudley, Wade G. *Splintering the Wooden Wall: The British Blockade of the United States, 1812–1815* (Annapolis, MD: Naval Institute Press, 2003).

Dudley, William S., ed. *The Naval War of 1812: A Documentary History*, 3 vols. (Washington, DC: Department of the Navy, 1992).

Duffy, Michael. *Soldiers, Sugar, and Seapower: The British Expeditions to the West Indies and War against Revolutionary France* (Oxford: Oxford University Press, 1987).

Dunn, Richard S. "After Tobacco: The Slave Labour Pattern on a Large Chesapeake Grain-and-Livestock Plantation in the Early Nineteenth Century." In John J. McCusker and Kenneth Morgan, eds., *The Early Modern Atlantic Economy*, 344–63 (New York: Cambridge University Press, 2000).

———. "Black Society in the Chesapeake, 1776–1810." In Ira Berlin and Ronald Hoffman, eds., *Slavery and Freedom in the Age of the American Revolution* (Urbana: University of Illinois Press, 1983): 49–82.

———. "A Tale of Two Plantations: Slave Life at Mesopotamia in Jamaica and Mounty Airy in Virginia, 1799 to 1828." *William and Mary Quarterly*, 3rd ser., 34 (Jan. 1977): 32–65.

Dunn, Susan. *Dominion of Memories: Jefferson, Madison, and the Decline of Virginia* (New York: Basic Books, 2007).

Egerton, Douglas R. *Charles Fenton Mercer and the Trial of National Conservatism* (Oxford University Press of Mississippi, 1989).

———. "Forgetting Denmark Vesey; or, Oliver Stone Meets Richard Wade." *William and Mary Quarterly*, 3rd ser., 59 (Jan. 2002): 143–52.

———. *Gabriel's Rebellion: The Virginia Slave Conspiracies of 1800 and 1802* (Chapel Hill: University of North Carolina Press, 1993).

Einhorn, Robin L. "Patrick Henry's Case against the Constitution: The Structural Problem with Slavery." *Journal of the Early Republic* 22 (Winter 2002): 549–73.

Elkins, Stanley, and Eric McKitrick. *The Age of Federalism* (New York: Oxford University Press, 1993).

Ells, Margaret, and D. C. Harvey, eds. *A Calendar of Official Correspondence and Legislative Papers, Nova Scotia, 1802–1815* (Halifax: Public Archives of Nova Scotia, 1936).

Ely, Melvin Patrick. *Israel on the Appomattox: A Southern Experiment in Black Freedom from the 1790s through the Civil War* (New York: Alfred A. Knopf, 2004).

Epstein, James. "Politics of Colonial Sensation: The Trial of Thomas Picton and the Cause of Louisa Calderon." *American Historical Review* 112 (June 2007): 712–41.

Ericson, David F. "Slave Smugglers, Slave Catchers, and Slave Rebels." In John Craig Hammond and Matthew Mason, eds., *Contesting Slavery: The Politics of Bondage and Freedom in the New American Nation* (Charlottesville: University of Virginia Press, 2011): 183–203.

Eshelman, Ralph E., and Burton K. Kummerow. *In Full Glory Reflected: Discovering the War of 1812 in the Chesapeake* (Baltimore: Maryland Historical Society Press, 2012).

Eshelman, Ralph E., Scott S. Sheads, and Donald R. Hickey. *The War of 1812 in the Chesapeake: A Reference Guide to Historic Sites in Maryland, Virginia, and the District of Columbia* (Baltimore: Johns Hopkins University Press, 2010).

Eustace, Nicole. *1812: War and the Passions of Patriotism* (Philadelphia: University of Pennsylvania Press, 2012).

Evans, Emory G. *A "Topping People": The Rise and Decline of Virginia's Old Political Elite, 1680–1790* (Charlottesville: University of Virginia Press, 2009).

Fedric, Francis. *Slave Life in Virginia and Kentucky: A Narrative by Francis Fedric, Escaped Slave* (Baton Rouge: Louisiana State University Press, 2010).

Fehrenbacher, Don E., and Ward M. McAfee. *The Slaveholding Republic: An Account of the United States Government's Relations to Slavery* (New York: Oxford University Press, 2001).

Feltman, William. *The Journal of Lieut. William Feltman of the First Pennsylvania Regiment, 1781–1782* (Philadelphia: Historical Society of Pennsylvania, 1853).

Fenn, Elizabeth Anne. *Pox Americana: The Great Smallpox Epidemic of 1775–82* (New York: Hill & Wang, 2001).

Fergus, Claudius. "'Dread of Insurrection': Abolitionism, Security, and Labor in Britain's West Indian Colonies, 1760–1823." *William and Mary Quarterly*, 3rd ser., 66 (Oct. 2009): 757–80.

Fergusson, Charles Bruce, ed. *A Documentary Study of the Establishment of the Negroes in Nova Scotia between the War of 1812 and the Winning of Responsible Government* (Halifax: Public Archives of Nova Scotia, 1948).

Field, Cyril. *Britain's Sea-Soldiers: A History of the Royal Marines*, 3 vols. (Liverpool: Lyceum Press, 1924).

Finkelman, Paul. "The Dragon St. George Could Not Slay: Tucker's Plan to End Slavery." *William and Mary Law Review* 47, no. 4 (2006): 1213–43.

Fithian, Philip Vickers. *Journal and Letters, 1773–1774: A Plantation Tutor of the Old Dominion* (Williamsburg: Colonial Williamsburg, 1943).

Flournoy, H. W., ed. *Calendar of Virginia State Papers and Other Manuscripts from January 1, 1808 to December 1, 1835*, 12 vols. (New York: Kraus Reprint, 1968; reprint of Richmond, 1890).

Foner, Jack D. *Blacks and the Military in American History: A New Perspective* (New York: Praeger, 1974).

Forbes, Robert Pierce. *The Missouri Compromise and Its Aftermath: Slavery and the Meaning of America* (Chapel Hill: University of North Carolina Press, 2007).

Ford, Lacy K. *Deliver Us from Evil: The Slavery Question in the Old South* (New York: Oxford University Press, 2009).

Ford, Paul Leicester, ed. *The Works of Thomas Jefferson*, 12 vols. (New York: G.P. Putnam Sons, 1904–5).

Ford, Worthington C., ed. "Letters of James Monroe." Massachusetts Historical Society, *Proceedings* 42 (1908–9): 318–41.

——, ed. "Letters of William Duane." Massachusetts Historical Society, *Proceedings* 20 (May 1906): 257–394.

Foreman, Amanda. *A World on Fire: Britain's Crucial Role in the American Civil War* (New York: Random House, 2010).

Freehling, William W. *The Road to Disunion: Secessionists at Bay, 1776–1854* (New York: Oxford University Press, 1990).

Frey, Sylvia R. "Between Slavery and Freedom: Virginia Blacks in the American Revolution." *Journal of Southern History* 49 (Aug. 1983): 375–98.

——. *Water from the Rock: Black Resistance in a Revolutionary Age* (Princeton, NJ: Princeton University Press, 1991).

Furstenberg, François. "Beyond Freedom and Slavery: Autonomy, Virtue, and Resistance in Early American Political Discourse." *Journal of American History* 89 (Mar. 2003): 1295–330.

Gaines, William H., Jr. *Thomas Mann Randolph, Jefferson's Son-in-Law* (Baton Rouge: Louisiana State University Press, 1966).

Geggus, David Patrick. "The Cost of Pitt's Caribbean Campaigns, 1793–1798." *Historical Journal* 26, no. 3 (1983): 699–706.

——, ed. *The Impact of the Haitian Revolution in the Atlantic World* (Columbia: University of South Carolina Press, 2001).

——. *Slavery, War, and Revolution: The British Occupation of Saint Domingue, 1793–1798* (Oxford: Oxford University Press, 1982).

George, Christopher T., ed. "The Family Papers of Major General Robert Ross, the Diary of Col. Arthur Brooke, and the British Attacks on Washington and Baltimore of 1814." *Maryland Historical Magazine* 88 (Fall 1993): 300–16.

——. "Mirage of Freedom: African Americans in the War of 1812." *Maryland Historical Magazine*, 91 (Winter 1996): 427–50.

——. *Terror on the Chesapeake: The War of 1812 on the Bay* (Shippensburg, PA: White Mane, 2001).

Gilje, Paul A. *Rioting in America* (Bloomington: Indiana University Press, 1996).

Gleig, G[eorge] R[obert]. *A Narrative of the Campaigns of the British Army at Washington and New Orleans* (London: John Murray, 1861).

Gordon, Armistead C. *William Fitzhugh Gordon, a Virginian of the Old School: His Life, Times and Contemporaries* (New York: Neale, 1909).

Gordon-Reed, Annette. *The Hemingses of Monticello: An American Family* (New York: W. W. Norton, 2008).

Gould, Eliga H. "The Making of an Atlantic Slave System: Britain and the United States, 1795–1825." In Julie Flavell and Stephen Conway, eds., *Britain and America Go to War: The Impact of War and Warfare in Anglo-America, 1754–1815*, 241–65 (Gainesville: University Press of Florida, 2004).

Grant, John N. "Black Immigrants into Nova Scotia, 1776–1815." *Journal of Negro History* 58 (July 1973): 253–70.

———. "Chesapeake Blacks Who Immigrated to New Brunswick, 1815." *National Genealogical Society Quarterly* 60 (Sep. 1972): 194–98.

———. "The 1821 Emigration of Black Nova Scotians to Trinidad." *Nova Scotia Historical Quarterly* 2 (Sep. 1972): 283–92.

Greenberg, Kenneth S. "Name, Face, Body." In Kenneth S. Greenberg, ed., *Nat Turner: A Slave Rebellion in History and Memory*, 3–23 (New York: Oxford University Press, 2003).

Greene, Jack P. "The Intellectual Reconstruction of Virginia in the Age of Jefferson." In Peter S. Onuf, ed., *Jeffersonian Legacies* (Charlottesville: University Press of Virginia, 1993): 225–53.

Grigsby, Hugh Blair. "Sketches of Members of the Constitutional Convention of 1829–1830." *Virginia Magazine of History and Biography* 61 (July 1953): 319–32.

Grimes, William. *Life of William Grimes, the Runaway Slave* (New York: Oxford University Press, 2008; reprint of New York, 1855).

Grossberg, Michael. "Citizens and Families: A Jeffersonian Vision of Domestic Relations and Generational Change." In James Gilreath, ed., *Thomas Jefferson and the Education of a Citizen* (Hanover, NH: University Press of New England, 1999): 3–27.

Gudmestad, Robert H. *A Troublesome Commerce: The Transformation of the Interstate Slave Trade* (Baton Rouge: Louisiana State University Press, 2003).

Gutzman, Kevin R. C. *Virginia's American Revolution: From Dominion to Republic, 1776–1840* (New York: Rowman & Littlefield, 2007).

Gwynn, Julian, *Frigates and Foremasts: The North American Squadron in Nova Scotia Waters, 1745–1815* (Vancouver: University of British Columbia Press, 2003).

Hadden, Sally E. *Slave Patrols: Law and Violence in Virginia and the Carolinas* (Cambridge, MA: Harvard University Press, 2001).

Hamilton, Phillip. *The Making and Unmaking of a Revolutionary Family: The Tuckers of Virginia, 1752–1830* (Charlottesville: University of Virginia Press, 2003).

———. "Revolutionary Principles and Family Loyalties: Slavery's Transformation in the St. George Tucker Household of Early National Virginia." *William and Mary Quarterly*, 3rd ser., 55 (Oct. 1998): 531–56.

Hamilton, Stanislaus Murray, ed. *The Writings of James Monroe: Including a Collection of His Public and Private Papers and Correspondence*, 7 vols. (New York: G. P. Putnam's Sons, 1901).

Hammond, John Craig. *Slavery, Freedom, and Expansion in the Early American West* (Charlottesville: University of Virginia Press, 2007).

———. "'Uncontrollable Necessity': The Local Politics, Geopolitics, and Sectional Politics of Slavery Expansion." In John Craig Hammond and Matthew Mason, eds., *Contesting Slavery: The Politics of Bondage and Freedom in the New American Nation* (Charlottesville: University of Virginia Press, 2011): 138–60.

Hammond, John Craig, and Matthew Mason, eds. *Contesting Slavery: The Politics of Bondage and Freedom in the New American Nation* (Charlottesville: University of Virginia Press, 2011).

Hansard, T. C., ed. *Parliamentary Debates from the Year 1803 to the Present Time* (London: Parliament of the United Kingdom, 1817).

Haulman, Clyde A. *Virginia and the Panic of 1819: The First Great Depression and the Commonwealth* (London: Pickering & Chatto, 2008).

Haynes, Sam W. *Unfinished Revolution: The Early American Republic in a British World* (Charlottesville: University of Virginia Press, 2010).

Hecht, Arthur. "The Post Office Department in St. Mary's County in the War of 1812." *Maryland Historical Magazine* 52 (1957): 142–52.

Hendrickson, David C. *Peace Pact: The Lost World of the American Founding* (Lawrence: University Press of Kansas, 2003).

Hening, William W., ed. *The Statutes at Large: Being a Collection of All of the Laws of Virginia from the First Session of the Legislature, in the Year 1619*, 13 vols. (Richmond: W. W. Hening, 1809–1823).

Hening, William W., and William Munford, eds. *Reports of Cases Argued and Determined in the Supreme Court of Appeals of Virginia* (Richmond: Samuel Pleasants Jr., 1807).

Herndon, George Melvin, ed. *William Tatham and the Culture of Tobacco* (Coral Gables: University of Miami Press, 1969).

———. *William Tatham, 1752–1819: American Versatile* (Johnson City: East Tennessee State University Press, 1973).

Hickey, Donald R. "America's Response to the Slave Revolt in Haiti, 1791–1806." *Journal of the Early Republic* 2 (1982): 361–79.

——. *Don't Give Up the Ship! Myths of the War of 1812* (Urbana: University of Illinois Press, 2006).

——. *The War of 1812: A Forgotten Conflict* (Urbana: University of Illinois Press, 1989).

Hilton, Boyd. "1807 and All That: Why Britain Outlawed Her Slave Trade." In Derek R. Peterson, ed., *Abolitionism and Imperialism in Britain, Africa, and the Atlantic* (Athens: Ohio University Press, 2010): 63–83.

Himmelheber, Peter. "Sotterley Plantation during the War of 1812." *Chronicles of St. Mary's* (St. Mary's County Historical Society, MD) 51, no. 4 (Winter 2003): 90–93.

Hinderaker, Eric. *Elusive Empires: Constructing Colonialism in the Ohio Valley, 1673–1800* (New York: Cambridge University Press, 1997).

Hoffman, Ronald. *A Spirit of Dissension: Economics, Politics, and the Revolution in Maryland* (Baltimore: Johns Hopkins University Press, 1973).

Hoge, William A. "The British Are Coming Up the Potomac." *Northern Neck of Virginia Historical Magazine* 14 (Dec. 1964): 1265–79.

Holton, Woody. *Forced Founders: Indians, Debtors, Slaves, and the Making of the American Revolution in Virginia* (Chapel Hill: University of North Carolina Press, 1999).

Horne, Gerald. *Negro Comrades of the Crown: African Americans and the British Empire Fight the U.S. before Emancipation* (New York: New York University Press, 2012).

Horsman, Reginald. *The Causes of the War of 1812* (Philadelphia: University of Pennsylvania Press, 1962).

House of Commons. *Papers Relating to the Slave Trade, Ordered by the House of Commons to be Printed, 4 July 1815* (London: House of Commons, 1815).

Howard, Rosalyn. *Black Seminoles in the Bahamas* (Gainesville: University Press of Florida, 2002).

Hughes, Sarah S. "Slaves for Hire: The Allocations of Black Labor in Elizabeth City County, Virginia, 1782–1810." *William and Mary Quarterly*, 3rd ser., 35 (Apr. 1978): 260–86.

Hume, Edgar Erskine, ed. "Letters Written during the War of 1812 by the British Naval Commander in American Waters (Admiral Sir David Milne)." *William and Mary Quarterly*, 2nd ser., 10 (Oct. 1930): 279–301.

Hunt, Gaillard, ed. *The First Forty Years of Washington Society: Portrayed by the Family Letters of Mrs. Samuel Harrison Smith (Margaret Bayard)* (New York: Charles Scribner's Sons, 1906).

——, ed. *The Writings of James Madison*, 9 vols. (New York: Charles Scribner's Sons, 1900–1910).

Iaccarino, Anthony A. "Virginia and the National Contest over Slavery in the Early Republic, 1780–1833." Ph.D. dissertation, University of California at Los Angeles, 1999.

Inscoe, John C. "Carolina Slave Names: An Index to Acculturation." *Journal of Southern History* 49 (Nov. 1983): 527–54.

Janson, Charles William. *The Stranger in America* (New York: Press of the Pioneers, 1935: reprint of London, 1807).

Jarvis, Michael J. *In the Eye of All Trade: Bermuda, Bermudians, and the Maritime Atlantic World, 1680–1783* (Chapel Hill: University of North Carolina Press, 2010).

———. "Maritime Masters and Seafaring Slaves in Bermuda, 1680–1783." *William and Mary Quarterly*, 3rd ser., 59 (July 2002): 584–622.

Jefferson, Thomas. *Notes on the State of Virginia*, with an introduction by Peter S. Onuf (New York: Barnes & Noble; 2010; reprint of 1785 original).

Jenkins, Brian. *Henry Goulburn, 1784–1856: A Political Biography* (Montreal: McGill-Queens University Press, 1996).

Jennings, Paul. *A Colored Man's Reminiscences of James Madison* (Brooklyn: George C. Beadle, 1865).

Jeter, Jeremiah Bell. *The Recollections of a Long Life* (Richmond: Religious Herald Co., 1891).

John, Richard R. *Spreading the News: The American Postal System from Franklin to Morse* (Cambridge, MA: Harvard University Press, 1995).

Johnson, Michael P. "Denmark Vesey and His Co-conspirators." *William and Mary Quarterly*, 3rd ser., 58 (Oct. 2001): 915–76.

———. "Reading Evidence." *William and Mary Quarterly*, 3rd ser., 59 (Jan. 2002): 193–202.

Johnston, James Hugo. *Race Relations in Virginia and Miscegenation in the South, 1776–1860* (Amherst: University of Massachusetts Press, 1970).

Jordan, Daniel P. "John Randolph of Roanoke and the Art of Winning Elections in Jeffersonian Virginia." *Virginia Magazine of History and Biography* 86 (Oct. 1978): 389–407.

———. *Political Leadership in Jefferson's Virginia* (Charlottesville: University Press of Virginia, 1983).

Jordan, Winthrop D. *White over Black: American Attitudes toward the Negro, 1550–1812* (Chapel Hill: University of North Carolina Press, 1968).

Joynes, Thomas R. "The Burning of the Richmond Theatre, 1811: A Letter from Thomas R. Joynes to Levin S. Joynes." *Virginia Magazine of History and Biography* 51 (July 1943): 297–300.

Kamoie, Laura Croghan. *Irons in the Fire: The Business History of the Tayloe Family and Virginia's Gentry, 1700–1860* (Charlottesville: University of Virginia Press, 2007).

Kastor, Peter. "'Motives of Peculiar Urgency': Local Diplomacy in Louisiana, 1803–1821." *William and Mary Quarterly*, 3rd ser., 58 (Oct. 2001): 819–48.

Kaye, Anthony E. *Joining Places: Slave Neighborhoods in the Old South* (Chapel Hill: University of North Carolina Press, 2007).

Kennedy, John P. *Memoirs of the Life of William Wirt*, 2 vols. (Philadelphia: W. J. Neal, 1834).

Kettner, James H. *The Development of American Citizenship, 1608–1870* (Chapel Hill: University of North Carolina Press, 1978).

Kierner, Cynthia A. *Scandal at Bizarre: Rumor and Reputation in Jefferson's America* (New York: Palgrave Macmillan, 2004).

Kingsley, Zephaniah. *A Treatise on the Patriarchal, or Co-operative System of Society, as It Exists in Some Governments, and Colonies in America, and in the United States, under the Name of Slavery, with Its Necessity and Advantages* (n.p.: no pub.,1829).

Kirk, Russell. *John Randolph of Roanoke* (Indianapolis: Liberty Press, 1978).

Kirtland, Robert. "George Wythe." In John A. Garraty and Mark C. Carnes, eds., *American National Biography* (New York: Oxford University Press, 1999): vol. 24: 92–94.

Kulikoff, Allan. *Tobacco and Slaves: The Development of Southern Cultures in the Chesapeake, 1680–1800* (Chapel Hill: University of North Carolina Press, 1986).

———. "Uprooted Peoples: Black Migrants in the Age of the American Revolution." In Ira Berlin and Ronald Hoffman, eds., *Slavery and Freedom in the Age of the American Revolution* (Urbana: University of Illinois Press, 1983): 143–71.

Lambert, Andrew. *The Challenge: America, Britain, and the War of 1812* (London: Faber & Faber, 2012).

Laurence, K. O. "The Settlement of Free Negroes in Trinidad before Emancipation." *Caribbean Quarterly* 9 (Mar. 1963): 26–52.

Lavery, Brian. *Nelson's Navy: The Ships, Men, and Organisation, 1793–1815* (London: Conway Maritime Press, 1989).

Lawson, Mrs. William. *History of the Townships of Dartmouth, Preston and Lawrencetown, Halifax County, N.S.* (Halifax: Morton, 1893).

Lee, Henry. *Memoirs of the War in the Southern Department of the United States*, 2 vols. (Philadelphia, 1812).

Lee, Jean Butenhoff. *The Price of Nationhood: The American Revolution in Charles County* (New York: W. W. Norton, 1994).

Lee, Sidney, ed. *Dictionary of National Biography*, 22 vols. (London: Smith, Elder, 1899).

Leichtle, Kurt E., and Bruce G. Carveth. *Crusade against Slavery: Edward Coles, Pioneer of Freedom* (Carbondale: Southern Illinois University Press, 2011).

Leonard, Cynthia Miller, ed. *The General Assembly of Virginia, July 30, 1619– January 11, 1978: A Bicentennial Register of Members* (Richmond: Virginia State Library, 1978).

Lester, Malcolm. "Sir John Borlase Warren." In H. C. G. Matthew and Brian Harrison, eds., *Oxford Dictionary of National Biography* (Oxford: Oxford University Press, 2004): vol. 57: 485–88.

Lewis, Jan. "The Problem of Slavery in Southern Political Discourse." In David Thomas Konig, ed., *Devising Liberty: Preserving and Creating Freedom in the New American Republic* (Stanford, CA: Stanford University Press, 1995): 265–97.

———. *The Pursuit of Happiness: Family and Values in Jefferson's Virginia* (New York: Cambridge University Press, 1983).

Lewis, Michael. *A Social History of the Navy, 1793–1815* (London: George Allen & Unwin, 1960).

Lindsay, Arnett G. "Diplomatic Relations between the United States and Great Britain Bearing on the Return of Negro Slaves, 1783–1818." *Journal of Negro History* 5 (Oct. 1920): 391–419.

Lipscomb, Andrew A., and Albert Ellery Bergh, eds. *The Writings of Thomas Jefferson*, 20 vols. (Washington, DC, 1903–4).

Lobb, John, ed. *Uncle Tom's Story: An Autobiography of the Rev. Josiah Henson, 1789–1876* (London: Frank Cass, 1971; reprint of London, Ontario, 1881).

Looney, J. Jefferson, ed. *The Papers of Thomas Jefferson, Retirement Series*, 9 vols. to date (Princeton, NJ: Princeton University Press, 2005–).

Lossing, Benson J. *Pictorial Field Book of the War of 1812* (New York: Harper & Brothers, 1869).

Loux, Jennifer R. "John Hartwell Cocke, Jr." In Sara B. Bearss, ed., *Dictionary of Virginia Biography* (Richmond: Library of Virginia, 2006): vol. 3: 330–31.

Lovell, William Stanhope. *Personal Narrative of Events from 1799 to 1815* (London: William Allen, 1879).

Lowrey, Charles D. *James Barbour: A Jeffersonian Republican* (Montgomery: University of Alabama Press, 1984).

MacNutt, W. S. *New Brunswick: A History: 1784–1867* (Toronto: Macmillan of Canada, 1984).

Madison, James. *A Message from the President of the United States, Transmitting Copies of a Communication from Mr. Russell to the Secretary of State* (Washington, D.C.: U.S. Congress, 1812).

Main, Jackson Turner. "Sections and Politics in Virginia, 1781–1787." *William and Mary Quarterly*, 3rd ser., 12 (Jan. 1955): 96–112.

Malcomson, Thomas. "Creating Order and 'Disorder' in the British Navy: The North American and West Indies Station, 1812–1815." Ph.D. dissertation, York University, Toronto, 2007.

———. "Freedom by Reaching the Wooden World: American Slaves and the British Navy during the War of 1812." *The Northern Mariner*, vol. 22 (Oct. 2012): 361–92.

Malone, Dumas. *Jefferson and His Time: The Sage of Monticello* (Boston: Little, Brown, 1981).

——. *Jefferson, the President: Second Term, 1805–1809* (Boston: Little, Brown, 1974).

Manning, William R., ed. *Diplomatic Correspondence of the United States: Canadian Relations, 1784–1860,* 4 vols. (Washington, DC: Carnegie Endowment for International Peace, 1940–45).

Marine, William M. *The British Invasion of Maryland, 1812–1815* (Baltimore: Society of the War of 1812 in Maryland, 1913).

Martell, J. S. *Immigration to and Emigration from Nova Scotia, 1815–1838* (Halifax: Public Archives of Nova Scotia, 1942).

Mason, Matthew. "The Battle of the Slaveholding Liberators: Great Britain, the United States, and Slavery in the Early Nineteenth Century." *William and Mary Quarterly,* 3rd ser., 59 (July 2002): 665–96.

——. "Necessary but Not Sufficient: Revolutionary Ideology and Antislavery Action in the Early Republic." In John Craig Hammond and Matthew Mason, eds., *Contesting Slavery: The Politics of Bondage and Freedom in the New American Nation* (Charlottesville: University of Virginia Press, 2011): 11–31.

——. *Slavery and Politics in the Early American Republic* (Chapel Hill: University of North Carolina Press, 2006).

Mason, Thomas A. "The Luminary of the Northern Neck: Walter Jones, 1745–1815." *Northern Neck of Virginia Historical Magazine* 35 (Dec. 1985): 3978–83.

Masur, Louis P. "Nat Turner and Sectional Crisis." In Kenneth S. Greenberg, ed., *Nat Turner: A Slave Rebellion in History and Memory* (New York: Oxford University Press, 2003): 148–61.

Mathias, Frank F. "John Randolph's Freedmen: The Thwarting of a Will." *Journal of Southern History* 39 (May 1973): 263–72.

Matthewson, Timothy, ed. "Abraham Bishop, 'The Rights of Black Men,' and the American Reaction to the Haitian Revolution." *Journal of Negro History* 67 (Summer 1982): 148–54.

Mayer, David N., ed. "Of Principles and Men: The Correspondence of John Taylor of Caroline with Wilson Cary Nicholas, 1806–1808." *Virginia Magazine of History and Biography* 96 (July 1988): 345–88.

McColley, Robert. *Slavery and Jeffersonian Virginia* (Urbana: University of Illinois Press, 1964).

McConville, Brendan. *The King's Three Faces: The Rise and Fall of Royal America, 1688–1776* (Chapel Hill: University of North Carolina Press, 2006).

McCoy, Drew. "James Madison and Visions of American Nationality in the Confederation Period: A Regional Perspective." In Richard Beeman and Stephen Botein, eds., *Beyond Confederation: Origins of the Constitution and American National Identity* (Chapel Hill: University of North Carolina Press, 1987): 226–58.

McCoy, Drew R. *The Last of the Fathers: James Madison and the Republican Legacy* (New York: Cambridge University Press, 1989).

McDaniel, Lorna. "Memory Spirituals of the Ex-Slave American Soldiers in Trinidad's 'Company Villages.'" *Black Music Research Journal* 14 (Autumn 1994): 119–43.

———. "Memory Spirituals of the Liberated American Soldiers in Trinidad's 'Company Villages.'" *Caribbean Quarterly* 40 (Mar. 1994): 38–58.

McDonell, Michael A. *The Politics of War: Race, Class, and Conflict in Revolutionary Virginia* (Chapel Hill: University of North Carolina Press, 2007).

McGarvie, Mark Douglas. "Transforming Society through Law: St. George Tucker, Women's Property Rights, and an Active Republican Judiciary." *William and Mary Law Review* 47 (Feb. 2006): 1393–1425.

McLean, Robert Colin. *George Tucker: Moral Philosopher and Man of Letters* (Chapel Hill: University of North Carolina Press, 1961).

McPherson, Elizabeth G., ed. "Letters of William Tatham." *William and Mary Quarterly*, 2nd ser., 16 (Apr. and July 1936): 162–91, 362–98.

Meade, Bishop William. *Old Churches, Ministers and Families of Virginia*, 2 vols. (Philadelphia: J. B. Lippincott, 1857).

Meaders, Daniel, ed. *Advertisements for Runaway Slaves in Virginia, 1801–1820* (New York: Garland, 1997).

Meriwether, Robert C., ed. *The Papers of John C. Calhoun*, 28 vols. (Columbia: University of South Carolina Press, 1959–2003).

Miller, Stephen F., ed. *Memoir of General David Blackshear* (Philadelphia: J. B. Lippincott, 1858).

Millett, Nathaniel. "Britain's 1814 Occupation of Pensacola and America's Response: An Episode of the War of 1812 in the Southeastern Borderlands." *Florida Historical Quarterly* 84 (Fall 2005): 229–55.

Moore, John Bassett. *History and Digest of the International Arbitrations to Which the United States Has Been a Party*, 6 vols. (Washington, DC: Government Printing Office, 1898).

Moore, John Hammond. "A Hymn of Freedom—South Carolina, 1813." *Journal of Negro History* 50 (Jan. 1965): 50–53.

Morgan, Philip D. "Conspiracy Scares." *William and Mary Quarterly*, 3rd ser., 59 (Jan. 2002): 159–66.

———. "Ending the Slave Trade: A Caribbean and Atlantic Context." In Derek R. Peterson, ed., *Abolitionism and Imperialism in Britain, Africa, and the Atlantic* (Athens: Ohio University Press, 2010): 101–28.

———. "Interracial Sex in the Chesapeake and the British Atlantic World, c. 1700–1820." In Peter S. Onuf and Jane Ellen Lewis, eds., *Sally Hemings and Thomas Jefferson: History, Memory, and Civic Culture* (Charlottesville: University Press of Virginia, 1999): 52–84.

——. *Slave Counterpoint: Black Culture in the Eighteenth-Century Chesa-peake and Lowcountry* (Chapel Hill: University of North Carolina Press, 1998).

Morgan, Philip D., and Andrew Jackson O'Shaughnessy. "Arming Slaves in the American Revolution." In Christopher Leslie Brown and Philip D. Morgan, eds., *Arming Slaves from Classical Time to the Modern Age* (New Haven, CT: Yale University Press, 2006): 180–208.

Morriss, Roger. *Cockburn and the British Navy in Transition: Admiral Sir George Cockburn, 1772–1853* (Columbia: University of South Carolina Press, 1997).

Morton, Louis. *Robert Carter of Nomini Hall: A Virginia Tobacco Planter of the Eighteenth Century* (Charlottesville: University Press of Virginia, 1964).

Mullin, Gerald W. *Flight and Rebellion: Slave Resistance in Eighteenth-Century Virginia* (New York: Oxford University Press, 1972).

Murphy, Pleasants. "Pleasants Murphy's 'Journal and Day Book.'" *William and Mary Quarterly*, 2nd ser., 3 (Oct. 1923): 231–38.

[Napier, Charles]. "Narrative of the Naval Operations in the Potomac." *Colburn's United Service Journal*, no. 53 (Apr. 1833): 469–81.

Napier, Edward H. D. E. *The Life and Correspondence of Admiral Sir Charles Napier, K.C.B., from Personal Recollections, Letters, and Official Documents*, 2 vols. (London: Hurst & Blackett, 1862).

Napier, Priscilla. *Black Charlie: A Life of Admiral Sir Charles Napier, KCB, 1787–1860* (Norwich, England: Michael Russell, 1995).

——. *Henry at Sea: Part One of the Life of Captain Henry Napier, R.N.* (Norwich, England: Michael Russell, 1997).

Nash, Gary B. *The Forgotten Fifth: African Americans in the Age of Revolution* (Cambridge, MA: Harvard University Press, 2006).

Nash, Gary B., and Jean R. Soderlund. *Freedom by Degrees: Emancipation in Pennsylvania and Its Aftermath* (New York: Oxford University Press, 1991).

Nevins, Allan, ed. *The Diary of John Quincy Adams, 1794–1845* (New York: Charles Scribner's Sons, 1951).

Newman, Richard S. *The Transformation of American Abolitionism: Fighting Slavery in the Early Republic* (Chapel Hill: University of North Carolina Press, 2002).

Newman, Simon P. "American Political Culture and the French and Haitian Revolutions: Nathaniel Cutting and the Jeffersonian Republicans." In David Patrick Geggus, ed., *The Impact of the Haitian Revolution in the Atlantic World* (Columbia: University of South Carolina Press, 2001): 72–89.

Nicholls, Michael L. "Passing through This Troublesome World: Free Blacks in the Early Southside." *Virginia Magazine of History and Biography* 92 (Jan. 1984): 50–70.

——. "'The Squint of Freedom': African-American Freedom Suits in Post-Revolutionary Virginia." *Slavery and Abolition* 20 (1999): 47–62.

——. *Whispers of Rebellion: Narrating Gabriel's Conspiracy* (Charlottesville: University of Virginia Press, 2012).

Norris, Walter Briscoe, Jr., ed. *Westmoreland County, Virginia, 1653–1983* (Montross, VA: Westmoreland County Board of Supervisors, 1983).

Norton, Mary Beth, Herbert G. Gutman, and Ira Berlin. "The Afro-American Family in the Age of Revolution." In Ira Berlin and Ronald Hoffman, eds., *Slavery and Freedom in the Age of the American Revolution* (Urbana: University of Illinois Press, 1983): 175–91.

Oakes, James. "Conflict vs. Racial Consensus in the History of Antislavery Politics." In John Craig Hammond and Matthew Mason, eds., *Contesting Slavery: The Politics of Bondage and Freedom in the New American Nation* (Charlottesville: University of Virginia Press, 2011): 291–303.

——. *Freedom National: The Destruction of Slavery in the United States, 1861–1865* (New York: W. W. Norton, 2012).

——. *Slavery and Freedom: An Interpretation of the Old South* (New York: Vintage, 1990).

Oberg, Barbara B., ed. *The Papers of Thomas Jefferson*, 36 vols. to date (Princeton, NJ: Princeton University Press, 1950–).

Onuf, Peter S. "Domesticating the Captive Nation: Thomas Jefferson and the Problem of Slavery." In Thomas J. Knock and John Milton Cooper Jr., eds., *Jefferson, Lincoln, and Wilson: The American Dilemma of Race and Democracy* (Charlottesville: University Press of Virginia, 2010): 34–60.

——. "Federalism, Republicanism, and the Origins of American Sectionalism." In Edward L. Ayers, Patricia Nelson Limerick, Stephen Nissenbaum, and Peter S. Onuf, eds., *All over the Map: Rethinking American Regions* (Baltimore: Johns Hopkins University Press, 1996): 11–37.

——. *The Mind of Thomas Jefferson* (Charlottesville: University of Virginia Press, 2007).

Onuf, Peter S., and Jane Ellen Lewis, eds. *Sally Hemings and Thomas Jefferson: History, Memory, and Civic Culture* (Charlottesville: University Press of Virginia, 1999).

Owsley, Frank Lawrence, Jr. *The Struggle for the Gulf Borderlands: The Creek War and the Battle of New Orleans, 1812–1815* (Gainesville: University Press of Florida, 1981).

Owsley, Frank Lawrence, Jr., and Gene A. Smith. *Filibusterers and Expansionists: Jeffersonian Manifest Destiny, 1800–1821* (Tuscaloosa: University of Alabama Press, 1997).

Pack, James. *The Man Who Burned the White House: Admiral Sir George Cockburn, 1772–1853* (Emsworth, Hampshire, England: Kenneth Mason, 1987).

Padgett, James A., ed. "Letters from Thomas Newton." *William and Mary Quarterly*, 2nd ser., 16 (Apr. 1936): 192–205.

Papenfuse, Eric Robert. *The Evils of Necessity: Robert Goodloe Harper and the Moral Dilemma of Slavery* (Philadelphia: American Philosophical Society, 1997).

Parkinson, Richard. *A Tour in America in 1798, 1799, and 1800*, 2 vols. (London: J. Harding, 1805).

Parkinson, Robert G. "'Manifest Signs of Passion': The First Federal Congress, Antislavery, and Legacies of the Revolutionary War." In John Craig Hammond and Matthew Mason, eds., *Contesting Slavery: The Politics of Bondage and Freedom in the New American Nation* (Charlottesville: University of Virginia Press, 2011): 49–68.

Parramore, Thomas C. "Covenant in Jerusalem." In Kenneth S. Greenberg, ed., *Nat Turner: A Slave Rebellion in History and Memory* (New York: Oxford University Press, 2003): 58–76.

Pasley, Jeffrey L. *"The Tyranny of Printers": Newspaper Politics in the Early American Republic* (Charlottesville: University of Virginia Press, 2001).

Pearson, Ellen Holmes. *Remaking Custom: Law and Identity in the Early American Republic* (Charlottesville: University of Virginia Press, 2011).

Perkins, Bradford. *Prologue to War: England and the United States, 1805–1812* (Berkeley: University of California Press, 1963).

Peterson, Norma Lois, ed. *The Defence of Norfolk in 1807 as Told by William Tatham to Thomas Jefferson* (Chesapeake, VA: Norfolk County Historical Society, 1970).

Petrides, Anne, and Jonathan Downs, eds. *Sea Soldier: An Officer of Marines with Duncan, Nelson, Collingwood, and Cockburn: The Letters and Journals of Major T. Marmaduke Wybourn, RM, 1797–1813* (Tunbridge Wells, Kent, England: Parapress, 2000).

Pitch, Anthony S. *The Burning of Washington: The British Invasion of 1814* (Annapolis, MD: Naval Institute Press, 1998).

Porter, Kenneth W. "Negroes and the East Florida Annexation Plot, 1811–1813." *Journal of Negro History* 30 (1945): 9–29.

——. "Negroes and the Seminole War, 1817–1818." *Journal of Negro History* 36 (July 1951): 249–80.

Pybus, Cassandra. *Epic Journeys of Freedom: Runaway Slaves of the American Revolution and Their Global Quest for Liberty* (Boston: Beacon Press, 2006).

——. "Jefferson's Faulty Math: The Question of Slave Defections in the American Revolution." *William and Mary Quarterly*, 3rd ser., 62 (Apr. 2005): 243–64.

——. "Thomas Jefferson and Slavery." In Francis D. Cogliano, ed., *A Companion to Thomas Jefferson* (Malden, MA: Wiley-Blackwell, 2012): 271–83.

Quimby, Robert S. *The U.S. Army in the War of 1812: An Operational and Command Study*, 2 vols. (East Lansing: Michigan State University Press, 1997).

Quincy, Edmund. *Life of Josiah Quincy of Massachusetts* (Boston: Ticknor & Fields, 1867).

Quincy, Josiah. *Figures of the Past* (Boston: Little, Brown, 1926).

Raboteau, Albert J. "The Slave Church in the Era of the American Revolution." In Ira Berlin and Ronald Hoffman, eds., *Slavery and Freedom in the Age of the American Revolution* (Urbana: University of Illinois Press, 1983): 193–213.

Randolph, Thomas Jefferson. *The Speech of Thomas J. Randolph in the House of Delegates of Virginia on the Abolition of Slavery* (Richmond: Samuel Shepherd, 1832).

Ratcliff, Donald J. "The Decline of Antislavery Politics, 1815–1840." In John Craig Hammond and Matthew Mason, eds., *Contesting Slavery: The Politics of Bondage and Freedom in the New American Nation* (Charlottesville: University of Virginia Press, 2011): 267–90.

Richardson, Ronald Kent. *Moral Imperium: Afro-Caribbeans and the Transformation of British Rule, 1776–1838* (New York: Greenwood Press, 1987).

Richter, Daniel K. *Before the Revolution: America's Ancient Pasts* (Cambridge, MA: Harvard University Press, 2011).

Riley, Padraig. "Slavery and the Problem of Democracy in Jeffersonian America." In John Craig Hammond and Matthew Mason, eds., *Contesting Slavery: The Politics of Bondage and Freedom in the New American Nation* (Charlottesville: University of Virginia Press, 2011): 227–46.

Risjord, Norman K. *Chesapeake Politics, 1781–1800* (New York: Columbia University Press, 1978).

——. *The Old Republicans: Southern Conservatism in the Age of Jackson* (New York: Columbia University Press, 1965).

Roberts, Kenneth, and Anna M. Roberts, eds. *Moreau de St. Mery's American Journey, 1793–1798* (New York: Doubleday, 1947).

Robinson, Ralph. "New Light on Three Episodes of the British Invasion of Maryland in 1814." *Maryland Historical Magazine* 37 (Sep. 1942): 273–90.

Robson, David W. "'An Important Question Answered': William Graham's Defense of Slavery in Post-revolutionary Virginia." *William and Mary Quarterly*, 3rd ser., 37 (Oct. 1980): 644–52.

Rockman, Seth. *Scraping By: Wage Labor, Slavery, and Survival in Early Baltimore* (Baltimore: Johns Hopkins University Press, 2009).

Rothman, Adam. *Slave Country: American Expansion and the Origins of the Deep South* (Cambridge, MA: Harvard University Press, 2005).

Rothman, Joshua D. "James Callender and Social Knowledge of Interracial Sex in Antebellum Virginia." In Peter S. Onuf and Jane Ellen Lewis, eds.,

Sally Hemings and Thomas Jefferson: History, Memory, and Civic Culture (Charlottesville: University Press of Virginia, 1999): 87–113.

———. *Notorious in the Neighborhood: Sex and Families across the Color Line in Virginia, 1787–1861* (Chapel Hill: University of North Carolina Press, 2003).

Rouse, Parke. "The British Invasion of Hampton in 1813: Reminiscences of James Jarvis." *Virginia Magazine of History and Biography* 76 (1968): 318–36.

Rowley, Peter, ed. "Captain Robert Rowley Helps to Burn Washington, D.C., Part 1." *Maryland Historical Magazine* 82 (Fall 1987): 240–50.

———, ed. "Captain Rowley Visits Maryland: Part II of a Series." *Maryland Historical Magazine* 83 (Fall 1988): 247–53.

Royster, Charles. *Light-Horse Harry Lee and the Legacy of the American Revolution* (New York: Alfred A. Knopf, 1981).

Rucker, Walter C. *The River Flows On: Black Resistance, Culture, and Identity Formation in Early America* (Baton Rouge: Louisiana State University Press, 2006).

Rugemer, Edward B. "Caribbean Slave Revolts and the Origins of the Gag Rule: A Contest between Abolitionism and Democracy, 1797–1835." In John Craig Hammond and Matthew Mason, eds., *Contesting Slavery: The Politics of Bondage and Freedom in the New American Nation* (Charlottesville: University of Virginia Press, 2011): 94–113.

Runge, William. "Isaac A. Coles." *Magazine of Albemarle County History* 14 (1954–55): 49–60.

Sarson, Steven. "Yeoman Farmers in a Planters' Republic: Socioeconomic Conditions and Relations in Early National Prince George's County, Maryland." *Journal of the Early Republic* 29 (Spring 2009): 63–99.

Saunders, Robert M. "Crime and Punishment in Early National America: Richmond, Virginia, 1784–1820." *Virginia Magazine of History and Biography* 86 (1978): 33–44.

Schama, Simon. *Rough Crossings: Britain, the Slaves, and the American Revolution* (New York: HarperCollins, 2006).

Schermerhorn, Calvin. *Money over Mastery, Family over Freedom: Slavery in the Antebellum Upper South* (Baltimore: Johns Hopkins University Press, 2011).

Schmidt, Fredrika Teute, and Barbara Ripel Wilhelm. "Early Proslavery Petitions in Virginia." *William and Mary Quarterly*, 3rd ser., 30 (Jan. 1973): 133–46.

Schoen, Brian. "Calculating the Price of Union: Republican Economic Nationalism and the Origins of Southern Sectionalism, 1790–1828." *Journal of the Early Republic* 23 (Summer 2003): 173–206.

———. *The Fragile Fabric of Union: Cotton, Federal Politics, and the Global Origins of the Civil War* (Baltimore: Johns Hopkins University Press, 2009).

Schwarz, Philip J. "Gabriel's Challenge: Slaves and Crime in Late Eighteenth-Century Virginia." *Virginia Magazine of History and Biography* 90 (1982): 283–309.

——. "George Boxley." In Sara B. Bearrss, ed., *Dictionary of Virginia Biography*, vol. 2: 164–65 (Richmond: Library of Virginia, 2001).

——. *Migrants against Slavery: Virginians and the Nation* (Charlottesville: University Press of Virginia, 2001).

——. *Slave Laws in Virginia* (Athens: University of Georgia Press, 1996).

——. *Twice Condemned: Slaves and the Criminal Law of Virginia, 1705–1865* (Baton Rouge: Louisiana State University Press, 1988).

Scott, James. *Recollections of a Naval Life*, 3 vols. (London: Richard Bentley, 1834).

Scully, Randolph Ferguson. *Religion and the Making of Nat Turner's Virginia: Baptist Community and Conflict, 1740–1840* (Charlottesville: University of Virginia Press, 2008).

Shade, William G. *Democratizing the Old Dominion: Virginia and the Second Party System, 1824–1861* (Charlottesville: University Press of Virginia, 1996).

Shalhope, Robert E. *John Taylor of Caroline: Pastoral Republican* (Columbia: University of South Carolina Press, 1980).

Shammas, Carole. "Black Women's Work and the Evolution of Plantation Society in Virginia." *Labor History* 26 (Winter 1985): 5–28.

Sheldon, Marianne Buroff. "Black-White Relations in Richmond, Virginia, 1782–1820." *Journal of Southern History* 45 (Feb. 1979): 27–44.

Shepperson, Archibald Bolling. *John Paradise and Lucy Ludwell of London and Williamsburg* (Richmond: Dietz Press, 1942).

Shomette, Donald G. *Flotilla: Battle for the Patuxent* (Baltimore: Johns Hopkins University Press, 2009).

Sidbury, James. *Ploughshares into Swords: Race, Rebellion, and Identity in Gabriel's Virginia, 1730–1810* (New York: Cambridge University Press, 1997).

——. "Saint Domingue in Virginia: Ideology, Local Meanings, and Resistance to Slavery, 1790–1800." *Journal of Southern History* 63 (1997): 531–52.

Skeen, C. Edward. *John Armstrong, Jr., 1725–1843: A Biography* (Syracuse, NY: Syracuse University Press, 1981).

Smith, G. C. Moore, ed. *The Autobiography of Lieutenant-General Sir Harry Smith, Baronet of Aliwal on the Sutlej, G.C.B.*, 2 vols. (London: J. Murray, 1902).

Smith, Gene A. *The Slaves' Gamble: Choosing Sides in the War of 1812* (New York: Palgrave Macmillan, 2013).

Smith, Gene A., ed. *A British Eyewitness at the Battle of New Orleans: The Memoir of Royal Navy Admiral Robert Aitchison, 1808–1827* (New Orleans: Historic New Orleans Collection, 2004).

Sobel, Mechal. *The World They Made Together: Black and White Values in Eighteenth-Century Virginia* (Princeton, NJ: Princeton University Press, 1987).

Spray, W. A. "The Settlement of the Black Refugees in New Brunswick, 1815–1836." *Acadiensis* 6 (Spring 1977): 64–79.

Stagg, J. C. A. *Mr. Madison's War: Politics, Diplomacy, and Warfare in the Early American Republic, 1783–1830* (Princeton, NJ: Princeton University Press, 1983).

——, ed. *The Papers of James Madison: Presidential Series*, 5 vols. to date (Charlottesville: University Press of Virginia, 1984–).

Stanley, Linda, ed. "James Carter's Account of His Sufferings in Slavery." *Pennsylvania Magazine of History and Biography* 105 (July 1981): 335–39.

Stanton, Lucia C. *"Those Who Labor for My Happiness": Slavery at Thomas Jefferson's Monticello* (Charlottesville: University Press of Virginia, 2012).

——. "'Those Who Labor for My Happiness': Thomas Jefferson and His Slaves." In Peter S. Onuf, ed., *Jeffersonian Legacies* (Charlottesville: University Press of Virginia, 1993): 147–80.

Stanton, Lucia C., and James A. Bear Jr., eds. *Jefferson's Memorandum Books: Accounts, with Legal Records and Miscellany, 1767–1826*, 2 vols. (Princeton, NJ: Princeton University Press, 1997).

Stephen, James. *The Crisis of the Sugar Colonies . . . to Which Are Subjoined Sketches of a Plan for Settling the Vacant Lands of Trinidada* (London: J. Hatchard, 1802).

Stevenson, Brenda E. *Life in Black and White: Family and Community in the Slave South* (New York: Oxford University Press, 1996).

Steward, Austin. *Twenty-Two Years a Slave and Forty Years a Freeman* (Canandaigua, NY: A. Steward, 1867).

Stokes, William E., Jr., and Francis L. Berkeley Jr., eds. *The Papers of Randolph of Roanoke: A Preliminary Checklist of His Surviving Texts in Manuscript and in Print* (Charlottesville: University of Virginia Library, 1950).

Sutcliff, Robert. *Travels in Some Parts of North America, in the Years 1804, 1805, and 1806* (York, England: C. Peacock, 1811).

Sutton, Robert P. "Nostalgia, Pessimism, and Malaise: The Doomed Aristocrat in Late-Jeffersonian Virginia." *Virginia Magazine of History and Biography* 76 (Jan. 1968): 41–55.

Swem, Earl G., and John W. Williams, eds. *A Register of the General Assembly of Virginia, 1776–1918* (Richmond, 1918).

Taylor, Alan. *The Civil War of 1812: American Citizens, British Subjects, Irish Rebels, and Indian Allies* (New York: Alfred A. Knopf, 2010).

Taylor, John. *Arator, Being a Series of Agricultural Essays, Practical and Political* (Georgetown [DC]: J. M. & J. B. Carter, 1813).

Thomas, William H. B. "Poor Deluded Wretches! The Slave Insurrection of 1816." *Louisa County Historical Magazine* 6 (1974): 57–63.

Thrift, C. T. "Thomas Ritchie." *John P. Branch Historical Papers of Randolph-Macon College* 3 (Richmond: Everett Waddey, 1903): 170–87.

Torrence, Clayton. "War's Wild Alarm." *Virginia Magazine of History and Biography* 49 (July 1941): 217–27.

Torrey, Jesse. *A Portraiture of Domestic Slavery in the United States* (Philadelphia: J. Biorden, 1817).

Tragle, Henry Irving. *The Southampton Slave Revolt of 1831* (New York: Random House, 1971).

[Tucker, George]. *Letters from Virginia, Translated from the French* (Baltimore: Fielding Lucas Jr., 1816).

———. *Letter to a Member of the General Assembly of Virginia, on the Subject of the Late Conspiracy of the Slaves; with a Proposal for their Colonization* (Baltimore: Bonsal & Niles, 1801).

Tucker, Robert W., and David C. Hendrickson. *Empire of Liberty: The Statecraft of Thomas Jefferson* (New York: Oxford University Press, 1992).

Tucker, Spencer C., and Frank T. Reuter. *Injured Honor: The Chesapeake-Leopard Affair, June 22, 1807* (Annapolis, MD: Naval Institute Press, 1996).

Tucker, St. George. *A Dissertation on Slavery: With a Proposal for the Gradual Abolition of It in the State of Virginia* (Philadelphia: Mathew Carey, 1796).

———. *Reflections on the Cession of Louisiana to the United States, by Sylvestris* (Washington, DC, 1803).

———. "The Tucker Letters from Williamsburg." *Bermuda Historical Quarterly*, vol. 3, no. 1–vol. 9, no. 4 (Jan. 1946–Nov. 1952).

Turlington, S. Bailey. "Richmond during the War of 1812: The Vigilance Committee." *Virginia Magazine of History and Biography* 7 (Jan. 1900): 226–27, 408–9.

United States Congress. *Report of the Committee of Elections on the Petition of John Taliaferro, Contesting the Election of John P. Hungerford, Returned to Serve in the Thirteenth Congress as a Representative for the State of Virginia* (Washington, DC: Roger C. Weightman, 1814).

Van Cleve, George William. "Founding a Slaveholders' Union, 1770–1797." In John Craig Hammond and Matthew Mason, eds., *Contesting Slavery: The Politics of Bondage and Freedom in the New American Nation* (Charlottesville: University of Virginia Press, 2011): 117–37.

———. *A Slaveholders' Union: Slavery, Politics, and the Constitution in the Early Republic* (Chicago: University of Chicago Press, 2010).

Varon, Elizabeth R. *Disunion! The Coming of the American Civil War, 1789–1859* (Chapel Hill: University of North Carolina Press, 2008).

Waldstreicher, David. "The Nationalization and Racialization of American Politics: Before, Beneath, and Between Parties." In Byron E. Shafer and Anthony J. Badger, eds., *Contesting Democracy: Substance and Structure in*

American Political History, 1775–2000 (Lawrence: University Press of Kansas, 2001): 37–64.

———. *Slavery's Constitution: From Revolution to Ratification* (New York: Hill & Wang, 2009).

Walker, Clarence E. *Mongrel Nation: The America Begotten by Thomas Jefferson and Sally Hemings* (Charlottesville: University of Virginia Press, 2009).

Walker, David. *David Walker's Appeal, in Four Articles* (New York: Hill & Wang, 1965, reprint of Boston, 1829).

Walker, James W. St. G. *The Black Loyalists: The Search for a Promised Land in Nova Scotia and Sierra Leone, 1783–1870* (Halifax: Dalhousie University Press, 1976).

———. "Myth, History, and Revisionism: The Black Loyalists Revisited." *Acadiensis* 29 (Autumn 1999): 88–105.

Wallace, Adam. *The Parson of the Islands; a Biography of the Rev. Joshua Thomas* (Cambridge, MD: Tidewater, 1961; reprint of Philadelphia, 1870).

Walsh, Lorena S. "Rural African Americans in the Constitutional Era in Maryland, 1776–1810." *Maryland Historical Magazine* 84 (Winter 1989): 327–41.

———. "Work and Resistance in the New Republic: The Case of the Chesapeake, 1770–1820." In Mary Turner, ed., *From Chattel Slaves to Wage Slaves: The Dynamics of Labour Bargaining in the Americas* (Bloomington: Indiana University Press, 1995): 97–122.

Walsh, Lorena S., and Lois Green Carr, "Economic Diversification and Labor Organization in the Chesapeake, 1650–1820," In Stephen Innes, ed., *Work and Labor in Early America* (Chapel Hill: University of North Carolina Press, 1988): 144–88.

Waterhouse, Benjamin, ed. *A Journal of a Young Man of Massachusetts, Late a Surgeon on Board an American Privateer* (New York: William Abbott, 1911).

Watts, Steven. *The Republic Reborn: War and the Making of Liberal America, 1790–1820* (Baltimore: Johns Hopkins University Press, 1987).

Weeks, Barbara K. "This Present Time of Alarm: Baltimoreans Prepare for Invasion." *Maryland Historical Magazine,* 84 (Fall 1989): 259–66.

Wehjte, Myron F. "Opposition in Virginia to the War of 1812." *Virginia Magazine of History and Biography* 78 (1970): 65–86.

Weiss, John McNish. "Cochrane and His Proclamation: Liberator or Scaremonger?" (Anglo-American War of 1812 Conference paper, London, July 2012).

———. "The Corps of Colonial Marines 1814–1816: A Summary." *Immigrants and Minorities* 15 (1996): 80–90.

———. *The Merikens: Free Black American Settlers in Trinidad 1815–16* (London: McNish & Weiss, 2002).

Wharton, James. *Corotoman: Home of the Carters* (Kilmarnock, VA: Rappahannock Record, 1948).

Whitehill, Walter Muir, ed. *New England Blockaded in 1814: The Journal of
Henry Edward Napier, Lieutenant in H. M. S. Nymphe* (Salem, MA: Pea-
body Museum, 1939).

Whitelaw, Marjory, ed. *The Dalhousie Journals*, 3 vols. (Ottawa: Oberon Press,
1978).

Whitfield, Harvey Amani. *Blacks on the Border: The Black Refugees in British North America, 1815–1860* (Hanover, NH: University Press of New
England, 2006).

———. "The Development of Black Refugee Identity in Nova Scotia, 1813–
1850." *Left History* 10 (Fall 2005): 9–31.

———. *From American Slaves to Nova Scotian Subjects: The Case of the Black
Refugees, 1813–1840* (Toronto: Pearson/Prentice Hall, 2005).

Whitman, T. Stephen. *Challenging Slavery in the Chesapeake: Black and White
Resistance to Human Bondage, 1775–1865* (Baltimore: Maryland Historical
Society, 2007).

———. *The Price of Freedom: Slavery and Manumission in Baltimore and Early
National Maryland* (New York: Routledge, 2000).

Wiencek, Henry. *Master of the Mountain: Thomas Jefferson and His Slaves*
(New York: Farrar, Straus & Giroux, 2012).

Wilson, W. Emerson, ed. *Plantation Life of Rose Hill: The Diaries of Martha
Ogle Forman, 1814–1815* (Wilmington: Historical Society of Delaware,
1976).

Winks, Robin W. *The Blacks in Canada: A History* (Montreal: McGill-Queen's
University Press, 1997).

[Wirt, William]. *An Argument in Support of the Chesapeake Claims in Reply
to the Argument of James Hamilton and Others* (Washington, DC, 1828).

Wolf, Eva Sheppard. "Early Free-Labor Thought and the Contest over Slavery
in the Early Republic." In John Craig Hammond and Matthew Mason, eds.,
*Contesting Slavery: The Politics of Bondage and Freedom in the New Ameri-
can Nation* (Charlottesville: University of Virginia Press, 2011): 32–48.

———. *Race and Liberty in the New Nation: Emancipation in Virginia from the
Revolution to Nat Turner's Rebellion* (Baton Rouge: Louisiana State University Press, 2006).

Wood, Donald. *Trinidad in Transition: The Years after Slavery* (New York:
Oxford University Press, 1968).

Wood, Gordon S. *The Radicalism of the American Revolution* (New York:
Alfred A. Knopf, 1992).

Wright, Louis B., ed. "William Eaton Takes a Dismal View of Virginia." *William and Mary Quarterly*, 3rd ser., 5 (Jan. 1948): 106–7.

Wyatt-Brown, Bertram. *Southern Honor: Ethics and Behavior in the Old South* (New York: Oxford University Press, 1982).

Wyllie, John Cooke, ed. "Observations Made during a Short Residence in Virginia: In a Letter from Thomas H. Palmer, May 30, 1814." *Virginia Magazine of History and Biography* 76 (Oct. 1968): 387–414.

Zaborney, John J. "Slave Hiring and Slave Family and Friendship Ties in Rural Nineteenth–Century Virginia." In John Saillant, ed., *Afro-Virginia History and Culture* (New York: Garland, 1999): 85–107.

Zimmerman, James Fulton. *Impressment of American Seamen* (Port Washington, NY: Kennikat Press, 1966).

ACKNOWLEDGMENTS

As an author, my debts are many, but a pleasure to acknowledge. This project began in the mid-1990s during a visit to the Nova Scotia Archives, where I first encountered the records of black refugees from the Chesapeake, revealing a story entirely new to me. At that archives, I benefited greatly from the assistance of Barry Cahill; from the sage advice of my friend and fellow researcher David Jaffee; and from the generosity and hospitality of Marian Binkley and Jack Crowley. More recently, Dr. Henry Bishop and Dr. Afua Cooper provided insights drawn from their own work with the records and legacy of the refugee communities. Lieutenant Colonel (retired) Bruce Gilchrest provided splendid hospitality, including a revealing tour of the Halifax Citadel Army Museum.

Fifteen years passed before I could return to the intriguing tale of the Chesapeake refugees. Thanks to the University of Richmond, I had the good fortune to hold the Douglas Southall Freeman Professorship during the fall of 2010, which enabled me to explore the archives and libraries of Virginia, where I found a surprising wealth of documentation, making this book possible. At the University of Richmond, I enjoyed great support from the president, Ed Ayers; the best of chairs, Hugh West; and wonderful colleagues, especially Joanna Drell, Woody Holton, Robert Kenzer, Manuella Meyer, John Pagan, Carol Summers, and Doug Winiarski. My sojourn in Richmond was also enriched by the generous friendship of Mark and

Lynn Valeri. Mark McGarvie helped to kick start my work by sharing his own interests in St. George Tucker and Chinese food.

I received great assistance from the staff at the Virginia Historical Society, particularly Canan Boomer, Jamison Davis, Bill Obrochta, and Katherine Wilkins; and from the archivists at the Library of Virginia, especially Brent Tarter and Minor Weisiger. I am especially grateful to Brent for sharing his formidable knowledge of Virginia history and its sources. A trip to the special collections at the Duke University Library proved especially rewarding thanks to the staff, particularly Josh Larkin-Rowley. I also enjoyed the hospitality of Kathleen DuVal and Marty Smith, although I did suffer a steady string of humiliating defeats at board games invented or adapted by their sons Quinton and Cal.

My research and writing benefited enormously from a fellowship at the Robert H. Smith International Center for Jefferson Studies in Charlottesville, where I received extraordinary support from Christa Dierksheide, Mary Scott Fleming, and Mary Mason Williams. I never lacked for sources thanks to the work of the librarians Anna Berkes, Jack Robertson, and Endrina Tay. Laura Voisin George, Jeff Looney, Cinder Stanton, and Gaye Wilson provided valuable research leads and suggestions. I am also grateful to the center's director, Andrew Jackson O'Shaughnessy, for arranging the fellowship and sharing his own expertise.

My sojourn in Charlottesville proved especially pleasant thanks to the generous hospitality and great, good spirits of my amigos Pedro and Kristen Onuf and new friends Alice and Jon Cannon. I enjoyed an especially memorable and revealing visit to Bremo, John Hartwell Cocke's former plantation, thanks to Andrea Cumbo, who shared her insights into slavery. At the University of Virginia, Max Edelson, Gary Gallagher, John Stagg, and Liz Varon generously gave of their time and expertise.

I proceeded to the C.V. Starr Center for the Study of the American Experience at Washington College in Chestertown, Maryland, where I spent two rewarding weeks as the Frederick Douglass Fellow, for which I thank the generous and able director, Adam Goodheart, and his staff: Michael Buckley, Lois Kitz, and Jill Ogline Titus. During my visit to Chestertown, I also enjoyed the friendship and hospitality of Donna and Kenny Miller, who graciously arranged a townball match. Despite having the teams stacked against me, justice and decency prevailed in a victory that would have thrilled Quinton DuVal Smith. I also thank Joan and Richard Ben Cramer for offering the best of company during my sojourn.

While in Maryland, I had the good fortune to research at the Maryland Historical Society, where I received able guidance from Katherine Gallagher, Dustin Meeker, and Francis O'Neill. At the Maryland State Archives, I enjoyed generous support from the archivist, Edward C. Papenfuse, and his staff, particularly Maya D. Davis, Rachel Frazier, and Owen Lourie. I owe my greatest Maryland debt to Ralph Eshelman, who shared his extraordinary knowledge of the local history and geography. I spent a delightful and revealing day exploring the Patuxent Valley with Ralph and his wife, Evelyn, who kept us on the right roads. Ralph, Burt Kummerow, and Gerry Embleton also helped me locate and obtain key illustrations.

Once again, I thoroughly enjoyed my research at the Library Archives Canada in Ottawa, thanks to the extraordinary friendship and generosity of Sheila McIntyre, Michael Von Herff, and their children Lucy, Silas, and Will—although they continued their threats to take me to the "Experimental Farm."

My study of the Colonial Marines benefited enormously from my fellow travelers Thomas Malcomson and John Weiss, who generously shared research leads, their own intriguing work, and helpful comments on drafts of my chapters. Tom has taught me much about the Royal Navy in the past and Thai restaurants in the present. John and Althea McNish Weiss illuminated the past and present of Trinidad and led me to the best West Indian and Chinese restaurants in London. During my visit to Oxford University, Peter Thompson proved the finest of hosts and provided an opportunity for me to present this project to the American history seminar. I am also grateful to Richard Carwadine and Jay Sexton for helping to arrange my visit. My visit to the University of Edinburgh proved memorable thanks to the generosity and friendship of Frank Cogliano and Mimi Kalman. I benefited both from Frank's exemplary work on Thomas Jefferson and from the opportunity to present this project to his seminar.

Mark McGarvie, Peter Onuf, Annette Gordon Reed, Brian Schoene, Clarence Walker, and Harvey Amani Whitfield generously improved several draft chapters with their close readings and insightful advice. John Smolenski provided helpful advice. Ari Kelman reviewed the entire draft with an extraordinary attention to both detail and the bigger picture, and this book is far the better for his generosity. Critical support for my research came from my friend and department chair, David Biale, and from the dean of social sciences at the University of California, Davis, Ron Mangun. I reaped spiritual guidance on bicycling, pool, and life from Pablo Ortiz (as corrected by Ana Peluffo and Isa and Cami Ortiz). Sam Warren manifested his passion for Canadian history hidden deep beneath a cover of classicism. That passion owes much to nurturing by his talented parents, Louis and Spring Warren. And as always, I am grateful to Kevin Convey for sharing his expertise on pirate culture, to the study of which he has devoted his life. And Carole and Marty Goldberg have enriched my life.

I completed this study at the Huntington Library, thanks to a fellowship arranged by Steve Hindle and in honor of my longtime friend and mentor, Robert C. "Roy" Ritchie. One of the greatest honors and pleasures of my career has been to hold the Ritchie Distinguished Fellowship with Roy as my office neighbor. For assistance at the Huntington, I also thank Molly Gipson, Juan Gomez, Carolyn Powell, Jason Sharples, Jaeda Snow, and Olga Tsapina. And I'm grateful to Steve Aron, Amy Green, Carla Pestana, Craig Yirush, Michael Meranze, Peter Mancall, Lisa Bitel, Bill Deverell, and Jennie Watts for their friendship during my sojourn in southern California.

At the Wylie Agency, I again benefited from representation by Andrew Wylie and his assistants. Shepherding this book to publication depended on my editor at W. W. Norton & Company, Steve Forman, who carefully nurtured the project with enthusiasm and professionalism. His assistant, Justin Cahill, helped with innumerable details, especially in sorting out the illustrations. Mary Babcock expertly and carefully copyedited the manuscript.

I have dedicated this book to my dear and talented friends Alessa Johns and Chris Reynolds and their son (and my godson) Gabriel, who has shared many journeys on two continents with us. My work and morale have often benefited from Alessa's infectious energy and enthusiasm. Chris's keen wit is exceeded only by his generosity. He also earned this dedication by his insistent devotion to "states rights," which strangely comes out when playing pool. And Gabriel has kept me honest at both chess and table tennis. Completing this group is Gabriel's godmother, Emily Albu, who remains the kindest and most lovely and interesting person on this or any other planet. She made this book possible in too many ways to list.

I have also dedicated the book to the memory of Emory Evans: an exceptionally gracious and encouraging scholar. My encounters with him were relatively few but always extraordinarily helpful, for Emory was a true gentleman of the old school in the very best sense. To my great regret, he died just as this project began and before I could again seek out his expertise on the eighteenth-century Chesapeake. Including him in the dedication also seems fitting because he had his ashes interred at Christ Church in Irvington, Virginia: the parish church for Corotoman Plantation, which looms so large in this book.

INDEX

Accomack Co., Va., 260–61, 275–76, 283–84, 321, 413–14

Adams, John, 95, 97, 103

Adams, John Quincy, 357, 430, 431

Addison, Kendall, 203

African colonization, 8–9, 42, 78, 83, 87, 99, 400–4, 425

African-Americans, 72, 128, 138
culture of 2–3, 5, 36, 58, 94, 95, 256–58
families of, 6–8, 26, 46–52, 55–60, 212, 235–41, 247–48, 252–59, 280, 330, 362, 364, 374–75, 400
free, 8, 37–40, 100–102, 103–4, 119–20, 127, 260–61, 363, 399–404, 413, 419, 434
as soldiers and marines, 30, 108, 117–18, 208–9, 323–26, 416–17, 419
see also "Colonial Marines"

agriculture and agricultural reform, 17–18, 48, 62–66, 152, 163, 222–24, 228, 320, 421–26

Alabama, 359, 405, 432

Albemarle Co., Va., 82–83

Albion, HMS, 192, 255, 275–76, 313

Alexander I, Czar, 431

Alexandria, Va., 18, 56, 73–74, 75, 100, 304, 322

Allen, James, 92

Amelia Co., Va., 19, 164

American Revolution, 6–7, 13–52, 56, 99, 101, 108–10, 179, 184, 219–20, 273, 324, 366–67, 430

Ambrister, Robert, 347

Amherst Co., Va., 218, 429

Anacostia River, 300

Anglicans, 29, 115–16

Annapolis, Md., 192, 306

Anne Arundel Co., Md., 359, 381

Anti-Federalists, 35

antislavery, 41, 115–20, 229–30, 390, 398–99, 400–9, 414

Apalachicola River, 340

Appomattox River, 15, 18, 31, 39

Arbuthnot, Alexander, 347

Archer, Col. S. B., 393

Archer, Thomas, 256, 267

Armistead, Lucy Baylor, 55–56

Armstrong, John, 305, 325, 393–96

Asbury, Francis, 41

Badger, Thomas, 441
Bahamas, 328, 342, 351, 355
Baker, Anthony St. John, 334, 353
Ball, Charles, 59–60, 66, 69, 248–49, 265
Ball, Spencer, 39–40
Ballard, Elizabeth, 262
Baltimore, Md., 183, 186–88, 208, 287, 290, 294, 307–10, 311, 325, 332–33, 364, 383, 419
Bannister, Rachael, 250
Baptists, 29, 36, 38, 41
Barbados, 346, 361, 377
Barbour, James, 146–47, 149, 153–54, 155, 158–59, 160–62, 164–65, 166, 169, 195, 260, 277, 319, 392, 394–95, 408
Barney, Joshua, 287, 291–93, 299, 300, 325
Barraud, Dr. Philip, 135, 230, 309, 319, 392, 397
Barrie, Capt. Robert, 196, 203–4, 247, 284, 310–12, 327, 328, 332, 358
Barron, James, 122
Barrow, David, 36
Bathurst, Earl, 200–201, 203, 204, 209, 212, 299, 354, 369, 373, 376
Baton, Canada, 236, 239, 422
see also "Beaton, Kennedy"
Bayly, Thomas M., 113, 338
Beanes, Dr. William, 304, 309
Beaton, Kennedy, 239, 284
see also "Baton, Canada"
Beckwith, Sir Sidney, 180, 185, 194, 195, 201
Bedford Co., Va., 102
Beech Hill, N.S., 369, 373
Bendall, James, 318
Benedict, Md., 281, 292, 294, 295, 297, 299, 383
Beresford, Sir John, 277

Berkeley, Sir George Cranfield, 122, 141–42
Bermuda, 13, 14, 30, 31, 181, 196, 205–7, 280, 305, 327, 336, 338, 342–45, 354–55, 357, 358, 360–61, 366, 368, 377, 419, 433
Berry, William, 382
Billups, John, 166
Birkbeck, Morris, 413
Bizarre Plantation, 31, 38, 39
Blackburn, Thomas, 16
Blackshear, Gen. David, 329
Blackstone, Sir William, 21
Bladensburg, Md., battle at, 300, 305, 325
Blow, Richard, 46
Bolivar, Simon, 376–77
Boush, William, 249
Boxley, George, 398–99, 400
Boyers, William, 411
Brand, Captain Benjamin, 81–82
Bremo Plantation, 63–64
Brent, James, 270
Brewer, Holly, 452n77
British Empire, 1–2, 3, 19–28, 34, 367
    abolishes the slave trade and ame-
        liorates slavery, 115–21
    diplomacy with the United States,
        121–31, 139–42, 176–77, 332–33,
        338, 348, 429–32
    Orders in Council of, 177
    see also "Royal Navy" and "War
        of 1812"
Broadnax, Lydia, 105, 106
Brooke, Col. Arthur, 305, 308
Brooke, John J., 176, 267–68
Brougham, Henry, 116
Brown, Jacob, 393
Brown, Joe, 233
Brown, John, 238
Brown, John Thompson, 416

Brown, Michael, 105
Brown, Sukey Saunders, 238
Brown, Lt. Col. Thomas, 279–80
Bruce, Jim, 254
Buckingham Co., Va., 76
Burwell, Nathaniel, 155
Bush, Betsy, 238
Butler, Harry, 281
Butler, Pierce, 329–30
Byrd, Richard W., 134

Cabell, Joseph C., 6, 64–65, 151–52,
    216, 218–43, 257, 258, 265, 266,
    267, 268, 351–53, 357, 381, 394–
    95, 415, 420–29, 434–35
Cabell, William H., 76, 125–26, 127,
    151–52, 218, 220–21, 222, 324,
    333, 428, 429
Cadin, Minty, 254
Calvert Co., Md., 176, 248–49, 250,
    252–53, 254, 262, 282, 287–95
Campbell, David, 322
Campbell, John, 135, 138, 145–48,
    150, 155, 161, 162, 319, 322, 392
Campbell Co., Va., 60
Canada, American invasions of, 149,
    154, 178, 276, 291, 300, 392, 393
Canning, George, 120
Cape Henry, 198
Carleton, Sir Guy, 28
Caroline Co., Va., 164
Carr, Dabney, 406–7
Carroll, Charles, 306
Carter, Charles, 33, 217, 222, 228–34,
    236–37, 239, 241, 258, 338, 420–
    21, 426–27, 434, 435
Carter, Charles B., 254
Carter, Dick, 215–16, 237, 238, 258,
    434
Carter, George, 33, 217, 240
Carter, James, 55–56
Carter, Landon, 55–56

Carter, Rebecca Parke Farley, 426
Carter, Robert, of Nominee Hall, 25,
    38, 39–40, 59
Carter, Robert "King", 217
Carter, Sukey Saunders, 238
Carter's Creek, 216, 233, 235–36
Castlereagh, Viscount, 136
Caulk's Field, battle of, 306
Chamberlain, Theophilus, 371, 372
Chambers, Ezekiel, 264,
Champ, Anthony, 358
Chaptico, Md., 293
Charles Co., Md., 293
Charles, Peter, 382
Charlestown, Md., 192, 193
Charlotte Co., Va., 31, 138
Chesapeake Bay, 1–3, 15–16, 24–25,
    27, 52, 69, 89, 121–22, 126, 159,
    177–80, 182–83, 185, 190, 196–
    98, 213, 216, 247, 250, 260, 269,
    271–72, 283, 287–290, 310–11,
    327, 332, 337–39, 349, 377, 381
Chesapeake Claimants, 432–34
Chesconessex Creek, 276, 284
Chesterfield Co., Va., 31
Chestertown, Md., 306
Cheves, Langdon, 432, 433
Chrystie, Thomas, 66
Chub, John, 231
Civil War, 416–17
Claiborne, Nathaniel H., 161
Clark, Archibald, 382, 383, 384, 387
Clavell, Capt. John, 327, 337–38
Clay, Henry, 7, 131
Clinch, Col. Duncan, 341
Clinton, DeWitt, 396
Coalter, John, 219, 242
Cochrane, Sir Alexander, 209–13,
    276, 280, 283, 286, 299, 307–8,
    311, 327, 328, 331, 353
    proclamation by, 211–13, 340, 342,
    369, 372

Cockburn, Sir George, 5–6, 178–79,
    182, 183, 188–98, 199, 200, 203,
    205, 206–7, 211, 212–13, 246–47,
    248, 271, 274–75, 276, 277, 279,
    280, 282–303, 308, 311, 313–14,
    327–32, 335–38, 339–40, 343,
    348, 360, 366, 419, 430
Cockburn, James, 305, 343–44, 355,
    360, 419
Cocke, John Hartwell, 63–64, 77, 79,
    230, 233, 415, 425
Codrington, Edward, 179–80, 189,
    200, 290, 291, 305, 307
Coleman, Seth, 371–72
Coles, Isaac A., 151, 393, 406
College of William and Mary, 14, 33,
    218, 229
Collins, Peggy, 202
Colonial Marines, 5–6, 248, 251–52,
    262, 263–64, 276, 279–86, 299,
    302, 307, 308, 310, 312–14, 327–
    32, 336, 342–45, 360–61, 373,
    377–78, 400, 422
  non-commissioned officers
    among, 282, 284–85
communication, 19, 103–4, 382–87
Company Towns, Trinidad, 378–80
Connecticut, 390
conspiracy theories, 355, 357
Cook, Betty Saunders, 240
Cook, Jim Bully, 240
Cooper, Rebecca, 268
Corbin, Henry, 427
Corbin, Richard, 233
Cornick, Jeremiah, 92
Cornwallis, Lord Charles, 27–28, 179
Corotoman Plantation, 6, 215–18,
    222–43, 258, 284, 338, 381, 419–
    27, 434–35
  slave community at, 223–43,
    437–40
Cowper, John, 92, 258

Cox, Franky, 239
Cox, Hostler Joe, 239
Craney Island, battle at, 194, 195, 197
credit and debt, 19–20, 60–62
Creeks, 328
Cross, Oliver, 412, 414
Croxton, Philip, 66–67
Cuba, 90
Culpeper Co., Va., 85
Cumberland Island, 327–32, 332,
    336–38, 360, 430
Currie, Ellison, 426

Dalhousie, Lord, 372–74
Dallas, Alexander J., 322–23
Daniel, Peter V., 161
Dare, William, 248
Davenport, David P., 385
Deadman's Bones, 235, 236
Denmark, 124
Devastation, HMS, 358
Dick, Alexander, 389
disease, and disease environments,
    16–17, 26–27, 151–52, 163, 165,
    318–20
Ditcher, Jack, 95
Dixon, William, 345
Dorsey, Clement, 297
Douglas, Capt. John Erskine, 126–27
Douglass, Frederick, 71, 176
Downman, Raleigh W., 358
Dragon, HMS, 280, 385–86
Duane, William, 9, 393
Dungeness Plantation, 328, 336, 337
Dunmore, Lord, 23–27, 30, 34, 44,
    98, 259
Dunn, Robert, 253

Early, Peter, 328–29
Easter Rebellion, 346, 377
Eastern Shore, 209, 250
    of Maryland, 182, 191–93, 198, 208

of Virginia, 15, 27, 37, 51–52, 89–90, 163, 201–2, 203, 260–61, 275–78, 413–14, 441
Easton, Md., 198
Eddins, Langley B., 167–68
Edgewood Plantation, 221, 222, 427–28
Edinburgh, University of, 245
Edmondson, Henry, 113–13
Edwards, Jesse, 281
Eglinton, Lord, 277
Elizabeth City County, 47–48
Elizabeth River, 27
embargo, 130–31
England, 20–21, 383
entail and primogeniture, 6, 43–46, 51–52, 219, 426–27, 452n77
environment, 17
Essex Co., Va., 253, 358
Eustis, William, 149
Evans, Andrew Fitzherbert, 206–7, 342
Evans, Robert J., 406
Eyre, John, 255, 413

Fall Line, 18
Fairbanks, Rufus, 371, 374–75
Farnham Church, Va., 312
Faulcon, John, 79–80
Faulcon, Nicholas, 268
Fauquier County, Va., 48
Fay, Lt. H. A., 306
Federalists, 35, 95, 102–3, 129, 130–32, 154–55, 160–61, 167, 179, 183, 184, 186–88, 190, 192, 275, 291–94, 296, 304, 323, 324, 389–90, 392, 405, 430
Fedric, Francis, 48, 70
Fincastle Co., Va., 25
Fithian, Philip Vickers, 59, 72
Florida, 328–29, 331–32, 335, 375
Floyd, John, 113–14

Floyd, John K., 255
Fluvanna Co., Va., 63, 415
Forbes, Francis, 361
Forbes, John, 331–32
Forester, Robert, 253
Forester, Toby, 383, 384
Fort Albion, 277–78
Fort Bowyer, 359
Fort McHenry, 308, 325
Fort Powhatan, 148, 393–94, 395
Fort Washington, 304
Fossett, Peter, 60
Francisco, Peter, 13
Fraser, Lt. John, 339
Frederick Co., Md., 159
Frederick Co., Va., 163
Fredericksburg, Va, 18, 55–56, 63, 399
Fredericktown, Md., 191–92
freedom, 13–14, 20–25, 30, 35–42, 100–2, 106, 107–10, 198–99, 262, 265, 266, 373, 399, 425, 426
French Empire, 115, 116, 122, 130
French Revolution, 42
Fuller, Maria, 373

Gabriel's revolt, 94–97, 100, 134, 400
Gales, Joseph, 302
Gayle, Col. Leaven, 166–67, 168, 170, 171
gender relations, 193–95, 218–22, 257
George, Ben, 260–61
Georgetown, Md., 191–92
Georgia, 48, 51, 57, 227, 327–32, 335–37, 342, 358, 360, 361, 365, 377, 379, 380, 430, 432
Ghent, Treaty of, 332–38, 357, 429–31
Giles, William Branch, 401, 407, 410
Gillett, Sci, 155–56, 160, 344–45
Gilmer, Francis Walker, 407
Gleig, Lt. G. R., 339
Gloucester Co., Va., 75–76, 155

Gooch, Claiborne W., 323
Goode, William, 416
Goodchild, Billy, 155, 156
Goosley, James, 386–87
Gordon, Capt. James, 304
Goulburn, Henry, 212
Grammar, Frederick, 359
Granger, Gideon, 103–4
Great Dismal Swamp, 76, 415
Great Jenny, 239–40, 243, 284, 422
Grecian, the, 170
Greenhow, Robert, 1, 141, 164
Grenville, Lord, 115
Grenville, Thomas, 176
Gresham, George, 217, 218, 223, 224,
    227–28
Griffin, Robert, 386–87
Griffin, Major Thomas, 256, 351–52,
    385–86
Grimes, William, 49, 57, 70, 71, 77
Gumby, Dadda Thomas, 59
Gwynn Island, Va., 26, 247

Haggeman, Mary Ann, 159
Haiti, 7, 103, 376
    see also Saint-Domingue
Halifax Co., Va., 72
Halifax, Nova Scotia, 122, 176, 181,
    195, 196, 280, 354, 355, 357, 360,
    361–75, 381, 383, 384, 385–87,
    433, 434
Hall, Addison, 434, 437, 498n49
Hall, Gabriel, 350–51
Hall, John, 358
Hall, Mary K., 247
Hall, Thomas L., 354–55, 357
Hallidan, Patrick, 199
Hamilton, John, 125–28
Hammond, Capt. William, 279, 284,
    286, 312, 337–38
Hammonds Plains, N.S., 369–74
Hampton, Va., 125, 194–95, 196, 197,
    198, 247, 250, 351, 395

Hanover Co., Va., 66, 81–82, 94, 164,
    411
Hanson, Alexander Contee, 187
Harding, Michael, 283–84
Hardy, Capt. Thomas M., 127–28
Harper, Robert Goodloe, 187
Harris, Thomas M., 262
Hartford Convention, 323
Havannah, HMS, 246, 337–38
Havre de Grace, Md., 186, 191–92,
    193, 195–96
Haynes, Lemuel, 138
Hemings, Sally, 77, 79
Henderson, Capt. William, 296
Henrico Co., Va., 94
Henry, Patrick, 7, 8, 23, 29, 35, 36
Henson, Josiah, 58, 62, 70, 71
Hillhouse, William, 414
Honor, 391–95
Hooe, Abraham, 1–3, 384–85
Hopkins, Samuel, 323
Hudgins, Houlder, 106, 167–68, 172,
    268
Wrights v. Hudgins, 106, 108–10, 167
Hull, Gen. William, 154
Humphreys, Salusbury, 121–22
Hungerford, Gen. John P., 270, 286,
    297, 298, 313
Hunt, Gilbert, 112–13

Illinois, 425
impressment, 122–25, 130, 131,
    136–38, 177
Indiana, 399
Indians, American, 5, 10, 48, 106, 108,
    121, 131, 138, 177, 328
Ireland and Irish-Americans, 121,
    185–86, 196, 198–99, 325, 348
Ireland Island, Bermuda, 206–7, 344,
    360, 366
Ironmonger, Edward, 354–55
Isle of Wight Co., Va., 134, 399
Israel Hill, Va., 39

Jaboe, Capt. James, 312–13, 354
Jackson, Andrew, 334, 335, 347, 396–98
Jackson, Henry, 127
Jackson, Lewis, 358
Jackson, Samuel, 253–54
Jacob, Arthur, 255–56
Jamaica, 354, 355, 383
James, Charles, 239
James City Co., Va., 157–58, 202
James River, 15, 18, 27, 47, 96, 134, 148, 156, 163, 201, 207, 243, 255, 320, 393–94
Jamestown, Va., 156
Jasseur, HMS, 215, 236
Jefferson, Thomas, 6, 8, 9, 19, 20, 22, 27, 28, 29, 30, 34, 42, 43–46, 57, 59, 60, 64, 77, 78, 82–83, 86–87, 110, 140, 163, 245, 305, 317, 320–21, 322, 389, 393, 408
  and the Declaration of Independence, 14, 104
  and his plan for gradual emancipation, 87, 403
  as president and presidential candidate, 95, 97, 98–99, 102–4, 123–24, 126, 128, 129–31, 149, 400
Jeter, Jeremiah Bell, 102
Johnson, Harriot, 364
Johnson, Sergeant, 284–85, 339
Jones, Caleb, 251
Jones, Walter, 145, 150, 162, 204, 245–46, 264–65, 296, 312, 322, 361–62, 441
Joynes, John G., 261, 275–76, 413–14

Kelley, James, 434, 437, 498n49
Kemp, Sarah, 320
Kempt, Gov. James, 374
Kennon, Elizabeth, 134–35
Kent Co., Md., 264
Kent Island, Md., 192, 198, 199, 391
Kentucky, 48, 132, 172

Key, Francis Scott, 293, 309–10
Kilgour, William, 263
Kindelan, Sebastian, 331
King, Miles, 68–69
King, Roswell, 329–30, 358
King, Thomas B., 293
King and Queen Co., Va., 55, 73
King George Co., Va., 319–20, 382
Kinsale, Va., 245, 246, 296–97
Kinsman, Maj. Andrew, 343, 377–78

Laidloe's Ferry, Md., 1
Lake Porter, N.S., 370, 371
Lancaster County, Va., 6, 159, 216, 217, 227, 234–35, 247, 261, 269, 270, 358, 425, 434
Lane, Joe, 253
Latrobe, Benjamin Henry, 16, 19, 63, 93
law, 20–21, 35, 40, 43–46, 67–68, 80–82, 105–6, 183, 399
Lee, Henry, 51–52, 187–88, 324
Lee, Ludwell, 88
Lee, Richard E., 126
Lee, Richard Henry, 14
Leopard v. Chesapeake, 121–22, 125, 129, 130, 132, 137, 175
Liberia, 403
liberty, see freedom
Lingan, James, 187–88
Lipscomb, Benjamin, 81
Liverpool, Lord, 431
Loker, George, 337, 338
Lomax, John Taylor, 298, 313
Loney, Ezekiel, 236, 238
Loney, Gabriel, 238
Loney, Nancy, 238
Loney, Nelly Marx, 238
Loney, Sam, 238
Louisa Co., Va., 94, 398–99
Louisiana, 97, 103, 129, 375, 432
Lovell, Capt. William Stanhope, 139–40

Lynchburg, Va., 164–65, 243
Lynnhaven Bay, 175, 197, 269

Madison Co., Va., 74
Madison, James, 22–23, 28, 35, 43, 51,
    102, 123, 147, 245, 395, 400–1,
    403, 404
  as president, 131–32, 138, 149,
    160–62, 183, 189, 197, 211, 287,
    291, 293, 300, 301–2, 305, 323,
    324, 325, 338, 351–52, 389–90,
    393, 395–96, 397
Magruder, Eli, 360, 361
Maid of the Isles, 344–45
Maine, the great state of, 129, 392, 408
malaria, 17, 163, 235, 318, 425
Malcolm, Sir Pulteney, 205, 211, 252,
    310, 327
Malcomson, Thomas, 442
Mansfield, Lord, 20–21
Marshall, John, 401
Maryland, 48, 58, 182, 186–88, 345,
    373, 383, 385
  War of 1812 in, 190–93, 203, 204–
    5, 208, 234, 247, 248–53, 254,
    262–64, 281, 282, 284, 287–95,
    296, 299–310, 312–14, 337, 391
masculinity, 95, 189, 193, 195, 220–21
Mason, Benjamin, 267–68
Mason, George, 29, 86
Massachusetts, 390, 393, 408
Massey, John, 382, 384
Mathews, John, 68
Mathews, Thomas, 126, 127
Mathews Co., Va., 47, 68–69, 89, 106,
    155–56, 157–59, 160, 166–73,
    176, 260, 266, 268, 270, 271,
    344–45, 410–11, 453n86
Matoax Plantation, 27, 31, 32
Maud, James, 92–93
McCarty, Bartholomew, 255, 503n23
McCroskey, Widow, 61

McNamara, Timothy, 270
Melville Island, 368
Memory Spirituals, 380
Menelaus, HMS, 381
Mercer, Charles Fenton, 319, 334,
    400–1, 403
Merikens, 375–80
Methodists, 29, 36, 41–42, 47, 115,
    193, 279, 376
Middle Atlantic states, 396
Middlesex Co., Va., 321
Midway Plantation, 429
migration, 17–18, 48–49, 400–4
Minor, John, 97, 100–1, 322, 392
Mississippi River, 404–5, 406
Missouri Crisis and Compromise, 9,
    405–9, 425
Mitchell, Robert, 378
Monroe, James, 92, 96, 97, 98–99,
    160, 271, 305, 312, 324, 325–26,
    334, 352–57, 360, 362, 363, 365,
    387, 393, 395, 397, 400–1, 430
  as President, 347, 403, 408
Montgomery Co., Md., 187, 303
Montgomery Co., Va., 113–14
Monticello Plantation, 45–46, 60, 77,
    82
Moore, John, 308–9
Murphy, Pleasants, 334

Naparima, Trinidad, 375–80
Napier, Sir Charles, 194, 208–9
Napoleon Bonaparte, 115, 116, 117,
    124, 129, 139, 176, 177, 179, 277,
    332
Nassau, Bahamas, 351, 355
National Intelligencer, 183, 211, 251,
    302, 326, 346–47, 357, 391
nationalism, American, 396–98
Neale, Augustine, 258, 360, 361–65,
    387
Negro Fort, 340–42, 347

Nelson, Lord Horatio, 178
Nelson Co., Va., 221–22, 224, 243,
    415, 422, 427–28
New Brunswick, 3, 368
New England, 130–31, 154, 160–61,
    323, 333, 389–92, 395, 397–98, 414
New Orleans, La., 327, 329, 334, 335,
    347, 383, 396–98
New Point Comfort, 168–69
New York City, 27, 28, 192, 361
New York (state), 325–26, 413
Newell, Capt. Thomas M., 336–37
Newton, Thomas, 318
Nicholas, Peggy, 133, 136
Nicholas, Wilson Cary, 133, 136, 319,
    321, 392, 428–29
Nicolls, Major Edward, 328, 329,
    340–41
Nomini Ferry, Va., 296–98
Nonsuch, USS, 363–64
Norfolk, Va., 15–17, 18, 26, 58, 73,
    77–78, 89, 92, 96, 125–28, 133,
    148, 149, 151–52, 155, 160–66,
    194, 258, 259, 281, 295, 318–19,
    321, 353, 355, 394, 397, 398
North Carolina, 134
North Point, battle of, 307–8
Northern Neck, 37, 38, 162, 164,
    240, 245–46, 272, 287, 295–98,
    313–14, 318, 319–20, 383, 395,
    415, 441
Northampton Co., Va., 51–52, 89–90,
    94, 141, 203, 253, 255, 270–71,
    382, 412, 413–14
Northumberland Co., Va., 253,
    295–98, 359
Nottingham, Md., 383
Nourse, Capt. Joseph, 212, 262–64,
    266, 292, 298
Nova Scotia, 3, 28, 343, 354, 355, 358
    black refugees in, 361–75, 382–87,
    434

Ohio, 132
Old Dick, 39–40, 49, 50, 71
Oneill, John, 186
Orange Co., Va., 147
overseers, 60, 62–66, 70, 79, 82–83,
    157, 158, 223–28, 255–56,
    421–27
Oxford Iron Works, 60–61

Palmerston, Lord, 348
Paradise, Lucy Ludwell, 157
Parker, Gen. Alexander, 318
Parker, Jacob G., 381
Parker, Col. Richard E., 284–85, 295,
    298, 306
Parker, Gen. Thomas, 393
Parkinson, Richard, 65, 66, 70, 71
Parrott, John, 247
Patapsco River, 308
Patriots, American, 13–14, 37, 108, 245
Patterson, John, 156, 169, 344–45
Patuxent River, 247, 251–52, 262,
    284, 287, 289, 290, 294, 298, 303,
    304–5, 314, 339, 383
Pennsylvania, 101, 405, 413
Perks, Thomas, 256
Petersburg, Va., 18, 92, 101
Philadelphia, 56, 354
Picton, Thomas, 121
Piedmont region, 17–19, 23, 28–29,
    34, 63, 148, 153, 162–64, 271–73,
    398, 407, 409–10, 411, 414, 416
Pinckney, Gen. Thomas, 355
Plantagenet, HMS, 269
Plater, John Rousby, 251–52, 293
Pleasants, James, 432, 433
Pleasants, Robert, 38
Port of Spain, Trinidad, 373, 377
Potomac River, 1–2, 15, 25, 37, 203–4,
    234, 247, 248, 254, 285, 289, 290,
    294, 295, 296, 298, 304, 310, 314,
    338, 358

Poverty, 17
Powhatan Co., Va., 82, 160
Prentiss, William, 430
Presson, Capt. William, 412
Preston, N.S., 2, 369–74, 384
Primrose, Thomas, 254
Prince Edward Co., Va., 31, 38, 39
Prince Frederick Town, Md., 282
Prince George's Co., Md., 262, 293, 303, 383
Prince William Co., Va., 16, 39–40
Princess Anne Co., Va., 125–27, 152, 162–63, 175–76, 202, 249, 259, 269
privateers, American, 156–57, 177, 197, 202, 419
pro-slavery ideology, 391, 404, 412
Prosser, Thomas Henry, 94
Pumphrey, James, 387
Pungoteague Creek, 283–84
Pybus, Cassancra, 26

Quakers, 37, 38, 42, 75, 86, 100, 108, 115
Quincy, Josiah, 390

race and racial concepts, 5–10, 30, 40–42, 58–59, 65, 77–78, 80–81, 102, 105, 106–10, 118, 136–42, 205–6, 242, 256, 257, 310, 330, 376, 401
Randolph, Francis Bland, 31, 32
Randolph, John, 7–8, 19, 31, 32, 45–46, 49, 57–58, 65, 79, 90–9, 96–97, 105, 132, 163, 321, 401, 402, 403–4, 405, 408, 410
Randolph, Richard, 31, 32, 38–39
Randolph, Theodorick, 31, 32
Randolph, Thomas Jefferson, 15, 318, 416–17
Randolph, Thomas Mann, Jr., 75, 82–83, 403

Rappahannock River, 15, 18, 216, 253, 255, 311–12, 327, 358
Regulus, HMS, 327, 368
religion, Christian, 15, 29–30, 36, 38, 100, 115–16, 184, 380, 387, 398–99
    see also Anglicans, Baptists, Methodists, Quakers
Republicans, 95, 102–4, 123, 129–32, 136–38, 140–41, 149, 179, 183, 184, 186–88, 190, 192, 195, 210–11, 275, 293, 296, 304, 322, 324, 334–35, 390, 405
republicanism, 29–30, 43–46, 94–95, 125–26, 132, 137–39, 150, 165–66, 322
Richardson, John, 153
Richeson, Henry, 422
Richeson, John, 232–33, 235, 236, 237, 238, 421–23
Richmond, Va., 13, 18, 27, 32, 75, 94–96, 99, 104–6, 113, 132, 133–35, 145–46, 150, 155, 157, 164, 168, 195, 222, 242, 260, 268, 295, 319, 333, 393–94, 397, 410, 411
    theater fire in, 114, 135, 147
Richmond Co., Va., 255, 281
Richmond Enquirer, 138, 146, 195, 198, 240, 245, 259, 311, 319, 323, 335, 347–48, 391, 395, 397, 408–9
Ripley, John, 155–56, 176
Ritchie, Thomas, 146–47, 311, 408–9
Roane, Spencer, 109, 406, 407
Roanoke Plantation, 31, 46
Roberts, George R., 418–19
Roberts, Jonathan, 405
Robertson, George, 225–28, 231–33, 423–24
Robertson, Thomas B., 100, 101
Roots, Sam, 247–48
Ross, Capt. Charles B. H., 255, 283, 284

Ross, David, 60–61
Ross, Edward, 320, 323
Ross, Richard, 256
Ross, Gen. Robert, 281, 298–302, 304, 306–8
Ross, William "Rolla," 381
Rowley, Capt. Robert, 285, 290, 304–5, 311
Royal Navy, 1–2, 4–6, 115, 121–28, 348, 366
  desertion from, 122–25, 128, 169, 184, 198–200, 294, 308, 312
  officers' views of Americans, 139–40, 178–79, 185–86, 188–90, 209–11, 277, 298, 307, 339–40
  raids along the Chesapeake shores, 155, 162–63, 166–70, 177–81, 189–98, 287–314, 317
  raids along the Georgia coast, 327–32
  runaways and the, 170, 175–76, 200–13, 234–37, 246–52, 261–68, 269–71, 275–314, 327–32, 335–44, 351–59, 365–66, 367, 430–31
  treatment of free women, 193, 194–95, 291, 293, 302–3
Ruby, HMS, 206
Rule, John, 371
Russell, Col. Gilbert C., 359
Russell, Jonathan, 136

Saint-Domingue, 7, 42, 86, 103, 116, 317, 346, 349, 394, 398, 413
  see also Haiti
St. George's Island, Va., 338, 358
St. John, N.B., 368
St. Mary's, Ga., 328
St. Mary's Co., Md., 251, 262–63, 281, 287–95, 312–13, 337
St. Memin, Charles B. J. F. de, 85
Sarus, the, 156–57
Scotland, 383, 384

Shaler, William, 353
Saunders, Charles, 238, 239
Saunders, Fanny Loney, 238, 239
Saunders, Hannah Marx, 238, 240
Saunders, Tom, 236, 238
Sceptre, HMS, 203
Scott, Lt. James, 175, 180, 181, 183, 188, 192, 193, 199, 205, 207–8, 248, 250, 255, 266, 275–76, 281, 285, 290–91, 294, 297–98, 299, 303, 312–13
Sea Islands, Ga., 327–32, 360, 377, 380
Seale, Ignatius, 251
Seawell, Henry, 432, 433
Seminole Indians, 342, 347
Sergeant, John, 405
Serle, Ambrose, 21
Shanklyn, Bartlett, 2–3, 384–85
Shaw, John, 261
Sherbrooke, Gov. Sir John, 366–70, 372
Shiner, Michael, 301
Sierra Leone, 367, 370, 372
Singleton, James, 163
Skinner, John, 253
Skipwith, Col. Henry, 233
Skipwith, Sir Peyton, 33, 240
slave patrols, 73–74, 90, 91–92, 99, 207, 268–69
Slaves (African-American), 2, 6–10, 13–14, 20–23, 28–29, 34–52, 80–83, 366, 442
  conjurors among, 72–73, 114
  diet of, 64, 69–70
  emancipation and manumission of, 8–9, 35–42, 78, 83, 87–89, 93, 98–102, 105, 229–31, 415–17, 427
  escapes by, 1–5, 6–7, 24–28, 74–76, 127, 157, 160, 169–73, 175–76, 200–5, 215–17, 234–41, 245–56, 271–73, 303–4, 329–31, 335–42, 413–14, 424–25

Slaves (African-American) (*continued*)
  families of, 55–60, 74, 82, 95,
    101–2, 212, 235–41, 242, 247–48,
    252–59, 262–63, 272–73, 280,
    330, 362
  as house servants, 78–80, 218,
    226–27, 239–40, 245–46, 256
  look to the British as liberators,
    21, 24, 52, 110, 114–15, 120,
    121, 127, 128, 141–42, 156–57,
    175–76, 234–35, 334, 349, 362
  material conditions of, 71
  migration of, 48–49, 404–9
  mixed race, 76–78, 106–10, 255–56,
    258, 503n23
  naming practices of, 256–58
  nocturnal lives of, 69–74
  as outliers, 75–76, 158, 202, 227,
    228, 269
  prices of, 47, 158, 432
  punishment of, 25–26, 57, 59, 62,
    64, 66–69, 73, 75, 76, 82–83, 90,
    92, 94, 96, 97, 137–38, 156–60,
    225–27, 231, 233, 399, 422
  religion of, 36
  rental of, 47–48
  resistance by, 64–65, 70–72, 75,
    225–28, 231–33, 235, 421–25
  revolts by feared, 22–23, 26, 37,
    40, 49, 51–52, 67, 74, 89–97, 129,
    132–36, 140–42, 151, 159–60,
    161, 163–64, 200, 204, 212,
    300–1, 346–48, 379, 389, 391,
    398–402, 410–17
  sale of, 46–52, 55–62, 104, 107,
    225–26, 233, 242, 261–62, 272,
    400, 402, 404–9, 442, 453n86
  sexual relations with, 54–55, 64,
    65, 76–79, 228, 255–56
  work of, 62–66, 223, 225, 228,
    421–26
  see also "African-Americans"
smallpox, 26–27

Smith, Rev. Armistead, 47, 155, 169,
  170, 171, 267, 268, 271
Smith, George William, 135, 147
Smith, Isaac, 358
Smith, John Tabb, 351–53
Smith, Lewis, 381, 385–87
Smith, Margaret Bayard, 301, 303
Smith, Gen. Samuel, 308
Smith, Sydney, 348
Smith, Gen. Walter, 301
Smyth, Alexander, 154
Snead, Col. Smith, 90
Somerset, James, 20–21
Somerset v. Stuart, 19–23, 35, 41,
  265–66, 331, 366
Somerville, Capt. Philip, 328
Sotterley Plantation, 251–52, 293
South, American, 277, 326, 396–98,
  403–9
  the lower (or Deep), 49, 56, 57–58,
    261–62, 327, 400, 402, 404, 432–
    33, 442
  the upper, 51
South America, 376–77
South Carolina, 349, 355, 432
Southampton Co., Va., 414–15
Southside, Virginia, 17–18
Spalding, Thomas, 336–37, 340, 341,
  360–61, 442
Spanish Empire, 118, 331, 376–77
Spesutie Island, Md., 182, 198–99
Spilman, James, 358, 361, 362
Spotsylvania Co., Va., 398–99
Star-Spangled Banner, 293, 309–10
Starke, Col. Bowling, 411
Stephen, James, 118, 120
Steward, Austin, 48, 70, 72
Steward, James, 358–59
Stokeley, Col. John, 153
Stratton, Peter, 82
Stuart, Charles, 20–21
Stuart, Gen. Philip, 313
Surry Co., Va., 268

Sutcliff, Robert, 85
Sweeney, George Wythe, 105–6
Swift, Col. John, 394

Talley, Elkanah, 81
Tallmadge, James, Jr., 405
Taney, Michael, 292, 293–94
Tangier Island, Va., 277–79, 280, 282, 283, 306, 338, 357–58, 430
Tappahannock, Va., 311–12
Tatham, William, 126, 141, 144–45
Taylor, Col. John, 8, 62, 78, 102, 154–55, 223, 225, 232, 334
Taylor, Robert Barraud, 128, 141, 161, 165–66
Texas, 347, 409
Tidewater of Virginia, 2, 6–7, 15–18, 24–25, 28–29, 34, 37, 43, 45, 52, 68–69, 72, 148, 153, 161–73, 180, 201–2, 207–8, 271–73, 312–14, 318, 407, 409–16, 452n77
Tippecanoe, battle of, 131
tobacco, 17, 62, 224, 228, 287, 294
Tomlin, John W., 81
Tompkins, Christopher, 166–71, 410
Tompkins, Daniel D., 396
torpedoes, 190, 276
Torrey, Jesse, 50, 72, 316–17
transportation, 19
Trant, Captain, 364
Trinidad, 3, 118–21, 340, 353, 357, 372, 373, 374, 375–80, 434
Triumph, HMS, 127
Tucker, Ann Frances, 32, 107, 219
Tucker, Elizabeth, 32
Tucker, George, 58, 71, 73, 77, 97–98, 110, 324
Tucker, Henry, 419
Tucker, Col. Henry, 13–14
Tucker, Henry St. George, 32, 58–59, 79, 229, 321–22
Tucker, John G. P., 185

Tucker, Lelia Skipwith Carter, 33, 214–15, 217–22, 230, 231, 232, 234, 239–40, 241, 422, 427–28
Tucker, Nathaniel Beverley, 32, 107, 320, 393, 406
Tucker, Mary (Polly) Carter, 33, 151, 217–22, 232, 241, 427
Tucker, St. George, 6, 13, 14, 19, 27, 28, 30–33, 35–36, 38, 42, 43–46, 58, 61, 78–79, 84–87, 152, 215, 351–53, 422, 423
    death of, 427–28
    family relations of, 31–33, 107, 217–22,
    gradual emancipation plan by, 87–89, 106–7, 109–10, 231
    as a judge, 107–10
    during the War of 1812, 185, 305, 321, 332, 333–34, 392, 397, 398, 419–20
    and management of Corotoman Plantation, 222–42, 419–26
Tucker, Theodorick Thomas Tudor, 32
Tucker, Thomas, 185, 305,
Turberville, John, 204, 254
Turner, Nat, 113, 414–15
Turner, Samuel, 281
Tyler, John, 401, 407–8

United States, 1–2
    abolishes foreign slave trade, 49, 104, 115
    Anglophobia in, 121, 129, 136–41, 311, 345–49, 392, 396–98
    Claims Commission for runaway slaves, 431–35, 441–42
    crisis of 1814–1815 in, 321–26
    diplomacy with the British Empire, 123–25, 176–77, 332–38, 429–32
    Federal Constitution of, 34–35, 104, 395, 406

United States (*continued*)
  sectional relations in, 9–10, 97,
    104, 130–32, 154, 160–62, 323,
    333, 389–98, 404–9, 414, 416–17
  special agents of, 360–65
  western expansion of, 10, 99,
    347–48, 404–9
Upper Marlboro, Md., 304, 383
Urmstone, Lt. George C., 312–13

Vermont, 131, 138
Vesey, Denmark, 349
Virginia, 4, 6–10, 14–19, 361, 385
  American Revolution in, 21–32,
    324
  class relations within, 29–30, 34,
    151–54, 166, 167, 171–73, 227–28
  Council of State, 34, 145, 148, 155,
    157, 158, 161, 164, 166, 167, 168,
    261, 270, 322, 412
  fear of slave revolts in, 85–102,
    132–36, 140–42, 155, 157–61,
    163–64, 173, 200, 204, 394,
    407–8
  interstate slave trade and, 104,
    404–9
  manumission of slaves in, 35–42
  militia of, 126–27, 146, 148–55,
    160–70, 180–81, 189, 197, 234,
    295–98, 318–21, 333, 398–99,
    411–15
  peace welcomed in, 333–34
  post-war depression in, 402, 407,
    420, 428–29
  relations with the federal govern-
    ment, 34–35, 149, 160–62, 166,
    172–73, 323–24, 391–98, 403–9
  sectional tensions within, 33–34,
    148, 152–54, 161–64, 172–73,
    409–10
  state constitution of, 33–34,
    409–10

slavery in, 54–83, 419–29
War of 1812 in, 145–73, 275–89,
    295–98, 310–314, 317–27, 389–
    98, 477n44

War of 1812, 1–7, 9
  atrocities of, 194–96, 197, 200–1,
    297–98
  British operations in the Ches-
    apeake during the, 176–213,
    234–35, 275–314
  civil war aspect of, 181–88, 291–
    93, 392–93
  declaration of, 131–32, 135,
    145–46
  escapes by the enslaved during the,
    245–73
  military preparations in Virginia
    during, 145–73
  myth of British selling the run-
    aways, 259–62, 263, 266, 351–57,
    362, 536n12
Walker, David, 349
Warminster, Va., 221
Warren, Sir John Borlase, 139, 174–
    78, 179, 181, 183, 184, 186, 188,
    193–96, 203, 204, 208, 209
Warwick Co., Va., 253, 412
Washington, D.C., 5, 50–51, 209,
    287, 295, 298, 299, 322, 334, 400,
    431
  British capture of, 301–5, 313–14,
    383
Washington, Bushrod, 401, 402
Washington, George, 25, 27, 28, 29,
    69, 85, 402
Washington, Nathaniel, 263
Wayles, John, 20
Webster, Joseph, 358, 362, 364
Weems, Mason Locke, 36
Welford, Dr. Horace, 281
Wellington, Lord, 194, 300, 309

West, Jeremiah, 384, 385
West Indian Regiments, 117–19, 141, 279–80, 327–28, 343, 376, 377
West Indies, 7, 25, 26, 42, 99, 115–21, 140, 177, 200, 259, 260, 266, 280, 327, 348, 354, 355, 364, 373, 375–80
Westmoreland Co., Va., 254, 270, 284–85, 286, 295–98, 313
Whiddington, William, 383–84, 385
White, James J., 236
Whitefield, Harvey Amani, 374
Wilkinson, George, 262
Williams, Lewis, 75
Williams, Patrick, 351–53, 355, 357, 385
Williams, William, 325
Williamsburg, Va., 14–15, 23, 31, 32–33, 91, 107, 157, 217, 218–22, 226, 227, 231, 240, 333–34, 353, 422, 427, 428
Willis, Capt. Perrin, 354
Willis, Simon, 358
Wilson, Martha, 248–49
Winchester, Va., 58–59, 229
Winder, Levin (of Md.), 292, 300, 306
Winder, Levin (of Va.), 253

Winder, Gen. William H., 300, 306
Winks, Robin, 545n89
Winston, John, 101
Wirt, William, 148, 434
women, 7–8, 31, 32, 49, 55–60, 61, 64–65, 73, 82, 95, 152, 159, 163–64, 193–95, 202, 218–22, 236–37, 250, 253–56, 268, 280, 290, 302–3, 320, 380, 509n68–510n68
Wood, Holland, 434
Wood, Thomas, 434
Woodford, Sir Ralph, 375–80
Wrights, Jacky, 106, 108–9
Wybourn, Major Marmaduke, 182, 186, 189, 190, 192, 193, 198–99, 246
Wythe, George, 14, 33, 104–6, 108

Yeatman, Thomas R., 266
Yeocomico River, 285, 296
York Co., Va., 150
York River, 15
Yorktown, Va., 27, 194, 209, 256, 267, 381, 385
Young, Peregrine, 251

Zane, Noah, 153